CARIBBEAN
PATTERNS

A young coffee plantation in the San Andrés Valley. The author (right) with Señor Mario González, director of the Development Project there.

CARIBBEAN PATTERNS

A political and economic study of the
contemporary Caribbean

by

Sir Harold Mitchell Bt. Dr ès sc. pol.

Research Professor of Latin American Studies,
Rollins College, Florida

Second Edition

A HALSTED PRESS BOOK

JOHN WILEY & SONS
New York   Toronto

Published in the U.S.A., Canada and Latin America
by Halsted Press, a Division of
John Wiley & Sons, Inc., New York

ISBN 0 470-61165-0
Library of Congress Catalog Card No.: 72-7741

Printed and bound in Great Britain
by T. & A. Constable Ltd, Hopetoun Street, Edinburgh

For MARY-JEAN

CONTENTS

LIST OF ILLUSTRATIONS

LIST OF MAPS

PREFACE

The historical links of the Caribbean with Europe, the United States of America and parts of Latin America have affected the modern world more than might be expected from the area of its land surface and the number of its inhabitants. In the sixteenth century it was the spring-board for Spanish Conquest in the Americas: more than four hundred years later, it was nearly the detonator of the first atomic war.

In *Europe in the Caribbean*, I compared the policies of Great Britain, France and the Netherlands towards their West Indian territories in the present century. The book was limited to a group of territories with a population substantially less than that of Haiti and the Dominican Republic which together share the single island of Hispaniola. In *Caribbean Patterns*, first published in 1967, I extended my field of view to include the Latin American republics in the Antilles, and also Puerto Rico.

The favourable reception and reviews of *Caribbean Patterns* have encouraged me to revise and update the book. I have been by no means dissatisfied with my interpretations in the first edition, but in the inter-vening five years significant developments have occurred, and these I have felt bound to take into account. In fact this has entailed a con-siderable extension of the text, and while the format of the book has been retained, almost every chapter has received substantial alteration and addition. Over 30,000 words—amounting to about one-fifth of the original book—have been added or rewritten.

Nationalism has surged in the Caribbean. Inevitably this has led to increasing pressure for participation in or control of major enterprises, not least in those countries which have recently attained independence. Black Power, so strongly manifested in the United States, lessens its sometimes abrasive force in countries which in fact have a black majority electing a black government. In the outcome the newly independent countries of the Commonwealth compare very favourably in the art of successful democratic government with many old-established Latin American republics.

The entry of Trinidad, Barbados and Jamaica into the Organisation of American States has widened their political orientation. At the same time the need for closer economic cooperation within the area has led to the creation of CARIFTA, a Commonwealth Caribbean idea envisaging possible extension.

The future of the Caribbean may turn more on economics than politics. The small size of island markets remains the major problem. Despite the real effort being made in some of these countries to control the birthrate, the limited area of good agricultural land increasingly threatens full employment. As in other parts of the world, people pour in ever greater numbers into the cities, while unemployment soars. Indeed only Fidel Castro professes to see no problems of population in Cuba, aided of course by an exceptionally large army and a work system verging on the compulsory, linked to a far from modern system of labour demanding sugar cane culture.

These current problems have been brought together in Chapter XIV dealing with Agriculture and in Chapter XV with Industry, together with a newly written Conclusion.

The break-up of the West Indies Federation has been considered in revised Chapter VI which throws light on the precipitate granting in London of permission for the holding of the Jamaica referendum of 1961 without prior consultation with the Governor General: a decision which proved the death warrant of the West Indies Federation.

The Anguilla affair provides an interesting example of the troubles of latter day colonialism and transfer of power. It has been considered in Chapter VIII, with a new map prepared by John Bartholomew and Son.

Lecturing and researching over the past twelve years at Stanford University and Rollins College on Latin America (with a strong emphasis on the Caribbean) has given me the advantage of discussion with faculty, students and others interested in this rapidly changing area. Nothing aids interpretation more than perceptive question and comment, something I first learnt as a young man when seeking the suffrages of electors in Great Britain. Farming and industrial participation in four Caribbean and Central American countries as well as in Brazil and Canada has helped me to appreciate the practical problems of tropical agriculture and its markets: an apprenticeship which began in 1936.

In revising and updating this edition I have referred whenever possible to documents and works in addition to editorials and articles in many responsible publications, reflecting varying opinions. My views have been influenced by many meetings and conversations with people responsible for Government policy.

The research for this revised and updated edition has not been confined to the Caribbean. The Library of the Royal Institute of International Affairs in London has again proved cooperative and helpful, as has that of Canning House. The West India Committee has unfailingly and patiently aided my search for source materials. In addition, in The Hague, the Ministries concerned with the Netherlands Antilles and Surinam, and in Paris, both the Ministry for the Overseas Departments and the Economic Planning Centre, have given me a generous measure of their time and much useful advice. Valuable information has been provided by Government Departments in the Caribbean and in London and elsewhere, by banks, public and private companies and individuals. To all of them I express thanks. I have also benefited from my own library, probably one of the largest private collections of books and documents on today's Caribbean. Some 450 published works have been added to the original bibliography: an increase of about 50 per cent. The book also includes 32 new photographs.

I am particularly grateful to my Research Assistant, Miss Joy Martin, M.A., for her patience in helping me update this book, including the many notes and cross references, over a period of five years. Her work has been tireless in the search for source material, something of particular difficulty in the Caribbean, itself fragmented and affected by so many countries in the Americas, Europe and beyond.

Once again, I have had perceptive advice and encouragement from Professor Ronald Hilton of Stanford University. My thanks are also due to Mrs. Thomas Bolton, M.A., in regard to Puerto Rico and the Virgin Islands of the United States. To Mr. Peter McIntyre I am indebted for undertaking the formidable task of making a second index.

I hope that this book may prove of use to students who today comprise people of diverse ages. It may also interest a different group: businessmen who contemplate investment in the area. The increasing complexity of international trade and finance compels the intelligent entrepreneur to take into account political considerations.

No Caribbean country has a chance of effective economic expansion to provide work for an increasing population, demanding an ever higher standard of living, except with the assistance of massive investment by the developed countries, both from Government and private sources. On a successful partnership with foreign countries and their investors will turn the future prosperity of the Caribbean.

CHAPTER I

INTRODUCTION

"The Caribbean" is a loose yet convenient term to describe the islands and the sea which contains them. It lies between parts of North, South and Central America. European powers as well as mainland neighbours have influenced its history. It is the result of three centuries of inter-mittent strife. With the conflict of divided loyalties, mixed races and a variety of cultures arose. The calypso, the eighteenth-century Dutch colonial architecture of Willemstad, a skyscraper in San Juan, a Spanish chapel, an English cricket-bat or a virgin jungle still unmapped are each in their way a typical feature of some part of the Caribbean. This diversity extends to coinage and weights and measures, language, constitutions, traditions and ways of life. However, similarities as well as contrasts exist. Frequently recurring is the problem of limited effective land and increasing transport difficulties for export-import trade. These difficulties are due to small and inefficient harbours unsuited to modern commerce, although improvement is taking place. One reason for the failure of the West Indies Federation was that the economies of the different islands did not complement one another.

Geographically, the Antilles comprise the islands stretching from Florida and Yucatán to the Venezuelan coast, a distance of some 1,500 miles. The formation consists of a series of archipelagos; the Bahamas alone are made up of 700 islands, the great majority uninhabited. Describing the Caribbean, Professor G. J. Butland writes: "... no comparable area of Latin America has such a variety or complexity of physical or human geography".[1] Some of the islands, such as the Bahamas and the larger part of Cuba, consist of limestone platforms. Others are partially submerged mountain ranges, separated by deep ocean trenches. In total height from mountain summit to the adjacent ocean bottom, they exceed the Himalaya peaks.

Unfortunately, except for Cuba and parts of the Dominican Republic, much of the land in consequence is too uneven for mechanical cultiva-tion. Even the level limestone plateaux often have too little soil for successful cultivation. On the other hand there are areas which pro-duce magnificent crops.

[1] *Latin America: A Regional Geography* (London, 1960), p. 96.

Rainfall varies with the location of the land, particularly in the mountainous areas. The trade winds bring a plentiful supply of rain to the north-east areas, but the south-east or leeward coast may suffer from a shortage. The parish of Portland in north-east Jamaica may be lush and green, with a rainfall in some areas exceeding 200 inches per year, when 30 miles across the mountains, Kingston may be parched and rationed for water.

Another climatic hazard which the Caribbean farmer faces is the hurricane. These circular storms, which usually move slowly, often altering course, can reach such intensity as to bring severe damage to buildings and agriculture. In many cases the flimsily constructed houses, such as those of Anguilla and Martinique and the wooden-built dwellings on stilts in British Honduras, do not easily withstand hurricanes and the flooding from river or sea which may accompany them. After the 1951 hurricane in Jamaica much of Kingston was severely damaged. In August 1970, Hurricane Dorothy cost Martinique N.F. 191 million in damage.

Many Caribbean crops can be affected by high winds well below hurricane velocity. Bananas inevitably are blown down and will take a year to fruit again; sugar cane is flattened and twisted, which hinders the harvest and is likely to affect the yield. Coconut trees, although resistant, may be uprooted. New trees may take eight years to reach full production.

The rehabilitation necessitated by a hurricane frequently results in improvement to housing and other buildings, but the capital cost is high and the interruption to business expensive. Hurricane Flora brought disaster to Haiti and seriously affected Cuba's economy by damage to the sugar crop; neither country could afford to meet the cost of repairing the damage.

Yet notwithstanding these variations of climate, Professor Preston James considers that in the Antilles are found the true temperate climates of the world.[1] That the public is in agreement, the rising volume of the tourist trade demonstrates. The golden beaches to which visitors throng have proved to be of more lasting value than the treasure sought by Columbus and his followers. Yet behind every golden beach is another picture of the Caribbean, on which the tourist's camera seldom focuses—a disused sugar mill in Antigua, the shack dwellings on the outskirts of Kingston, the undernourished peasants of Haiti indoctrinated with Voodooism, and the problem that faces Curaçao with almost a quarter of its working population unemployed. These are only a few examples of the dual nature of life in the Caribbean, where the gap between rich and poor is vividly depicted and where,

[1] *Latin America* (New York, 1959), p. 745.

ironically, scientific progress often produces hardships of its own which may not easily be overcome.

The problems of the Caribbean are extremely complex but of the greatest interest, since they provide a preview of the mounting differences between the developed and underdeveloped nations. Narrow markets due to small populations add further complications. Yet, paradoxically, the rapid growth in numbers only worsens the situation, since limited natural resources are inadequate to match this increase. The result is an ever-increasing impoverished population with an ever-diminishing purchasing-power attempting to overcome the extremely costly problem of education.

Located at the approaches to the heart of the Western Hemisphere, the Antilles command the sea routes. Narrow passages between the islands have historically limited penetration. Cuba is separated by less than 100 miles from Florida and 45 miles from Haiti. The Mona Passage between the Dominican Republic and Puerto Rico is 45 miles. The same pattern can be found to the south and east. In consequence, fortified bases have existed since the seventeenth century. The Panama Canal route added to the importance of the islands in the twentieth century.[1] Today, however, the position has altered because of jet transport and nuclear warfare, but their importance continues.

Politically the Antilles have been linked to outside countries. Spain centralized the government of its territories in the Sovereign. His representative, the Viceroy at Mexico, in turn controlled, at least nominally, the Spanish islands in the Caribbean which defended the trade routes between Spain and its American Empire.

Other European powers recognized the importance of the Caribbean. The Dutch, fighting for survival against Spain, occupied and fortified Curaçao originally for strategic reasons. Britain and France seized different islands and built forts on them. The struggle between the European powers reached a climax in the eighteenth century. Events in the Caribbean had a bearing on the American War of Independence. In the twentieth century, the Caribbean has continued to be affected by outside influences. The dominance of Great Britain from the end of the Napoleonic wars has been succeeded by that of the United States.

The international aspect of the Caribbean must always be borne in mind, even when dominance has seemed to rest with one outside power. Independence of the countries may in due course modify this position. However, it can still be said that "the Caribbean is the American

[1] Cf. Fred A. Carlson, *Geography of Latin America*, 3rd edition (Englewood Cliffs, N.J., 1952), pp. 437-8.

3

Mediterranean in a strategic as well as a climatic sense".[1] Yet there is a strong desire amongst Caribbean countries to run their own affairs and thus avoid becoming merely a pawn of any of the larger powers. Independence is one of their main objectives. Nevertheless, such power as they may exert will always be limited. The growing number of small nations has little relevance to their influence in the world of power politics. Their admission to the United Nations as members of the General Assembly may give them the semblance rather than the reality of power.

In practice, power today rests with countries which are effectively developed, with a large and virile population, and therefore in the first place with the United States and the Soviet Union. The Western European powers continue to exert influence. Communist China's strength remains relatively unknown and untested, probably still limited although atomic research may alter this position. Undoubtedly a certain size favours industrialization. Nevertheless, some of the smaller democracies, including Switzerland, Sweden, the Netherlands and Belgium, have extremely high incomes *per capita*. They are fortunate in so far as they have wider markets with land rather than ocean boundaries. Much of their success, however, must result from their traditional neutrality.

Although the limited size and resources of most Caribbean countries underline their difficulties, it is significant that a powerful neighbour like Mexico, historically linked to the Greater Antilles, should find it so hard to overcome the same problems: too many people, and too limited natural resources. Industrialization alone cannot quickly provide a solution. It reinforces the argument for concentration on a slowly increasing and better educated population which will stay at home where it is most needed rather than emigrate to the developed countries.

None of the Caribbean countries can aspire to substantial international influence except by building up a moral and intellectual position of leadership and mediation, as Switzerland has done. The utility of their armed forces is not obvious except as an adjunct to their police forces. Otherwise the military may simply become the decisive factor in never-ending power struggles illustrated by the history of Hispaniola and other parts of Latin America. The hope of these nations must rest more and more on international agreement.

The most significant economic development in the Caribbean has been the establishment of the Caribbean Free Trade Association by the

[1] Samuel E. Morison and Henry S. Commager, *The Growth of the American Republic*, 4th edition (New York, 1950), Vol. I, p. 48.

major Commonwealth countries. The purpose of CARIFTA is to encourage trade between the members and particularly the establishment of suitable industry. The successful commencement of CARIFTA may one day lead to closer association with the Commonwealth countries and Latin America. The entry into the O.A.S. of Trinidad, Barbados and Jamaica suggests closer political links in the area. The Commonwealth connection continues and the problems created by Great Britain's entry into the E.E.C. seem likely to be surmounted on a basis acceptable to the Commonwealth Caribbean although not ideal.

The major dilemma in the area becomes more acute: a rise in population more rapid than any apparent opportunities of development. The solution of this problem will be a major task for the 1970's and beyond. Undoubtedly it will involve the developed countries in investment, carefully planned with those countries less developed, to achieve results agreeable to both sides.

Chapter II

CUBA

THE POLITICAL PATTERN

Alone of Spain's American possessions, Cuba and Puerto Rico remained under Spanish rule after all of the mainland territories had won independence. The reasons for this anomaly are varied. The government of Ferdinand VII was no more enlightened in Cuba than in any other part of his dominions. Nor did matters materially improve with his successors. Yet many of the leading citizens of Cuba, planters and officials alike, were very conscious of the disasters of the Haitian revolution, including the perpetration of atrocities and the wrecking of the agricultural economy of that island. This, in turn, may have continued to influence Great Britain, which had intervened, albeit ineffectively, against the Haitian disturbances. Moreover, France had no desire to see a spread of Negro revolt to its remaining Caribbean territories where slavery existed as it also did in the British islands. The Treaty of Vienna had prohibited the slave trade, but the major Caribbean powers did not wish to encourage emancipation in each other's colonies. Thus the *status quo* was upheld.

Naval supremacy in the Caribbean and indeed in the world during most of the nineteenth century gave Great Britain little interest in a change of Cuba's status. Already Britain was beginning to find that its own sugar-producing islands presented problems at a period when the former mercantilist system of a protected market was coming under rising attack from the newer theories of the liberal economists.

Notwithstanding the influence of refugee French planters from Haiti, many of whom had settled in Cuba's Oriente province, and of other refugees from the former Spanish mainland territories who favoured the continuance of Spanish rule, criticism gradually began to increase among Cubans. The dominance of peninsular officials in high administrative positions was a grievance, as it had been earlier in other Spanish territories. Of more significance, Cuba, which in former days had been mainly a supply and garrison base for Spanish America, was beginning to expand its agricultural products, particularly sugar. As the nineteenth century progressed, Cuban output increased, thanks to the large areas of flat land which were suitable for the new system of

6

larger central factories often supplied by light railways. Since Great Britain and France traditionally traded with their own colonies and Europe was expanding sugar beet production, Cuba's natural market was the United States. Spanish interference, often inept, in Cuba's trade with the United States ultimately brought colonial resentment to a head.

The statecraft which had led to the acquisition of Louisiana in 1803 and of Florida in 1805, sought its logical conclusion in Cuba. Many Americans regarded a southward thrust into the Caribbean as inevitable. Under rising pressure against their slave economy, the southern states were attracted to the idea of acquiring a new island similarly organized, which might strengthen their position.

Sporadic and unsuccessful invasions of liberating bands[1] had been followed by the bitter Ten Years' War (1868–78) which settled nothing. Spain was still strong enough to throttle rebellion. Despite the efforts of patriots including José Martí, its grip was not loosened until the armed intervention of the United States proved decisive in the brief Spanish-American War of 1898.

The destruction of Spanish rule in Cuba left the United States in a position of dominance. It had accomplished in less than a year what the weak and ill-armed revolutionaries had failed to achieve in half a century of invasions and rebellion. Despite the announcement by the United States that it would not exercise sovereignty or control over Cuba, the disorganized condition of the island seemed to justify the period of American military control which followed, especially as Leonard Wood proved to be an exceptionally capable governor.

Notwithstanding an overwhelming victory, the Spanish-American War had convinced the United States of the weakness of a fleet split between the Atlantic and the Pacific. If the answer was to be a trans-isthmian canal, Cuba's significance was obvious. The writings of Admiral Alfred T. Mahan emphasized the strategic importance of the Caribbean.[2]

The Platt Amendment to the Army Appropriation Bill of March 1901 established the pattern of U.S. relations with Cuba. Formulated by Elihu Root, Secretary of War, the Amendment made certain that no foreign power other than the United States could tamper with the destiny of the island. In it, the United States reserved the right to intervene in Cuba to protect life, property and individual liberty, and to

[1] Narciso López, a Venezuelan, organized from the United States three quixotic invasions of Cuba in 1848, 1850 and 1851. Cf. Hubert Herring, *A History of Latin America*, 2nd edition, revised (New York, 1961), pp. 403-4.
[2] *The Influence of Sea Power upon History* (Boston, 1894).

preserve the independence of the island to facilitate the defence of the United States including the creation of U.S. naval bases. At first these terms were rejected by Cuba. However, assurances by Root that intervention would take place only in the event of foreign threat or domestic disturbance caused a reluctant Cuba to change its mind. After a new Cuban Government had been formed in May 1902, the Platt Amendment was incorporated in the Cuban Constitution and embodied in the 1903 Treaty between the United States and Cuba. The Treaty also included mutual preferences and incidentally gave Cuba valuable access into the United States for its principal crops, including sugar.

For the United States the Platt Amendment marked "an era of protective imperialism focussed on the defense of an Isthmian canal . . . vital to its naval communications and to its security".[1] While the United States in effect guaranteed the new Republic against outside interference, its provisions imposed a severe limitation on Cuba's sovereignty.

From 1902 to 1934 the Platt Amendment continued to be the dominating factor in Cuba's national affairs and Cuban Presidents were inevitably diverted from the problems of government by the need to keep a watchful eye on the attitude of the American Embassy at Havana. The United States intervened in Cuba from 1906 to 1909 and again in 1912 and 1917. The result was widespread resentment against U.S. control of Cuban affairs. Finally, after the misrule of President Gerardo Machado (1925–33) led to his fall, President Franklin D. Roosevelt, who had Sumner Welles as his adviser in Havana, negotiated a treaty in 1934 abrogating the Platt Amendment, though the provision for a U.S. Naval Base at Guantánamo Bay was retained.

The end of U.S. tutelage proved to be as difficult as it did in the neighbouring republics of Hispaniola. What should have been the beginning of an era of democratic freedom proved to be the prelude to the dictatorship of Fulgencio Batista, even if at first his government gave promise of better things.

The weakness of the civil and military forces in Cuba alone made possible the unlikely advancement of a sergeant clerk in the Army to the position of dictator of Cuba. When Batista's stripes were changed to a colonel's stars, all over the country similar promotions of non-commissioned officers took place. At first moving with discretion, he

[1] Samuel Flagg Bemis, *The Latin American Policy of the United States* (New York, 1943), p. 140. Julius W. Pratt emphasizes that the dominant note in the Caribbean policy of the United States was not "financial imperialism" but "clearly political and strategic rather than economic". *A History of United States Foreign Policy* (Englewood Cliffs, N.J., 1955), p. 413.

Cuba: Cuban troops in action against the mercenary invasion at the Bay of Pigs, April 1961.

Cuba: Fidel Castro just before launching the final attack, Bay of Pigs.

Associated Press

Cuba: the American destroyer *Barry* (foreground) pulls alongside the Russian freighter *Anosov* (presumably carrying a cargo of withdrawn missiles) for inspection in mid-Atlantic, November 10, 1962. Overhead an American patrol plane.

Kosygin welcomed by Castro to Havana, 1967, p. 24.

Associated Press

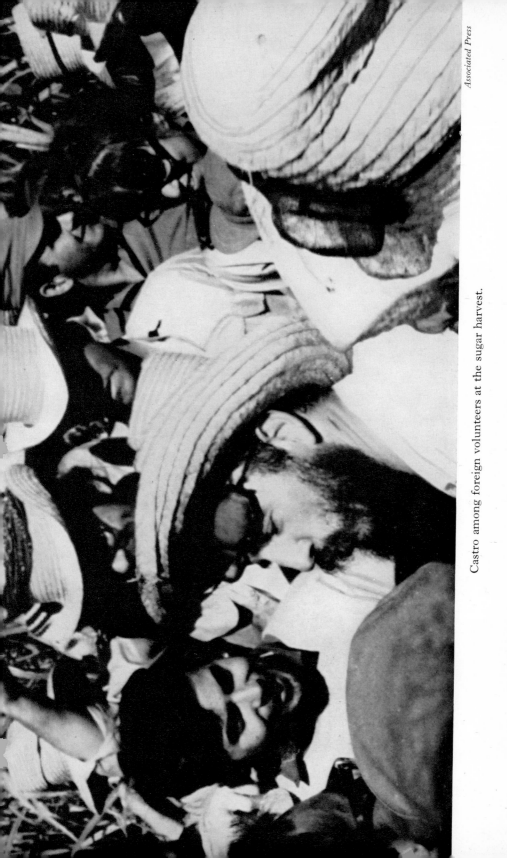

Castro among foreign volunteers at the sugar harvest.

The literacy campaign in Cuba increased the demand for newspapers, pp. 45-47.

relied on the support of the new officers of the Army. Concentrating on public works, he gave Cuba a better government than it had formerly had.[1] He retired in 1944 on completion of his term of office, being succeeded by Ramón Grau San Martín and Carlos Prío Socarrás.

Against a background of dissatisfaction in the island arising from increasing corruption, Batista staged a *cuartelazo* (barracks revolt) and seized the presidency once more in 1952. Although he claimed to advocate democracy, age and experience had not improved Batista's presidential qualities. His second period of rule (1952–59) was marked by tyrannous oppression combined with press censorship. The development of large-scale gambling allied to American organizers enabled Batista to amass a vast fortune. Corruption quickly spread within his regime. Batista and his associates shared in the profits of the new hotels with casinos which opened in the capital. State lotteries, in which the police also had their cut, were extended.[2] As the quality of Batista's rule steadily deteriorated, the traditionally changeable Cuban population ripened for revolution.

On July 26, 1953, a group of students led by Fidel Castro attempted to capture the Moncada barracks at Santiago. The failure ended in the death or capture of its leaders: the survivors were brought to trial. Castro, a lawyer, conducted his own defence when he made a celebrated speech in which he set forth the ideas and objectives of his group. He justified his attempted revolution on the grounds of the right of the people to revolt against injustice while he set out in general terms his philosophy of government, derived more from the Paris of the French Revolution than from modern Moscow.[3] His initial failure might be compared with that of Martí and other nineteenth-century revolutionary leaders.

Castro, imprisoned at the Isle of Pines off Cuba, was subsequently released by Batista. He was thus enabled to collect in Mexico a band of followers for another revolutionary attempt. His December 1956 landing with a small group of companions in Cuba's Oriente Province and his two-year struggle in the Sierra Maestra mountains have certain epic qualities. The story was effectively publicized by Herbert L.

[1] Herring, *op. cit.*, p. 413.

[2] "Certes, Batista n'a pas introduit la corruption dans l'île, mais il l'a organisée au profit de l'armée et de la police, les deux seules forces qui pouvaient faire régner la terreur pour sauvegarder leurs privilèges." Claude Julien, *La Révolution Cubaine* (Paris, 1961), p. 36. The author, who visited Cuba in 1958, formed a similar opinion of the corruption in the island at that time.

[3] "La Historia me Absolverá" (Havana, 1964), Fidel Castro's defence speech at his trial at Santiago de Cuba.

Matthews of *The New York Times*, who interviewed him at his base.[1] That Batista could not destroy the handful of insurgents in the Oriente Province, who at first had very limited public support, displayed the feebleness of the Cuban Government. Even arms supplied by the United States to Cuba, as to many other Latin American countries, were of no avail without men trained and prepared to use them.

Sensing that public opinion was rapidly moving in his favour, Castro's forces dramatically marched through the island towards Havana, encountering little effective resistance. Castro himself remained in the Oriente. On December 31, 1958, Batista fled to the Dominican Republic and his government collapsed. A week later, Castro entered Havana in triumph.

Both Cuban and world opinion hailed Castro as the overthrower of a tyrant. His 26th of July movement made a promising start. Manuel Urrutia Lleó, a former Cuban judge whose independence had brought him into conflict with Batista, was installed as President with Castro as Premier. Although executions of some of the worst of Batista's followers shocked foreign opinion, the promise of honest and democratic government created optimism. Unfortunately, impetuosity and lack of experience soon led into difficulties the new government, largely composed of young men whose chief claim to office rested on a few years of guerrilla warfare in the Cuban mountains.

To implement promises made during the years of Castro's struggle in the Oriente, the National Institute of Agrarian Reform was set up in May 1959. Laws were passed to make it illegal for sugar-mills to own land for growing cane. The size of properties was drastically curtailed. Payments for expropriated holdings would be in Cuban Government bonds. As expropriation was also extended to public utilities, which were often American-owned, as were many of the sugar-mills, relations with the U.S. Government steadily deteriorated.

President Eisenhower would probably have gone a considerable way to reach agreement with the new rulers of Cuba. Too much support for Batista had undoubtedly been given to the dictator by the United States Embassy at Havana. Military supplies had been cut off in March 1958, but a U.S. military mission remained in the island.[2] Stories of the Batista corruption in Cuba had penetrated the United

---

[1] New York, February 24, 25 and 26, 1957. Cf. Herbert L. Matthews, *The Cuban Story* (New York, 1961), pp. 33-9.

[2] A similar apparent inconsistency occurred in Haiti in 1963 when the United States, in protest of the policies of President Duvalier's Government, withdrew its Marine training mission but left its Air Force mission. *Vide* p. 56.

States. Moreover, the image of young men fighting a hated dictator appealed to the American public.

Castro came to the United States in April 1959. The visit was not a State one and there is some disagreement as to how he was received by officials in Washington. However, considerable goodwill was accorded to him by the American public. To the surprise of the Americans, Castro soon made it clear that he had not come for the purpose of discussing aid. Batista had left a bare treasury, but Castro may have decided that he did not wish to become involved in any deals with the United States.

The views of the Castro Government favoured State as opposed to private enterprise. In particular, foreign investment was looked at askance by the new regime as something linked to a colonialism which it was dedicated to abolish. However, Cuban-owned industry and large estates also came under government intervention.

Subsequent pressure against foreign companies, principally American, brought Cuba into collision with the United States. Foreign-owned oil-refineries in Cuba rejected a demand that they process a proportion of Russian oil. Castro's Government replied by taking over the refineries in August 1960.

The seizure of sugar-mills and public utilities further hurt U.S. citizens, by far the largest group of foreign investors. Not unnaturally, the United States protested strongly. Had it failed to do so, a tacit invitation to follow the same confiscatory course would have been extended to other countries in Latin America and beyond.

The Eisenhower Government believed that the standard of living in Latin America could be most quickly raised by foreign investment, including making use, at least in the first stages, of technical skill and knowledge from abroad. American and European capital had made striking contributions to the development of countries from Canada and Mexico to Brazil and Argentina.

The whole basis of continuing investment depends on the confidence of investors, who are the main source of future investment. Apart from those economists who believed that the capitalist system should be replaced by a socialist all-controlling state, the rest of the western democracies broadly agreed with the concept of the Government of the United States. John F. Kennedy's views were not far different on this topic from those of his political opponents. Addressing a Puerto Rican audience in December 1958, just before Fidel Castro overthrew Batista, he said: "Ninety-eight cents of every American dollar spent to purchase sugar from Cuba, for example, is spent by the Cubans to buy American exports. And we can be certain that any vacuum we leave through the instability of our own foreign trade policies will be swiftly filled by the Soviet Union".[1]

A poor island at the end of the nineteenth century, Cuba had advanced rapidly under increased U.S. investment after the overthrow of Spanish rule. Roads and railways were constructed; public utilities were financed. In relation to the period and the potentialities of Cuba, massive capital had been introduced to the island.[2]

Cuba's income *per capita* in 1958 ranked fourth in Latin America; a continuing rise was indicated. As in other Latin American countries, the distribution of wealth was bad because of an inefficient system of taxation. Only in 1870 had Cuba abolished slavery. The lot of the *guajiros* (agricultural peasants) was still one of desperate poverty. Yet, unlike its neighbours Haiti and Jamaica, Cuba had the striking advantage of not being overpopulated.

In short, the Eisenhower Government, orthodox in economic thinking and cautious in action, became increasingly alarmed over events in the island where it had so many historic ties. Vice-President Richard M. Nixon summed up its views: "Recently, there has been much concern expressed from time to time over the danger of Communism, in Cuba particularly, but also elsewhere in the American hemisphere. . . . For Communism to come to any one of the American republics is the very foreign intervention to which the Monroe Doctrine referred."[3]

The expropriations of American property exacerbated relations. Ambassador Philip Bonsal, carefully chosen after the Revolution as an experienced diplomat in what was obviously a key post, made every effort to stem the deterioration of relations.[4] In spite of Bonsal's efforts, relations between the two countries steadily worsened. The patience of the Ambassador reflected U.S. policy: not until July 1960 was drastic action taken by the suspension of the balance of Cuba's U.S. sugar quota for the year. Diplomatic relations were broken in 1961, just before Kennedy took office.

At the same time Cubans were constantly leaving the island for

---

[1] Senator John F. Kennedy, *The Strategy of Peace* (New York, 1960), p. 141.

[2] Cf. Charles A. Gauld, *The Last Titan*, Institute of Hispanic American and Luso-Brazilian Studies, Stanford University, Stanford, 1964, p. 37.

[3] *The Challenges We Face* (New York, 1960), pp. 102-3.

[4] Cf. Philip W. Bonsal, "Cuba, Castro and the United States", *Foreign Affairs*, Vol. 45, No. 2, Council on Foreign Relations, New York, January 1967, pp. 268-9. The author, who had a conversation with him at his Embassy some months after his appointment, was impressed with his fair-minded approach towards the new regime and his friendliness to Castro notwithstanding the difficulties that he had in even seeing him.

exile, often in Miami, a convenient city for them both geographically and climatically. Nixon had suggested in 1959 that the exiles might be used against Batista. It was not, however, until 1960 that the Eisenhower Government directed the Central Intelligence Agency to attempt the organization of the exiles into a body of opposition. By this time the point of view of the Cubans in exile was being modified from that of the original pro-Batista groups by the arrival of disenchanted former supporters of Castro's Revolution. Ultimately some five groups were persuaded to form the vague Frente Revolucionario Democrático.

Following Castro's own successful example of guerrilla warfare, the C.I.A. promoted anti-Castro guerrillas in the Escambray Mountains of Southern Cuba. It was, however, challenging a government which did not lack expertise in the problems of rebellion. Ernesto ("Che") Guevara has brilliantly analysed guerrilla warfare, stressing the need for the opponents to achieve the destruction of each of the components of the guerrilla band.[1] Despite the activity of the guerrillas and the efforts of the C.I.A. to keep them supplied, success was limited.

The C.I.A. needed a more effective plan. Doubtless bearing in mind the experience of the Arbenz affair,[2] the Guatemalan Government, strongly anti-Communist, was persuaded by the C.I.A. to allow the military training of a refugee force to proceed. Clearly secrecy was desirable. Roberto Alejos, who was friendly with President Ydígoras Fuentes of Guatemala, arranged for the installation of a training camp at his Helvetia property, one of the largest coffee estates in Guatemala. He was able to arrange that Guatemalan troops would act as guards to keep out intruders. Money was not lacking any more than it had been in the former C.I.A. affair in Guatemala. To improve the airstrip at near-by Retaluheu, originally used for light passenger planes, $1,200,000 was expended by the C.I.A.[3] Transportation of the Cubans was carried out from airstrips in Florida to Retaluheu as required.

The original plan, for which pilots had been recruited, was to drop small parties of Cubans to reinforce the ailing guerrillas in the Escambray. Practice was not far off, for in November 1960 a portion of the Guatemalan Army revolted and captured Puerto Barrios, Guatemala's principal Caribbean port. The C.I.A.'s B-26s bombarded the rebels, a prelude to the Cuban affair. At least on this occasion the intervention was successful and the revolt suppressed.[4]

[1] *Guerrilla Warfare* (New York, 1961), p. 21.
[2] *Vide* p. 407.
[3] David Wise and Thomas B. Ross, *The Invisible Government* (London, 1965), p. 28.
[4] *Ibid.*, p. 33.

The guerrillas in the Escambray Mountains were making little progress. Instead a project of invasion by the exile troops was canvassed. Meanwhile the veil of secrecy was pierced by Professor Ronald Hilton of Stanford University.[1] Other newspapers in the United States followed, expanding the story of the training camps. Notwithstanding the lack of information in the United States, the existence of the bases was common knowledge in Guatemala.

When John F. Kennedy took office as President, one of his first assignments was a briefing by the C.I.A. on the Cuban project, Eisenhower's parting gift to his successor. The fantastic plan was already in full swing. The hazards were both military and diplomatic. At some future date the trainees would be transported by trucks and planes to a Nicaraguan port where they would remain on another property said to belong to the President of Nicaragua. The omnipresent C.I.A., which had provided air transport from Miami via Retaluheu in Guatemala to Nicaragua, would then assemble its chartered fleet to transport the trainees to the Cuban beach for the invasion attempt. To add verisimilitude to this improbable project, the U.S. Joint Chiefs of Staff of the Services, as well as Allen W. Dulles, Director of the C.I.A., had given qualified approval to the project. Perhaps the most amazing fact is that this plan of invasion was ultimately mounted, more or less as planned.

Kennedy gave deep thought to the project. A shrewd judge of politics, he perceived at once the obloquy which might well arise involving both the United States and his own administration.[2] He insisted that there must be no U.S. military intervention. The President also tried to give a new look to the Cuban refugee groups, more in keeping with his own democratic views. Finally, at the prodding of the C.I.A., the rival Cuban factions selected Dr. Miró Cardona as provisional president. He had been Castro's Ambassador designate to Washington but had resigned.

The President clearly had misgivings over the project both from the practical standpoint of success and still more from the probable international repercussions. However, Dulles pointed out that the Cubans were already trained and determined to go to their homeland. If they were disbanded, they would either disperse, disgruntled, spreading the tale all over Latin America; or else they would have to be brought back to the United States, where the results would be equally embarrassing. Kennedy finally gave his consent for the invasion to proceed.

[1] *Hispanic American Report*, Vol. XIII, p. 593.
[2] An excellent account of Kennedy's meetings over the Cuban invasion project is given by Arthur M. Schlesinger Jr., *One Thousand Days* (London, 1965), pp. 211-70.

Numerous problems arose. The original site proposed for landing was at Trinidad, a small port on the south coast of Cuba. If plans went wrong, the nearby Escambray Mountains afforded a possible asylum for the troops. Ultimately, the remote Bay of Pigs, surrounded by swamps and with only two approach roads, was selected.

The Cuban forces were transported by trucks and air to Puerto Cabezas on the Caribbean coast of Nicaragua. Its Government, no lover of Castro, facilitated the expedition. Meanwhile the C.I.A. assembled its fleet of some half-dozen transports, chartered from a Cuban shipping company in exile. The operation was planned for April 1961, after earlier postponement. Castro, who had knowledge of the preparations and was rapidly expanding his air force with Russian aid, provided the C.I.A. with an argument for swift action. The increasing reluctance of Guatemala to permit the continuation of troop training underlined the need for speed. Open disagreement was expressed in Guatemala in the press and on radio over the invasion project.

A basic part of the plan was the destruction of Fidel Castro's small air force. On April 15, a force of exile-piloted planes attacked with partial success aerodromes where Castro's planes were located. Kennedy cancelled a second strike on April 17, the day of the invasion, at the urging of his foreign policy advisers, despite strong objections from the C.I.A.[1] The B-26s were already lined up at Puerto Cabezas in the small hours with six of Castro's airbases as targets pinpointed by U-2 photographs.[2] Later in the day, Kennedy changed his mind and reinstated the strike; but by then the clouding of the weather prevented the attack. In consequence, the Cuban air force, which included two or three rocket-equipped T-33 jet trainers, did major damage to the invaders. A large part of the ammunition supply was sunk on the freighters *Río Escondido* and *Houston*, laden with supplies. The 1,400 Cuban invaders fought tenaciously against a force which may have reached 20,000. Inevitably they were repulsed and many taken prisoner. The invasion became a fiasco. Probably it never had a chance without strong U.S. support, something which Kennedy from the start had overruled.

In its objectives and execution, the scheme was more suited to the filibustering days of William Walker and "Commodore" Vanderbilt than to the government of the world's major power. It was foisted on an unwilling President in his first months of office when he was working with a team strange to him. Moreover, when he sought to abandon

[1] Theodore C. Sorensen, *Kennedy* (London, 1965), p. 301.
[2] Cf. Wise and Ross, *op. cit.*, p. 53.

the project, he was warned of the adverse publicity involved in pulling out.

The C.I.A. seemed to have organized the training efficiently, but lacked the staff to plan the military invasion. Certainly Kennedy's indecision contributed to a defeat which would probably in any event have occurred. His advisers completely misjudged the strength of Castro in the estimation of the Cuban people. Far outnumbering the critics and defectors from the regime were the thousands who believed in the Revolution personified by their leader. Cuba's army, which was beginning to receive aid from across the Iron Curtain, was probably the most effective military force in Latin America.

Castro had plenty of notice of the preparations for the attack, although he may not have known the exact form it would take, or the precise location selected. The air strike designed to cripple the Cuban air force not only failed to do so but also alerted Castro.

The Bay of Pigs was the biggest disaster of Kennedy's short but distinguished presidency. He courageously accepted full responsibility for the affair. However, he also used the experience to reassess his team. Without the Bay of Pigs, he might have been less well equipped to meet his greatest crisis a year later when he confronted the Soviet Union.

Victory at the Bay of Pigs greatly strengthened Castro's position. He had proved strong enough to crush an attack which had been promoted and clandestinely aided by the United States. The Cuban people had stood behind him. His armed forces had proved their worth. The invasion threat had also enabled Castro to take action against his opponents in Cuba. Many were held under arrest.[1] All were disheartened. The prisoners captured at the Bay of Pigs proved effective hostages in Castro's future negotiations with the United States. Kennedy in particular felt, with justification, a strong personal responsibility for their fate. When Castro threatened to execute his captives, Kennedy exerted the strongest pressure to prevent it. Probably Castro had also now realized that the public executions of certain of his political opponents in 1959 had shocked world opinion, notwithstanding the criminal records of some of them under the Batista regime.

In May 1961, Castro proposed an exchange of the surviving Bay of Pigs prisoners for 500 bulldozers valued at $28 million. The Government of the United States clearly could not be a party to such a deal. However, with Presidential goodwill, a Tractors for Freedom Committee was organized. Political controversy in the United States led to

[1] The Cuban police quickly arrested some 200,000 people in Havana. Schlesinger, op. cit., p. 248.

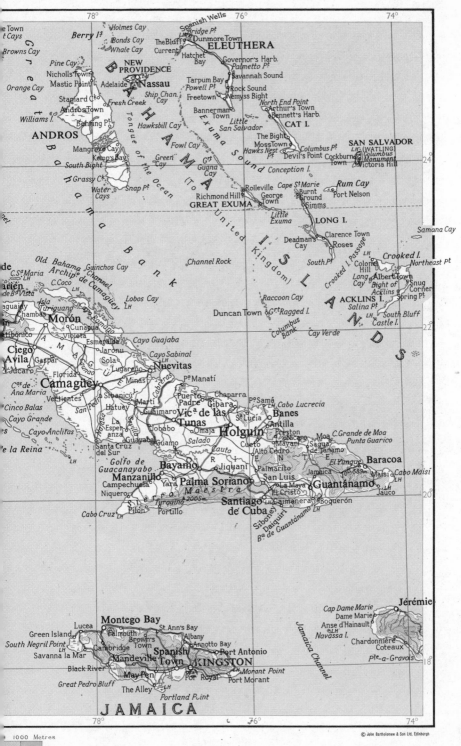

e Town
t Cays
Browns Cay

78°

Holmes Cay
Berry I$
Bonds Cay
Whale Cay

The Bluff
Current

Spanish Wells 76°
Bridge Pt
Little
Dunmore Town

Hatchet
Bay

ELEUTHERA

Governor's Harb.
Palmetto Pt
Savannah Sound

74°

Pine Cay
Nicholls Town
Mastic Point
Adelaide

NEW
PROVIDENCE
Nassau

Tarpum Bay
Powell Pt
Freetown

Rock Sound
Wemyss Bight

Orange Cay
Stanard Ck°
Andros Town

Fresh Creek
Behring Pt

Ship Chan.
Cay

Bannerman
Town

Little
San Salvador

North End Point
Arthur's Town
Bennett's Harb.

CAT I.

Williams I.

ANDROS

Hawksbill Cay

Fowl Cay

Green
Cay

The Bight
Moss Town
Hawks Nest

Columbus Pt
Devil's Point

Cockburn

SAN SALVADOR
(WATLING)
LH Columbus
Monument

24°

Mangrove Cay
Kemp's Bay
South Bight
Grassy Ck.
Water
Cays

Snap Pt

Rolleville
Richmond Hill
GREAT EXUMA

George
Town

Gt
Guana
Cay

Conception I.

Cape St Marie
Burnt
Ground
Simms

Rum Cay
Port Nelson

Victoria Hill

Channel Rock

Little
Exuma

LONG I.

Samana Cay

Deadman's
Cay

Clarence Town
Roses

Old Bahama
Archip.

de
C.Sta Maria
de Bª Vista
LH
C.Coco

Guinchos Cay
Channel
de Camaguey

Lobos Cay
LH

Raccoon Cay

South Pt

Colonel
Hill
Long
Cay

Crooked I. Passage

Crooked I.
Northeast Pt

Bight of
Acklins

Snug
Corner
Spring Pt

arién
aguayi
Isla
Turiguano
Chambas

C.Romano

Duncan Town

Grt Ragged I.

ACKLINS I.
Salina Pt

South Bluff
Castle I.

MORÓN

Cayo Guajaba

Columbus
Bank

Cay Verde

Cunagua
Vibleta

Ciego
Avila
Jucaro
Florida

Gaspar

Esmeralda
Jaronu
Sola
Lugareño

Cayo Sabinal
LH

Nuevitas

Cª de
Ana Maria
Cinco Balas
Cayo Grande

Vertientes

Cayo Anclitas
e la Reina

Minas
Sibanicú
Hatuey

Marti

Camaguey

Guaimaro

Pº Manatí

Puerto
Padre
Guamo

Chaparra
Gibara

Pº Samá
Sta Lucia

Cabo Lucrecia
Banes

La
Esperanza
Guayabal

Vª de las
Tunas

Omaja
Salado

Holguín

Antilla
Preston
Nicaro
Mayarí

Moa
Sagua
de Tánamo

C. Grande de Moa
Punta Guarico

Santa Cruz
del Sur

Jobabo
Cauto

Alto Cedro
Cueto

Baracoa

Golfo de
Guacanayabo
Manzanillo
Campechuela
Niquero

Bayamo

Jiguaní

Palma Soriano

Palmarito
San Luis
La Maya
El Cristo

Jamaica
El Yunque

Maisi
Cabo Maisí

Guantánamo

Cabo Cruz

Pilon
Portillo

Turquino
2005m

Santiago
de Cuba

Siboney
Daiquiri
Bª de Guantánamo

Boquerón
Jauco

Jérémie

Montego Bay
Lucea
Green Island
South Negril Point
Savanna la Mar

St. Ann's Bay
Falmouth
Brown's
Town
Cambridge
Mandeville

Albany
Annotto Bay
Spanish
Town
KINGSTON

Port Antonio

Cap Dame Marie
Dame Marie
Anse d'Hainault
Navassa I.

Chardonnière
Coteaux

Black River
May Pen
Great Pedro Bluff
The Alley

Port Royal
Morant Point
Port Morant

Jamaica Channel

Pte-a-Gravois

18°

Portland Point

JAMAICA

78°

76°

74°

© John Bartholomew & Son Ltd, Edinburgh

1000 Metres

0 3280 Feet

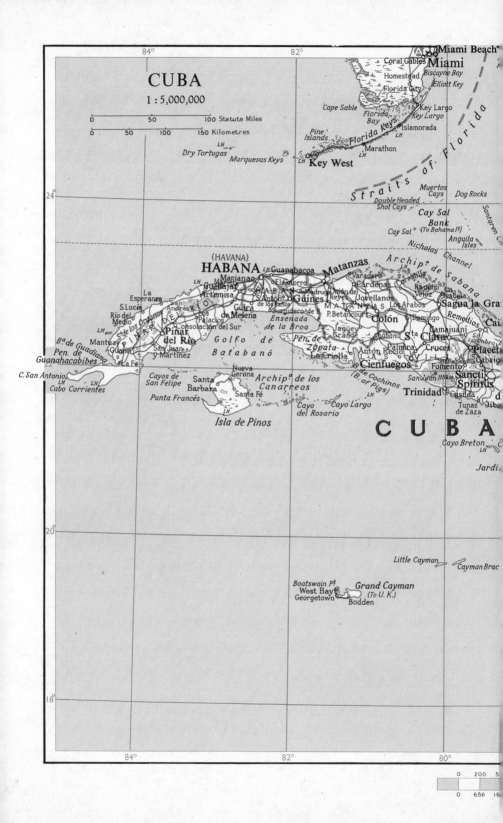

its abandonment. The prisoners were put on trial in March 1962 and finally freed in December of that year in exchange for $52 million of drugs and medical equipment. The series of negotiations had the flavour of ransoms in the Middle Ages. At least a discreditable chapter was at last closed.

Inevitably Castro turned towards the Communist countries. The commercial blockade, instigated by the United States and pressed, not always successfully, on its reluctant allies, compelled a major economic change in Cuba. Castro quickly translated this into politics, using mass meetings as a forum for his views. Meanwhile the Soviet Union encouraged closer relations with Cuba resulting in the military build-up of Russian weapons and personnel in the island.

Nikita S. Khrushchev appears to have decided that the installation of Russian missiles in Cuba would restrain the United States from precipitous military action against Castro's Government at a time when the Cuban economy was clearly deteriorating.[1] The much-heralded policy of industrialization with Soviet aid seemed to be floundering. For both Khrushchev, who was footing the bill, and for Castro, who had declared it to be the cornerstone of his policy, the position was ominous.

About this time, the suggestion of erecting Russian missile sites in Cuba must have been discussed. Castro may have considered they bolstered his defence against possible U.S. attack although the nature of the weapons, six sites for medium-range and three for intermediate-range ballistic missiles, suggests other considerations. Clearly the I.R.B.M.s, with a range of 2,200 miles, double that of the M.R.B.M.s, could cover the larger part of the United States and much of Latin America, as President Kennedy did in due course publish to the world. In all, forty-two missiles, "each one capable of striking the United States with a nuclear warhead twenty or thirty times more powerful than the Hiroshima bomb", were dispatched to Cuba.[2]

The more likely explanation would seem to be that Khrushchev was making a strategic bid to improve his nuclear position vis-à-vis the United States. Ringed by the missile sites of his opponents supplemented by Polaris submarines, the secret installation of a powerful deterrent less than a hundred miles from the United States had obvious attractions. The very dependence of Cuba on Russian aid put Khrushchev in a strong bargaining position. How far he had to use his powers of persuasion to achieve his purpose is not revealed.[3] Castro, however, later told Claude Julien that the Soviet Union had

---

[1] *Khrushchev Remembers*, ed. Edward Crankshaw, (London, 1971), p. 493-4.
[2] Sorensen, *op. cit.*, p. 668.
[3] *Khrushchev Remembers*, pp. 494-5.

made the proposal, not to aid Cuba's defence but to strengthen world socialism.[1]

In July 1962, Raúl Castro, Cuban Minister of the Armed Forces, had visited Moscow. Probably the suggestion to instal missiles was made about this time by the Russian to the Cuban Government.[2] The significance of the decision was increased by the fact that the Soviet Union had never before placed nuclear missiles in any other country, not even in its own satellites. Russian personnel and equipment began to arrive in Cuba at a faster rate.

Every effort to preserve secrecy was maintained during the autumn of 1962 when the sites were being erected. Even when the missiles were on their way to Cuba, Ambassador Andrei A. Gromyko denied to President Kennedy that the Soviet Government had given any assistance to Cuba with offensive armaments while Khrushchev had practised a similar deception on Foy Kohler, the American Ambassador in Moscow.[3]

Kennedy's handling of the crisis was diplomatic, shrewd and well thought out. The erection of the sites was identified from U-2 photographs taken by the U.S. Air Force. On October 16, Kennedy received the alarming information. When the President learnt that a number of Soviet ships were on their way to Cuba carrying offensive weapons, he had various alternatives, including that of mounting an air strike against Cuba.

Ultimately he chose the course of imposing a quarantine on all offensive military equipment under shipment to Cuba. In his announcement of his action, he added that any missiles launched from Cuba would be regarded as an attack by the Soviet Union on the United States, requiring full retaliation upon the Soviet Union. Air surveillance of Cuba would be intensified. The Organization of American States would be convened to discuss the threat to hemisphere security and the Security Council of the United Nations would meet to consider the threat to world peace.

The President's decision was a subtle one.[4] In the Caribbean the United States had overwhelming predominance in conventional military force. If the Soviet vessels continued, they would be stopped by the U.S. fleet. Doubtless the missiles would be seized or at least thoroughly

---

[1] "Ce n'était pas pour assurer notre propre défense, mais d'abord pour renforcer le socialisme à l'échelle internationale." "Sept heures avec M. Fidel Castro", *Le Monde*, Paris, March 22, 1963.

[2] Schlesinger, *op. cit.*, p. 680.

[3] Sorensen, *op. cit.*, pp. 690-1.

[4] Kennedy may have had information which facilitated his decision, *vide* p. 409.

examined, something not desired by the Russians. Khrushchev had no reply except to resort to a nuclear attack on the United States or to move against West Berlin. He dared do neither. His only alternative was to order his ships home.

On October 28, 1962, Khrushchev offered to cease work on the missile sites and to withdraw the offensive armaments to Russia. Moscow had underestimated the speed and intensity of Washington's reaction. The bungling of the Bay of Pigs affair may have given a false impression of Kennedy's capacity for decisive action.

One of the most significant facts in the missile crisis appears in the direct negotiations between the Soviet Union and Kennedy.[1] When the two great powers stood on the brink of war, the Cuban Government appeared to be brushed aside.

Castro, with some justice in the context of international law, was infuriated at a settlement which involved the removal of his major "defences" by an agreement between two other Powers without his concurrence. He declared that he would not accept the settlement without the withdrawal of the United States from its base at Guantánamo in Eastern Cuba. He also refused to permit inspection of the missile sites. U Thant, Secretary General of the United Nations, thereupon proceeded to Havana to confer with Castro on October 30 and 31. At least Cuba's position as an independent country had received belated acknowledgement in the affair.

Castro remained adamant in refusing inspection of the sites. In this he was successful, but at the price of the United States withdrawing the guarantee it had been prepared to give against a future invasion of Cuba.

Events however were too strong for Castro. He could not afford to break relations with the Soviet Union as he had with the United States. Clearly he was not going to make the same mistake twice.[2] The alternative of drawing closer to China offered no solution. A détente with the United States would have contradicted all that he had said. Indeed, the interests of both the Soviet Union and Cuba dictated putting the best face on an even greater fiasco than the Bay of Pigs. The President's personal restraint in victory may have helped to assuage the disappointment of his opponents.

For Kennedy the result of the missile crisis was the apogee of his

[1] The importance of rapid direct contact between the two major nuclear powers was later emphasized by agreement to instal a direct teletype line between Moscow and Washington. Cf. *Khrushchev Remembers*, p. 497.

[2] Cf. Theodore Draper, "Castro and Communism", *The Reporter*, New York, January 17, 1963.

statesmanship: for Castro, in the words of two American writers sympathetic to his regime, "it represented the most humiliating and dangerous point of his leadership of the revolution".[1]

Russia too had suffered. Khrushchev was superseded in the Soviet Union in 1964, to which the Cuban fiasco may have contributed. That Castro survived was a major tribute to the affection and regard in which very many Cubans held him.

In his wrath at the turn of events, Castro had the support of China. For a time he seemed attracted to that country. In the controversies that developed between the Soviet Union and China, Castro displayed considerable skill in remaining unaligned for so long. For the Soviet Union to write off Cuba was not politically practicable, though such a policy might well have had economic attractions at the time. Instead, Anastas Mikoyan, Soviet First Deputy Premier, made a prolonged visit to Cuba in November 1962, to restore damaged relations.

In April 1963, Miró Cardona resigned as chairman of the Cuban Revolutionary Council, the principal body co-ordinating the work of Cuban exiles in the United States. He sharply criticized the United States for its policy of co-existence with Cuba. President Kennedy made clear his views, namely that he did not propose to use military force to overthrow the Castro Government.[2] Commenting from Puerto Rico, where many Cubans had sought asylum, *The San Juan Star* noted the basic differences between the point of view of the exiles who felt that the only way they could return to Cuba was through U.S. military action, and the American Government which was fully conscious of its international responsibilities over this matter which had already in 1962 brought the world to the brink of a nuclear war.[3] The influence of the exiles appeared to have diminished substantially since the Bay of Pigs disaster in 1961.

Cuba moved into closer association with the Soviet Union, but cautiously: the overdependence on the United States before the Revolution had not been forgotten. As a counterpoise, Castro encouraged

[1] Robert Scheer and Maurice Zeitlin, *Cuba: An American Tragedy* (Harmondsworth, England, 1964), p. 249.

[2] Convention of the American Society of Newspaper Editors, Washington, D.C., April 19, 1963.

[3] April 20, 1963. In an interesting article on Miró Cardona's resignation, *Expreso* compared the attitude of the Cuban exiles to that of the Spanish exiles who were prepared to see a world war to displace Franco after his victory in the Spanish Civil War. Lima, April 30, 1963. Cf. *Hispanic American Report*, Vol. XVI, pp. 346-7.

friendly relations with China, although for the period 1961–64 Chinese trade accounted for only some 10 per cent. of Cuba's total foreign trade compared with the Soviet Union's 45 per cent.

As early as 1962, Cuba's economic difficulties had aroused concern in Russia. The chance of establishing a nuclear base in Cuba may have held off pressure by the creditor country. In January 1964, Castro visited Moscow. The time had come for Cuba to concentrate on sugar production and reduce the industrialization drive. Since the U.S. market was closed, sugar purchases by Russia and its allies were crucial.

As the rift between Russia and China deepened, Cuba found it increasingly difficult to continue the neutral position that Castro probably at heart desired. In March 1965, Raúl Castro travelled to Moscow to represent Cuba at the Moscow meeting of Communist parties, an indication of Cuba's alignment.

Increasingly Castro seemed to dominate and lead Cuba's policy. The humiliation of the missile crisis had passed, although it had long rankled. Castro displayed perception of a changing international situation. He was greatly aided by having little permanent attachment to dogma. In some ways he might be compared to an honest *caudillo* in a modern setting, adjusting his own position as circumstances necessitated, yet at the same time managing to give his country an essentially practical lead. Graham Greene wrote of him: "Fidel is a Marxist, but an empirical Marxist, who plays Communism by ear and not by book. Speculation is more important to him than dogma, and he rejoices in the name of heretic."[1] Theodore Draper commented on him: "As a personality he could easily fit into the most contradictory movements, from the extreme Left to the extreme Right, as long as it was *his* movement and the future seemed mortgaged to it".[2] Hernán Cortés, who also launched his career from Santiago de Cuba, would have understood him.

An obstacle to improved relations with the Soviet Union had been the attitude of Guevara, for long second only to Castro in the Cuban hierarchy. He had favoured closer ties with China, an active revolutionary policy in Latin America, and had been highly critical of Russian policy after the missile crisis. In April 1965, he vanished from the Cuban scene. "Guevara's disappearance was a contribution to the resolution of the controversial issues that kept Cuba and the Soviet Union apart."[3] He had been an advocate of the strong line taken by

[1] "Fidel: An Impression", *Weekend Telegraph*, London, December 2, 1966.
[2] "Castro and Communism", *The Reporter*, New York, January 17, 1963.
[3] Daniel Tretiak, *Cuba and the Soviet Union: The Growing Accommodation*, The R.A.N.D. Corporation, Santa Monica, California, 1966, p. 19.

China against the West, while Castro increasingly appreciated the need for bringing Cuba nearer to Soviet policy.

As Cuba drew nearer to the Soviet Union, its relations with China inevitably cooled. Hopes of other Cuban-type revolutions which the Chinese had shared with Castro seemed to have faded. Cuba became increasingly isolated from Latin America.[1]

The success of Castro at the Bay of Pigs had raised his prestige to a point where the moment was suitable to transform the internal organization of Cuba. The opposition had largely been liquidated. Relations between Castro and the Partido Socialista Popular, the pre-Revolution Communist Party, had been ambivalent. When Castro, as head of the guerrilla forces in the Sierra Maestra, had tried in 1958 to call a General Strike against the Batista Government, the Communists had given little support. Only at the end, when Castro was clearly winning, had the P.S.P. openly supported him.

However, Cuba's move towards the Iron Curtain countries suggested the desirability of a single party instead of the loose Twenty-sixth of July Movement manned largely by Castro's comrades in arms and the P.S.P. The new Organización Revolucionaria Integrada was set up for this purpose. It soon became dominated by former P.S.P. members, particularly Aníbal Escalante. The take-over by the old Communists caused considerable discontent among Castro's personal followers and others. By March 1962, Castro, always closely in touch with opinion, decided that the new set-up was working badly. He abruptly exiled Escalante to Czechoslovakia. Castro's strength was shortly afterwards more strikingly displayed when he suddenly forced the withdrawal of Sergei Mihailovitch Kudryavtsev, the Soviet Ambassador to Cuba.

Castro's answer to his internal problems was to organize the new Partido Unido de la Revolución Socialista. Late in 1965 P.U.R.S. became the official Cuban Communist party. Castro's purpose was to weaken the hold of the old Communists by dilution of the membership. Notwithstanding his interest in ideologies, he had also come to realize the importance of having in key positions men who were personally dedicated to him.

In January 1966, the Tricontinental Conference took place at Havana to mark the seventh anniversary of the Cuban Revolution. Official delegations attended from all the Communist countries except Yugoslavia, and some from uncommitted countries, including Algeria. Many delegates of underground and guerrilla organizations were amongst the fifty delegations. The Conference emphasized the split in

[1] *Ibid.*, p. 36.

22

ideology between the Soviet Union and China in regard to the propagation of Communism. If the Cubans hoped, as hosts, to play a mediating role, they were disappointed. Castro originally had favoured militant Communism, much more akin to the Chinese concept. However, for economic reasons, he had moved increasingly towards Moscow, vital financially to his country.[1] Nevertheless, Castro made a considerable impression on the delegates outside the two major Communist countries by his personification of the revolutionary ideal.[2]

In regard to the spread of Communism in Latin America, the Conference did not convey any major advance. The Chinese appeared to be making limited headway in penetrating Latin American Marxism, not necessarily to the satisfaction of the Russians.[3] On the whole, however, progress appeared to be difficult, particularly in Guatemala, Venezuela and Colombia, where the support of the peasants, on whose help the guerrillas had to rely, was often hesitant because of their lack of political organization.[4] Probably the strategy of violence advocated by the Chinese had, in conservative Latin America, only strengthened dictatorial and oligarchical tendencies.[5]

On January 15, 1966, Castro closed the Conference claiming that it had achieved great success. In his militant speech, he denounced strongly the United States for its action in Vietnam and in the Dominican Republic. He also went out of his way to refute the suggestion made in countries hostile to Cuba that Guevara had left Cuba because of disagreement over Cuba's policy towards China. Guevara, he said, had always maintained that when the struggle was completed in Cuba he would have other duties to fulfil in another place. Cuba had promised that it would not hinder him from carrying out that wish.

[1] "Whereas Cuba is not economically dependent on China, she is dependent on Russia: this dependence sets limits to revolutionary nationalism which Castro resents." Raymond Carr, "Cuban Dilemmas", *The World Today*, Vol. 23, No. 1, The Royal Institute of International Affairs, London, January 1967, p. 41.

[2] "Il n'est pas douteux que le chef suprême de la Havane incarne beaucoup mieux que ceux de Moscou ou de Pékin l'idéal révolutionnaire vers lequel tendent les leaders du 'tiers monde' qui n'ont pas encore accédé au pouvoir." *Le Monde*, Paris, editorial, January 18, 1966.

[3] Cf. "Chinese Efforts in Latin America", Latin American Correspondent, *The Times*, London, January 5, 1966. Marcel Niedergang, "A la Conférence de la Havane", *Le Monde*, Paris, January 18, 1966.

[4] Cf. Norman Gall, "Mao-type War in the Andes", *The Observer*, London, January 16, 1966.

[5] Philippe Nourry, "Conférence Précontinentale de la Havane", *Le Figaro*, Paris, January 24, 1966.

In August 1967, following Premier Alexei Kosygin's brief visit in June, Cuba was the scene of the first conference of the Latin American Solidarity Organization. Stressing the slogan that "the duty of a revolutionary is to make revolution", Castro made no attempt to hide his strong support for the guerrilla movements in Latin America and elsewhere. In doing so, he stressed Castroism as an independent force in contrast to more orthodox Communist policy such as presented in Venezuela.[1]

The lack of success of Guevara's exploits in Bolivia followed by his death in October 1967 at the hands of the Bolivian Army symbolized the failure to create revolution in rural Latin America on the Sierra Maestra pattern. Guevara was hailed as a martyr in Cuba but to many revolutionaries outside his missionary zeal spelt only hardship and suffering with little chance of success.[2] The publication of Guevara's Bolivian Diaries instead of glorifying his expedition as it intended actually suggested the futility entailed in attempts by foreigners to launch a revolution in any country.[3] In fact the Bolivian peasants were instrumental in Che's destruction by providing information to their army.[4] The impetus for change by violence moved from the country-side to the cities, inspired by the writings of the Brazilian Carlos Marighella.[5]

Doubts as to the loyalty of former P.S.P. members resulted in another purge in early 1968. Escalante, who had returned to Cuba in 1964, was charged with consistently plotting against the Party leadership, by organizing a microfaction opposed to the Castro Government. He and his followers were accused of having sought support from Soviet, East German and Czech diplomats, not, it appeared, without some justification.[6]

Castro's attitude towards the Soviet Union during 1967–68 did little to suggest to his followers any sort of return to the Soviet fold. Yet surprisingly in August 1968 he supported Russian intervention in

[1] Kevin Devlin, "The Permanent Revolution of Fidel Castro", *Problems of Communism*, Washington, January-February, 1968, pp. 6-7. Cf. Hugh Thomas, *Cuba or the Pursuit of Freedom* (London, 1971), p. 1478 and *The Guardian*, London, editorial, August 11, 1967.

[2] "Bolivia will sacrifice itself so that conditions [for revolution] can be created in neighboring countries. We have to make [Latin] America another Vietnam, with its center in Bolivia." *The Complete Bolivian Diaries of Ché Guevara and Other Captured Documents*, ed. Daniel James, (New York, 1968), p. 16.

[3] Cf. Thomas, *op. cit.*, pp. 1478-9.

[4] *The Complete Bolivian Diaries of Ché Guevara*, pp. 54-55. *Vide* p. 58.

[5] *Minimanual of the Urban Guerrilla*, Spade, n.p., n.d.

[6] Cf. Thomas, *op. cit.*, pp. 1468-9.

Czechoslovakia.[1] During 1969 relationships with the Soviet Union continued to improve. Intense concentration on the ten million ton sugar crop in Cuba gave Castro less time to contemplate further revolution in Latin America. In June the Cuban delegate to the World Conference of Communist Parties in Moscow declared that in any "decisive confrontation" Cuba would be "unyieldingly at the side of the U.S.S.R."[2] In July the visit of a Soviet naval squadron to Havana caused considerable unease. The Soviet Defence Minister, Marshal Andrei Grechko, also went to the island. Fears of a possible Russian naval base in Cuba continued despite denials from Moscow.[3] In October 1971, after his tour of Canada, Kosygin returned to Cuba. He spent four days in the island, and, unlike 1967, was enthusiastically received. Both the Cuban and Latin American pictures had radically changed.[4]

Although he continued to attack apathy and idleness at home, Castro found it difficult to sustain the revolutionary spirit of earlier days. The glamour had worn thin.[5] In addition he was aware of the growing criticism of over-centralization of power. On the Tenth Anniversary of the Committees for the Defence of the Revolution he clearly acknowledged the need to give greater balance to Cuban society.[6] The C.D.R., a unique creation of the Castro regime, to a large extent carried out the numerous campaigns on which the Cuban political and social system depended.[7] Nearly every other adult citizen belonged to a Committee which functioned at a number of different levels. Castro had

[1] Cf. K. S. Karol, *Guerrillas in Power* (London, 1971), pp. 511-12.

[2] Carlos Rafael Rodríguez, June 10, 1969.

[3] A statement was issued by Tass on October 13, 1970, refuting the allegations of a base in Cuba. Foreign Minister Andrei Gromyko speaking at the 25th Session of the U.N. General Assembly stated: "With no grounds whatsoever a propaganda campaign has been mounted about some kind of invented Soviet arrangements in Cuba allegedly jeopardizing the security of the United States. That fabrication has fallen flat too." October 21, 1970.

[4] *The Guardian*, London, editorial, October 30, 1971.

[5] "...motivation without qualifications, youth without experience, enthusiasm without discipline, may make a revolution, but cannot make a state." *The International Herald Tribune*, Paris, editorial, July 28, 1970.

[6] Havana, September 28, 1970. Leo Huberman and Paul M. Sweezy suggested that one of two possibilities open to Castro "would be an attempt to change the character of the relationship between the leadership and the people to the sharing of power and responsibility, in other words, a turn to the Left". They concluded such a course would be difficult involving the mutual breaking of traditional habits and an attack on bureaucratic methods of government such as the Cubans had never known. *Socialism in Cuba*, (New York, 1969), pp. 218-9.

[7] Such as the 1961 literacy drive, health campaigns and lectures, salvage operations, etc.

come to the conclusion that he would have to use these "mass organizations" as a watchdog on the Communist Party itself.[1]

The crux of so many of Castro's problems is that his idealism has
clashed with the materialism of his people. For them such progress
was a basic priority of revolution. Yet the continued effect of Castro's
charisma, increased by his own honest admission of failure in July 1970,
turned to a large extent on his own emotional involvement in his cause.[2]
He remained the "boss" of the peasants and felt tied to them in a very
special way.[3]

Few leaders of our day have received more analytical attention than
Fidel Castro. An extrovert, he enjoys speech-making, meeting people,
and public controversy. By the sheer force of his personality, had he
been born in any other country, he would probably have made his mark
in politics. He will readily stop his car to converse with a group of
admirers in the street in Havana or discuss world politics with a foreign
journalist in the small hours. Castro's magnetic personality has continued to fascinate Cubans; his belief in himself has aided him in
overcoming opposition. He has always believed that he knew best the
course for Cuba to follow. However, Herbert Matthews, a sympathetic
critic, considers that Castro "had no concept of the true meaning of
freedom and democracy and was never to have one".[4]

Angel Castro, Fidel's father, had come to Cuba as an immigrant from
Spain. At first he worked on a United Fruit Company plantation.
Thanks to traditional Galician shrewdness and hard work, he became
prosperous. An interesting comparison is afforded by Cheddi Jagan,
whose father was also an immigrant, and who also worked for an
overseas company. Both Jagan and Castro grew up with strong
antagonism to foreign enterprise in their countries, an antagonism
which may later, when they wielded power, have distorted their judgment. Both were indifferent to economics, depending for their power
on their charismatic qualities and dramatic leadership.

Castro in the Sierra Maestra almost certainly was not a Communist.
True he had, as a young man, participated in the "Bogotazo" riots in
1948, but nothing then or in his Sierra Maestra days suggests that he

[1] Cf. Hugh O'Shaughnessy, "Castro curbs the Party", *The Financial Times*,
London, October 1, 1970, and Charles Vanhecke, "M. Fidel Castro entreprend
de 'démocratiser' la révolution", *Le Monde*, Paris, October 17, 1970.

[2] *Vide* p. 43.

[3] Cf. "Is Cuba a Typical Soviet Satellite?" *Report, An Analysis of Develop-
ments*, ed. Ronald Hilton, The California Institute of International Studies
Vol. 1, No. 2, January 1971, p. 48. A comparison with the late President
Duvalier of Haiti may be made.

[4] *Op. cit.*, p. 163.

was contemplating crossing the Iron Curtain. To the public he had promised elections; to the peasants, land distribution. His views, even in his famous speech at his trial in October 1953, which in its published form may have been rewritten during his prison term at the Isle of Pines, were moderate, advocating a government of popular election.[1]

For some years the United States had bungled its Cuban relations. Batista, whose first administration had some merit, deteriorated disastrously during his second. Unfortunately the United States, with its special relationship to Cuba going back to the Spanish-American War, continued to support the dictator. Some would claim that a similar pattern could be observed in its attitude at different times to dictatorships in the Dominican Republic, Nicaragua, Haiti and elsewhere in Latin America. Professor Frank Tannenbaum perceives here a fatal flaw in the Cuban policy of his country.[2] Theodore Draper comes down cautiously on the same side.[3] He considers it a myth that American policy in 1959 pushed Castro into the arms of the Communists. Perhaps correctly, he suggests that the real flaw in U.S. policy was ineffectiveness.[4]

Some other writers sharply attack American policy of the period. Herbert Matthews states categorically: "United States policy towards Cuba since early in 1960 has been to destroy the Castro regime. This is the key factor around which relations between Cuba and the United States have revolved."[5] He considers that the policy was unwise and without a correct understanding of the situation in Cuba and the extent to which U.S. intervention would be resented in Latin America. C. Wright Mills acidly criticized the United States as being responsible for forcing a Castro who sought to be "olive-green" neutral into the red, white and blue or the red camp.[6]

Varied and often critical comment has come from abroad. An interesting Canadian point of view is put forward by Professor Leslie Dewart, who sees in the Cuban policies of the Eisenhower and Kennedy administrations the overarching purpose to prevent at all costs Cuba's autonomy. He considers that "American diplomacy has preferred

---

[1] Cf. Draper, *Castroism, Theory and Practice* (New York, 1965), pp. 5-8.

[2] *Ten Keys to Latin America* (New York, 1964), pp. 189-90.

[3] Draper comments: "From 1953 to the middle of 1957, the American Ambassador in Cuba was an unabashed admirer and ardent abettor of Batista. His successor was gullible enough to bank on a pledge of Batista to hold 'honest elections' in 1958." *Castro's Revolution: Myths and Realities* (New York, 1962), p. 162.

[4] *Ibid.*, p. 164.

[5] *Op. cit.*, p. 231.

[6] *Listen, Yankee* (New York, 1960), pp. 99-100.

27

Cuba's Communism over Cuba's full emancipation".[1] Perhaps the answer may be that effective and complete independence for a small nation, not least in the Caribbean, is nearly unattainable in our day.

Once Castro had overturned the Cuban Government, a dramatic change had taken place. Undoubtedly the United States, not unsympathetic to Batista's overthrow, none the less failed to adjust its policy to the new situation. The anti-U.S. flavour of the Revolution made the task of Washington hard. To be fair to the Eisenhower Government and subsequent administrations, America had made immense efforts, principally in Europe, to restore the economy of a war-damaged world. Despite the success of the Marshall Plan, animosity to the United States was too often displayed by the very countries which had received aid. Whatever mistakes the United States had made over Cuba in the past, it had at least destroyed Spanish rule, something that, despite the gallantry of a few, the Cubans had been unable to do for themselves. American control of Cuban affairs through the Platt Amendment was an affront to Cuban independence. On the other hand, the economic progress of Cuba in the context of the Latin America of the period was impressive. The United States, however, was learning, as Great Britain had been compelled to do at an earlier date, that world leadership and international popularity rarely go together.

It is at least problematical whether a more dynamic or "golden" approach by the United States would have achieved any better results. Castro was no ordinary political leader. Clearly he did not realize the difficulties which the expansion of Cuban economy presented. His very sincerity of purpose combined with egotism blinded him to the problems; nor was his own lack of experience compensated by the political and commercial knowledge of his principal colleagues.

The passing of more than twelve years since Fidel Castro stormed his way to power makes it possible to survey his country in some measure of perspective. Influenced by its proximity to the United States since the days when some Americans sought to incorporate it in their dream of "manifest destiny", in recent years Cuba has become a political shuttlecock.

To the United States, dedicated leader of the West during the years of cold warfare, the danger of Cuba may have assumed unreal proportions, even if in 1962 the island nearly provided the spark for a world conflict just as had both Serbia and Poland earlier in the twentieth century. Yet that very clash seemed to take some of the heat out of the

[1] *Christianity and Revolution: The Lesson of Cuba* (New York, 1963), pp. 253-4.

confrontation, bringing home to the adversaries the dangers and the futilities of their attitudes. The turning back of the Russian ships in mid-Atlantic was symbolic. President Kennedy, who might have maintained his blockade of Cuba, since his conditions for terminating it had not been fulfilled, in the outcome withdrew it, which caused *The Economist* to say that the President knew not only "how far to go but precisely when to stop".[1]

It would be reasonable to assume that the climax of the U.S.-Russian conflict, so far as it centred on Cuba, has been passed. The reduction in tension occurred at a time of change in the ideological struggle between the East and the West. Russia has run into severe and continuing difficulties with some of its partners, while the N.A.T.O. powers have experienced not inconsiderable problems of their own, touched off by President Charles de Gaulle.

Much of Castro's glamour, which at first he succeeded in projecting far beyond Cuba, has worn thin. The shock of the discovery of rocket sites within range of Latin America as well as of the United States proved a strong antidote to Latin American euphoria, previously induced by the Bay of Pigs affair. More decisive, however, in creating disillusionment was the outcome of Castro's policy. In sharp contrast to the graft and corruption of the Batista administration, the honesty of the Castro Government has been generally acknowledged, as has its effective concentration on education. Nevertheless, the censorship of newspapers, the refusal to hold elections, the lack of a permitted opposition within the country, and the forced-labour camps, have made it clear that his Revolution has not introduced democracy to Cuba.

The Russian and Cuban concepts of revolution are different, even if circumstances press them together. Throughout, Castro, not necessarily less ardent than the Soviet Union in seeking to extend his Revolution beyond his island's shores, has sought to maintain political independence. The memory of the Platt Amendment is embedded in Cuban minds. No less basic are the different points of view of the Cuban and the Russian. In the early days of the Revolution, Jean-Paul Sartre perceived that Cuba took neither Russia nor China as its model.[2] Castro expressed a similar attitude claiming the importance of Cuba developing its own criteria.[3] No one would deny that he is a frank and outspoken critic on all topics and all countries.

[1] London, November 3, 1962.
[2] "Mas, de *forma alguma*, não se deve confundir esta transformação social com aquela que levou Lenine ao poder, nem mesmo com a que forjou a China de Mao Tse-tung." Introduction to the Brazilian edition, *Furacão Sôbre Cuba* (Rio de Janeiro, 1960), p. 8.   [3] Havana, August 29, 1966.

Politically Castro has continued to survive, notwithstanding the distance from his Soviet base. He has even managed to retain a bridge with Communist China, despite the fact that Russian financial aid has kept his island afloat. How much the Soviet Union has gained from its continuing and costly support is questionable. In some ways, the position might be compared to that of a semi-beleaguered West Berlin.

To assess Castro's present popularity is difficult. In typical Communist fashion he uses the mass media simply to bolster the reputation of his regime and to denounce enemies and rivals. His policy of permitting disillusioned Cubans to depart to the United States has certainly in the short run reduced the numbers of his bitter critics.

Castro's youth when he came to power in 1959 has stood him in good stead. He can still pose as a vigorous man in an age which adulates youth. For anyone who has watched him among the public, his electioneering talent is outstanding. In a country notoriously fickle towards its leaders, he remains ensconced in power. Yet time may erode his greatest asset—the contrast of the honest leader as opposed to the Batista image.

How far his much vaunted educational development has succeeded is hard to verify. The campaign to eliminate illiteracy was dramatic and well publicized. Yet the long-term development of Cuban higher education in an increasingly technical age appears to move slowly.

In the realm of foreign affairs, Guevara's dramatic failure in Bolivia marked a turning-point in guerrilla warfare. The deified warrior has oddly brought about a complete change in revolutionary methods. How far the activities of the urban guerrillas will result in regimes more sympathetic to Cuba remains to be seen. The failure of the Alliance for Progress and the weakening of U.S. influence may result in a climate more favourable to Cuba. Chile renewed diplomatic relations with Cuba in 1970 and some other Latin American countries may follow.[1] The economic importance of such renewed relations would necessarily be limited.

Prime Minister Eric Williams of Trinidad and Tobago suggested a renewal of economic ties with Cuba.[2] The possible interest in some Commonwealth Caribbean countries in establishing closer relations with

[1] *Vide* p. 429. Those Latin American countries opposed or at least ambivalent to the easing of sanctions against Cuba included Argentina, Brazil, Guatemala, Paraguay, Uruguay and Venezuela.

[2] Inter American Economic and Social Council Meeting, Caracas, February 3, 1970. Cf. Neville Linton "Regional Diplomacy of the Commonwealth Caribbean", *International Journal*, Toronto, Spring 1971, pp. 415-6.

Cuba has arisen partly through the problem of a substantial number of their nationals resident in the island.

Basically the United States and the Soviet Union appeared to continue the unwritten agreement following the missile crisis of 1962. The United States replaced its sugar imports from Cuba with a minimum of difficulty. To buy once more from Cuba would present far greater problems, for the Cuban quota has been parcelled out among many needy countries.

The blatant democratic failure of Cuba which did not even pretend to have a system of elected government, and which had a rigidly controlled press with prison camps in the background, effectively thwarted any attempts to extend the Castro Revolution even to neighbours so poorly administered as Haiti. For the present Castro reigns supreme as a modern *caudillo*, but his popularity with a large part of the population of Cuba seems to have diminished, quite apart from the thousands who have left the island. He has made no adequate provision for his succession.

Probably more than in any other Communist country, the army dominates Cuba. It is Castro's instrument of power. Almost symbolically, his brother, Raúl, heads it. In size it is over 100,000 strong, exceeded in Latin America only by Brazil and Argentina, both vastly larger in area and population. In arms it is well equipped. Castro, who normally appears in uniform, clearly uses it as a political balance to prevent the Cuban Communist Party from impinging on his power. Even the not over-effective Central Committee of the party is well flavoured with army veterans. Perhaps inevitably, the Spanish tradition, implanted in Latin America, of government based upon and linked to the army in support of a dictator has emerged from the turmoil of the revolution which was originally set in motion to bring democratic power to the people and to protect the peasant. The bond with Russia became a necessity because of economic weakness.

The image of Cuba as a modern Socialist country continues to fade. Failure of the public to participate in the country's government, combined with economic failure, has compounded the disillusionment. More and more the impression of one man Government has emerged even if its presentation to the world is under a modern guise. The United States has adopted towards Cuba an attitude of indifference. Its tourists moved to Puerto Rico or the Commonwealth Caribbean. The Soviet Union, which has the thankless and unprofitable task of financing Cuba, appears to be disillusioned. It has attempted to press more economic guidance upon the island. Recognition by some Latin American countries might improve Cuba's political image, but any

31

significant commercial gain in trade would seem to be unlikely. At best the outlook for Cuba remains obscure.

THE ECONOMIC PATTERN

The importance of colonial Cuba derived mainly from its geographic position covering the approaches to the Panama mule-route and the gulf ports of Mexico, particularly Veracruz, and nearby Florida. Precious metals, not farming, obsessed the minds of the Spaniards. Cuba had little to offer, though Havana provided a market for agricultural produce. Not even the spectacular success of nearby Saint Domingue's sugar plantations caused the Spaniards of the eighteenth century to emulate their French neighbours. Spain preferred to leave international trade to others. The selling of sugar on a world scale had little appeal. In any event the mercantilist system of the day imposed severe restrictions.

The brief occupation of Havana by the British, which had temporarily broken the Spanish trade monopoly with the island, had made Cuba aware of the commercial advantage of international shipping, but restricted trade returned with the resumption of Spanish rule two years later. French immigrants who left Haiti after the slave uprising of 1791 to settle in Cuba's Oriente helped to stimulate agriculture. The growing market for sugar in the United States during the nineteenth century encouraged Cuban trade and fanned the island's rising dissatisfaction with the centralized rule of Spain.

American investments in Cuba greatly increased after the Spanish-American War, and the period of American dominance over Cuba was economically productive. Aided by a protected position in the American market in return for which Cuba gave preference to U.S. goods, the large centralized sugar-mills made Cuba the world's greatest exporter of sugar. Excessive reliance on one commodity unbalanced Cuba's economy, particularly as the sugar market maintained its fickle and erratic tradition; yet without the injection of foreign capital, Cuba's economy could not have expanded so rapidly.[1] Containing more than half the land area of the Antilles, much of it reasonably level, the island's agriculture nevertheless should have been more diversified.

The corruption which stained the island's administration involved foreign companies as well as Cuban nationals, yet Cuba can hardly

---

[1] In 1900 Cuba produced less than half a million tons of sugar. By 1919, aided by World War I, it had increased to 4 million tons, rising by 1930 to 5 million tons. The economic crisis of 1931 reduced this to 2 million tons in 1933. James, *op. cit.*, p. 765.

Cuba: Plaza de la Revolución, Havana, January 2, 1967: the Eighth Anniversary of the Revolution.

Associated Pres

Castro, accompanied by President Salvador Allende, acknowledges an enthusiastic reception on his arrival in Chile, November 1971.

Cuba: a new school, part of the San Andrés Valley development, Pinar del Río. The Secretary General of the local Communist Party (right) with the author and a group of school children.

Autho

lay the major blame for its economic shortcomings on foreigners. The Cuban people failed to provide an effective system of taxation, an honest civil service, or an imaginative economic policy to diversify its economy, including agriculture. Many underdeveloped *latifundia* contributed to the difficulties. But despite these shortcomings, industry continued to expand and new factories were opened.

In assessing the take-over of Cuba by Castro, it is important to appraise pre-Revolution Cuba. From an economic point of view, the island had, prior to the Revolution of January 1959, one of the highest standards of living in Latin America, even if by U.S. and Western European standards it was low. Wealth, however, was very unevenly distributed among the population.[1] Certainly the country depended far too much on sugar; unfortunately, most underdeveloped small countries tend to be monocultural, not least in the Caribbean. Sugar-mills normally work for about half the year only, although cane cultivation requires substantial labour even out of crop. Moreover, Cuban capital in the sugar industry was increasing at the expense of American capital, which from having controlled 55 per cent. of the total production in 1940 had already fallen to 40 per cent. on the eve of the Revolution. Compared to the problems which countries such as India and Brazil had to resolve, Cuba's problems were relatively simple.[2] However, to the revolutionary elements, Cuba's economy with its wealth, tourists and gambling was the symbol of plutocratic foreign domination. To the youth of Cuba, mainspring of the Revolution, the anti-Yankee cry appealed. Although the overthrow of a cruel and ruthless dictator was the apparent objective of the Cuban Revolution, it was in fact also a declaration of independence from the United States; as it were, the expression of the views of José Martí in the context of the twentieth century.[3]

The development of the Cuban tourist industry presents interesting

[1] The income *per capita* in pre-Castro Cuba in 1955 was about $365. *Ibid.*, p. 764. Cf. Boris Goldenberg, *The Cuban Revolution and Latin America*, Library of International Studies (New York, 1965), pp. 132-3.

[2] Raymond Aron, "Fidel Castro et sa révolution", *Le Figaro*, Paris, March 7, 1961.

[3] The idea of liberation from U.S. dominance was increasingly stressed by Castro and his colleagues in subsequent years. In an interview given by Castro to P. Satiukov, the chief editor of *Pravda*, and to A. Adzhubei, the editor of *Izvestia*, he was asked: "What Comrade Prime Minister, are the greatest results of the three-year growth of the Cuba Revolution?" The answer was: "The chief, the most important . . . is the national liberation, complete national sovereignty. Cuba was liberated from the tutelage of American imperialism. This is the most important achievement of the revolution." *Pravda*, Moscow, January 29, 1962.

features. Prohibition in the United States gave tourism a strong forward urge, although its repeal in 1932 ended this impetus. In the post-war years, the National Tourist Commission of Cuba provided statistics indicating an increasing tourist trade which rose to $39 million in 1949. On the other hand, the International Bank Report[1] agreed with travel business experts that the Tourist Commission estimates were too optimistic and that tourism was static or even receding in the period 1946–49. Much of the Cuban tourist accommodation outside of Havana and Varadero Beach was unsuitable for foreign tourists. Some of the most beautiful parts of the island such as Pinar del Río and Oriente had very limited accommodation.[2] The report stressed that, despite a perfect winter climate and some of the finest beaches in the world, Cuba had failed to develop sufficiently what it had.

However, these considerations were soon to become academic. The Revolution, followed by the almost complete severance of air routes with North America and the heavy drop in cruise ships calling at Cuban ports, put an end to the tourist business. Instead, the luxury hotels of Havana were filled with delegations, often from Iron Curtain countries.

The advent of the Castro Government had the most far-reaching effect on Cuba's economy. In the first place, the new government was dominated by young men, mostly without experience of economics. Castro himself was a lawyer. Guevara, his right-hand man, was a medical doctor from Argentina. Raúl Castro had had no economics training. The team technically was not a strong one.

Economic considerations were subordinated to political aims. The new rulers believed that the influence of the United States had to be broken quickly and regardless of consequences. The implications of this policy were not fully perceived. As tension between the neighbouring countries deepened, with no improvement resulting from the change of U.S. administration, the impact of this quarrel on Cuba's trade increased. Before the Revolution, Cuba's exports to the United States had been 63 per cent. of its total, with the United States providing 74 per cent. of Cuban imports. The island clearly had to consider the re-orientation of its trade, implicit in Castro's Havana speech of December 2, 1961.

Following negotiations with the Iron Curtain countries, Cuba had

---

[1] *Report on Cuba, 1950*, International Bank for Reconstruction and Development (Johns Hopkins Press, Baltimore, 1951).

[2] "In a great many cases, sanitary arrangements, cleanliness and food would not be acceptable in a sub-standard American hotel." *Ibid.*, p. 767.

since 1960 initiated a policy of establishing new industries, purchasing machinery from behind the Iron Curtain. As always in an under-developed country, the choice of the most suitable ones proved trouble-some. Soon the experiment ran into great difficulties. Mistakes arose from lack of precise understanding of the technological and economic factors necessary in the new factories installed. The need for substitut-ing imports and for providing employment led the Cuban Government to acquire a large number of factories. Guevara later frankly admitted the failure of his plans.[1] "We found that in many of these plants the technical efficiency was insufficient when measured by international standards, and that the net result of the substitution of imports was very limited, because the necessary raw materials were not nationally produced."[2] As the deals were largely on a barter basis, hard currency, formerly available to Cuba from sugar sales to the United States, became scarce. Most countries supplying machinery wished cash against shipment. A few transactions were aided by Government credit guarantees, as in the case of Great Britain, but these were exceptional. Castro was learning that the path of a small country seeking to industrialize is a thorny one, especially when it is separated by great distances from its political friends and on bad terms with a powerful neighbour.

The Castro Government, fresh from its revolutionary successes against the Batista regime, found itself in accord politically with the active and aggressive Chinese policy. Economics, however, were probably decisive in causing Cuba ultimately to side with Russia in the ideological quarrel which began to rage between the two Iron Curtain countries. China lacked the financial resources and the industrial skills of Russia and its European satellites. Cuba, nevertheless, for long showed great dexterity in steering a middle course between the two major Communist powers.[3]

By the beginning of 1962, Cuba's economic problems were becoming clearer after the near chaos of the first three years of Revolution. The island's budget estimated expenditure at 1,853 million pesos. Since 400 million pesos were unaccounted for, the missing figure might be for defence. Education had an appropriation of 238 million pesos.

Feeling perhaps that the time had come to reduce his detailed work, Prime Minister Fidel Castro gave up to Carlos Rodríguez, one of

[1] *Hispanic American Report*, Vol. XV, p. 707.
[2] Ernesto ("Che") Guevara, "The Cuban Economy", *International Affairs*, Vol. 40, No. 4, The Royal Institute of International Affairs, London, October, 1964, pp. 595-6.　　　　　[3] *Vide* p. 20.

Cuba's top Communists, the post of President of the Instituto Nacional de Reforma Agraria.[1] The change may have lacked significance since already in 1961 I.N.R.A.'s industrial functions had been transferred to the Ministry of Industries.

Meanwhile shortages of foodstuffs and other commodities had begun to appear in the summer of 1961.[2] The Cuban economic picture further darkened on February 8, 1962, when President Kennedy imposed a complete embargo on U.S. trade with Cuba, apart from medical supplies and certain foodstuffs. The effectiveness of the American action, however, was weakened by Kennedy's failure to persuade his N.A.T.O. allies to align their policies with that of the United States. Western Europe and Japan supplied about one-fifth of Cuba's imports. In the first ten months of 1961, Canada's exports to Cuba had been $24 million, or double the 1960 figure. Quite apart from reluctance to abandon profitable trade, some of these countries, including Great Britain, France and Canada, were sensitive to criticism of being deemed subservient to U.S. policy. Indeed, continuing disagreements over economic policy towards Cuba may have contributed to the problems which were increasingly to cause dissension between members of N.A.T.O.

In March 1962, Castro was forced to announce rationing of vegetable oil, butter, rice and beans, which he attributed to the U.S. economic blockade.[3] Some of Cuba's problems were, however, directly attributable to internal errors of judgment. Guevara, always outspoken, pinpointed the shortcomings of Cuba's economic planning. He claimed that the targets set up had been absurd, and the programme overwhelmed by bureaucracy.[4] The mistakes were not surprising considering the youth and inexperience of Castro's comrades in arms, though some of the old-guard Communists in the Government had previous administrative training in Batista's first administration.

In a report written in March 1962, Guevara insisted on more discipline in industry and attacked absenteeism. He also criticized inferior quality goods and low production in the rubber, shoe, clothing and other industries.[5] At Havana he called for 40,000 technical workers during the coming four years and again stressed the need for better

---

[1] Rodríguez had been editor of the Havana daily *Hoy*. In 1961 he had been appointed head of the Junta Central de Planificación, Cuba's central planning commission.

[2] Draper, *op. cit.*, p. 133.

[3] Lard and fats had already been rationed in July 1961.

[4] *Hispanic American Report*, Vol. XV, p. 225.

[5] *Ibid.*, p. 707.

quality manufactured goods.[1]   Relentlessly he demanded efficiency, especially from the nation's youth.[2]

Claiming that the public appreciated the need for rationing and supported it, the Cuban press urged increased agricultural production.[3] Although noting that Cuban leaders had been criticizing errors committed in the development of agriculture, *Pravda* congratulated Cuba, the "first free territory of Latin America", as being a magnificent example of a country which had ended "Yankee imperialism" to become master of its own destinies.[4]   Nevertheless, the dangerously monocultural economy of Cuba was moving into a crisis which threatened the nation's stability.

At the National Cane Workers meeting at Santa Clara in May 1962, Guevara admitted that the harvest, hampered by sabotage in the canefields, had been bad. He also commented on the manpower, technical and mechanical difficulties in the sugar-mills and the overall disorganization in the industry.[5]   In anticipation of a poor crop, Cuba was holding back a half-million tons of sugar originally destined for Eastern Europe. Serious technical difficulties arose due to the nationalization of sugar-mills and large farms which involved changes in management. The loss of skilled personnel was added to ever-growing problems over the replacement of worn-out machinery and the obtaining of spare parts. The psychological effect of the Government's policy of rapid agricultural diversification, which drew off cane-cutters, had damaged the morale of Cuba's largest and formerly most efficient industry.[6]

Mistakenly believing that new industries would quickly solve Cuba's commercial problems, Guevara was engaged in establishing new factories imported from Soviet-bloc countries. Although he remained

[1] "Sin calidad no se puede competir en el mercado mundial donde simplemente ahí va lo mejor a precio de competencia; pero además calidad es lo que tenemos que darle a nuestro pueblo." *Hoy*, Havana, April 17, 1962.

[2] This theme dominated his speech on the eleventh anniversary of the Juventud Cubana at Havana. *Revolución*, Havana, October 22, 1962.

[3] "El pueblo entero ha comprendido que nuestra tarea esencial es incrementar aceleradamente la producción—en primer lugar la producción agropecuaria—y se dá a ella con entusiasmo y decisión." *Hoy*, Havana, April 7, 1962.

[4] Moscow, April 11, 1962.

[5] La Plenaria Provincial Azucarera de la Habana decided to press the mobilization of cane-cutters to overcome the daily shortfall of production in the Province of La Habana. *Hoy*, Havana, April 7, 1962.

[6] In a frank and critical speech to the Plenaria Nacional Azucarera, on July 18, 1962, Carlos Rafael Rodríguez analysed in detail the mistakes which had contributed to the poor harvest, including lack of attention to cane cultivation.

optimistic over Cuba's economy and talked of developing a steel industry with the aid of Soviet credit as well as nickel, petroleum, electric power and shipping projects, he admitted the lack of training and organization in industry. At Havana University in May, Guevara urged the importance of training students in technology who could work for the Ministry of Industries while continuing their studies.

With a production of 4,800,000 tons, the 1962 sugar crop, nearly 2 million tons below that of 1961, confirmed the predictions of the pessimists. Castro criticized irresponsible officials for taking small farms away from their owners, while Rodríguez blamed the exodus of workers to better paid city jobs.[1] The Cuban Government banned 150,000 street vendors, although it promised to subsidize them until they found new jobs. The speculations of this group were held to aggravate scarcity and raise prices.

Mounting agricultural problems turned the active minds of the Cuban leaders to basic problems of the land. Whatever might have been said in Sierra Maestra days about distributing land for peasant holdings, the difficulties of such a programme were becoming increasingly obvious.[2] The Cuban Government had organized a dual system of State farms which were normally large, and of co-operatives for the peasant smallholders. In a period of rapidly changing agricultural techniques, survival in world markets depended on efficient production. The small co-operative producer of sugar or other crops could never be competitive in the revolution which since World War II had not only transformed, but had also complicated, tropical farming. The importance of the individual farmer, recognized in Western Europe and also in many Caribbean countries as a stabilizing political factor, made little appeal to Rodríguez or Guevara, both convinced Marxists. The initial land distribution had been a political gesture to fulfil the promises of the Revolution.

Cuba's international difficulties were reflected in the economic field. Its request in August 1962, to be admitted to membership of the Latin American Free Trade Association, met with strong opposition from five of the nine members. Undoubtedly the increasing participation of Soviet-bloc countries in Cuban trade was making an impact on both Latin American and U.S. opinion.[3]

[1] In Matanzas province, for example, fifty-five small farms had been nationalized under the Castro regime. *Hispanic American Report*, Vol. XV, p. 511.

[2] *Vide* pp. 327-8.

[3] For example, in August 1962, Cuba signed an agreement with the U.S.S.R. under which the U.S.S.R. would train 2,000 Cuban fishermen with the aid of five 750-ton Soviet fishing-boats.

Cuba's trade was largely carried on by ships flying the flags of America's allies. For example, in August 1962, Greek, British, Norwegian and West German ships provided 61 per cent. of the individual voyages. Denmark, Japan, Spain and Sweden were also significant participators in this trade.[1] The United States quietly kept pressure on its N.A.T.O. allies to stop shipments to Cuba, but only West Germany, Turkey, and finally Greece were responsive. Great Britain and Norway said that they could not control private shipping. In the United States, however, flag-of-convenience shipping companies with their Liberia and Panama registered vessels, promised to end trade with Cuba.

Notwithstanding the difficulties of 1962, President Osvaldo Dorticós claimed, in January 1963, that Cuba's economic growth since the 1959 Revolution had been 30 per cent. One-half of the country's arable land was under some form of socialist cultivation, while industrial production was 90 per cent. nationalized. The President claimed a fall in the numbers unemployed from half a million in 1958 to 220,000 in 1962.

In fact, U.S. policy towards Cuba was steadily changing from military pressure to the stepping up of economic sanctions. Pressure was increasingly exerted on foreign shipowners to abandon trade with Cuba under the threat of ineligibility to carry U.S. Government cargoes.[2] Inevitably Cuba turned more and more to the Iron Curtain countries as the largest and most reliable available source of economic aid and market for its exports. However, Western European countries continued to trade on a restricted scale with Cuba, as did Canada and Japan.

Notwithstanding a measure of success from Castro's visit to Russia in April 1963, his country's difficulties mounted. In July, the U.S. Government froze Cuban assets in the United States and prohibited dollar transactions with Cuba. The United States was pursuing a policy of making the support of Cuba by Iron Curtain countries as expensive as possible.[3] Cuba was believed to be costing Moscow a million dollars a day to support. The expanding black market was moreover tarnishing Castro's claim to have replaced the corruption of the Batista regime with one of honesty. If Russia had aided Cuba

---

[1] Henry J. Taylor, "Our Allies should Think Twice", *New York World Telegram and Sun*, New York, October 10, 1962. Cf. *Hispanic American Report*, Vol. XV, p. 802.

[2] "Blacklist Amended to Aid Shipowners", *Journal of Commerce*, New York, December 17, 1963.

[3] Henry Raymont, "U.S. Allies Resist Strong Cuba Curb", *The New York Times*, New York, July 16, 1963.

by increasing the price it paid for sugar, it was also pressing its Cuban debtor to reorganize the faltering island economy. Former President Manuel Urrutia Lleó claimed that as socialism advanced in the island, national production had declined, and that this was responsible for shortages and rations.[1]

Perhaps the most important result of Castro's first visit in 1963 to Russia was that he returned apparently more than ever convinced that the policy of rapid industrialization in Cuba had failed dismally and must be delayed at least for several years. Castro was in effect echoing the point of view first put forward by Guevara who although clearly appalled by the initial difficulties and failures in Cuba's industrialization policy, yet foresaw opportunities for success in the future. No doubt the Russians too were becoming increasingly apprehensive over the mounting Cuban problems which left them in the uncomfortable and costly position of being the major creditor in an enterprise five thousand miles away which was floundering.[2]

Castro may also have been disappointed with the support which he had been receiving from the Soviet bloc. True, he had obtained aid without which his regime must have collapsed; but countries like Ghana, Egypt and Algeria had been able to obtain financial support from both sides of the Iron Curtain. Algeria in particular seemed to interest Castro; and President Ahmed Ben Bella visited Cuba. The policies of the two countries had much in common, although Algeria had been subtler in its diplomacy with the two great power blocs.[3]

The lessening of Soviet interest in Cuba was manifested in the limited aid offered by Russia to Cuba after its eastern provinces of Oriente and Camagüey had been devastated by a hurricane in 1963. Food supplies were seriously damaged, causing intensified problems of rationing.[4] Of greater significance, Russian personnel in Cuba had dropped by the autumn of 1963 from more than 20,000 to below 10,000. So far, a Communist experiment of over four years had brought little satisfaction to anybody. To the United States it had been a period of

---

[1] "Cuba está en ruinas", *Diario Las Américas*, Miami, July 7, 1963.

[2] Sanche de Gramont, "Cuba al Borde del Desastre", *Listín Diario*, Santo Domingo, Dominican Republic, December 11-16, 1963.

[3] Jean Daniel compares the two countries from the political and economic standpoint. "Ben Bella and Castro", *The New Republic*, Washington, D.C., October 5, 1963.

[4] "Cubans Wait for Their Number to come up", The Latin American Correspondent, *The Times*, London, November 28, 1963.

continued and costly trouble punctuated with crisis. To the U.S.S.R., financial backer of Cuba, it had involved pouring money into the apparently bottomless abyss of Castro's disorganized economy. For a large part of the Cuban people, especially in the cities, the Revolutionary years had involved hardship and disappointment, including the frustrating change of dependence from one foreign master to another.[1]

Apart from that of Mexico, Latin American diplomatic missions in Havana had departed. To Switzerland fell the task of representing many countries which had broken relations with Cuba. Airline traffic evaporated until only one uncertain service to Mexico remained on the many air routes which had formerly linked Cuban airports with the Americas. Visitors to Cuba might even find it quicker to travel to Madrid or Prague in order to reach Havana.

Prime Minister Fidel Castro made a lengthy speech in Havana on January 2, 1964, commemorating the fifth anniversary of the Revolution. While defiant towards the United States, he made it clear that he would be prepared to trade with it. No response being forthcoming, Cuba signed in May of the same year a supplementary commercial protocol agreement with the U.S.S.R. which would raise trade between them to $750 million per year, an increase of more than 40 per cent. over 1961. Russia would supply industrial and agricultural equipment, wheat, maize, beans, fats, canned meat and milk, as well as petroleum derivatives, metals, chemical products and textiles.

By the end of 1964, the economic pattern of Cuba's development had become clearer. Notwithstanding intense effort and effective propaganda, the plan for the swift industrialization of the island had failed. After five Revolutionary years, the island's efforts to extricate itself from the toils of an economy of monoculture dominated by a foreign power had not succeeded. The United States had indeed been discarded. Nevertheless, Cuba's former principal trading partner seemed to be heading for ever greater expansion and affluence while Cuba continued to tighten its belt. The attempt of the island to escape from its agricultural strait-jacket had clearly failed. The U.S.S.R., which had attained a position of economic dominance on the island not less than the former American hold, was clearly perturbed at the cost of financing Cuba. In the outcome Moscow had advised concentration at least for the present on agriculture, which meant in practice a return to sugar.

Of even more importance, Cuba's propagandistic value in spreading Marxist doctrines in Latin America seemed to be fading. Cuba's

[1] Cf. Tad Szulc, "Cuban Confrontation—A Look One Year Later", *The New York Times*, New York, October 20, 1963, and Joseph Alsop, "Soviet Exodus from Cuba", *The New York Times*, New York, November 13, 1963.

neighbours had not been impressed with its programme. Nearby Haiti, with probably the lowest *per capita* income in Latin America, remained unresponsive. Commonwealth independent Caribbean countries remained aloof. Jamaica even made a military pact with the United States and offered to authorize a base if one were requested, clearly with an eye on its neighbour to the north.[1] Communications between the two neighbouring islands had largely ceased apart from clandestine arrivals in Jamaica of occasional parties of Cuban refugees in small boats.

The most significant economic occurrence emerging from the Cuban Revolution has been the inability of Cuba to move from an agricultural economy leaning heavily on sugar to a system of industrialization. Castro has now accepted that the central work of the Revolution at present lies in agriculture.

He seems, however, to have modified his views on small agricultural holdings. Problems of labour shortage have arisen. One hundred thousand share croppers, squatters and tenant farmers who prior to the Revolution used to work part of the year as hired labourers have since devoted their time to the lands that they had received from the Government. Castro stresses that the solution must be found in rapid mechanization.[2]

In January 1969, Castro introduced sugar rationing. The 1968-69 sugar crop proved disappointing, yielding some 4·7 million tons; yet on July 14, 1969, Castro launched a 10 million ton target for the year ahead.[3] Making it a matter of honour for every Cuban citizen he appeared to stake everything on achieving an unlikely result.[4] Indeed Castro hoped to restore the confidence in his movement swept away by all the unkept promises.[5] Christmas celebrations were postponed until the following July; in February 1970 groups of U.S. youths set out to help in the Cuban canefields, to be followed by volunteer brigades from North Korea and

---

[1] *Vide* p. 137.

[2] Havana, August 29, 1966. In a visit to the San Andrés Valley in April 1967, the Secretary of the local Communist Party informed the author that Government policy was to help the small farmers in the valley, many of whom before the Revolution had been share croppers. Notwithstanding this, some in the San Andrés Valley had already sold their holdings to the Government and had obtained housing accommodation in the village. The reason was the expectation of better economic conditions. The secretary doubted if living on a small-holding would make any appeal to the next generation.

[3] Puerto Padre, Oriente Province.

[4] " . . . a goal which, because of the innate unwisdom of relying on the production of a large quantity of an already far from scarce commodity, would once have seemed so foolish as to be absurd." Thomas, *op. cit.*, p. 1436.

[5] Cf. Karol, *op. cit.* p. 535.

Bulgaria. Despite a record sugar crop of some eight and a half million tons, Castro was forced to admit failure.[1]

On the 17th anniversary of the attack on the Moncada Castro shouldered the blame for Cuba's continuing economic problems in an important speech. He admitted that the cost to the people of learning economic construction had been too great: the Revolutionaries had found it more difficult than they had imagined.[2]

The 1971 target of seven million tons also fell short; unlike 1970, Castro did not move workers from other industries to assist the short sugar harvest. For the moment Cuba's markets for sugar are assured.[3] Possibly the introduction of mechanisation, which Castro expects to be completed by 1975, will help to raise the industry's efficiency.

Cuba can certainly expand its cane industry, but much remains to be done. Roads by Caribbean standards are good; however, transport, a very important factor in cane farming, is backward. The heavy trucks and trailers of some other countries are often absent. Much of the cane is transported by light railways, a system that avoids the need for trucks but which many modern cane farmers would regard as less satisfactory and slower than road haulage. However, the reduction in the number of vehicles facilitates the upkeep of the highways. Some of the factory machinery is very antiquated.

In the smaller islands of the Caribbean, the displacement of the workers by mechanization has presented great problems and has even in some instances resulted in legislation to restrain it.[4] Sugar production in some islands has ceased. Cuba's position may well prove to be different. Its larger population, about the same as that of Venezuela, and the extensive resources of the island hold more possibilities of diversified employment than do those of some of its neighbours. Significantly, Cuba has not expressed any anxiety over a too rapid increase of population perhaps having in mind the substantial outflow to the United States and elsewhere.[5]

The Cuban economy after such a massive effort concentrated on a single agricultural product has received a serious reverse. Industrialization had already failed in Cuba; now agriculture presented a second economic disaster to the Cuban Government.

[1] The final total was 8,535,281 million metric tons. *Granma*, Havana, August 9, 1970.

[2] Havana, July 26, 1970.

[3] The Soviet Union pays the equivalent of £56 a ton for Cuban sugar. Great Britain's price to the Caribbean under the Commonwealth Sugar Agreement was raised in December 1971 from £47.50 to £61 a ton.

[4] *Vide* pp. 146-7 and 163.

[5] *Vide* p. 364.

In addition to the failure of the sugar crop, setbacks had occurred in beef, milk, fertilizer, fuel, tyre, rubber and other industries.[1] Castro failed to offer much hope for 1971, the Year of Productivity.[2] However in his July 26, 1971 speech, he claimed many of the setbacks had been reversed: both light and heavy industry, for example, showed signs of improvement. Significantly Castro made no mention of the Soviet Union which was financing Cuba at the rate of some one million dollars a day.

The cattle industry has for long been of importance in Cuba since colonial days when the island found a market in the provisioning of passing Spanish ships. Prior to the Revolution, good Brahman herds had been established while the celebrated U.S. King Ranch had large estates for its Santa Gertrudis breed. After the Revolution, the cattle industry concentrated on limiting the slaughtering of cows, the use of artificial insemination, the cross breeding of pure-bred Holstein bulls with high milk yield Zebu cows and diet improvement. Severe rationing emphasized the domestic meat shortage.

Some agricultural projects started under the Revolution proved successful. The Cordon de Habana, a farm belt round the capital, after two years began to show promising results. For several years Cuba had imported rice from China. Failure to meet requirements had led to a cooling-off of relations between Cuba and China in 1966. The rice plan, begun in 1967, made full use of mechanization, which is not the case in countries such as Vietnam. A high yield enabled the Cubans to crop twice a year.

Cuba has experienced increasing success in the development of its fishing industry. Some of the fishing is in the Gulf of Mexico; other vessels fish northwards to Greenland and southwards off Argentina. Aided by funds from Moscow, a modern processing plant has been erected near Havana, and a fleet of some 3,000 vessels built up. In 1969 the acquisition of two refrigerator ships, enabling some 10,000 tons of fish to be carried in each, helped Cuba to reach its $15 million annual sales total.[3]

In 1971 rationing was down to subsistence level. It included meat, poultry and dairy products. Petrol rationing had been introduced in 1968. A 45 per cent. cut in the 1971 tobacco crop, because of a severe

---

[1] Fidel Castro, Havana, July 26, 1970.

[2] Cf. *Granma*, Havana, editorial, March 10, 1971. Cf. George Volsky, "Castro sees little hope for Cuban Economy in '71", *The New York Times*, New York, January 2, 1971.

[3] Cf. James Nelson Goodsell, "Cuba goes fishing—for food and profit", *The Christian Science Monitor*, Boston, October 4-5, 1970.

drought, halved the domestic ration. Few consumer goods appeared in the shops.

Transportation remained a problem. Constantly Castro blamed perishing foodstuffs on a lack of transport. Britain, the first to recognize a potential market for vehicles, was swiftly followed by other European countries and then Japan.[1] Japanese exports to Cuba rose to some $40 million in 1970 making that country a contender for the title of Cuba's leading non-Communist supplier.[2]

Absenteeism and low worker output constituted another of Castro's recurring problems. Since a month's rations cost approximately a week's pay, little incentive remained for the worker to try to earn more.[3] Castro continually emphasized in his speeches that economic targets were not met because of "loafing". In March 1971, he passed a Law on Loafing which stipulated that all men from 17 to 60 and women from 17 to 55, presuming they were fit, should work. Rehabilitation camps were to be set up for those guilty of loafing with a maximum term of two years.[4]

Prior to the Revolution, education in Cuba was limited. Of the population aged 10 years or older in 1953, one-quarter had never attended school. Only 1 per cent. of the population over 10 had completed instruction in a professional school and 2 per cent. in pre-university training.[5]

As in other Latin American countries, university education had over-concentrated in the Arts. In consequence there was a shortage of engineers and technicians, although the supply of doctors and dentists was adequate. A total number of some 21,000 Cubans had graduated before the Revolution.

The Constitution of 1940 stressed the importance of education and laid down eight years of primary schooling. Nevertheless, insufficient advance was made, partly through corruption at the Ministry. Some

[1] "The lorry makers do battle for sales", *The Financial Times*, London, January 8, 1971.

[2] *The Japan Times*, Tokyo, May 13, 1971.

[3] Cf. Richard Beeston, "Cuba plans work camps for loafers", *The Sunday Telegraph*, London, January 31, 1971. Advocating Marxist development throughout Latin America, Teresa Hayter commented that for Cuba: "It provides all Cubans with a minimum wage which is more than enough to buy everything that is available on the ration, and therefore to provide adequate food and clothing for many who were previously without them, and to have money left over for travel and restaurants." *Aid as Imperialism* (Harmondsworth, 1971), p. 178-9.

[4] *Granma*, Havana, March 28, 1971.

[5] Richard Jolly, "Education", *Cuba, The Economic and Social Revolution* (University of North Carolina Press, 1964), p. 164.

teachers even drew salaries whether they taught or not.[1] As in other parts of the Caribbean, teaching lagged in the rural areas.

The Revolutionary Government placed education in the forefront of its objectives. Castro constantly stressed its importance. About one-fifth of the adult population was illiterate, a number not exceptional in a Latin American context but nevertheless a serious handicap for a country which sought rapid material advance.

The most striking feature of the campaign to eliminate illiteracy which Cuba launched in 1961 was its speed. A year was allocated to the task; the timetable was met. Success was due to several causes. Very large numbers of persons were enrolled for teaching. Although television and radio were used to advertise and popularize the campaign, teaching was entirely personal. The U.N.E.S.C.O. Report points out that the organization was the masterpiece of the campaign; it also became an instrument of revolutionary integration. The Report also stressed that the success of the campaign could be found in personal contact.[2]

The campaign had the advantage of being spearheaded by many young men and women convinced supporters of the Government. From the official angle, it provided an exceptional opportunity of explaining the purpose of the Revolution to people all over Cuba, including the most remote villages. A study of the textbooks widely used makes this clear.[3] Effective use was made of the pronouncements of Castro. Probably the campaign did more than anything else to consolidate the image of the Revolution in the minds of the Cuban people.

The intention of the campaign was not that it would come to an end, but rather that it should be a first step towards further study. Its significance can best be appreciated by a visit to the building which houses its records at the Centro Escolar in Havana. On the average young people learnt to read and write in about one and a half months; the older illiterate person took substantially longer.

Revolutionary Cuba maintained its educational fervour, with a strong emphasis on youth. Higher education was seen as a means of overcoming underdevelopment.[4] Adult educational systems became an integral

---

[1] Cf. Herbert Matthews, *Cuba* (New York, 1964), p. 34.

[2] *Methods and Means Utilized in Cuba to Eliminate Illiteracy* (U.N.E.S.C.O. Report), Editora Pedagógica, Havana, 1965, p. 73.

[3] Cf. *Manual Para el Alfabetizador*, Ministerio de Educación, Havana, and *Venceremos*, Comisión Nacional de Alfabetización, Ministerio de Educación, Imprenta Nacional de Cuba, Havana, 1961.

[4] *Vide* pp. 369-70.

part of the national education system. At an Education Seminar held in December 1970, Dr. Raúl Roa, Minister of Foreign Relations, praised Guevara as the epitome of the new, multi-dimensional man Cuban education was attempting to form.[1] In April 1971 Castro himself presided over the first National Congress on Education and Culture.

*　　*　　*　　*

Cuba's growing economic problems meant ever greater dependence on Soviet resources. As a result the Russians sought increasing control over the planning and administration of the island's economy. Discussions by the Cuban-Soviet Commission for Economic, Scientific and Technical Collaboration, created in 1970 to study ways of boosting the Cuban economy, led to the signing of an agreement in September 1971.[2]

More than a decade of Marxist rule had failed to bring prosperity to Cuba, despite its pre-eminence in the Caribbean as the island with the best agricultural possibilities. Its sugar industry at the outset was as efficient as any in the area. Castro's desperate effort to achieve the harvest of 10 million tons of sugar underscored the weakness of Cuba's economy. The original programme of co-operatives for small farmers proved equally unproductive. The state farms turned out to be poor substitutes for the former efficient, if often foreign-owned, enterprises. Severe rationing indicated to any visitor the economic weakness of the regime.

Distance compounded Cuba's problems, cut off as it was from most of its former markets in the Americas. Difficulties of replacing equipment, originally purchased in the United States, increased with the years. The limited traffic on the roads illustrated this, as did the problem of machinery in many of the sugar mills.

Castro's lack of economic success at home damaged his prospects of promoting revolution in Latin America. Despite the failure of the Alliance for Progress, few believed that Cuba had found a better solution. Although aid continued from across the Iron Curtain, the loss of foreign—largely U.S.—expertise in addition to markets had proved deadly. Notwithstanding the willingness to trade displayed by Great Britain, France and other Western countries including Franco's Spain, as well as Japan, economic progress, which had earlier eluded Guevara, continued to be conspicuous by its absence. There is no indication

[1] "A man capable of uplifting the human race on an individual and collective basis". *Granma*, Havana, December 27, 1970.

[2] To assist the mechanization of sugar cane, the Soviet Union promised to build 1,600 trailers for hauling sugar in Cuba and to supply combine harvesters. *Granma*, Havana, September 19, 1971.

47

that work in the cane fields is any more popular in Cuba than elsewhere in the Caribbean, although the introduction of cane-cutting machinery may cause a change of attitude.

The international currency crisis of 1971 suggested that the United States might move more towards a policy of self-sufficiency, aid to underdeveloped countries being temporarily reduced. There was no evidence that the resumption of trade with Cuba was likely to be a high priority in U.S. diplomacy. The economic outlook remained unpromising.

Cuba's economy has crumpled under the weight of the U.S. boycott. Guevara optimistically thought that he could re-establish it by rapid industrialization, which in the event proved to be a failure. Later, prodded by his Soviet paymasters who were tiring of the large subsidies needed to keep Cuba afloat, Castro undertook his reorganization of the sugar industry. He himself admitted its failure. His economic record in this respect is worse than that of the Batista Government.

Castro's popularity has waned though he remains without a rival in his country. In a Latin America which is changing rapidly and in some cases under a cloak of nationalism seeking to lessen its dependence on the United States, is it possible that Cuba may seek to mend its fences with the United States? If it be argued that Cuba has been the main loser in the unequal contest, nevertheless for the United States the advantages are also obvious. For the Soviet Union, Cuba has been a costly experiment: a pupil in Communism far from docile or easy precisely to indoctrinate. Far-reaching events are presaged during the coming years, particularly between the super powers who may be beginning to learn that at least a minimum of co-operation has become vital if twentieth-century civilization is to survive. A Soviet outpost in the Western World could prove as troublesome as Western "fortresses" on the frontiers of Communist countries.

Haiti: Former President Duvalier delivers his inaugural address for his second term of office, 1963. Madame Duvalier stands beside him.

Jean-Claude Duvalier, appointed President for Life on his father's death in April 1971.

CHAPTER III

HAITI

THE POLITICAL PATTERN

The first country in Latin America, and second in the Western Hemisphere, to obtain independence, Haiti won the added distinction of being the world's first Negro republic; at the same time, it provides a depressing example of a country which has failed dismally to order its political affairs. Turbulence has been the characteristic of its government. After the successful struggle to achieve and maintain independence under such leaders as Toussaint l'Ouverture and Jean-Jacques Dessalines, the small country split into two separate states, the north ruled by the despotic King Henri Christophe and the south by the more enlightened Alexandre Pétion. Haiti's internal struggles were as unprofitable as those of Bolivia after independence. The despotic Faustin Soulouque (1847–59) would be a candidate for the worst dictator that Latin America has produced. Maladministration and corruption reduced the state to penury.

For almost a hundred years after independence, Haiti's record had been one of dictatorship, destitution and civil strife. Ninety-five per cent. of the population was illiterate. The mulatto elite constituting perhaps 2 per cent. of the population lived comfortably in the few towns, oriented towards French education and culture, but with lessened political influence since the days of Presidents Alexandre Pétion and Jean-Pierre Boyer. Even language separated them from the patois-speaking peasantry.

In 1902 President Tiresias Sam resigned, discredited when Haiti had to apologize and pay an indemnity to the German Government for alleged improper treatment of a German subject. His rule was marred also by scandals over a French 50-million franc loan. A civil war followed between rival political factions, resulting in General Pierre Nord Alexis, a former Minister of War, becoming President. He, in turn, was ejected from office by the near-illiterate General Antoine Simon, who became involved with further French loans of 65 million francs, much of which never reached the Haitian treasury. Simon also encouraged the establishment of the French-sponsored Banque Nationale de la République d'Haïti. He was overthrown in 1911.

D   49

Cincinnatus Leconte succeeded to the presidency, only to be killed in an explosion in the presidential palace.

After further political struggles, the climax came in 1915. Vilbrun Guillaume Sam, who had recently assumed the presidency by capturing Port-au-Prince at the head of a *caco*[1] army, imprisoned a large number of his political opponents, including leading citizens of the capital. After 167 of them had been slaughtered with Sam's connivance, a surge of fury against the President swept Port-au-Prince; Sam was forced to take refuge in the French Legation. When the mob learned where he was, they forced their way into the building, seized Sam and tore him to pieces in the street.

Although such treatment may have been merited, it provoked international outrage. France sent naval units to protect its embassy. The United States took still more drastic action. It not only landed troops but compelled the Haitian regime to sign the treaty of November 11, 1916, placing the supervision and control of the national finances in the hands of the United States: a control which was to last nineteen years and which penetrated even deeper than in Cuba.

In justification of the American action, Haiti had clearly shown itself for years to be incapable of honest or even tolerable government. Moreover, the United States, mindful of the Monroe Doctrine, may have feared lest other countries should intervene in the faction-torn republic. However, there were also cynics who pointed out that an American bank had obtained virtual control of the French Banque Nationale de la République d'Haïti, which in turn dominated the finances of Haiti, including the railways.[2] Moreover, with World War I at its height in Europe, the United States was very conscious of its own strategic problems in the Caribbean. It was particularly anxious that the Germans should not establish a coaling station in Haiti, a country in which they had interfered politically in the past.[3]

The U.S. Administration was tough—some 2,000 Haitians in revolt were shot by Marines[4]—but it was also efficient. The Americans reorganized the country, imposing the rule of law with a Haitian police

---

[1] *Cacos* are "peasants living along the northern part of the frontier between Haiti and the Dominican Republic". Dana G. Munro, *Intervention and Dollar Diplomacy in the Caribbean* (Princeton, 1964), p. 330.

[2] "Dans la gestion de leurs finances publiques, tous ces petits Etats sont empressés à recourir aux services des banques de l'Union. A Cuba, à Panama, à Haïti et à Saint-Domingue, la dette publique se trouvait déjà, en 1919, entièrement dans les mains de ces banques." *Histoire des Relations Internationales*, ed. Pierre Renouvin, Vol. VII (Paris, 1957), p. 324.

[3] Munro, *op. cit.*, pp. 330 and 339.

[4] *Ibid.*, pp. 372-4.

force which they trained. The chaotic finances were put in order;[1] graft was reduced; sanitary and medical services were improved.[2]

Nevertheless, to the Haitians, the occupation simply represented the loss of the freedom for which more than a century earlier they had fought.[3] Presidents Philippe Sudre Dartiguenave, Louis Borno, and Sténio Joseph Vincent, enlightened mulattoes, ruled only in name. The power was in the hands of the American officials backed by the Marines.

With the adoption of Franklin D. Roosevelt's Good Neighbour Policy in 1934, America handed Haiti back to the Haitians. Unfortunately, democracy did not flower when the Marines marched out. The island's subsequent history proved to be a succession of thinly veiled dictatorships, sometimes ending in the overthrow of the President, who would then retire to spend his remaining days in expatriate luxury.

Elie Lescot, a mulatto, made a successful President (1941-46) until he was ousted by the Negro masses in favour of Dumarsais Estimé. Already it had become clear that power lay in the hands of the Garde d'Haïti, trained by the Americans, and that this situation was to continue. In 1950 Estimé was unseated and replaced by U.S. instructed Colonel Paul Magloire. Although a capable chief of state, he too was overthrown in 1956. François Duvalier, a country doctor, succeeded him.

Following an election of dubious legality, Haiti entered in 1957 into one of the grimmest dictatorships of even its chequered history. With quiet but ruthless skill, Duvalier consolidated his power. His medical training may have contributed to his perceptive judgment of his countrymen. A realist, he early concentrated on destroying the power of Haiti's small armed forces. If the destruction was hardly a cause for grief, the new police force which he recruited to bolster his regime and extend his power throughout the country soon gave the people cause to regret that there was no longer a body which could spark a change of government. With great assiduity, arms were collected for the Milice Civile, Duvalier's personal force, which became known as the Tonton Macoute.[4] The presidential palace itself was turned into

[1] The public debt was $31 million in 1915. By 1927 it was under $20 million.

[2] Despite the improved medical services, the life expectancy in 1966 was only 33 years.

[3] For a balanced American view, see Herring, *op. cit.*, pp. 431-2.
For a critical view by a neutral, see Richardo Pattee, *Haiti* (Madrid, 1956), pp. 200-3.

[4] Duvalier's creation of the Tonton Macoute as his private police force was not dissimilar to the Secret Police created by President Arnulfo Arias of Panama (1949-51). These men supported the President against the National

an arsenal for this private army as well as a prison where those arrested were "examined".

For the first two years of Duvalier's Government, Haiti was of relatively little importance to the United States. The situation, however, began to change with the advent of the Castro regime in Cuba and the deterioration of relations between that island and the United States. Castro had repeatedly expressed his desire to extend his system to other parts of Latin America. Separated from Cuba by only fifty miles of water, Haiti was Cuba's nearest neighbour. In August 1959, the landing in south-western Haiti of some thirty men who apparently hoped to lead an insurrection against Duvalier aroused anxiety in the United States. Although increasingly embarrassed by the dictatorial methods of Duvalier, the American Government was even more concerned at what might happen were the invasion to succeed, since the expedition had sailed from a Cuban port.

The Haitian armed forces succeeded in killing or capturing most of the handful of invaders. The affair, nevertheless, was regarded as sufficiently serious for the Organization of American States to send, at Haiti's request, a five-man team, led by U.S. Ambassador John C. Dreier, to investigate the invasion. The prisoners identified themselves as members of the Cuban Army who had been told that they were going on an expedition to an undisclosed destination. Perhaps encouraged by the failure of the invasion, the U.S. military mission of forty Marines, which had arrived in Haiti in January 1959, subsequently announced progress in the training of the Republic's armed forces of some 5,000 men.

Duvalier, meanwhile, pursued his consolidation of personal power by expelling, on October 10, 1959, six of Haiti's twenty senators. In December his whole Cabinet, only eight months old, resigned to permit its reorganization by the President. Only three members were reappointed.

The United States was now to pursue a policy of vacillation. It was influenced by its desire to aid the economic advance of Haiti, mindful of its own period of nineteen years' control of the island. Doubtless, it wished to see the former U.S. occupation justified by political

---

Police in the Revolution of May 1951, which ended in the overthrow of Arias. Professor Larry L. Pippin, *The Remón Era*, special issue, *Hispanic American Report*, 1964, pp. 67, 74-6. "Tonton Macoute" in Creole means "bogyman", implying Duvalier's play on voodooism. It was trained by the Haitian armed forces, which in turn received training from the U.S. Marine Corps Mission.

stability combined with a rise in the standard of living of the population.[1] To these disinterested aspirations was added the increasing fear that, if it abandoned Haiti, Fidel Castro might pick the republic as a ripe if indigestible plum. The political and economic difficulties of Haiti heightened the risk of a Communist take-over. The possibility of Communism in Haiti appeared ever more menacing after the failure of the Bay of Pigs invasion in 1961,[2] while the consequent coolness of many Latin American countries towards the United States made the maintenance of U.S. influence in the Organization of American States more difficult. Haiti's role, therefore, assumed a deeper significance.

The U.S. need for votes in its struggle to obtain the expulsion of Cuba from the O.A.S. at the Eighth Meeting of Consultation of Foreign Ministers held at Punta del Este, Uruguay, on January 22, 1962, provided the Haitian delegation with just the opportunity it sought. To exploit the situation, the Haitian vote was withheld until the last moment, when hesitation was overcome by the U.S. offer of an airport and a hospital.[3]

Meanwhile, on the domestic side, the President was clearly building up a dictatorship as ruthless as that of Rafael Leonidas Trujillo next door in the Dominican Republic. Whether or not Duvalier personally sympathized with voodooism, he sought to lacquer this cult with Roman Catholicism in the churches of the country. The attempt was strongly resisted by the Church. In November 1960, Duvalier, as ruthless in ecclesiastical as in political matters, expelled French-born Archbishop François Poirier, Haiti's highest prelate. Two months later he exiled native-born Bishop Rémy Augustin, who had taken over Poirier's duties, together with four other Roman Catholic priests. No reasons for the expulsion were given. The Catholic newspaper *La Phalange* was also seized.

The Vatican reacted swiftly. It issued a blanket anathema (*latae sententiae*), which automatically excommunicated anyone connected with the expulsions. Although no one was named in the decree, Duvalier, who had signed the order, was clearly included.

In May 1962, the Papal Nuncio Monsignor Giovanni Ferrofina also left the island, apparently in protest against the expulsions. The entire diplomatic corps assembled to bid him farewell. The episode

[1] According to a budget enquiry conducted in 1954 among 574 families (2,815 persons: about 5 persons to a family) in 24 selected rural areas, the total average family income was 1,608 gourdes. The average urban family was probably worse off. *Bulletin Trimestriel de Statistique*, Institut Haïtien de Statistique, Port-au-Prince, March 1957.

[2] *Vide* pp. 15-17.

[3] *Hispanic American Report*, Vol. XV, p. 36.

recalled the withdrawal of support by the Vatican just prior to the collapse of the regimes of Perón in Argentina and of Trujillo in the Dominican Republic.

The Vatican's opposition did not deter Duvalier. A month later, Bishop Paul Robert of Gonaïves was forced by demonstrators to leave his diocese after Duvalier's Government had recommended that he resign. In November 1962, together with three other priests, Robert was finally expelled from Haiti for crusading against the Haitian Government's policy of imposing voodoo practices on the Catholic Church. In the eyes of Duvalier and his supporters, the Catholic Church had remained foreign and had allied itself too closely with the mulattoes.[1]

If Haiti's diplomatic relations with the Vatican had turned stormy, they were also tempestuous with some other countries. Following disputes with Great Britain over the death of Cromwell James, a Negro from Grenada,[2] and the arrest at Jacmel, a port on Haiti's southern coast, of Francis Brenton, a British yachtsman, Haiti recalled its Ambassador from London and requested the recall of British Ambassador Gerald T. Corley Smith. Apparently the reason was that on November 17, 1961, Corley Smith, dean of the diplomatic corps, had headed a group of Ambassadors protesting against the extortion of contributions from nationals by the Tonton Macoute for a housing project at Duvalierville.

The right of political asylum, to which Latin American countries attach particular importance, has been the cause of numerous incidents in the Caribbean. During the Duvalier regime, many Haitians, fearing for their lives on political grounds, had sought asylum in various embassies at Port-au-Prince.[3] Great difficulty was encountered in obtaining for asylees safe-conduct passes to leave Haiti.

In June 1962, a diplomatic quarrel between Haiti and Venezuela erupted, reminiscent of the antagonisms of earlier years between Presidents Trujillo of the Dominican Republic and Rómulo Betancourt of Venezuela. Three Haitians, including a four-year-old child, received asylum in the Venezuelan Embassy at Port-au-Prince. After

[1] "In 1963, among 416 secular and religious priests, only 113 were Haitians. There were 180 French, 26 Americans, 37 Belgians, etc. The scant number of native clergy reveals that the Church has not taken root in the population of Haiti, despite a hundred years of tireless, and often heroic, apostolate." The English Periodical Service of the Center of Intercultural Documentation, Cuernavaca, Mexico, October 16, 1964.

[2] He was beaten to death in jail at Port-au-Prince.

[3] In May 1963, 103 Haitians were in asylum in Latin American embassies at Port-au-Prince, including those of Venezuela, the Dominican Republic, Brazil, and Ecuador. *Hispanic American Report*, Vol. XVI, p. 460.

a refusal by the Duvalier Government to grant them safe-conduct passes as required by the Caracas agreement of 1954, the Venezuelan Government threatened to denounce Haiti before the O.A.S. Finally Duvalier gave way and the safe-conduct passes were granted.

However, the hard-pressed Venezuelan Embassy soon had new guests. On August 9, 1962, Chief of Staff Brigadier-General Jean-René Boucicaut, with his wife and four children, sought asylum. The State Department and the Pentagon, through Colonel Robert D. Heinl who commanded the U.S. Marine Mission, had suggested to Duvalier and Defence Minister Boileau Méhu the abolition of the Tonton Macoute, a suggestion which Boucicaut had supported. Duvalier had immediately replaced him.

In March 1963, lack of space caused the Venezuelan Embassy to arrange the transfer of some Haitian asylees in their embassy to the Dominican Embassy, which led the Duvalier Government to request the recall of the Venezuelan chargé d'affaires, Francisco Millán Delpretti. He became the fourth Venezuelan chargé d'affaires since 1959 to be declared *persona non grata* by the Haitian Government.[1] The Venezuelan Embassy was permanently surrounded by militiamen, recalling the prolonged Peruvian-Colombian quarrel of 1949-54 over Víctor Raúl Haya de la Torre.

The Haitian Government's refusal to issue safe-conduct passes applied particularly to requests from the Dominican Republic. In April 1963, two Tonton Macoutes in search of political refugees entered the chancellery of the Dominican Embassy during the temporary absence of the Dominican chargé d'affaires. On his return he ordered the police out. Anticipating an ultimatum from the Dominican Republic, Haiti broke diplomatic relations.

The Dominican Republic then commenced moving troops and warships into battle positions on the Haitian frontier. Its military forces were larger and better equipped than those of Haiti. President Juan Bosch concentrated 4,000 troops, supported by tanks, at Elías Piña and at Jimaní near Lake Enriquillo, only 40 miles from Port-au-Prince. In Haiti, antagonism to the Dominican Republic was easily aroused: the 1937 massacre of some 10,000 Haitian immigrants along the border, at the instance of President Trujillo, had left bitter memories.[2]

---

[1] *Hispanic American Report*, Vol. XVI, p. 256.
[2] The number of Haitians killed varies. Herring puts it at between 10,000 and 20,000. *Op. cit.*, p. 434. Dr. Jean Price-Mars says reports varied between 12,000 and 25,000 but that a reasonable estimate would be about 12,000. *La République d'Haïti et la République Dominicaine*, Vol. II (Port-au-Prince, 1953), p. 312. *Vide* p. 386.

With war clouds gathering over Hispaniola, the U.S. State Department announced that it was withdrawing its Marine training mission, though the U.S. Air Force Mission and a Military Assistance group remained in Haiti. A U.S. task force steamed past the Gulf of Gonaïves into the Saint-Marc Channel, just outside Haitian waters. British and French naval units were also sent to protect their nationals. It was reminiscent of the days when another asylum incident had led to the U.S. occupation of Haiti.[1]

Although pressure for U.S. intervention was voiced both in Congress and in the press, the handling of the confrontation was placed in the hands of the O.A.S. A five-member O.A.S. investigating committee was dispatched to Port-au-Prince and Santo Domingo.[2] As a result, the Dominicans withdrew their troops from the frontier, while Haiti acquiesced to the extent of granting safe-conduct passes for asylees. The fall of Duvalier had been taken for granted; yet he survived. Indeed his position may even have been temporarily strengthened by the Haitians' animosity towards the Dominicans.[3]

Notwithstanding economic difficulties, Duvalier's hold over Haiti was remarkable. An explanation might be found in his image as "Father" of his people. His subtle appeal to voodooism—a religion, as Francis Huxley reminds us—increased his influence with the Negro masses.[4] To them he was the symbol of the Haiti that had successfully revolted against France. The peasants backed their country doctor against the city elite.[5]

"Papa Doc", unlike some dictators, appeared to be able to command the loyalty of his armed forces. His success lay in his appeal to the championship of the Haitian Negro. Certainly the rebel invasions in 1963 and again in 1964, instigated by General Léon Cantave, were easily defeated by the troops of "Le Rénovateur de la République". Arrests and executions of those suspected of aiding the invasion

---

[1] *Vide* p. 50.

[2] The committee was composed of representatives of Bolivia, Chile, Colombia, Ecuador and El Salvador.

[3] *Vide* p. 75.

[4] "Haiti's Search for a Social Order", *The Times*, London, May 1, 1963.

[5] "Sans doute le petit peuple voit-il encore en Papa Doc une protection contre l'éventuel retour au pouvoir de la classe des mulâtres, particulièrement brimée sous l'ordre nouveau." "Une Crise Permanente", *Le Monde*, Paris, September 25, 1963. Michael Faber comments: "Dr. Duvalier himself is black like the peasant farmers, while the privilege caste that most hates him is mulatto. No anti-Duvalier revolution could be founded upon the sort of support that made possible Castro's overthrow of Batista", *The Observer*, London, September 29, 1963.

followed as a matter of course.[1] Nevertheless, like Nkrumah in his latter days, Duvalier shut himself up behind guards in his palace, with an occasional outing to some function in an armoured car. Perhaps Graham Greene with his novelist's perception of an incredible situation summed it up when he remarked "some strange curse descended on the liberated slaves of Hispaniola".[2]

In its long, cynical, diplomatic tug-of-war with Haiti, the United States continued on the horns of a dilemma. Unwilling to follow its convictions of opposition to a ruthless dictatorship, it felt there was some justification for arms and aid, including military missions, to Haiti.[3] Yet in 1962 the United States by ceasing economic aid had tried to topple Duvalier and failed. The relative weakness of the world's most powerful nation was clearly demonstrated. Instead, the dictator of Haiti was being kept afloat with sporadic U.S. financial aid.[4]

The *Hispanic American Report* commented editorially: "Honorable men cannot help being appalled by the opportunism which characterizes the United States policy in Latin America. The consensus is that the rule of President François Duvalier of Haiti is perhaps the most despicable and corrupt in the world. . . . Our reaction to the Duvalier regime was at first one of loathing, the U.S. Government broke relations, but such is our determination to undermine the Castro regime in Cuba at all costs that we have begun to cultivate Duvalier as we cultivated Trujillo (who, by comparison, was an admirable individual). It is as though the police made a deal with the worst of the Harlem gangs, to which the Duvalier regime has a clear resemblance."[5]

In 1963 Duvalier succeeded himself in office without the formalities

[1] "Le régime haïtien devant l'orage", *Le Monde*, Paris, August 24, 1963.

[2] "Nightmare Republic", *The Sunday Telegraph*, London, September 29, 1963.

[3] "Unofficially they (the United States) recognize that their aid is helping nobody much except the President and his bogymen, but their occasional efforts to control the use of their money have been paralysed so far by Duvalier's threat that he will turn to Moscow if Washington will not play." David Holden, "Bogymen of Port-au-Prince", *The Guardian*, London, April 26, 1962. Roscoe Drummond also believed that Duvalier was desperate enough to take the risk of inviting into Haiti the Castro-Soviet Communists. *The New York Herald Tribune*, New York, May 3, 1963.

[4] "Until interrupted at the end of 1962 as a sign of displeasure at the regime's corruption, violence and inefficiency, American aid had amounted to more than $100 million since 1945. For humanitarian reasons, the United States has continued to finance malaria control and provide Food for Peace shipments distributed by private agencies." Jonathan Randal, "Duvalier Retains Tight Grip in Haiti", *The New York Times*, New York, May 9, 1966.

[5] Vol. XVII, p. 293.

of an election.   The following year he had himself installed as President of Haiti for life.   Referring to predecessors Jean-Jacques Dessalines, Henri Christophe and Faustin Soulouque, *The New York Times* commented that his action was "in a long tradition".[1]   Although the United States sharply criticized Duvalier's 1963 extension of his presidential term of office, its policy appeared to change when faced with the fact of his dictatorship for life.   Instead of the previous policy of boycotting Duvalier's anniversary celebrations, Benson L. Timmons, recently appointed as U.S. Ambassador, attended in May 1964 a High Mass to commemorate Duvalier's second anniversary as self-appointed ruler.   The Mass was followed by a drill display outside the presidential palace, by some 10,000 blue-uniformed members of the Tonton Macoute.   The friendliness of the U.S. Embassy to the Haitian Government drew caustic comment from opponents of the Duvalier dictatorship and from diplomats in Port-au-Prince.[2]

The President succeeded in re-establishing relations with the Vatican at the end of 1966 with the reappointment of a Papal Nuncio.   On the other hand, the continuance of opposition to Duvalier was demonstrated by the abortive attempt to invade Haiti from Florida by a party of Haitians, Cubans and Americans in January 1967.

Guerrilla attacks instigated by exiles, similar to those in 1963, 1964 and 1967, recurred during the period 1968–1970.   Like these earlier attempts, poor organization and a total lack of support from the peasants led to failure.[3]   Duvalier's response was characteristically brutal: in 1967 he personally supervised the shooting of nineteen officers; five Ministers were dismissed and over a hundred Haitians exiled.   The collapse of the so-called "invasion" of Cap Haitien in May 1968 met with equally harsh reprisals.   Rumours of C.I.A. participation circulated in Port-au-Prince.[4]   Duvalier was by no means immune to opposition

[1] April 3, 1964.

[2] Cf. Henry Raymont "U.S. Quietly Seeks Better Haiti Ties", *The New York Times*, May 24, 1964, and Richard Eder "U.S. Said to Lose Prestige in Haiti", *The New York Times*, December 6, 1964.   Marcel Niedergang wrote caustically: "Il semble que l'administration Johnson ait décidé de soutenir sans réserve le gouvernement de Port-au-Prince, qui professe habilement et officiellement un anti-américanisme de principe.   Cette attitude lui permet d'émarger confortablement au budget de l'Alliance pour le progrès.   Tout en regrettant peut-être le caractère policier et totalitaire du régime Duvalier, Washington estime sans doute que 'Papa Doc en vaut bien un autre', reprenant ainsi le point de vue de son représentant à Port-au-Prince."   "Haïti continue de connaître la terreur et l'arbitraire", *Le Monde*, Paris, January 23, 1965.

[3] Cf. Bernard Diederich and Al Burt, *Papa Doc* (London, 1970), p. 316.

[4] *Le Monde*, Paris, June 26, 1968.

from within his family: both his exiled son-in-law and his nephew plotted against him. The dictator's apparently failing health caused increasing speculation, particularly during the early summer of 1969.

In April 1970, the pattern changed when Duvalier faced his first internal revolt. Ships of Haiti's coastguard, after unsuccessfully shelling Port-au-Prince, had to seek asylum in Puerto Rico. Alleging Communist infiltration from Cuba, Duvalier appealed in vain to the United States to intervene. The inevitable executions of suspects followed.

Behind Haiti's welcome for Governor Rockefeller during his ill-fated Latin American tour in July 1969 lay hopes of a changed attitude towards the island by the United States. Optimism increased when the Rockefeller Report, although not specifically mentioning Haiti, made no moral judgement on authoritarian regimes.[1]

In January 1971, Parliament amended the Haitian Constitution to allow persons of 18 years of age to assume the presidency, thus enabling Duvalier to appoint his 19-year-old son, Jean-Claude, as his successor.[2] On April 22, the day of the month Duvalier considered his most auspicious, his death was announced. At once Jean-Claude Duvalier was named as Haiti's new "President for Life". His sister, Marie-Denise, seemed likely to prove his most serious rival. However by August 1971 the first political crisis occurred: Marie-Denise resigned as private secretary to her brother after a disagreement with Luckner Cambronne, the strongly conservative Defence Minister, and a loyal supporter of Duvalierism. Both she and her husband left Haiti. The outlook remained uncertain.

*   *   *   *

Duvalier's career remains astonishing. The country doctor practising among the peasantry, often without payment, became the dictator who ruled Haiti longer than any other. For much of his fourteen years in office his power was absolute.[3] Though Haiti's proximity to Castro's Cuba proved a strategic advantage, he showed he could play his cards coolly and with judgement. The U.S. aid so badly required in his

[1] *The Rockefeller Report on the Americas* (Chicago, 1969).
[2] The previous minimum age was 40.
[3] ". . . the essence of Duvalierism was power for power's sake. It had failed to foster progress. It was the most nakedly absolutist of the remaining regimes of dictatorial cast." Robert I. Rotberg, with Christopher K. Clague, *Haiti, the Politics of Squalor* (Boston, 1971), pp. 256-57.

near-bankrupt country materialized sufficiently to enable him to meet his needs, even with a little on the side for his own private overseas bank accounts to meet the emergency of exile—something that never arose.[1] He could even trade a vote at Punta del Este for an airfield.[2]

Haiti had no oligarchy: Duvalier operated alone.[3] His ability to disrupt any organization which might challenge him was remarkable.[4] To overcome the traditional risk of an army coup he even collected and stored the U.S.-provided arms in the cellars of his capacious palace. His Tonton Macoute served as a counterpart to both army and police. Ruthlessly he dismantled the limited organization of Haiti to consolidate his own personal power.

A Catholic, he quarrelled with the Church, but in due course relations were re-established. He exploited his lack of principle, changing his views when it suited. Even in domestic matters he always carried the day. When his daughter married a popular army officer whom Duvalier thought might become dangerous, he arrested a large group of associates of Colonel Max Dominique, accused them of plotting against the regime and personally conducted their execution before a firing squad with the unfortunate son-in-law an unwilling spectator. Then he immediately packed off his daughter and her husband to take over the Haitian Embassy in Madrid.

Duvalier remains an enigma. He exploited everything in voodooism which appealed to so many of his people. A Black Negro, he received much support from the negro population in the country districts. Although they did not benefit in any way he was however one of them.[5] The fact that he had worked as a country doctor and was not a military man aided his image.

---

[1] Cf. Ian Ball "Exquisite cruelty of Papa Doc's dictatorship", *The Daily Telegraph*, London, April 23, 1971.

[2] *Vide* p. 53.

[3] Cf. Rotberg, *op. cit.* p. 344.

[4] ". . . Duvalier has simply replaced experienced administrators with large numbers of devoted followers, giving new emphasis to the old truth that governmental employment in Haiti is not a matter of public administration but a form of national income distribution." Robert D. Crassweller, "Darkness in Haiti", *Foreign Affairs*, Council on Foreign Relations, New York, January 1971, p. 319.

[5] "The most significant ideology is that of *négritude*. Since 1929 Duvalier himself has been associated with that group of intellectuals who have emphasized the African roots of Haitian culture rather than the French." David Nicholls, "Embryo-Politics in Haiti", *Government and Opposition*, London, Vol. 6., No. 1, Winter 1971, p. 78.

Haiti has shown none of the usual signs of national progress. The Haitian people have suffered too long for any mere change of President, or Government, to overcome decades of neglect and misrule.

THE ECONOMIC PATTERN

Haiti presented at the end of the eighteenth century one of the most advanced examples of technical development and organization in the field of agriculture. The achievements of the French there might be compared to the earlier work of the Dutch in developing the sugar plantations of north-east Brazil. However, in the great slave revolt of 1791 the French plantation owners were killed or fled the country, and many of the buildings and irrigation systems, vital to the successful cultivation of the Plaine du Nord, were destroyed. The great estates were divided among the peasants; this fragmentation of the land resulted in the decay of Haiti's agriculture.[1]

Dessalines endeavoured to restore discipline in the disorganized plantations, but the impulse to revert to the primitive agriculture of Africa was too strong. Moreover, when Alexandre Pétion became President in the south, he encouraged the parcelling of the land which still remains a feature of the Haitian economy.

Prolonged political disturbances, combined with extreme nationalism, discouraged the investment of outside capital. At times Haiti was almost as isolated from the outside world as was Paraguay under José Francia, himself a life dictator like some of Haiti's rulers. Agriculture slipped backwards; erosion of the hillside land, consequent on the cutting down of forests, stimulated flooding in the valleys; the hardwoods, once a useful source of revenue, were not replanted. A steady decrease took place in the production of the peasant plots. With the advent of the American occupation in 1915, Haiti's primitive agriculture received its first effective organization since the destruction of the French plantations. Orderly government and honest finance led to economic improvement. Large-scale plantations were established, financed and organized by Americans, and the banana industry expanded, though

---

[1] "After the extinction of the cruellest and most successful of the colonial regimes, while at the height of its prosperity, the ex-slaves razed the plantations, and destroyed the irrigation systems that had cost the labour of a century to construct. Then they settled themselves to a future of implacable poverty and a life that was the memory-image of the ancestral existence of the forests of Guinea." Norman Lewis, "Haiti—the Caribbean Africa", *The Sunday Times*, London, February 16, 1958.

the agricultural development was not on the scale of that in Cuba.[1] As a result of settled government and improved conditions the population rose from 2 million in the 1920's to over 2·5 million in 1936. But for this increase the material benefits from the period of American rule, including health improvement, would have been even more obvious.[2]

Coffee gradually replaced sugar as Haiti's principal export. As a peasant crop, it proved more suitable than sugar cane. Although Haiti's link with France was broken politically, it continued nevertheless on a cultural and economic basis. France remained the principal buyer of Haitian coffee. The commodity proved subject to sharp market fluctuations. In the decade before World War II, coffee prices slumped, with Brazil even on occasion burning part of its huge crop. The Haitian peasant holdings on which half-wild coffee was grown had also to compete against highly organized Central American and Colombian plantations. Cheap labour remains a major consideration in the growing of coffee. This factor enabled Haiti's industry to survive since the peasants received a pitifully low return for their work. Although coffee prices soared in the 1940's, once again world overproduction caused the inevitable fall.

Even greater difficulties had beset the once promising banana industry. In 1935, reversing the policy of excluding foreign capital and land ownership, the Government signed a ten-year contract with the Standard Fruit and Steamship Company of New Orleans, granting the company the right to run Haiti's banana export trade. The Company established its own plantations, mainly in the Artibonite Valley. It also purchased the production of independent planters, who had been encouraged by technical assistance from the Department of Agriculture.

Aided by an organized shipping service, vital to the export of bananas, production rose sharply. During World War II, the Republic's banana exports held up in volume and value, unlike the position in the British islands where no shipping was available. In the year 1944-45, bananas became Haiti's second largest export. Unfortunately, politics in Haiti were to ruin this promising industry. The Lescot Government

[1] "A few new foreign agricultural enterprises were started in Haiti, most of them after 1921, but only one or two were ever profitable". Munro, *op. cit.*, p. 537. In 1924 the Council of State of President Borno set up a Central School of Agriculture. It created six technical departments under U.S. officers. Cf. Raymond L. Buell, "The American Occupation of Haiti", *Foreign Policy Association Information Service*, Vol. V, Nos. 19–20, New York, n.d., p. 362.

[2] The World Health Organization reported in 1955 that a five-year campaign had practically eliminated yaws, previously Haiti's most serious health problem. *Hispanic American Report*, Vol. VIII, p. 468.

zoned the banana industry, allotting the south to several small companies. In 1947, the leading producers—the Standard Fruit Company and the Haytian Banana Exports, S.A.—harassed by the interference of the Estimé administration, ceased operations. The result was catastrophic to the Haitian economy. Banana exports for the year 1946-47 had provided nearly 20 per cent. of the value of Haiti's total exports. Three years later they had fallen to under 4 per cent., and the decline continued.[1]

Despite substantial aid from the United States, Haiti remained in the direst financial stress. What was in the eighteenth century the richest territory in the Caribbean, had become, by the middle of the twentieth century, one of the poorest. Nor had independence produced statesmanship to grapple with the problems facing a country with the lowest *per capita* income in Latin America and with a population whose expansion threatened still graver consequences.

The post-war development of the Artibonite Valley in central Haiti represented one of the most important developments in the Antilles. Financed by the Government of Haiti in conjunction with an Import-Export Bank loan, it was estimated to cost some $20 million. The project envisaged a planned development of the lower valley of the river, which suffered both from flooding and from insufficient rainfall. The development of rice production was designed to replace imports. Leaf tobacco, cotton and vegetables were to be grown and livestock extended. A barrage was constructed at Peligre to control the Artibonite river and provide irrigation water for some 35,000 hectares (86,485 acres). At the same time the dam was to generate electricity to meet the shortage in Port-au-Prince. The electrical part of the scheme was separate from the irrigation works and was exclusively in the hands of the Government of Haiti.[2] Although the barrage and irrigation works were largely completed, the electrical project was seriously delayed. Moreover, friction with the United States developed when the Haitian authorities insisted on the right to hire and fire personnel without the approval of U.S. officials.

Conditions in Haiti when Duvalier took over were showing some signs of improvement. Like its Caribbean neighbours the Republic was endeavouring to attract new industries; a law giving tax concessions had been enacted.[3] Although exports had dropped, the tourist trade continued expanding. In the first quarter (the winter season) of 1955,

[1] "The peasants, disappointed and defrauded by local companies, simply ceased growing bananas". Rotberg, *op. cit.*, p. 287.

[2] *Plan and Program for Development of the Artibonite Valley* (Port-au-Prince, 1952).

[3] The tax concession was 100 per cent. for the first year and 20 per cent. for the next five.

25,000 had visited the country, 5,000 more than the annual total for any year prior to 1953. As a general rule the length of stay was not more than three days; less than half the tourists arrived by air.[1] However, disturbed internal conditions in Haiti began to discourage tourists to the island. In 1964, Duvalier created an Office National du Tourisme, in an attempt to bolster up and expand the industry. In December 1970 Haiti went into the foreign divorce business in an effort to increase tourism. Weakness in coffee prices causing Haiti's exports to drop underlined tourism's importance. Clearly the Haitian economy required all the financial help possible from the United States as well as from international agencies. As the largest contributor to these organizations, the United States was well placed to interest them in Haiti's problems.

With an infinite capacity for reversing its policy towards Haiti,[2] the United States in June 1962 renewed its annual contributions of $7·25 million, in addition to new loans amounting to nearly $6 million under the Alliance for Progress programme. This financing took place despite American criticisms of the general malversation of $18·5 million during the first four years of Duvalier's Presidency from 1957, including a defalcation in a previous $3·4 million road-building fund. In September 1962, Congress reverted to its policy of sharply reducing Alliance for Progress funds to Haiti. However, at the end of September, the International Monetary Fund announced a stand-by arrangement authorizing Haiti to draw up to $6 million over a twelve-month period. Apparently the complaints of Paul Blanchet, Haitian Secretary of Information, who had declared that the U.S. conditions attached to further aid violated Haiti's sovereign right of choosing its own policy, had influenced the decision of the International Monetary Fund.

In October 1962, Haitian Secretary of Agriculture André Théard announced that the American aid reduction had made it necessary to cut the annual budget of the uncompleted Artibonite irrigation project from $400,000 to $80,000. There was, however, apparently no reduction in the allocation of $40,000 to the Tonton Macoute for salaries, uniforms and transportation.

Once again changing its policy, the United States announced in the same month the offer of a $2·8 million loan for the construction of a jet airport at Port-au-Prince.[3] The loan was defended on the grounds that Haiti needed the airport whether or not Duvalier remained in power. The confusion in U.S. economic policy over Haiti was matched only by its cynicism.

[1] Paul Moral, *L'Economie Haïtienne* (Port-au-Prince, 1959), p. 134.
[2] *Vide* pp. 52, 57 and 59-60.
[3] *Vide* p. 53.

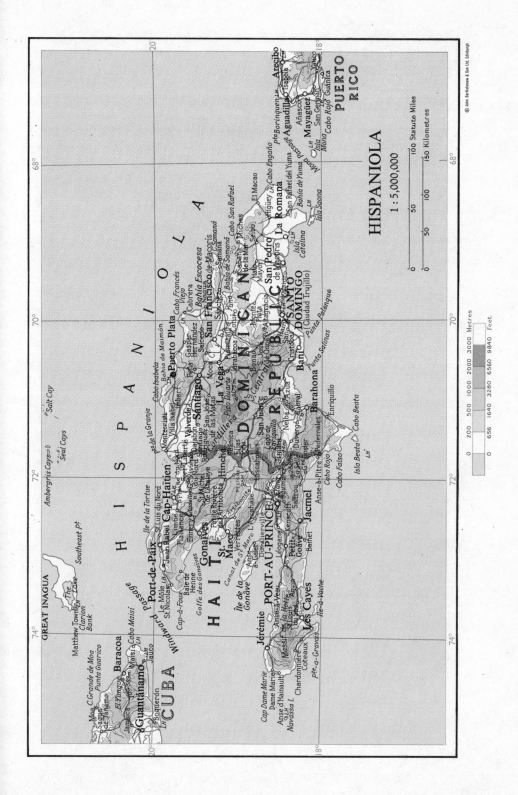

HISPANIOLA

1 : 5,000,000

The gloomy political, financial and economic picture which the country had almost consistently presented had continued. Its deterioration had hardly ceased since the French plantations in the Plaine du Nord, the Artibonite Valley and the Cul de Sac were destroyed or permitted to run down.[1] Poverty had become endemic. Politics enmeshed in graft dominated commerce. The impoverished population could provide only a minimum market even if the country were to attempt serious industrialization. Competition from African and other territories even endangered Haiti's traditional exports of coffee to France.

Thanks to the United Nations' concern with underdeveloped countries, Haiti was able to obtain outside development aid. Political mismanagement, however, wrecked any chance of success. Advancing years in independence were not matched with increasing political integrity.

A population density of 430 persons to the square mile, of whom 89·5 per cent. are illiterate,[2] and a falling income *per capita* of $60, results in most Haitians in the rural areas living outside the money economy.[3] So they have existed for generations in primitive dwellings often on arid and eroded hillsides which comprise so much of Haiti. Not enough good-quality level land exists to provide the base for a modern agricultural system. Far from improving, the condition of the peasants is deteriorating. The very success of the medical and sanitation programme initiated by the American military government (1915 to 1934), which resulted in a sharp population rise, doomed the country to endemic unemployment. No agricultural or industrial development has appeared likely to make an impression on the grim poverty. As in many other Caribbean countries, accurate figures of unemployment are lacking. Some fifteen thousand Haitians have in recent years illegally entered Nassau in the Bahamas, transported by unscrupulous captains who have held out tales of well-paid employment. The immigrants swim or wade ashore at night. Despite large sums of money spent by the Bahamas Government in rounding up and disposing of these unfortunate people, paradoxically the economy depends to some extent

[1] A good description of sugar conditions under the French colonial system, the change to peasant agriculture, and the difficulties of instituting a modern system of central sugar factories is set out by Paul Moral, *op. cit.*, pp. 104-9.

[2] Census of 1950. *Statistical Yearbook*, 1964, U.N.E.S.C.O., Paris, 1966, pp. 20 and 38.

[3] Eighty-seven per cent. of the population is rural, the highest percentage in Latin America.

on this Haitian labour which undertakes work undesirable to local inhabitants.[1]

Haiti's economy remains perilously poised on exports of coffee, sisal, and a little sugar and cacao. All are products which have fluctuated considerably since World War II. The setting up of light industries by U.S. and Canadian companies has eased unemployment, but capital comes from, and profits go, abroad. Bauxite appears to be the only mineral of commercial significance within the country. The future of Haiti's swelling population, estimated at 4·6 million in 1968, appears to be dim.

When Haiti won independence in 1803, no public schools existed. By 1954, 3,660 public and private schools functioned, a considerable improvement. Not withstanding the advance, the illiteracy rate remains one of the highest in the world. Education, traditionally modelled on that of France, has remained the monopoly of the elite. Its attitude to extending education has too often exhibited indifference, linked to the tradition that an educated man should do no manual work. Peasants, themselves illiterate, show little enthusiasm for learning; they encourage their children to seek employment at an early age rather than to further their education. Moreover, the Haitian curriculum has always tended to be literary rather than practical.[2] The peasants speak Creole; yet most classes are given in French,[3] spoken by some 10 per cent. of Haitians, which is, in the words of Professor Leyburn, "as different from that tongue as Dutch from German".[4] Illiteracy is more rampant in the country districts than in the towns: in 1950 it was highest in the Department of the Artibonite and, as might be expected, lowest in the Department of the West, which contains Port-au-Prince.[5]

[1] Cf. Ian Scott, "Haiti refugees a big social problem", *The Financial Times*, London, April 1, 1969. In 1968 the number of work permits granted to Haitians in the Bahamas was second only to those granted to Americans. *Statistical Abstract 1969*, Commonwealth of the Bahamas, Department of Statistics, Nassau, Bahamas, October 1970, p. 29.

[2] "Teachers trained in this tradition might teach Racine and Montaigne, but not soil conservation and new methods of planting." James G. Leyburn, *The Haitian People* (Yale University Press, New Haven, 1941), p. 279. *Vide* p. 284.

[3] Maurice A. Lubin of the Institut Haitien de Statistique in Port-au-Prince draws attention to the success of primary instruction in Creole as opposed to French. "Il convient de signaler qu'à la phase primaire, l'enseignement se donne en créole (Méthode Lauback ou méthode traditionnelle). N'importe. L'individu qui peut lire du noir sur du blanc est alphabétisé." "Où en sommes-nous avec l'élite intellectuelle d'Haïti." *Journal of Inter-American Studies*, University of Florida, Gainesville, January, 1961, p. 129.

[4] *Op. cit.*, p. 279.

[5] 92·2 per cent. in the Artibonite and 86·5 in the West. *World Illiteracy at Mid-Century*, U.N.E.S.C.O., 1957, p. 56.

Since 1950 some improvement has taken place in primary school education due to the expansion of private schools. In the decade 1950-60 the number of primary school children at private schools increased by 15 per cent. Nevertheless, in 1960, out of 993,000 children of primary school age in both rural and urban areas, only 25 per cent. attended school, either public or private.[1] The theory that primary schooling is both compulsory and free is far from being the case.[2] Secondary schools cater more for the wealthy who are better able to pay for a good primary education, thus enabling their children to pass the necessary entrance examination. In 1961 out of 18 public and 50 private secondary schools, only four were in the countryside.[3]

University education follows the Latin American pattern.[4] Students prefer to study law and medicine rather than agriculture or engineering. In consequence, a surplus of lawyers and doctors has been created, as in other Latin American countries, particularly in the urban areas where the earning power is greater.

In 1961 educational centres known as "écoles d'analphabétisation" for adults came under the Office National de Développement Communautaire, and by March 1962 there were 88 of these, of which 33 were in rural areas. According to Professor Brand, they have not been a success due to a rapid and continuing fall in attendance, linked to a lack of qualified teachers and equipment.[5]

The high cost of providing good education is the obvious stumbling-block to progress in Haiti. In the rural areas the cost is borne by the Ministry of Agriculture, which has less funds at its disposal for this purpose than the Ministry of Education responsible for the urban areas. In 1962 rural education received another blow when as a result of the reduction in U.S. aid, the allocation for the construction and maintenance of rural schools was reduced by 85 per cent. According to the budget for 1966, the Haitian Government's expenditure on military forces was more than double that on education.[6] The 1968–1969

---

[1] W. Brand, *Impressions of Haiti* (The Hague, 1965), pp. 48-9, 52.

[2] By the Constitution of 1950, education became the responsibility of the national and muncipal governments.

[3] Brand, *op. cit.*, p. 53.

[4] The University of Port-au-Prince was created in 1944 out of several independent schools and institutions. In 1960 it was reorganized by decree.

[5] *Op. cit.*, p. 52.

[6] $7 million was to be spent on Defence and Interior and $3 million on Education. *Cuba, Dominican Republic, Haiti, Puerto Rico, Quarterly Economic Review*, Economist Intelligence Unit, London, January 1966.

economic plan allocated 4 million gourdes to education out of a total of 65 million.[1]

* * * *

Haiti's economy recalls parts of Africa; its proximity to the prosperity of the United States underlines the effects of more than a century and a half of bad and arbitrary government. International aid has spasmodically been extended. Yet until the basic question of the nation's illiteracy has been solved the future of Haiti in a Western Hemisphere, or even in a Caribbean context, is unpromising. However, Haiti cannot afford to remain isolated from current trends towards economic unity in the Caribbean, although the advantages to the other territories of Haitian membership in any economic community may be hard to justify.[2]

The relatively small number of educated Haitians face a gloomy outlook. Just as Fidel Castro has encouraged the emigration of Cubans opposed to his regime, François Duvalier made little effort to utilize the skills of technically qualified Haitians, many of whom preferred to seek a career in other countries, including the Congo. Both probably have felt that the deportation of critics would contribute to stability. Jean-Claude Duvalier, in an immediate attempt to improve Haiti's international image, declared an amnesty for all Haitian political exiles, except known Communists. Whether many will avail themselves of the opportunity to return remains uncertain.

The small elite groups in the capital still look culturally to France. Yet culture and religion for the peasant majority remain basically African. Perhaps the whole attempt to Westernize Haiti was ill-advised. It raises the question of how far one civilization may be imposed upon another. The developments in different parts of Africa in coming years may well shed light on Haiti's problems.

François Duvalier's interest was in nationalism, not economics. He seemed to look back to the Haiti of Dessalines, now regarded as its greatest hero: an African state without whites or mulattoes. We must turn to South Africa to find a parallel philosophy today. In the final phase, he isolated himself in his fortified palace at Port-au-Prince in the glow of a voodoo nationalism amidst the remnants of Haiti's shattered economy. Well did Graham Greene name his satire on Haiti, *The Comedians*.[3] Yet with a new regime led by a young President the possibility of economic advance appeared as a challenge.

[1] *Plan d'action économique et sociale 1968–69*, Conseil National de Planification, Port-au-Prince, 1969.
[2] Cf. Gérard R. Latortue "Haiti et les institutions économiques Caraïbéenes", *Caribbean Studies*, Vol. 10, No. 3, Institute of Caribbean Studies, University of Puerto Rico, October 1970.   [3] (London, 1966.)

CHAPTER IV

THE DOMINICAN REPUBLIC

THE POLITICAL PATTERN

If Haiti's history had been grim, that of the Dominican Republic was not less tragic. Haiti had preserved, at least, the façade of independence since its successful revolution from the rule of France. After two successful rebellions, the first against the French in 1809, the second against Ferdinand VII, the Dominican patriots declared their independence in 1821 and endeavoured to secure association with Simón Bolívar's Gran Colombia. However, President Jean-Pierre Boyer of Haiti invaded the Dominican Republic in 1822 and imposed a harsh Negro rule on the Spanish-speaking, largely Creole, population. The principal governmental posts were filled by Haitians, supported by a Negro army of occupation. Economically the country deteriorated, like Haiti had done after independence, as a result of confiscatory taxes. From the cultural angle Haitian rule was equally disastrous, with the closing of the University of Santo Domingo, the third oldest in the Americas, and the severance of papal relations.[1]

In 1843-44 the Dominicans, taking advantage of a civil war in Haiti, regained their freedom, but it was freedom in name only, for the Republic was normally ruled by corrupt and ruthless dictators. Pedro Santana, who alternated with Buenaventura Baez as President, arranged in 1861 with the Government of Queen Isabel II of Spain that his country should return to Spain as a colony, which he then administered as captain-general. The Dominicans, however, moved back to independence in 1865. Spanish rule had been disastrous, but the renewed freedom produced no improvement.

Under the presidency of Ulises Heureux (1882-99) the Dominican Republic became involved in fraudulent foreign loans.[2] As a result, in

[1] Although founded by decree in 1538, the University did not function at once. The University of Mexico, which began in 1553, and the University of San Marcos at Lima, which commenced in 1571, appear in fact to have functioned earlier.

[2] Professor Julius W. Pratt aptly comments: "The government of the Dominican Republic, or Santo Domingo, since that state won its independence from Haiti in 1844, had been a dictatorship generously tempered by revolution". *Op. cit.*, p. 417.

1904 European creditors threatened the Dominican Republic with the seizure of its custom-house to enforce payment.[1] However, the U.S. Government itself, which also had claims of its nationals to look after, intervened and took over the custom-house. This action led to the announcement of the celebrated doctrine which became known as the "Roosevelt Corollary".[2] As an addendum to its insistence on the inviolability of the Americas in terms of the Monroe Doctrine, the United States announced that it might be forced to collect debts owing to other countries by Latin American governments which had failed to recognize their contractual obligations.

In 1904 the United States appointed an agent to take over the custom-house at Puerto Plata on the north coast of the Dominican Republic. When later in the year France threatened a similar move on the capital and Italy dispatched a cruiser, President Carlos F. Morales asked for United States help.[3] After protracted negotiations, a convention was approved in 1907 under which the American President appointed customs receivers for the creditors. Following the assassination in 1911 of Ramón Cáceres, who had succeeded Morales as President, President William Howard Taft sent Marines temporarily to the capital to protect the custom-house. In 1916 with disorder continuing and no solution in sight, President Woodrow Wilson again sent Marines to inaugurate what proved to be an eight-year takeover of the government of the republic. Despite Wilson's strongly expressed liberal views, his administration intervened in the internal affairs of Caribbean countries more than any of its predecessors.[4]

As in the case of Cuba and Haiti, considerable material benefits accrued from the advent of U.S. military government.[5] The U.S. Marine rule terminated, however, in 1924, when the American diplomat Sumner Welles arranged the withdrawal. Prior to the ending of the occupation, an election was held in which Horacio Vázquez was again chosen President. His rule was undistinguished but reasonable.

---

[1] More than $30 million was owing to nationals of France, Belgium, Germany, Italy, Spain and the United States.

[2] President Theodore Roosevelt proposed this doctrine to the Senate on February 15, 1905.

[3] In 1905 all custom-houses in the Dominican Republic were administered by an American receiver of customs appointed by President Theodore Roosevelt, the proceeds being divided in the proportion of 55 per cent. to the foreign creditors and 45 per cent. to the Republic's Treasury. Graham H. Stuart, *Latin America and the United States*, 5th edition (New York, 1955), pp. 267-8.

[4] Munro, *op. cit.*, p. 269.

[5] *Vide* pp. 90-1.

However, when he sought re-election illegally in 1930, it became clear that the American-trained constabulary force, the counterpart of the Garde d'Haïti in the sister republic, was the real power in the Dominican Republic.[1] Rafael Leonidas Trujillo, head of that force, became the strong man of the Dominican Republic. He was to rule it either as President or through puppets for the following thirty-one years.

Unlike some of his predecessors, Marine-trained Trujillo displayed drive and efficiency. After a severe hurricane had wrecked the city of Santo Domingo in 1930, the capital was rebuilt and renamed Ciudad Trujillo in his honour.[2] However, Trujillo's executive record was increasingly marred by growing corruption and his determination to retain power at all costs. Control of the police and armed forces was a simple matter for the self-styled generalissimo. Even when he relinquished the presidency for short periods to Jacinto B. Peynado and Manuel de Jesús Troncoso de la Concha, and later to his brother Héctor Bienvenido and to Joaquín Balaguer, in order to preserve an appearance of democracy, he retained control of the armed forces and continued to run the country as before. His title of the "Benefactor" applied more aptly to the good he did himself, his family and his friends than to that he did the country. Corruption became almost an institution. The dictator's personal fortune was prodigious, though some asserted that his associates were even more predatory.

Beneath a façade of law and order, the very effectiveness of the dictatorship led to the total suppression of liberty. The vanity of Trujillo compelled Dominican orators and writers to laud the dictator on every occasion. In the press and radio, which Trujillo controlled directly or indirectly, no criticism was permitted. Police control made even personal conversations dangerous. Enemies of the President were ruthlessly eliminated. While some were imprisoned, others might be found shot in automobiles or would simply disappear. The long arm of the dictator extended beyond the borders of his country. In an episode which attained international notoriety, Jesús de Galíndez, a Spanish refugee who had been employed by Trujillo and who disagreed with the dictatorship, had fled to the United States. As a lecturer at Columbia University, he wrote a highly critical doctoral dissertation entitled *La Era de Trujillo*.[3] After threats to his life, he suddenly disappeared one evening in New York City. The mystery was never cleared up, though the matter was pressed in the U.S. Congress. It seems probable that Galíndez had been kidnapped and taken to the

[1] *Vide* p. 51.
[2] *Vide* pp. 90-1.
[3] Posthumously published as *La Era de Trujillo* (Santiago de Chile, 1956).

Dominican Republic for torture and execution or had been killed on a Dominican merchant ship which sailed from New York shortly after his disappearance.

By the end of Trujillo's rule the Dominican Republic was one of the more efficient countries in Latin America from the angle of communications, trade and tourism. The construction of roads, harbours, airfields and public buildings testified to his capability. Trujillo might have said in his defence that to expect a democracy to flourish after years of maladministration, corruption and inefficiency was impossible, even with the interlude of U.S. Marine administration. Be that as it may, it cannot excuse the ever-increasing censorship, the stifling of human rights, and the curtailment of all means of expression.

When Fulgencio Batista fled from Cuba in January 1959, Trujillo gave him asylum in the Dominican Republic. The country was dubbed the hemisphere's hospitable zoo for ex-dictators, since Juan Perón of Argentina was also there, while earlier Marcos Pérez Jiménez of Venezuela had received Dominican asylum before he unwisely left for the United States.

Relations between the Dominican Republic and Cuba rapidly deteriorated, culminating by June 1959 in the landing of 150 persons, including Dominicans, Cubans, and Puerto Ricans, at Maimón Bay on the north coast of the Republic. Troops under the personal command of Trujillo, aided by the local peasantry, easily defeated the invasion attempt; the victory was celebrated by a fiesta at Santiago. As a protest against the Dominicans' alleged killing of their prisoners, and also because of the Dominican Republic's refusal to extradite Batista, Cuba severed diplomatic relations with the Dominican Republic.

Trujillo, who already possessed a small-arms factory at San Cristóbal near the capital, had begun to arm his country against what he termed the threat from Castro's Cuba. The cost of the armament soon resulted in a mounting financial crisis in the Dominican Republic. With rising hostility in Latin America towards the Dominican dictatorship, the United States was also becoming increasingly critical, notwithstanding its earlier support of Trujillo. In December 1959 it withdrew its naval mission to the Dominican Republic, and the following month it announced that it would supply no more military aid.

The thirty-one-year rule of the dictator ended on May 30, 1961, with his assassination while driving to his country home at San Cristóbal. In some ways, Trujillo may be compared to the Venezuelan dictator, Juan Vicente Gómez, who ruled Venezuela from 1908 to 1935. Both men came from humble origins. Both seized power and held it by ruthless force combined with qualities of organization. Development

Dominican Republic: Brigadier-General Elias Wessin y Wessin, the rightist military leader, with troops in the early days of the Revolution, May 1965.

United Press International

Dominican Republic: rioting Dominicans forced to pick up rubbish which they had thrown at U.S. soldiers of the Inter-American peace force.

Dominican Republic: Brazilian troops under O.A.S. command in defensive positions at the National Palace, Santo Domingo.

Dominican Republic: former President Juan Bosch.

Dominican Republic: Joaquín Balaguer, later President, campaigning at Santiago de los Caballeros.

marred by corruption took place during each of their dictatorships. Both men were sadistically savage to those who opposed them. Both were successful on the whole in their foreign relations with major powers, including the United States. Under Gómez's regime, the foreign oil companies opened Venezuela's Maracaibo basin. Similarly the Dominican sugar industry was greatly developed by Trujillo, partly with foreign aid. Both men had an absolute disregard for the human and civil rights of their subjects. The Dominican Republic and Venezuela were police states under these two dictators. Oddly, while the one started life as a policeman, the other gained his early experience as a smuggler.

Neither Trujillo's son Ramfis nor his brother Héctor had the ability to follow him, especially as the free world had latterly held the dictator's regime in such contempt.[1] After more than a year of political manœuvres, the Dominican Republic's first free elections in thirty-eight years were held in December 1962.[2]

The election aroused interest far beyond the country's boundaries, since "La Era de Trujillo" had earned international opprobrium. The violence of the regime within and even beyond its borders had aroused increasing hostility in the United States and in several Latin American countries. To mark the importance of the coming electoral contest, the Organization of American States sent a three-man advisory group to observe the election, which was regarded as a test for the survival of democracy in Latin America.[3]

For the novel task of choosing on December 20, 1962, a President, Vice-President, 27 Senators and 74 Deputies, no less than 28 political parties appeared, though only eight campaigned and nominated candidates. However, these eight claimed between them a total membership exceeding nine million persons—about three times the total population of the Dominican Republic.[4]

The most distinguished candidate for the Presidency was Juan Bosch, Chairman of the Partido Revolucionario Dominicano. A novelist and political scientist who had spent nineteen years of his life in exile, he carried his campaign to the countryside and impoverished villages.[5] To

---

[1] Cf. Gerald Clark, *The Coming Explosion in Latin America* (New York, 1963), p. 286.

[2] General Horacio Vázquez became President in 1924 as the result of a free election.

[3] The O.A.S. advisory group were joined by Secretary-General José A. Mora and a team of 28 observers.

[4] *Hispanic American Report*, Vol. XV, p. 1013.

[5] Aged 53, Bosch was the son of a Catalan immigrant with German and Italian blood. His exile had been spent in Cuba, Costa Rica and the United States.

these people his slogan was "Land and Dignity", a reference to his party's promise to settle 70,000 families on seventeen-acre farms over the coming four years. For the intellectuals in the towns his cry was "Dignity against money", in which he hit at the traditional graft among the establishment in the capital.

Bosch also advocated a move from the dominance of sugar in the economy to diversification by the development of livestock farming. The transformation into co-operatives of the government-owned sugar properties, which had been taken over from Trujillo, was also part of his platform.

Although he had to meet attacks both from the right and the left, Bosch proved his mettle as an electioneer. At a critical point towards the end of the election, he refuted charges that he was a Communist in a television debate with Laútico García, a priest and one of his leading critics. The nation watched fascinated as Bosch's transparent honesty overcame his opponent. His sincerity at this confrontation had an influence which may be compared with the Kennedy–Nixon debates in the United States' 1960 election.

Bosch defeated his nearest rival, Viriato Alberto Fiallo of the conservative Unión Cívica Nacional, by about two to one.[1] The size of his victory was surprising as Fiallo appeared to be the candidate favoured by the U.S. Government. That a genuinely free election had been held was a remarkable achievement following on thirty-one years of dictatorship.[2] Moreover, some 65 per cent. of the electorate was illiterate. The result was widely welcomed. Bosch visited the United States shortly after his election, meeting President Kennedy, Secretary of State Dean Rusk, and Teodoro Moscoso, Co-ordinator for the Alliance for Progress. He also visited London, doubtless having in mind that Great Britain was his country's second best customer.

Whatever reservations it may have held during the Dominican election, the United States welcomed Bosch as President. Vice-President Lyndon B. Johnson represented his country at the inauguration ceremony at Santo Domingo, while Rafael E. Bonelly, President of

---

[1] Bosch polled 628,495 votes, Fiallo 315,877. The total poll was 1,050,867. The Partido Revolucionario Dominicano won 23 out of 27 seats in the Senate, and 52 out of 74 seats in the Chamber of Deputies. The Unión Cívica Nacional, later the principal opposition party, obtained 4 Senate and 21 Chamber of Deputies seats.

[2] Cf. Henry Wells, "The O.A.S. and the Dominican Elections", Orbis, Vol. VII, No. 1, Foreign Policy Research Institute, University of Pennsylvania, Spring 1963.

the interim Council of State, was praised by the U.S. State Department for making possible the orderly transition of government.[1]

As a liberal, the new President's position was far from easy. On taking office, he was faced with a $45 million deficit in the national finances. He set a good example by reducing government salaries, including his own and those of his ministers. Moreover, the United States, glad to see the end of the dictatorship, indicated its willingness to continue the substantial aid which had recently been afforded under the Alliance for Progress to the Dominican Republic. The purpose was to make it a showcase; since the fall of Trujillo, nearly $50 million in loans and grants had been made. A boom in sugar prices should also have favoured the Dominican economy, since the State, as a result of taking over the Trujillo holdings, was now the largest producer of this commodity in the country.[2]

In April 1963, the new President faced a crisis which nearly led to war with Haiti. A diplomatic quarrel between the two neighbours flared when pressure was exerted on the Dominican embassy at Port-au-Prince alleged to be giving asylum to 24 refugees.[3] On May 7, in a nation-wide speech, Bosch declared: "Duvalier must go. . . . The Dominican Republic is a lake of gasoline beside a keg of gun-powder."[4] Applied in either order, the simile was apt. As events turned out, however, Bosch would be the first to go.

Criticism of Bosch for his leftist views had been increasing, particularly from his unsuccessful opponents. Germán E. Ornes, editor of the nationally influential *El Caribe* of Santo Domingo, made charges of censorship against the Government, also asserting that it was waging a campaign against his paper with a view to expropriating it.[5] Bosch vigorously rebutted the accusation, claiming that no act of persecution by his Government against the paper could be cited.[6]

In an atmosphere of mounting criticism of Bosch, inevitable when the glamour of a successful election had begun to wear off, Fiallo,

[1] After the end of the Trujillo dictatorship, the capital had reverted to its former name.

[2] However, State ownership proved difficult. *Vide* p. 93.

[3] *Vide* p. 55.

[4] *Hispanic American Report*, Vol. XVI, p. 461.

[5] *El Mundo*, San Juan, Puerto Rico, April 6, 1963. A former editor of *El Caribe* under the Trujillo regime, Ornes had quarrelled with the dictator. In exile, he published a scathing attack entitled *Trujillo: Little Caesar of the Caribbean* (New York, 1958).

[6] *El Mundo*, April 23, 1963. However, in an editorial it had earlier expressed concern at the progress of events in the Dominican Republic, asserting that already there was suppression of liberty of speech and news. San Juan, Puerto Rico, April 8, 1963.

leader of the conservative opposition, asserted that the President favoured Communism. Radio commentator Rafael Bonilla Aybar, who had been charged with embezzling funds belonging to the government newspaper *La Nación* was arrested: released on bail, he declared that the Bosch Government could "rely on the full support of international Communism". That these attacks were having an effect was apparent when U.S. Representative Armistead Selden, Chairman of the Foreign Affairs Committee of the House of Representatives, criticized Bosch on the ground that he had permitted to return to the Dominican Republic 150 Communists exiled during the Cuban crisis in 1962.[1] However, Senator Hubert Humphrey retorted that Bosch was a target not only of Radio Havana, which claimed that he was an imperialist, but also of the enemies of reform who assaulted him from the opposite angle. Humphrey likened the attacks to those which had been made on President Rómulo Betancourt of Venezuela.[2]

Opposition to Bosch increased. In July 1963, at San Isidro Air Base, high-ranking military officers demanded that he suppress leftist activity. He replied that he would sooner quit office than yield to pressure. The following month a mass meeting of some 40,000 persons was held at the Puerta del Conde in Santo Domingo. Principal speakers were Bonilla Aybar and General Belisario Peguero Guerrero, Chief of Police. Both were warmly applauded, while the President's name was received with jeers. Notwithstanding the impropriety of Peguero's attack on his head of state, he was not dismissed. The President seemed to be losing his grip. Anti-Bosch meetings followed in the Cibao, to the north of the Republic. Thousands of the strongly Catholic peasants rallied to the cry "Cristianismo sí, Comunismo no". Labour troubles added to the President's difficulties with successive strikes of workers at the La Romana sugar-factory.

On September 25, 1963, the President was overthrown by a military junta. His opponents alleged that he had been working to introduce Communism into the country: this Bosch emphatically denied. The ouster was widely criticized.[3] The democratically elected President, chosen by an overwhelming majority less than a year before, left his country to resume exile which had for so long been his lot.[4] His fall

---

[1] May 31, 1963. [2] June 10, 1963.

[3] Cf. Theodore Draper, "Bosch y el Comunismo", *Cuadernos*, Paris, January 1964, pp. 29-35.

[4] Bosch, who first sought asylum in Guadeloupe, was brought by a Puerto Rican Government plane to San Juan. In an editorial, *The San Juan Star* commented on the curious situation of a government plane being sent to a foreign country to transport a newly deposed President. Puerto Rico, October 2, 1963.

at first aroused little protest. Later demonstrations were firmly put down by his successors.

Despite his many talents, Bosch lacked the strength and determination vital to success. He took over a country that had been in the grip of a dictator for thirty-one years. He had no trained civil servants other than those of "La Era de Trujillo", an immense disadvantage to an incoming President committed to the quick implementation of an ambitious programme. Bosch's land reforms, though only incipient, aroused hostility among his opponents. Many who accepted that Bosch was not a Communist believed that he would pave the way for Communism as Fidel Castro had done in Cuba.

Nor could the President's ministers supply the experience and talent he required. He could rely on neither his armed forces nor his police. His long exile abroad resulted in his having few influential friends. Unorganized, Bosch's peasant supporters were powerless to help him. It was far easier for his opponents to promote a shop strike in Santo Domingo which aided the overthrow of his Government.

The issue of the Bosch administration was whether the *petite bourgeoisie*, which under Trujillo's patronage had come to rival the economic and political power of the traditional aristocracy, was strong enough to govern. At the recent election they had largely sided with Bosch. In Norman Gall's view, the Dominican Republic was being run by a group of half-educated, unsure, fearful men who were chiefly provincial lawyers and merchants with political experience, conditioned by the thorough corruption of the Trujillo regime and the perpetual jealousy and jockeying of splintered groups in exile at San Juan, Caracas, Havana, New York and Miami.[1]

In a farseeing evaluation of the Dominican situation shortly after the 1962 election, Dom Bonafede described Bosch as "a white-haired, silver-tongued political mystic" who could be grouped with the Latin American Social Democratic leaders Rómulo Betancourt, Luís Muñoz Marín, Víctor Raúl Haya de la Torre, and José Figueres, all in search of a social revolution. He added that the internal conflict between artist and politician plagued Bosch since his administrative capabilities were clearly open to question.[2] Certainly Bosch's success with the peasant voters could be compared with that of Muñoz and Haya.

A lack of administrative experience, combined with electoral promises which he appeared unlikely to fulfil, and a failure to take action against

[1] "Ferment in the Caribbean", *The New Leader*, New York, June 10, 1963, p. 9.
[2] "Freedom after Trujillo: The Dominican Elections", *The Nation*, New York, January 12, 1963.

77

opponents proved Bosch's undoing. However much his culture and liberal sentiments may be admired, they were unlikely to prove an "open sesame" to the governance of one of the most unruly states in Latin America's turbulent history. Bosch himself had no doubt as to the reasons for his downfall. He placed the blame fairly and squarely on the shoulders of the military and civilian oligarchy whose machinations to defeat democracy had succeeded.[1]

The revolution of September 25, 1963, placed in power a triumvirate consisting of Emilio de los Santos (President), former Chairman of the Electoral Board, Manuel Tavárez Espaillat, a former Secretary of State prior to the election, and Ramón Tapia Espinal, former Secretary of Industry and Commerce. Effective power, however, rested with the military. In October, student riots in favour of Bosch were put down by police aided by troops.

The contradictions in U.S. policy, very apparent in the case of Haiti, could also be detected in its reactions to the Dominican *coup d'état*. At first the United States expressed its disapproval of the new regime and withheld recognition, a course which was followed by Costa Rica, El Salvador, Honduras, Nicaragua and Venezuela. However, Great Britain, for reasons of trade, and perhaps no more willing to follow blindly the United States' lead in the Dominican Republic than in Cuba, quickly gave its recognition. By November, nine Western European nations had followed this lead, as had Japan and the Philippines.

Notwithstanding the difficulties which the Triumvirate soon encountered, the United States reversed its policy and afforded recognition in mid-December. The real reasons for this change of attitude must remain a matter for speculation because of its complexity. Was the United States fearful lest delay might lead to a loss of its political influence in the Dominican Republic?[2] Was it loath to abandon the economic projects undertaken by the Alliance for Progress, work which had been halted since Bosch's fall? Pressures from U.S. commercial interests in the Dominican Republic may also have been strong. Moreover, the Pentagon fully appreciated the importance of the Dominican Republic in the strategy of the Caribbean. Probably a combination of these forces influenced President Kennedy and Dean Rusk. Obviously the early British recognition given to a Caribbean

---

[1] Juan Bosch, "Why I was Overthrown", *The New Leader*, New York, October 14, 1963.

[2] The United States had followed a somewhat similar policy in the case of the Peruvian *coup d'état* of July 18, 1962, when it immediately severed diplomatic relations but gave recognition on August 17, 1962.

country in an area where it had traditional influence had carried great weight.

In December 1963 a state of emergency together with the suspension of civil rights was declared, following guerrilla outbreaks which were firmly suppressed. Perhaps opposed to the harshness of the measures being put in force, Emilio de los Santos resigned as President of the Triumvirate. He gave no reason for his action. Donald Reid Cabral replaced him and a reconstruction of the Cabinet followed. Before the year was out, the Triumvirate survived an attempted *coup d'état* organized by Peguero, Commander of the 12,000-strong National Police Force. During a crisis in April 1964 within the Triumvirate itself, Tapia was forced to resign when the army chiefs protested that he had infringed their prerogative. In his place, Reid nominated Ramón Cáceres Troncoso, Ambassador to Italy. With labour disputes in the capital and mounting economic problems, the outlook for the Dominican Republic and its government seemed precarious.

In May 1964, serious disputes reminiscent of those which had occurred before the fall of Bosch took place in the capital. The taxi drivers, an important factor in Santo Domingo's transport, staged a strike in what appeared to be a political attempt to overthrow yet another government. Bus drivers, teachers and students supported the strike.[1] In three days of disorder, 548 persons were arrested.

Addressing the nation on radio and television, Triumvir Reid branded the strike as a Communist attempt to overturn the government, with the assistance of members of the extreme Right. He reminded the strikers that he had power to recruit them for military service, though adding that he did not wish to use it. Four radio stations were closed for expressing approval of this strike. Two thousand troops were used to re-establish order in the capital. In the end the strike collapsed. *The New York Times* said that Reid had handled the crisis with firmness and good sense. The newspaper commended the austerity measures of the Triumvirate, made more urgent since the United States had cut off all aid at the time of President Bosch's ouster.[2] Clearly, however, no permanent solution had as yet been found for the

---

[1] The strikers' demands included the right to hold union meetings, the withdrawal of police power to seize their driving licences for any infraction, and the revocation of the duty on vehicles and parts used in public transport.

[2] New York, May 7, 1964. By this action Reid's chances of success were gravely prejudiced during the first three months of his government because the United States continued to withhold all economic aid. It also withdrew its military and Alliance for Progress missions. Nevertheless, during the remainder of 1964, the United States disbursed $26 million in Alliance for Progress aid.

79

political dilemmas of the Republic. As had happened elsewhere in the Caribbean, the policy of the United States displayed ambivalence.

The Triumvirate appeared to be governing the Dominican Republic with limited success, bearing in mind the country's depressing political background. Whereas Bosch had pursued a weak economic policy, Reid attempted to steady an economy now seriously unbalanced. His austerity measures, however, combined with dismissals of military officers, probably accelerated his downfall.[1] He had also sacked Police Chief Peguero for embezzlement. With neither the prestige of popular election nor the force of traditional dictatorship, the well-intentioned Triumvirate was unable to cope with the rising tide of poverty and discontent. Bosch, who had foretold in June 1964 its overturn "within a year's time" proved a true prophet.[2]

On April 24, 1965, the Triumvirate collapsed before a rising of army officers, made possible by the attitude of the army's tank commander, Brigadier-General Elías Wessin y Wessin, who now withdrew his support from Reid. The generals were motivated by the fear that Reid would honour the Triumvirate's promise to hold elections on September 1, 1965. Reid was quickly confined in the Presidential Palace "for his own safety". Rafael Molina Urena, nominated as Acting President, called on Bosch to return from his exile in nearby Puerto Rico. Bosch, however, failed to come. Had he done so, it is at least possible that he would have been reinstated. Since the United States had only a year and a half before protested his overthrow, it could hardly have done other than accept him. Meanwhile, on April 27 General Wessin y Wessin launched from the San Isidro Air Base a powerful counter-attack against the new regime. Molina resigned and sought asylum in the Colombian embassy. After fierce fighting, the Molina forces were pressed into a limited area in the northern part of the city of Santo Domingo.

Meanwhile President Johnson, anxiously watching the drama, announced that he would dispatch U.S. troops since American citizens were in danger.[3] Two thousand paratroops were landed at San Isidro Air Base on May 1 while American warships patrolled off the coast. However, two days later, convinced that the Revolution presented a

---

[1] "One suspects the real reason for the revolt to be the fact that Donald Reid, the strong man in the overthrown Government, had cut down the military establishment in February and dismissed a number of officers. Moreover Mr. Reid had instituted several necessary austerity measures, which made him unpopular and hence vulnerable." *The New York Times*, New York, editorial, April 26, 1965.

[2] Cf. *The New York Herald Tribune*, New York, editorial, April 28, 1965.

[3] The President set forth his views in a broadcast address, May 2, 1965.

Communist risk, Johnson increased the build-up of American troops to 14,000. Within a few days the U.S. forces totalled over 20,000 troops, together with 9,000 sailors on warships off the cost. A truce was signed on May 5, to be interrupted, however, by intermittent fighting and sniping.

To replace Molina, his supporters proclaimed Colonel Francisco Caamaño Deñó Provisional President. In opposition, a five-man military junta which directed the "government" forces set up a Government of National Reconstruction headed by General Antonio Imbert Barreras, which claimed to be in control of all twenty-six of the Dominican provinces and 90 per cent. of the capital district. Intermittent fighting, occasionally fierce, continued in Santo Domingo, despite attempts at outside mediation. However, on May 21, another brief truce was accepted by both sides. U.S. and later O.A.S. forces attempted to separate the adversaries by the occupation of a strip of Santo Domingo. Charges brought by the Caamaño faction, which asserted that the Imbert faction had executed a number of prisoners, further exacerbated the situation.

The weighty intervention of the United States had altered what might have been regarded as simply another *coup d'état* in a small Latin American country into something loaded with international significance. President Johnson had been faced with the decision of taking an immediate action which involved his contravening Articles 15 and 17 of the Charter of the O.A.S.[1] The Charter was not, however, drafted to facilitate rapid decision in an emergency. Nor was the record of former Marine occupations of the Dominican Republic and of Haiti likely to inspire confidence, even if full credit is given to the much greater understanding that the U.S. Government of today has of similar situations compared with that of its predecessors in the earlier part of the century. The issue, therefore, became not only a legal but a moral one which divided world opinion.

[1] Article 15: "No State or group of States has the right to intervene, directly or indirectly, for any reason whatever, in the internal or external affairs of any other State. The foregoing principle prohibits not only armed force but also any other form of interference or attempted threat against the personality of the State or against its political, economic and cultural elements."

Article 17: "The territory of a State is inviolable; it may not be the object, even temporarily, of military occupation or of other measures of force taken by another State, directly or indirectly, on any grounds whatever. No territorial acquisitions or special advantages obtained either by force or by other means of coercion shall be recognized."

Cf. Walter Lippmann, "Solidarity of the Americas", *The New York Herald Tribune*, New York, May 7, 1965.

Strong criticism from the Iron Curtain countries was inevitable, and may be considerably discounted. At a meeting of the U.N. Security Council called for by the Soviet Union, Nicolai T. Fedorenko accused the United States of "trampling under foot the fundamental principles of the United Nations and the universally recognised principles of international law". Replying for the United States, Adlai E. Stevenson retorted that the American nations would not permit the establishment of another Communist government in the Western Hemisphere. The United States had summoned the entire Hemisphere to prevent Communism from gaining control of the Dominican Republic.[1] Put to the vote, the Soviet-sponsored motion condemning the United States action in the Dominican Republic failed to win the support of any of the other ten member-countries of the Council.

Among the allies of the United States, the British Government approved its action in the Dominican Republic, as it had done in the case of Vietnam, perhaps bearing in mind the importance of American aid in the financial difficulties which beset Great Britain at that time. The British press was less convinced. In France, President Charles de Gaulle was sharply critical of the U.S. intervention[2] and the French press was equally unsympathetic.[3]

Latin America, annoyed at the United States' initial by-passing of the O.A.S., took strong exception to the American intervention. President Raúl Leoni of Venezuela protested to the O.A.S. that the U.S. landings were a unilateral violation of O.A.S. principles. The Venezuelan Congress unanimously endorsed its President's views. In Lima, Foreign Minister Fernando Schwalb López Aldaña condemned the intervention as interference against the personality of the State. The Peruvian Senate called for the withdrawal of U.S. troops in the name of American solidarity, while the Mexican Government hoped that the Marine intervention would be as brief as possible. Unable to secure unanimity, the O.A.S. scraped together a token force to which Brazil was the major contributor. The United States placed its troops in the Dominican Republic under the O.A.S. commander, General Hugo Panasco Alvim of Brazil. Thus an O.A.S. façade was established.

[1] United Nations, New York, May 3, 1965.
[2] De Gaulle's attack on U.S. policy in the Dominican Republic brought strong editorial comment from *The Times*, which claimed that the French President had broken new and dangerous ground in an area where no major French interest was involved. London, May 7, 1965.
[3] Marcel Niedergang claimed that U.S. action in the Dominican Republic had provoked growing anger in Latin America, even in countries traditionally faithful to Washington. *Le Monde*, Paris, May 9-10, 1965.

Notwithstanding generally unfavourable and often hostile foreign comment on the United States' intervention, the U.S. public for the most part supported the President.[1] Former President Dwight D. Eisenhower shared the sentiments of the majority of Americans in backing the Government's policy.[2] However, an influential minority, strongly represented by the liberals in Congress, in the Universities and by some sections of the Press, was sharply critical.[3]

Lengthy negotiations took place to find a solution to the Dominican impasse by setting up an interim government as a prelude to the holding of elections. The greatest difficulty arose in selecting a suitable Dominican leader. With memories of Castro's move towards the Iron Curtain, any leftist was suspect to the United States. On the other hand, three decades of Trujillo's dictatorship had provided no training-ground for democratic government and had tainted many leaders of the armed forces and civil service.

After much discussion and manœuvring, on August 31, 1965, Hector García Godoy was proposed by the O.A.S. for the post of provisional President until elections could be held. A member of one of the oldest families in the country, he was an industrialist and former diplomat. Aged 44, he had served for eighteen years in the Foreign Service under Trujillo and in 1963 had become Foreign Minister in Bosch's

---

[1] George Gallup estimated that nearly 80 per cent. of persons interviewed at a survey were aware of the Dominican crisis, and that 76 per cent. favoured President Johnson's move, while 17 per cent. opposed it and 7 per cent. had no opinion. "U.S. Majority Favors Policy in Santo Domingo", *The New York Herald Tribune*, New York, June 2, 1965.

[2] Press interview, April 30, 1965, Harrisburg, Pennsylvania. From the angle of international law a strong defence of the U.S. intervention was made by Leonard C. Meeker: "We recognized that, regardless of any fundamentalist view of international law, the situation then existing required us to take action to remove the threat and at the same time to avoid nuclear war. In the tradition of the common law we did not pursue some particular legal analysis or code, but instead sought a practical and satisfactory solution to a pressing problem." Meeker also argues that without the U.S. troops, the O.A.S. would have had no foothold for constructing multilateral action and peacemaking efforts. "The Dominican Situation in the Perspective of International Law", *Department of State Bulletin*, Washington, D.C., July 12, 1965, p. 64.

[3] "One line of anti-Johnson talk is that Thomas C. Mann, Under Secretary of State for Economic Affairs, is turning out to be a 'czar' of U.S. policy in the Western Hemisphere. From an embittered 'liberal' came this assertion: 'Johnson doesn't know Latin America. All he has is the Texas border outlook on Latin Americans—a decidedly negative one. But Mann does know Latin America and obviously sold Johnson on invading at the drop of a hat.'" "The 'Liberal' Break with Johnson", *U.S. News and World Report*, Washington, D.C., May 24, 1965.

Government. He thus had qualifications which might prove acceptable to both of the warring factions.

Although Caamaño's Government was prepared to accept the O.A.S. proposal, Imbert claimed that his was the provisional government which should rule the country until a general election could be held. With strong pressure from the O.A.S. and also from the United States, García Godoy was finally appointed President of the Provisional Government. His task was an unenviable one, since he took over a divided and frustrated country with an empty treasury. Moreover, he would have to depend largely on foreign troops and aid. Yet the very installation of a President was at least a gain, even if the weather ahead still presaged storms.

Perhaps the most subtle task of García Godoy, as Provisional President, was to move the top military leaders to suitable employment outside of the Dominican Republic. Fortunately plenty of precedents could be quoted for these sort of situations in Latin America. The normal "asylum" in such a case was a diplomatic post, although Wessin y Wessin had already refused such an appointment in the United States, and near-force had been necessary to get him out. Commodore Francisco Rivera Caminero and his associates of the right refused to leave until Colonel Caamaño Deñó and his group had departed. Finally honour was satisfied. Caamaño went to London as Military Attaché and Rivera Caminero to Washington. Others went as military attachés to Canada, Chile and Belgium.[1] Nevertheless, the President continued to be harried in turn by both sides.[2]

Meanwhile the 1966 electoral campaign was commencing in a tense situation. Juan Bosch as a candidate criticized the Provisional President on the grounds that he had not got all of the right-wing military leaders out of the country.[3] As a former President who had been honestly elected, Bosch was regarded as a likely winner.

Precautions were taken to organize a fair election. García Godoy expressed his confidence that the polling would be orderly, honest and free. The O.A.S. provided a team of 42 observers assigned to check against fraud at selected stations. A further group of 70 from the United States and Latin America also arrived to observe the voting. Voters had to dip the index finger in red ink as a check against double voting.

As the June election drew near, pessimism mounted. One solution

[1] Altogether a total of 34 officers from both sides left the country in January 1966. Cf. *The New York Times*, New York, editorial, February 16, 1966.

[2] Cf. Rowland Evans and Robert Novak, "The Dominican Headache", *The New York Herald Tribune*, New York, March 1, 1966.

[3] *The New York Times*, New York, editorial, March 3, 1966.

suggested was another provisional government to be headed jointly by Bosch and his principal opponent, Balaguer, since "both are intellectuals who might have the capacity for mutual understanding".[1] To most people, however, it must have sounded an odd and unlikely team.

Bosch had the support of all the left. His own views have been compared to those of Rómulo Betancourt of Venezuela and José Figueres, namely moderate left of centre. Three and a half years previously, Bosch had won the election, polling 63 per cent. of the total votes cast.

Balaguer, moderate right of centre, represented the most important anti-socialist elements in the country. A professor of law at Santo Domingo University, he had been Trujillo's Vice-President from 1957 to 1959. He then became the dictator's nominee as President.

Rafael Bonnelly stood as the third candidate, supported by the rightist National Civic Union. He had served as Minister of the Interior and Minister of Justice under Trujillo. From the outset of the campaign the contest clearly lay between Bosch and Balaguer.

The United States in 1962 had favoured Bosch's candidacy, but in 1966 the position had changed. The Johnson administration regarded Bosch as too tolerant of Communism. On the eve of the poll, *The Guardian* summed up the U.S. position: "The United States has been, for the past year, in the position of an unwilling colonial Power. Her troops have kept order in a reluctant and embarrassed fashion; her technical advisers have supplied the skill; her treasury has supported the currency; and her pro-consul—in the person of Mr. Ellsworth Bunker, the leader of the three-man commission provided by the Organization of American States—has tried to restore political peace."[2]

When the votes were counted, Balaguer won with a majority of 241,000 votes. Bosch carried the capital, Santo Domingo, but not with the plurality he had obtained in 1962. Balaguer swept the countryside, including Santiago de los Caballeros, his hometown and second city in the Republic. His victory was attributed to his personal campaign all over the country. Balaguer may also have been aided by the extension to women of the right to vote without the need for an enrolment carnet. This theory postulates that the woman voter is more conservative than the man.[3] A small poll for Bonnelly suggested that some of his supporters may have swung to Balaguer as being more likely to defeat Bosch.

[1] *The New York Herald Tribune*, New York, editorial, March 12-13, 1966.
[2] Editorial, London, June 1, 1966.
[3] J. Halcro Ferguson, *Observer Foreign News Service*, London, No. 22710, June 3, 1966.

The division of the voting between Santo Domingo, the only large city, and the rest of the Dominican Republic which is dominantly rural, symbolized the dichotomy in the country at the time of the Revolution. The same pattern has clearly appeared in Jamaica, in Guyana and in Surinam, although in the two latter countries, racialism influences the voting.

Both Balaguer and Bosch had in their election campaigns called for the withdrawal of the Inter-American Peace Force, by then composed of about 8,000 men, dominantly U.S. troops, but under O.A.S. command. The time had clearly come for a phased withdrawal of foreign troops, notwithstanding that many believed the election of a Dominican Government to be less difficult than its retention in office. Finally the O.A.S. voted to withdraw its forces from the Dominican Republic over a ninety-day period. Appropriately July 1, 1966, was selected for the beginning of the operation since it was also the day of the swearing in of President Balaguer.

The extensive U.S. Embassy at Santo Domingo had during the fourteen months of U.S. intervention expanded its U.S. personnel from 47 to 115 and the local employees from 42 to 286.[1] Much of the increased U.S. activity centred in the Agency for International Development, whose personnel had risen from 23 to 131. A.I.D. expenditure increased from $12 million in 1964 to $130 million in the fourteen months following the Revolution.[2]

In true Latin American tradition Balaguer relied for support on the alliance of Church, army and landowners. He brought more stability to the Dominican Republic than originally anticipated, at the price of dictatorship and austerity. In early 1969, he announced his intention of running again in the elections scheduled for May 1970. This by no means popular move, although constitutionally permissible, created major tensions in a country still mindful of Trujillo. The proposed boycotting of the election by seven non-Communist parties including the P.R.D. removed all hope of a democratic election. In April 1970, Godoy, the only candidate who might have challenged Balaguer, died. Bosch, who had returned to the Dominican Republic for the election, did not run for the Presidency although he attracted considerable attention. Wessin y Wessin, who had also returned, stood as a candidate at the head of the Partido Quisqueyano Democrático.

Despite growing fears of a repetition of the events of 1965 and an increase of violence, election day passed off peacefully. The O.A.S.

[1] Paul L. Montgomery, "U.S. Vastly Expands Embassy in Santo Domingo", *The New York Times*, New York, June 19, 1966.
[2] *Ibid.*

sent a three-man observer mission to the island. With 55 per cent. of the vote, Balaguer emerged as the clear winner. However, large numbers abstained, despite army propaganda to the effect that those who failed to go to the polls would be considered as Communists and might risk losing their jobs.[1] Whether all these abstainers would have voted for the P.R.D. candidate remains questionable.

In an attempt to reconcile the warring political factions Balaguer sought to establish a "Government of national unity", but only the National Conciliation Movement agreed to serve. In a period of three months, rivalry between Bosch's and Balaguer's supporters accounted for some 200 known deaths and the disappearance of another 30 people.[2] In July 1971 Wessin y Wessin, whose party had refused to join the new government, was exiled. Failure to solve the political problems further aggravated the economic troubles of the island.

One of the strangest features of the Dominican crisis was Bosch's failure to return to the Dominican Republic when the uprising took place. He had the prestige of a President legitimately elected and he had consistently denounced those who had overthrown him. From the outset, the insurgents had hailed him as their leader. Yet he vacillated and his moment passed. Bosch conducted his election campaign from the seclusion of his own house, under the protection of guards. His appeal was made to the people on the television screen. His withdrawal damaged his electoral prospects. Many must have doubted his qualities as leader of a country critically divided.

A detached idealist, Bosch had been perhaps too long in exile to grapple with the problems of his country. Nor would there have been much likelihood that in a further period of office he would have proved more capable of tackling the thorny problems which remained.[3]

The Dominican Republic presents at its most tragic the failure of a democracy. Depopulated as a result of the Spanish conquest, Santo Domingo, first Christian city in the Americas, which should have been

[1] Cf. " 'Statu Quo' et terreur à Saint-Domingue", *Le Monde*, Paris, May 19, 1970.

[2] Cf. Jo Beresford "The legacy of violence", *The Financial Times*, London, July 9, 1971.

[3] Theodore Draper concluded that in Bosch's mind it was clear that the United States did not wish him to return, and an anti-Bosch campaign there was attributing to him all sorts of unworthy reasons for not wishing to do so. "A difficult political decision was transformed into a simple failure of nerve." "The Dominican Crisis, a Case Study in American Policy", *Commentary*, Vol. 40, No. 6, American Jewish Committee, New York, December 1965, p. 57.

a beacon of Europe's influence in the New World, had become instead a caricature. Ceded to France by Spain at the Treaty of Ryswick at the end of the seventeenth century, it was submerged by the Haitian revolution at the turn of the eighteenth century. Later it became a prey to its own dictators.

The island of Hispaniola recalls in its ruthless barbarities the complex political changes in England during the fourteenth and fifteenth centuries. Little more than half the size of England and Wales, it has a population nearly three times that of England before the Black Death. Professor Jan Kott writes brilliantly of the "Grand Mechanism" in Shakespeare's History plays.[1] It is not hard to decipher a similar Hispaniolan pattern from Toussaint l'Ouverture, Dessalines and Christophe to Faustin Souloque, Trujillo and Duvalier.

By the twentieth century, a cycle appeared established. Corrupt dictatorship led to foreign pressure. Finally, U.S. military government replaced local despotism. Sound finance was introduced; public works were undertaken. Ultimately the occupying country handed back power, and withdrew. Carefully supervised elections were held to ensure fairness as far as possible in a largely illiterate electorate unused to democracy. A suitable President was chosen, hailed at home and abroad. However, democracy proved to be only a veneer. Soon a "strong man" would take over the Presidency, maybe Marine-trained, as were Trujillo, and Magloire in Haiti. Rule becomes ever more despotic, throttling the seedling democratic plant. Gradually the repression worsens until finally the tyrant is assassinated, as in the case of Trujillo. Otherwise the despotism may continue until the despot dies in bed, like Juan Vicente Gómez in Venezuela. With a sigh of relief the democrats return from exile and take over. Attractive electoral promises are made. Yet the machinery to fulfil them fails, partly through lack of a competent civil service, partly through ineffective leadership. The promises cannot be financed and chaos follows. Regimes are short-lived; uncertainty prevails; anxiety mounts. The United States fears for its influence lest another power intervene, whether France or Germany in the second decade of the twentieth century or Cuba and the Soviet Union in the seventh. Once more the Marines arrive. If the pattern has been most pronounced in

[1] "Emanating from the features of individual kings and usurpers in Shakespeare's History plays, there gradually emerges the image of history itself, the image of the Grand Mechanism. Every successive chapter, every great Shakespearian act is merely a repetition." *Shakespeare Our Contemporary* (London, 1964), p. 7. Cf. E. M. W. Tillyard, *Shakespeare's History Plays* (London, 1961), p. 321.

Hispaniola, it may be traced elsewhere, particularly in the countries in or fringing the Caribbean.

Hispaniola's future remains obscure. In the 1965 Dominican Revolution no man emerged a winner. Apart from costs involved, the United States damaged its public relations over the issue, particularly the goodwill it endeavoured to generate in Latin America through the Alliance for Progress.[1] To the O.A.S., U.S. policy appeared suspect; tepid support was only with difficulty obtained as in the case of the Punta del Este meeting of 1962.[2] The latest variant of the Monroe Doctrine implied that action, hopefully through the O.A.S., would be taken against any similar Communist threat arising in the New World; but it included the implicit corollary that if O.A.S. support was not forthcoming, the U.S. reserved the right to take whatever action it judged necessary to its own security.[3]

Yet the successful second election of President Balaguer could qualify as a measure of victory for U.S. policy, although probably extremism in the Dominican Republic prevails more today than in 1965. Balaguer must retain army support. By allowing the decision on Wessin y Wessin's fate to be taken by the armed forces' commanders, Balaguer yielded to their desire for power at little cost to himself. His reshuffling of the army in July 1971 made good use of sympathizers of the late García Godoy.

Should the U.S. cut its sugar quota, which is possible, Balaguer might seize the opportunity of exploiting the widespread anti-U.S. feeling in his country, turning himself into a Right-wing nationalist leader with the backing of the country.[4] Meanwhile to the people of the

[1] Cf. Jerome Slater, *Intervention and Negotiation: the United States and the Dominican Revolution* (New York, 1970) pp. 210-11.

[2] *Vide* p. 53. Cf. Gordon Connell-Smith, "For the present the Dominican crises has re-emphasized what the Cuban problem had already demonstrated: that the issue of Communism divides rather than unites the American states." "Inter-American Relations Today", *Quarterly Review*, Vol. VI, No. 2, Bank of London and South America Limited, April 1966, p. 71.

[3] "All of this is now history. But it is history that could repeat itself—with appropriate local variations—in other countries of Central America and the Caribbean. In Haiti, for instance, or in Guatemala or in Honduras. These are countries that lie within a sphere the United States regards as being of vital importance: under no circumstances will their capture by Communist regimes be permitted. The device of preventive intervention, employed by the United States in the Dominican case, could be employed again. Whether it will be employed, or should be, is another matter." John N. Plank, "The Caribbean: Intervention, When and How", *Foreign Affairs*, Vol. 44, No. 1, Council on Foreign Relations, New York, October 1965, pp. 37-8.

[4] Cf. *Latin America*, London, Vol. V., No. 28, July 9, 1971, p. 218.

Dominican Republic, as to their neighbours in Haiti, the Grand Mechanism grinds on inexorably. The population increases but not the standard of living. Unemployment coupled with a heavy drift of population from the countryside into the city continues. If frustration remains the people's lot, it also continues to embitter the relations between the Dominican Republic and the United States.

THE ECONOMIC PATTERN

Although France had developed Saint-Domingue (Haiti) during the eighteenth century into the world's most valuable sugar-exporting territory, and the world's richest colony after Java, Spain had taken little interest in the colonization of the eastern two-thirds of Hispaniola. With a Viceroyalty established at far-off Mexico City, and Havana and San Juan heavily fortified, the importance of Santo Domingo had faded. In its underdeveloped condition, the need for slaves was small compared to the demands of the plantations in Haiti. Two official languages have added to the barrier which still keeps Haiti and the Dominican Republic apart, mutually suspicious and hostile.

In 1916 the United States' intervention in the Dominican Republic, resulting in military government, provided certain material benefits. Fiscal reforms were introduced. Roads and bridges were built; sanitation was improved, a vital matter where disease-carrying mosquitoes spread death. On the other hand, to prevent criticism of the government, press censorship was introduced, and trial by military courts instituted. Suspicion rankled that foreign-owned sugar-plantations received preferences over local business interests.

Trujillo took power shortly after the end of the U.S. Marine occupation (1916-24). In the accepted condemnation of Trujillo for tyranny, corruption and vanity, his policy should nevertheless be examined objectively. While the U.S. rule had greatly improved the finances and communications, the general development of the country still remained backward. Undoubtedly influenced by his Marine training, Trujillo, rough but efficient, displayed in many directions outstanding organizing capacity. Shortly after he took office, he revealed this ability when Santo Domingo was struck by one of the worst hurricanes ever recorded in the West Indies.[1] With an empty treasury and a storm-wrecked countryside, he required $3 million per year to service his country's

[1] More than 2,500 persons were killed and 8,000 injured in the city of Santo Domingo. The flimsy buildings in the crowded poorer sections of the city were destroyed.

bonds. In 1931 revenue fell to less than half of the 1930 figure. However, using the hurricane as a telling argument, he persuaded the United States to reduce sinking-fund payments on loans. Moreover, he slashed internal expenditure. He could thus rebuild the devastated areas. So successful were Trujillo's measures that by 1940 he was able to end the convention by which the United States controlled revenue from the Dominican customs. Santo Domingo was renamed Ciudad Trujillo in his honour.

The new President's financial methods were ruthless. Although he began the development of industry, the mechanization of agriculture and improved communications and the electricity supply, he prevented any rise in real wages by a widespread system of indirect taxation which fell with crushing force on the poor. If the industrial revolution had been harsh in Great Britain, the lot of the working man was infinitely worse in the Dominican Republic. Nevertheless, the money from this taxation aided the rapid expansion of the Dominican Republic's economy. The regime concentrated on roads and public works. New hotels were constructed to develop a tourist industry. An industrial estate was created in the capital and a shipyard constructed at nearby Río Haina.

Nearly twice the area of Haiti, the Dominican Republic had a population substantially less than its neighbour. Trujillo gave limited encouragement to immigration. Agriculture remained the principal activity, with sugar of first importance. To expand the industry, Trujillo did not hesitate to borrow from foreign banks, thus enabling him to gain personal control of most of the sugar-mills which he proceeded to modernize. He could be criticized for overemphasizing the development of sugar; nevertheless he created an efficient industry. His Río Haina factory with tandem mills became one of the largest in the world. The other leading producer was the American-owned South Puerto Rico Sugar Company, an important complex also on the south coast.[1] The very fact that the Dominican Republic's quota with the United States was small may have encouraged efficiency since, unlike the larger part of the Antillean sugar of the day, much of the crop had to be sold on the open market. The cheapness of Dominican labour was a major factor in the low cost of the product.

Trujillo participated financially in many other enterprises, notably the tobacco monopoly, while he was believed to divert the cacao export tax of $2.10 per bag to his own purposes. His other interests within the

[1] Conjunto Azucarero Haina, formerly owned by Trujillo, produced 55-60 per cent. of Dominican sugar. La Romana (South Puerto Rico Sugar Company) provided 30 per cent.

country's economy were diverse and his financial greed enormous.[1] The country was also saddled with the activities of the dictator's family. One brother controlled the export of bananas, another the charcoal monopoly and the third, Romeo, the concession for prostitution.[2]

How much of the vast fortune of the Trujillo family was sent abroad is unlikely ever to be known. However, the roads, bridges, electricity grid, airfields, sugar factories and new industries remained. Despite the speculation and peculation of the President, and a few failures such as the grandiose International Fair opened in 1955, the economy of the country had been strengthened by solid industrial development.

Following on the diplomatic pressure exerted on the Dominican Republic by the Organization of American States, and in the face of threats of attack from Cuba, Trujillo increased his defence forces.[3] Denied supplies of U.S. arms, he purchased wherever he could, thus straining his country's finances. Strict currency control had to be imposed. Moreover, the tourist trade, a valuable source of foreign exchange, had already begun to fall off sharply because of the disturbed conditions in the northern Caribbean.[4]

The altered political situation after the assassination of Trujillo caused a drastic reshuffling and reappraisal of ideas. Trujillo's huge holdings, now taken over by the State, presented the latter with a major problem. He had owned no less than fifty-seven enterprises constituting some 43 per cent. of the industry of the country. To handle these concerns, the Corporación de Fomento Industrial was formed.

The change-over should have been highly beneficial to the national concerns which were no longer being milked by Trujillo, but many complications arose. The financial position had deteriorated, as has been seen, during the last years of his rule. Inflation caused a sharp

[1] Rafael Leonidas Trujillo's wealth as revealed by official sources appeared to include the following percentage figures of the total Dominican assets in the following industries: bank deposits 22 per cent., money in circulation 25 per cent., sugar production 63 per cent., cement 63 per cent., paper 73 per cent., paint 86 per cent., cigarettes 71 per cent., milk 85 per cent., wheat and flour 68 per cent., together with ownership of the only national airline, its leading newspapers, radio and television stations. *Hispanic American Report*, Vol. XV, p. 1114. According to Ornes: "Trujillo and his associates control three-quarters of the country's means of production and maybe a greater share of the national income." Ornes, *op. cit.*, p. 258.

[2] Selden Rodman, *Quisqueya: A History of the Dominican Republic* (Seattle, 1964), p. 141. Cf. Ornes, *op. cit.*, pp. 224-5.

[3] *Vide* p. 72.

[4] *Vide* p. 357.

rise in wages. Moreover, industrial strife which had been prevented by the strong measures of the Trujillo government now became frequent. Despite financial help from the United States under the Alliance for Progress, on a scale far above the average being given in Latin America, the Dominican balance of payments became adverse, aggravated by inflationary spending.

President Bosch was no financier. His $150 million agrarian reform plan, launched during his election campaign, had raised expectations which he was unable to satisfy. The original scheme aimed at settling 5,500 families on 90,000 acres by the end of 1963; a further 25,000 families on one million acres by the end of 1968; and 70,000 families on the total of two million acres of former Trujillo-owned lands by 1970. The plan was effectively stalled by owners who had been dispossessed by Trujillo claiming title to their former property. Substantial time-consuming litigation ensued.

The new President also proposed free entry to tourists, without the need for passports or other documents. He sought the development of a resort area on the north coast.[1]

The Bosch Government brought no reduction of labour disputes. For example, in July 1963 a strike occurred at the La Romana mill. The owners had to negotiate with no less than fifteen different unions. Next month a stoppage occurred at the Ozama mill belonging to the same company, while a strike of electricity workers threatened the national economy. The effect of labour disputes was shown in September when the Río Haina mill reported a loss of $7·5 million, a fantastic figure in view of the booming sugar economy.

The Triumvirate which succeeded Bosch, providing stronger if less democratic government, took a firmer line against strikes. In the autumn of 1964 the Government claimed that its three-month-old stabilization plan had liquidated $54 million in national debts. Higher taxes on luxury items such as cigarettes, rum, automobiles and gasoline, and increased employers' contributions to the security fund, were partly responsible for the result. With a serious decline in world sugar prices, Reid, President of the Triumvirate, refused to pay harvest bonuses to sugar-workers.[2] At least an attempt to steady the economy was being made.

[1] When Bosch visited the United States shortly after his election, he discussed these plans with Juan Trippe, president of Pan-American World Airways. *Hispanic American Report*, Vol. XVI, p. 40.

[2] Reid declared: "People must realise that the time of the give-away is gone. You don't build anything on a permanent basis by giving away things. The Alliance for Progress is useless if citizens do not work hard." Santo Domingo, November 15, 1964.

Education began to receive more attention. Although it had been for a long time free and obligatory for everyone up to 14 years of age, in 1961, 40 per cent. of the population of 15 years or more was illiterate and only 25 per cent. of the school-age population attended elementary schools. Despite a twenty-year campaign against adult illiteracy, about 65 per cent. of the population was still illiterate in 1964.

The schools generally were understaffed and overcrowded, a problem which recurred throughout much of the Caribbean. By 1970, nearly 5,000 primary, 75 secondary and 500 other schools existed in the country.

The civil strife disrupted the Dominican economy. As in most Latin American republics, the capital dominated the rest of the country not only politically but also economically. In a report to the Security Council, Secretary General U Thant estimated that, of the 3·5 million inhabitants of the Dominican Republic, 1·4 million were economically active, and of these 25 per cent. were unemployed. Even before the hostilities the gross national product for 1965 had been estimated at $830 million compared with $875 million the previous year, a decline of 5·4 per cent., attributed to a six months' drought which had affected agricultural produce, while at the same time sugar prices had fallen and credit contracted.[1]

Political troubles continued to be reflected in the economy although the comparative calm after 1965 and the austerity programme begun by Balaguer when he took office in July 1966 began to take effect. Early in 1968 five international companies formed a consortium, at first to develop parts of the Dominican Republic agriculturally and then to move into industries based upon agricultural raw materials.[2] In addition, Shell International announced the construction of a refinery and Nestlé's a milk-processing plant. The largest mining enterprise in the country's history began construction at Bonao in 1969–70. The Falcondo project, a $U.S.200 million ferro-nickel mine and processing plant, backed by the Falconbridge Nickel Company of Canada aided by U.S. capital, was expected by 1993 to produce some $U.S.325 million in foreign exchange earnings and about $U.S.185 million for the Santo Domingo Government. The World Bank made its first ever loan to the Dominican Republic of $U.S.25 million to provide electric power and related facilities for the operation of the plant.[3]

Despite its size, Falcondo, as a fully automated plant, will do little

[1] United Nations Security Council, s/6408, June 3, 1965.
[2] Cf. *The New York Times*, New York, January 22, 1968.
[3] *Caribbean Business News*, Toronto, March 1970.

to ease the unemployment rate, estimated at some 25 per cent. The 3·6 per cent. population growth rate further aggravates the problem, notwithstanding an active National Population and Family Council. Of nearly four million people, 47 per cent. are less than 15 years old: those leaving school add to the unemployment level.

The tourist industry, which had virtually ended in 1965, remains minimal. Unless the country becomes politically more stable, it seems likely to remain so. However, in many ways the relatively undeveloped Dominican Republic holds more appeal to tourists than neighbouring Puerto Rico. Yet even the facilities for quick divorce, afforded by the Dominican Republic in place of those offered by Mexico, were affected by the political unrest in the island.

Agriculture, basic to the economy of the Dominican Republic, was badly disrupted throughout most of the 1960's. If Trujillo had run the country as a private farm for the benefit of himself and his friends, at least he had some appreciation of the need for modernizing agriculture. His cattle-breeding operations with imported bulls could have improved cattle farming throughout the island. Neither Bosch, an intellectual, nor Reid, a merchant, had any understanding of the land. The slaughter of many of Trujillo's pedigree stock after his assassination and the losses suffered by the State sugar-mills under the Bosch regime, at a time when sugar was enjoying a boom, were symbolic of the Dominican leaders' lack of understanding of agricultural problems, curiously similar to the attitude of the Castro regime during its early years, when it had liquidated the operation of the King ranch in Cuba and had disrupted the island's all important sugar operations.

The prolonged Dominican crisis of 1965 still further disorganized agriculture. However Balaguer's Government undertook extensive work on roads and dams to assist agricultural development. Four years of comparative stability, and the end of the drought, which lasted for 22 months, resulted in an agricultural revival. The 1969 sugar harvest exceeded that of 1968 by some 25 per cent. The export of tropical fruits, winter vegetables and tobacco increased.

Economic developments have prompted the Dominican Republic to seek some sort of link with CARIFTA, or less likely, with Puerto Rico. Certainly the effect of the Dominican Republic on the CARIFTA markets would be considerable.[1]

*　*　*　*

The history of the Dominican Republic caricatures the worst features

[1] *Vide*, pp. 353. Dominican Republic membership would be of advantage to neighbouring Jamaica as a counter-balance to Trinidad, far away, and one of its main competitors.

95

of Spanish and Latin American government. The country's nine-teenth-century failure to provide itself with reasonable government after it had belatedly secured its freedom was matched by its twentieth-century fiasco. Abject poverty face to face with great wealth, family feuds, Sicilian in their intensity, the Spanish cult of *personalismo* allied to the worship of courage for its own sake: all this produced chaos. If lip service had been paid, in the rare moments of tranquillity, to the principle of freedom of thought and expression, the public had so far not been prepared to make the immediate sacrifices necessary to establish a liberal regime.[1]

Professor Ronald Hilton, who was at Santo Domingo when Bosch fell, wrote: "It may be that no regime can save the Dominican Republic. A ride across the country bears graphic evidence of what we know from vital statistics. There may be no country in the world where one sees such a high proportion of children, most illegitimate, for whom there is no prospect of education, training and jobs. Perhaps the example of Puerto Rico offers some hope. Otherwise within 50 years the Dominican Republic will be another Haiti."[2]

The basic economic difficulties of the Dominican Republic are largely man-made. Certainly much of the island is rugged and infertile. Yet with competent and forward-looking administration, the country could be developed for agriculture and limited industry, including tourism.

In examining the evolution of the first two Antillean republics, Haiti and Santo Domingo, we may well ask whether they might have had a better political and economic chance if their independence had been delayed. The emergent countries of Jamaica, Trinidad and Barbados, and the self-governing Netherlands Antilles with fewer natural resources, inherited the advantages of a better administration and of long exposure to the democratic process. The Dominican Republic's other neighbour, Puerto Rico, which had accepted autonomy within the United States, also afforded the example of the country with the highest standard of living in Latin America.

[1] A striking vignette of the spirit of the Dominican Revolution is provided by Max Clos who illustrates the *personalismo* which characterized the struggle. "The Four Musketeers of the Dominican Revolution", *The Guardian*, London, June 8, 1965. (By arrangement with *Le Figaro*, Paris.)

[2] *The New York Times*, New York, October 1, 1963.

Puerto Rico: El Morro, historically one of the strongest fortresses in the Caribbean, today a tourist attraction.

Puerto Rico Information Serv

Puerto Rico: Plaza of San Germán, which has fine examples of colonial architecture.

Chapter V

PUERTO RICO

THE POLITICAL PATTERN

Puerto Rico is the island fulcrum of the Caribbean. Westward for more than a thousand miles the Greater Antilles stretch to Cape San Antonio. Cuba's western provinces control the entrance to the Gulf of Mexico. To the east and south the Lesser Antilles curl over 600 miles to Trinidad, which almost touches the South American coast. Thus from Florida to the mouth of the Orinoco River, the Antilles form a bridge of islands between the Americas roughly parallel to the mainland connection.

With superb geographic judgment, Spain concentrated on the essentials since it lacked the manpower to occupy all of the islands. Puerto Rico commanded the vital eastern approaches where the sailing-ships, borne by the trade-winds, entered the Caribbean.[1] From the sixteenth century onwards, Spain, partly financed with funds from Mexico, strongly fortified the small island upon which San Juan, Puerto Rico's capital, stands. El Morro, with the adjacent fortress of San Cristóbal, flew the Spanish flag without interruption until it yielded to the United States in 1898. The nearest rival to this record of continuity in government in the Antilles is the British island of Barbados, which was settled more than a century later.

The history of Puerto Rico under Spain was essentially that of a garrison fortress. Under its Captain-General, normally an army officer, whose authority was limited only by the laws of the Indies and by the remote control of a Viceroy in Mexico, agricultural development, apart from providing food for the garrison, was not of prime importance. The more ambitious Spaniards passed on to the mainland colonies where fortune had more to offer.

The strong peninsular influence present in the Puerto Rico garrison, an important factor in the economy of the island, had the effect of discouraging revolt, just as earlier in the century somewhat similar conditions made Peru's liberation difficult. The very success of the wars of independence in other parts of Latin America resulted in

---

[1] To the south, Spain held Trinidad until it was ceded to Great Britain at the close of the Napoleonic Wars.

thousands of loyalist refugees coming to Puerto Rico, including many from Venezuela. The situation might be compared to the exodus from the Thirteen American Colonies after Independence to parts of Canada, where, as in Puerto Rico, the new influx for long exerted political influence. Moreover, the newly formed Latin American Republics, beset by internecine feuds, lacked the naval power necessary to attack a distant Spanish island on the fringe of the Atlantic Ocean. Although Great Britain, whose sea power was then dominant in the Caribbean as elsewhere, had shown its sympathy with the newly established nations of Latin America, it had friendly relations with Spain and was a colonial power with possessions of its own in the Caribbean. Like France, it had no desire to disturb the Antillean settlement reached in the Treaty of Vienna. It was certainly not prepared to convoy a revolutionary expedition to liberate Puerto Rico, especially as Puerto Rico was a potential competitor in the weakening sugar market and not a promising outlet for British goods. In due course, the Monroe Doctrine became an additional deterrent to interference in the Western Hemisphere.

In between minor rebellions, Puerto Ricans aimed at constitutional reform. In 1869 the island received from Spain the rank of a province. Although this status was withdrawn in 1874, it was restored three years later. Relations with Spain improved with the liberal Prime Minister Práxedes Mateo Sagasta in power in Spain and Luis Muñoz Rivera leading the island's autonomist party. In 1897, Spain granted self-government to Puerto Rico, though precisely how this system would have operated remains a matter of speculation since the Spanish-American War broke out in the following year.

Under the Treaty of Paris of 1898, Puerto Rico was ceded by Spain to the United States, whose invading forces were warmly received by many of the inhabitants. At the same time, the population had envisaged independence. The island, however, had to commence afresh the move towards self-government which had already begun, if in modest degree, under Spain. Rooted in almost four centuries of Spanish rule and customs, the Puerto Ricans did not take easily to Anglo-Saxon concepts of government and law. The Puritan tradition of the United States ill matched the Catholicism of Spain.

As in Cuba, military government, at first inevitable, was soon replaced by civil government. The Foraker Act of 1900 established a popularly elected Lower House with a nominated Executive Council, of which at least five members had to be Puerto Ricans. Effective control, however, remained in the hands of the American officials nominated by the President. The Puerto Ricans were not satisfied; to many of them the sole change seemed to be one of colonial masters. Finally, in 1917

Congress passed the Jones Act, which established Puerto Rico as a Territory of the United States and granted the islanders U.S. citizenship. A legislature with elected senators and representatives was set up, though the principal executive officers were still appointed by the President of the United States.[1] The Jones Act was a step forward, but it did not offer autonomy.

Despite prosperity during World War I, the post-war slump in the price of sugar and the depression of the early 1930's, aggravated by a hurricane, seriously disrupted the island's economy. Political criticism followed, as it did in the British islands.[2]

Although they were citizens of the United States, Puerto Ricans were ineligible to vote in the U.S. Congressional elections. On the other hand, remembering its own early colonial problems, the United States remained true to its principle of no taxation without representation. Thus Puerto Rico was absolved from contributing to the Federal services which played a major part in the development of the island's economy. Not only was Puerto Rico relieved of the costs of its defence, but the large naval, military and air bases, which the United States had established in Puerto Rico and the offshore island of Vieques, made a substantial contribution to the economy through the expenditures of the troops stationed there. Puerto Ricans were liable for military service, but in a community faced with heavy unemployment, this provided an outlet, and one which was well paid in comparison with the wage rate to be found in any of Puerto Rico's neighbours. Moreover, those unable to find a job in Puerto Rico could move without restriction to the continental United States. If unemployment increased in the island, the problem could be partially exported.

The advance from colonialism toward self-government accelerated in the years following World War II. Yet in this regard Puerto Rico presented difficulties, especially as its use as a United States strategic base continued in importance. The precise method of constitutional progress caused deep anxiety in Washington, for Puerto Rico had as neighbours the long-established republics of Haiti and the Dominican Republic, the British Virgin and Leeward Islands, the Netherlands Windward Islands, and the French West Indies. Not one of these territories was even moderately prosperous.

The victory in 1941 of the Partido Popular Democrático, or Popular Party, organized by Luis Muñoz Marín, son of Luis Muñoz Rivera, was

[1] The powers of the Governor of Puerto Rico, however, were very restricted compared with the authority of British Colonial Governors. Cf. Gordon K. Lewis, *Puerto Rico, Freedom and Power in the Caribbean* (New York, 1963), p. 156.
[2] *Vide* p. 122.

99

accompanied by the appointment of Rexford Tugwell as Governor of Puerto Rico (1941-46), who proved to be an enlightened, far-seeing administrator. The new island government introduced further political and economic reforms. It tackled the problem of housing, which was in many parts deplorable. A Transportation Board Authority was established, while the development of the island's hydro-electric resources was accelerated by the United States' engagement in a World War. The crisis, however, complicated both the question of island defence and that of food supply from the mainland.

In the years following World War II, the question of status had continued to be one of primary political importance to Puerto Rico. Cautiously and gradually the United States Congress amended Puerto Rico's constitution. Between 1947 and 1952, the Organic Act which governed the island was altered to allow a greater degree of self-government. In future the Governor of Puerto Rico would be elected by popular vote of the islanders, thus giving Puerto Ricans the same voice in the election of their executive branch as they already held in that of their legislative. The Governor in turn would appoint the heads of departments in consultation with the Puerto Rican Senate. In 1952, Puerto Rico was declared an *Estado Libre Asociado* or Commonwealth.

Tugwell, the last Governor appointed by the United States, was succeeded in 1949 by Muñoz Marín, the first Puerto Rican to be elected Governor. In Tugwell's view, Muñoz Marín had persuaded and cajoled the United States into giving Puerto Rico the best of both worlds, namely rights to the benefits of U.S. citizenship, together with virtual independence. "His Commonwealth was, I really believe, a genuine claim to be rated as a first class political device—one to be ranked with our Federal Union and with the British Commonwealth."[1]

Half statesman, half poet, Muñoz had the business acumen which commands respect in the United States together with the literary and intellectual calibre so highly regarded by a Latin American electorate. Installed in La Fortaleza, at San Juan, he rapidly expanded his influence. To both the United States and Puerto Rico he was the one man who could resolve the tangled skein of their association. Under his direction, Puerto Rico moved towards leadership in Latin America as the country with the highest standard of living. From many parts of the world individuals and delegations came to study Puerto Rico and its accomplishments. Its dramatic transformation included the development, at Río Piedras near San Juan, of the largest university in the Caribbean.[2] Yet the very ability of Muñoz, which resulted in all awkward problems

[1] Rexford Tugwell, *Art of Politics* (Toronto, 1958), p. 68.
[2] *Vide* p. 369

being submitted to him for solution, may have distorted the constitutional balance of the island. There were some who wondered whether, as a consequence, the power of the Executive was growing at the expense of the Legislature.

The Commonwealth solution had great economic attraction. Negotiating with adroitness, Puerto Rico had achieved inclusion in the United States without paying the normal price. But certain doubts about the settlement still lingered. Agitation for revision quickly followed. The term "Commonwealth" was itself ambiguous. The word had occurred in the early history of some American states. In a different sense it had succeeded "Empire" in the designation of the relationship between the components of Britain's former Empire. If Commonwealth was vague, the Spanish equivalent used, *Estado Libre Asociado*, was also inexact. Puerto Rico was not free in the sense that it had sovereign status, nor was the term "associated" an accurate expression of its link with the United States. Thus it was that criticism of the constitutional settlement increased. The Partido Estadista Republicano, the leading opposition party, sought incorporation as a state within the Union, the status which Alaska and Hawaii were to attain in 1959. Supporters of this view believed that the Muñoz solution might not survive. Although adopted by one Congress, the solution could in theory be reversed by another. Moreover, since Puerto Rico was not an independent country, no treaty sanctified by international law could be drawn up. The underlying fear of the P.E.R. group was that the United States might find it convenient to sever the link with Puerto Rico. Such critics argued that though Puerto Ricans served in the United States Armed Forces, they did not enjoy full rights of citizenship since they still could not participate in the election of a President or return members of Congress. Others took a diametrically opposed view. The Partido Independencia Puertorriqueño advocated complete separation from the United States as the only acceptable solution, claiming that, alone of Spain's former colonies in the Americas, Puerto Rico had remained in a condition of colonialism. These critics also stressed the rapid advance of U.S. business interests in the island which would, in their view, quickly obliterate its Spanish inheritance and crush its individualism. To these people, the cultural background, including the Spanish language, was of major importance. How Puerto Rico, separated from the United States, could continue its expansion, ever more vital as population increased, was not explained. The appeal was to nationalism rather than to economics.

In July 1962, Muñoz and President Kennedy agreed that this unique association between the United States and Puerto Rico should be clarified in order to silence the accusation that it was merely a new variant of colonialism. Muñoz then requested the Puerto Rican legislature to ask the United States Congress to approve a plebiscite to determine island opinion on the three alternatives of commonwealth, statehood or independence. A bill was subsequently proposed in the House of Representatives to establish a Status Commission to study the current relationship between the island and the United States and to make recommendations for improvement. After the Commission had reported, Congress would then consider its conclusions and indicate its attitude in regard to independence or statehood. There was no legal obligation for Congress to act on the Commission's report. However, if it did, the issue would then be referred back to the island for settlement by plebiscite.[1]

Initial difficulty arose over who were to be appointed as members of the Commission so as to ensure that it would be representative of Puerto Rican views. Progress was very slow.[2] In February 1964 President Johnson finally signed the Status Commission Bill, requiring the Commission to report to Congress, which it eventually did in August 1966.[3] The Commission felt that whereas politically Puerto Rico was fully equipped to take on either Statehood or Independence, any immediate or abrupt change in political status would seriously dislocate the economy of the island. The time would come when economically Puerto Rico might "absorb the impact of a change to Statehood or Independence".[4] The Commission concluded that a declaration by the people themselves should precede any attempts to change the existing status.[5] A plebiscite was set for the summer of 1967.

That a solution was in any way possible stemmed from the dynamism

[1] Cf. A. W. Maldonado, "Status Commission", *The San Juan Star*, San Juan, February 25, 1964.

[2] ". . . it is beyond doubt that Congress is unable and unwilling to engage in Commonwealth 'culmination' efforts. The cold fact is that Commonwealth, as well as Puerto Rico's entire status problem is 'peanuts' to a Congress deeply and permanently involved in such earth-shaking issues [as] nuclear test treaties and such vital domestic issues as civil rights for Negroes." A. W. Maldonado, "Commonwealth and Congress", *The San Juan Star*, San Juan, August 24, 1963.

[3] Cf. Henry Wells, "Puerto Rico's Association with the United States", *Caribbean Studies*, Vol. V, No. 1, Institute of Caribbean Studies, University of Puerto Rico, Río Piedras, April 1965, pp. 6-22.

[4] *Stacom Supplement*, *The San Juan Star*, San Juan, August 1966, p. S-3. The economist representing the Independent Party estimated that it might take as long as twenty years to ensure satisfactory economic adjustment after independence.

[5] *Ibid.*

of Muñoz Marín who was a link between two cultures. He was educated in the United States where his father was Puerto Rico's first Resident Commissioner. Thus he had the inestimable advantage of understanding both the American and the Puerto Rican viewpoint. Returning to his homeland at the age of 28, he devoted his life to politics. The popular party, of which he had become the leader, steadily improved its position at elections. By 1952 it was polling 65 per cent. of the votes. Even more remarkably, Muñoz had succeeded in imposing on his party honesty in electioneering. With this achievement he transformed the political climate of Puerto Rico.

Muñoz entered politics at a time when three situations menaced the well-being of Puerto Rico: the stranglehold of sugar, the natural poverty of land and people, and a runaway population growth. To analyse Muñoz's political views precisely is well nigh impossible. Although he claimed to belong to the Democratic left, it would be more accurate to dub him a far-seeing and pragmatic Puerto Rican; one of his characteristics was his acute political foresight. At his inaugural speech he referred to colonization as obsolescent. Subsequent years soon corroborated his judgment.

The party's choice of the name Popular had been felicitous. The designation, in Spanish as in English, had the advantage of being indefinite. Although he professed to be a socialist, much of Muñoz's work was directed nevertheless into other channels. Professor Robert J. Alexander places his party in what he terms the *Aprista* group, which includes the original Aprista Party of Peru and the Democratic Action Party of Venezuela. He describes all three as ". . . socialistic in a general sense, nationalistic in economic matters, and democratic in their political aspirations".[1]

Power stemming from his ability enabled Muñoz to interpret the aspirations of his countrymen. He stood for honest politics in an island, and indeed an area of the world, where corruption was widespread. From certain angles he had the appeal of a Fidel Castro or an Eric Williams. Muñoz matched his emotional and nationalistic side with a practical grasp of what was possible in politics. He was far-sighted enough to realize that on its own Puerto Rico would be doomed to penury. For confirmation he needed to look no further than across the Mona Passage to Hispaniola.

The attitude of the United States is an outstanding example of generosity shown by a great power toward a tiny island, not even composed

[1] "Organized Labor and Politics", *Government and Politics in Latin America*, ed. Harold E. Davis (New York, 1958), p. 175.

of its own race. The continuing endorsement of Commonwealth status by the majority of Puerto Ricans has attested to the soundness of the arrangement. More than just a happy solution to a troublesome colonial problem, the subsequent Operation Bootstrap has attracted to Puerto Rico economists and political scientists from all over the world. No better laboratory for these important social and economic experiments could have been found.[1]

Certainly the economic revolution has not solved all Puerto Rico's problems. An attempt to break up the large corporation-owned sugar-estates met with disappointment. Although Puerto Rico diversified its agriculture, the inability of the island to take full advantage of its valuable U.S. sugar quota was an economic loss which was offset only through its commercial progress in other directions.

Muñoz showed great ability in surrounding himself with talented associates. Teodoro Moscoso, who had spearheaded Puerto Rico's economic development, was later transferred to the greater field of the fledgling Alliance for Progress: no small compliment to Puerto Rico. Rafael Picó, President of the Government Development Bank, had much of the responsibility for pressing forward Puerto Rico's development and yet keeping the finances sound.

The impact of the Cuban Revolution must be borne in mind in considering the future of Puerto Rico. Both islands had remained under Spanish government for some three-quarters of a century longer than the rest of the Spanish American colonies. Although Cuba had not been a U.S. colony, nevertheless Puerto Ricans were sharply aware of the Platt Amendment which had for thirty-two years limited the island's independence.[2]

Reaction to the Cuban Revolution was mixed. The arrival of many exiles created an attitude of hostility to the Castro Government. As conditions worsened in Cuba, the prosperity of Puerto Rico appeared in ever sharper focus. On the other hand, the relatively few supporters of independence were stimulated by Castro's break from the United States.[3]

After sixteen years of leadership of the Commonwealth of Puerto Rico, Muñoz requested his Partido Popular Democrático at its meeting

[1] Rafael Picó opens his interesting dissertation on *The Geographic Regions of Puerto Rico* by stressing the "surprising diversity in its physical environment and in the uses that man makes of its resources". (University of Puerto Rico Press, Río Piedras, 1950), p. 1.

[2] *Vide* pp. 7-8.

[3] Cf. Manuel Maldonado Denis, "Efectos de la Revolución Cubana en la Política Puertorriqueña", *Revista de Ciencias Sociales*, Vol. VIII, No. 3, University of Puerto Rico, Río Piedras, pp. 271-8.

in August 1964, at Mayagüez, to permit him to resign office for the sake of democracy in Puerto Rico. By that gesture he recognized that his unique position as the island's pilot, steering between statism on the one hand and independence on the other, had centred enormous power in the office of the Governor. The very quality of Muñoz's statesmanship had alerted him to this danger which would be further aggravated were he to serve for another term. His party, with his approval, nominated Roberto Sánchez Vilella to succeed him. His wide experience, including his deputation for Muñoz when the latter was abroad, made the choice an obvious one, and he was duly elected. The Muñoz era had ended: a new one opened which promised to be no less challenging.

Sánchez Vilella continued the programmes initiated under Muñoz Marín. However, the difficulties of assuming the position previously held by such an international figure became increasingly apparent and the inevitable challenges to his authority grew evident beneath the surface. In the spring of 1967, Sánchez Vilella announced that he would not, for personal reasons, run for re-election in 1968, thus throwing open to question the leadership and future strength of the P.D.P.[1]

By early 1967 the approaching plebiscite on Puerto Rico's status dominated the island's politics. The P.D.P. began campaigning for continuation of the "free associated state" while its main rival, the P.E.R., split over the issue. One section of the party, under the P.E.R. leader Senator Miguel-Angel Garcia Méndez, decided to boycott the referendum as it was "a mere popularity contest".[2] However, Luis Ferré, brother-in-law of the Senator and several times P.E.R. presidential candidate, broke away, formed the United Statehooders, and participated in the pre-plebiscite campaign. Similarly, the third party in size, the P.I.P., experienced internal dissension regarding the referendum, but by April had launched its own pro-independence campaign.[3]

An overwhelming majority approved maintaining some form of close

[1] Luis Negrón López, leader of the Senate, was mentioned as a possible replacement. Cf. *The San Juan Star*, April 6, 1967. The problem of the character of the P.D.P. after Muñoz had already been raised by various people including T. G. Mathews. "En adición a su joven edad de escasamente 27 años existe el hecho de que la definición de sus principios y programa dependen demasiado de la habilidad de su líder y fundador." Thomas G. Mathews, "La Próxima Década en la Política Puertorriqueña", *Revista de Ciencias Sociales*, Vol. IX, No. 3, University of Puerto Rico, Río Piedras, September 1965, p. 279.

[2] Henry Giniger, "Puerto Rico vote will split 3 ways", *The New York Times*, New York, March 20, 1967.

[3] *The San Juan Star*, San Juan, April 6, 1967.

relationship with the United States in the July plebiscite.[1] In the election the following year, Ferré's pro-statehood Partido Nuevo Progresista (P.N.P.) won the governorship and control of the House. Ferré's success, however, could not be looked upon as a national endorsement of statehood as the principal thrust of his campaign was the need for change after 19 years of P.D.P. leadership.[2] In addition, the P.N.P. was aided considerably by the P.D.P.'s refusal to endorse Sánchez Vilella for re-election. As of 1971, the P.D.P. still had not been able to unite behind a single candidate which left the P.N.P. in quite a strong position for the election of 1972.[3]

Further developments in the complex relationship between Puerto Rico and the United States came in the spring of 1970 when a 14 member committee (7 Stateside and 7 Puerto Ricans) was named to study the feasibility of giving Puerto Ricans the right to vote for the President and Vice President of the United States. The P.N.P. was the only party supporting the study, and an affirmative decision would require an amendment to the U.S. Constitution.[4] Then in June 1971 the Puerto Rican Resident Commissioner in Washington, D.C., received the right to vote in congressional committees for the first time.[5]

The status question did not disappear from the political arena after the 1967 plebiscite—as the riots at the Río Piedras campus of the University of Puerto Rico in early 1971 underscored.[6] Indeed, the growing

[1] 66·3 per cent. of all registered voters participated. Of those, 60·4 per cent. favoured retaining Commonwealth status, 39 per cent. favoured statehood, and only ·6 per cent. advocated independence. Puerto Rico Water Resources Authority, *Electric Revenue Bonds (Series 1971)*, December, 1970, p. 23.

[2] Ferré received 45 per cent. of the vote compared with 41·8 per cent. received by the candidate of the P.D.P. *Puerto Rico, International Economic Survey*, Chemical Bank, International Division, New York, June, 1970, p. 3.

[3] Cf. Frank Ramos, "Collision Course", *The San Juan Star*, San Juan, June 13, 1971.

[4] *Monthly Economic Report, Puerto Rico*. First National City Bank, New York, May, 1970. The committee had studied expert reports and started to hold public hearings by March, 1971. *Ibid.*, March, 1971.

[5] *The San Juan Star*, San Juan, June 11, 1971.

[6] "The plain truth is that there can be no end to the debate about political status so long as Commonwealth lasts. But this is one of the best features of Commonwealth status, an advantage seldom noticed by Puerto Ricans themselves. The Puerto Rican political community is deeply split on the status question, almost the only divisive issue in Puerto Rican politics. If either one of the truly final solutions (statehood or independence) was to be accepted, the new entity would have to contend with thousands of citizens intransigently opposed to its existence. The upshot would almost certainly be political instability and turbulence, or possibly even civil war. Under the Commonwealth formula, by contrast, the very lack of permanent solution to the status problem

social and cultural problems resulting from Commonwealth status will undoubtedly attract increasing political attention.[1]

* * * *

Has Puerto Rico paid too high a price for its unique status? Some nationalists will claim that it has indeed sacrificed its traditions and personality. Certainly the American way of life has invaded Puerto Rico just as it has appeared, if not so strongly, in other parts of the Caribbean. However, on the other side must be set the advantages of much higher wages, better public services, good communications and improved services of health and education. In addition, unrestricted entry into the United States for those seeking work is at least a safeguard for the economic future of the island.

THE ECONOMIC PATTERN

Historically Puerto Rico, like other Spanish colonies, was permitted no trade except with Spain, although this limitation had in practice been tempered by widespread smuggling facilitated by the proximity of foreign territories.[2] In 1804 Spain opened some of its colonial ports on the Atlantic, thus further denting its trade monopoly which had already been breached at Buenos Aires.

At the end of the period of Spanish rule in Puerto Rico, Spain was purchasing one-quarter of the island's exports and Cuba almost another quarter. The United States, France and Germany each took 10 per cent. Coffee, the leading export, went to Spain and Cuba; sugar, next in importance, was shipped to the United States, Spain and Great Britain. Tobacco found a market in Spain and Cuba. Of the island's imports, one-third came from the mother country; of the remainder, half was shared between the United States and Great Britain.

Under U.S. rule, the trade of Puerto Rico changed sharply. Aided by freedom of entry into the American market, sugar and tobacco, both tariff-

---

enables even the extremists at both ends of the political spectrum to live together with a minimum of discord and violence. . . . " Henry Wells, *The Modernization of Puerto Rico, A Political Study of Changing Values and Institutions.* (Cambridge, Mass., 1969), pp. 262-3.

[1] A problem with growing implications is the inability of the Puerto Ricans returning to the island to speak Spanish. In August 1971 the Government planned to implement a special Spanish instruction programme in various island schools. *The New York Times*, New York, May 23, 1971.

[2] Arturo Morales-Carrión, *Puerto Rico and the Non-Hispanic Caribbean* (University of Puerto Rico Press, Río Piedras, Puerto Rico, 1952), p. 138.

protected crops, were rapidly developed. As in the case of Cuba, capital from the United States flowed to the island in the years after the Spanish American War, attracted by its favoured position in the U.S. market.

Modern central factories replaced the old small mills of the former regime. Annual sugar production, which had been 57,000 tons under Spanish rule, rose in five years to 300,000 tons, and to 900,000 tons in 1930. Tobacco-growing also expanded, aided by the establishment of new factories. Banking, which had hardly existed, became firmly established. The United States financed roads, schools and public utilities. In 1930, the Brookings Institution estimated that in the thirty years of United States rule, $120 million had entered the island for agricultural and manufacturing development.[1] The protected American market provided the foundation for economic advance, though the field of activity was still narrow.

The slump of the early 1930's caused severe hardship in the island. Moreover, the very excellence of the American-sponsored health services was contributing to the steady growth of population. The labour force was increasing by 10,000 persons per year, while agricultural employment had become static. The sugar industry provided basically seasonal work; Puerto Rican coffee, unprotected in the United States market, was hard hit by the fall in the world price.

From 1933 to 1941, the Puerto Rican Emergency Relief Administration[2] spent $72 million on a variety of projects designed to provide work and development, including hydro-electric plants, factories, re-afforestation and the building of schools. During these years an additional $230 million was spent on relief and rehabilitation. Yet the problem remained unsolved. Moreover, only some 845,000 acres out of 2,100,000 were suitable for permanent agriculture, while of this amount a considerable portion required complex and costly measures of soil conservation. By the 1940's Puerto Rico had a population of about two persons per acre of tillable soil, or just half an acre per habitant, compared with the United States which had three acres per person and was also more highly industrialized.

World War II, which temporarily ruined Europe, brought prosperity once again to Puerto Rico as to some other parts of the New World. The sugar industry, with its by-product rum, prospered from free entry to the United States market. Besides the benefit of exemption from Federal income tax, the island was handed back the considerable excise duty collected by the United States on Puerto Rican rum. In

[1] Victor S. Clark and Associates, *Porto Rico and its Problems* (Washington, D.C., 1930), p. xxii.
[2] Succeeded by the Puerto Rican Reconstruction Administration.

the post-World War II years, Puerto Rico found difficulty in fulfilling its United States sugar quota.

Unlike Latin American countries which had also benefited from the war-time boom but squandered the proceeds, Puerto Rico was to succeed in channelling its new-found fortune into expanding affluence of a permanent character. The architect of the new Puerto Rico was Luis Muñoz Marín, backed by his Partido Popular Democrático.[1] Putting to active use the revenue arising from Puerto Rico's favoured treatment by the United States, Muñoz Marín used the capital available to his Government to pump-prime a new programme of industrialization, often referred to as "Operation Bootstrap".

The post-war Puerto Rican Government pressed forward by every means at its disposal the industrialization of the island. A State owned and operated plant would be established to introduce a new industry. The plant could later be sold to private enterprise. Otherwise, the State would build a factory to be leased to a promising new industry. To encourage industrial development, the Puerto Rican Government introduced tax exemptions usually for a ten-year period. As a measure of the success of the programme, 171 new manufacturing industries commenced business in 1957 and 122 in 1958. Although some of these industries were small, altogether they contributed to alleviating the unemployment situation.[2] Nevertheless, a rising unemployment rate of 12·3 per cent. in 1966 emphasized the seriousness of the problem.[3] During the 1950's large numbers of Puerto Ricans had migrated to the United States, although by 1965 these numbers had considerably decreased.[4]

[1] Vide pp. 99-102

[2] In the year 1939-40, the unemployed numbered 112,000; in 1957-58, 82,000. For the same period the figures of those employed had risen from 512,000 to 555,000. Emigration to the United States had averaged 45,000 per year for the years 1951-58.

[3] Rafael Picó, "Growing with Tight Money", Progress in Puerto Rico, Banco Popular de Puerto Rico, Vol. II, 4, 1966. In 1960 the general level of unemployment stood at 11·6 per cent. In 1961 it had risen to 12·5 per cent., but dropped to 12·3 in 1962, to 11·3 in 1963 and to 10·7 in 1964, rising again in 1965 to 11·3 per cent. Bulletin of Labour Statistics 1966 (2nd quarter), International Labour Office, Geneva, table 4, p. 20.

[4] Between 1941 and 1950, 18,794 Puerto Ricans migrated to the United States. Between 1951 and 1960 this figure had more than doubled to 41,212, but showed signs of dropping off during the 1960's since figures for the first five years showed that only 6,319 had migrated to the United States. A Summary in Facts & Figures 1964/1965, Migration Division, Department of Labor, Commonwealth of Puerto Rico, New York, p. 15. Cf. Oscar Lewis, "The Culture of Poverty", Scientific American, Vol. 215, No. 4, New York, October 1966, pp. 19-25.

To suggest that the pump-priming of Operation Bootstrap was un-complicated would be untrue. There were examples of companies, including textiles, whose tax concessions ran out and whose profits were marginal; it was necessary for them either to close or ship their plant out of the island.[1]

As long as the number of new industries is considerably larger than those that cease operation, no great damage will be done, even if psychologically a closed business is a bad advertisement. In one month alone, twenty industrial projects were scheduled to begin operations.[2] The size of the multi-million dollar plant proposed by the Phillips Petroleum Company to process oil imported from Venezuela will alone have a substantial impact on the Puerto Rican economy.[3] The complex might stimulate further industrial expansion as had happened in Trinidad and the Netherlands Antilles.

Puerto Rico, like other Caribbean countries, has been faced with the too rapid expansion of its capital, San Juan. Since the heart of the old city is built on an island, overcrowding has been accentuated. In 1953 the San Juan Metropolitan Area contained more than half of the new plants and nearly half the employment in Fomento factories;[4] since then a serious attempt has been made to mitigate the situation. In-centives have been offered to encourage the location of new factories in the smaller towns. Substantial financial concessions have been made to those which have accepted including a differential scale of rents. The Government claimed to have cut in half the proportion of new jobs created in the metropolitan area in favour of those in other parts of the island.[5]

In June 1963, Muñoz Marín, worried over the continuing drift of

[1] Ruth Gruber, "Puerto Rico Oils Its Economy", *The New York Herald Tribune*, European Edition, Paris, August 25, 1965.

[2] Announced by Rafael Durand, Director of Fomento, *The San Juan Star*, San Juan, April 1, 1967.

[3] "The Phillips company received the oil import allocation it requested of 50,000 b/d, effective January 1, provided that it has its $45 million plant in operation within 21 months. The allocation is for 10 years, and the petroleum must come from the western hemisphere." *Cuba, Dominican Republic, Haiti, Puerto Rico, Quarterly Economic Review*, The Economist Intelligence Unit, London, January 1966.

[4] The Economic Development Administration, created by Muñoz Marín in 1950, together with the Puerto Rico Industrial Development Company and the Puerto Rico Ports Authority are responsible for Fomento programmes. Cf. William H. Stead, *Fomento—The Economic Development of Puerto Rico*, National Planning Association, Washington, D.C., 1958, *passim*.

[5] Economic Development Administration, Office of Economic Research, San Juan, Puerto Rico, February 6, 1958.

rural workers into the metropolitan area of San Juan, pressed his drive to attract industries into the less-developed areas of the island by granting thirteen years of tax exemption instead of the usual ten. He also called for better roads and an improved telephone service in the interior of the island. Time alone will determine the success of this experiment in the use of differential taxation. At least it showed courage in contrast to the failure of many countries to establish industries where they were most needed.[1]

Sánchez Vilella has tried to encourage industrial development in the southern part of the island. As the effect of location on industry goes far beyond economic policy, the Government aims at widening the geographic area of industrial activity.[2] In a small island, an oversize city must cause a national imbalance. Difficult as population movements are to control, the Government of Puerto Rico at least tackled a problem which confronts a large part of the world. The problem recurs in Kingston, Port-of-Spain and in all Latin America from Mexico City to Buenos Aires.[3]

Island movements of population have complicated schooling in Puerto Rico. In the past two decades, primary and secondary education has progressed considerably in both quantity and quality. Between 1940 and 1964, the percentage of school-age children attending school rose from 40 to over 90. Much improvement is still needed, although the illiteracy rate had fallen to 11 per cent. in 1965.[4] Attendance figures are deceptive as many children work half-day while school conditions are often crowded. Perhaps in reaction to conditions in public schools as well as an indication of improving economic circumstances, the number of private schools in Puerto Rico is increasing. One most successful educational institution has been the junior secondary school which

[1] The Puerto Rican Planning Board announced in December 1961 a six-year economic programme to accelerate the production of sugar and coffee, road construction, and loans for housing construction. Eduardo Rivera, the Board's programming director, said that the Governor of Puerto Rico would make recommendations to correct the exaggerated emphasis on the development of the San Juan area compared with that of the rest of the island. *Hispanic American Report*, Vol. XIV, p. 1099.

[2] "Puerto Rico se enfrenta en este momento a uno de los más dramáticos cambios en su desarrollo. El ritmo de crecimiento urbano es extraordinario. El país está cruzando el umbral del urbanismo. En muy poco tiempo seremos un país más urbano que rural." Sánchez Vilella, San Juan, February 2, 1966.

[3] Cf. Charles M. Haar, "Latin America's Troubled Cities", *Foreign Affairs*, Vol. 41, No. 3, Council on Foreign Relations, New York, April 1963, pp. 536-49.

[4] Oscar Lewis, *La Vida* (New York, 1965), p. xiv.

concentrates on practical skills such as shop, agriculture and weaving.[1] The large number of university places in Puerto Rico reflects the progress of the island.[2]

Tourism has played an important part in Puerto Rico's development. Six new hotels were opened for the 1962-63 season alone, and four more in the following season. Puerto Rico's attractions have been actively promoted, in the United States and elsewhere. The Cuban crisis, which adversely affected some other areas in the Caribbean, helped Puerto Rico, since American tourists felt a greater sense of security there than elsewhere in the Antilles. Income from tourism rose from $58,100,000 in 1960 to $84,788,000 in 1963.[3]

In 1961-62, for the first time, the beef-poultry-dairy industry, with a revenue of $100 million, surpassed that of sugar, an indication of Puerto Rico's changing agriculture. One sugar-mill closed and others ran into difficulties. In June 1962, the Bull Lines ended fifty years of service to Puerto Rico because of losses in shipping sugar, despite an appeal by the Commonwealth Government and five sugar companies heard before the Federal Maritime Commission, to keep the service going.[4]

Sugar production clearly was not holding its own, notwithstanding the attraction of a protected market at a substantial price. The policy of breaking up the larger estates had not paid off. After several years of shortfall, Puerto Rico's sugar quota in the United States was cut in 1962 from 1·23 to 1·14 million short tons, a small but significant reduction. In an effort to arrest this decline, the Puerto Rican Government allocated $1 million to encourage farmers to plant new cane-fields. In the case of workers left jobless by mechanization, a new unemployment law extended compensation from 16 to 52 weeks to provide for their retraining in fresh skills. The provision of this law did not solve the problems of the sugar industry. Growers, using the case of Hawaii as an example, claimed that only by mechanization could production be

[1] Gordon K. Lewis, *op. cit.*, p. 446.

[2] *Vide* p. 369.

[3] In 1964 tourist expenditure was $97,516,000 and in 1965 it was $119,278,000. Puerto Rico Planning Board, Bureau of Economic & Social Planning, June 1966.

[4] In October 1962, President Kennedy, under pressure from U.S. lumber companies who were unable to compete with Canadian lumber companies, agreed that U.S. traders could appeal to the Federal Maritime Commission to permit foreign-flag ships to operate in the domestic trade normally closed to them. This permitted an amendment to the Shipping Act of 1920 for a one-year trial period. The income from their Puerto Rican trade was $3 million annually.

Associated Press

Shack buildings (*above*) which have now been replaced by a fine low rent housing project
(*below*) at San Juan, a striking example of the changing face of Puerto Rico.

Puerto Rico: Muñoz Marín (right) congratulates Sánchez Vilella, his successor, on his victory, November, 1964.

increased and wages raised. The powerful unions, however, opposed mechanization until displaced sugar-workers were adequately protected.

Muñoz Marín announced in November 1963 a $30 million plan to provide farmers with credit for mechanization. Probably the decline of 18,319 tons in the 1963 sugar production, compared with that of the previous year, influenced him in this course of action.[1] Moreover, in 1963, 4,000 acres of land in sugar cane had remained uncut primarily because the rural unemployed had migrated to the cities.

The coffee industry continued depressed, competing as it had to against larger and more efficient plantations in Latin America using cheaper labour. Many plantations had run down. Despite a Puerto Rican subsidy, the future for coffee growing in the island appeared bleak.

As in other Caribbean islands, much of the food had always been imported. Rising U.S. transportation costs began to raise prices. In 1961, the Commonwealth Department of Agriculture launched a new programme to stimulate the island's fruit and vegetable industry. Food-processing firms which used more than 51 per cent. of local products would receive tax benefits. An authority was also set up to encourage small farmers to grow fruit and vegetables.[2]

At the same time, supermarkets were replacing the former *colmados* (grocery stores). If these small shops were finally squeezed out, it would affect the employment of nearly 30,000 owners and workers. As in other parts of the world, the more economical use of labour was creating problems of employment.

The handling of the problem of land in Puerto Rico proved more difficult than that of industry. In the spring of 1962 a Commonwealth Land Administration was established after bitter criticism from the opposition Partido Estadista Republicano. The Bill provided for a Government agency which could buy real estate from private individuals and resell it at lower prices or hold it for Government use. The

---

[1] 1962: 913,454 metric tons, raw value. 1963: 911,132 metric tons, raw value. In 1964 it went down further to 884,954, and in 1965 further still to 815,978. *Sugar Year Book 1965*, International Sugar Council (London, 1966), p. 268.

In 1967, "Science and Technology in Support of the Puerto Rican Economy", a report prepared by mainland experts at the request of the Commonwealth Government, cited lack of technological improvement as the continuing principal problem of the sugar industry. One obstacle to technological improvement was the law limiting private farms to 500 acres. Although the law was not strictly enforced, fear of it discouraged individual efforts to mechanize. *The San Juan Star*, San Juan, March 31, 1967.

[2] *Hispanic American Report*, Vol. XIV, p. 222.

Government's purpose in sponsoring the Bill was to prevent excessive rises in prices from the action of private realtors as demand for land spiralled with the population increase.

The Land Administration of Puerto Rico functions as a public corporation with wide duties and powers. These include the acquisition of land, normally by negotiation but if necessary by use of its compulsory powers. The Administration is concerned with urban development and housing schemes for low income groups. Its aim is to facilitate family purchases of homes. The Administration is also charged with the planning of residential and industrial areas. By June 1966 it had acquired 5,610 *cuerdas* of land at a cost of over $34 million.[1] The housing shortage continued, however, despite considerable construction. The Government estimated that approximately 26,000 housing units had been built by the State and 63,000 by private enterprise between 1960 and 1966. To increase the pressure against speculation, a tax increase from 25 per cent. to 75 per cent. on capital gains on land sales was proposed.[2]

The Puerto Rican Government planned to keep wages below those of the United States, though rising in phase with those of its powerful partner.[3] Efforts were made to explain the policy to labour, especially to island union leaders, though the incursion into the island of established mainland unions critical of this wage policy, caused certain complications.

The locally organized unions faced competition for members from the powerful U.S. unions who sought to widen their stake in Puerto Rico. Some thought that the mainland unions were partly motivated by the wish to avoid the keen competition of Puerto Rican products in the United States due to the island's lower wage rates. On the other hand, the drive for membership on the part of the mainland unions may have been the normal desire for expansion.

Of all the unions, the Brotherhood of Teamsters, headed by James Hoffa in the United States and by Frank Chávez in Puerto Rico, displayed most activity. Hoffa set out to mould trade union policy in

---

[1] Cf. *Informe Anual, 1965-1966*, Administración de Terrenos de Puerto Rico, Santurce, Puerto Rico, p. 4. One *cuerda* = 0·9712 of an acre.

[2] Sánchez Vilella, San Juan, February 2, 1966.

[3] Sánchez during his administration stressed the necessity of establishing different minimum wages for each industry geared to its level of development. However, the growing strength of mainland unions in Puerto Rico with their demand for the federal minimum wage was a disruptive force in the island's economic development. Cf. William R. Frye, "Operation Bootstrap Suffers from Some Foot-Dragging", *The Hartford Courant*, Hartford, Connecticut, March 5, 1967.

Puerto Rico. In October 1961, the Teamsters won an election which gave the union control of seven waterfront hauling companies formerly under the jurisdiction of the Seafarers International Union. At that time Chávez stated that his union had invested $800,000 since 1958 in an organization drive in the island.

In the hotel industry, struggles between competing unions increasingly disrupted the labour situation. On occasion, charges of malpractice on the part of the Teamsters had been alleged.[1] In March 1962, a meeting of the island hotel workers voted to sever relations with the mainland Hotel and Restaurant Employees Union. However, the Teamsters established a five-year mutual aid pact with this organization; without consulting the Puerto Rican leaders or members, they installed their own representative as trustee of Local 610, thereby affecting three of San Juan's largest hotels.[2] The Puerto Rican Senate investigated and criticized the arrangement. In the quarrel which developed, Chávez strongly attacked the island government for trying to indoctrinate and control labour and for impeding union growth.

As the decade progressed, the island's economy continued to expand, bringing with it the advantages and problems not unfamiliar to other industrializing nations.[3] Operation Bootstrap quietly subsided into the background after realizing $2 billion of industrial investments, approximately 2,000 new plants and about 150,000 new jobs.[4] In 1970 the Puerto Rican Planning Board announced the development of an Industrial Master Plan "to provide guide-lines for industrial development and the location of industries on the Island".[5] Then in 1971, the Economic Development Administration launched a new programme aimed at attracting $4 billion of additional industrial investments by 1980.[6]

[1] In April 1962, the Teamsters were found in contempt of court by the U.S District Court for not complying with a court order. The issue was illegal picketing and vandalism at La Concha Hotel at San Juan. The union was also ordered to stop coercing workers of the Valencia Baxt Express Company. *Hispanic American Report*, Vol. XV, p. 137.

[2] *Ibid.*, p. 232.

[3] "During the Sánchez administration . . . tourism, construction, and all other sectors of the insular economy except agriculture set new growth records every year." Wells, *op. cit.*, p. 324.

[4] *The New York Times*, New York, April 8, 1971.

[5] First National City Bank, *op. cit.*, October, 1970. During 1970, 271 new industries established themselves on the island or indicated plans to do so and 138 others expanded operations. Government Development Bank for Puerto Rico, *Annual Report 1970*, p. 14.

[6] According to the new director, Manuel A. Casiano, Puerto Rico ranks among the top 20 industrial areas of the world and is the United States' fifth-largest overseas market. *The New York Times*, New York, April 8, 1971.

The manufacturing sector had now become the main prop of the island economy.[1] The petrochemical industry was growing dominant with investments of up to $1,058 million (up from $96,328,000 in 1960) anticipated by the Government.[2] Food processing, pharmaceuticals, textiles and apparel industries were increasing. The Industrial Incentive Act of 1963 was amended in 1969 and entitled qualifying firms to tax holidays of 10, 12, 15 or 17 years depending on the industrial zone in which they were situated. The law will expire in 1973 but is likely to be extended.

Two serious obstacles, however, continued to hamper outside investment. Capital intensive industries require skilled labour which was in great shortage despite training efforts by mainland corporations. In addition, unions increased pressure to raise the minimum wage which was established by a tripartite committee representing labour, the public and industry.[3] The attraction of cheaper island labour began to lessen while Ferré negotiated urgently with union leaders in an effort to maintain some wage advantage over the mainland.[4]

The island's economy became increasingly hurt by the sharp decline in agricultural output, reflected in the continuing trade deficit.[5] There was an increase in the production of beef cattle, poultry, eggs and milk, but the cash crops of sugar, tobacco, and coffee continued to suffer.[6] In the decade between 1960 and 1970, 15 sugar mills had ceased operation leaving only 14, of which 5 were Government owned.[7] The Puerto

[1] The Chase Manhattan Bank, N.A., *World Business-14-Country Reports: Puerto Rico*, January, 1969, p. 17.

[2] Puerto Rico Water Resources Authority, *op. cit.*, p. 24.

[3] *The San Juan Star*, San Juan, June 13, 1971. First National City Bank, *op. cit.*, May, 1971.

[4] "Ferré Sees Labor OK for Wage Exemptions", *The San Juan Star*, San Juan, June 8, 1971.

[5] The deficit reached $1·4 billion in 1970. Ralph Ober, "Island Trade Deficit Grows Serious", *The San Juan Star*, San Juan, May 31, 1971.

[6] Agriculture's share of net income went from 24 per cent. in 1950 to 6 per cent. in 1970. Chemical Bank, *op. cit.*, pp. 5-6.

In 1971, in the first renewal of the Sugar Act since 1965, the House of Representatives voted to cut Puerto Rico's sugar quota for three years. The provision would reduce the quota by 285,000 tons each of the next two years and restore half of that in 1974. Puerto Rico produced 450,000 tons in 1970 and had not met its quota of 1·14 million tons in 15 years. Ed Konstant, "Badillo Hits House OK of Sugar Slash", *The San Juan Star*, San Juan, June 11, 1971.

[7] First National City Bank, *op. cit.*, August 1970.

Rico Government launched in 1970 a $100 million programme to rehabilitate the sugar industry.[1]

The accompanying shift of rural labour force into the urban areas aggravated existing problems there and increased unemployment. Migration to the mainland which had helped to alleviate that problem in the past diminished sharply by 1971 as the United States itself moved into recession.[2] Unemployment stood at 13·2 per cent. in January, 1971.

Tourism, previously a growing source of income, decreased substantially at the same time. By the spring of 1971, receipts from tourism were down an estimated 7 per cent. from 1970. Several large hotels were forced to close. The Government created the Tourism Development Corporation in an effort to rescue the industry. The official programme included the centralization of hotel reservations and the creation of a hotel management school.[3]

In the overall economic planning a change of emphasis first apparent in the last years of Muñoz's administration became more pronounced during the regimes of Sánchez and Ferré. Education, health, and public safety began to assume greater importance in relation to the production of wealth.[4] The continued rapid population increase reaching nearly 3 million in 1971 was forcing its attention on Government planning.[5] The consideration of the quality of life would most likely assume increased importance in the future development of the island's economy.

[1] *Ibid.*, Sept. 1970. According to Thomas D. Curtis in his able study: "The problem in the agricultural sector is not one of increasing supply but one of increasing the world's demand for the island's cash crops." "Employment and Land Reform in a Labour-Surplus Economy: A Case Study of Puerto Rico", *Land Economics*, Vol. 43, No. 4, Madison, Wisconsin, Nov. 1967, p. 453.

The sugar industry "due to climate, topography and soil conditions . . . has the highest per unit cost of production of any major sugar producing country in the Caribbean". *Ibid.*, p. 452.

[2] In the year ending June 30, 1971, net migration dropped to 1,811, except for 1969, the lowest in 29 years. *The New York Times*, New York, September 12, 1971.

[3] First National City Bank, *op. cit.*, May 1971.

[4] Wells, *op. cit.*, p. 325. In 1968, 1969, 1970 approximately 47 per cent. of the Government expenditures went to education and health. Puerto Rico Water Resources Authority, *op. cit.*, p. 24.

[5] The 1970 preliminary census showed a population of 2,688,289. The birth rate was 18·4 per 1,000 in 1970 according to the *Informe Económico Al Gobernador*, Oficina del Gobernador, Junta de Planificación – area de planificación económica y social – negociado de planificación económica. San Juan, Feb.

With some justification, Puerto Rico is often presented as an example of development potential inherent in other Caribbean islands which are today as poor as Puerto Rico was before its rise to the position of the Latin American country with the highest standard of living.[1] Other countries, especially some in the Caribbean, have been strongly influenced by Puerto Rico's methods.[2] Tax holidays and incentives on the Puerto Rican model continue to proliferate, often with success. Puerto Rico's grasp of the technique of widescale advertising, yet another example of the impact of the United States on the island's life, has made a rewarding contribution to its economy.[3]

The very rapidity of the island's development, however, demands a dispassionate examination of its success, to ascertain whether it has discovered a real technique which will facilitate the industrialization of similar small underdeveloped countries.

The prosperity in Puerto Rico is artificial, based upon a disguised subsidy from the United States. In 1959, Dr. Rafael Picó estimated the value to Puerto Rico of the remission of United States Federal Taxes at not less than $50 million. In 1970, the Puerto Rican Economic Development Administration evaluated the Tax remittances at $261 million. Moreover, Puerto Rico has benefited economically from the U.S. bases on the island in much the same way as Germany has prospered from the American and British troops stationed there. The island's unique status, which gave it the benefits of the United States' protection and diplomatic representation at no cost, contributed to the

---

[1] Incomes *per capita* have shown a dramatic rise during the period 1940 to 1965:

1940	$121	1950	$279
1960	$585	1965	$900

Selected Indices of Social and Economic Progress: Fiscal Years 1939-40, 1947-48 to 1964-65, Bureau of Economic and Social Analysis, Puerto Rico, Planning Board, San Juan, Puerto Rico. Governor Sánchez Vilella hoped *per capita* incomes would exceed $1,000 during 1967. "Puerto Rico's Growth in Fiscal 1967 to Approach 11%", *American Banker*, New York, February 3, 1967. By 1970 income *per capita* had risen to $1,340.

[2] *Vide* p. 123.

[3] Puerto Rico ". . . is to start a long-range advertising campaign that will present Puerto Rico to the world in the image which inspires us all—an image of Puerto Rico in renaissance. . . . Ted Moscoso and Governor Muñoz accepted this proposal, and we launched the campaign which is still running, nine years later. It has had a profound effect on the fortunes of Puerto Rico. It is, I believe, the only instance of an advertising campaign changing the image of a country." David Ogilvy, *Confessions of an Advertising Man* (New York, 1964), p. 67.

prosperity. Only a very rich nation with an uneasy conscience over "colonialism" would have pursued this policy.

* * * *

It has been seen that Puerto Rico enjoys a special position, through the generous financial treatment which it receives from the United States. If at first some of the U.S. aid was poorly directed, the persuasive ability of Muñoz Marín and his associates not only used the aid to great effect but increased it. Puerto Rico did not simply pull itself up by its bootstraps: rather it skilfully used American aid for this domestic purpose. Professor Gordon K. Lewis estimates that the island received benefits from every one of the federal services and programmes made available.[1] The full weight of U.S. subsidies, to some extent concealed, or at least not obvious, may not be readily appreciated by many Puerto Ricans. It is only natural that any government will arrogate the credit for improvements made during its term of office. Similarly, foreigners may fail to comprehend the extent to which U.S. aid to Puerto Rico has contributed to the excellence and speed of results. The integration of Puerto Rico's economy with that of the United States will continue to increase as the island develops, provided its Commonwealth status prevails.

Yet the result may be the distortion of Puerto Rico's economy. The small island must conform to its great associate's pattern of industry and agriculture. Should Puerto Rico one day opt for independence, the fresh orientation which would result would present profound complications. Probably the advantages of Puerto Rico's existing status far outweigh any change. By choosing statehood, it would have to compete on even terms with the United States, thus losing its special tax advantages. The issue amounts to one of economics versus nationalism.

In considering the development of the Caribbean islands associated with Great Britain, the Puerto Rico success story may be looked at as an inspiration: nevertheless, it must be accepted only with many reservations as a pattern of what is possible in other countries. Dr. Jaime Benítez, President of the University of Puerto Rico, while justly commending his island's policy, pointed out that Puerto Rico's solution to its internal problems was not intended for export.[2]

[1] *Op. cit.*, p. 183.
[2] "I regard Commonwealth as our own peculiar expression of social and political life wrung from our own tribulations and vicissitudes, a result of our own history and preferences, one of the many forms of endeavoring to live, work and achieve in peace, freedom and tranquility in the modern world. I do not regard our Free Associated State as a product for exportation." "Developing Nations in the International Arena", Caribbean Conference on International Affairs, University of the West Indies, Jamaica, March 17, 1966.

Despite Puerto Rico's spectacular success since World War II, it may prove difficult to maintain the rate of growth. Much will turn on the continuance of the special arrangement with the United States over the island's status. But even if that endures, the island must still grapple with the problem of its swelling population and limited usable land.[1] Although the island government is aware of the implication of the population explosion, the problem has not been effectively tackled. It is unlikely that even Puerto Rican bootstraps can indefinitely continue to lift such a heavy load.

Some, however, fear lest the very development of the island's economy will more and more deliver its trade and commerce to absentee ownership. Certainly Puerto Rico will undergo increasing pressure. Moreover, problems may arise through the fault of management which, being remote, may not understand local problems.[2]

The world is moving into an era of ever larger businesses, despite attempts in some countries to legislate against monopolies—not always with success. On the whole, competition with American-owned companies is likely to remain sufficiently keen to eliminate any risk of Puerto Rico being trammelled with unfair prices or inefficient services. In this regard, the island is differently placed compared with independent Antillean countries which can protect local industries even if they are inefficient. Its public has much to gain from the retention of effective outside competition. The change in Puerto Rico's way of life may be regretted, but the contribution to its prosperity from the American link cannot be gainsaid. The economic bond with the United States is even more vital to Puerto Rico than that which links the English-speaking islands to Great Britain, partners in another and different Commonwealth.

[1] *Vide* pp. 372-3
[2] Gordon K. Lewis, *op. cit.*, pp. 210-11.

CHAPTER VI

THE ISLANDS OF THE COMMONWEALTH INTO FEDERATION

At the termination of the Napoleonic Wars, Great Britain's powerful fleet dominated the Caribbean. With a garrison in Jamaica and a heavily fortified naval base at English Harbour, Antigua, no challenge to its power remained. Although Britain had not made the great territorial demands at the Treaties of Vienna which were customary for a victor in those days, significantly it had added Trinidad to its Antillean possessions. Spain's former position, controlling the Caribbean with forts, had been outmoded by the British system, supported by the world's strongest navy.

British Colonial administration, based on the British system of government, was politically, at least, in advance of the other powers. The Governor was appointed by the Crown; an Upper House was nominated by the Crown through the medium of the Governor; a Lower House was elected on a property franchise. Since the Crown could not legislate in Council, the powers of the Lower House were considerable. So effective had been the opposition to official policy by the elected members of the older colonies on occasions that when further colonies like St. Lucia and Trinidad were ceded to Britain, they did not receive the representative government of the original model.

The weakness of the old colonial system was the narrowness of the franchise, but it must be remembered that in Great Britain itself the electorate was very restricted despite the Reform Bills of 1832 and 1867 and it was not until 1918 that full adult franchise for men first came into force and not until 1928 for women.

In consequence of the political power struggle between some of the colonies and London, combined with a weak economy in many of the islands, Great Britain persuaded and pressed the different island legislatures to relinquish their elective Assemblies. Despite the gradual widening of the British franchise with the Reform Bills, the same policy was not adopted in the colonies, partly because of complications arising from the large slave population.[1]

---

[1] Indeed, as late as 1928 the constitution of Guyana—outside the Antilles, but usually regarded in the past as a West Indian colony—was abrogated. Crown colony government was substituted with very full powers in the hands of the Governor. Cf. Sir Harold Mitchell, *Europe in the Caribbean* (London, 1963), p. 141.

Indeed, Britain's failure to introduce a more representative government by extending the franchise may be one of the most valid criticisms of its colonial rule. The three British colonies in the Caribbean and North Atlantic which maintained their original constitutions, Barbados, the Bahamas and Bermuda, proved among the more successful from the economic standpoint despite limited resources.

Abolition of the slave trade, sponsored by Great Britain at the Peace of Vienna, was followed by the freeing of the slaves after 1834. William Wilberforce just lived to see the fulfilment of his dream, the most important and far-reaching legislation ever advocated by a Private Member in British Parliamentary history.

However, if political advance in the Caribbean may be described as slow during the nineteenth century, economic expansion in the widest sense was non-existent. Development had earlier taken place, especially in the cultivation of sugar cane. Yet the entrepreneur spirit which made vital contributions to the economies of Canada, Australia and New Zealand could find little scope to express itself in the Caribbean. Railways were impractical and the idea of industrialization had not emerged. London and Glasgow, not Kingston and Port of Spain, would manufacture the goods which the colonies needed. When sugar began to decline, bananas were successfully expanded. Cacao and coffee provided further diversification, though on a scale which could not replace the decay in sugar, the major crop. Economic stagnation, extending into the first part of the twentieth century, characterized the era.

The elimination of yellow fever and the improved control of malaria and other diseases played their part in the increasing population which in turn created problems of employment.[1] Many West Indians began to migrate to help build the Panama Canal, and to harvest the sugar cane of Cuba. The prosperity, due to a rise in commodity prices during World War I, was soon offset by the depression that followed in the post-war period.

Disillusionment with conditions led to serious rioting in several of the islands in the years before the outbreak of World War II. Trinidad, Jamaica and St. Kitts all experienced severe trouble. Out of these disputes arose the trade union movement which was to influence politics profoundly in Jamaica, Trinidad and other islands. Equal in importance to the rise of trade unionism was the upsurge of nationalism, which emerged from World War II, and was closely linked to the weakening of "old colonialism".

With the decline of the colonial concept, more and more attention was devoted towards finding new outlets for employment. Colonialism

[1] *Vide* pp. 362-3.

was effectively attacked as economic thraldom of the underdeveloped colony to the colonial power. Certainly the policies of Europe and the United States had not encouraged the development of industries in overseas territories.

Puerto Rico provided an early example of a change in thought. The success of Operation Bootstrap reverberated through the Caribbean.[1] Fortunately in the post-World War II years opportunities appeared which diversified the economies of some of the other territories. The economic progress which took place in Jamaica and Trinidad was almost as significant as the political development. Faced with agricultural difficulties which had plagued the Caribbean for more than a century and a half, not surprisingly the new nationalism in the islands turned to industrialization as a solution. While acknowledging the success of the Puerto Rican technique, the situation of these islands was very different. They had no free market for their produce comparable to that of Puerto Rico with the United States.

Even at the time of the federation of the British Antillean colonies, the home market of 3·5 million persons stretched across a thousand miles of sea with limited shipping services and harbour facilities to serve it. Poor communications often militated against successful factory operations in regard to both the import of raw materials and the export of finished goods.

Yet in an era when President Franklin D. Roosevelt's leadership placed "freedom" in the forefront, many obstacles to federation, such as geography, were overlooked. The Report of the Moyne Royal Commission had breathed caution and the Labour Government of Clement Attlee had indicated that a progressive policy toward Caribbean countries obtaining independence would be followed.

Reasonably enough, many people both in the Caribbean and in Britain believed that federation or at least some form of union was essential for the creation of a viable state.[2] An interesting feature was the large measure of agreement between the Labour Government and the Conservative opposition on colonial policy.[3]

[1] *Vide* pp. 109-10.
[2] A small measure of federation had been attempted in the nineteenth century when the Leeward Islands became a federal colony in 1871. However, an attempt to federate Barbados with the Windward Islands five years later was abandoned when riots commenced in Barbados. Nevertheless, following on the report of the Royal Commission of 1882-83, the Windwards were federated. *Report of the Royal Commission appointed to inquire into the public revenues, expenditures, debts and liabilities of the Islands of Jamaica, Grenada, St. Vincent, Tobago and St. Lucia and the Leeward Islands* (1884).
[3] Mitchell, *op. cit.*, pp. 47-8.

In 1947, a conference on the West Indian colonies was held at Montego Bay, Jamaica. Although the difficulties of distance between the colonies began early to emerge, the principle of a decentralized federation on the model of Australia met with acceptance. Further conferences took place at London in 1953 and 1956 and in Jamaica in 1957. The question of where the capital was to be sited caused much argument. The final choice of Trinidad displeased Jamaica, a thousand miles away. The mainland territories of Guyana and British Honduras had declined to join in federation.[1]

In 1958, Princess Margaret on behalf of Queen Elizabeth II inaugurated the West Indies Federation. The newly elected federal legislature consisted of a House of Representatives or Lower House of 45 members, of whom 17 were from Jamaica, 10 from Trinidad, 5 from Barbados and 2 each from Antigua, St. Kitts-Nevis, St. Lucia, Grenada, St. Vincent and Dominica, and 1 from Montserrat, all elected by adult suffrage. The 19-member Senate comprised 2 members of each territory except Montserrat, which had 1. The senators were appointed by the Governor-General of the West Indies Federation in consultation with the Prime Minister. The system was modelled on the former colonial legislatures, in turn influenced by the British system of two Houses of Parliament.

The hereditary composition of the House of Lords was replaced in the colonies by Crown nomination. Although the system may have had merit in an earlier era, its value was more doubtful in the middle of the twentieth century. Lack of popular election greatly weakened the influence of the West Indian Senate.

The finance of the Federal Government in a group of far from wealthy islands proved difficult to arrange. Ultimately a levy on unit governments was adopted. Of the total, Jamaica contributed 43 per cent., Trinidad 39 per cent. and Barbados 9 per cent.

From the outset the Federation met with mounting difficulties. At the Federal General Election of 1958, the Federal Labour Party which had been formed with Premier Norman Manley of Jamaica as leader and Sir Grantley Adams as deputy leader, and was supported by Dr. Eric Williams, Premier of Trinidad, all of whom headed powerful parties in their islands, was expected to score an easy victory. To the surprise of many, the opposition Democratic Labour Party, led by Sir Alexander

---

[1] Although only 300 miles from Trinidad, Guyana under the leadership of Cheddi Jagan decided not to enter the Federation. Fears of upsetting the racial balance of Guyanese of Indian and African stock may have influenced the majority party. With 83,000 square miles of territory, compared with Jamaica's 4,400, which was half of the Federal area, opportunities of development existed.

Bustamante of Jamaica and the opposition Democratic Labour Party in Trinidad, won a majority of seats in both territories. Consequently, the Federal Labour Party only scraped a majority by its victories in the small islands. The electorates in the two large islands had shown themselves antipathetic to the Federation.

The result of the General Election focused attention on the influence of the Leeward and Windward islands, arising out of the structure of the constitution. These small islands, with only 9 per cent. of the population, elected 11 members or nearly a quarter of the Lower House. No member of either Federal House was permitted to serve on the executive or legislative council of any territory. Certainly the great distances between some of the islands and the capital made this provision a reasonable one. On the other hand, island leaders were faced with a dilemma. Very often the leader's personality had played a large part in the success of his party. To detach men like Manley and Bustamante from their parties would weaken their influence. In fact, they both decided to remain in island politics, as did Williams in Trinidad.

Thus Manley, the elected leader of the winning Federal Labour Party and therefore the natural choice for Prime Minister of the West Indies, could not serve. Instead the appointment fell to Sir Grantley Adams, painstaking but pedestrian. Many of the likely candidates for office in Jamaica and Trinidad had been defeated at the polls. In consequence too many ministerial posts had to be filled from the small islands. They could not supply the talent. Had Manley moved from Jamaican to Federal politics, the field of speculation would have become fascinating. Undoubtedly with his immense prestige and influence in Kingston, he could easily have achieved election to the Federal Parliament. He was personally popular, especially in the urban areas which had benefited under his administration. Sore over the inequalities of federal voting and taxation and frustrated by the selection of Trinidad for the capital, when with some justice it believed a better site beside the new University at Mona was available, Jamaica might well have assuaged its disappointments in its satisfaction at the choice for first Prime Minister of its distinguished son. As Federal Prime Minister, Manley would have been less easily talked into a referendum, which was in any case not provided for in the West Indies constitution. Even if the referendum had taken place, Manley's prestige as Federal Prime Minister might well have turned the narrow adverse majority into a favourable vote.

As it was, in Jamaica, Manley and Bustamante who had alternated in heading Jamaica's Government since World War II, remained locked in political strife.   The opposition Jamaica Labour Party lost no opportunity in claiming that the constitution discriminated against its island.   Jamaica had half the population as well as half the land area of the West Indies Federation; with some justice it had a claim to half the seats.   With around one-quarter of the Federation's population, Trinidad was expected to find 39 per cent. of the revenue; yet it had only 22 per cent. of the representation in the Lower House.[1]

A wiser arrangement might have been the granting of representation in the Lower House according to population.   Had this been combined with an elective Senate on the basis of 2 senators from each island, Montserrat retaining 1 by reason of its size, the small islands would have retained a more effective check and one more easily defensible. The system of nomination in modern Commonwealth constitutions has much less to recommend it, for the implication is that the Crown— which in fact means the Prime Minister—will nominate better men than the electors will choose: a dangerous assumption for democracy.

Inter-island quarrels continued with the Federal Government coming under increasing attack from Jamaica and Trinidad.   Grantley Adams, though personally popular, proved an ineffective Prime Minister with little influence outside Barbados.   Even in his own island his party was ultimately defeated.   Adams sparked an unfortunate quarrel with Manley when he hinted that he might introduce later on a retroactive income tax to raise revenue.   The constitution precluded this tax being imposed in the first Parliament.

Divisions of opinion also occurred between the islands over fiscal policy.   Jamaica since 1952 had through its Industrial Development Corporation promoted many new industries, such as textiles, footwear and glass bottles, designed to replace imports.   It was reluctant to subject these new industries, usually sheltered by a substantial tariff, to increased competition.   However, a Federation without free trade amongst its members was an anomaly; nevertheless, Jamaica strongly pressed its point.   Trinidad, which had a similar industrialization programme and the strongest economy within the Federation, feared lest its prosperity be injured by excessive immigration from the impoverished nearby islands of the Eastern Caribbean.

Both Jamaica and Trinidad instinctively felt that the Federal Government, which depended for its slender majority on the votes of members from the Leeward and Windward Islands, might be more

[1] Cf. David Lowenthal, "Two Federations", *Federation of the West Indies, Social and Economic Studies*, Vol. 6, No. 2, ed. H. D. Huggins, Institute of Social and Economic Research, University College of the West Indies, Jamaica, June 1957, pp. 188-9.

sympathetic to them than to themselves. Jamaica sought a weak Federation with limited powers, while the small islands clung to their constitutionally entrenched position. The sagacious Williams kept Trinidad between the two; though he appeared to be increasingly pessimistic over the outcome of Federation.

Weakened by a financial structure which ever since World War II had caused anxiety to successive governments, Great Britain sought to hand over independence to the West Indies Federation. The continuing pattern of grants-in-aid discouraged Whitehall. In a forthright speech Governor-General Lord Hailes declared that the goal of independence could only be attained if the West Indies became self-financing. An independent nation would have the added burden of defence and representation abroad which Great Britain was bearing.[1] An Inter-Governmental Conference on Federal Constitution Revision began in Trinidad in September 1959. Following a General Election in Jamaica in 1959, which Manley won but in which both his People's National Party and the opposition Jamaica Labour Party had sharply criticized the Federal constitution, the Jamaican delegation to the Conference insisted on the settlement of the controversial issue regarding the number of representatives which each territory would have in the Federal House of Assembly. Unable to obtain a satisfactory compromise, Manley left the Conference and took the Jamaican delegation home.

To further exacerbate the relations between the Federal and the Island governments, Williams opened direct negotiations with Venezuela over customs problems.[2] Technically this was a breach of sovereign rights since Great Britain, through its ambassador, represented the West Indies Federation at Caracas. Trinidad finally announced that its discussions with Venezuela were suspended, but the incident had not aided the smooth functioning of the Federation. Provision for alteration of the Federal constitution, necessary though it might be, also led to controversy between the members. The sea-keeping qualities of the Federal ship were increasingly exhibiting serious defects. Misgivings began to be expressed, not only within the Federation but also in Great Britain.[3]

Trinidad's traditional fears of excessive immigration were expressed by police action to deport illegal immigrants at the rate of twenty-five per week. Criticized for this action by Chief Minister Ebenezer

[1] Jamaica, October 13, 1959.
[2] *Vide* p. 157.
[3] Cf. *The Times* and *The Daily Telegraph*, London, editorials, October 9, 1965.

127

Joshua of St. Vincent, Patrick Solomon, Home Affairs Minister of Trinidad, claimed that 13,000 immigrants had illegally entered his island.[1] The Trinidad police blamed them for the high incidence of crime.

Iain Macleod, who had recently been appointed Secretary of State for the Colonies, announced in October 1959 that he could not agree to any date for independence for the West Indies until the Conference on Federal Constitution Revision had reached agreement. He added that he would invite to London representatives of the territorial governments to settle the constitution's final shape.

Opposition to continuance of the West Indies Federation grew when Bustamante announced that his powerful Jamaica Labour Party would advocate Jamaica's secession. He crystallized his opposition by resigning as leader of the Federal Democratic Labour Party, whilst retaining the leadership of the Jamaica Labour Party. His party also refused to contest a Federal by-election in St. Thomas, Jamaica.

Shortly afterwards, Morris Cargill, deputy opposition leader in the Federal House of Representatives resigned his St. Mary, Jamaica, seat, declaring that he could no longer accept the taxpayers' money for something which he considered harmful to Jamaica. Manley, realizing the strength of the opposition in Jamaica, announced a Referendum in 1961 to test public opinion as to whether or not Jamaica should secede from the Federation.[2] Surprisingly the Governor General was not consulted or informed before this vital decision was taken.

The signs of disintegration became more ominous. For example, Eric Williams advocated at a Port of Spain conference in July 1960 that Guyana should join the Federation, to which Jamaica's Trade Minister, Wills Isaacs, retorted that he would never agree to Jamaica remaining in a Federation if a Marxist-dominated country were to enter it. Great Britain could do little to overcome the numerous inter-territorial disputes. The early establishment of a Federation with full independence was a major British objective, but one which was delayed by disputes between the territories. However, when Prime Minister Harold Macmillan visited the West Indies in March 1961 to address a joint meeting of the Federal Senate and the House of Representatives at Port of Spain, he declared that there was no doubt in the minds of the British Government over its success. He urged the territories to

[1] *Vide* pp. 364-5.
[2] "All the vast political, national and international consequences which would flow from such a decision were weighed and measured by one man in one hour." John Mordecai, *The West Indies: The Federal Negotiations* (London, 1968), p. 224.

compose any differences and to go ahead as a united West Indian nation. Although the British Government may have had doubts, presumably Macmillan felt he had to take a hopeful stance.

Certainly two years before, Julian Amery, Parliamentary Under-Secretary for the Colonies, had declared at a press conference that he had not met anyone in Jamaica or in any other Caribbean island he had visited who was opposed to Federation.[1] At this time the press in Great Britain and in the West Indies was expressing the danger looming for the Federation. If Macmillan's views may seem in retrospect optimistic, allowance must be made for his proper desire to indicate Great Britain's support for the Federation at a moment of crisis. The Inter-Governmental Conference at Port of Spain in May 1961 tried to secure agreement. Jamaica pressed the reallocation of seats on a basis of population in each territory, which was heavily weighted in favour of the small islands. A Conference to approve a final draft amending the West Indies constitution followed in London. Financial disagreement nearly wrecked it. Macleod, however, showed skill in obtaining agreement by permitting both Federal and unit governments to legislate in financial matters provided there was unanimous consent of all territories. Jamaica was satisfied, although other territories had misgivings. The new constitution further weakened the Federation since the establishment of movement and customs union were both to be phased over a period of nine years.

Only the Jamaican referendum on the island's attitude towards continuing within the Federation remained. Although not posed as a party question, it soon became clear that the issue would be fought on party lines. Manley had won two successive General Elections; his popularity, however, had waned, partly due to his equivocal position as a theoretical supporter of Federation and at the same time a powerful critic. The far-reaching concessions made to Jamaica had been extracted from the other members of the Federation largely through his skill and persistence.

In the outcome, the referendum took on the character of a general election. A variety of issues probably influenced the voters. The Manley Government symbolized too much the dominance of Kingston in the island; just as Federation with a capital some thousand miles away in Trinidad suggested a remote and alien rule. Under Manley's administration much had been done to advance industrialization,

---

[1] Kingston, Jamaica, May 31, 1959. "A visiting Minister naturally follows a carefully arranged programme and meets selected people, but it seems almost incredible that Amery's itinerary allowed him to form an opinion so wide of the mark." Mitchell, *op. cit.*, p. 54.

particularly in the Kingston area. To a lesser extent the smaller towns had also benefited. Yet this prosperity was not shared by the country districts where unemployment was heavy, even if no exact statistics were available to measure it.

A wave of optimism, arising from the concessions made to Jamaica at the London Conference, caused opinion in Trinidad and in other parts of the Federation and also in official circles in the West Indies and Great Britain to believe that Jamaica would vote to remain in the Federation. On September 19, 1961, at the commencement of the count after the poll, this view appeared to be justified. The "yes" votes from Kingston and other urban areas provided a comfortable majority for continuance. As the night wore on, the picture changed. Steadily the "no" votes from the country parishes began to diminish the early trend. The unpopularity of the People's National Party in the rural areas was being expressed. The majority of nearly 39,000 votes adverse to continuing in the Federation, namely 54 per cent. of those who voted on a 60 per cent. poll, was small; nevertheless, it was sufficient to topple the Federation. Manley refused the Opposition demand for an immediate General Election but announced that his Government would proceed with the preparations for the attainment of independence by Jamaica.

In December 1961, Williams won a General Election in Trinidad. He then announced that Trinidad too would seek independence and that his country would be prepared to enter into political association on a unitary basis with any of the smaller islands which sought this solution. The knell of the Federation had been sounded.

To Reginald Maudling, newly appointed Secretary of State for the Colonies, fell the disappointing task of a further conference in London with Manley and Bustamante to draw up the future constitution of Jamaica. As the leaders of the two Jamaican political parties had reached substantial agreement, a constitution patterned on that of other modern Commonwealth constitutions proved readily acceptable. A Senate of 21 members would be appointed by the Governor-General, of whom the Prime Minister would nominate 13 and the Leader of the Opposition 8. Revision of electoral boundaries was provided for: membership was restricted to a maximum of 60. Single member constituencies were provided on a basis of adult franchise.

A General Election followed in 1962. Jamaica recorded the highest poll in its history, namely 71·6 per cent. The result followed the pattern of the referendum with Manley, represented as "the man with a plan", comfortably winning in Kingston. Once again the agricultural constituencies, where the Bustamante Industrial Trade Union was strong, carried the day for the Jamaica Labour Party. The rural voters had outvoted the urban areas, just as had occurred in a different context in the Guyana General Election of 1961. The image of the Manley Government had been damaged by unemployment in Jamaica estimated at 18 per cent., a figure which threatened to be accentuated by immigration restrictions imposed by Great Britain.[1]

The country areas had developed less than the small towns.[2] Kingston had moved ahead faster than anywhere else. Significantly the most striking urban victory of the Jamaica Labour Party was that of Edward Seaga in West Kensington, the poorest and roughest area of the city. *The Nation*, organ of the Trinidad People's National Movement, claimed that the results of Jamaica's pre-independence elections showed that the referendum result was as much against the Manley Government as against Jamaica's continuance in the Federation.[3] Without doubt the failure of the People's National Party Government to find a solution for the problems of the rural areas had led to its defeat.

Bustamante had, in effect, brought to an end the West Indies Federation, convinced that he was pursuing the course which was best for his island. At the age of 78 he had changed the course of Jamaica's history. At midnight on August 6, 1962, the black, green and gold flag of the new nation replaced the Union Jack. After three centuries of government, Great Britain handed over to the people of Jamaica the responsibility of Government. Within the month Trinidad had followed suit. Barbados, the third largest member of the Federation, was quick to opt out of any further federation with the smaller islands; it too was on the road to independence.[4]

In the case of the two major Commonwealth islands, independence signified in reality that federation was unworkable. The failure was rooted in the Caribbean's past history when previous attempts had met

[1] *Hispanic American Report*, Vol. XV, p. 327. *Vide* pp. 365-6.

[2] "First, the swing of group votes towards the J.L.P. strikingly reflects the degree to which various areas tended to believe that they had not benefited from their proper share in the course of economic development. The country areas developed less than the parish towns, which in turn grew less fast than Kingston. There are strong economic forces which tend both towards centralization and towards the faster growth of the industrial and commercial than of the agricultural sector. The failure of the P.N.P. government to mitigate these forces may have been partly responsible for their defeat." Michael Faber, "A 'Swing' Analysis of the Jamaican Election of 1962: A Note", *Social and Economic Studies*, Vol. 13, No. 2, Institute of Social and Economic Research, University of the West Indies, Kingston, Jamaica, June 1964, p. 309.

[3] Port of Spain, April 13, 1962.

[4] *Vide* p. 173.

with opposition. From the earliest days each colony had looked to the Mother Country for guidance, defence and commerce. Inter-island trade was of little account. Even when steam replaced sail and in turn when the jet rivalled steam, communications still remained stretched. Rivalry rather than partnership characterized the attitude of one island to the other.

To each component of the Federation, loyalty was first to itself; a West Indian nation remained a mirage, with few enthusiasts. Political suspicions contributed to separation. The over-representation of the small islands in the House of Representatives played an important part in building up antagonism, particularly in Jamaica. The mistake, for which London must bear some share, appeared at its worst when the chances of the ballot box resulted in the establishment of the first—and last—West Indies Federal Government with an administration which was heavily loaded with small-island Ministers, ill-equipped for the job. Nor did its leader, Grantley Adams, succeed in inspiring enthusiasm for Federation by personally carrying the torch of federalism to the member territories.

A subtle danger existed in the granting by Britain of increasing independence to Jamaica and Trinidad during the process of forming the Federation and even after it was formed. Undoubtedly Jamaica's claim to independence was strengthened by the measure of autonomy which it had already received. When Manley ultimately asked Macleod to sanction a plebiscite, his request was accepted, despite the fact that there was no provision for a plebiscite in the Jamaica constitution. Albert Gomes and others bitterly criticized the Secretary of State for the Colonies.[1]

If the political omens had been unpromising, the economic prospects were worse. A group of islands of which all but four were grant-aided colonies came into federation.[2] Unquestionably, Great Britain had decided that the continuance of its former colonial system was impossible. Irked by the persistent financial problems of the islands, independence suggested an ultimate way out, though British opinion realized that financial aid must for long continue.

Anxiety to launch the Federation may have caused Great Britain, more experienced than the advisers of any of the island governments, to gloss over the economic problems which were to play so large a part in undermining federation. The financial burdens placed on Trinidad and to a lesser extent on Jamaica, much heavier than was justified by

[1] Gomes was Minister of Labour, Industry and Commerce in Trinidad from 1950 to 1956.

[2] Jamaica, Trinidad, Barbados and St. Kitts were not grant-aided.

their populations, could be defended on the grounds of their greater development. The impoverished and grant-aided smaller islands could not make large contributions. Moreover, the industrial developments expected from federation were more likely to favour the two major islands.

For reasons of equity and balance, the federal capital might have been sited in Barbados or one of the other small islands; instead, Trinidad was chosen, notwithstanding its lack of an immediately available site.[1] Temporary buildings in Port of Spain did not contribute to the success of the Federal venture. Moreover, the hot and humid climate made it far from ideal, affecting the capacity to work of persons whether of African, Indian or European origin. Brazil, in changing its capital from Rio de Janeiro to Brasília, was considerably influenced by the same climatic consideration, as well as by the desire to secure a more central location, something which Trinidad did not have in relation to the Federation. Jamaica, which might have acquiesced in a small island solution for the capital, felt that the selection of Trinidad was an additional reason for leaving the Federation.

The awkward fact that not one of the federated islands had an internal market extensive enough to support large industry handicapped development. The Federal Government failed to appreciate the vital importance of pressing the integration of the Federation. Despite its economic weakness, the Government could at least have put forward plans for commercial development.[2]

Not all the blame for the collapse of the West Indies Federation can be placed on economic causes. Political failure may be clearly discerned in the refusal of Manley and Bustamante in Jamaica and Williams in Trinidad to abandon island politics to enter the Federal Parliament. Unless a Federation can produce leaders, it is likely to fall apart.[3] On

[1] The American base at Chaguaramas proved to be the only site in Trinidad suitable for the permanent capital. The United States, having established this base at great cost, was disinclined to give it up, especially at a time of international tension. Consequently, the Federal Government had to be squeezed into an already overcrowded Port of Spain. After prolonged negotiations, a solution was reached in 1961 whereby the United States relinquished 21,000 acres of the land it had acquired in Trinidad under the 1941 bases-for-destroyers agreement made with the United Kingdom Government. *Hispanic American Report*, Vol. XIII, p. 885.

[2] Cf. Hugh V. Springer, "Reflections on the Failure of the First West Indies Federation", *Occasional Papers in International Affairs*, No. 4, Harvard University, Center for International Affairs, July 1962.

[3] "The Federation was destroyed by poor leadership rather than by the intractability of its own internal problems." Mordecai, *op. cit.*, Epilogue, W. Arthur Lewis, p. 461.

the rim of the Caribbean, the ill-fated Central American Confederation of the nineteenth century had collapsed. The splintered Republics have only lately drawn together with the powerful aid of a U.S.-sponsored Common Market. Both Canada and Australia have experienced serious constitutional problems, some of which remain unsolved. More recently, Africa has been rent with federal failures.

Not one of the mistakes alluded to would by itself have been fatal to the continuance of the West Indies Federation, if enthusiasm to build a new nation had existed. Nationalism, one of the most powerful forces in the twentieth century, operated not to support the Federation but rather to bolster up island loyalties which ultimately destroyed the federal image. Thus the Federal ship, overloaded with controversy, inadequately manned by industry and lacking in effective leadership, sank with its crew. The political "wise men" had remained on shore in their islands or disembarked in time.

CHAPTER VII

INDEPENDENCE IN THE COMMONWEALTH ISLANDS

JAMAICA

THE POLITICAL PATTERN

Both Jamaica and Trinidad entered into independence in August 1962, nearly sixty years after Panama, the last country in the Western Hemisphere to do so, had attained independence. The speed and ease with which the change was accomplished contrasted with the tortuous history of the West Indies Federation which in the stormy four years of its existence had not succeeded in reaching that status.

Jamaica had assimilated British institutions and customs since its capture from Spain by Oliver Cromwell's forces in 1655, even if the island had unobtrusively modified and adjusted them to suit its own conditions. It moved into independence with many advantages. Already it had established self-government anchored to a well-tried two-party system which had existed since 1944. In Bustamante and Manley the new country had leaders of experience and capability who had successfully alternated in office. This democratic rivalry proved an enormous gain to Jamaica. The Civil Service which had over the years replaced British by Jamaicans, was experienced and competent, with a standard of efficiency far above that of most Latin American countries which had been independent for more than a century.

However, despite an excellent record, the Civil Service had only a limited number of fully trained personnel; Manley had stressed this in 1958,[1] yet Sangster six years later highlighted it as one of the biggest problems still facing the service.[2] A shortage of staff prevailed,[3]

---

[1] House of Representatives, April 8.
[2] Annual General Meeting of the Jamaica Civil Service Association, March 12, 1964.
[3] Cf. B. L. St. John Hamilton, *Problems of Administration in an Emergent Nation*, Præger Special Studies in International Economics and Development (New York, 1964), pp. 176-90.

sometimes complicated by Ministers who failed to delegate work adequately.[1]

Statutory Boards offering better salaries and working conditions proliferated.[2] From time to time frictions developed as some members of the Boards complained of excessive Government interference whilst the Government in turn claimed that its rightful functions were being usurped.[3]

Despite these problems, Jamaica was fortunate in its administration. Its Civil Service was incomparably more experienced than that of most of the newly independent countries in Africa and Asia. The judicial system was highly respected and the police efficient. Although complaints had been launched by each party against the other over corruption at the polls, at least the electors had been able to secure changes of Government through the ballot box. Nothing emphasized the strength of British tradition in the island more than the pendulum swing between the Jamaica Labour Party and the People's National Party.[4]

The Jamaica constitution, joint work of the two main political parties, in many respects bore the marks of the Colonial Office which had probably drafted in the space of two decades more constitutions than even Napoleon. A graceful compliment by Jamaica to Great Britain was the retention of Sir Kenneth Blackburn, last Colonial Governor, as first Governor-General. In November 1962, he handed over to the first Jamaican Governor-General, Sir Clifford Campbell, who had been Speaker of the Jamaican House. The choice proved a very happy one.

The principle of a nominated Senate which had been a feature of the defunct Federal Upper House was retained. The constitution could only be changed by a vote of each House with a two-thirds majority.[5] Since the leader of the Opposition nominated enough members to

[1] *The Daily Gleaner*, Kingston, editorial, April 28, 1964.
[2] Such as the Agricultural Development Corporation, the Industrial Development Corporation, the Tourist Board, the Jamaica Broadcasting Corporation and the Agricultural Marketing Board.
[3] *Memorandum on Statutory Boards*, Farquharson Institute of Public Affairs, Kingston, July 1, 1965, p. 1.
[4] Cf. Sir Hilary Blood, "And Now—Jamaica", *New Commonwealth*, London, August, 1962. Philippe Decraene commented: "Faite de libéralisme et de conservatisme mêlés, la vie politique, elle aussi, emprunte beaucoup à la tradition anglaise". "La plus anglaise des Antilles", *Le Monde*, Paris, August 7, 1962.
[5] Section 49, *The Jamaica (Constitution) Order in Council 1962* (H.M.S.O., London, 1962).

MR N W MANLEY

Jamaica moved into independence with the support of both Government and Opposition. Mr. Norman Manley (left), then Premier, shares a joke with Sir Alexander Bustamante after the formal signing of the Independence Conference Report, Lancaster House, February 1962.

The Jamaica Parliament after Independence: question time. Mr. Donald Sangster (centre left), then Finance Minister, with Prime Minister, Sir Alexander Bustamante on his right, who faces Opposition leader. Mr. Norman Manley, Q.C., M.P.

Jamaica: the Morissa Shoe Factory outside Kingston. An example of Jamaica's policy of encouraging industrialization by far-seeing legislation, p. 145.

Jamaica: the Blue
Lagoon,   near
Port Antonio, an
important   resort
area on the north
coast.

Anne Bolt

Jamaica: the campus of the University of the West Indies at Mona, including administrative buildings, lecture halls and student hostels.

Jamaica: Kingston's busy port is one of the largest natural harbours in the world. In the background, the Caribbean Cement factory.

Gleaner Co. Ltd.

Former Prime Minister Hugh Shearer a[t] Andrews Memoria[l] Hospital, Kingston.

Jamaica: Michael Manl[ey] congratulated by S[ir] Clifford Campbell on [his] election victory, 1972

Gleaner Co. L[td.]

defeat a Bill of this character, some believed that a valuable safeguard had been included, though history past and present might make a student of politics chary of pinning too much faith to a constitution however carefully worded.

Besides the welcome into the Commonwealth, symbolized by Princess Margaret representing Queen Elizabeth II at the Independence celebrations, the presence of Vice-President Lyndon B. Johnson betokened the good wishes of the United States of America. These two countries seemed likely to continue as Jamaica's principal supporters even if their relative influence on Jamaica might change.

With the intuitive understanding of his countrymen's feelings which had helped to win him political power, Bustamante encouraged a measure of informality which permitted everyone, even in the poorest homes, to participate in the independence of their country. Each town and village had its celebration. Thus it was that each parish capital on August 6 had its own ceremony of lowering the Union Jack and replacing it with the bold green, gold and black flag of the new nation.

Bustamante, who had always stressed his attachment to the British connection, was careful soon after independence to visit both London and Washington. Indeed, his country would need help from any friendly quarter for there were many who still believed that Jamaica had made an error in opting out of the Federation.

In a Caribbean that was far from tranquil, Jamaica had for neighbours Cuba, Haiti and the Dominican Republic, all three under dictatorships, all three hostile to one another. Britain, which had during three centuries garrisoned Jamaica, now was happy to hand over this task to the newly independent nation which could not afford to ignore its defence problems. Jamaica lost no time in expanding its defence force, descendant of the historic West India Regiment.

Conscious of the impact which American bases had had in the Caribbean, Bustamante offered base facilities to President Kennedy.[1] Although the proposal was not taken up, an agreement was shortly afterwards signed with the United States under which Jamaica received American aid for improving defence services.[2] The action was criticized by the Opposition Leader, Norman Manley, on the grounds that it might have implications involving Jamaica's sovereignty; nevertheless, the agreement seemed to be in accordance with Jamaica's declared policy of aligning itself with the Western powers.

As a small nation in a world of power blocs, Jamaica sought to make

[1] *Hispanic American Report*, Vol. XV, p. 721.
[2] Washington, June 6, 1963.

friends internationally while retaining its sovereignty and independence. This would be achieved by its support of the United Nations and the objectives of the Charter. Seeking the ending of colonialism, it opposed all forms of discrimination based on race, sex, colour or religion. Jamaica was not in favour of any form of political federation, believing that co-operation in the Caribbean would best be achieved on a national and not a supra-national level.[1] As a small nation strongly opposed to the use of force to settle international disputes, Jamaica in 1969 joined the Organization of American States.

The first election after independence took place in February 1967, and provided as it were a shop-window for the Government and its critics to display their respective wares. Apart from controversy over the method of registering voters, which involved photographing and fingerprinting to avoid fraud and resulted in some 300,000 fewer persons being placed on the voting roll, most of the major issues were economic.[2] The Jamaica Labour Party fought on its five years' record. It was able to point to very marked expansion of both the bauxite and tourist industries. A large number of new industries had been started, particularly in the Kingston area.

The Opposition People's National Party attacked the Government on the ground that one in five persons of working age and one in three young persons were out of work. It advocated the establishment of Trade Training Centres and Agricultural Schools. The plantation system was to be ended. Grants and loans to work the land would be made together with a three-year guarantee of good prices. A National Health Service would be established together with increased social security.

The Election was marred by considerable violence, particularly in West Kingston where partisans of both parties used firearms. A number of people were injured and killed during the campaign. In the rest of the country, the contest was comparatively orderly.

The result followed closely the pattern of the Referendum on the Federation and the General Election of 1962. The early results on February 21, 1967, seemed favourable to the Opposition. However, as the evening wore on, the pattern changed. In the final result the J.L.P. won 30 seats against 20 for the P.N.P. The Government party received most of its support from the rural areas. It had, however, improved its position in the urban area of Kingston. Despite the

[1] Statement laid on the Table of the House of Representatives, Kingston, June 30, 1964.
[2] Cf. "Effects of New Registration System on Elections", *The Daily Gleaner*, Kingston, February 27, 1967.

decisive majority of the J.L.P., the poll was very close. As often happens, the British two-party system with single member constituencies had exaggerated the size of the majority.

Despite illness which had kept him out of politics for a year, Sir Alexander Bustamante had influenced the result. His image as the father figure of independent Jamaica was effectively publicized during the election campaign by J.L.P. speakers. Bustamante did not seek re-election. Hugh Shearer, who had been Leader of Government Business in the Senate and Minister without Portfolio in the previous Government and who had headed the organization of the Bustamante Industrial Trade Union, successfully contested the Prime Minister's Clarendon seat. Bustamante announced his retirement after twenty-three years in politics. He had been Jamaica's most colourful political leader. His immense personal prestige, particularly in the country districts, had established the trade union which bears his name and also the Jamaica Labour Party. His supporters claimed the election result as a birthday present since two days later he was 83.

Donald Sangster, who became the new Prime Minister, had acted in that role for Bustamante during a year's illness. As Finance Minister, he had earned the confidence of the public of Jamaica and also of those overseas who had backed Jamaica financially, both in the public and private sphere. In contrast to Bustamante, Sangster was urbane and cautious. Long political experience had made him an expert on the complex problems which faced Jamaica.

At the same time, the island was fortunate in having an effective Opposition led by Norman Manley, who had headed the Government when his party had been in office. Most of the P.N.P. leaders had been elected, together with Michael Manley, the Opposition leader's son, who was also a principal executive of the National Workers Union. Jamaica had successfully completed its first parliament in independence. The closeness of the election suggested the vigour of Jamaica's democracy, badly needed in the Caribbean where so many failures had occurred.

Tragedy came to Jamaica when its new Prime Minister, struck down by illness only a month after he had led his party to victory at the polls, died on April 18, 1967. Born in 1911, Sir Donald Sangster[1] was still a comparatively young man in terms of politics. His grasp of finance had been of immense value to his country during a period of rapid

---

[1] A few days before his death, Sangster received a knighthood from Queen Elizabeth II.

expansion. A cautious and shrewd statesman "Donald Sangster grew and grew in service of his nation and his people".[1] On April 18, 1967, Hugh Shearer was appointed Prime Minister.

Lacking the charisma of a Bustamante (although he was his personal choice), Shearer took several months to win confidence as the nation's leader and suffered a series of internal party struggles. Norman Manley died in September 1969 having resigned in March from the leadership of the opposition. His son, Michael, took over and quickly achieved considerable success, as he had done earlier as Island Supervisor in the National Workers' Union. Both party leaders, now in their mid-forties, with similar backgrounds, retained effective union control. Jamaica thus continued its strong two-party system. Shearer's defeat by Manley in the February 1972 election was considerably heavier than predicted. With 35 seats to Shearer's 17, Manley ended the ten year rule of the Jamaica Labour Party.[2]

Jamaica has also had its share of world political problems. In October 1968, riots, organized for the first time in Jamaica by Black Power militants, followed protest demonstrations at the University of the West Indies against the expulsion from Jamaica of Walter Rodney, Guyanese Professor of African History. Rodney's *The Groundings with my Brothers*, aimed at Jamaica, appeared to envisage revolution.[3] The Rodney affair was weakly handled and the police not sufficiently supported by the Government. But it occurred at a time when Prime Minister Shearer was concerned with rifts in his Cabinet, and Norman Manley was nearing retirement.

Inspired perhaps by the "back to Africa" movement of Marcus Garvey in the 1930's, Black Power in Jamaica later drew its strength from economic conditions. Despite record sums of foreign capital pouring into the island, the gap between rich and poor was growing. The feeling this aroused was also reflected by *Abeng*, a radical weekly newspaper whose articles were directed particularly against the foreign-owned bauxite companies. Although successful initially, it later ceased publication.

Basically Jamaica was trying to industrialize as fast as possible, linking this to a policy of "Jamaicanization", the stressing by Jamaicans of their own industry. This could be interpreted not only as a natural reaction

---

[1] *The Daily Gleaner*, Kingston, editorial, April 19, 1967.

[2] "Mr. Shearer had become too remote. Mr. Manley's strong suit is the personal contact with the people which he had forged in his years of trade union organization." *The Times*, London, editorial, March 3, 1972.

[3] (London, 1969), pp. 30-1, 65.

to colonialism but also as a response to the promptings of Black Power. Nevertheless Jamaica strongly criticized the form of nationalization being carried out in Guyana.[1]

Jamaica's representation overseas increased. A new embassy to serve future Common Market needs opened in Bonn. After attending the conference of non-aligned nations in Zambia in September 1970, Jamaica, pressurized by public sentiment, opened an embassy in Ethiopia—its first in Africa. Nearer home, the appointment of an ambassador to Haiti and the Dominican Republic was of particular significance, since either might become members of CARIFTA and the Caribbean Development Bank. The visit of Dr. Aristides Calvani, Venezuela's Minister of Foreign Relations, to Kingston in May 1970, led to editorial speculation in Jamaica over increased trading possibilities with Latin America.[2]

After the uneventful visit of Rockefeller to Jamaica during his 1969 Latin American tour, in August 1970 Prime Minister Shearer went to the United States. Shearer's task lay in formulating a U.S.-Caribbean policy, recognizing that Jamaica's interest should lie "with the United States rather than with Russia, or China or even with the United Kingdom".[3] Although it welcomed the broadening of international contracts, *The Daily Gleaner* expressed concern lest a possible fusion of Caribbean with Latin American objectives should prove detrimental to the former.

THE ECONOMIC PATTERN

On the political side Jamaica had entered independence with few apparent major problems. No serious racial problems existed. The new nation was homogeneous and tolerant and a well-organized two-party system of government was established.

The real problems were economic, though the weight of them had been masked by recent rapid industrial growth combined with massive emigration which, however, had proved to be short lived. Since World War II, its economy had been revolutionized by the exploitation of bauxite for which it had become in the space of a few years the world's largest source, exporting bauxite mainly to the United States and alumina to Canada and Norway.[4] The policy of industrialization

---

[1] *Vide*, p. 242-3. Cf. Dennis Topping, "Alcan plays it cool", *The Times*, London, October 28, 1971.

[2] *The Daily Gleaner*, Kingston, May 14, 1970.

[3] *The Daily Gleaner*, Kingston, editorial, May 14, 1970.

[4] By 1966 Jamaica had four bauxite developments, three owned by U.S. companies and one by a Canadian company.

was making steady progress; many commodities, formerly imported, were now manufactured in the island; moreover, a valuable tourist industry was developing. In a period when industry throughout the world was becoming ever more integrated and complex, Jamaica was fortunate in having the new University of the West Indies, where training for administration and industry at the higher levels was available. Well situated for world trade, particularly with the United States, Jamaica has good natural harbours, even if much required to be done before Kingston, the principal port, could be considered efficient.[1]

By international standards Jamaica was far from poor, whether the yardstick of national income or actual wage rates is used. Most Asian countries had infinitely greater poverty, as had some countries of South and Central America. The fact of Jamaica's propinquity to the United States, the world's richest country whence came the larger part of Jamaica's tourists, may by contrast have given an unduly unfavourable impression of Jamaica's economic position.

Difficulties, however, existed. In earlier centuries Jamaica had been repopulated from Africa after the near elimination of the Amerindian population. The position, however, had dramatically altered. The slow rate of population growth under slavery began to change after emancipation in 1834. Improved medical skill and knowledge of hygiene in later years played their part in stimulating the growth. By the twentieth century, Jamaica already had a population beyond the economic needs of the day. After 1952 there had been a rise in the level of emigration, which not only helped to provide an outlet but also caused significant amounts of capital to flow back into the island from abroad. Unfortunately, it also meant a loss of skilled workers. In recent years Jamaica had been a leader in the flow of emigrants to Great Britain until this was sharply curtailed in the very year Jamaica obtained independence.[2] The United States, which had used surplus West Indian labour for seasonal farm work, also largely closed this outlet due to political pressure.

As the population growth exceeded 2 per cent., even the rapid expansion of the Jamaican economy could not provide sufficient jobs. In the past Jamaica had been extravagant in the use of labour, and wages had been low. On the plantations there was a tradition of

---

[1] The Jamaica bauxite industry found it necessary to construct port facilities and to operate its own shipping, a course open only to the industrial giant.
[2] By the *Commonwealth Immigrants Act, 1962* (H.M.S.O., London, 1962). Cf. Mitchell, *op. cit.*, pp. 84-90.

spreading out work over a larger number of persons than was really necessary.

The impact of highly mechanized bauxite companies on a somewhat archaic economy was dramatic. With wages a relatively small part of the cost of production and with expensive equipment imported from the United States to operate, and above all, used to American labour rates and trade union practice, they made substantial inroads into the limited pool of skilled labour.[1] The direct effect on the employment figure was limited, although in due course the production of alumina, first stage towards aluminium, provided more work.[2] Of greater importance, the bauxite companies established wage rates which were often beyond the capacity of other employers to match, with the result that they recruited heavily from other industries. Due to the high degree of mechanization, the numbers they employed were relatively low. A highly paid elite group of workers emerged which may have been a mixed blessing for the island.[3] This became particularly difficult when, in order to meet Government regulations, to replace the material they were abstracting and to rectify the inevitable temporary damage to the countryside, these companies were engaging in large-scale agricultural operations on land whose mineral value was their primary concern. Although figures were not available to show the exact farming results, a fair assumption would be that the profitability of bauxite mining to a large extent carried the agricultural operations.[4] This arrangement was reasonable from the companies' angle, whilst

---

[1] "With the development of the bauxite industry by three American aluminum companies in 1951, the United Steel workers of America, AFL-CIO gave financial aid to the National Workers Union for the organization of the bauxite workers. Kenneth Sterling, formerly an organizer of the People's National Party, was employed by the steel workers and did an outstanding job in the organization of bauxite workers and his development of a union along traditional lines. In this task he was helped by the technical assistance of the Steelworkers Union; by the bauxite companies who wanted a shop-steward system for the orderly processing of grievances—and by the fact that the cream of the Jamaican labor force, many with union experience in the United States, had been hired by the aluminum companies. The bauxite-workers division became the backbone of the union. . . ." William H. Knowles, *Trade Union Development and Industrial Relations in the British West Indies* (University of California Press, Berkeley and Los Angeles, 1959), p. 73.

[2] The bauxite companies employ over 5,400 persons, but of these only about 3,300 are engaged in mining operations. *Five-Year Independence Plan 1963-1968*, Government Printer, Kingston, 1963, p. 13.

[3] *Vide* p. 340.

[4] Cf. "Jamaica Pasture Land Pays Off in Bauxite", *Business Week*, New York, April 19, 1952.

also suiting the Jamaica Government. Yet the outside effects were not at first appreciated by other farmers on marginal land. The greater contribution of alumina than bauxite to the country's revenue from 1960 onwards emphasized the need to process more alumina.[1]

Kaiser Bauxite opened a £12·5 million development at Port Rhoades, Discovery Bay, on Jamaica's north coast. In March 1970, the Alpart alumina plant, the first undertaking by American firms in the alumina industry, was officially opened, representing an additional investment for Jamaica of some $J.60 million. Although various problems still prevented aluminium production, the conversion of more and more bauxite (an ever diminishing asset) into alumina within the island was essential.[2] In 1969, bauxite and alumina exports totalled $J.118 million, an increase of 25 per cent. over the preceding year.[3]

Jamaica faces union difficulties as each of the major trade unions, the Bustamante Industrial Trade Union and the National Workers Union, has political associations : one to the Jamaica Labour Party and the other to the People's National Party. An interesting event in connection with the never-ending inter-union struggles in Jamaica was an agreement entered into in May 1963 between the Bustamante Industrial Trade Union and the National Workers Union. Under the new arrangement, neither union would try to improve its membership at the expense of the other for two years. Membership in either union was signified by the check-off—an arrangement whereby the worker authorizes his employer to deduct his union dues at source.

Frequent criticism was voiced over disputes which stemmed from inter-union competition, something that has occurred in other countries during the development of a trade union movement. The rivalry appeared in a variety of industries. In 1963, Sir William Stevenson, the chairman of the Caribbean Cement Company, made strong criticisms on this subject, declaring that it created abroad an unfavourable image of Jamaica which he feared might lead to a slump in confidence on the part of investors.[4] After a strike in 1965, which had compelled *The Daily Gleaner* to suspend publication, the editor castigated inter-

---

[1] In 1955 out of 2,666,000 tons of bauxite produced, 433,000 tons were converted into alumina. By 1961 the amount of bauxite produced had more than doubled, whereas alumina converted had multiplied almost four times. *Commonwealth Development and Its Financing No. 8, Jamaica* (H.M.S.O., London, 1964), p. 32.

[2] Cf. *The Daily Gleaner*, Kingston, editorial, March 12, 1970.

[3] *Economic Survey Jamaica 1969*, Central Planning Unit, Kingston, 1970, p. 75.

[4] Kingston, January 18, 1963.

union rivalry as the source of the dispute.[1] The problem of inter-union disturbances has not been solved, though it might be a mistake to regard it as more than a phase in the growth of a trade union movement still comparatively young.

As a result of the success of industrialization in Jamaica, the quality of labour available improved, partly through trade and technical education projects. By 1964 Jamaica had, apart from its sugar industry, over 800 registered manufacturing establishments, including a cement factory, cigarette factories, breweries and bottling plants, textiles, clothing factories and plants producing soap, margarine and edible oil.[2] New industries continue to be established and a small but highly efficient oil refinery was completed in 1963.[3]

Despite the rapid expansion of the Jamaican economy, recessions have taken place. Although considerable success had been attained in attracting new industries to Jamaica, the announcement in October 1962 that the plant of Jamaica Woolens in Kingston would shut down was a severe blow to the Jamaica Industrial Development Corporation which had backed the company. The loss amounted to £500,000. Production had commenced in 1961 and the capacity of the plant was one million blankets per year. It was the largest undertaking which the J.I.D.C. had financed. In addition to a late start, two strikes had interrupted the factory's short career. In an editorial sharply critical of the management of the I.D.C., *The Daily Gleaner* compared the event to the severe loss of the Colonial Development Corporation in its early years.[4]

In consequence of rapidly rising wages and no comparable rise in either the production or the price of agricultural commodities, which in some cases were Government controlled, agriculture often fared badly. Only a relatively small part of the land was first class and suitable for mechanical cultivation. Most of this was under sugar cane and bananas.

---

[1] *The Daily Gleaner* commented in its editorial: "Through the years the *Gleaner* establishment has been a battleground between unions who regard representation of Gleaner workers as a special plum. Stoppages in past years have been caused by one union or another seeking to gain ascendancy over a rival union." Kingston, February 19, 1965.

[2] *Commonwealth Development and its Financing, No. 8, Jamaica* (H.M.S.O., London, 1964), p. 9.

[3] Crude oil is imported from Venezuela and oil is refined at the rate of 26,500 barrels a day.

[4] October 3, 1962. For the difficulties of the I.D.C. in the Caribbean, *cf.* Mitchell, *op. cit.*, p. 80 and pp. 166-7. In a second editorial, *The Daily Gleaner* claimed that the heavy losses of the J.I.D.C. should never have arisen, adding "This has been an example of intemperate enthusiasm suffocating elementary business acumen". Kingston, November 20, 1962.

Much land was marginal, often hilly or with outcrops of rock, which frequently precluded mechanical cultivation. Agriculture was, however, still by far the largest source of employment.[1]

In 1952 the International Bank for Reconstruction and Development reported that there was no doubt that "the available land can be made to yield far more than at present".[2] Amongst other things, the report suggested agricultural techniques might be improved. Various schemes were put into operation: one of the most recent, the Farmers' Production Programme, formed part of the *Five-Year Independence Plan 1963-1968*.[3] Agricultural research, education and marketing were developed.

The success of the sugar industry depended both on favourable climatic conditions and on the fluctuations of the world market. By 1963 Jamaica had built up a market in the United States, although the bulk of its sugar production continued to be sold under the Commonwealth Sugar Agreement.[4]

Faced with heavy unemployment, the Jamaican Government in 1962 had prohibited the importation of mechanical equipment for loading sugar cane, except under licence involving agreement between employers and trade unions. The advantages of mechanization had already been demonstrated in other sugar-growing areas like Hawaii. The wage increases recommended by the Goldenberg Report had accelerated the change.[5] Inevitably the subject proved highly controversial. In spite of an extremely low price for sugar on the world market during 1964 and 1965, Jamaica faced an even deeper crisis.[6] Not even the protected market of the Commonwealth Sugar Agreement was enough to cover the costs of sugar production. Wholesale mechanization was no panacea for the ills of the sugar industry, because of the resultant impact of

[1] Nearly four out of every ten members of the labour force are in this sector. *Jamaica Today, A Brief Survey*, Jamaica Information Service (Kingston, n.d.).

[2] *The Economic Development of Jamaica* (Johns Hopkins Press, Baltimore, 1952), p. 10.

[3] Kingston, 1963, pp. 88-94.

[4] Out of a total sugar production of 496,706 metric tons in 1965, Jamaica exported 80,198 tons of sugar to the United States and 350,761 to the United Kingdom and Canada. International Sugar Council, *op. cit.*, p. 137. *Vide* pp. 323-7.

[5] *Report of the Commission of Enquiry on the Sugar Industry of Jamaica, January 1960*, p. 85.

[6] In 1963 (a peak year for sugar) the average London daily price for sugar was £71·70 and the Commonwealth Sugar Agreement negotiated price was £46, 0s. 10d. By 1964, the average London daily price had dropped to £51·13 and by 1965 to £21·51, whereas the Commonwealth Sugar Agreement negotiated price was £46, 0s. 10d. and £42, 0s. 0d. respectively. Cf. International Sugar Council, *op. cit.*, p. 345.

redundant workers on the unemployment figures. The Sugar Enquiry Commission in 1967 advocated mechanization to reduce production costs together with training schemes to cushion displaced labour.[1] Their findings were largely ignored. However in 1969, Prime Minister Shearer emphasized his belief in mechanization stressing, nevertheless, its serious effect on the labour force.[2]

Continuous difficulty beset the Jamaica banana industry involving it in long negotiations with the Fyffes Group who shipped the bulk of the fruit to Great Britain. Finally in December 1969, Fyffes terminated its Jamaica contract. After further meetings a temporary arrangement was reached to cover the position into the latter part of 1970. The long-term position, which was likely to be affected should Great Britain enter the E.E.C., remained undetermined. In the meantime Jamaica was striving to improve the quality of its fruit which had come under criticism.

Historically Jamaica had imported food which was paid for by the proceeds of sugar exports. To assist the numerous small peasant farms earning a minimum income, the Government helped to establish the Jamaica Agricultural Society. In association with the Ministry of Agriculture, extension officers of the Society toured the country in an endeavour to teach better farming practices. Effective results were few.[3] Food imports rose from over $J.40 million in 1965 to nearly $J.60 in 1969. Despite the protection of locally produced consumer goods enforced after 1965, the demand for imported items, largely created by rising incomes, continued.[4]

Without doubt the development of the tourist industry directly and indirectly provided more employment than any other change in the post-World War II years, and as a dollar earner it surpassed even sugar. Legislation encouraged the construction and extension of hotels, allowing the importation of building materials and equipment free of customs duties and permitting the rapid depreciation of capital for income tax relief. In 1954 a Tourist Board was set up. After a setback in 1960 when visitors were kept away from the island by exorbitant prices and lack of organization in the industry, the Government appointed John Pringle, a talented young Jamaican, as Director of

[1] *Report of the Sugar Enquiry Commission (1966) Jamaica,* Kingston, October 1967, pp. 123 and 225.

[2] Kingston, February 1969.

[3] *The Daily Gleaner* attacked the political parties which sought "to enable seeds to grow by Acts of Parliament and crops to be reaped by ministerial regulations". Kingston, February 6, 1965.

[4] Among the food items placed on the restricted list were frozen vegetables, sweets and biscuits, fruit juices, confectionery and peanuts.

Tourism. Assisted by political stability and under careful direction, the industry made a remarkable recovery.[1] Intensive and well-diversified advertising in North America and Great Britain, together with considerable effort at home not only to improve facilities but also to make the public conscious of the importance of tourism, accounted for much of Pringle's success. Because of its proximity to North America, the majority of visitors came from the United States and Canada (88 per cent.). Hotel construction benefited both from the Hotels (Incentive) Act of 1968 and the establishment of a Development Department to screen projects. Cottage and apartment accommodation gained in popularity. Tourist expenditure increased from £13·1 million in 1962 to £39 million in 1969.[2] As the largest single earner of foreign exchange, the industry steadily increased as a major force in the economy. Kingston commenced a ten year modernization programme of its water-front. Limited airport terminal facilities (despite expansion) and deterioration of roads in many parts presented urgent problems. Great difficulties were experienced with the telephone service, particularly in country districts. However in 1971, a reorganised and improved system came into use.

Notwithstanding the spectacular advance in Jamaica's economy since the end of World War II, much of this gain has been lost by the population increase.[3] The problem is one of education rather than of employment. Despite the advantage of being the seat of the University of the West Indies, educational services, particularly in the rural areas, were poor. Crowded schools made the task of teaching extremely difficult. A substantial percentage of illiteracy or near-illiteracy[4] increasingly complicated the employment of workers required in an era when better education was growing more and more necessary.

Sir Philip Sherlock, Vice-Chancellor of the University of the West Indies, stated that the most hopeful thing about the state of education in Jamaica was that it stimulated widespread interest.[5] After 1950 great improvements had been made: secondary school enrolment almost trebled, and the output of teachers from enlarged training

[1] Jamaica has benefited from disturbed political conditions in islands such as Cuba, Haiti and the Dominican Republic. *Vide* p. 357.

[2] *Economic Survey Jamaica 1969*, p. 20.

[3] Between 1943 and 1960, Jamaica's population increased by almost half a million.

[4] In 1953, according to a sample survey, the figure was 23·0 per cent. This had fallen to 18·1 per cent. in 1960. U.N.E.S.C.O., *op. cit.*, p. 38.

[5] "Crisis in Education", *The Times Supplement on Jamaica*, London, February 21, 1966, p. vii.

colleges also trebled.[1] Nevertheless, the Five-Year Independence Plan made little provision for the 90,000 children of infant school age.[2]

Junior and All-age schools also presented a problem, due to an increase in the birth rate and an inadequate number of places. To cope with the number taking their secondary education 9,000 more places would have to be found in the High Schools during the period of the Plan. Emphasis was put on a technical programme, and on improving General Certificate of Education results.[3] In September 1966, the World Bank approved a $9·5 million loan to Jamaica for the development of education: the United Nations Educational, Social and Cultural Organization assisted the Jamaican Government in the preparation of the project.[4] Paradoxically, within a year of receiving this aid, Jamaica was denied another source of educational subsidy. For many years the British Council has trained and staffed libraries, supplied books and offered other valuable services to many developing countries. Early in 1967, the British Council announced that at the British Government's request it would withdraw completely from Jamaica, where its current budget was £15,000.[5]

The University of the West Indies by 1969 was firmly established with 2,500 students in the Mona campus compared with 150 in 1950.[6] Its medical faculty had a very strong influence on the island. Despite the break-up of the West Indies Federation, the University had held together and steadily expanded. Besides the original campus at Mona, Trinidad had a flourishing campus as had Barbados. Under its

[1] In 1961 output from teachers' colleges totalled 230; in 1970 it was expected to reach 1,000 and by 1975, 1,400. Cf. E. L. Allen, Minister of Education, *A Teacher's Guide to Jamaica*, Introduction, Ministry of Education, Kingston, 1970.
[2] To the existing 36 Infant Schools and Departments (enrolment 8,500) it was proposed to add 300 new places each year during the succeeding five years. 26,000 pupils of this age-group attended Basic Schools and Infant Centres where facilities were poor and teachers untrained. *Five-Year Independence Plan 1963-1968*, p. 159.
[3] Fifty per cent. of the pupils in existing High Schools failed to secure three G.C.E. subject passes. *Ibid.*, p. 160.
[4] The World Bank Loan would cover about 50 per cent. of the total $19·4 million cost of the project. $1·3 million would be provided from bilateral sources for technical assistance and the Government of Jamaica would finance the rest. International Bank for Reconstruction and Development, Washington, D.C., Press Release, September 21, 1966, p. 3.
[5] As part of British Government saving, a similar withdrawal would take place by the British Council from Trinidad and Barbados.
[6] *Vide* p. 369.

eminent new Chancellor, Sir Hugh Wooding, the U.W.I. would play a vital role in the future of higher education in the Caribbean.

Family Planning found a place in the Five-Year Independence Plan but was not as strongly emphasized as some might have wished.[1] Dr. Herbert Eldemire, Minister of Health and a leading medical practitioner in the island, had stated that his Government would make available facilities for birth control, including literature on the subject; clinics were established for the use of the public. Eldemire made it clear that the policy was in no way being forced on the country: he stressed that the matter was one for the individual to decide for himself.[2] The Jamaica Family Planning Association conducted intensive campaigns to encourage the use of birth control methods.[3]

After nearly a decade of independence Jamaica had preserved its democratic system of government with a well-entrenched two-party system. Its interest in world affairs was demonstrated not only by its membership of the United Nations but also by its entry into the O.A.S. It had avoided major internal disturbances aided by a well established judicial system and an efficient police force.

Its major difficulties were economic. Unemployment at an unofficial figure of perhaps 20 per cent. remained the darkest cloud on the horizon.[4] Industrial development had advanced lately aided by the establishment of CARIFTA. Heavy investment from outside had taken place and the important bauxite industry further expanded. The Jamaica Government, although its ultimate aim might be to acquire at least a majority Jamaican participation in all the main financial institutions in the country, appeared anxious to avoid Guyana's course of action.[5] Tourism, despite problems, continued to expand. Agriculture presented a major problem with the outlook for both sugar and bananas, and to some extent citrus, serious, compounded by the probable entry of Great Britain into the Common Market.

[1] "The Government will encourage the spread of information on, and technique for, the spacing or limitation of families for the benefit of those persons who desire them." p. 53.

[2] Savanna-la-Mar, July 29, 1964.

[3] "Islandwide Birth Control Drive Launched", *The Daily Gleaner*, Kingston, March 18, 1965. The most significant work was carried out by Dr. Lenworth Jacobs.

[4] Professor Doxey estimated that between 107,000 and 214,000 new jobs would have to be created to achieve immediate full employment in the Western sense. *Survey of the Jamaican Economy*, Kingston, July 1969, p. 18, paragraph 53.

[5] Cf. *Caribbean Business News*, Toronto, December 1970.

TRINIDAD AND TOBAGO

THE POLITICAL PATTERN

As in Jamaica, political parties evolved steadily in Trinidad. After the constitutional reforms in 1956, the People's National Movement led by Dr. Eric Williams moved quickly ahead to win in that year a majority of the elected seats in the Legislative Council.[1] The opposition Democratic Labour Party was formed after the 1956 General Election. Largely East Indian in composition, it became the principal alternative party. In 1961, Trinidad received full internal self-government.

With the nearing of independence, the Trinidad Government made a novel approach to consideration of the country's future constitution. In April 1962, it organized a three-day conference for this purpose. Representatives of different interests and groups were invited to attend. The Press was excluded from the conference, but the proceedings were broadcast and in due course published verbatim.

The constitution of independent Trinidad provided for a nominated Senate with Government representation increased from 12 to 13 and Opposition from 2 to 4. The remaining 7 members represented religious, economic and social bodies. Whereas previously this group had been nominated by the Governor after consultation with the bodies themselves, under the new constitution the Governor-General appointed them on the advice of the Prime Minister.[2] Clearly the change greatly strengthened the Government's power in the Senate.

The new constitution for independent Trinidad contained safeguards with regard to the civil liberties of the citizen. Entrenched clauses provided that alteration would require a two-thirds majority in both Houses of Parliament.[3] However, if Trinidad and Tobago was engaged in war, a public emergency could be declared by a two-thirds majority of both Houses or by Proclamation of the Government.

On August 31, 1962, Williams made his first broadcast as Prime Minister of Trinidad and Tobago to celebrate independence. His theme for the new nation was Discipline, Production and Tolerance, words of value for the whole Caribbean and beyond. He stressed also the constitutional rights of the parliamentary opposition. Doubtless noting

[1] Cf. Ann Spackman "Constitutional Development in Trinidad and Tobago", *Social and Economic Studies*, Vol. 14, No. 4, Institute of Social and Economic Studies, University of the West Indies, Kingston, December 1965, p. 289.

[2] *The Trinidad and Tobago (Constitution) Order in Council 1962*, Article 23 (c) (H.M.S.O., London, 1962), p. 21.

[3] For Jamaica's solution, *vide* pp. 136-7.

the rough lot of democracy in some other parts of the Antilles and beyond, Trinidad like Jamaica had endeavoured to protect its constitution.

Much of Trinidad's future would turn on Williams, its dynamic leader. He had left the Caribbean Commission in 1955 to form the new People's National Movement. Combining integrity, something that had been lacking in Trinidadian politics, with energy and debating skill, he had won every political contest in which he engaged. He soon built a reputation as an astute and resolute bargainer for his country. Yet most striking of William's gifts was his tolerance, supremely important in a country composed of races which were only beginning to merge. He advocated this quality to his P.N.M. supporters in his Woodford Square addresses. Williams' outstanding success had been his ability to avoid racial conflict which had torn Guyana apart. A Negro himself, Williams headed a government of a country whose 870,000 population was 47 per cent. African, 35 per cent. Indian, 3 per cent. European and the balance mixed. Despite the disruption caused by the collapse of the West Indies Federation, Trinidad and Tobago had succeeded in consolidating its different racial components into a nation.[1] Deeply conscious of history, Williams traced most of Trinidad's problems to its past. His criticisms of British Colonial Office policy and administration emerge sharply in his published works and speeches.[2]

Holding a Doctor's degree from Oxford University, Williams' grasp of international politics led him to envisage the future of the Caribbean far beyond the boundaries of his own small country. Although he had pulled out the final props which had brought down the West Indies Federation after Jamaica had voted to secede, he continued to advocate co-operation between different parts of the Caribbean. In early 1964, Williams undertook an extensive tour to eleven African countries, the Middle East and Europe. In London he had meetings with Duncan Sandys, Secretary of State for the Colonies, and he met also Prime Minister Sir Alec Douglas-Home and Opposition Leader Harold Wilson. Williams formed a pessimistic view over the future of the Commonwealth, claiming that Trinidad had more in common with countries like the United Arab Republic or Yugoslavia. However, his despondency may have been tinged by his belief that financial aid from

[1] Charles Archibald commented with justice, "Trinidad-Tobago can claim to have been as well-prepared for sovereignty as any other British ex-colonial territory. The people rallied swiftly from the shock of their Federation's failure and followed with commendable discipline the firm course forward which the Government subsequently charted". "Trinidad . . . Cross Roads of the Caribbean", *New Commonwealth*, London, November 1962.

[2] Cf. Eric Williams, *Capitalism and Slavery* (London, 1964), pp. 143-4.

Students at the Institute of International Relations, Trinidad, attached to the University of the West Indies.

Trinidad: the Imperial
School of Agriculture, since
1960 part of the University
of the West Indies at
St. Augustine.

Port of Spain, Trinidad's
capital, from the air.

Anne Bolt

Riots in Port of Spain, April 1970.

Britain had been inadequate. A pugnacious and effective critic, he realized that sometimes a well-timed protest might produce results, as he had already demonstrated by his bouts with the U.S. Government over the Chaguaramas base.[1] At the same time, by undertaking his tour comparatively soon after Trinidad's independence, Williams displayed his conviction that a well-organized small country must set aside any idea of living in isolation.[2] He had been one of the first to realize the weakness of the defunct West Indies Federation, but he was too much of a realist to believe that Trinidad could flourish alone.

In the autumn of 1966, Prime Minister Eric Williams led his People's National Movement to a decisive victory at the polls. At the previous general election in 1961, the P.N.M. had won 20 seats against 10 held by opposition parties. On this occasion, 6 new seats had been created. Williams kept his two to one ratio by winning 24 seats. However, the Opposition, which in 1961 had been split, was now consolidated in the Democratic Labour Party led by Dr. Rudranath Capildeo who won the remaining 12 seats. Neither the Liberal Party nor the Workers and Farmers Party won a single seat. Once again the British system of a single seat a single vote had reinforced the two-party system of government. Whether it might later result in a racialist approach in Trinidad will remain to be seen. In Guyana a desperate deadlock partly caused by this very system had led a Conservative Secretary of State in the United Kingdom to introduce proportional representation.[3]

The success of the P.N.M. in Trinidad, which might be compared with that of the governing Jamaica Labour Party some weeks later, suggested that the two first Commonwealth countries in the Caribbean to attain independence had justified the attainment of statehood. In each case, moreover, a vigorous opposition existed to provide an alternative Government.

---

[1] Cf. Mitchell, *op. cit.*, pp. 64-65.

[2] "Will you accept the fragmentation and go off on your own by yourself? Or will you look at what has gone on in the area, learn from the mistakes, see the objective economic necessities and put forward the clarion call to the entire Caribbean, that the entire Caribbean, dwelling together in colonialism for four and a half centuries, should hereafter seek like other parts of the world to dwell together in unity?" From the Premier's speech on Independence delivered to a Special Convention of the People's National Movement, January 27-28, 1962. Commenting on the tour, *The Nation*, organ of the P.N.M., wrote: "Realizing that his country is a part of the whole, he [Williams] has correlated its problems with other places and has caused them to be viewed not merely as peculiar to the West Indies, but as affecting the world at large". Port of Spain, May 8, 1964.

[3] *Vide* p. 231.

Inevitably the losers in both countries blamed the system of voting. Defective voters lists in Jamaica could be compared with criticism against voting machines in Trinidad. Nevertheless, in each case the result was convincing. Democracy appeared to be well entrenched in the Commonwealth Antilles.

Unfortunately, however, the two-party system of government led to racial cleavage in Trinidad, even if the Guyanese situation was temporarily avoided. The Negroes, (some 43 per cent. of the population) identified themselves with the P.N.M. whereas the East Indians (about 38 per cent. and with a higher birth rate) backed the Democratic Labour Party. Despite ill-health, frequent absences abroad and a movement inside the party to depose him, Capildeo remained in nominal control.

Williams, a pragmatist, tended to encourage both political and economic nationalism as it suited him. His attitude resembled that of Shearer in Jamaica.[1] Long years in power had taught the Trinidad Prime Minister that foreign investment was vital to the development of his country: anything which deterred it could be disastrous. At the same time, he sought greater Trinidadian involvement in his country's industry and commerce. In March 1970, the Government took over the Bank of London and Montreal in Trinidad, turning it into the proposed National Bank of Trinidad and Tobago. Williams' autocratic style offended some of his younger followers, such as Arthur N. R. Robinson, former Minister of Finance, who resigned in 1970 as Minister of External Affairs. Robinson proved the most formidable opponent Williams had yet encountered.

Aware of the power of the mass media, in 1969 Williams' Government took over the television station and one of the two radio stations, arguing that this would instil "a national consciousness" and eliminate harmful advertising.[2] To his opponents this had a hollow ring.

Williams' political skills were severely challenged in April 1970. A series of demonstrations which had started in February demanded the release of ten Trinidadian Black Power followers who were on trial in Montreal accused of destroying the computer centre at the Sir George Williams University. Although Jamaica had already experienced trouble from Black Power,[3] events in Trinidad were much more serious. Heavy unemployment, estimated by some as touching 20 per cent., particularly affected the younger section of the work force. Criticism

[1] *Vide*, pp. 140-1.
[2] Cf. *Draft Third Five-Year Plan, 1968-1973*, Port of Spain, pp. 402-404.
[3] *Vide*, pp. 140 and 389-90.

of the Government, which was encouraging overseas investment, mounted.[1] As early as 1967, Williams had barred Trinidad-born Stokely Carmichael, U.S. Black Power leader, from entry into the island, a move which angered his supporters.

Attacks in Port of Spain on Canadian and British property followed. On April 21 the National Joint Action Committee, a militant body headed by Geddes Granger, urged stronger action. Mob violence erupted in the centre of the capital, which resulted in the police opening fire on the rioters. Threatened by a wave of strikes, the Government declared a state of emergency, imposing a curfew throughout the island. By April 22, the revolt was intensified by the mutiny of a handful of soldiers in Trinidad's tiny army. The United States and Great Britain sent warships to the vicinity, ostensibly to evacuate their nationals if matters grew worse. An attempt by the mutineers to send arms to the Port of Spain mob was foiled by fire from a coastguard vessel which commanded the only coast road leading from the army base to the capital. This action may have been decisive in the defeat of the uprising.

In due course the revolt was quelled, partly by negotiation. A number of mutineers were brought to trial, military judges being brought in from abroad, and prison sentences were in some cases imposed. The Government may have sought to stress the army rising in order to distract attention from the general dissatisfaction among the poorer workers in the island.

Williams announced a national reconstruction plan which envisaged greater local participation in banking, advertising, commerce and industry.[2] He aimed at even stronger Government hold on the economy. However in October 1970, Williams suffered another setback when his stringent Public Order Act, designed to prevent repetition of earlier riots, had temporarily to be withdrawn.

The General Election of May 1971 took place in the aftermath of the uprising in the previous year. The state of emergency had been ended in the autumn and the traditional Winter Carnival had passed off without incident. Yet the drawn-out trials of the soldiers accused of mutiny, high-lighted by the addition of officers from African countries to the courts-martial, continued the feeling of apprehension. The number of soldiers put on trial for mutiny—some 60 in an "army"

[1] "Both parties have failed to build up effective youth sections, and the absence of young people from party politics has been a striking feature of Trinidad life in recent years." David G. Nicholls, "East Indians and Black Power in Trinidad", *Race*, London, April, 1971, p. 446.
[2] Port of Spain, June 30, 1970.

of under 1,000 men—suggests that matters had gone seriously wrong.[1]

The main opposition party, headed by Arthur N. R. Robinson and Vernon Jamadar, had resulted from a merger between the Democratic Labour Party and the Action Committee of Dedicated Citizens, founded by Robinson. They concentrated on attacking the Government as corrupt and the voting machines as rigged.

The traditional party line-up of Negroes versus East Indians became blurred. Instead an image of Black Power arose: the poor and unemployed of both races versus the well-to-do, again of both races, who tended to support Williams. To some extent it was an ominous protest against the moderate policy of Williams trying to encourage industrialization, substantially by foreign investors, in Trinidad's ailing economy. In a way the election reflected the revolt of the year before. The destruction of the computers in Montreal symbolized Black Power opposition to the establishment: even when as in Port of Spain the Government itself was Black.

In the outcome the General Election was unreal. The more powerful and vociferous opposition groups did not run candidates. The only parties to oppose the Government were the weak Democratic Liberation Party, a break-away group from the Democratic Labour Party, and the African National Congress. The very fact that Williams had won all the 36 seats in the House emphasized the hollowness of the victory.[2]

As a result of the election boycott, only 41 per cent. of the electors voted compared to 66 per cent. at the previous election. Had the opposition parties, disunited as they were, entered candidates, Williams would still most probably have won. At the same time the younger generation, many without jobs and increasing rapidly in numbers, suggested that change was in the air.[3]

THE ECONOMIC PATTERN

Half the size of Jamaica and with about half its population, Trinidad is a wealthier island largely because of its natural resources in oil; limited in size and often faulted, its oilfields have proved sufficient not only for valuable production but also as a magnet to attract allied industry.

[1] Cf. *The Financial Times*, London, March 30, 1971 and *The New York Times*, New York, April 2, 1971.

[2] *The Financial Times*, London, May 26, 1971.

[3] Cf. James Nelson Goodsell, "Support wanes for Trinidad and Tobago chief?" *The Christian Science Monitor*, Boston, May 27, 1971.

Purchase of a substantial part of these oilfields by the Texas Company accelerated their development. Moreover, the W. R. Grace Company established a large fertilizer plant in 1960.

Although Trinidad's trade is worldwide, Williams has taken great pains to extend trade with Trinidad's neighbours, including Guyana and Surinam. Traditionally trade with Trinidad's nearest and most important neighbour, Venezuela, only ten miles off its eastern shore, has been bedevilled by historical trading disputes, sometimes linked with smuggling. Venezuela has set up long-standing tariffs directly aimed at Trinidad and the Netherlands Antilles.[1]

Trinidad and Tobago entered independence with a government reputed for its integrity and one of the strongest economies in the Caribbean. If Jamaica had half the population of the defunct Federation of the West Indies, Trinidad had half the revenue. Agriculture was developed and diversified between sugar, cacao, coconuts and other crops. Despite a higher standard of living than most other Caribbean territories, Trinidad and Tobago faced serious economic problems. The rising population showed little sign of deceleration: employment was unlikely to keep pace with the annual increase of workers into industry unless there was continued and extensive industrial expansion. Moreover, sovereignty would impose additional burdens of defence and overseas representation. Apart from Commonwealth aid, outside help from the Organization of American States and the United States might be necessary.[2]

The British custom of giving a "golden handshake" to former colonial territories on their attaining independence caused hard words in the case of Trinidad. While Jamaica had also been disappointed with what it had received from Great Britain, Williams was offered a much smaller sum than he had requested, partly in kind.[3] With perhaps a measure of justice, he added in reference to the West Indies, "I don't know of any area where so much money has been spent to so little purpose". Referring to his country's association with Great Britain, he continued "It is Commonwealth for the United Kingdom

---

[1] Mitchell, *op. cit.*, p. 57.

[2] "Neither Jamaica nor Trinidad, nor especially the Little Eight, can support the appurtenances of sovereignty, even within the British Commonwealth, without outside help. The O.A.S. as a whole, and the United States in particular, should and must look to their welfare." *The New York Herald Tribune*, New York, editorial, September 2, 1962.

[3] A credit of £1 million for British goods and services together with the unspent portion of the former Colonial Development and Welfare Fund (about £250,000) and a gift of four Viscount aircraft that the Trinidad airline had on loan made up the offer.

and common poverty for Trinidad and Tobago".[1] Certainly Williams was addressing a West Indian student gathering on a Saturday night and perhaps should not be taken too literally. The comment of *The Economist* was "if you tip, tip high!"[2] Not that the requests of Trinidad and Tobago from the British Government were small: in addition to a £5 million loan for housing, they included defence, the redevelopment of the town of Scarborough in Tobago, the completion of arrangements for the smaller islands of the Eastern Caribbean to become partners in Trinidad's British West Indian Airways, finance for the Trinidad Telephone Service and for extension of University of the West Indies facilities in Trinidad. Clearly, if Great Britain were to provide loans for these projects, it could not refuse similar requests to other territories emerging from colonialism. As later events would shortly demonstrate, Great Britain's financial resources were becoming over-strained, which precluded satisfaction being given to Trinidad and Tobago. In retrospect, Britain could claim that the financial crisis which shook its economy a few years later justified its caution.

Without any doubt the astutest of the West Indian political leaders was far from being satisfied with a purely Commonwealth role for his country. Williams had toured the European Economic Community in an endeavour to expand Trinidad's trade with the Common Market, and was frustrated by his dependence on the tortuous attempts of Britain to enter the Common Market.

The Prime Minister took a middle position between State and private enterprise. Appreciating the importance of new industries, he offered, as did other Caribbean countries, tax concessions to attract suitable investment. To potential capitalists in the United States he commended his country as a desirable and stable development centre. In his efforts to attract new industries, Williams made use of the Industrial Development Corporation, which was continued after independence. At the same time, he was prepared for the Trinidad Government to engage in industry where necessary. Already in 1960 he had nationalized the telephone service in Trinidad; the next year he had purchased a controlling interest in British West Indian Airways from the British Overseas Airways Corporation. To some he appeared to be aiming at a mildly socialized state on the Swedish model.[3] The Second Five-Year Plan emphasized that Independence meant local owners of capital

[1] *The Times*, London, Commonwealth staff, November 26, 1962.
[2] *The Economist* also pointed out that Britain was being credited with a policy of getting out of the West Indies as cheaply as it could. London, December 1, 1962.
[3] *The Weekly Review*, Cheltenham, England, February 8, 1963, p. 5.

were obliged to invest in their own island. The plan pointed out that 60 per cent. of the average annual total of gross private capital came from abroad.[1]

Williams was very conscious of the widening of the gaps between the have and have-not nations. He also felt that among the underdeveloped countries, little powers might be overlooked compared with giants like Brazil.[2] During a tour of Africa in 1964, he stressed the need for a league of small countries.[3] Williams believed that Trinidad's relatively high gross domestic product of U.S.$656 *per capita* made it difficult to obtain economic aid in comparison with some other newly independent countries.[4]

In a debate in the Trinidad House of Representatives, Government and Opposition members sharply criticized industrial strife. In the absence of Williams, Acting Prime Minister Patrick Solomon declared that unions in the United States had set aside millions of dollars for the deliberate purpose of interfering in the affairs of other countries. "If they can ensure that the cost of production of any commodity is as high as or higher than the cost of production in the United States, then there would be no inducement for the U.S. investors to leave the United States and invest in Trinidad. They send delegates abroad and boast of their successes. They have deliberately set out to insure that investments remain in the United States and provide employment for workers there."[5] He attributed to this strategy the current spate of strikes which were likely to discourage overseas investors from participating in Trinidad's development.[6] Solomon also hit out at subversive

[1] "Local capital must accept and play a far more important role than hitherto in the economic life of the country if assurance is to be had that the nation's economic future will be guided by people with a permanent stake in the Independence of the country and its people." *Draft Second Five-Year Plan 1964-1968*, National Planning Commission, Trinidad, 1963, p. 4.

[2] *The Nation*, Port of Spain, April 24, 1964.

[3] Cf. I. K. Merritt, "That 'Safari' ", *The Nation*, Port of Spain, April 3, 1964.

[4] Among the Commonwealth Caribbean territories, Trinidad ranked first. Jamaica in comparison had $417, although Puerto Rico, aided by the United States, was higher at $825. More striking, Trinidad surpassed in Europe, Portugal ($279), Spain ($322), Greece ($394) and Ireland ($641). It approached Italy with $688. In Asia, Trinidad exceeded Japan's $504. Williams also stressed that it was not the high *per capita* gross domestic product alone which dictated Britain's "total lack of interest to the point almost of a vendetta against Trinidad and Tobago" but also lack of strategic interest. His figures were quoted from U.N. 1963 statistics. "Together We Have Achieved, Together We Must Aspire", *The Nation*, Port of Spain, August 28, 1964.

[5] Port of Spain, November 23, 1962.

[6] *Vide* pp. 114-5.

elements advocating a foreign ideology. Both sides of the House agreed that an enquiry into the causes of unemployment and labour unrest be set up. The *Sunday Guardian* commented on interference of American unions in local industrial relations, which it felt was only one aspect of the difficulties which were distracting industry.[1] In a thoughtful editorial, *The Nation* recalled unjust treatment to labour in the past. It pinpointed the rare qualities required of union leadership in modern society, complicated by an industrial cake which was small and whose major ingredients—capital, entrepreneurship and managerial skills—came from abroad.[2]

Union conflicts which had caused so much difficulty in Jamaica were also apparent in the Trinidad canefields: three unions strove for power.[3] Following the series of strikes in the sugar industry during 1962, the commission presided over by Sir George Honeyman confirmed part of Solomon's warning over subversion, although its conclusion was guarded.[4] The Commission recommended the retention of collective bargaining in opposition to any system of compulsory arbitration or the creation of a statutory body to adjudicate on claims.

In March 1965, the Williams Government passed the Industrial Stabilization Act which required Government employees and workers in essential services to give notice to the Minister of Labour before taking strike action. An Industrial Court presided over by a High Court Judge was set up to whom the Minister could refer disputes. The court's decision was binding. Naturally the measure was attacked as a restriction of the basic freedom of the employee to withhold his work. The Government's purpose in placing the measure on the statute book was economic: strikes were destroying its revenue, largely

---

[1] Port of Spain, editorial, November 25, 1962.

[2] Port of Spain, November 16, 1962.

[3] The All-Trinidad Sugar Estates and Factories Workers' Trade Union led by Bhadase Maraj, the Amalgamated of Woodrow Sutton and the National Union of Sugar Workers. An editorial in the *Sunday Guardian* called attention to the "Sugar Cloud" which threatened the industry. The newspaper warned that increased wages would speed mechanization. Port of Spain, January 5, 1964.

[4] "Without explicitly stating that Communist infiltration is widespread in Trinidad, the Commission has given a clear warning which we should be foolish indeed to ignore. Here we have a plausible explanation of the startling fact that this country in the past three years has lost more than half a million man-days by strikes, and that in only one of the 76 strikes up to November last year [1962] was recognised grievance procedure fully invoked before the workers walked out. Surely there was much more in this than meets the eye." *Sunday Guardian*, Port of Spain, editorial, March 31, 1963.

derived from industry. Even more serious was the damage in the eyes of prospective investors to Trinidad as a centre for new industries. Labour was not unanimous in condemning the new Act. The powerful Trades Union Congress attacked it; the National Federation of Labour gave it tepid approval.

One aspect of the legislation was to compel a more sophisticated approach to wage bargaining. In consequence, important bodies such as the Oilfield Workers' Trade Union expanded their staff to provide the necessary negotiating skills. Smaller unions seemed likely to be absorbed.[1] At a time when Trinidad faced many difficult problems, the case for an ordered attempt to replace stoppages by negotiation was strong. Other Caribbean countries would watch with interest a courageous experiment by an intelligent government.[2]

Yet despite these labour disputes, affecting at different times sugar, oil, telephones and other industries, Trinidad continued to attract investment. More far-seeing than some developing countries, Trinidad had between 1958 and 1962 spent more than $125 million on public improvements which contributed to this end. Schools, roads and bridges were built or improved. A World Bank loan of $23·5 million helped expand the island's electric power system using cheap natural gas. Industrial estates in both Trinidad and Tobago were set up. With wages about one-fifth of U.S. rates, the country was distinctly competitive.[3] The willingness of international companies to establish new plant expansion, and new industries in Trinidad acted as a practical long-term testimonial to world confidence in the country's stability.[4] However, the very international nature of these companies presented problems both for Government and labour. Certainly oil, comprising 85 per cent. of Trinidad's exports in the late 1960's, and produced at a high cost, was in a state of dangerous imbalance, accentuated by the fall-off in production together with management and union disputes. However in November 1970 finds of oil off the east coast and, later, of natural gas off the north coast injected new optimism into

[1] E.g., The Cement Workers of South Trinidad dissolved their union to join O.W.T.U. *Caribbean Monthly Bulletin*, Vol. 3, No. 12, Institute of Caribbean Studies, University of Puerto Rico, Río Piedras, October 1966.

[2] Trinidad's strike free record since 1965 has impressed other countries. The Burnham Government, in a country which had been rent by major industrial disputes, announced that it was studying the Trinidad experiment. Ministry of Information, Georgetown, April 16, 1967.

[3] Cf. Cyril A. Merry, "Trinidad-Tobago Attract Investors", *International Trade Review*, New York, May 1963, pp. 73-4.

[4] Shell, B.P., Unilever, Tate & Lyle, and the Metal Box Company are among the "big-names" in the manufacturing business in Trinidad.

the industry.[1]   In addition the petrochemical industry developed rapidly during the 1960's: exports rose from $T.T.12·6 million in 1963 to $T.T. 115 million in 1970.   Texaco at Pointe à Pierre and W. R. Grace at Point Lisas concentrated on normal paraffins and ammonia.

With a measure of prosperity and a great advance in the standard of living, Trinidad and Tobago nevertheless faced formidable economic problems.   On the whole its industries were all high-cost producers. The sugar industry had to mechanize or perish.   For many that meant a lost job.   In the five years to 1963, a net reduction of nearly 2,500 jobs had occurred in oil and asphalt.   Prices which had fallen by 25 per cent. over the previous six years had compelled the oil companies to economize, with serious consequences for the island.   Between 1964 and 1968 the problem of redundancy became more acute than ever.[2] Fears that the Government had not prepared itself sufficiently to over-come the unemployment problem appeared to be justified.   By mid-1966 unemployment stood at about 14 per cent. of the labour force and remained static.[3]   Between 1968 and 1973 the number was ex-pected to increase by 48,000 at a rate per annum of 2·5 per cent., although the new activity in the oil industry may help reduce these figures.[4]   Unemployment became one of the main issues of the Third Five-Year Plan: urgent measures such as massive housing and con-struction programmes were planned.   Youth camps were to be estab-lished for training young people in productive skills, especially those of an agricultural nature.[5]

Agriculture in Trinidad was well organized, particularly in sugar manufacturing and cane farming, the most important section.   This industry, dominantly in large units, had an assured outlet for a large part of its products.[6]   Certainly the Commonwealth Sugar Agreement

[1] Natural gas is of particular interest to the United States, whose reserves and explorations have declined rapidly.   Cf. "Valuable finds of natural gas", *The Financial Times*, London, May 19, 1971.

[2] Since 1956 when 20,000 were employed in the oil industry, there has been a steady decline.   By 1964 only 4 per cent. of the labour force were employed in oil.   From 1964 to 1968 employment decreased while production of crude oil increased.   Cf. Vernon C. Mulchansingh, "The Oil Industry in the Economy of Trinidad", *Caribbean Studies*, Vol. 11, No. 1, Institute of Caribbean Studies, University of Puerto Rico, April 1971, pp. 92-93.

[3] Between 1960 and 1968 the number of unemployed had increased from 37,000 to 53,400.   *Draft Five-Year Plan 1969–1973*, Government of Trinidad and Tobago, p. 175.

[4] *Ibid.*, p. 182.

[5] *Ibid.*, pp. 16, 106-7.

[6] "We in the West Indies, in fact, regard the sugar preference as a sort of compensation, however limited, to the people of the West Indies them-

provided a stabilizing price for a major part of Trinidad's production, but part had to be disposed of on the world market. In competition with countries such as Brazil which had substantially lower costs of production, Trinidad producers sought to lower costs by the introduction of mechanical harvesters, each capable of doing the work of 88 men together with self-loading trailers. The Industrial Court agreed to the phased mechanization proposal of Caroni, Trinidad's largest producer, notwithstanding Trade Union opposition.[1] In the long view, the decision could hardly be other than wise, the more so as the Commonwealth Sugar Agreement would not continue indefinitely should Britain succeed in its efforts to enter the European Common Market.[2] A wage increase for sugar-workers for 1967 and 1968 was financed by an increase in the retail price for sugar in Trinidad which had been unchanged for sixteen years. At a time when sugar was being purchased by Great Britain and the United States at prices far above that of the world market, for Trinidad to make its own contribution to the support of sugar prices was politically wise.

Citrus had been efficiently developed on co-operative lines by the Citrus Growers' Co-operative Association. Moreover, Trinidad is one of the few Caribbean islands with a fair amount of unused and under-utilized cultivable land.[3]

Third in size, having surpassed cacao in the value of its exports, the coffee industry presented a contrast. The quota, under the International Coffee Agreement, ratified in 1968, stood at about 69,000 bags (1 bag = 132 lb.) with an expected increase to 100,000 bags by 1973. Despite lack of local organization and the use of unsuitable soils, which characterized the industry, increased output in 1968 was due mainly to better methods of crop cultivation. Robusta coffee, suitable for low-lying country, made up 90 per cent. of the crop. The balance was mainly Arabica coffee selling at a price 60 per cent. higher.

Cacao farmers were beginning to realize that central fermentaries must be established to improve quality and therefore the price. More

selves for the preferential position which the United Kingdom has enjoyed for centuries in the markets of the West Indies." L. Marconi Robinson, Trinidad Minister for Agriculture, Industry and Commerce at the World Trade Conference, Geneva, April 1964. *The Jamaican Weekly Gleaner*, Kingston, April 10, 1964.

[1] Cf. "The Finance Bill and Sugar Mechanization stimulate Controversy in Trinidad", *Chronicle of the West India Committee*, London, September 1966, p. 483.

[2] Cf. James O. Whitmee, Chairman, West Indies Sugar Company, Montego Bay, March 6, 1967.

[3] *Draft Second Five-Year Plan 1964-1968*, p. 61.

and more manufacturers of confectionery were beginning to demand properly fermented cacao free from moulds, damaged "shells" and insect infestation. The larger unit fermentaries would also save man-hours, and could become a centre for stimulating better farming practices. The system would fit in with the Government's agricultural extension services, thereby expanding the education of the cacao farmers. Although it ranked behind coffee, the cacao industry was better organized with a Cocoa Planters Association and a Cocoa Industry Board, whose produce was highly regarded in the United States. A stronger world market led to an increase in exports of some 3 million pounds in 1968 over 1967. A wider use of fertilizers and more effective pruning contributed to this result.

With the probability of increasing trade between Latin America and the United States, Trinidad might benefit. Already international air-lines connecting the United States and South America made use of its airport. Trinidad was also used as a trans-ship point of bauxite coming from Guyana.

While recognizing like other Caribbean islands the potential of the tourist industry, particularly in Tobago, Trinidad sought controlled development.[1] It has not shown any desire to seize a significant share of the American tourist market, perhaps partly because it is one of the farthest islands from North America. Considerable efforts were made by the Government to stimulate the industry, including hotel construc-tion, when during the period of the First Five-Year Plan (1958 to 1962) a total of $15·3 million was spent.[2] In 1962 it was estimated that a total of 3,000 jobs were generated of which as many were indirect as direct. The industry suffered a severe setback during the hurricane season of 1963, when many hotels were damaged and the islands received a great deal of overemphasized adverse publicity.[3]

Diversification of the economic base was one of the main objectives of both the Second and Third Five-Year Plans: the potential of tourism was fully recognized although Trinidad resisted its development at the expense of the rights, or the animosity, of its citizens. Casinos were banned, disproportionate alienation of land by foreigners was guarded

[1] "Unlike most of its Caribbean neighbours, Trinidad and Tobago does not lean heavily on its tourist trade. Rather the government allows it to develop at the same time exercising a firm control". Alan Bowden, "A Vast Potential", *New Commonwealth*, London, No. 9, 1965.

[2] This figure included the sum of $13 million for the construction of the Trinidad Hilton Hotel.

[3] Lee Sanowar, "Plan to win back Tourists", *Sunday Guardian*, Port of Spain, February 2, 1964.

against and everyone had right of access to all hotels and beaches. By 1967 the number of visitors to Trinidad and Tobago totalled over 230,000 compared with 192,000 in 1962. Tourist expenditure rose from $T.T.15·8 million in 1962 to $T.T.27·8 million in 1967. Nearly 4,000 people found employment in the hotel and allied industries. The Third Five-Year Plan aimed at doubling guest accommodation in the island. Out of a total budget of $T.T. 355 million, $T.T. 4 million were to be devoted to tourist development.[1]

Naturally as the tourist industry grew, Trinidad's import bill rose but between 1963 and 1967 total net imports changed little. Government policy in import-substitution in food manufacture had proved partially successful.

Trinidad's income *per capita* remained high in an international context.[2] Family planning although still in its early stages seemed to be taking effect. The birth rate fell rapidly after 1964.[3] The voluntary Family Planning Association formed in 1965 was given Government support in 1967 by the appointment of a Population Council under the Ministry of Health. $T.T. 1 million will be spent on family planning during the period 1968–73. Emigration removed many Trinidadians of child-bearing age, but at the same time robbed Trinidad of many with valuable skills the loss of which could be ill-afforded, such as doctors, nurses, engineers and, more recently, students graduating from the technical schools.

Trinidad's primary and secondary education had largely come under religious management financed, however, with funds provided by the Government. Following on the advice of the Maurice Committee and with independence pending, education was considerably reorganized. In 1961 it was made free at all levels both in Government and in Assisted Schools. By 1962 the number of places in both primary and secondary schools had greatly increased. The recurrent expenditure on education had increased from $12·2 million in 1957 to $24·4 million in 1963.[4] The Education Act passed in 1965 aimed at a national system of education. In 1956 about 7,000 children attended public secondary

[1] Cf. *Draft Five-Year Plan 1968–73*, pp. 76–77, 321.
[2] In 1967 it had risen to $T.T. 1,230. Cf. *Draft Five-Year Plan 1968–73*, p. 127.
[3] In 1964 the birth-rate was 2·9 and in 1968, 1·0. *Ibid.*, p. 166. Cf. Jack Harewood, Director of the Trinidad and Tobago Statistical Service, "Population Growth in Trinidad and Tobago in the Twentieth Century", *Social and Economic Studies*, Vol. 12, No. 1, Institute of Social and Economic Research, University of the West Indies, Jamaica, March 1963, p. 1. *Vide* p. 368 n. 3
[4] This did not include the sum contributed to the University of the West Indies by the Government.

schools.[1] In 1968 the number had reached 26,000. From 1969 to 1983, a fifteen year period, it was proposed to spend more than $T.T. 171 million on education: primary school places were to be greatly increased and the junior secondary school would eventually accommodate all 12–14-year-olds, thus providing a fully integrated system from the age of five upwards.[2] National and branch libraries were to be set up throughout the island.

Technical education had in the past been neglected in Trinidad by the Ministry of Education, which did not appear to be aware of the problems of industry. The bulk of the training had been for the most part carried out by a handful of the largest firms. The importance of a skilled and employable labour force was recognized by both the Second and Third Five-Year Plans. The John Donaldson Technical Institute, Port of Spain and the San Fernando Technical Institute provide technical education at an advanced level.

Higher education until the time of the setting up of the University College of the West Indies in 1948 was obtained abroad. The failure of nationals to return after graduating overseas frequently took place. Trinidad's problems occur elsewhere in the Caribbean. The College of Arts and Science of the University of the West Indies at St. Augustine offers free tuition to Trinidad and Tobago nationals. Following its general policy, the Third Five-Year Plan encouraged the University to specialize for local needs.[3] The establishment of the Institute of International Relations linked to the Graduate Institute of International Studies at Geneva has proved a valuable addition to the University of the West Indies on its Trinidad Campus. It makes a substantial contribution to the training of students who seek to enter the field of diplomacy.

*　　*　　*　　*

The riots of April 1970, exploited by Black Power insurgents, and successfully overcome by Williams, sounded a warning note. Perhaps fortunately, occurring at a time when the oil companies were heavily involved in promising exploration, their effect was less than it might otherwise have been. Although pressurized by the turn of events, Williams took care to emphasize that his Government intended public participation and not, as in the case of Guyana, state ownership of industry. In this way he shrewdly endeavoured to attract the foreign investor.

[1] Both Government and assisted.
[2] *Draft Five-Year Plan 1968–1973*, pp. 334-335.
[3] *Ibid.*, p. 340.

BARBADOS

Isolated from the rest of the Antilles, Barbados lies in the Atlantic about 100 miles east of St. Vincent and St. Lucia. British settlement of the island dates from the early seventeenth century. It has had parliamentary institutions since 1639, only nineteen years after Bermuda's first Parliament met at St. George's. In 1663 an earlier patent given to Lord Carlisle was surrendered to the Crown. Barbados obtained the earliest system of parliamentary government in the British Caribbean territories. Never invaded, the island preserved its valued constitutional rights with limited modification until it obtained independence in 1966.

With a population of 250,000 giving it a density of 1,500 persons per square mile, Barbados was the largest of the remaining units of the West Indies Federation after the withdrawal of Jamaica and then Trinidad. Barbados had provided in Sir Grantley Adams the Federation's Prime Minister. Many of his ministers came from the smaller islands.

Hopes of a successor Federation led by Barbados to include the colonies in the Leeward and Windward Islands did not materialize. A conference of the islands, postponed in 1963, took place in London in 1964. Agreement in principle was reached on the desirability of federation, but in 1965 negotiations ended. Economic considerations played a major part in the failure, just as they had in the demise of the West Indies Federation. The desire for the maximum of autonomy was also strong within each island, despite the financial cost. The economic advantages were even less than they had been in the defunct West Indies Federation. A unitary state which might have afforded administrative economies was anathema to all. Trinidad did indeed offer such a status to any territory which would join it, but although Grenada examined the proposal it did not accept.

Ultimately Barbados decided to move into independence apart from its smaller neighbours. In the long-term management of its own affairs, the island had had adequate preparation for this step and had more than proved its political qualities. Two major parties assured the electors of a governmental choice. Once again the British parliamentary system had formed a two-party pattern.

Once Barbados had decided to abandon the attempt to create an Eastern Caribbean Federation, the move to independence proved simple.[1] In 1951 adult suffrage had been instituted, followed three

[1] Cf. *The Federal Negotiations 1962-1965 and Constitutional Proposals for Barbados*, The Barbados Goverment Printing Office, Barbados, n.d.

years later by ministerial government. Self-government had come in 1961.

Under the new constitution, many existing features were retained, including a preamble based on the rights and privileges of the inhabitants set forth in the 1652 Charter of Barbados, a tribute to the enlightened colonialism of Great Britain in the seventeenth century. The Senate continued to be composed of 21 members nominated by the Governor-General. Of these, 12 were appointed on the advice of the Prime Minister, 2 on that of the Leader of the Opposition; in addition 7 represented economic, religious or other interests. The House of Assembly consisted of not less than 24 elected members. Entrenched clauses could be altered only by a two-thirds majority of both Houses. The Governor-General appointed as Prime Minister the member of the House of Assembly who in his view was best able to command a majority. On the advice of the Prime Minister, he also appointed 5 other members drawn from the two Houses to complete the Cabinet, which had to include the Attorney-General. After consultation with the Prime Minister, the Governor-General also named the Privy Council. Its duties included advising the Governor on the exercise of the prerogative of mercy.

The opposition parties expressed disagreement at the 1966 Constitutional Conference in London over the method of altering the entrenched provisions notwithstanding a united opposition. They advocated the method adopted in the Jamaica Constitution.[1] However, the objection was not accepted.

Immediately prior to independence, a General Election was held. For the 24 Assembly seats, 59 candidates were nominated. In the person of Errol Barrow the Democratic Labour Party had a leader who was closely in touch with the needs of the people. At 46 he was younger than most West Indian politicians, yet his experience as both the Vice-President of the Barbados Transport and General Workers Union and also as a lawyer, enabled him to grasp firmly the problems that faced the island in independence. His victory of 14 seats against Sir Grantley Adams' Barbados Labour Party's 8 and the right-wing Barbados National Party's 2 gave him a narrow working majority.

Notwithstanding its small size, Barbados entered independence as one of the most politically mature and best educated communities in the Caribbean. It had a well-established Civil Service, a competent Judiciary and above all a sophisticated electorate. Its main problems were likely to be economic rather than political.

[1] *Report of the Barbados Constitutional Conference 1966*, Cmnd. 3058 (H.M.S.O. London, 1966), p. 4. *Vide* pp. 136-7.

Trinidad: part of the oil refinery at Pointe à Pierre, the largest in the Commonwealth.

Trinidad's new Port Lisas, where facilities for bulk loading are provided, p. 162.

Anne Bolt

Trinidad: a gaily decorated Hindu temple at San Fernando. East Indians form an important part of Trinidad's population.

Barbados: the quay at Trafalgar Square, Bridgetown: small schooners for inter-island trade.

Barrow maintained effective control by assuming the role of Minister for External Affairs and Finance. In 1967 Barbados joined the Organization of American States. During a successful tour in 1968 which included Britain, Canada and the United States, Barrow made it clear that the interests of his country now included membership of the O.A.S.

On the retirement of Grantley Adams, Bernard St. John, a London-trained barrister, became the new leader of the opposition Barbados Labour Party. In September 1971 Barrow's D.L.P. won a landslide victory with 18 of the 24 seats.[1] New electoral boundaries had divided the island into 24 single-member constituencies. St. John lost his seat; his place as Opposition leader was taken by J. M. G. Adams, son of Grantley Adams.

In the first General Election since it attained independence, Barbados like Jamaica, Trinidad and Guyana returned the incumbent Government, despite the wind of change that had led to the displacement of long-standing Governments elsewhere in the Caribbean. Barrow's carefully drawn up manifesto to the electors had been accepted against the critical but vaguer appeal of the Barbados Labour Party.[2]

THE ECONOMIC PATTERN

Barbados was originally developed largely by smallholders, mostly from Britain, who grew crops such as tobacco. From the middle of the seventeenth century the rising importance of sugar cane profoundly changed its economy, as it did that of other islands. Many of these peasant farmers left Barbados, unable to make a living.[3] The island's economy became a monoculture based on the growing of sugar cane with slave labour for the manufacture of sugar, molasses and rum, mainly for export.

Sugar has continued as the principal export industry and largest employer of labour which during 1967 paid $E.C.18·99 million in wages. Through its Agricultural Development Corporation, the Government had become a considerable land-owner although peasant farmers who owned plots varying from ten acres to half an acre supplied some 50 per cent. of the cane to the factories. As in other sugar-growing areas of the Commonwealth Caribbean the need to mechanize and reorganize the industry became urgent.

[1] Barrow's victory was seen in the Caribbean as an endorsement of his Government's commitment and support for CARIFTA, cf. *Guyana Graphic*, Georgetown, editorial, September 11, 1971.

[2] Cf. *Sunday Advocate News*, Bridgetown, editorial, September 12, 1971.

[3] Cf. J. H. Parry and P. M. Sherlock, *A Short History of the West Indies* (London, 1960), pp. 66-7.

Ground provisions and green vegetables began to be produced on a considerable scale, largely by smallholders. The expanding population increasingly compelled the intensive use of the land, an example to some other Caribbean territories. Encouraged by the Government, local food production to replace imports has created greater diversification, which has spread to the development of beef and dairy cattle. Between 1961 and 1968 the value of local agricultural production rose by $E.C.12 million.

Limited opportunities of industrialization have led Barbados to concentrate on its tourist development. Tourist expenditure rose from $E.C.10·4 million in 1958 to some $E.C.55 million in 1969. For the period 1969 to 1972 the Government allocated $E.C.3 million to the tourist industry. Its progress was the most advanced in the Eastern Caribbean.[1] Membership of the O.A.S. may one day attract the tourist from South America.[2]

Bridgetown Deep Water Harbour, opened in 1961, has greatly facilitated the commerce of Barbados. By 1970 there were 129 industries in the island. As a member of CARIFTA Barbados seeks actively to industrialize as a necessary balance to the uncertain future of its sugar industry. The attraction of Barbados as a centre for light industry has been aided, through the Barbados Industrial Development Corporation, by the concessions offered in "Operation Beehive", which include a 10-year tax holiday, duty free raw materials and industrial estates.

With headquarters in Bridgetown, a United Nations fisheries project has promoted fishing in Guyanese waters, partly for the Barbados market.[3] By its provision of cold storage the Barbados Marketing Corporation has greatly aided the export of shrimps.

Efficient education has for long characterized Barbados, which claims a literacy standard estimated at 98 per cent. Just under half of the population is under 20 years of age. In addition to the provision of technical education within the island, the University of the West Indies College of Arts and Sciences, opened in 1963, affords opportunities for higher education. Teacher training is provided at Erdiston with an enrolment in 1970–71 of over 200.

The population density of 1,807 to the square mile remains a problem in Barbados; the available land has been substantially developed. Notwithstanding industrial development, unemployment as in other parts

[1] *The Future of Tourism in the Eastern Caribbean*, Zinder and Associates, Inc., Washington, May 1969, p. 106.

[2] *Barbados Development Plan 1969-1972*, St. Michael, 1969, p. 98.

[3] Cf. Anthony Sylvester, "Caribbean imperatives", *The Scotsman*, Edinburgh, January 19, 1972.

of the Caribbean remained high, estimated at 13 per cent. The pace of emigration has perforce slowed down. The population had grown from about 232,000 in 1960 to almost 240,000 in 1970, although the increase rate had dropped to 0·9 per cent., the lowest in the hemisphere. The decline was due to a large extent to Barbados' Family Planning Programme, one of the oldest and most efficient in the Caribbean, fully supported by the Government.

Despite limited natural resources Barbados had succeeded in moving into independence. With the longest tradition of Parliamentary Government it continued to make the most of its limitations. Agriculture was being diversified and industry and fishing promoted while tourists increasingly favoured it as one of the most attractive countries in the world for a vacation.

The proposed entry of Great Britain into the Common Market called in question the future of West Indies sugar.[1] Although the arrangements made provide some measure of assurance for the future, at the same time industrial development linked to Barbados' membership of CARIFTA assumed greater significance. Together with tourism these two industries would supply the basis for the future prosperity of the island.

[1] *Vide* pp. 323-6.

CHAPTER VIII

THE LEEWARD AND WINDWARD ISLANDS

The smaller islands of the Caribbean present profound problems of interpretation within the total framework. Any consideration of their political and economic role is necessarily linked to the limits imposed by geography. Such a consideration becomes fragmented and disjointed. The charm of these small islands resides in territorial bounds. Most of them cast a backward glance to a past of drama; in the wars of the seventeenth and eighteenth centuries they changed hands like pawns on a chess board. Linked historically to European powers rather than to each other, there is little communal spirit. Differences in language and religion early separated them. The imported slaves could not communicate with one another from island to island. As the islands developed, far from these gaps narrowing, they tended to widen with the introduction of currencies linked to Europe, different banking systems, different flags and different rates of economic growth. In the mid-twentieth century the original commercial dominance of Spain is fast being revived by another single power, this time the United States. Gradually the dollar has replaced the piece of eight.

This chapter covers the British Leeward and Windward Islands,[1] which neither took independence nor moved successfully into further federation after the failure of the West Indies Federation in 1962. The British and U.S. Virgin Islands, the Cayman Islands, Turks and Caicos Islands, the Bahamas, Margarita and the Bay Islands are dealt with separately.[2] The Leeward Islands cover an area of 342 square miles, whereas the Windward Islands cover an area twice that size.

When the West Indies Federation collapsed, the small British islands in the Eastern Caribbean ended up the greatest losers. Together they had dominated its destiny through the chance of the ballot box in the 1958 General Election which resulted in the Federal Labour Party depending for its slender majority on the support of their representatives. In fact, Sir Grantley Adams' administration was a "small

---

[1] Antigua, St. Kitts-Nevis-Anguilla and Montserrat in the Leeward group and Dominica, St. Lucia, St. Vincent and Grenada in the Windward group.

[2] *Vide* Chapter IX.

islands" government. When Jamaica and Trinidad moved smoothly into independence after the collapse of the Federation, Barbados together with the remainder of the colonies, grant-aided in most cases by Great Britain, had to replan their future. Barbados chose independence, which was economically impossible for the other smaller, less-developed islands. Their choice, therefore, was threefold: to continue as colonies of Great Britain, which hurt their sense of nationalism, further federation, or entry into a unitary state with Trinidad. The first choice was never really considered, the second attempted but fruitlessly, and the third only weighed up by Grenada.

At first the idea of a new Federation led by Barbados was canvassed. However, it soon became plain that each territory was determined to keep its territorial government more or less intact: thus any chance for the economic success of the proposed federation began to vanish. Nothing had been learnt from the previous disaster.[1] Had such a federation been formed, it would have been far weaker than its deceased predecessor. However, important links between the former Federation members survived. Much the most significant was the University of the West Indies, which had campuses in Jamaica, Trinidad and Barbados, and was spreading its teaching throughout the Caribbean and beyond. The influence of its graduates, who would inevitably hold more and more of the chief executive posts in the islands and would become the political and commercial leaders, could not fail to be a factor for inter-island co-operation. The projected expansion of the University would accelerate the process.

In the smaller islands, politics tended to revolve round a leader dominating a party, often linked to a trade union. Economic problems took first place, for most of the territories were unable to balance their budgets without outside aid. Although agriculture had been the traditional base and had been directly responsible for the introduction of slaves in earlier days, the sugar industry appeared increasingly unpromising in these islands. Cacao and copra were becoming ever more precarious, while the export of long staple cotton was suffering from the competition of synthetic fibres.[2] In a world of fluctuating prices, these small territories could exert no significant influence on

[1] "For one thing they [the political elites in the British Caribbean] have been and are attempting to establish a pre-World War II federal government to administer a post-World War II society." M. S. Joshua, "Government and Politics of the Windward Islands", *Politics and Economics in the Caribbean*, Special Study No. 3, Institute of Caribbean Studies, University of Puerto Rico, Río Piedras, 1966, p. 255.

[2] *Antigua, Report for the years 1959 and 1960* (H.M.S.O., London, 1963). p. 2.

markets; to make matters worse, they were usually high-cost producers, and were further handicapped by indifferent port and shipping facilities. In the Windward Islands, where the sugar outlook was even more unpromising than in the islands to the north, an intensive drive to develop the banana industry for the British market was put in hand. So successful has it been that nearly half of that market has been captured, mainly at the expense of Jamaica which formerly dominated this trade. Competition between the two groups has been fierce and has tended to depress prices. However, the replacement of the Gros Michel banana by the Lacatan has enabled the islands of the Eastern Caribbean as well as Jamaica to recover from the disasters of Panama disease which had wiped out their former plantations.[1] Banana cultivation in the Caribbean, as elsewhere, remains speculative. The liability of disease, including leaf spot (Sigatoka), which involves continued spraying, results in heavy costs. The possibility of serious damage from wind is always present.[2]

Great Britain had expected to find a solution in Caribbean federation. As in the case of the Central African Federation, Malaysia and East Africa, its hopes had been frustrated. Even in Nigeria they appeared to be tottering. The ancient Caribbean colonies had incomparably wider political experience than many of the countries attaining independence but their weakness lay in the size and economic instability of each unit.

Colonialism remained under fire at the United Nations and beyond. It symbolized exploitation, alien government and oppression, even if the attack was often greatly exaggerated. By the 1960's, the units of the Leeward and Windward Islands had substantial self-government. Such disagreements as arose, for example in Grenada and St. Vincent, were usually associated with local financial failures which had compelled British intervention. Britain had a considerable financial stake at risk.

Finally a solution was hammered out in a series of conferences in London between the British Government and individual island governments.[3] The new pattern of government decided on was in each case

[1] *Vide* p. 327.
[2] The hazards of banana growing are examined by Stacy May and Galo Plaza, *The United Fruit Company in Latin America* (Washington, D.C., 1958), pp. 92-4.
[3] *Report of the Antigua Constitutional Conference, 1966*, Cmnd. 2963, (H.M.S.O., London, 1966). *Report of the Windward Islands Constitutional Conference, 1966*, Cmnd. 3021 (H.M.S.O., London, 1966). *Report of the St. Kitts-Nevis-Anguilla Constitutional Conference, 1966*, Cmnd. 3031 (H.M.S.O., London, 1966).

similar. The existing colonial relationship with each territory would be replaced by full self-government. The United Kingdom would retain responsibility for external affairs and defence. No British Act of Parliament passed subsequent to the new association would extend to the territory without its express consent; nor could Great Britain amend, suspend or revoke the territory's constitution.

The association of the two parties could be terminated unilaterally. In the case of the territory, termination would involve a two-thirds majority vote in the House of Assembly and a similar majority in a referendum. No referendum would be necessary in the case of a territory uniting or federating with another Commonwealth country in the Caribbean. On its side, Great Britain agreed not to terminate the association without giving six months' notice. Provision in the new constitutions would be made for safeguarding the fundamental rights and freedoms of the individual, as had already been adopted in the case of the first two Commonwealth countries to obtain independence, Jamaica and Trinidad.

The Legislature would be elective on the basis of adult suffrage at the age of 21. Parliaments would have a normal life of five years on the British pattern, with power to the Governor to prorogue or dissolve the Legislature at any time on the advice of the Premier.

The Governor would appoint as Premier the member of the House of Representatives who in his opinion was best able to command the confidence of a majority of the members in the House. Other Ministers would be appointed on the advice of the Premier.

At the proposal of the British Government, a Regional Supreme Court of Judicature was set up to determine whether the laws or executive acts were inconsistent with the constitutions. The Court had power to enforce orders to ensure compliance with the constitutions. The President of the Court would be appointed by the Lord Chancellor.[1]

The plan provides for self-government without independence. The impossibility of independence without financial viability is tacitly admitted. Great Britain will continue for the present, as far as it deems it necessary, to give financial aid. Should the territory believe at any time that it will fare better by joining with another territory, or by seeking full independence, it has complete freedom to carry out these actions.

The relationship allows rather more self-government than in the

[1] *Constitutional Proposals for Antigua, St. Kitts-Nevis-Anguilla, Dominica, St. Lucia, St. Vincent, Grenada*, Cmnd. 2865 (H.M.S.O. London, 1965), p. 4. Cf. "New Status of Association with Britain for Six Eastern Caribbean Islands", Colonial Office, Information Department, May 26, 1966.

case of Puerto Rico and the U.S. Virgin Islands, in so far as Great Britain cannot affect a territory by legislation without its consent. On the other hand, the financial advantages are much less. The territories have not the representation in London that the partners in the Tripartite Kingdom of the Netherlands have at The Hague, where their own Ministers attend Cabinet meetings on matters affecting their interests. They have, however, a far greater measure of autonomy than do the French Overseas Departments, but they will not receive the costly educational and social services enjoyed by Guadeloupe and Martinique nor have they unrestricted right of entry to Britain.

Inhabitants of the territories retain the citizenship of Great Britain and the colonies. Great Britain as it were accepts a moral responsibility for the future welfare of these small countries. Leadership in the islands has defeated any immediate likelihood of their successful federation.[1] The constitutional solution is a clever refutation of colonialism, since an attack against the scheme as being "colonialism" must face the retort that any dissatisfied territory can vote for immediate independence at any time.

ANTIGUA

Discovered by Columbus in 1493 during his second voyage to the West Indies, Antigua was not successfully colonized until 1632 by the British. From then onwards it remained in British hands. By 1970 the population of Antigua and its island dependencies of Barbuda and tiny Redonda was estimated at more than 67,000, giving a density of over 350 to the square mile.

A visit to the fortified heights which command English Harbour in Antigua, Britain's strongest fortress in the eighteenth-century Caribbean, illustrates the great changes which occurred in the area over a century and a half. The ruined buildings and powder magazines contrast with the harbour that once served warships but today provides a basin for pleasure yachts.

Similar changes may be observed in the countryside. The individual windmills which characterized each small property finally gave way to a central factory. Lack of water, worsened by a series of years when the rainfall was inadequate, eventually forced the sugar mill to cease operations in 1966. Antigua faces the necessity of growing more of its own foodstuffs, despite its difficulties over water, so vital to intensive farming.

[1] Cf. Professor Sir Arthur Lewis, *The Agony of the Eight* (Barbados, n.d.), p. 38.

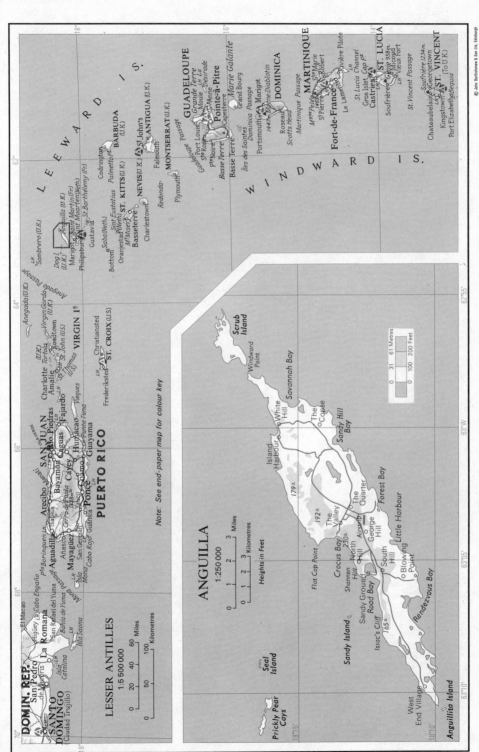

LEEWARD IS.

WINDWARD IS.

Anegada Passage

Anegada (U.K.)
Sombrero (U.K.) LH

Dog I.
(U.K.)
Anguilla (U.K.)
Saint Martin (Fr.)
St. Maarten (Neth.)
St. Barthélemy (Fr.)

Virgin Gorda
(U.K.)
Tortola (U.K.)
Road Town (U.K.)
St. John (U.S.)
St. Thomas (U.S.)
Charlotte
Amalie (U.S.)
Christiansted
Frederiksted ST. CROIX (U.S.)

VIRGIN IS.

Mango
Philipsburg

Bottom
Saba (Neth.)
Oranjestad (Neth.)
Sint Eustatius
ST. KITTS (U.K.)
Basseterre
Charlestown
NEVIS (U.K.)

BARBUDA
(U.K.)

Codrington
Palmetto Pt.
St. John's
Guadeloupe ANTIGUA (U.K.)
Falmouth

GUADELOUPE
Grande Terre
Port Louis
Ste Rose
Pte Noire
Basse Terre
Anne
La Désirade
Moule

Pointe-à-Pitre

Redonda
Plymouth
MONTSERRAT (U.K.)

Marie Galante
Grand Bourg
Capesterre

Iles des Saintes
Dominica Passage

Portsmouth
Margot
Roseau
Scotts Head
Morne Diablotin
DOMINICA

Martinique Passage

Mme St. Marie
St. Pierre
St. Robert
Le Lamentin
Rivière Pilote
FORT-DE-FRANCE

MARTINIQUE

St. Lucia Channel
Gros Islet, Cap Pt
Castries
Soufrière 958m.
ST. LUCIA
Micoud
Vieux Fort

St. Vincent Passage

Chateaubelair
Kingstown
Soufrière 1234 m.
Georgetown
ST. VINCENT
(To U.K.)
Port Elizabeth, Bequia

St. Vincent Passage

© John Bartholomew & Son Ltd, Edinburgh

DOMIN. REP.
El Macao
San Pedro
de Macorís
Higüey
La Romana
San Rafael del Yuma
Bahía de Yuma
Isla Saona

SANTO
DOMINGO
(Ciudad Trujillo)

La Altagracia, Cabo Engaño

Boriquén LH
Aguadilla
Mayagüez
Añasco
San Germán
Cabo Rojo
Guánica
Isla
Mona

Arecibo
Bayamón
Caguas
Ponce
Cerro de Punta

SAN JUAN
Río Piedras
Cayey
Juana Díaz
Guayama
Humacao

Fajardo
Vieques
Punta Tuna

PUERTO RICO

Note: See end-paper map for colour key

LESSER ANTILLES
1:5 500 000

0   20   40   60 Miles
0   50   100 Kilometres

ANGUILLA
1:250 000

Heights in Feet

0   1   2   3 Miles
0 1 2 3 Kilometres

0   31   61 Metres
0   100   200 Feet

Scrub Island

Windward
Point

Savannah Bay

White
Hill
The
Copse
Sandy Hill
Bay
Island
Harbour

Sandy Ground
179 ▲
192 ▲
The
Valley
The Quarter
Forest Bay
Little Harbour

Flat Cap Point
Crocus Bay
Shannon
Hill
North
Hill
230▲
Airport
George
Hill
South
Hill
Blowing
Point
165▲
Issac's Cliff
Road Bay

Sandy Island

Seal
Island

Prickly Pear
Cays

West
End Village

Rendezvous Bay

Anguillita Island

Warfare, which had brought employment to eighteenth-century Antigua through the building of a naval base, once again provided work when the United States constructed a large air base during World War II. The existence of a fine airfield has now made possible the development of the island's tourist industry. Its gleaming beaches have attracted interesting hotel developments, mostly of a small size. Today Antigua has a series of attractive tourist resorts. Ironically, the very lack of rain, which makes sugar cane growing unremunerative, produces a climate which the tourist from the northern winter seeks. Notwithstanding balance of payment problems, arising out of heavy imports which affect the finances of Antigua like other tourist centres, tourism may well prove less speculative than the growing and processing of sugar cane in competition with countries whose costs of production are much less. The industry would also provide a market for the enterprising agriculturist.[1]

Antigua's traditional position as a strategic base in time of war resulted in a final dividend when the U.S. Government agreed in 1961 to hand back to the Antigua Government a large portion of the area which it had taken over under the Leased Bases Agreement of 1941. It further made a grant to the Antigua Government of $350,000 to assist in the economic development of the island.[2]

Antigua, like other British colonies, had its constitutional status changed to that of a Crown Colony. The poverty of the island made it particularly subject to pressure from Great Britain. Its story is one of a decaying sugar industry. The collapse of the West Indies Federation finally led it to seek a new political status.

In consonance with Great Britain's new policy in the Caribbean, Antigua's new constitution was quickly agreed. It became, together with Barbuda and Redonda, an Associated State in 1967.[3]

For nearly 35 years, Vere Cornwall Bird dominated Antiguan politics, first as leader of the original island trade union, then, after Associated Statehood, as Prime Minister. His union split in 1967 and George Walter founded the rival Workers Union which later became the Progressive Labour Movement. In the 1971 elections Bird was ousted by Walter, whose party gained 13 seats to the Antigua Labour Party's 4. The P.L.M. manifesto stressed the importance of education, the

---

[1] Cf. Hugh O'Shaughnessy, "Prospects for agriculture the brightest ever", *The Financial Times*, London, March 12, 1970.

[2] Cf. Mitchell, *op. cit.*, pp. 64-5.

[3] *Vide* pp. 174-6. Cf. *Report of the Antigua Constitutional Conference 1966*, Cmnd. 2963 (H.M.S.O., London 1966), *Constitutional Proposals for Antigua, St. Kitts-Nevis-Anguilla, Dominica, St. Lucia, St. Vincent, Grenada*, p. 3.

development of Barbuda and the reappraisal of tourism. Aided by its excellent airport which functions as a thoroughfare for the whole Caribbean, the number of visitors has rapidly increased. The victory of the P.L.M. ended an historical epoch for Antigua. Under Bird's leadership Antigua had acquired effective trade unions and a status of semi-independence. However the election of a new government with a young leader once again demonstrated the strength of the two-party system in the Commonwealth Caribbean, one of the better legacies of the British system.

ST. KITTS-NEVIS-ANGUILLA

St. Kitts and Nevis are both formed by the tops of submerged mountains, separated by a three-mile-wide strait. Each has a peak reaching almost to 4,000 feet, whose summit of 2,000 feet is covered by forest, although this is not considered commercially exploitable. Anguilla, situated some 60 miles north of St. Kitts, is formed by a coral mass on the foreland of the same submerged range and is flat in comparison with the two other islands. St. Kitts and Nevis are both volcanic. All three islands lie in the hurricane belt, though often only one island is struck during the course of a storm.[1] Their total area is 139 square miles with a population of 60,000, of whom some 16,000 live in Basseterre, the administrative capital, on St. Kitts.

On his second Caribbean voyage in 1493, Christopher Columbus discovered St. Kitts and Nevis. The first British settlers arrived in St. Kitts in 1624 and 1625; together with the French, they drove out the Caribs and defended the island from Spanish attack. Following this, the island was divided between the French and the British and gradually became known as the "Mother of the Antilles" as more and more settlers left St. Kitts for neighbouring islands. In 1628, some of the English from St. Kitts settled in Nevis. From 1666 to 1783, St. Kitts was far from peaceful, although Nevis enjoyed comparative prosperity.[2]

From the time of the Treaty of Versailles in 1783, both St. Kitts and Nevis have remained British. Anguilla, on the other hand, suffered at the hands of both the French and other marauders, but did not capitulate, and remained British from the time of its colonization in 1650.

The population of St. Kitts and Nevis had by the mid-seventeenth

[1] St. Kitts was struck in 1889, both St. Kitts and Nevis in 1924, and Anguilla in 1960.
[2] The fortress of Brimstone Hill in St. Kitts stands as a monument to the Anglo-French struggles.

century grown to 20,000. The early settlers were smallholders who concentrated on growing food for themselves and tobacco, cotton, ginger and indigo for export. After 1650, with the introduction of sugar cane, this pattern changed. The sugar plantations grew at the expense of the smallholdings; African slaves were introduced and had increased ten times by 1836, when they were emancipated. Indentured labourers were then introduced from Madeira and India, but few remained. In 1911, a central sugar-factory was set up near Basseterre to grind the island crop. Cane was also shipped to it from Nevis. Sugar production in St. Kitts has increased both in acreage and production since that date. Most of the arable land, situated on the lower slopes of the hills, is privately owned.[1] The volcanic soil of St. Kitts, if skilfully fertilized, grows excellent sugar cane.

St. Kitts depends on the export of sugar cane and molasses for some 90 per cent. of its foreign earnings, and has consequently been at the mercy of world sugar prices, despite its quota under the Commonwealth Sugar Agreement.[2] In 1963, St. Kitts was described as the wealthiest of the small islands, but with an economy "strongly suspected of having a tendency towards stagnation".[3] There was no growth in the *per capita* income and the population increase was about 2 per cent.: too high for the rising gross domestic product to counteract. By 1966 it was found that the "economy of St. Kitts has been marking time for the past 10 years".[4] Tourism was, however, one sector in which economic growth could be achieved, perhaps with Government assistance.

Nevis, on a tiny scale, dramatizes the problems of many of the smaller islands of the Caribbean. In the eighteenth century, when its cane was ground in small wind-driven mills and the sugar shipped in hogsheads on small sailing-ships to Bristol and London, the island flourished. Clustered on the slopes of central Nevis Peak, the estates, small in the context of modern sugar cultivation, were ideally suited to the needs of the time. Many had sea frontage, which aided shipping. Although little of the island is level, animal transport to the point of shipment was downhill.

However, when each small estate became an uneconomic unit during

---

[1] Forty-nine estates own some 15,000 of the 16,000 acres of land under sugar cane.

[2] *Vide* pp. 323-6.

[3] Dr. Carleen O'Loughlin, *A Survey of Economic Potential and Capital Needs of the Leeward Islands, Windward Islands and Barbados*, Department of Technical Cooperation (H.M.S.O., London, 1963), p. 17.

[4] *Report of the Tripartite Economic Survey of the Eastern Caribbean, January-April 1966* (H.M.S.O., London, 1967), p. xiii.

the latter part of the nineteenth and the twentieth centuries, Nevis' difficulties grew. St. Kitts solved its problem, as did Antigua for a time, by centralizing the grinding of cane in a single factory. Nevis lacked sufficient cane production to support a modern factory, nor did its hilly lands lend themselves to mechanization. A little cane could be shipped to the St. Kitts factory, but transport costs made the business unpromising; nor was the yield of cane as good as in St. Kitts.

Sea-island cotton, grown by peasants, is the chief export from Nevis, but due to share-cropping agreement or one year only rentals, there is little incentive to improvements and yields are low. Much of the land has reverted to scrub, which provides reasonable grazing for stock. Probably the brightest spot in the Nevis economy is its position as supplier of foodstuffs to St. Kitts. With more and more land turned over to sugar in St. Kitts, Nevis has an expanding market in the supply of foodstuffs. Peasants farm a substantial area of land in Nevis, which makes the Nevis market a very suitable outlet for their produce.

Nevis presents a sad picture. Ruined Great Houses and sugar-mills testify to by-gone prosperity. Yet the beauty of the island and the courtesy of its inhabitants suggest that it may yet find recovery in attracting overseas visitors, just as it did in the eighteenth century when its mineral springs were famous.

The Anguilla Secession

Anguilla is an island of 35 square miles, situated some 69 miles north-west of St. Kitts. The majority of its population of about 5,000 are peasant cultivators and farmers. At the beginning of the nineteenth century, together with St. Kitts and Nevis, it belonged to the British Leeward Islands Federation; again from 1958–1962, these islands constituted part of the ill-fated West Indies Federation.

After five years of indefinite status, in February 1967, St. Kitts, Nevis and Anguilla became a State in voluntary association with Great Britain. Some four months later two hundred and fifty armed Anguillans, rebelling against the unpopular union with St. Kitts-Nevis, forced the dozen policemen on the island to flee to St. Kitts. Telecommunications between Anguilla and St. Kitts were broken. Dubbing the revolt illegal, Premier Robert Bradshaw asked Britain to send troops to quell it. On July 11, 1967, Anguilla held a "referendum" on its continued association with St. Kitts-Nevis. By 1,813 votes to 5 it chose independence, the result refuting the St. Kitts contention that the rebellion was the work of a small minority.[1]

[1] Cf. James Nelson Goodsell, "Anguilla votes for independence", *The Christian Science Monitor*, London edition, July 18, 1967.

With a primitive agriculture, no electricity or telephone system and poor roads, the island's future as a separate unit seemed dim. The high cost of goods imported from St. Kitts aroused discontent. Part of the problem stemmed from Anguilla's location: far in small-boat terms from Basseterre, the capital of St. Kitts, it lies nearer both to its prosperous tourist-oriented neighbours, the U.S. Virgin Islands, which have the highest income *per capita* in the Caribbean, and to the British Virgin Islands, which are less successful, but which enjoy the beginnings of tourist expansion. On the other hand, Anguilla possesses good but undeveloped beaches. As seamen, the Anguillans understand their position. They feel no benefit from the sugar industry, the mainstay of St. Kitts, and they see that only 12 miles away, the tourist industry of St. Martin (part Dutch part French), of tiny St. Barthélemy (French), and of Saba and St. Eustatius (Dutch) is going ahead.

In July 1967 in Barbados, representatives of Great Britain, Barbados, Trinidad and Guyana met to end Anguilla's secession. Together with Peter Adams, the only Anguillan M.P. in the three-island legislature, Bradshaw signed an agreement which, although it stipulated the return of Anguilla to constitutional relations with St. Kitts-Nevis, provided for a local council. The arrangement was short-lived. Adams, set aside by the islanders, was replaced by one of their well-known personalities, Ronald Webster, a Seventh Day Adventist pastor. Under his leadership Anguilla reaffirmed independence.

Great Britain, with no diplomatic representation in St. Kitts, was poorly informed of developments.[1] In December 1967, it appointed Anthony Lee as Administrator to act in a liaison capacity between St. Kitts and Anguilla. However in January 1969, Anguilla resumed full independence. In March, William Whitlock, Parliamentary Under-Secretary at the Commonwealth Office, visited Anguilla in an unsuccessful attempt to restore Lee, but was forced to leave.[2] A few days later Michael Stewart, Secretary of State for Foreign Affairs, defined Great Britain's policy as a search for a long-term solution "acceptable to all concerned", something that seemed unlikely and in the outcome proved impossible.[3]

On March 19 at the request of Bradshaw the British Government ordered troops into Anguilla. They took over the island without resistance. The intervention, well intentioned as it was, aroused a

[1] Cf. Charles Smith, "Anguilla looks for a partner", *The Financial Times*, London, June 20, 1967.
[2] *Hansard*, March 17, 1969, Col. 41 and March 25, 1969, Col. 1555.
[3] *Hansard*, March 18, 1969, Col. 207.

storm of criticism.[1]   Caribbean reaction was divided and conflicting. If Great Britain could have obtained for the invasion token forces from the Commonwealth Caribbean countries which favoured intervention, the action would have lost much of its "colonialist" overtones.   As it was, the psychological damage done far exceeded any success achieved in Anguilla. British troops avoided bloodshed, but on March 21 Webster demanded their immediate withdrawal. Lord Caradon, British representative at the United Nations intervened, but the agreement reached on March 31 was short-lived.   Webster, accusing Britain of treachery, pressed for the recall of Lee.   Lord Caradon returned to the island, and after further negotiation Lee was replaced by John Cumber, a former administrator of the Cayman Islands.   A Committee of Enquiry was set up consisting of four members selected by the British Government and the Government of the Associated State, presided over by Sir Hugh Wooding, the distinguished Trinidadian jurist.   By August 1969, almost all British troops had left, leaving 84 British policemen and about 140 soldiers, costing some £1 million a year to maintain.[2] In March 1971 only 55 Royal Engineers and 20 policemen remained. In 1972 a British-trained local force took over.

The Wooding Committee recommended substantial local control for Anguillan affairs but within St. Kitts-Nevis-Anguilla.[3]   Bradshaw accepted the proposals but Anguilla totally rejected them.   At the General Election of May 1971 in St. Kitts-Nevis-Anguilla no polling took place in Anguilla.   The Bradshaw Government was victorious.

Following the visit of Joseph Godber, Minister of State, Foreign and Commonwealth Office, to St. Kitts-Nevis-Anguilla in June, 1971, Britain reluctantly resumed full control of Anguilla including defence. A caretaker period of five years with a governor as administrator would be followed by a referendum.   If then the people rejected union with St. Kitts-Nevis, the island was likely to be given Crown Colony status. The Act contained a clause which gave the British Government the right, if deemed expedient, to separate Anguilla by Order in Council from the Associated State of St. Kitts-Nevis-Anguilla should that

[1] *The Times* of London criticized British policy in a series of editorials; *The Economist* called it "a suitably silly ending to a melodrama that has been going on for over two years"; *The New York Times*, *The Washington Post* and *The Chicago Tribune* were strongly critical of Britain, as were *Le Monde* and *Le Figaro* of Paris.   Only in the independent *Algemeen Dagblad* of the Netherlands was there any sympathy for Britain's position.

[2] Cf. Neil Marten, M.P., *The Times*, London, March 16, 1970.

[3] *Report of the Commission of Inquiry appointed by the Governments of the United Kingdom and St. Christopher-Nevis-Anguilla to examine the Anguilla problem.* Cmnd. 4510, H.M.S.O., London, November 1970, p. 59.

territory terminate its status of Association with the U.K., and to provide a constitution for Anguilla.[1]

Webster's Anguilla Council accepted the British proposals; neither Bradshaw nor the six Associated States Council of Ministers agreed. A measure of criticism from the Caribbean was inevitable.[2] The *Trinidad Guardian* expressed concern editorially that secession was being legalized and raised the possibilities of it happening elsewhere in the Caribbean.[3]

Britain's undoubted error in its original attempt to unite incompatible territories had been compounded by four years of tortuous negotiations, during which one near-calamity had occurred. For three hundred years Britain had done little for Anguilla; the cost of paying past debts was, as it were, belatedly met by the decision to develop the island with Great Britain paying the bill.

The size of a territory such as Anguilla need not necessarily be a disadvantage. Bermuda affords an excellent comparison: in size some 21 square miles compared with Anguilla's 35. Their climates are comparable: probably Anguilla's is less humid in summer and more acceptable in winter. There is no future for agriculture in either, although Anguilla has somewhat better land. During their long associations with Great Britain, neither has received significant economic assistance.

Now that Britain has resumed, albeit temporarily, its colonialist mantle, the infrastructural improvements made since 1969 should be turned to advantage. Anguilla should be given a chance to achieve, if not the success of Bermuda, at least the growing prosperity of neighbouring St. Martin, whose jet airport has aided tourist development. Politically Anguilla may be back at the beginning; economically this could be its point of take-off.

MONTSERRAT

Half-way between Nevis and Guadeloupe, Montserrat is formed of three volcanic masses, part of the inner volcanic arc of the Lesser Antilles. Its 32 square miles are broken up by three main mountain ridges, of which the Soufrière Hills, in the south, attain 3,000 feet. In 1970, the population amounted to some 14,500 people.

Like St. Kitts and Nevis, Montserrat was discovered by Columbus in

[1] *Anguilla Act*, H.M.S.O., London, 1971.
[2] Cf. *Guyana Graphic*, Georgetown, editorial, June 19, 1971.
[3] Port of Spain, June 16, 1971.

1493. In 1632 it was colonized by settlers from St. Kitts.[1] During a century and a half it changed hands between Britain and France. British sovereignty was ultimately established in 1783.

The economic development of Montserrat may be compared with that of Nevis. The sugar plantations declined at the end of the nineteenth and early twentieth centuries, when sea-island cotton replaced sugar. Unfortunately, the cultivation of this crop involved clearing the ground of weeds, which resulted in erosion of the soil. The higher slopes have been cleared for food crops. The change from sugar cane, excellent for retaining the soil, has caused in this hilly island serious problems.

Notwithstanding that about a third of the land is under cultivation, agriculture has decayed.[2] During the 1960's some 40 to 60 per cent. of those employed in agriculture emigrated. Neither the systems of share-cropping nor rentals have encouraged the development of the cotton industry of the peasants. A central ginnery at Plymouth, the capital, collects and processes the cotton. Earnings from cotton exports fell between 1962 and 1967: Hurricane Inez in 1967–68 compounded the difficulties.

As in Nevis, a central sugar factory could not be established through lack of sufficient level land to grow cane for its supply. The hilly land prevents mechanization. Other crops include a variety of fruits and vegetables, notably tomatoes. Montserrat could benefit from the tourist trade in neighbouring Antigua and Barbados by supplying top quality nursery produce. However this would mean sacrificing the possibility of high land prices for building purposes to the interests of agriculture. Moreover the prestige of the agricultural worker is as depressed in Montserrat as in some other areas of the Caribbean.

Until the early 1960's the island took little interest in tourism. Since then the industry has had considerable impact on the island. In order to boost the building trade, Montserrat has been promoted as a place for retirement rather than a resort for the itinerant tourist.[3] Many tourists find the beaches, which are of dark volcanic sand, strange but nevertheless pleasing. The Antilles Radio Corporation established in 1963 has provided effective advertising in the Caribbean.

In December 1970 the Progressive Democratic Labour Party, headed by Austin Bramble, son of the Prime Minister W. H. Bramble, won all

---

[1] In this case they were Irish and were sent from St. Kitts to prevent quarrels between Protestants and Irish Catholics.

[2] *Report of the Tripartite Economic Survey of the Eastern Caribbean, January-April 1966*, (H.M.S.O., London, 1967), pp. xiii and 126-7.

[3] Cf. *Montserrat Development Plan 1966-1970*, Plymouth 1966, pp. 45-46.

A group of villagers round a well.
Antigua is one of the drier islands
in the Lesser Antilles.

Antigua: picking sea island cotton,
a possible alternative to sugar
which is in decline.

Antigua: English Harbour, once Britain's strongest base in the Antilles—today a pleasure yacht basin. Behind, the arid mountains illustrate the problems of Antillean agriculture, Chapter XIV.

St. Kitts: historic Brimstone Hill, once one of the strongest fortresses in the Antilles: today a tourist attraction.

Nevis: one of the smaller islands in the Eastern Caribbean is now linked to its neighbours by air.

"President" Ronald Webster leads protesting Anguillans after the landing of British troops, March 1969.

Lord Caradon greeted on his arrival in Anguilla, p. 182.

British paratroopers land in Anguilla,
March 1969.

Associated Press

Montserrat: spraying limes, a crop for which the island is famous.

Anne Bolt

St. Lucia: hand loading: often now being replaced by mechanization in the Caribbean.

St. Vincent: loading bananas by conveyor belt.

R. A. Calvert, Grena

Grenada: the charming harbour of St. George's.

Fishermen going to sea on Grenada's leeward coast.

Anne B

seven seats in the Legislative Council, thereby displacing the Montserrat Labour Party which had held uninterrupted power for eighteen years.

The small size of Montserrat rules out major agricultural and industrial development. It was not included in Associated Statehood with Great Britain and remains a Crown Colony. The membership of CARIFTA which it enjoys is vital to its economy. Already recognizing the importance of tourism, the island may seek development more on the lines of Bermuda, the Bahamas and the Cayman Islands.

DOMINICA

Discovered by Columbus during his second voyage in 1493, Dominica for long continued as a Carib island. Britain and France agreed to leave the Caribs in possession in the Treaty of Aix-la-Chapelle in 1748. Notwithstanding this, the French commenced settlements. Britain in turn obtained sovereignty of it after the Seven Years' War. The French recaptured the island during the American War of Independence, but Britain regained permanent possession in 1783. From 1871 to 1939, Dominica was federated with the Leeward Islands to the north. In 1940 it was incorporated in the Windward Islands.

Although Dominica is the largest of the Lesser Antilles, it has a population of only some 72,000 persons.[1] Between 1960 and 1961 there was even a small decrease due to emigration to Great Britain. Still today, the Carib population is significant.

The Constitution is on the traditional lines of a Crown Colony moving into autonomy, with an established two-party system. In 1951 the Dominica Labour Party won the General Election, defeating the Dominica United People's Party which had provided the previous Government. Its leader, E. O. Le Blanc, became Chief Minister.

After the collapse of the West Indies Federation, Dominica took part in conferences held at Port of Spain and London in 1962. When hopes of a federation of the "Little Eight" faded, Dominica followed with the other smaller islands into autonomous association with Great Britain.

The economy of Dominica depends almost totally on agriculture, especially bananas. Exports doubled during the 1960's under the expert management of Geest Industries even though production costs remained above world market levels. Geest owned three large estates in the island, but 9,000 peasant farmers, most with less than 1½ acres of land under bananas, were responsible for the major part of a high

---

[1] 1968 estimate.

quality crop. Handling methods and transport seemed likely to improve following the construction of a new deepwater harbour at Roseau, the siting of boxing facilities throughout the island, a wider use of fertilizers and better access roads to the plantations. However the British market remains a vital outlet in any future process. A heavy responsibility rests on the British Government when negotiating entry into the E.E.C. to safeguard the sales outlet of this industry, so skilfully built up in the Windward Islands.[1]

Limes, faced with strong competition and falling prices, declined in importance during the sixties, although a replanting programme and a potential British market might reverse the trend during the next decade.[2] Exports of cocoa which had declined in the sixties were boosted by the signing of the former Oils and Fats Agreement, by all CARIFTA members, which stipulated that the purchase of copra and coconut oil should take place within the agreement. Other agricultural products, such as mangoes and avocado pears, exported to regional markets, also achieved promising results.

Membership of CARIFTA should continue to act as a stimulus for industry, however small, to develop from the island's natural resources. Fast-growing forests and a wide variety of different woods encouraged Dom-Can Timbers, a Canadian company, to start a logging operation in 1968. Pumice, handled by an American company, found a regional market in the building industry. Minor industries made a contribution, however small, to the diversification of the economy.

Tourism developed in Dominica largely because of the rise of the industry in the rest of the Caribbean particularly during the 1960's. Tourist arrivals rose from 2,000 in 1960 to 10,000 in 1969. The Government attitude towards the industry changed slowly, leading to a greater allocation to the Tourist Board in 1970.

Prime Minister Le Blanc and the Dominica Labour Party were still in power twenty years later although with a reduced majority.[3] Dominica's economic success was immeasurably greater during the sixties than might have been forecast at the start of the decade. Nevertheless its dependence on agriculture kept it extremely sensitive to overseas demand.

[1] Cf. Hugh O'Shaughnessy "Bananas the mainspring of the economy", *The Financial Times*, London, August 21, 1970. *Vide*, p. 333 n. 2

[2] In 1960 lime exports totalled $E.C.330,000; eight years later they dropped to $E.C. 226,000. Cf. Tony Crozier, "Rising exports of a wide range of crops", *The Financial Times*, London, August 21, 1970.

[3] In October 1970 Le Blanc's majority in the House of Assembly was reduced from 10-1 to 7-4. The remaining seats were divided amongst three other parties. Cf. *The Advocate-News*, Barbados, October 28, 1970.

ST. LUCIA

St. Lucia, second largest of the Windward Islands, has an area of 233 square miles and a population of almost 112,000. A volcanic island whose highest peak reaches over 3,000 feet, it has a varied topography which favours diversified agriculture.

After the first European settlers had been driven out by the Caribs in 1605 and again in 1638, St. Lucia changed hands fourteen times. The small harbour at Castries, considered one of the finest in the Caribbean, became of considerable military importance. By the Treaty of Paris in 1763 the island was ceded to France. However, in 1778 the British seized St. Lucia and in 1782 Admiral Rodney sailed from its shores to win the Battle of the Saints. By the Treaty of Versailles in 1783 St. Lucia was restored to France. During the last decade of the eighteenth century, the struggle between the British and the French continued, until the Treaty of Amiens in 1802 reconfirmed French ownership. The island was again captured by the British in 1803 and, following confirmation of this at the Treaty of Paris in 1814, it has remained British.

St. Lucia, however, did not receive the colonial pattern of constitution given to some of the older colonies. It was administered by a Governor directly responsible to the Colonial Office from 1814 to 1838, when it was annexed to the Government of the Windward Islands. Since 1960, St. Lucia has been administered as a separate unit. Two U.S. bases were established in 1940. Beane Field now handles medium-sized jets, of great importance to the growing tourist industry. Associated Statehood, attained in 1967, provided St. Lucia with time to recover from the break-up of the West Indies Federation and to plan for the future.

From the middle of the eighteenth century, sugar increased in importance, but its development was slow. Sugar cane did not replace tobacco, ginger and cotton as the main crop in St. Lucia until a century after this change had occurred in Barbados and the Leeward Islands. Emancipation enhanced the difficulties of the weakening nineteenth-century economy. The planters were slow to turn to the production of vegetables, ground provisions, and stock raising.[1] Some of the

[1] W. K. Marshall, "Social and Economic Problems in the Windward Islands, 1838-1865", *The Caribbean in Transition*, Second Scholars Conference, Mona, Jamaica, April 14-19, 1964, Institute of Caribbean Studies, University of Puerto Rico, 1965, p. 236.

freed slaves emigrated to the goldfields of Guyana and to other parts of South America. Sugar production dropped from 5,000 tons in 1830 to 2,260 in 1843. East Indians were brought in but they did not remain on the plantations and quickly found other work. Of four sugar centrals, only the Roseau factory remains. Cane growing is confined to the Roseau and Cul de Sac valleys: the output sometimes fails to meet the required quota.

With the advent of the steamship, Castries acquired new importance as a coaling station. Coal was imported from the United States and Britain and stored for loading as required, affording work to many. The rates of pay for this work were considerably higher than for agricultural work. Half the island's income was earned in this manner between 1880 and 1920. However, the advent of oil-burning vessels resulted in ever fewer ships calling at Castries.[1] Further employment was created by the building of the U.S. bases and the rebuilding of Castries after its destruction by fire in 1948. After this, St. Lucia came to rely solely on agriculture for its income.

Like Dominica, St. Lucia exemplifies the changing Caribbean. In agriculture, the island has rapidly increased its production of bananas shipping a record 84,762 tons of fruit to Great Britain in 1969. Yet to illustrate the hazards of banana growing, 1970 proved a disastrous year for St. Lucia, largely because Hurricane "Dorothy" destroyed 30 per cent. of the crop.[2] Confidence in the future is displayed by the project of setting up in St. Lucia an industry to make boxes for bananas which should also benefit neighbouring Dominica. The finance will be provided by a Venezuelan concern in conjunction with the Governments of CARIFTA Eastern Caribbean producing islands. Nevertheless bananas have surpassed sugar growing and have balanced the falling production of spices and cacao. Coconuts continue to prosper in contrast to shortages elsewhere in the Caribbean. Inter-planting of coconuts with bananas has greatly increased copra production. The signing by CARIFTA members of the Oils and Fats Agreement, suggested by St. Lucia, is likely to provide a further boost.[3]

Tourism in St. Lucia soared significantly from under 6,000 visitors in 1961 to over 25,000 in 1969. Calls by cruise ships rose from 15 in 1964 to 120 in 1969.[4] A deep-water harbour at Castries, presently under consideration, would enable the port to accept even the largest vessels. A major development in the south of the island at Vieux Fort

[1] In 1911, 139,000 tons of coal were sold; in 1938 only 22,000.
[2] Cf. *West Indies Chronicle*, London, January 1971, pp. 19, 21.
[3] *Vide*, p. 186.
[4] *West Indies Chronicle*, London, January 1971, pp. 25-27.

has been projected for 1975, aided by a nearby airport at Beane Field, planned to take Jumbo jets.[1]

The economic progress enjoyed by St. Lucia during the 1960's will continue only if the banana industry can rely on access to the British market. The potentials for St. Lucia to benefit from ever-closer co-operation through CARIFTA and its offshoot, the Eastern Caribbean Common Market, remain strong.

ST. VINCENT

Although Christopher Columbus named St. Vincent, he made no attempt to establish sovereignty for Spain. He was too shrewd to take a small island with limited agricultural possibilities and populated with fierce Caribs. The first settlements were made by the French. Declared neutral by the Treaty of Aix-la-Chapelle in 1748, St. Vincent was ceded to Britain in 1763. During the American War of Independence, France seized the island, but it was restored to Britain at the end of the war. In 1795 the Caribs, encouraged by the French settlers in the island, revolted. They were finally defeated and many were deported to the Bay Islands off the coast of Honduras.[2] The treatment of the Caribs makes a grim story. For the next century and a half St. Vincent continued as a Crown Colony.

At the end of 1966 a violent dispute flared up between the Administrator, Colonel Lionel Chapman, and Chief Minister Theodore Joshua. A new constitution conferring self-government on St. Vincent was planned to take effect in February 1967. However, following the General Election of August 1966, which Joshua's party had won with a majority of 5 of the 9 seats, four election petitions were lodged: two of them by the St. Vincent Labour Party, who were the losers, and two by the People's Popular Party. In view of the narrow result, the British Government, acting through the Administrator, refused to proceed with the constitutional advance before the hearing of the election petitions. In view of the possibility of trouble arising from the dispute, a British warship was sent in December 1966 to lie off St. Vincent.[3]

After considerable unrest, Joshua was dismissed, new elections held

[1] The Commonwealth Development Corporation is likely to be involved in these developments. *C.D.C. Partners in Development 1970*, London, n.d. p. 3.
[2] *Vide* pp. 215-6.
[3] Cf. Ian Colvin, "Warship sent to West Indies Island", *The Daily Telegraph*, London, December 24, 1966.

in May 1967 and Milton Cato's Labour Party returned with a 6-3 majority. The British Government now sought to expedite Associated Statehood; in addition it had promised further elections before the end of 1968. As a result Cato tried to delay Associated Statehood whereas Joshua, a powerful, charismatic Opposition leader pressed for the 1968 elections. The final report of the St. Vincent Constitutional Conference in June 1969 suggested that the next election be held after the granting of Associated Statehood, and on the basis of 13 constituencies instead of the existing 9.[1] Thus St. Vincent became an Associated State over two years after the other territories.

St. Vincent administrates as a dependency the northern Grenadine Islands from Bequia to Union Island. Fishing is an important local industry with a fish-collecting station established at Canouan. The catch is exported to St. Vincent, St. Lucia and Dominica.

The economic history of St. Vincent is similar to that of the other islands. Sugar, once the main crop, had no chance once the day of small plantations was ended. Emancipation of the slaves produced a labour shortage, which was met by introducing Portuguese from Madeira. Sugar struggled on until 1962 when the last factory shut.

Entirely dependent on agriculture, St. Vincent like other islands in the Windward group successfully expanded its cultivation of bananas. In 1969 the island sold over $E.C.4·5 million worth of fruit to Britain.[2] Damage from hurricanes continued as a major hazard.

Arrowroot ranks next to bananas as the principal export, bringing in over $E.C.1 million of revenue in 1968. Efforts are being made to increase and widen the production of foodstuffs for local consumption, including the expansion of livestock. Membership of CARIFTA may stimulate progress in marketing techniques.

Tourism particularly in the Grenadines, a yachtsman's paradise, has shown marked success; new hotels are being constructed and a cruise-ship terminal planned.[3] Like other Caribbean islands St. Vincent faced the problem of a better system of roads where much still remains to be done. The 1966-70 Development Plan allocated $E.C.337,000 to the tourist industry over the whole period.[4]

A territory of under 93,000 persons is very small for independence,

---

[1] *The Saint Vincent Electoral Provisions Order 1969*, (H.M.S.O., London, August 1969.)

[2] *Vide* p. 333.

[3] *The Future of Tourism in the Eastern Caribbean*, H. Zinder and Associates, Washington, May 1969, p. 254.

[4] *St. Vincent Development Plan 1966-1970*, Government Printer, 1968, pp. 41-43.

notwithstanding that some countries of similar size have already attained that status.[1] The crux of the problem is how to raise the standard of living of the people; or at the least to prevent it from falling. Emigration has taken place to Great Britain; and from the Grenadines to the Netherlands Antilles. In the latter case, many of the emigrants have had to return.[2] Perhaps the descendants of the unfortunate Caribs, so cruelly deported, who later moved to British Honduras, have fared better than those who remained behind.

GRENADA

Grenada, the smallest of the Windward Islands, is similarly volcanic. Its dependencies include the island of Carriacou to the north and the islets lying between known as the Grenadines.[3] A backbone of mountains runs down the length of the island and the indented south coast has many harbours. In 1970 the population was estimated to be over 92,000.

After the discovery of Grenada by Columbus in 1498, the Carib inhabitants were left in undisturbed possession of the island for over a century. In 1626 and 1627 both the French and the British theoretically claimed Grenada but not until 1650 did the French land in the island and successfully take it over from the Caribs who proved easier to subdue than those in the more mountainous Dominica and St. Vincent. In 1664 Grenada became the possession of the French West India Company and, when that was dissolved in 1674, of the French Crown.

Following the island's capture by Admiral George Rodney in 1762, British rule was established by the Treaty of Paris in the following year. The island was governed as a unit with Dominica, St. Vincent and Tobago. In 1776 it became a separate colony with Tobago. The French recaptured and held Grenada from 1779 to 1784 when the Treaty of Versailles finally awarded it to Britain. Under British rule the population increased rapidly following the importation of slaves and migration from the Leeward and other islands to work in the expanding sugar industry.

In 1833, Grenada was included in the Windward Islands. Crown

---

[1] The Maldive Islands in the Indian Ocean have a population of about 70,000. British Honduras, not much larger in population than St. Vincent, is moving into independence.

[2] *Vide* p. 302.

[3] Grenada covers an area of some 120 square miles and Carriacou some 13 square miles.

Colony government with a Legislative Council composed of an equal number of official and nominated members followed in 1877. During succeeding decades the Constitution underwent several changes. In 1951 the form of the Legislative Council was changed to include 3 nominated and 8 elected members. Universal suffrage was introduced in the same year. In 1959 a new provision for the Government of Grenada was drawn up. An Administrator, appointed by the Queen, presided over an Executive Council consisting of the Chief Minister, 3 other Ministers, a member without portfolio and the principal law officer. The Legislative Council consisted of 1 *ex-officio* member, 2 nominated and 10 elected members.

As in the other islands, sugar declined in importance and cacao took its place until the 1920's, when disease and low prices caused a setback. Nutmeg and mace, for long cultivated, became the major crop. Sugar cane was confined to a small area south of St. George's, the capital, where a central factory was built in 1935.[1] Cotton is grown only on Carriacou and the entire crop sold to Trinidad. Many labourers, particularly from Carriacou, emigrated to Curaçao and Aruba to work in the thriving oil industries.[2]

When Trinidad withdrew from the West Indies Federation and moved into independence, Prime Minister Eric Williams offered to admit any of the smaller British Islands of the Eastern Caribbean into association with his country on the basis of a unitary state.[3] Only Grenada showed interest.

With cacao, nutmeg and mace as principal exports, Grenada's economy was precarious. Acute political controversy added to the problems. Chief Minister Eric Gairy, who was also Minister of Finance, was strongly criticized by a Commission of Enquiry on the grounds that he had contravened the laws and regulations controlling expenditure and had destroyed the morale of the Civil Service by undesirable interference and by improper threats against the security of office; this had induced the Civil Service to commit or condone improprieties or irregularities in public expenditure.[4]

[1] By 1964 the Grenada Sugar Factory even failed to supply enough sugar for the home market. Cf. *Grenada, Report for the Years 1963 and 1964* (H.M.S.O., London, 1966), p. 24.

[2] *Vide* pp. 302 and 364.

[3] *Vide* p. 130. Notwithstanding Williams' offer, Ashford Sinanan, leader of the opposition claimed that Trinidad should take on no additional burdens in view of its unemployment situation.

[4] *Report of the Commission of Enquiry into the Control of Public Expenditure in Grenada During 1961 and Subsequently*, Cmnd. 1735 (H.M.S.O., London, 1962).

In consequence, the British Government suspended Grenada's Constitution in June 1962, and both the Legislative and Executive Councils were dissolved. Less important than the suspension of Guyana's Constitution nine years earlier, the event nevertheless adversely affected the chance of any federation of the "Little Eight". At a General Election which followed, Gairy's Grenada United Labour Party was defeated by Herbert A. Blaize's Grenada National Party. Blaize, who became Chief Minister, won a narrow victory on a platform of union with Trinidad and Tobago in a unitary state. The defeat of Gairy may have relieved the British Colonial Office of embarrassment, but the policy of his successor augured ill for the federation of the smaller islands.[1]

Although Blaize claimed that his victory cleared the name of Grenada from "squandermania",[2] the correspondent of *The Nation* cynically concluded that local reaction to the Gairy extravagances as disclosed by the Report signified little to either party. "This uncomplicated attitude stems from the vision of politics conveyed to your correspondent by a native, provoked into the spurious intimacy brought on so easily by the local brew. 'You ever been near to so much money in your life!' Here is a sort of remorseless logic."[3] This depressing conclusion was corroborated by Leigh Richardson, to whom Blaize had admitted that he could not get support from the electorate on the issue of squandermania; he had been forced to rely on the "join Trinidad" issue to win the day. The writer clearly concluded that Gairy, employing the technique of candlelight sessions, hymn singing and near-evangelical speech-making on election eve, remained a powerful force in Grenada's politics.[4] Modern democracy still seemed far away.

Meanwhile the prospect of joining Trinidad began to recede. Many influential groups in Trinidad feared the addition of Grenadians, especially as considerable unemployment existed in that island.[5] As the implications of the proposed union with Trinidad were examined, the difficulties loomed greater. Apart from the integration of a poorer colony into a wealthier state, heavy emigration from Grenada to Trinidad seemed inevitable. Nor was it probable that expected

[1] Cf. *The Times*, London, September 15, 1962.

[2] Broadcast, Grenada, September 14, 1962.

[3] "Grenada Personages and Politics", Port of Spain, September 21, 1962.

[4] "Uncle Gairy Still Casts a Long Shadow", *Sunday Guardian*, Port of Spain, September 23, 1962.

[5] Ken Hill, "Comment", *The Nation*, Port of Spain, December 7, 1962. Out of a working population of some 23,000 persons, nearly 10,000 were employed for less than ten months per year, with about 1,700 looking for their first job.

aid of $B.W.I.60 million from Great Britain would be substantially increased.[1]

In 1966 Grenada received a constitution similar to those of the other Commonwealth islands in the Leeward and Windward group. Like Antigua, the Parliament of Grenada would consist of a Governor appointed by the Queen, a Senate and a House of Representatives. In the Senate 5 of the 9 members would be appointed by the Governor on the advice of the Premier, 2 on the advice of the Premier after he had consulted other organizations on the island, and 2 on the advice of the Leader of the Opposition. The House of Representatives would consist of 10 elected members. Grenada's new free and voluntary association with Great Britain came into force in March 1967.

At elections held later in 1967 Gairy was unexpectedly returned to office with 7 of the 10 seats in the House of Representatives. By now he was firmly entrenched politically as Head of Government, Minister of Home Affairs, Minister of Agriculture and leader of the only recognized union on the island. Gairy did little to alter his former reputation exercising power both directly and indirectly. In February 1972 Gairy was again returned to power with a convincing 13 of the 15 seats in the Legislature.[2]

Gairy was also popular with U.S. business men interested in his island whom he hoped to cajole into buying the former site of Expo '69, held to publicize CARIFTA. Few benefited from this expensive venture which cost the Grenada taxpayer several million dollars.

Grenada's products, spices and cacao, had been seriously damaged by Hurricane Janet in 1955, a much more serious affair for orchard crops than for cane or bananas which normally recover in a year. Complete rehabilitation had not been achieved almost ten years later.

Tourism, however, increased more than four times during the sixties. Grenada boasts some of the most spectacular scenery in the Caribbean, not unlike Jamaica's north coast. The Grande Anse beach, reminiscent of Grand Cayman, is one of the finest in the Caribbean. Grenada is gradually changing its economic emphasis from agriculture to tourism, although the dangers of development along the lines of the Bahamas are obvious, but hopefully, avoidable.

*　　*　　*　　*

The political solution for the Commonwealth Leeward and Windward Islands is an ingenious plan worked out by Great Britain which has had more experience in drafting constitutions than probably any

[1] *Sunday Guardian*, Port of Spain, editorial, February 7, 1965.
[2] *The Times*, London, March 1, 1972.

country in history. Near but not complete independence has been given to the territories. Great Britain continues to accept responsibility for their defence and foreign relations. The new territories can at any time unilaterally vote to terminate the association. If a thread of colonialism still exists, it is a slender one. The West Indies Associated States do not have diplomatic relations with sovereign bodies, including the United Nations, though they may participate in some of its Committees.

Although legally nothing prevents the British Government from responding to a request for assistance from an Associated State, it would obviously be reluctant to do so since it has disclaimed all responsibility for internal affairs. Unfortunately the situation in Anguilla in March 1969 compelled the British Government to intervene: a step which since 1967 it had consistently refused to take at the request of the St. Kitt's Government.[1] In other words, Britain technically gave its support to the legal government of St. Kitt's yet simultaneously it admitted moral responsibility towards Anguilla which did not concur with the constitutional position: a dilemma impossible of satisfactory solution.

The Anguilla crisis sorely tested the delicate fabric of Associated Statehood. For Anguilla it had signified an even closer association with St. Kitt's, already strongly resented. As in the case of the West Indies Federation, this was yet another example of the continuing, if well intentioned, attempts by the United Kingdom to impose political integration and uniformity upon the West Indian islands, without due regard to their political and economic differences and to the strong antipathies which held them apart.[2]

From the British Government's point of view, Associated Statehood was an unsatisfactory compromise which was never envisaged as a permanent solution.[3] Ultimately a new federal grouping might develop on the initiative of the islands themselves. Leaders such as Grenada's

[1] *Vide*, pp. 181-2.

[2] Cf. George C. Abbott, "Political Disintegration: the Lessons of Anguilla", *Government and Opposition*, London, Winter 1971, pp. 64 and 70. Abbott blames slavery for the destruction of the essence of corporate existence in the islands, adding that they "have never really felt the need for each other as is perhaps natural among peoples of a common social, cultural and ethnic origin". p. 69.

[3] "Associated Statehood was intended to represent an acceptable compromise between the political expectations and the economic realities of the region to which it was applied. Historically it was a third preference compromise . . ." K. R. Simmonds, "Anguilla—an interim settlement", *The International and Comparative Law Quarterly*, Vol. 21, Part 1, London, January 1972, p. 156.

Gairy clearly urged political as well as economic union.[1] In St. Vincent a crisis had been averted by delaying the granting of Associated Statehood until after the change of Government in the island. However without waiting for further progress in the political integration of these West Indian territories, there was sufficient evidence for the urgent need to set up machinery whereby local conflicts could be settled on a regional basis.[2]

It may be questioned how wise the Colonialism Committee of the United Nations has been in its continued attacks against the former colonial powers.[3] Great Britain, the United States, France and the Netherlands all have associations with Caribbean territories which are not fully independent. In every case the connection involves substantial financial contributions, including grants and soft loans. Should public opinion in these countries, all of them developed nations and major providers of international finance, become soured over the continuing attacks from the Afro-Asian bloc, the task of obtaining the necessary aid may become increasingly difficult. That public opinion in Great Britain has been aroused in this matter appears clear.[4] Present indications suggest that financing underdeveloped countries is meeting with increasingly limited support.[5]

Should the Afro-Asian group of countries at the United Nations press into independence small territories which have no likelihood of economic survival without continuing outside subsidy, they may alienate the public of the countries which have a moral responsibility

---

[1] Cf. *The Grenada Declaration, 1971, on West Indian Political Unity*, Commonwealth Caribbean Regional Secretariat, Press Release, No. 46/1971, October 30, 1971. *Vide* p. 355.

[2] Cf. Yves Collart, "Regional Conflict Resolution and the Integration Process in the Commonwealth Caribbean", *Regionalism and the Commonwealth Caribbean*, Institute of International Relations, University of the West Indies, Trinidad, n.d., p. 187.

[3] Shortly after Dominica, Grenada, St. Kitts-Nevis-Anguilla and St. Lucia entered into associated statehood with Great Britain, seven countries, Afghanistan, Iraq, Mali, Sierra Leone, Syria, Tanzania and Yugoslavia, tabled a resolution regretting Britain's failure to implement the U.N. declaration on the granting of independence to them. The critics were not an especially influential group, but opponents of colonialism were expected to continue to voice their objections to the solution.

[4] "The Colonialism Committee [of the U.N.] . . . is grossly biased against Britain, and has consistently striven, either for abstract doctrinaire reasons or out of sheer malice, to make the solution of knotty colonial problems even more difficult. Its attitude to the associate status of the tiny West Indian Islands, to Gibraltar and to Australian Nauru are cases in point." *The Daily Telegraph*, London, editorial, April 4, 1967.

[5] *Vide* pp. 349-51.

for continuing aid.   No one who has sought election in a modern democracy is unaware of the public pressure for expenditure on local as opposed to international projects.   Should the links between the former colonial territories be severed, the economic results may in many cases create major hardships.

CHAPTER IX

OTHER ISLANDS

In endeavouring to group the islands of the Caribbean, there are a few that do not fall easily into any of the previous chapters, either for geographical or political reasons. For convenience they have been considered in the following sequence:

> The British Virgin Islands
> The Virgin Islands of the United States
> Turks and Caicos Islands
> The Bahamas
> The Cayman Islands
> Bay Islands
> Margarita

THE BRITISH VIRGIN ISLANDS

Separated by the wide Anegada Passage from the Leeward Islands, the British Virgin Islands consist of thirty-six islands covering fifty-nine square miles and with a population of more than 7,000.[1] Although constitutional government was established in 1773 with an elective House of Assembly and a Legislative Council partly elected, the constitution was surrendered in 1867 as in other British West Indian colonies.[2] When the West Indies Federation was formed in 1958, the British Virgin Islands declined to join.

Election of members to the Legislative Council was introduced in 1950. Further constitutional advance took place in 1954 when the number of elected members was increased from four to six. As was inevitable in a grant-aided colony not commercially viable, power

---

[1] England occupied Tortola, the largest island, in 1666. Six years later the Governor of the Leeward Islands formally annexed the group.

[2] On a minute scale, the failure to prepare the British Virgin Islands for democratic advance may be compared to the tardiness of other West Indian colonies such as Guyana. Cf. Mitchell, *op. cit.*, pp. 141 and 171-2. From 1902 power to legislate for the British Virgin Islands passed to the Legislature of the Leeward Islands.

dominantly resided in the Administrator who was, from 1960, directly responsible to London.

With increasing anxiety in Great Britain over the Colony's future development,[1] Dr. Mary Proudfoot was appointed Constitutional Commissioner in 1965 to enquire into the working of the British Virgin Islands' political system and to make recommendations for any constitutional changes. Her report criticized the Government for being out of touch with the public.[2] It recommended the introduction of a ministerial system of government while leaving substantial powers in the hands of the Administrator. A gradual advance to self-government was envisaged, leading to a full, if small, ministerial system.[3]

A lack of soil and water has handicapped the development of farming. The former plantations have been replaced by smallholdings which yield a scanty living. Tourism undoubtedly offers the greatest promise in an area where industrialization would seem impossible. Tax holidays of up to twenty years are offered to hotel developers; a big increase in the number of hotel beds available has quickly resulted. Laurence S. Rockefeller's hotel at Little Dix on Virgin Gorda has proved successful amongst wealthy Americans, although its continued losses illustrate the high costs of running a successful hotel in the Islands.[4] Many of the recent developments are British. The British Virgin Islands are also emerging as a new kind of tax haven, offering a low rate of tax rather than none at all.

Nevertheless, much heart searching over the future continues among the islanders. A plebiscite in the United States Virgin Islands and the British Virgin Islands might result in both cases in a vote in favour of union. Already 10 to 15 per cent. of the population of the British Virgin Islands find regular employment in the U.S. Virgin Islands; remittances are a significant contribution to the economy of the British Islands.[5] Moreover, the much higher wages and standard of living in the American islands are an added attraction to such a solution. Since 1959, the U.S. dollar has been the normal currency in the British islands.

The taking over of a British territory might provoke criticism from

---

[1] Cf. M. S. Staveley, Administrator, *The Times*, London, April 29, 1963.

[2] *British Virgin Islands, Report of the Constitutional Commissioner 1965* (H.M.S.O., London, 1965), p. 8.

[3] *Ibid.*, p. 11.

[4] Cf. Douglas Skelton, "A more profitable approach comes to tourism", *The Financial Times*, London, August 12, 1969.

[5] *British Virgin Islands, Report of the Constitutional Commissioner 1965*, p. 6.

other countries through the United Nations. On the whole union would at present seem unlikely.

THE VIRGIN ISLANDS OF THE UNITED STATES

Together with the British Virgin Islands, from which they are separated by the Sir Francis Drake Strait, the Virgin Islands of the United States form an archipelago to the east of Puerto Rico. Ownership of the islands has fluctuated; the flags of Spain, the Netherlands, France, and the Knights of Malta have flown over islands in this group.

The principal islands of St. Thomas, St. Croix and St. John were purchased by the United States from Denmark for strategic reasons in 1916-17. Half-way between New York and the Panama Canal, they dominate the Anegada Passage leading to the Caribbean. A U.S. air-base was constructed on St. Croix and a submarine-base on St. Thomas. Together with the bases in Puerto Rico, Culebra and Vieques, they contribute substantially to the U.S. defence of the Panama Canal and control of the Caribbean. For similar reasons, Spain had built its mighty fortress of El Morro at San Juan, Puerto Rico.

The Virgin Islands of the United States have a colonial status with a measure of self-government. Until 1931 they were administered by the Navy Department. In 1936 they were given an Organic Act followed by universal suffrage in 1938. A further devolution of power to the group was made by a new Organic Act in 1954 which vested power in nine executive departments under the supervision of a Governor nominated by the President of the United States. The islands have no direct representation in the United States, though they have citizenship. The relationship to the United States is that of a colony or dependency without a long cultural tradition as in the case of most of the British, French and Netherlands Caribbean territories. Notwithstanding the dominance of nationalism in the Caribbean, the majority of the inhabitants, who are mainly of African origin, clearly wish to remain associated with the United States, though with an extension of self-government. Ralph M. Paiewonsky, first native to be appointed Governor, has pressed for greater autonomy.

The popularity of the link with the United States stems directly from the successful economic position of the islanders. The income *per capita* is considerably more than that of Puerto Rico. The contrast with the poverty-stricken British Islands adjacent to them is still more marked. Free entry of the islanders to the United States is permitted:

Anne Bolt

Jetty at Roadtown, Tortola, capital of the British Virgin Islands.

Governor Ralph M. Paiewonsky (left) of the U.S. Virgin Islands making payment for lands on St. Thomas which his government have acquired from the U.S. Federal Government as part of the island's development programme.

Margarita: ancient fortifications overlooking Pampatar.

Dirección de Turismo, Ministerio de Fomento, Venezuela

Bahamas: Prime Minister Prindling welcomes Lord Shepherd, British Minister of State for Commonwealth Affairs, January 1968, p. 210.

New hotels at Freeport, Bahamas.

many have sought employment there. In turn, men from the British Virgin Islands have replaced them.[1]

Agriculture has only restricted possibilities, despite the favourable U.S. market for sugar.[2] The prosperity of the U.S. Virgin Islands arises from a well-organized tourist trade. In 1964, tourist expenditure amounted to $48 million, almost double the purchase price paid by the United States to Denmark. The proposed construction of a jet airport at St. Thomas, where the capital of the group, Charlotte Amalie, is situated, will still further add to the visitors.[3]

An active programme of introducing new industries has been encouraged by fiscal and other inducements, facilitated by the favoured tax position of the Virgin Islands themselves in relation to the United States. Some 57 industries are already in operation.[4] A population of over 35,000 persons sharply limits the local market. In short, the U.S. Virgin Islands provide an example of prosperity brought to a small territory by the intelligent injection of capital added to U.S. military expenditure.

In November, 1970, the Virgin Islands elected their first Governor. Dr. Melvin Evans, who had been appointed by the U.S. President to replace Paiewonsky in 1969, won a four-year term by 52·5 per cent. of the vote in a run-off election. Representation in the islands' unicameral legislature, which had previously been totally Democratic, split 3 ways with 6 Democrats, 6 Independents, and 3 Republicans.[5] The political emphasis in the campaign showed for the first time a shift from inter-party to inter-island conflict.[6]

The elected Virgin Islands representative to Washington, D.C. still had no congressional privileges. In 1971 the House Interior and

[1] *Vide* p. 199.

[2] Governor Ralph Paiewonsky wished to eliminate the sugar industry. He advocated instead the development of citrus. *Hispanic American Report*, Vol. XVI, p. 877.

[3] Cf. Ronald Walker, "St. Thomas has its eye on Jet Airport", *The New York Times*, New York, October 25, 1964.

[4] Some of these industries benefit from the right to ship duty-free to the United States articles containing up to 50 per cent. of foreign materials. Cf. Jeanne P. Harman, "Businessman-Governor Spurs Commerce in the Virgin Islands", *The New York Times*, New York, January 6, 1964.

[5] Cf. Darwin D. Creque, *The U.S. Virgins and the Eastern Caribbean*, (Philadelphia, 1968).

[6] Al Bill "St. Croix and St. Thomas . . . Squabbling Sisters?" *The Home Journal*, St. Thomas, June 6, 1971. The preliminary 1970 census figures showed a population of 58,719 (St. Croix: 31,187; St. Thomas: 25,798; St. John: 1,734). *Monthly Economic Report: Virgin Islands*, First National City Bank, New York, September, 1970.

Insular Affairs Committee recommended giving him non-voting representation in Congress. But the question of committee voting rights, a privilege Puerto Rico's resident commissioner received in 1971 for the first time, was left open.[1]

The economic difficulties experienced by the United States in the late 1960's and early 1970's adversely affected the islands' own economy. Revenue from the tourist industry, the mainstay of the economy and the islands' largest source of employment, exceeded $107,000,000 in the fiscal year 1970, down $12 million from 1969.[2] It fell again 25 per cent. by mid-1971[3] compared with pre-season estimates.

The manufacture of rum and the watch industry still remained important components of the islands' economy. By 1970 there were 15 watch companies operating with a work force of over 1,200 persons. As a result of the industrial incentives programme, 81 persons, firms or corporations held tax exemptions and subsidy certificates. Hotels and guest houses accounted for about half and small businesses the rest.[4]

Despite the slump unemployment was minimal. About 47 per cent. of the labour force were aliens, providing the vast majority of workers in construction and tourist related industries as well as domestic work. Although this influx relieved surplus labour in the neighbouring islands, it caused concern to the Virgin Islands who had to house, feed, and educate them and also provide medical assistance.[5]

In March, 1971, the Governor launched a 9-point programme to deal with the sagging economy. He proposed greater efficiency of all Government personnel, increased tax collection, new tax incentives to

[1] *The San Juan Star*, San Juan, June 11, 1971.
[2] *Virgin Islands 1970 Annual Report to the Secretary of the Interior*, U.S. Government Printing Office, Washington, D.C., p. 8.
[3] *The Home Journal*, St. Thomas, June 9, 1971. Despite the slump in the economy family income averaged $4,000 per year.
[4] *Annual Report, op. cit.*, pp. 74-75.
[5] Oliver Oldman and Milton Taylor, "Tax Incentives for Economic Growth in the U.S. Virgin Islands", *Caribbean Studies*, Vol. 10, No. 3 University of Puerto Rico, October, 1970, pp. 182-94. The New Manpower Administration programme went into effect in 1970 and from May 1970 to April 1971, 11,810 aliens were bonded to work in the islands. Their origin by place of birth broke down partially as follows:

Anguilla, St. Kitts, and Nevis	32·0
Antigua	19·7
St. Lucia	14·4
Trinidad and Tobago	12·5

The Daily News, St. Thomas, June 1, 1971.
In 1970, a U.S. District Court judge ruled that alien children were entitled to attend the islands' public schools. First National City Bank, *op. cit.*, August 1970.

encourage industrial growth, faster tourist promotion, a stepped-up Government housing programme, a new Government centre to eliminate high rentals, an expanded road programme, an accelerated vocational education programme,[1] and extension of the business community beyond the high rent areas.

That the Virgin Islands have surpassed in *per capita* income the larger Caribbean islands, including Puerto Rico, is a remarkable achievement. No other territory so small in numbers can approach this measure of success. For a comparative achievement, beyond the scope of this study, Bermuda with a somewhat larger population (over 53,000 persons) might suggest itself. On a wider view, the immense advantage of the association of a miniscule group of islands with a strong partner must submerge any arguments put forward for their independence which might result not in prosperity but indigence.

The Virgin Islands of the United States make an interesting comparison with Puerto Rico. Ethnically they have a population more Negro than that of Puerto Rico. The two territories have different histories: Puerto Rico had a link with Spain only equalled by that of Cuba, whereas the archipelago of the Virgin Islands had a confused and turbulent past in which France, England and even the Knights of Malta were involved. At a time when Denmark was under pressure from Germany, during World War I, it ceded the islands to the United States, who for strategic reasons were anxious to purchase.

Puerto Rico has given careful thought to an independence status, although so far the large majority clearly prefer the existing Commonwealth (*Estado Libre Asociado*) status, while a substantial number would prefer statehood as part of the United States. Those who seek independence are fewer, although active. The Virgin Islands look for increasing devolution of government. However, to enter the United States as a state with an extremely small population in relation to any of the existing states would appear impracticable. Independence would be disastrous since the advantages of U.S. citizenship and internal trade would be lost. Notwithstanding this small population and exiguous natural resources, the standard of living is higher than that of Puerto Rico, in turn the highest of any major Caribbean country.

TURKS AND CAICOS ISLANDS

Associated first with the Bahamas and from 1873 with Jamaica, from which it is separated by 450 miles of sea, Turks and Caicos Islands had to face the severance of either its tie with Jamaica or its link to

[1] The College of the Virgin Islands became a 4-year institution in 1969.

Great Britain when it became obvious in 1961 that the West Indies Federation was likely to disintegrate. The Turks and Caicos trade largely consisted of exporting salt and sisal in return for essential supplies. Commercial routes linked it to the neighbouring Bahamas Islands and to the United States rather than to Jamaica through the Windward Passage. The islanders were also reluctant to give up British nationality and passports, since many of them sought work in the Bahamas, the United States, and also as seamen; they feared lest a change might prejudice their chances of employment.[1] In April 1962, the Legislative Assembly expressed its gratitude to the Government of Jamaica for past assistance; but it also stressed the population's preference for remaining a British colony. The decision was an interesting commentary on the often-criticized British colonial system.

Under a constitution introduced in 1962, Turks and Caicos Islands received a Legislative Assembly of 9 elected members, of not less than 2 or more than 3 official members, and not less than 2 or more than 3 nominated members, over which the Administrator appointed by the British Government presides. The Executive Council consists of 2 official, 1 nominated and 2 elected members of the Assembly.

The population of 5,688 in 1960 had decreased since 1943 by 10 per cent. The provisional 1970 figure of 6,000 showed a minimal increase. Significant male emigration was responsible for this decline.[2] The birthrate remained high. Primary school education, available for all, failed to match the standards of similar schools in other Commonwealth Caribbean countries. Unemployment does not exist and the *per capita* income reaches some £500.

Difficult trading conditions adversely affected the salt industry, before 1963 the principal employer of labour and main source of export earnings. Now subsidized by the Government it employs some 50 people on Salt Cay. The U.S. Guided Missile base and other naval facilities helped to cushion the effects of this declining industry.[3] Seafood, particularly crawfish and to some extent conchmeat (dried and exported to Haiti), forms the basis of the colony's only profitable export industry. Everything else is imported and the cost of living is consequently high.

[1] *Turks and Caicos Islands, Report for the years 1961 and 1962* (H.M.S.O., London, 1963), p. 4.

[2] Between 6,000 and 8,000 Turks and Caicos Islanders live overseas, mainly in the Bahamas.

[3] *Economic Survey and Projection, Turks and Caicos*, British Development Division in the Caribbean, Ministry of Overseas Development, November 1969, p. x.

Turks and Caicos Islands highlights the problems of colonialism which occur in the Caribbean. Great Britain provides an annual grant-in-aid which in 1970 exceeded £500,000. In March 1970 a British Government working party concluded that good prospects existed for the territory to achieve a balanced budget by the mid-1970's thus eliminating the need for aid.[1] This would be achieved by a judicious balance of tourist and property development. The report also advocated the setting up of the Turks and Caicos Islands as a tax haven. Although at first the direct benefits for the islanders might be few, the indirect advantages would be substantial, including improved communications.[2] However, the outcome of implementing the proposals would be that within 15 years immigrants would numerically equal local inhabitants and even in due course outnumber them. The report stressed the need for careful yet sensible control of immigration.[3]

The islands may benefit from the experience of the Bahamas (with whom they share a Governor) and Bermuda (also with very limited natural resources) in regard to the possibilities of tourism and tax legislation providing a means of increasing their prosperity.

THE BAHAMAS

The near 700 islands of the Bahamas archipelago stretch for a distance of 760 miles. Grand Bahama and Bimini lie about 50 miles off the Florida coast; to the south-east Great Inagua is about the same distance from Cuba's coast and 70 miles from that of Haiti. One of the Bahamas, San Salvador or Watling Island, is generally accepted as the first land in the New World to be sighted by Columbus. The Spaniards took little interest in these somewhat bare islands beyond transporting many of the Amerindian population to work in the mines and plantations of Hispaniola. British involvement in the group dates from a Charter granted in 1629 to Sir Robert Heath. The first effective colonization came from Bermuda in the mid-seventeenth century.

Piracy marred the early history of the islands. However, a representative assembly was summoned in 1729. The government continued except when the colony was briefly captured by the Americans in 1776 and when it surrendered to the Spaniards in 1782. A Legislative Council was created in 1841.

---

[1] *Property and Tourist Development in the Turks and Caicos Islands,* (Sir Derek Jakeway), London, March 1970, pp. 27-28.

[2] *Ibid.,* Appendix 2, pp. 3-5.

[3] *Ibid.,* pp. 29-30.

Unlike most of the Caribbean islands, the Bahamas constitution remained intact. In the 1962 General Election universal male suffrage was introduced throughout the colony; votes were also extended to women. Traditionally the House of Assembly had been controlled by the white "Bay Street" minority in Nassau. Contrary to the forecasts of many, the United Bahamian Party, representing the point of view of those who had previously been responsible for the policy of the colony, won a victory over the Negro Progressive Liberal Party. For the first time the pattern of the defeat of white colonialists in some twenty British colonies which had obtained full or partial independence since World War II was reversed. Although some attributed the result to the votes of the women electors, more conservative than the men, probably the main reason was the high degree of prosperity in the islands, the result of very successful government planning.

In May 1963 a Constitutional Conference was held in London. Out of it a new constitution for the Bahama Islands was promulgated which came into force in 1964.[1] To the 15-member Senate presided over by a President, the Governor appointed 8 members of his own choice after consultation with the Premier, 5 on the advice of the Premier and 2 on the advice of the leader of the Opposition. The 38-member House of Assembly was elected by adult suffrage from twenty-one years of age. The Cabinet, collectively responsible to the Legislature, consisted of a Premier and not less than 8 other Ministers, one of whom had to be the Minister of Finance.[2]

The most interesting feature of the constitution was the wide power reserved to the Governor, who remained responsible to the British Government which had chosen him. In addition to external affairs and defence, always reserved until independence has been attained by a territory, the Governor appointed a Police Service Commission of three persons which he was empowered to remove.[3] In contrast, the 1966-67 Constitutions of the Commonwealth territories in the Leeward and Windward Islands vested control of the police force, a vital matter in any country, in the Island Executive. The contrast became greater when the Governor's control over the Bahamas Senate appointments was compared to the position in the islands of the Eastern Caribbean where he nominated on *advice* (not simply *after consultation*). It was

[1] *The Bahama Islands (Constitution) Order in Council 1963* (H.M.S.O., London, 1964).
[2] A combination of the powers of the head of the government and Finance Minister in one individual, which had been so disastrous in Grenada, appears to be prevented. *Vide* p. 192.
[3] *The Bahama Islands (Constitution) Order in Council 1963*, Clause 100.

difficult to justify the reason for giving lesser responsibilities to a successful colony than to those grant-aided.[1] A comparison with political improprieties in St. Vincent and Grenada was especially striking.[2] Certainly British political thinking in the devolution of authority had progressed in the interval of some two years between the drafting of these Constitutions.

The Bahama Islands represent one of the most successful examples of economic progress in a small territory during the last two decades. Difficult to administer by reason of the numbers of small communities, separated by considerable distances, nature has not aided them with an abundance of fertile soil or water. Hurricanes add to the hazards.

Far removed from Great Britain—in some cases offshore islands in relation to the United States—they have moreover depended largely on North America for their imports, exports and particularly their tourist trade. Although former prosperity stemmed from seafaring, transformed between the two world wars into rum-running, the colony has later concentrated on the dynamic development of tourism. The accessibility of Nassau, the Bahamas capital, to Miami in Florida, combined with excellent international air services, has encouraged the increasing flow of visitors, winter and summer. Although the scenery of the islands lacks the spectacular beauty of some of the Caribbean islands, the sandy beaches and beautiful lagoons teeming with fish have proved an enormous draw. Skilful and persistent advertising, particularly in North America and Great Britain, has produced rewarding results.

Figures indicate most effectively the growth in the number of tourists who have visited the Bahamas. In 1949, 32,000 tourists came to Nassau, more than half by ship. By 1959 the figure had risen to 244,000, and by 1969 to 725,572.[3] Although the pattern fluctuates, by 1969 nearly two-thirds came by air as opposed to sea.[4] In addition the rise in tourists to the Out Islands has been even more spectacular: from 20,000 in 1959 to over 600,000 in 1969. Despite the predominance of Grand Bahama (Freeport) in these figures, the outward spread of tourism from Nassau to Eleuthera and Andros and to other poorer islands in the group provided encouragement.

During the 1960's the percentage of visitors from the United States

[1] Cf. *Report of the Windward Islands Constitutional Conference 1966*, Cmnd. 3021 (H.M.S.O., London, 1966), pp. 28 and 34-5.

[2] *Vide* pp. 189 and 192-3.

[3] *1969 Bahama Islands Visitor Statistics*, Ministry of Tourism, Nassau, n.d., Table No. 8, p. 12.

[4] *Ibid.*, Table No. 3, p. 7.

remained consistently high, although those from Canada and the United Kingdom fluctuated.[1] In 1970 tourist figures for the Bahama Islands dropped for the first time; from 1,332,396 in 1969 to 1,298,344. Adverse publicity, following outbreaks of civil unrest throughout the Caribbean, was partly responsible together with continuing economic recession in North America.[2] Criticism of the attitude of local people towards tourists persisted; Prime Minister Pindling laid blame on some of the clientele, attracted to the casinos at Freeport, who alienated the Bahamians. Despite the 2·6 per cent. drop in total visitor arrivals, those coming by sea to Nassau and the Out Islands, other than Grand Bahama, increased.[3]

In October 1970, partly as a result of poor tourist returns, the Bahamas suffered a severe setback when the operations of Bahamas Airways suddenly ended. The national airline had been operating at an annual loss of more than $4 million.[4] Not only was the sudden closure a blow to island confidence but also it adversely affected investment in the area. Provisional figures, however, for the first six months of 1971 showed an 11 per cent. increase on the previous year: the fall in tourist figures in one year may not be a recurring factor.

The economy of the Bahamas has been greatly expanded not only by tourism itself but also by the interest that many wealthy tourists have taken in investing in the Bahamas. Tourism has acted as a shop window for other enterprises.[5] Moreover, the fiscal system of the islands, attractive to overseas investors, has encouraged many visitors to become whole or part-time residents. They form a valuable and permanent extension of the tourist trade. A background of exemption from personal income tax, favourable estate taxation at death, and in

[1] The percentage of visitors from the United States was 88·3 per cent. in 1960 and 87·5 per cent. in 1969; from Canada, 6·6 per cent. in 1960 rising through 12·0 per cent. in 1963 and falling to 5·1 per cent. in 1969; from the United Kingdom, 2·1 per cent. in 1960 and 1·4 per cent. in 1969. *Ibid.*, Table No. 17, p. 28.

[2] Cf. *Report of the Royal Commission appointed on the Recommendation of the Bahamas Government to Review the Hawksbill Creek Agreement*, Vol. 1, Report, (H.M.S.O., London, 1971), p. 69.

[3] Bahamas Ministry of Tourism, *Monthly Visitor Report*, December 1970.

[4] Cf. *The Times*, London, October 16, 1970.

[5] "It is important to point out the fact that it is the tourist industry which has created the underlying facilities necessary to make the Bahamas attractive to business enterprises. Without the tourist industry, the Bahamas could not support the fine and frequent air transportation from New York, Miami and Palm Beach." Report by the First Research Corporation, Miami, quoted by E. Brownrigg, "Bright Future Forecast for Bahamas", *New Commonwealth*, London, February 1962.

some cases tax holidays for new enterprises, have combined to expand the commerce of the Bahamas.[1]

A lack of suitable soil frequently limits agriculture, as Neville Chamberlain found when, to the disappointment of his father, Joseph Chamberlain, he failed to make a success of growing sisal on Andros Island. Nevertheless, a large-scale production of cucumbers and tomatoes has been established in the Bahamas making use of modern mechanization. The introduction of pangola grass, one of the most important developments in tropical stock-raising, has been introduced in Cat Island. Dairy and poultry farming is expanding on Eleuthera. Tourism provides an ever-increasing market for top-grade local produce.

The high labour cost seems likely to limit the industrial expansion in the Bahamas, as in other parts of the Caribbean, such as Jamaica. However, spectacular development has taken place in the Grand Bahama. In 1955, the Government signed the Hawksbill Creek Agreement with the Grand Bahama Port Authority Limited to develop part of the island. Together with Canadian and American financial interests, the Port Authority formed in 1960 the Grand Bahama Development Company Limited to develop the resort and residential area of Lucaya. A deep-water harbour was constructed at Freeport, which is 81 miles east of Palm Beach in Florida and 145 north-west of Nassau. One of the largest bunkering installations in the Western Hemisphere was built capable of servicing four ships simultaneously. Some 150 ships a month are fuelled.

The main purpose of the scheme was to encourage industrial and commercial development. Very substantial long-term concessions were given by the Government of the Bahamas within the Hawksbill Creek Agreement. The Grand Bahama Port Authority and its licensees had the right of import free of duty until 2054, and also exemption from property taxes and income taxes until 1990. The Bahama Cement Company, a subsidiary of United States Steel Corporation, has erected a cement plant at an estimated cost of £18 million, which was opened in 1965.[2]

The Freeport concession has been criticized as too generous, but it must be remembered that a previous tourist development on the Grand Bahama, sponsored by Sir Billy Butlin, was unsuccessful. The island had few natural resources: its development by Mr. Wallace Groves and his associates was an act of courage which appears to

---

[1] Cf. William Davis, "A place in 'paradise' and it's tax free", *The Guardian*, London, January 24, 1966.

[2] Cf. *The Nassau Guardian*, Nassau, March 18, 1965.

be bringing profit not only to themselves but to the colony as a whole.

The tourist and commercial life of Nassau and Providence Island had been dominated until 1967 by the white "Bay Street Boys" who at the same time maintained a feudal-capitalist hold over the island's political life. Lynden Pindling learnt his political trade by fighting this group and with the slogan "Honesty in Government" successfully won the General Election in 1967. This slogan had a particular meaning for the Bahamas since the United Bahamian Party had had to face serious allegations of corruption levelled at them by the Press.[1] A report, commissioned by Sir Ralph Grey, then Governor of the Bahamas, confirmed that Sir Stafford Sands and four other members of the Bahamas Executive Council had benefited personally in financial terms as a result of facilitating the establishment of gambling in the Bahamas.[2] Since 1964 the Lucayan Beach Hotel on Grand Bahama had been permitted to operate a casino. The suggested association of this establishment with American gangsterism became the centre of much controversy.[3] In 1965 Pindling had lodged a complaint on the subject with the United Nations and in the next year at the U.N. he levelled charges that the people of the Bahamas were being "sold out to gangsterism".[4] In January 1967 another casino had been opened in the vicinity of the King's Inn Hotel.

To some people Pindling's victory came as a surprise, although he had conducted an extremely active pre-election campaign whereas the United Bahamian Party of Sir Roland Symonette, certain of political success on the strength of its economic position, had tended to rest on its laurels. Pindling and Symonette each won 18 seats in the 38-member House of Assembly. The balance of power was held by Mr. Randol Fawkes, the Negro Labour Party leader, who in the outcome supported Pindling's Progressive Liberal Party.

Almost at once, Pindling's Government urged further constitutional advance; a Conference was convened for September 1968 in London. Meanwhile, at the request of the Premier, the House was dissolved and at the General Election in April 1968, the P.L.P. won 29 of the 38 seats. The Conference then agreed to change the Constitution to

---

[1] Cf. *The Wall Street Journal*, New York, October 5, 1966.

[2] Cf. *Report of the Commission of Enquiry into the Operation of the Business of Casinos in Freeport and Nassau*, (H.M.S.O., London, 1967).

[3] Cf. Richard Oulahan and William Lambert, "The Scandal in the Bahamas", *Life Magazine*, New York, February 3, 1967.

[4] "Bahamas: Trouble in Paradise", *The Economist*, London, October 15, 1966, pp. 282-3.

give the Government wider powers. The Bahamas became known as the "Commonwealth of the Bahama Islands". The new Constitution provided for a 16-member Senate, presided over by a President. The Governor appointed 9 members acting in accordance with the *advice of* (no longer *after consultation with*) the Prime Minister (formerly Premier), 4 on the advice of the leader of the Opposition and 3 after consultation with the Prime Minister and "such other persons as the Governor, acting in his discretion, may decide to consult."[1] Since all the members nominated by the Prime Minister provided a permanent majority until the House was dissolved, Government Bills seemed likely to proceed unhindered. The 38-member House of Assembly remained unchanged, as did the composition of the Cabinet, save for the Minister of Finance who was no longer specified as a member.

The most important issue at the Conference arose from the request by the P.L.P. for transfer of police control and internal security to Bahamas Ministers.[2] It was decided that a Minister appointed by the Prime Minister would discharge this responsibility. A Security Council composed of the Governor, the Prime Minister, another Minister and such other persons as the Governor might appoint after consultation with the Prime Minister, was set up to consult on external affairs and internal security.[3] The Governor was not obliged to accept the advice of this Security Council and the Commissioner of Police would continue to answer directly to the Governor: a somewhat complex compromise.

Tensions between the Government and the Grand Bahama Port Authority followed shortly after the change of Government in 1967, chiefly over the granting of permits for immigrant workers.[4] The Government feared an excessive increase in the expatriate population, particularly at Freeport. In consequence in March 1970 it abrogated the immigration concessions under the Hawksbill Creek Agreement thereby regaining full control over immigration.[5]

The dispute adversely affected both Freeport and the Bahamas as a whole. The Report of the Royal Commission criticized the Government for its failure to arbitrate as provided for under the Hawksbill

[1] *The Bahama Islands (Constitution) Order 1969*, No. 590, (H.M.S.O., London, 1969), Clause 30-(2)(c).
[2] *Report of the Bahamas Constitutional Conference, 1968*, Cmnd. 3792, (H.M.S.O., London 1968), Chap. 11, p. 2.
[3] *The Bahama Islands (Constitution) Order 1969*, 74(3), p. 51.
[4] Cf. *The Miami Herald*, Miami, February 18, 1968.
[5] *Official Gazette Bahamas*, Supplement Part 1, No. 4 of 1970, Nassau, March 16, 1970.

Creek Agreement.[1] The Commission found that complaints over the processing of applications for work permits were sufficiently well-founded to give rise to grave concern,[2] and also that investor confidence was badly shaken.[3] However, it also noted the Freeport boom might not have lasted much longer. It recommended that Freeport should continue as part of the Bahamas.[4]

Following mounting uncertainty, at the opening of Parliament in June 1971 Pindling stated that his Government intended to serve out its term of office and that the Commonwealth of the Bahama Islands should proceed to independence "after the next General Election but not later than 1973".[5]

The business expansion in the Bahamas has encouraged the entry into the colony of overseas banks, trust and insurance companies. The ease and speed of company formation in the colony has drawn much business from neighbouring countries including Middle America. With leading British, U.S. and Canadian financial institutions entering Nassau in increasing numbers, a highly competitive financial market has been created which stimulates business. The recurrent crises which have plagued sterling during the post-war years have been the only serious handicap in this field. The Bahama Islands changed from pounds, shillings and pence to decimal currency in 1966. Significantly, the Bahamian dollar equals about forty new pence, at the time of writing nearly the same as the United States dollar. How long the Bahama Islands will seek to remain in the sterling area may be questionable.

The Bahamas pioneered tourism in the Commonwealth Caribbean. The rise in the standard of living, at first in New Providence Island (Nassau), spread outwards not only to Freeport and Eleuthera but also to the many poorer islands, proving (as Bermuda has done) that intelligently administered islands may attain prosperity even when totally lacking significant agricultural land or other resources.

Yet the problem of racial relations has raised a question mark over the future of this country. Can the political change from the White dominated "Bay Street" administration be transformed successfully into a government where Black Power is a major motivation? The

[1] *Report of the Royal Commission appointed on the Recommendation of the Bahamas Government to Review the Hawksbill Creek Agreement,* Vol. 1, Report, 178, p. 60.

[2] *Ibid.,* 90, p. 64.

[3] "Capital is so sensitive that it will not tarry to find out who is in the right legally or who is in the wrong." *Ibid.,* 197, p. 66.

[4] *Ibid.,* 203, p. 68.

[5] Speech from the Throne, Nassau, June 14, 1971.

expertise of those who built up Nassau's fortunes must be commended notwithstanding justified criticism of some individuals. Yet, equally, a heavy responsibility rests on successor administrations.

The importance of tourism, often underrated, is linked to the rising number of people able to take holidays abroad, coming very heavily from the developed countries, particularly the United States. Tourists from any country may not always understand other countries or even behave wisely. Nothing, however, is more certain than that if local people in any country show antipathy to tourists the stream will dry up quickly. In the same way confidence over investments may readily be shaken by unwise antagonisms. Whether the striking success of the Bahamas, both over tourism and as a financial centre, will continue may turn largely on the wisdom of government combined with the sophistication of the public.

THE CAYMAN ISLANDS

The Cayman Islands, which consist of Grand Cayman, Cayman Brac and Little Cayman, lie midway between Jamaica's west coast and the Isle of Pines off Cuba's south coast. The territory was ceded by Spain to the British Crown by the Treaty of Madrid in 1670 at the same time as Jamaica. Never permanently occupied by the Spaniards, the islands were for long a haunt of pirates. The largest settlement was made from Jamaica in the eighteenth century. Early administration was conducted by Justices of the Peace appointed by the Governor of Jamaica; from 1832 elected Vestrymen participated in the government. Acts of the administration required the assent of the Governor of Jamaica; however, in 1898 a Commissioner was appointed to administer the islands.

When the West Indies Federation was formed, the Cayman Islands did not seek entry. In consequence, the colony ceased in 1959 to be a dependency of Jamaica, though the Governor of Jamaica continued as Governor of the Cayman Islands, an illogical but convenient solution.

Following the collapse of the West Indies Federation and the independence of Jamaica in 1962, a new constitution was set up for the Cayman Islands under an Administrator for the colony to replace the Governor of Jamaica. The Legislative Assembly had an elected majority over official and nominated members, though a minority on the Executive Council. During the following nine years, as the importance of the Cayman Islands both as a tax haven and as a tourist resort grew, the need for a more sophisticated administration became increasingly obvious. A Commission was set up to examine possible constitutional evolution stopping short of independence, which the islanders did not want.[1].

The population of 10,652 is composed of persons of mixed African and European origin. Seafaring has traditionally been the life of the male part of the population. Today many Cayman islanders serve on U.S.-owned merchantmen, often sailing under flags of convenience of Panama and Liberia. The remittances of these seamen, as in the British Virgin Islands, provide an important factor in the economy of the Cayman Islands.

In view of limited agricultural possibilities the tourist industry has already contributed to the partial displacement of small local industries such as thatch rope manufacture (now largely a female occupation) and the capture of turtle and shark.[2] A fleet of lobster boats operates out of Georgetown. The expansion of tourism is particularly welcome as the growing use of automation in ships reduces openings for employment.[3] Unlike the Governments of Jamaica, Barbados and even St. Lucia, the Government of the Cayman Islands has retained a cautious approach towards tourism, though it is now the most important industry in the island. The colony remains unspoilt: its fifteen miles of white, sandy beaches rank among the finest in the world. Good air links exist with the Americas and other Caribbean islands, but improvements in airport facilities at Georgetown have yet to be extended to the other two islands. Visitors have increased from some 4,000 in 1964 to over 19,000 in 1969.[4] Hotel building has resulted in soaring land prices.

The Cayman Islands have an economy differing substantially from most of the Caribbean. Unemployment does not exist. The future is intriguing. Will the colony follow the pattern of Bermuda, which has a standard of living at present exceeding that of Great Britain? The model though it has its dangers is not without attractions.

Increasingly the Cayman Islands' financial provisions attract companies and trusts.[5] The economic future may lie mainly in its develop-

[1] *Cayman Islands, Proposals for Constitutional Advance, Report by the Constitutional Commissioner, the Rt. Hon. the Earl of Oxford and Asquith, K.C.M.G.*, (H.M.S.O., London, 1971).

[2] Turtle farming has achieved some success. Cf. Michael Buckmaster "Tax-free-port and land the assets", *The Times*, London, August 8, 1970.

[3] The 1970 census estimated that some 1,500 to 2,000 male Caymanians were serving at sea.

[4] Cf. *Cayman Islands, an Economic Survey*, Barclays D.C.O., London, March 1971.

[5] In a few years nearly a thousand international companies have been registered and about four hundred trusts formed. Cf. John Bradley, "Modern legislation offers a complete tax haven", *The Financial Times*, London, February 6, 1969.

214

ment as a financial centre. If the islands preserve their traditional political stability, avoiding the lure of casinos and all that goes with them, they may rapidly move ahead as a peace haven as well as a tax haven.[1]

THE BAY ISLANDS

The archipelago known as the Bay Islands stretches for over 80 miles parallel to the north coast of the Republic of Honduras at a distance of 30 to 50 miles offshore. The small population of some 5,000 persons is mainly concentrated in the island of Roatán, whose centres are Roatán town (also known as Coxin's Hole) and Port Royal, the largest of the group. In size, it is 30 miles by 9. The other principal islands are Guanaja (or Bonacca) to the east of Roatán and Utila to the west.

Christopher Columbus discovered Guanaja during his fourth voyage in 1502. He named it Isla de los Pinos, for like its neighbours it was luxuriantly afforested. British traders developed the Bay Islands in the seventeenth century for the log-wood trade. When they proceeded to erect forts on Roatán, King Philip V of Spain instructed the Governor of Honduras to destroy them.

Probably sparsely populated by Amerindians, some of whom Columbus met, the island became a haunt of buccaneers. Later the log-wood industry was developed by British settlers, who also traded with the mainland.

After Spain had declared war on Great Britain in 1779, the Spanish Governor of Bacalar made a surprise attack on Belize which resulted in the destruction of the St. George's Cay settlement. Most of the inhabitants were taken as prisoners to Mérida and Havana. Others, including Baymen working in logwood centres, escaped to Roatán. Thus the Bay Islands received an increase of settlers, most of whom were of European stock.

The confused origins of the inhabitants of the Bay Islands also stretched to the eastern rim of the Caribbean. In 1675 the wreck on St. Vincent of a ship conveying a cargo of West African slaves was later to affect profoundly the far-off Bay Islands, some 1,700 miles away. The liberated Negroes intermingled with the Carib Indians of St. Vincent. For long the two groups occupied the island. Finally in 1796 British troops took over complete control of St. Vincent.[2] The "Black Caribs", as they had been termed, were then deported to Roatán, Bonacca and the Mosquito Coast, whence some of them moved to

[1] Cf. "Choice of a tax haven demands careful study", *The Financial Times*, survey, London, September 17, 1971.

[2] Cf. Stephen L. Caiger, *British Honduras* (London, 1951), pp. 109-10.

Belize and to Spanish mainland settlements. They proved capable workers both as woodmen and on plantations. In 1838 some liberated slaves from the Cayman Islands settled in the Bay Islands. The Negro population was thus increased and the English language further established. Notwithstanding protests from Honduras, Great Britain maintained possession.[1]

The Bay Islands had an historic association with the coastal Kingdom of Mosquitia which stretched from Río San Juan in southern Nicaragua to Cape Gracias a Dios and to Truxillo in Honduras. The area supplied to Britain logwood, mahogany, sugar and tobacco in exchange for cutlasses, ammunition and cloth.

Sovereignty of the islands remained indeterminate. For example, in 1835 and 1841, the British administrator of Belize landed on Roatán to displace the flag of Honduras by that of Great Britain. Colonial Spain, however, never recognized British sovereignty over the Bay Islands any more than it did over the Belize settlements. After independence, the Republic of Honduras, established after the collapse of the ill-fated Federation of Central America, claimed both the Mosquito Coast and the Bay Islands, taking over Spain's rights under the theory of *uti possidetis*.

In the Clayton-Bulwer Treaty signed in 1850 by John M. Clayton, U.S. Secretary of State, and Sir Henry Bulwer, British Minister to the United States, the two countries agreed to neutrality throughout Central America. The treaty provided for joint control by them of any canal or railway constructed in the area. However, British Honduras and its dependencies, which signified the Bay Islands, were excepted from the Treaty. Great Britain had exercised a protectorate over the Mosquito Indians of the Nicaraguan and Honduran coasts. In 1852 the Bay Islands were declared by Royal Warrant a British Crown Colony.

Following on diplomatic pressure from the United States against British rule in the Bay Islands, Great Britain signed a Treaty with the Republic of Honduras in 1859 under which it recognized the sovereignty of the Republic over the Bay Islands. The United States regarded the event as a triumph of the policy expressed in the Clayton-Bulwer Treaty, since it resulted in "the only voluntary withdrawal of Great Britain from any land over which the British flag had once flown".[2]

---

[1] Sir Alan Burns, *History of the British West Indies* (London, 1954), p. 691. Cf. R. A. Humphreys, *The Diplomatic History of British Honduras 1638-1901* (London, 1961), p. 50.

[2] Gordon Ireland, *Boundaries, Possessions and Conflicts in Central and North America and the Caribbean* (Harvard University Press, Cambridge, 1941), p. 317.

Professor Julius W. Pratt sees in Great Britain's restoration of the Bay Islands to Honduras and its acknowledgement of the sovereignty of Honduras and Nicaragua over the Indians of the Mosquito Coast, "the first real victory of the Monroe Doctrine".[1] Great Britain retained in practice a protectorate over the Bay Islands until 1903 when it formally resigned all jurisdiction.

The commerce of the Bay Islands has been varied. Buccaneering had been punctuated with logwood cutting. Later the islanders profited from the turbulent politics of mainland Republics, supplying contraband weapons as occasion offered.[2] In the days of prohibition in the United States, the Bay Islands like the Bahamas and other islands participated in the smuggling of liquor, or even of Chinese immigrants into Florida.

As the integration of Central America proceeds, despite the problems of its Common Market, the Bay Islands also will inevitably be merged ever more closely into the economy of Honduras. Agriculture and fishing will advance. Peter Keenagh's vivid description of the Bay Islands must fade.[3] As the jet plane sails over the islands, they appear as jewels set in the translucent waters of the Gulf of Honduras, a reminder of the tangled skein of Caribbean history which once gave them links with Great Britain, the Windward Islands, the Caymans and Belize.

MARGARITA

Venezuela has had traditional bonds with the Caribbean since the sixteenth century when the Spaniards reached it from the sea. Santo Domingo, Cuba and Puerto Rico were its links to the mother-country of Spain. Two series of islands front the northern shores of Venezuela in the Caribbean Sea. The northerly group comprises Aruba, Curaçao and Bonaire, forming part of the Netherlands Antilles.[4] The archipelagos of Islas de las Aves and Los Roques, La Orchila, Blanquilla and Los Hermanos are all related in geological origin. These islands, together with La Tortuga, are Federal dependencies of Venezuela.

The southern or continental islands include Margarita, a mountainous island whose highest peak, San Juan, attains over 3,000 feet, Cubagua,

[1] Op. cit., p. 290.

[2] "Captain Macdonald, in fact, declared that it was not uncommon for a schooner to carry contraband weapons for both sides in the same shipment, leaving half at one rendez-vous and sailing on to deliver the other half somewhere else." Peter Keenagh, Mosquito Coast (London, 1938), p. 66.

[3] Op. cit., pp. 55-6.   [4] Vide pp. 300-1.

Coche and various islets; together they constitute the state of Nueva Esparta. Despite the fact that the island of Cubagua, where Nueva Cádiz was founded in 1523, had claimed to be the cradle of the Spanish development of South America, Margarita, much the most extensive of the islands and with the largest population, has played the major role in the islands' history.

Columbus on his third voyage sailed past Margarita after coasting along the Gulf of Paria. As was his custom, he gave the island its name. He did not linger, however, to examine the pearl fisheries which the Amerindians had discovered, for he was seeking to return to Hispaniola.[1]

The comparative order of Spanish rule was brusquely interrupted in 1595 when Amias Preston and George Somers sacked the small island of Coche, and in 1662 when the Dutch brought destruction to Margarita. In 1811, the independence of Venezuela was declared in Caracas, ending three centuries of Spanish rule. A year later Juan Bautista Arismendi became Governor of the island for the new Republic. Four years later, General Pablo Morillo with a Spanish fleet reconquered the island but he pardoned Arismendi in the name of the King of Spain.[2] In 1817, once more the patriots took over control of Margarita.[3] After the war, Margarita settled down as one of the six states of Venezuela, named, with its dependent islands, Nueva Esparta because of its prowess in battle. Commerce was to take the place of war.

The pearl fisheries, especially of Coche, had become world famous. Similarly, commercial fishing had originated in Amerindian days. As early as the sixteenth century, Venezuela exported fish to Puerto Rico and Santo Domingo. Cubagua, besides pearls, also shipped salt fish to Hispaniola. Local production of salt facilitated the business, which two successive centuries of wars were to interrupt.[4]

In the nineteenth century, fishing continued to be a major source of employment for the people of Margarita and the neighbouring islands, many of whom were Amerindians. The small island of Coche became a fishing centre. The population of mainland Venezuela provided a useful outlet for the sale of fish, the more so as much of the land in the northern

[1] Cf. Samuel E. Morison, *Admiral of the Ocean Sea* (Boston, 1942), pp. 550-3.

[2] Cf. Salvador de Madariaga, *Bolívar* (Buenos Aires, 1959), pp. 507-8.

[3] Jesús Manuel Subero, *Cien Años de Historia Margariteña* (Caracas, 1965), p. 37.

[4] Arcila Farías, *Economía Colonial de Venezuela* (Mexico, 1946), pp. 65 and 177.

area was unsuitable for farming. Much of Margarita's fish catch was shipped to La Guaira, conveniently located for supplying Caracas. By the middle of the nineteenth century, when the Caribbean was politically tranquil, Margarita exported fish regularly to Trinidad. It also supplied the colonies in the Windward Islands. In 1873, unable to continue its salt-producing operation, Margarita handed over its salt works to the Venezuelan Government with the stipulation that it would supply the fishing industry of the islands with 400,000 kilograms of salt at an agreed price.[1] In the 1880's, Venezuela was supplying Germany, the United States and the Antilles with over 20,000 tons of fish annually, the major part from Margarita, although the mainland port of Cumaná had also an important fish trade.

Venezuela has today probably the largest fishing industry in the Caribbean. Currents from the Atlantic, mixed with the waters discharged by the Amazon, Maroni, Courantyne, Essequibo and Orinoco rivers, flow past the Venezuelan coasts and islands. A part of the South Equatorial Current passes between Trinidad and the Paria peninsula.[2] The effect of the rivers is to add to the sea plankton, which in turn supply food for fish. In Venezuela the fishing industry employs some 25,000 persons. During the quarter century up to 1962, the fishing catch increased from an average of 11,000 tons per year to nearly 100,000 tons. Margarita and the adjacent islands constitute one of the country's principal fishing centres.

The economy of Nueva Esparta is, however, becoming diversified. In September 1971 Margarita was established as a free port. This action was the more welcome since a similar project had previously been turned down.[3] Bonded warehouses were erected. The free zone will facilitate the manufacture of articles fabricated in Margarita from imported raw materials.

Active promotion of the tourist industry has been under way in recent years. Some thirty hotels provide accommodation and in addition to the attraction of long sandy beaches, the visitor from Caracas or abroad can inspect the ancient fortified towns and villages or embark on a day excursion to one of the small nearby islands. An hour by plane from Venezuela's international airport at Maiquetía, and provided with frequent air services, Margarita's future potential as a Caribbean resort holds great promise.

[1] Alberto Mendez-Arocha, *La Pesca en Margarita*, Estación de Investigaciones Marinas de Margarita, Fundación La Salle de Ciencias Naturales, Caracas, 1963.

[2] Levi Marrero, *Venezuela y sus Recursos* (Caracas, n.d.), pp. 401-2.

[3] *El Universal*, Caracas, September 17, 1966.

Chapter X

GUYANA

THE POLITICAL PATTERN

In the seventeenth century the Dutch developed the swampy strip of sea-coast of what is today Guyana[1] by establishing trading posts at Essequibo, Demerara and Berbice. Sugar cane plantations were established in the succeeding century. Men, often from Zeeland, used their native skill in constructing polders to reclaim low-lying land. African slaves were imported to work the plantations. At first the Dutch West India Company controlled the administration, until in 1792 the United Colony of Demerara and Essequibo was set up under the States-General of the Netherlands. Berbice remained a separate colony.

After continued dispute, in 1814 Demerara, Essequibo and Berbice were ceded by the Netherlands to Great Britain in the Treaty of London. Great Britain unified the three territories as the colony of British Guiana in 1831 with Stabroek renamed Georgetown as the capital. By the terms of the capitulation of the colonies to Great Britain in 1803, the former rights and privileges of the people, including the Dutch Constitution and Roman-Dutch law, continued to exist. Great Britain had experienced increasing difficulties with its own West Indian colonies which enjoyed for the period advanced constitutions.[2] This may have contributed to its willingness to try out another system. The legislature consisted of two bodies: a Court of Policy of 4 official members, together with 4 unofficial members chosen by the Kiezers, elected representatives of the planters; and a Combined Court composed of the Court of Policy with 6 representatives added by the Kiezers. The Combined Court controlled taxation and finance.[3] With minor alteration, the Dutch-devised constitution lasted until 1891, when the College of Kiezers was abolished and election to the Court of Policy became direct.

Meanwhile the decline in the prosperity of the sugar industry caused

---

[1] British Guiana is throughout termed Guyana, the name adopted after independence in 1966.

[2] *Vide* p. 121.

[3] Cf. Burns, *op. cit.*, pp. 608-9, and Raymond T. Smith, *British Guiana* (Oxford University Press, 1962), pp. 24-5.

the white population to diminish. The rising influence of the middle-class Negroes accentuated the differences between the Court of Policy which voted taxation and the Executive Council which the Governor controlled. In 1909, the electorate was increased to about 11,000 out of a total population of 300,000.[1]

The British Guiana Commission, appointed by the Secretary of State for the Colonies, produced in 1927 a critical report which called for fundamental constitutional changes.[2] Next year, a new constitution was imposed on the colony by an Act of the British Parliament against considerable local criticism. The traditional Court of Policy and the Combined Court were abolished and replaced by a Legislative Council composed of the Governor, Colonial Secretary, Attorney General, 8 nominated officials, 5 nominated unofficial members, and 14 elected members. In addition to having an effective government majority in the Legislative Council,[3] the Governor also obtained powers to over-rule it. An Executive Council of 12 was set up composed of officials, 3 nominated unofficial members and 2 of the elected members of the Legislative Council who were also nominated by the Governor. The franchise was extended to women, just as it had been in the same year in Great Britain. The limited voting qualifications were retained. Financial control had been obtained by London at the price of retarded political development.

Apart from greatly increasing the power of the Colonial Office in the colony, the new constitution resulted in the British controlled sugar industry and other commercial enterprises receiving representation on the Executive Council. The losers were the Guyanese middle-class, often Negroes, whose restraining influence of the veto under the former constitution had been weakened.

Certainly the dual system had been difficult to apply and had doubtless proved frustrating to the establishment. Plenty of precedents existed for the action. Jamaica had been persuaded to abolish its old-established constitution in 1865. Of the other British colonies in the Caribbean, only Barbados and the Bahamas retained their original representative systems.[4]

However strong the case for the nineteenth-century constitutional changes, it was substantially less convincing six decades later. Indeed, only two years after the ending of Jamaica's colonial constitution, the British North America Act was passed which led to the formation of

[1] Cf. *Guyana*, Central Office of Information (H.M.S.O., London, 1966), p. 7.
[2] *Report of the British Guiana Commission, April 1927*, Cmd. 2841.
[3] Unofficial nominated members were expected to support the Government.
[4] *Vide* p. 122.

the Dominion of Canada. An admirable opportunity existed for a modification of Guyana's constitution; not to give more power to the Colonial Office but to increase the participation in government of the new middle-class of the colony through the widening of the franchise. L. S. Amery, Secretary of State for the Colonies, had the responsibility of the decision. Intellectually able and exceptionally widely travelled in the British Empire, he was usually far-seeing in constitutional matters. On this occasion, the opportunity of training an increasing number of Guyanese in politics was thrown away. It is certainly arguable that a more liberal policy over the franchise and the powers of elected members would have greatly enlarged the chances of a peaceful transition in due course to independence. In the outcome, events could hardly have been more disastrous. Professor Raymond T. Smith noted that 1928 became known as the year of the rape of the constitution.[1]

As in other parts of the Caribbean, World War II activated political thought. But it also had delayed the holding of elections in Guyana. The prospect of a General Election in 1947 aroused great political interest. In 1946, Dr. Cheddi Jagan, the able son of an East Indian plantation foreman, who had received his education in the United States, formed the Political Affairs Committee, with its own publication, *The Bulletin*. It was the forerunner of the People's Progressive Party.

For the 14 constituencies at the 1947 General Election, 31 independent candidates stood, including members of the Political Affairs Committee which did not however fight as a party, 11 Labour candidates, 7 representing the Manpower Citizens Association, and Cheddi Jagan as Independent Labour. The victors were the Labour Party with 6 seats and the independents with 8. Cheddi Jagan was elected for Central Demerara, but his American-born wife, Janet, was defeated in Georgetown. The election demonstrated the weakness of political parties, which was illustrated by the substantial independent successes, a characteristic of countries in the early stages of political development. One reason for the failure of the Manpower Citizens Association to secure the election of any of its candidates could well be its name. The electors of Guyana, like those of other Caribbean countries, would respond more readily to a party whose name professed to be more widely based than one designating a particular trade union.

Janet Jagan had accurately assessed the existing political alignments. As editor of *The Bulletin*, she advocated with her husband a strong leftist policy against the alleged exploitation of workers by the bauxite and sugar companies. Rioting at Enmore sugar-estate in June 1948, when five people were killed and some ten wounded by bullets from

---

[1] *Op. cit.*, p. 55.

police, exacerbated feelings and aided the campaign of the Jagans for the betterment of the sugar workers' dismal conditions.[1]

In 1950 the Jagans actively promoted the People's Progressive Party. Forbes Burnham, a leading Negro barrister, became leader of the new party, and Janet Jagan, General Secretary. *The Bulletin* was transformed into *Thunder*, the organ of the new party. By concentrating on the very real poverty in Guyana, an effective platform was built which appealed to both East Indians and Negroes. The Jagans proved remarkably talented in constituency organization, something not previously attempted in this colony.[2] While Cheddi concentrated on research, public speaking and propaganda, Janet directed her attention towards administration.[3]

In 1950 the British Government appointed Sir John Waddington to head a commission to report on constitutional reform.[4] The new constitution which followed provided a House of Assembly of 24 elected members, with the addition *ex-officio* of the Chief Secretary, the Attorney General and the Financial Secretary. An independent Speaker was appointed by the Governor. The State Council, an Upper Chamber, consisted of 9 members of whom the Governor nominated 6. Two were appointed on the recommendation of the Executive Council and one by the Governor after consultation with minority groups.

At the 1953 General Election, the People's Progressive Party ran 22 candidates and the National Democratic Party 14. Two other small parties provided a handful of candidates. In addition, no less than 79 independent candidates went to the polls. The People's Progressive Party won 18 out of the 24 seats, obtaining just over half the votes cast. The Jagan organization in the constituencies, aided by the resentment over the Enmore riot, had achieved victory.

The dramatic win of the People's Progressive Party soon led to trouble. Forbes Burnham was already Chairman of the Party, a wise choice in view of the importance of the Negro vote in the urban areas. However, Cheddi Jagan, supported by Janet Jagan, believed that the preponderating East Indian support for the party pointed to Cheddi as the most effective leader. The matter was temporarily patched up with Burnham remaining in the Government under Cheddi Jagan's leadership, but the seeds of disaster had been sown.

[1] Cf. Peter Simms, *Trouble in Guyana* (London, 1966), pp. 90-5.
[2] Cf. Morley Ayearst, *The British West Indies* (London, 1960), p. 117.
[3] Cheddi Jagan, *The West on Trial* (London, 1966), p. 91.
[4] British Guiana Constitutional Commission, 1950-51, *Report and Despatch from Secretary of State of the Colonies, 6th October 1951* (H.M.S.O., London, 1951).

Probably the P.P.P. had not expected such an outstanding success at the polls. Indeed, the wording of the Constitution also seemed to imply that it was designed for a House of Assembly representing several minority parties. A group of inexperienced politicians, dominantly trained as critics, could not easily weld itself into a team to govern. Moreover, the change-over to a new type of constitution imposed heavy work on government officials. Notwithstanding that he was leader of the House of Assembly, Cheddi Jagan remained as President of the Sawmill and Forest Workers Union, while Dr. J. P. Lachmansingh, Minister of Health, continued as President of the Guiana Industrial Workers Union. A similar course was followed by Sir Alexander Bustamante, who when Prime Minister of Jamaica retained his position as President of the powerful Jamaica Trades Union which bears his name.

A dispute over giving recognition to the Guiana Industrial Workers Union by the Sugar Producers Association caused difficulties in view of the entrenched position of the rival Manpower Citizens Association. Inevitably a strike resulted during which some 1,900 tons of cane were burnt and left standing.[1] Guyana lost about £80,000.

More serious, People's Progressive Party ministers presented to the Executive Council a Labour Relations Bill which was published in the Official Gazette. Basically the measure gave wide authority to the Minister over union ballots. Unions other than those associated with the People's Progressive Party saw in it their destruction. The Governor took the same view.

By now the British Government was increasingly perturbed over events in Guyana. The Jagans were believed, probably correctly, to be sympathetic to the Communist point of view. On October 9, 1953, the Governor declared a state of emergency: at the same time the constitution was suspended. The People's Progressive Party ministers were dismissed from office.

Whether other reasons existed, such as pressure from the United States against the People's Progressive Party Government on the grounds of its alleged Communist leanings, will only be known in years to come. The British Government may also have had undisclosed information on the same subject which caused it to move quickly.

A period of Civil Service caretaker Government followed. Meanwhile the smouldering dissension between the Jagans and Burnham flared into a split in the People's Progressive Party. Finally, Burnham left, taking with him the Negro strength of the party and some of the intelligentsia of the Colony. The clash was partly ideological and partly

[1] Burnt sugar cane becomes useless unless milled within a short period.

Anne Bolt

Guyana: bauxite mine near Mackenzie.

Anne Bolt

Guyana: hydraulic removal of overburden 180 feet deep near Mackenzie.

Guyana: sugar barges on the canals.

personal. Much more serious, it was to lead to an upsurge of racialism in the country.

Burnham, an Oxford graduate and capable scholar, was oriented towards moderate socialism. A fluent and witty speaker, he had very considerable influence in Georgetown. Jagan, less able intellectually, had charismatic qualities on the electioneering platform. His charm influenced not only the East Indian sugar-workers and rice-farmers, who looked on him as their leader in the struggle for a full recognition of their rights of citizenship, but also swayed many in other groups.

Probably Jagan and Burnham could not have permanently worked together. Both men were ambitious. Moreover, Burnham considered that he had been promised the leadership of the Party. A combination of the Jagans and Burnham would have been undefeatable. Tragically the two major parties in the country swung into opposition based on racialism.

Government, in effect by the Colonial Office through the Governor and his nominees, continued until the British Government felt by 1956 that further constitutional progress could be made. In Sir Patrick Renison the Colony had an experienced and strong Governor. The Waddington constitution which had not stood up to the 1953 crisis was jettisoned. Instead, a new constitution provided for a legislative council of 14 elected members balanced by 3 *ex-officio* and 11 nominated members. Despite not unreasonable complaints by the political parties that the constitution was less advanced than the former one, the British Government remained adamant in its support.

At the elections which followed in 1957, the People's Progressive Party won 9 seats out of a total of 14, giving it a clear majority. The Burnham group carried 3 Georgetown seats and the National Labour Front 1. After considerable discussion with the Governor, it was agreed that the People's Progressive Party select 3 nominated members, which gave them a majority of 1 over nominated and opposition elected members. On the Executive Council, the People's Progressive Party obtained 5 members against 3 officials.

The new P.P.P. Government started much more auspiciously than its predecessor. Janet Jagan proved an efficient Minister of Labour, Health and Housing. Opposition to the P.P.P. was weak. Burnham, however, began to reorganize his supporters as the People's National Congress. Racialism was advancing. The National Labour Front and the United Democratic Party had largely lost any influence. However, Peter D'Aguiar, a substantial Georgetown businessman of Portuguese origin, built up a new multi-racial party called the United Force, which was strongly anti-socialist. Associated also with the

P

Daily Chronicle, a Georgetown newspaper, he drew support from some of the more prosperous East Indian and Negro elements and also from racial minority groups, including Portuguese and other Europeans and the Amerindians of the interior.

In 1960 discussions took place over the entry of Guyana into the West Indies Federation. Party opinion was sharply divided. Jagan wished to remain outside, Burnham to enter. With the composition of the Federation dominantly Negro apart from an East Indian minority in Trinidad, the P.P.P. feared lest entry might open the door to Negro immigration into Guyana. Similarly, Trinidad had displayed during the short history of the Federation the greatest reluctance to unrestricted inter-island movement of population.[1] In the outcome, Guyana chose to remain outside the West Indies Federation, thereby contributing to its downfall.

Constitutional changes, wearisome even to the student of political science, continued to take place in Guyana. In 1958 the Governor set up a constitutional committee to make recommendations for further political advance. Following a conference in London in March 1960, a new constitution was introduced conferring on the colony full internal self-government: only defence and external affairs remained the responsibility of the British Government. At the General Election of 1961 which followed these changes, the People's Progressive Party won 20 of the 35 seats in the Legislative Assembly, the People's National Congress 11, and the United Force 4. On an 88 per cent. poll, the P.P.P. obtained 42·6 per cent. of the votes cast, the P.N.C. 41 per cent. and the U.F. 16·4 per cent. Party antagonism, merged with racialism, may have been stimulated by the use of symbols by parties. The P.N.C. took as their symbol a broom, with the slogan "A broom to sweep them out and keep them out".[2] Aggressiveness in Georgetown had probably damaged Burnham's chances. Inter-racial harmony had vanished. The election aroused world-wide interest. Rising tension between the United States and Cuba had caused the contest to receive far more publicity in the United States than would normally be expected.

Faced with financial problems, Premier Jagan decided to visit the United States, probably believing that he could dispel anxiety. Like Castro's visit in the previous year, after the latter's successful take-over of the Cuban Government[3], Jagan's was inconclusive. Neither visit achieved what the visiting Head of State had hoped for.

[1] *Vide* pp. 126 and 127-8.
[2] Simms, *op. cit.*, p. 151.
[3] *Vide* p. 11.

226

In Jagan's case, there were some in the U.S. Government who felt that the Cuban situation had been mishandled. Financial help to Jagan might steer him from the Communist path. However, when Jagan appeared on television, he was naturally asked, not for the first time, whether he was a Communist. His answers were non-committal and produced strong letters of criticism from the U.S. audiences. In the outcome, President Kennedy cautiously promised to send a commission to Guyana which would advise on the possibility of aid.

With mounting budget problems, Jagan turned to Nicolas Kaldor of Cambridge University for advice. As a result, his Government introduced an austerity budget which drastically increased taxation on rich and poor. Its impact appeared likely to fall most heavily on Georgetown, the only substantial urban area. Duties were raised on rum, beer and cigarettes. A Property Tax, a Capital Gains Tax, and a Gift Tax were imposed, which were to prove beyond the ability of the undermanned Inland Revenue Department to administer equably.[1] New customs duties were imposed to stimulate the creation of local industries.

The budget in theory had much to commend it; but in practice the new legislation was unworkable in a small colony. The timing, perhaps unavoidable, was unfortunate, following closely on a bitter General Election in which the victorious party was believed by many to be led by a man sympathetic to Communism. Moreover, the new taxes could easily be presented as being aimed at Georgetown, racially largely Negro and opposed to the People's Progressive Party. Hostility was further augmented by violent attacks on the budget in the Georgetown papers.

Opposition political leaders fanned the mounting criticism. On February 9, 1962, Jagan moved a resolution to set up a constitutional committee in preparation for a London Conference to discuss Guyana's constitution in relation to independence. Burnham strongly attacked the proposal and also led his followers out of the House; D'Aguiar then denounced the proposal and departed with his supporters. Meanwhile a hostile crowd had collected outside. In the following days, disorder increased. The climax came on February 16, when hooligan elements in the crowds got out of hand and started fires in the Georgetown business centre. In all, 56 premises were burned down, 87 damaged, of which 66 were also looted. The heart of Georgetown was destroyed at an estimated loss of $B.W.I.11,405,236.

The Commission set up by Reginald Maudling, Secretary of State for the Colonies, to report on the disturbances came to the conclusion that they were not the result of a deliberate plan to overthrow the

[1] The levy was in 1964 declared illegal by the Courts.

Government; and that they did not stem directly from East Indian and Negro racial tension.[1] The Report listed factors contributing to the discontent in the city, including a feeling of insecurity among the commercial classes who believed that Jagan's political convictions were increasingly assuming a Communist pattern, which would manifest itself after independence. Civil servants were discontented because the Government had not removed their grievances over rates of pay. Added to that was the hostility of trade union leaders who had personal grievances against Jagan.

The Commission likened the outburst of February 16 to an act of spontaneous combustion. The riots were not drawn from one race or one class. It commented favourably on the police, who "had performed their extremely onerous and difficult task to the best of their ability and capacity".[2]

Both Burnham and D'Aguiar attacked the Government on the proposal to set up a Constitutional Committee in preparation for independence talks in London. Thus the conference to settle the future independent Guyana opened inauspiciously in October 1962. Although the two major parties both sought a republican form of government, they could not agree on whether the existing system of single-member constituencies should be continued as favoured by the People's Progressive Party, or proportional representation introduced, which both the People's National Congress and the United Force advocated. The People's Progressive Party wanted the voting qualification to be from 18; the other two parties from 21.

Duncan Sandys, Secretary of State for the Colonies, had the invidious task of trying to achieve agreement among the quarrelling groups. Consequent on failure to reach a consensus, the conference was adjourned. Unfortunately the interval proved to be a year of violence. Despite the disaster of the Labour Bill of 1953, which had contributed to the suspension of the constitution, the P.P.P. Government introduced a similar Bill. Dissension erupted in the colony. In April 1963, the British Guiana Trades Union Council protested by calling a General

[1] *Report of a Commission of Enquiry into Disturbances in British Guiana in February 1962* (H.M.S.O., London, 1962).

[2] "If they failed in maintaining law and order on February 16, 1962 [the day of the major riot and fire in Georgetown], they cannot be blamed, for in no country is it possible to have available a police force large enough to control a sudden and extraordinary outbreak of violence on such an extensive scale." *Ibid.*, p. 61. One policeman was killed by the rioters and 39 were injured. Four rioters were shot dead and 41 injured.

Strike. The Union feared lest the Bill would give the Government powers to force the recognition of opposition unions, particularly the newer Guyana Agricultural Workers Union, which supported the P.P.P. A feature of the inter-union struggle, sometimes overlooked but apparent in the sugar workers' strike the following year, was that the old-established Manpower Citizens Association retained a very large number of East Indian members. Richard Ishmael, an East Indian but bitter opponent of Jagan, led the M.P.C.A.[1] No one was placed in a more awkward position than the sugar producers as Sir Jock Campbell, Chairman of Booker Brothers and McConnell Ltd., was afterwards clearly to point out.[2] A state of emergency was declared and a British regiment, in addition to the garrison already in Guyana, hurried in by air. The emergency ended in July after the Government had agreed not to re-introduce the contentious Bill. During the strike, ten people, including a British soldier, had been killed.

The team of Cheddi and Janet Jagan and their P.P.P. associates had continued to prove its ability in political organization; equally it had once more evinced the ineptitude of its political judgment. At a time of great racial strain, the appointment of Janet Jagan as Minister of Home Affairs, which included the largely Negro Police Department, was hardly judicious.

Jagan defended his Labour Bill on the grounds that it was based on the U.S. Wagner Act. In support he claimed that he had endeavoured unsuccessfully to compromise on the drafting of the Bill which was designed to protect the rights of workers to decide by secret ballot the union of their choice. He declared that the real resistance was inspired by opposition political parties and business interests.[3] Strong support for Jagan was expressed by Jack Woddis[4] and Keith Miles[5] in *The Daily Worker*. Both saw the struggle as an attempt by Government to free the workers from company unions. Miles specifically attacked the Manpower Citizens Association as being notorious for its close collaboration with the big sugar companies.[6] On the other hand, the

[1] Cf. Frank Taylor, "Race Madness in the Sugar Belt", *The Daily Telegraph*, London, June 6, 1964, and Rita Hinden, *The Times*, London, June 4, 1964.

[2] *The Times*, London, June 6, 1964.

[3] *The New York Times*, New York, June 28, 1963.

[4] "Government and the Unions in British Guiana", London, May 13, 1963.

[5] "An unholy alliance in British Guiana", London, June 12, 1963.

[6] During the course of the strike the following year, Philomena Sahoye, General Secretary of the Guiana Agricultural Workers Union, set out fully her union's point of view. She claimed that the struggle was not racial. Her union opposed the Manpower Citizens Association on the grounds that it did not sufficiently support the claims of sugar-industry workers. *The Times*,

British Trades Union Congress early in the strike sent out their own representative, Walter Hood, to advise the British Guiana Trades Union Council. Later it dispatched a further emissary, Robert Willis, whose good offices contributed to the final settlement. The striking unions, which had been greatly aided by the co-operation of the Civil Service unions, gained most of their demands, particularly when Jagan agreed not to re-introduce the embattled Bill.[1]

The P.P.P. also made full use of their allies. Control of the Rice Marketing Board afforded them a jetty at Georgetown which helped to weaken the dockers' grip on the port. Also control of the Import-Export Corporation (Gimpex) enabled the Government to import Cuban oil and Russian grain to loosen the strikers' blockade.[2]

The 80-day stoppage, one of the longest of its kind in Trade Union history, caused major damage to the economy of Guyana.[3] Strike-bound Georgetown paralysed most of the country's export-import trade. Considerable destruction of property also occurred.

The widespread publicity given to the General Strike underlined the international importance attached to the struggle. To the United States, deeply disturbed by Cuban events, a Communist Guyana, which had frontiers with both Brazil and Venezuela, presaged further danger. The country was far too near the approaches to the Orinoco, an important iron-ore route, for the Americans to be indifferent. Venezuela was grappling with Communist problems and stood out as a target for Castro's Cuba.

The international angle to the Guyana crisis was also emphasized by advice to the striking unions from their U.S. counterparts and by aid which may have amounted to $80,000 a week. Creole fears that they might be exchanging British rule for another foreign ideology were matched by East Indian fears of Negro rule from Georgetown.

The background of strife was not favourable to the reconvened constitutional conference in London. The representatives of the three parties failed to compose their differences. Finally they asked the British Government to solve the issues, agreeing to abide by the

London, June 10, 1964. In reply to her letter, Professor B. C. Roberts of the London School of Economics pointed out that the Manpower Citizens Association had negotiated substantial increases for workers in the sugar-cane industry. *The Times*, London, June 16, 1964.

[1] Cf. Frank Pilgrim, "Guiana Strikers Agree to Go Back", *The Observer*, London, July 7, 1963.

[2] Special Correspondent, "Towards the Point of No Return", *The Times*, London, July 5, 1963.

[3] Cf. *The New York Times*, New York, editorial, June 14, 1963.

decision.[1] Racialism had destroyed any chance of a consensus in the colony.

At the end of the conference, Sandys announced the decisions of the British Government. In his view, party politics on racial lines had caused the basic friction in Guyana. To encourage inter-party coalitions and multi-racial groupings, a system of direct election by proportional representation would be introduced. The country would form a single constituency. In order to encourage the formation of new parties, no minimum percentage of the total votes polled would be necessary for any party to obtain seats. The voting age would remain at 21.

The solution was an interesting one. For long the two major political parties in Great Britain in principle have opposed proportional representation. The theory postulates that the result will favour a two-party system and will usually provide a working—and probably exaggerated—majority which will provide effective government. In the British tradition of compromise, based on give and take between parties, the system has worked satisfactorily, nor has it worked badly in other parts of the Commonwealth Caribbean, including Jamaica, Trinidad and Barbados. In Guyana, however, racialism had poisoned relations. Sandys had clearly come to the conclusion that the weary struggle to provide Guyana with a new constitution had failed to bridge the gulf between the quarrelling parties. The rules of democratic government had been transgressed by the P.P.P. in 1953 and again after their subsequent victory in 1961. No bridge between the major parties had been found. The experience in Europe, where systems of proportional representation had been widely used, suggested that this electoral system encouraged an increasing number of political parties.[2] To many, particularly in Great Britain and the United States, that constituted a major objection to the system. On the other hand, in the impasse of Guyana, with co-operation between the major parties ruled out by racialism, any loosening of party allegiance could be desirable.

At the end of February 1964, a delegation from Ghana arrived in Georgetown to make a further attempt at mediation. Both Burnham

[1] Letter to the Secretary of State for the Colonies, October 25, 1963, signed by Jagan, Burnham and D'Aguiar.

[2] Sir Robert Ensor, in writing on proportional representation in Europe, points out that a new constitutional feature is seldom apparent immediately. After World War I, no less than eight new republics in Europe adopted proportional representation. All of them developed parliaments with an unmanageable multiplication of parties. "Political Institutions in Europe: Political Issues and Political Thought", *The New Cambridge Modern History*, Cambridge University Press, 1960, pp. 79-80.

and Jagan retracted from their firmly entrenched positions and an agreement to form a coalition government was almost reached. Ultimately, stumbling-blocks caused the Ghanaian mission to founder, but the Guyanese leaders were nearer together than they had been before. In May 1964, during a visit to Trinidad, Jagan requested Prime Minister Eric Williams "to use his good offices to explore the possibilities of a settlement of the political deadlock in British Guiana".[1] Following Williams' acceptance, both Burnham and D'Aguiar travelled to Trinidad for talks with Williams. Despite his firm undertaking (and repeated requests from Williams) to return to Trinidad for further discussions, Jagan failed to do so, proposing alternative suggestions. Lack of confidence in Williams' efforts was further underlined by Jagan's appeal to the United Nations at the very time Williams had proposed joint discussions in Trinidad.

In June, Williams published a report, addressed personally to Jagan, emphasizing his belief in independence as the essential prerequisite of Guyana's development but declaring that it was nothing more than a catch-word in the country at that moment. Williams was strongly critical of a lack of urgency regarding the national situation on the part of Jagan and the other leaders and of their failure to forget personal feuds in the national good.[2]

*　*　*　*

The gloom of severe sugar strikes, reminiscent of similar inter-union struggles in Jamaica but fiercer, overshadowed Guyana.[3] In February 1964, the Guiana Agricultural Workers Union, which sought to replace the Manpower Citizens Association as the major union for agricultural workers, and which was linked politically to the Jagan Government, called a strike which affected villages serving 80,000 acres of sugar estates. Whereas the General Strike had mainly concerned Georgetown, perhaps the grimmest and most ominous aspect of this new strike was the spread of violence from the capital to the countryside.[4] Many of the villages were inhabited partly by East Indians, partly by Negroes,

[1] *Report from the Prime Minister of Trinidad and Tobago on his good offices Mission, to the Premier of British Guiana*, June 12, 1964, Appendix, p. 1.
[2] "There was no readiness on any side to subordinate sectional interests or personal antagonisms or ideological vagaries to the over-riding national interest." *Ibid.*, p. 4.
[3] *Vide* p. 144-5. The inter-union struggles in Jamaica, however, were political and not racial.
[4] *The Guardian*, London, editorial, May 25, 1964. Cf. Thomas Buckley, "Racial Hatred Deepens between British Guiana's East Indians and Negroes". *The New York Times*, New York, May 29, 1964.

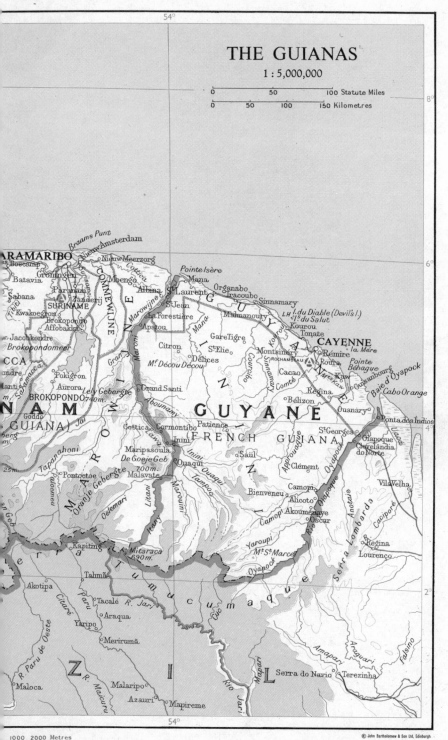

THE GUIANAS

1 : 5,000,000

| 0 | 50 | 100 | Statute Miles |
| 0 | 50 | 100 | 150 | Kilometres |

8°

Braams Punt
Nieuw Amsterdam

PARAMARIBO
Boscamp
Batavia
Groningen
Nieuw-Meerzorg
Cottica
COMMEWIJNE
Moengo
Albina
Pointe Isère
Mana
St Laurent
Organabo
Iracoubo
Sinnamary
6°
Sabana
Paramaka
SURINAME
St Jean
la Forestière
Malmanoury
LH
I. du Diable (Devil's I.)
I.s du Salut
Kwakoegron
Zanderij
GUYA
Kourou
Tonate
Tirti
Brokopondo
Affobakka
Aparou
Mana
GareTigre
St Elie
Montsinéry
ROCHAMBEAU
CAYENNE
la Mère
N. Jacobkondre
Brokopondomeer
Citron
Délices
Koura
Rémire
Roura
Pointe
Béhague
CCA
Mt. Décou Décou
Comté
Cacao
Kaw
Cabassou
ondre
Pokigron
Aurora
Lely Gebergte
740m.
Grand Santi
Régina
Baie d'Oyapock
Cabo Orange
Manti
Belizon
Bélizon
NAM
Aboumany
GUYANE
Goddo
(GUIANA)
Jai
Gottica
Cormontibo
Patience
Ouanary
Ponta dos Índios
4°
m.
Inini
FRENCH
GUIANA
St Georges
Oiapoque
Clevelândia
do Norte
Tapanahoni
Maripasoula
De Goeje Geb.
700m.
Malavate
Saül
Clément
Oyapock
Pontoetoe
Orange Gebergte
Ouaqui
Ouaqui
Camopi
VilaVelha
Litani
Tampoc
Bienvenu
Alicoto
Akoumékaye
Oscar
Serra Lombarda
Kapiting
Mitaraca
690m.
Marouini
Camopi
Yaroupi
Mt. St Marcel
Régina
Lourenço
Tahmã
Tumucumaque
Oyapock
2°
Akotipa
Paru
Tacalé
R. Jari
Araqua
Citaré
Caciporé
Yaripo
Merirumã
Amapari
Anguari
Falsino
Maloca
R. Paru de Oeste
Malaripo
Azauri
Mapireme
Rio Jari
Mapari
Serra do Navio
Terezinha

© John Bartholomew & Son Ltd., Edinburgh

1000 2000 Metres

3280 6560 Feet

54°

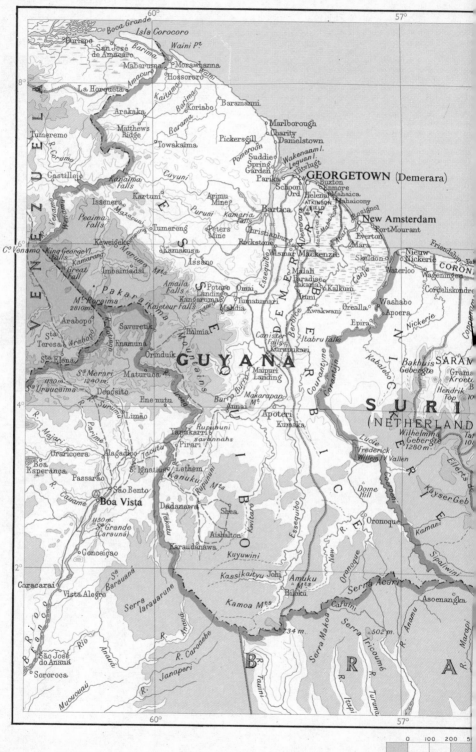

and much of the violence was caused by clashes between M.P.C.A. workers who wished to work and G.A.W.U. supporters who did not. As the strike progressed, an increasing number of attacks by majorities on minorities by both the racial groups caused destruction and death.[1] At the end of May, British troops were again sent out from England, and for the first time army units had to be moved to the countryside to restore order.[2] In June 1964, after 70 people had been killed and 400 to 500 injured, the Government assumed emergency powers.

Tragically the East Indian and the Negro were each learning to look on the other as the enemy. The concept of co-operation between races, whose forebears had often reluctantly entered the new land to change an empty tract of South American jungle into a viable country, had failed to take root. The strikes in Guyana were basically racial, but they also had an element of town versus country.

At the end of July the sugar strike was called off. It had lasted over five months and those killed numbered 159. To hold elections in such an aftermath of hate and fear presented a hazard. Yet the contest passed off quietly on December 7, 1964. A Commonwealth team of observers commented favourably on its conduct.

The P.P.P. came first with 45·88 per cent. of the votes cast and 24 seats; the P.N.C. obtained 40·5 per cent. and 22 seats, and the United Force 12·41 per cent. and 7 seats. The astonishingly high figure of 96 per cent. of the electorate of just under a quarter of a million persons voted. In the outcome the gamble which Sandys had taken to break the deadlock between the two large racial parties had been substantially justified. Neither major party could form a government without the United Force unless they sank their differences. Moreover, the substantial U.F. poll might well encourage the founding of further parties in the future. Whatever objections proportional representation may have in countries desiring a strong government, any change from single party control of Guyana had much to commend it. Treating the whole country as one constituency had also the by-product of discouraging the type of member who concentrated his major parliamentary work on obtaining favours for his own constituency.

---

[1] On June 1, 1964, Janet Jagan resigned from the Government, at the same time bitterly attacking the police force for discrimination against the East Indian community. At this moment peace talks between Jagan on the one hand and Burnham and D'Aguiar on the other were taking place. The two Opposition leaders promptly walked out and the talks collapsed.

[2] The entire East Indian population, totalling some 1,000 persons, under the protection of British troops had to be evacuated from villages in the Demerara River area. "More Troops Being Sent to British Guiana", Latin American Correspondent, *The Times*, London, May 27, 1964.

After consultation with the three party leaders, the Governor invited Burnham to form a Government. The P.N.C. leader agreed with D'Aguiar to form a coalition in which the 13-member cabinet had 3 U.F. representatives. D'Aguiar became Minister of Finance with Burnham as Premier. Jagan, however, refused to resign and the British Government had to secure his removal from office.[1]

Early achievement of an independent Guyana ranked as a priority for the new government. The conference to consider the constitutional forward move was held in London in 1965, presided over by Anthony Greenwood, Secretary of State for the Colonies. Six members each from the People's National Congress and the United Force attended, together with the representatives of the British Government. The People's Progressive Party refused to participate on the grounds that a state of emergency existed in Guyana; that political persons were in detention; and that the electoral system of proportional representation was unacceptable to a majority of the people.

Guyana was chosen as the name of the new country which would recognize the Queen as Head of State, represented by a Governor-General. After January 1, 1969, the Guyana Parliament could by a majority establish a republic modelled on the parliamentary system. Guyana would join the Commonwealth and would also apply for membership in the United Nations. The unicameral legislature was composed of a National Assembly of 53 members with a life of five years. Proportional representation would be maintained but could in the future be modified to provide for a measure of constituency representation.[2]

An interesting feature included the appointment, on the advice of the Prime Minister, of 4 ministers who did not require to be elected members of the Legislature but could sit as non-voting members of the Assembly. Despite the abolition of an Upper House, a neat method of appointing a minister who was not an elected member had been found. The method might well turn out to be an improvement on the system of a nominated Senate, adopted, for example, in Jamaica, where senior ministerial posts could only be held by members of the Lower House. The appointment of an ombudsman to be made by the Prime Minister

[1] "There is a strange tragi-comic atmosphere in British Guiana about this latest constitutional extravaganza. With the bland logic of one who confounds the English by simply not playing cricket, Dr. Jagan has dared them to remove him from office—a possibility which had never occurred to the legal brains which drafted and redrafted the Constitution." Frank Pilgrim, "Jagan fights to stop new Premier", *The Observer*, London, December 13, 1964.

[2] *Report of the British Guiana Independence Conference 1965*, Cmnd. 2849 (H.M.S.O., London, 1965), pp. 8, 9 and 12-15.

after consultation with the leader of the opposition was an interesting innovation. His duties would be to draw attention to administrative deficiencies rather than to criticize policy.[1]

The role of the United States in the continuing Guyanese crises merits consideration. Remote from the continental United States, the area might have seemed of secondary importance. Yet newspaper, radio and television comment make it clear that American interest has remained throughout at a high level.

The interest developed after the U.S. entry into World War II in 1941. The limited range of aeroplanes contributed to the establishment of the South Atlantic transport route via Brazil and Liberia to Cairo. At the American end, airfields were established in the Caribbean and Central America, manned by U.S. personnel. In South America, the Guianas were conveniently located and under Allied control.

A large airfield was constructed at Atkinson Field near the Demerara River south of Georgetown. The installation was impressive with a look of permanence even to the construction of a hydroponic garden to provide fresh vegetables for the station. So dense was the surrounding forest that the airfield commander remarked to the author that when a plane crashed just after take off, it had taken five days cutting through the bush to reach it, notwithstanding that the spot of the accident had been pinpointed from the airfield.

Peace came and in due course the United States withdrew its forces and the airfield was turned mainly to civilian use.[2] The interest of the United States in Guyana seemed to have dimmed.

Ironically it was re-activated by the education at two American universities of a young Guyanese student who was to marry an American girl of strong Marxist convictions. It is most questionable if the course of events in Guyana would have followed the course they did but for the great talent of Janet Jagan for political organization, something that no one with experience in that particular field can fail to notice.

[1] "By these and other explicit measures the Constitution seeks, as much as any constitution can, by guiding and shaping the Government's practices, to compel it to behave in keeping with the unwritten traditions of British parliamentarianism." B. A. N. Collins, "Independence for Guyana", *The World Today*, London, June 1966.

[2] A new agreement was signed on May 26, 1966. The United States was granted "contingency" rights to use the Atkinson Airbase over the next seventeen years. These rights included authority for U.S. Government aircraft to overfly Guyana and to use base facilities on a temporary footing. *Caribbean Monthly Bulletin*, Institute of Caribbean Studies, University of Puerto Rico, Río Piedras, Puerto Rico, September 1966.

American diplomacy since World War II had encouraged, and had sometimes appeared even to hustle, its British, French and Dutch N.A.T.O. partners towards colonial relinquishment. In Guyana pressure seems to have been applied in a contrary sense. All through the series of Guyanese crises, the American presence was admitted inside the United States and beyond.[1] Support by the strongly anti-Communist U.S. Trades Unions for the T.U.C. in Guyana confirms the U.S. attitude.[2]

British comment also tacitly accepted the existence of strong U.S. pressure.[3] Jagan, who may on this subject be biased, had no doubts. Just before the end of his Premiership, he wrote that it was no secret that the U.S. Government regarded his Government as a security risk in its main sphere of influence. He claimed that the U.S. attitude was backed by "subversive activities of various U.S. agencies" which had encouraged irresponsible opposition to his government and had made a compromise and settlement impossible.[4] Later, when in opposition, Jagan strongly attacked American policy during a visit to Havana, claiming the United States had financed opposition parties in Guyana.[5] A few days later Brindley Benn, Chairman of the P.P.P., claimed at a Cairo press conference that "U.S. imperialism" was giving financial and military support to the Guyana Government. He charged that it was paying one hundred thousand dollars a week to the reactionary trade

[1] Writing from Georgetown, Richard Eder comments, "Furthermore, United States policy, which weighs heavily here, is an unconditional rejection of Dr. Jagan and strong opposition to any participation by him in the Government. The United States Government believes that despite his rather confusing statements on the subject of Communism, Dr. Jagan is tied to international Communist movement." "Election Brings Guiana No Closer to Racial Unity", *The New York Times*, New York, December 16, 1964.

[2] Philip Reno sharply criticizes the attitude of the United States Government and that of the American Labour Unions in opposition to the Jagan Government. *The Ordeal of British Guiana* (New York, 1964), pp. 50-2.

[3] The Diplomatic Correspondent of *The Times* understood that the United States Government was urging the British Government to suspend the constitution of Guyana and revert to Colonial Government, London, June 29, 1963. H. A. Winslade, Special Correspondent, *The Daily Telegraph*, in an article quotes Cheddi Jagan as saying that the British Government was under very heavy pressure from the United States not to give Guyana independence. "Jagan says U.S. Pressure delaying Independence", London, July 1, 1963. Cf. Richard Scott, "U.S. Support for Britain over Guiana", *The Guardian*, London, July 13, 1963.

[4] Letter to *The Guardian*, London, September 11, 1964. Cf. Jagan, *The Weston Trial* (London, 1966), p. 441.

[5] *Hsinhua News Agency*, Peking, April 4, 1965. Cf. Cheddi Jagan, "British Guiana under U.S. Shadow", *The Daily Worker*, London, November 15, 1965.

unionist opponents of his former government.[1]   Others besides Jagan and his supporters were later to speculate on the part played in Guyana by the C.I.A.   In Britain the controversy even reached the House of Commons when Mr. Arthur Newens put a question to Prime Minister Harold Wilson on alleged C.I.A. infiltration of Guyana in 1964, which he parried by pointing out that he was not responsible for what happened prior to his Government taking office.[2]

Despite a boundary dispute which was settled in the nineteenth century,[3] Guyana historically had little contact with Brazil.   On both sides the boundaries remained sparsely inhabited, if at all.   Guyanese connections with other South American countries, apart from Surinam, were few.[4]   However, a problem arose after World War II due to Venezuela's revival of an earlier territorial claim on Guyana.   The dispute dated back to the nineteenth century.   In 1895 President Grover Cleveland presented the British Government with a near ultimatum when he announced that an American Commission would be appointed to settle the boundaries of Venezuela, which of course involved Guyana.   The moment was an inauspicious one for Great Britain, entangled in mounting South African difficulties and confronted with a hostile Germany.   Joseph Chamberlain, however, felt so strongly on the matter that after patient negotiation in London he travelled to the United States to discuss the matter personally with Secretary of State Richard Olney.   The Treaty of Washington of 1897 provided for a tribunal of five jurists[5] to adjudicate the dispute.   In 1899 the award was made based mainly on the Schomburgk boundary, a result very satisfactory to Britain but not to Venezuela.[6]

The prospect of constitutional advance in Guyana probably spurred the Venezuelan Government to press its claims since an independent Guyana might receive more sympathetic support in resisting a demand for revision than would a colony.   At his installation as President of Venezuela in March 1964, President Raúl Leoni announced that he

[1] *Hsinhua News Agency*, Peking, April 6, 1965.

[2] *Hansard*, April 18, 1967.   Cf. "How the C.I.A. got rid of Jagan", *The Sunday Times*, London, April 16, 1967.

[3] Cf. Gordon Ireland, *Boundaries and Conflicts in South America* (Harvard University Press, Cambridge, Mass., 1938), pp. 152-8.

[4] *Vide* pp. 311-12.

[5] Two from Great Britain, two from the United States, with the distinguished Russian international lawyer, Frederick F. Martens, as a neutral president.

[6] Sir Robert Schomburgk carried out exploration in southern and western Guyana on behalf of the British Government which led to a dispute over boundaries with Brazil.   Cf. Samuel Flagg Bemis, *A Diplomatic History of the United States* (New York, 1955), p. 420.

would press claims for about one-third of Guyana on the grounds that the commission in 1899 had exceeded its authority.

The Venezuelan case was put forward at the United Nations in 1965 in a full memorandum. It rested on the principle of *uti possidetis*. Venezuela claimed that the disputed territory "Guyana Essequiba" had always been part of the Captaincy General of Venezuela.[1] The British claim was founded on the cession of the settlements of Demerara, Essequibo and Berbice by the Netherlands to Great Britain in the Treaty of London 1814. Venezuela inherited all territory that was formerly Spanish on attaining its independence. The United States was in an embarrassing position. Plainly it had been a party to the boundary settlement of 1899. The controversy had the makings of a lengthy dispute.[2]

In May 1968 Venezuela again asserted its title to the disputed area, and by July hostilities threatened when President Leoni claimed a stretch of coastal waters off the disputed territory. In January 1969 a revolt of ranchers in the Rupununi district of Guyana, allegedly supported by the Venezuela Government, further aggravated the situation.[3] However the speedy air-movement of troops soon smothered the four-day uprising. In June 1970 the controversy finally reached the conference table in Trinidad at the instigation of Prime Minister Eric Williams. An agreement signed by Guyana, Venezuela and Great Britain put the affair into cold storage for twelve years.[4] The Protocol of Port of Spain inspired optimism in London, although Britain would have preferred to remain detached. In Guyana Jagan strongly criticized the moratorium as an act of betrayal by the Government. The

[1] United Nations General Assembly. *Implementation of the Declaration on the Granting of Independence to Colonial Countries and Peoples: Reports of the Special Committee: British Guiana*, Statement by the Representative of Venezuela at the Fourth Committee, December 7, 1965.

[2] Cf. Mitchell, *op. cit.*, pp. 16-17, 143. In February 1966, after discussion in Geneva between the Foreign Ministers of the United Kingdom and Venezuela and the Premier of Guyana, an agreement was signed whereby a mixed commission, consisting of members of both sides, was to present a report every six months. If, after four years, full agreement had not been reached, the matter would be referred back to the governments concerned and, if necessary, ultimately to an international organization or the United Nations. *British Guiana, Working Paper prepared by the Secretariat*, United Nations, April 25, 1966, p. 6.

[3] Cf. Forbes Burnham, Radio broadcast to the nation on disturbances in the Rupununi Savannahs, January 4, 1969.

[4] *Protocol relative to the Agreement to resolve the Controversy over the Frontier between Venezuela and British Guiana, signed at Geneva on 17 February 1966*, Port of Spain, June 18, 1970, Cmnd. 4446, (H.M.S.O., London, 1970).

likelihood that, in the event of a Communist Guyana, the United States would support Venezuelan claims seemed to recede.[1] Despite the moratorium, Guyana sought diplomatic support by strengthening relations with Brazil, which had virtually ceased to proclaim its territorial differences with Guyana.[2]

* * * *

In the 1968 General Election, Burnham won 29 out of the 53 seats in the Legislature, a somewhat larger majority than earlier predicted. For the first time all registered Guyanese living overseas could vote.[3] Of this very substantial number nearly all were of African origin, supporters of Burnham and mainly in Britain. Many had acquired citizenship and voting rights in their country of adoption and indeed never intended to return to Guyana.[4] Thus, despite the increased number of voters in the East Indian 21–24 age group, Jagan failed to make his return to power. Notwithstanding his allegations of a rigged election, Jagan's popularity waned after this setback. He visited Moscow in June 1969 to attend the World Communist Party Conference, and thereafter appeared to commit his Party more wholeheartedly to Communism. However, tension increased between him and his followers.[5]

This may indicate that, in future, politics in Guyana may be influenced less by racialism and more by ideology. The more bitter racial antagonisms are of recent making. Yet many citizens of all races and parties have come to realize the insupportable national loss suffered by the country, brought home by the violent destruction of property and life, especially in 1962 and 1964.

In February 1970, Burnham termed Guyana a "Co-operative Republic".[6] While actively encouraging overseas investment, Burnham

[1] Cf. Basil A. Ince, "The Venezuela-Guyana Boundary Dispute in the United Nations", *Caribbean Studies*, Vol. 9, No. 4, University of Puerto Rico, January 1970, p. 19.

[2] *The Daily Gleaner*, Kingston, editorial, January 7, 1971.

[3] *Representation of the People Act, 1968*, Georgetown, 1968. ". . . a device which secured 34,000 votes for the ruling People's National Congress as opposed to 1,003 votes for the People's Progressive Party." Raymond T. Smith, "Race and Political Conflict in Guyana", *Race*, London, April 1971, pp. 418-19.

[4] Cf. *The Times*, London, editorial, December 16, 1968.

[5] *Swiss Press Review and News Report*, Vol. X, No. 50, Berne, Switzerland, December 22, 1969.

[6] "What do we mean by Socialism in the context of Guyana? We mean, as we have said many times before, a rearrangement of our economic and social relations: a rearrangement which will give the worker, the little man, that substantial and preponderant control of the economic structure which he now holds in the political structure." Georgetown, August 24, 1969.

now sought simultaneously to gain control of foreign-owned concerns, particularly the bauxite industry. His dismissal of foreign volunteer workers from North America and the United Kingdom alarmed non-Negro groups. Furthermore Guyana established diplomatic relations with Russia. More than any other country in the Caribbean, except Cuba, Guyana has identified itself with the Third World.

The leaders in Guyana came to office as young men. The colonial system had resulted in their lacking previous administrative experience, a factor which probably contributed to the early split between Burnham and Jagan. Burnham had skilfully led his party to victory at the polls for the second time, countering Jagan's enthusiasm for Communism with a carefully considered approach to Moscow. Yet the more rapidly increasing East Indian section of the population may well obtain power in due course and stimulate the traditional tendency in Commonwealth countries for political change. How a Communist-oriented Guyana might fare in South America, with two powerful anti-Communist neighbours and a North America disillusioned by capital expropriation, remains an interesting speculation.

THE ECONOMIC PATTERN

Bounded on three sides by Surinam, Brazil and Venezuela, Guyana's effective communications are from its north-east coast which fronts the South Atlantic. Its size, 83,000 square miles, is approximately that of Great Britain, but its population is only about 714,000. It is nearly twice the area of Cuba, whose population exceeds 8,200,000, and is nearly twenty times the size of Jamaica, which has a population approaching two million.

The economic development of Guyana represents a struggle of man against nature. Never was the dream of an easy Eldorado to turn out less justified. The first Dutch settlers established trading-posts on the rivers which are navigable only for comparatively short distances from the sea. The Amerindians proved intractable for plantation work. As sugar prospects later developed, the Dutch planters imported slaves from Africa. An early rift between the races in the country may be observed in the tacit co-operation of the Amerindians with the planters to apprehend and return runaway slaves.[1] Unlike neighbouring Surinam, no bush Negro communities developed in the hinterland.

The early riverside plantations, mainly sugar and tobacco, began to be abandoned during the eighteenth century as the poor soil became exhausted. The basis of the modern agricultural economy of Guyana

[1] Simms, *op. cit.*, p. 34.

Guyana's Prime Minister, Forbes Burnham.

Savannah country in the Rupununi district on the borders of Guyana, p. 242.

Guyana: Dr. Cheddi Jagan addresses a political meeting.

rests on the strip of alluvial land, often below sea-level, which fronts the South Atlantic between the Essequibo and Courantyne rivers for some 150 miles.[1] The cultivation depth ranges from two to ten miles. Behind lies swamp and forest; in front a sea wall. The canals which intersect the cultivations serve to drain the land and to provide for the movement of barges which transport the cane to the factories. Originally grants to planters, each with sea frontage, comprised 250 acres. Today overseas corporations have taken over. Booker Brothers, the largest, is with its ancillary activities the major commercial concern in the country.

When viewed from a plane, the unusual system of cane cultivation is revealed and at once the pattern of the canals becomes apparent. The layout is highly efficient but costly to construct and maintain. Only large companies with ample resources could handle such an operation. The irrigated cane gives a high yield per acre; on the other hand, the sucrose content tends to be low. A climatic complication arises from two wet and two dry seasons involving two intervals of non-milling which is less convenient for the annual repairs and overhauls so essential in a sugar mill. Thus the advantage of controlling the cutting of the cane to provide a continuous supply to the mill throughout the year, a feature of some Peruvian irrigated plantations which have no rainy season, is lost.

The history of sugar production in Guyana is similar to that of the Antilles. The nineteenth century was a period of declining prosperity. Emancipation, which took place in 1834, was followed by the importation of indentured labourers from India. Many freed Negroes moved to the urban areas of Georgetown and New Amsterdam, or started agricultural smallholdings on their own account.

The lot of the indentured labourer was depressing. He occupied the former slave quarters and was tied for five years to the plantation where he worked. After completing ten years, he and his family could claim to be repatriated free of cost. The disparity in numbers of women compared to men, a third to a fifth, added to the hardship. The "ranges" of the houses could be compared to the "barracks" of the Antilles; insanitary, dismal and with a minimum of privacy; although to be fair, the situation in India which the immigrants had left was equally grim. Conditions for resident labour today have greatly improved in regard to housing, hospitals and community centres.

[1] "British Guiana is really like a West Indian island, sandwiched between the sea and the unoccupied interior. . . . The coastal strip is West Indian in its economy and problems, which are heritages of the days of slavery." Pierre Gourou, *The Tropical World* (New York, 1966), p. 149.

Rice cultivation has advanced rapidly in recent years. In the decade 1958–68 the tonnage exported more than quadrupled.[1] The crop is particularly valuable because it gives a livelihood to a large number of East Indian peasant farmers with holdings of 2 to 15 acres, and in some cases up to 500 acres. Two new rice development projects, the Black Bush Polder on the Courantyne coast and the Tapacuma scheme in the Essequibo area account for some 35,000 acres of the total 300,000 cultivated. The Guyana Rice Marketing Board disposes of all rice produced, both for local consumption and export.[2]

Cattle are raised in the coastal belt in swampy pastures. In the interior the Rupununi savannahs provide meagre pasture for a cattle industry which is further handicapped by having to transport the carcasses, often by air, to the Georgetown market.[3] Recent large-scale developments aim at supplying not only the home but also the Caribbean market.

Forest resources are large. However, the industry is handicapped partly by distance from suitable means of transport. As in Surinam and Guyane, road development is vital to future economic prosperity. In Guyana the few existing roads run in an east-west direction, broken by the rivers, although new roads are being driven into the forests. Even when a river is available, greenheart, the most marketable wood, is too heavy to float down the rivers except on rafts.[4] Moreover, the variety of timbers, a characteristic of tropical American forests, increases the cost and complexity of saw milling.[5] At best only 22,000 square miles of the forest areas covering 70,000 square miles or four-fifths of Guyana are considered to be at present economically exploitable.

Bauxite is Guyana's most important mineral product. In 1968 Guyana's exports of bauxite realized over £19 million. The production cost however is high due to the considerable overburden which has to be removed. Since 1969, in the free world, Guyanese output is surpassed only by Jamaica, Surinam and Australia. Reynolds Metals have mining operations at Kwakwani on the Berbice River. However, the most significant operation is that of the former Demerara Bauxite Company, associated with the Aluminum Company of Canada, which

[1] 1958—21,872 tons exported, 1968—95,729 tons exported.
[2] Cf. *Guyana, an Economic Survey*, Barclays Bank D.C.O., London, 1969, p. 16.
[3] Cf. *The Economic Development of British Guiana*, Report of a Mission organized by the International Bank for Reconstruction and Development at the request of the Government of British Guiana (Johns Hopkins Press, Baltimore, 1952), pp. 174-5.
[4] Greenheart is used for piles and wharves.
[5] *Vide* p. 256.

exports from its operations at Mackenzie on the Demerara River dried and calcined bauxite and aluminium. In December 1970 the Guyana Government entered into negotiations with Demba for majority participation in the company's undertakings in Guyana.[1] The talks later broke down, and in February 1971 Burnham announced the nationalization of Demba. Prior to this taking effect on July 15, 1971, an agreement was reached with the Government for $G.107 million compensation payable over 20 years and bearing a 6 per cent. interest rate. Such a confiscation was akin to similar action in Peru, Bolivia and Chile.

If the powerful restraining influence of overseas investment in the interests of the future prosperity of Guyana is removed and widescale nationalization takes place, a government which promotes such a policy might be disastrous for the country. Fears of possible repercussions from Burnham's takeover of Demba were widespread. Nothing can do more damage to the economy of a country than the ill-advised confiscation of foreign concerns. For Guyana to expand its economy, a full measure of help will be required over many years from more developed countries which alone can provide the funds necessary for industrial expansion. The Demba affair was sharply criticized editorially in Jamaica as having implications for the Caribbean that could be injurious.[2] Guyana faced not only the operation of the mines but also the sale of the mineral in a very complex and protected market.[3]

Manganese ceased to be mined in 1968 when the discovery of higher grade ore in other parts of the world forced the closing of operations. Diamonds in Guyana are the province of the small man: like alluvial gold, they have always attracted the adventurous individual. Guyana has sometimes rewarded the miner. In 1959 diamond production almost doubled, rising from 33,000 to 62,000 carats, due to a find in the Kurupung. By 1968 some 66,000 carats were produced, a useful contribution to the economy.

Gold, on the other hand, the dream of Sir Walter Raleigh, has so far proved a disappointment. The British Government, through the

---

[1] Demba denied claims that it had misused natural resources and provided foreign ownership with huge profits. Cf. *"Where did the money go"—The Demba Record in Guyana 1919-1969*, Demerara Bauxite Company Ltd., Guyana, September 1970.

[2] "The Caribbean countries have been receiving a great deal of bad publicity in recent years, and this new move might further undermine confidence in the area. . . . It is important to Jamaica's continuing progress that everything possible be done and said to let it be known that Mr. Burnham's thinking is not Jamaica's thinking." *Jamaican Weekly Gleaner*, Kingston, March 17, 1971.

[3] As from January 1, 1972, Phillipp Brothers of Switzerland became exclusive marketing agents for Guyana bauxite.

medium of the Colonial Development Corporation, helped to finance the expansion of the British Guiana Consolidated Goldfields and its subsidiary, the Potaro Hydro-Electric Company. Unfortunately the fixed price for gold and a very heavy rise in costs led to disaster.[1] Gold production fell from a peak of 138,528 ounces in 1893 to 4,000 ounces in 1968. Only individual miners, the "pork knockers", carried on the trade.

Conceivably the economic salvation of Guyana could come from mineral wealth. A large part of the country is closely comparable in geology with the metalliferous sections of the Canadian shield which makes a significant contribution to Canada's economy. The main difficulty has been the inability of detecting the minerals beneath weathered rock perhaps a hundred feet thick[2]; because of the same problem, Walter Link, chief executive of Petrobrás, recommended the search for oil in the Amazon be discontinued.[3] However, modern techniques are rapidly improving. It is hard to prophesy what the outcome of the search for base metals or oil will be. The author, who has been associated with mining in the Canadian West for more than thirty years, would hazard a guess that mining, including oil, represents the best—perhaps the only—chance of rapid economic progress for Guyana. Offshore oil investigation has recently been conducted, but results are not yet known.

Despite substantial cascades on its rivers, including the spectacular Kaieteur Falls, distance has so far impeded major development of hydro-electric power. The comparatively small labour force necessary for the exploitation of mineral wealth makes the need for the development of light industries, dependent in their turn on increased power resources, even more vital. The Government listed fourteen possible sites for power development as a result of reports by various concerns including the United Nations. In the coastal areas, the rough terrain and the cost of long-distance transmission has resulted in the employment of thermal fuels for electricity generation.

Political unrest together with the scarcity of good land, failure to develop enough new industries, mechanization of existing industries and a rapid population increase contributed not only to the growing rate of unemployment, which by March 1965 was estimated at 18·3 per

[1] The Colonial Development Corporation wrote off £1,200,000 over the project. *Colonial Development Corporation Report 1958*, pp. 7, 29-31.

[2] P. H. A. Martin-Kaye, Director Geological Survey Department, British Guiana, "Prosperous Future for Minerals", *The Financial Times, Supplement on Guyana*, London, May 26, 1966.

[3] Lecture at Stanford University, January 10, 1962. Notes taken by author when a member of the Stanford faculty.

cent. of the male and 27·7 per cent. of the female labour force,[1] but also to a declining *per capita* income. In 1966 the Government, in an effort to combat this situation, drew up the country's first development programme which was to run for a period of seven years. A team of experts from Guyana, the United Nations, the United States, Canada and Britain headed by Professor Sir Arthur Lewis took part in the drafting of the plan. Some $G.295 million needed to finance the plan was to be raised partly by soft and hard loans, partly by grants and partly by national effort.[2] One of the main aims of the programme was to move the country away from a heavy dependence on sugar, rice and bauxite. The Industrial Development Corporation, reorganized as the Guyana Development Corporation, was to promote new industries based on natural resources in an attempt to cut imports. All revenue-earning enterprises were to be put on a self-balancing basis and most would be expected to pay their way.[3] As an immediate step to reduce unemployment, the Government undertook sea defence projects and the building of roads and schools. The interior was to be opened up and possible new mineral deposits located.

The Development Programme brings out the wide possibilities of land development in Guyana. The Mahaica-Mahaicony-Abary Project is located in the eastern part of the Coastal Zone. The rivers which drain this area have too small a discharge capacity, causing flooding. At other times droughts occur. By major drainage and irrigation, an estimated 154,000 acres of additional farm land could be brought into use. At the same time the 140,000 acres at present under rice, sugar, coconuts, ground provisions and pasture would be improved. It was proposed to allocate $G.10·5 million for work in this area. The Canje area, some 979,000 acres, which is bounded by the Atlantic Ocean on the north and Berbice River on the east, could be drained and irrigated to improve existing farmlands and open additional ones.

The availability of these lands increases Guyana's future ability to export foodstuffs. To develop them, however, would involve finance far beyond the capacity of the country to supply.[4] (In 1964 a survey estimated that the total cost of the Canje Project would be not less than $G.100 million.) Moreover, the depressed prices for many agricultural crops discourage development. Nevertheless, the formidable increase

[1] *British Guiana (Guyana) Development Programme (1966-1972)*, The Government Printery, Georgetown, 1966, 1.I-8.
[2] *Ibid.*, p. 1.
[3] *Ibid.*, II-13.
[4] *Vide*, p. 243.

in world population may in due course justify the development of these lands using international finance.

* * * *

The origin of racial antagonism which has poisoned the recent life of Guyana is subtle. Certainly the Negro, forced into slavery, had a contempt for the Indian who had moved voluntarily into conditions not very much different. He may also have felt that his own bargaining position vis-à-vis the European employer had been weakened by the advent of an alternative source of labour. Although many Negroes moved from the hated plantations, some remained. The pattern, however, gradually developed, as it did in Surinam, with Georgetown and New Amsterdam dominantly Negro and the agricultural areas East Indian. However, both in the urban and rural areas segregation was far from complete.

Guyana prides itself, just as does Surinam, on being multi-racial. The Amerindian population lives in the little developed interior; the Europeans, Portuguese, Chinese and those of mixed race dominate the cities, where some East Indians also prosper in commerce. The depth of racial antipathies cannot readily be assessed. On the one hand the People's Progressive Party contains prominent Negro leaders, while there are East Indians who support the People's National Congress.

In his report which emphasized the disastrous position of British Guiana's finances, K. C. Jacobs clearly considered that the economic loss from the riots would not be confined to 1963 but would be "likely to go on as long as unrest engenders a lack of confidence". He added, "Crisis caused by continuing conflict and unrest clogs effort and the economy with it".[1] Nevertheless, the observers, including representatives from six Commonwealth countries who reported on the General Election of December 1964, which for the first time in Guyana was held under a system of proportional representation, stated that the elections had been fairly conducted. The poll had been "extraordinarily high" and in the opinion of the observers reflected the political conviction of the Guyanese electorate.[2]

The reasons for racial disharmony in Guyana are varied and elusive. Up to about 1950 little antagonism had emerged. The Negro population dominated the two urban areas. Education, as always in the Caribbean and beyond, tends to be better in the towns. The Negroes and those

[1] *British Guiana, Report on the Financial Position August, 1963* (H.M.S.O., London, 1964), p. 4.
[2] *British Guiana, Report by the Commonwealth Team of Observers on the Election in December 1964* (H.M.S.O., London, 1965).

of mixed parentage formed the natural source of recruitment for the Public Services, including the Civil Service and the Police.

Pioneer educational work was carried out in Guyana by the Churches. This was extended to secondary education which led to the establishment of Queen's College and Bishop's High School, acquired by the Government, as well as the Jesuit St. Stanislaus College and the Ursuline Convent School. As part of the plan to extend primary and secondary education, the Government is building a teachers' training college in the suburbs of Georgetown. Its enrolment capacity will be 300 and the Government has received from the United Nations Children's Fund a $G.50,000 grant for teacher training fellowships.[1] The University of Guyana, founded in 1963, is also being expanded. Buildings are planned on a site donated at the time of Independence by Booker Brothers near Georgetown.

The post-World War II development of effective malarial control revolutionized life in the country areas, mainly populated by East Indians. From being 40 per cent. of the population in 1891, the ethnic group advanced to 50 per cent. in 1960, aided by a rate of natural increase of 4·1 per cent. compared with 2·7 per cent. among the other components of the population.

At the same time, East Indians whose education was improving from better school facilities in the country naturally sought to play a more important part in the life of their country. The disproportionate number of better jobs held by those of other ethnic groups increasingly led them to criticize and complain.

Victory at the polls by the People's National Movement and the United Force in 1964, when proportional representation had altered, perhaps temporarily, the scales, caused the East Indians to press home their grievance of under-representation in the Public Services. Clearly racial imbalance exists in the Police Force, which led the International Commission of Jurists to recommend the accelerated entry of a higher percentage of East Indians[2]; however, the Guyana Police Force came through a remarkably testing period commendably well.[3] The standard of the Police Forces in the Commonwealth countries in the Caribbean is high: anyone who has come in contact with them would probably rate the force in Guyana as one of the most efficient.

The International Commission of Jurists stressed that racial disharmony was due in no small degree to the uncertainty and tensions of

---

[1] *British Guiana (Guyana) Development Programme (1966-1972)*, p. V-6.

[2] *Report of the British Guiana Commission of Inquiry* "Racial Problems in the Public Services", International Commission of Jurists, Geneva, 1965.

[3] *Vide* pp. 227-8.

a community passing from colonial tutelage to full independence. It went so far as to recommend that until an independent Guyana Government had an adequate and trained military force to cope with possible future disturbances, arrangements should be made for a peace-keeping force from outside the country to maintain order should the necessity arise.[1] The Commission did not specify whether this body should be supplied by the United Nations, the Organization of American States or the Commonwealth. Great Britain could hardly be expected, after Guyana's independence, to keep on hand a mercenary force for such a contingency. Bearing in mind the complications caused by the entry of foreign troops in the past to Caribbean countries, Guyana might be better advised to press forward expansion and adjustment of its own services.

*　　*　　*　　*

With the attainment of independence, Guyana is at the cross-roads in terms of economics as well as politics. Little investigation had been made to assess the country's economic potential.[2] The limited extent of its already developed resources is reflected in the high unemployment rate of its relatively small population.[3]

Taking account of the Guyana Government's propensity for nationalizing foreign-owned industry, and the even stronger views of the opposition party, the sugar industry may come under consideration for acquisition. Despite the complexity of sugar operation in Guyana[4] it became in 1969 the leading producer in the Commonwealth.[5] In a significant article a University of Guyana professor strongly advocated its nationalization.[6]

Guyana's links with the Commonwealth Caribbean rest on history rather than geography. As part of the South American continent and fronting the Atlantic, it has nevertheless retained its links with the Caribbean islands. Although it did not enter the West Indies Federation, it later actively supported the establishment of CARIFTA. While Guyana's membership may help to influence CARIFTA towards a

---

[1] *Op. cit.*, p. 118, paragraph (*b*), "Military Forces".

[2] An interesting comparison may be made with Guyana's neighbour, Surinam, which has already gone a long way in wise development of its natural resources. *Vide* pp. 312-17.

[3] In mid-1971, estimates of unemployment in Georgetown ranged from 12 to 20 per cent. of the labour force.

[4] *Vide* p. 241.

[5] *Booker News*, Georgetown, January 16, 1970.

[6] Horace B. Davis, "The decolonization of sugar in Guyana", *Caribbean Studies*, Vol. 7, No. 3, University of Puerto Rico, October 1967, pp. 35 ff.

British Honduras: fishing on the Belize River.

British Honduras: sawmill outside Belize.

The Citrus Company of British Honduras

British Honduras: grapefruit and orange plantations of the Citrus Company of Belize at Pomona in the Stann Creek Valley. The central factory shown in the centre of the photograph processes both its own fruit and that of other farms for export to Britain.

Anne Bolt

Belize City before the hurricane of 1961

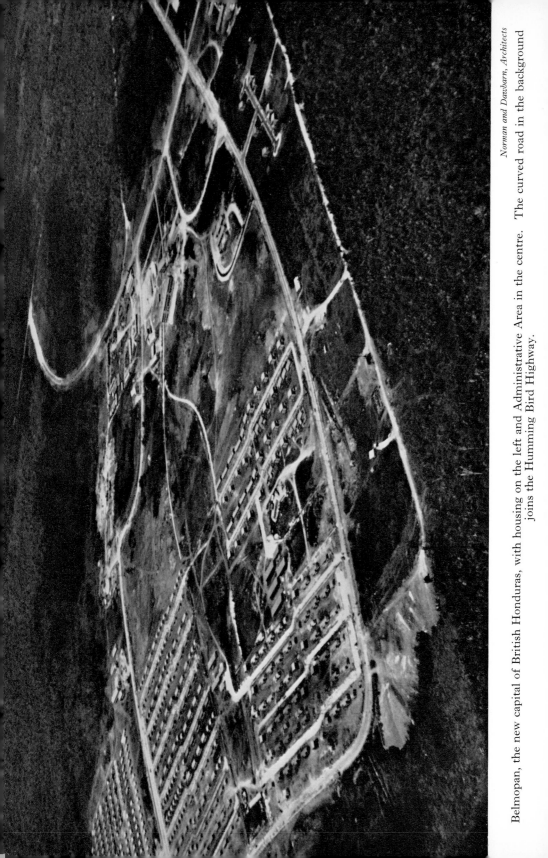

Norman and Dawbarn, Architects

Belmopan, the new capital of British Honduras, with housing on the left and Administrative Area in the centre. The curved road in the background joins the Humming Bird Highway.

measure of integration with Latin America, it remains a relatively small country in terms of population with limited development of its resources. Distance from its CARIFTA markets, including Jamaica, the largest member, involves added costs.

Guyana's two powerful neighbours, Brazil and Venezuela, have oriented their politics and economics towards the United States rather than the Communist bloc. Both countries follow capitalist systems of development. Its third neighbour, Surinam, constitutes part of the Kingdom of the Netherlands which is traditionally linked to international trade. Guyana's wisdom over its aggressive policy of nationalism, symbolized by the Demba takeover, may well be read as a warning to outside investors. Should new exploitable resources be discovered, rapid development is likely to turn on the attitude of investors from capitalist countries.

In the admirable supplement of *The Times* to mark the independence of Guyana on May 26, 1966, Guyana's new coat of arms was rightly given the place of honour. Below is the motto "One People, One Nation, One Destiny". More ominously, two jaguars rampant face one another. Perhaps each should have worn a party label. In the article which follows it is stated: "Whatever the political future of independent Guyana, her economy will still depend upon the mining of bauxite and the production of sugar".[1]

Guyana's way ahead is still open to question. Can two different racial groups drawn from two different continents and transplanted to a third, which they have in effect taken over from the indigenous Amerindians, work together, and organize the country, even with some measure of disagreement? On a workable solution may turn Guyana's future.

[1] *The Times, Supplement on Guyana to mark the Occasion of Independence,* London, May 26, 1966.

249

CHAPTER XI

BRITISH HONDURAS

THE POLITICAL PATTERN

The origins of British Honduras are wrapped in obscurity. From the sixteenth century, dyes made from logwood, which grows freely in many parts of the Caribbean, became a valuable commodity in the markets of Europe. Adventuresome British entrepreneurs commenced the cutting of logwood on the Yucatán peninsula. By the Treaty of Paris in 1763, England obtained certain ill-defined rights of cutting. Notwithstanding the eighteenth-century wars with Spain, the foothold on the Bay of Honduras was retained in areas not settled by Spain. Later Spain extended the logging franchise to mahogany. However, it was always careful to limit concessions to settlers to those of a usufructuary character, so that Great Britain should not obtain sovereignty over the territory. During the nineteenth century, Great Britain gradually began to establish government in the principal settlement which was at Belize, even before it claimed sovereignty. The Clayton-Bulwer Treaty of 1850 between the United States and Great Britain stated that neither party would exercise dominion over any part of Central America, which by then had broken away from Spain.

Guatemala, a new and weak state, was anxious to secure itself against interference from Great Britain on the one hand and the United States on the other. The boundary question was further complicated by Mexican claims. Mexico had claims on the boundaries to the west and north; Guatemala to the west. The whole area was thinly populated, as it still is today; the few inhabitants were Amerindians.

In 1859 a treaty was negotiated between Great Britain and Guatemala. Britain's purpose was to secure recognition by Guatemala of British sovereignty over British Honduras within defined boundaries, something which Spain had never given. Anxious to get the treaty concluded, Charles Lennox Wyke, the British negotiator, suggested the joint building of a road between Guatemala City, which is nearly 5,000 feet above sea-level, and a point near the Belize settlement on the Caribbean. The limited road-building facilities at this period made the project at best unpromising. Nevertheless, the construction of the road was provided for in the treaty although no money was in fact expended on it by either party.

Great Britain, however, had succeeded in getting its boundaries recognized by treaty, something of major significance in international law. On the other hand, Guatemala claimed that the provisions of the treaty had not been carried out. Meanwhile Mexico, like Guatemala a successor to Spain, made claims in 1865 during the imperial regime of Maximilian on the whole of British Honduras up to the river Sarstoon. Finally, a treaty was signed in 1893 between Great Britain and Mexico which defined the boundaries between the Republic and "the Colony of British Honduras". The northern boundary agreed was the River Hondo.

The Anglo-Guatemala Treaty of 1859 resulted in a change of British policy towards the Belize settlement. In 1862, at the request of the settlement's Legislative Assembly, Great Britain declared the settlement a Colony. The moment was opportune since the United States, a possible objector, was in the midst of civil war.[1]

In 1871 Great Britain, which had succeeded in replacing elected legislatures in most of the West Indian colonies by direct administration through a Governor, took over direct control of British Honduras when the Legislative Assembly abolished itself.[2] Crown Colony government was instituted. The same pattern of placing good administration above the political training of a colony, which was the gospel of the nineteenth-century Colonial Office in the Caribbean, was being meticulously followed.

Elections in British Honduras were restored in 1936 with reserve powers in the hands of the Governor. The franchise was severely restricted by a property or income qualification.[3] In 1954, for the first time, Great Britain conceded a constitution which could be termed democratic. Probably the weak financial position of the colony, combined with the traditional measure of Treasury control which accompanies financial grants, was the reason for this slow advance. Moreover, the scattered nature of the population in a country of poor communications, together with a substantial Spanish-speaking population, had retarded the extension of voting. Adult franchise was now conferred on all literate adults. The new constitution provided for

[1] The Anglo-Guatemala controversy is well described by Professor R. A. Humphreys, *op. cit.*, pp. 109-32 and 151-66.

[2] Cf. Mitchell, *op. cit.*, pp. 156-9.

[3] In 1945 there were only 822 registered voters; by 1950 this had risen to 3,695.

9 elected members, 3 official members, and 3 nominated unofficial members with a nominated Speaker. In the Executive Council, the control of the Governor was established. In addition to his reserve powers, he could rely on the support of the 3 official members and 2 nominated members, which gave a majority over 4 elected members.

Unfortunately, outside events had earlier disrupted the well-meant British intentions of political advance for British Honduras. Sterling was devalued in 1949.[1] British Honduras had maintained the parity of its own dollar with the U.S. dollar after the first devaluation of sterling during World War II. It continued to do so after the second devaluation. Although no other colonial territory did so, the reasons for holding the parity of its currency were important. Half of its imports, of which food was an important part, came from the United States; less than 12 per cent. of its imports originated in the United Kingdom. Agricultural implements and machinery and many other classes of manufactured goods were still difficult to secure from Great Britain. Due to the slow recovery from the war, deliveries were often very late. A further serious factor was the infrequent shipping services to Great Britain. In short, British Honduras was located in the dollar area.

Desperately short of dollars, Great Britain opposed the anomaly of one small colony's maintaining parity in its rate of exchange with the United States. In support of this argument, Great Britain could point out that the export trade of British Honduras was changing with an expanding citrus industry whose product was disposed of mainly in the sterling area, partly through sales to the British Government. Moreover, devaluation was likely to make the exports of British Honduras more competitive. As matters turned out, probably devaluation helped the future expansion of the sugar industry although this was not apparent at the time. However, opinion in the colony was strongly opposed to devaluation. The Governor was able to over-ride the opposition in the Legislature only by using his reserve powers.

Probably Great Britain made a political mistake. The public of British Honduras rightly felt that it had been over-ruled by London while the British handling of the final negotiations appeared clumsy. At a time when federation of the British Caribbean colonies was being actively considered and when British Honduras was one of the few territories that had substantial areas of suitable land for development, the quarrel was most unfortunate. By 1950 the newly formed People's United Party had obtained control of the Belize City Council. The

---

[1] From $4.03 = £1 to $2.80 = £1.

imprisonment of two of its leaders immediately enhanced the popularity of the party in a pattern that had already appeared in the Caribbean and beyond.

In the 1954 General Election, the People's United Party won 8 of the 9 seats on a platform advocating independence combined with strong criticism of Great Britain. Following the example of other British Caribbean territories, the party allied itself with labour through the medium of the General Workers Union.

A new group of enthusiastic young men with little experience had obtained a measure of power although this was still limited by the Constitution. Within the new party differences of opinion arose between the leading members. George Price and Nicholas Pollard quarrelled with Leigh Richardson who retained control of the General Workers Union. Some resemblance to the Jagan-Burnham split in Guyana may be seen in the power struggle.[1] At the 1957 General Election, the People's United Party led by Price and Pollard were the victors over the Honduran Independence Party which had been formed by Richardson. The decisive result which gave every seat to the winners was a tribute to the electioneering ability of Price, whose attractive personality, combined with his ability to address audiences fluently in either English or Spanish, made a major contribution to victory. The key issue had been Price's claim that Richardson, whose support was centred among the Negro population at Belize, had favoured entering the West Indies Federation. Again a strong similarity may be seen in the differing attitudes of Jagan and Burnham to joining the Federation.

A further complication arose in 1957 when Price led a delegation to London to discuss with the British Government the constitutional development and financial problems of British Honduras. Price was accused by Alan Lennox-Boyd, Secretary of State for the Colonies, of entertaining overtures from Guatemala through the Guatemalan Minister in London. The discussions were immediately broken off by the British Government, and Price, on his return home, was dismissed from the Executive Council. However, he still held the confidence of the elected members of the Assembly. Despite a break with Pollard, Price remained the leading political figure in the colony, with control of the People's United Party. He had the great ability of being able to make an appeal to people of all shades of opinion; not only in the Spanish-speaking country areas but also with the Protestant Negro population in Belize, notwithstanding that he was a Catholic. Again,

[1] *Vide* pp. 224-5.

making a comparison with the political pattern in Guyana, the ability of the population of British Honduras to avoid purely racial politics has undoubtedly strengthened the country.

The dispute with Great Britain over the devaluation of the British Honduran dollar antagonized public opinion in British Honduras which responded by opposing entry to the West Indies Federation.[1] In retrospect, the public of British Honduras may well have been right. British Honduras needed a heavy injection of outside financial help. The West Indies Federation required its money for other purposes. In the long run, British Honduras was likely to do better by getting help from Great Britain under the Commonwealth Sugar Agreement; and also from the United States, which had a profounder interest in the future of Central America.

In July 1963, an important conference was held in London at which a new Constitution for British Honduras was agreed. This took effect on January 1, 1964, and gave to British Honduras full internal self-government. The wide powers formerly exercised by the Governor were greatly reduced. They were confined to external affairs, defence and the safe-guarding of the terms and conditions of public servants. The country's government would be based upon a House of Representatives of 18 members elected by adult suffrage. The Speaker, however, who would be elected by the House, could either be one of its own members or from outside the House. A Senate of 8 members was nominated by the Governor. Five members would be appointed on the advice of the Premier, 2 on the advice of the leader of the Opposition and 1 after consultation by the Governor with such persons as he thought suitable.

In the past, Great Britain aided British Honduras with grants which involved Treasury supervision of the country's finances. At the end of 1966 it was freed from Treasury control.

In an attempt to settle the dispute between British Honduras and Guatemala, their respective Governments, together with that of the United Kingdom, called on the United States to mediate. In April 1968 a draft treaty, prepared by a well-known U.S. lawyer, proposed Guatemalan assistance to the Government of Belize in international relations and arrangements for external defence.[2] Not unexpectedly,

---

[1] Fear of increasing unemployment also contributed to this decision. In particular, concern was felt that the possible entry of large numbers of Jamaicans might depress wage rates.

[2] *Draft Treaty Between Great Britain and Guatemala Relating to the Resolution of the Dispute over British Honduras (Belize), submitted by the Mediator on 26th April 1968, Articles 13 and 14.*

although to the dismay of the United States, these proposals were firmly rejected by the Belize Government.

Price's P.U.P. returned to power in the 1969 Election with a convincing majority of 17 out of the 18 seats. A breakaway movement considerably weakened the opposition National Independence Party's chances of success.

British Honduras was expected shortly to move into independence, yet Britain still awaited a formal request for a constitutional conference. Prime Minister Price has emphasized his unwillingness to accept anything short of independence.[1] At present British Honduras enjoys a degree of internal and external autonomy. Yet the Guatemalan dispute, although not directly linked to independence, may affect Price's course of action, and he may well bear in mind the experience in Guyana in connection with the Venezuelan claim.[2]

*   *   *   *

British Honduras presents a striking example of the dilemma in which small detached countries find themselves. Geographically it is part of Central America. By the chances of history it was developed as an enclave of the Viceroyalty of Mexico and Captain Generalcy of Guatemala. Lack of communications cut it off effectively from Spanish territory. The presence of the early settlers or "Baymen" as they liked to be called, was tolerated by the Spaniards although Spain was careful to maintain its theoretical sovereignty over the Belize settlement.

Patient diplomacy enabled Great Britain to establish sovereignty over the territory notwithstanding tedious boundary disputes with Guatemala and Mexico. Belize, as British Honduras will be called when independence soon comes, presents intriguing problems. In area it is larger than several other independent countries, including, in the Caribbean, Jamaica and Trinidad, and beyond, Malta. But its population is minimal, barely 120,000 inhabitants. No minimum population for membership of the United Nations has as yet been fixed, but that of British Honduras is a small one to support representation in international affairs. From a defence angle, Belize might with advantage follow the example of Costa Rica by relying on a police force rather than embarking on the creation of an army.

---

[1] In an interesting article, Leigh Richardson, a former leader both of the P.U.P. and later the Honduran Independence Party, suggested that the logical step towards independence might first be some sort of Associated Statehood. "Three Choices for British Honduras", *The Daily Telegraph*, London, June 4, 1968.

[2] *Vide* pp. 237-9.

Nevertheless, to base an assessment of Belize's prospects only on the past would distort the view. In fact, the country has in all probability a much more viable future than have many other Caribbean countries. Overpopulation, the bane of the Antilles, does not exist. If a continuing investment of outside capital can be attracted, national prosperity may increase rapidly. The interest already shown in the country by large overseas corporations signifies their confidence.

Politically, the country, despite some internal quarrels of politicians and trade unions, has managed to avoid either racial discord or the pull between town and country so often noticeable in the Caribbean. Premier George Price, who more than any one man has influenced his country's political thought, might be compared to Trinidad's Dr. Eric Williams. Price seeks for British Honduras independence both as a Central American country and as one remaining in the Commonwealth. Although two apparently divergent concepts are involved, the Commonwealth is so elastic that he may achieve his purpose, particularly if an economic solution paves the way for a settlement of the boundary controversy with Guatemala.

THE ECONOMIC PATTERN

Twice the size of Jamaica, British Honduras comprises 8,866 square miles and has a population of some 119,000, of which one-third lives in the capital, Belize City. With the development of sugar and citrus offsetting the decline in forestry, the economy of British Honduras has undergone considerable change in recent years. Traditionally it had been built on the export of logwood, which, however, crumbled when aniline dyes were developed. Lumber was also important, particularly mahogany. The industry continues, mainly in the Cayo and Northern Districts, but much of the easily accessible lumber has been cut. The forests of British Honduras are costly to exploit because of the diversity of the timber which complicates saw-milling operations. Timber exports fell from \$B.H.3·521 million in 1960 to \$B.H.1·442 million in 1969.

The development of bananas in the Stann Creek Valley in Central British Honduras was ended by Panama disease, fatal to the Gros Michel variety intended for export to the United States. The Colonial Development Corporation invested considerable funds in trying to aid the economy of British Honduras after World War II. One of its projects was an attempt to re-establish banana plantations in the Stann Creek Valley, using the Lacatan variety which is resistant to Panama disease. The Lacatan fruit does not find a ready sale in the United

States but is popular in Great Britain and has been widely cultivated in the Caribbean. However, in British Honduras attacks of another disease, leaf spot, were so serious that Lord Reith, Chairman of the Corporation, announced in 1953 that the project was abandoned after more than £200,000 had been lost in the two years 1952-53.[1]

However, the fertile Stann Creek Valley, which contains some of the best land in the country, began to be developed for citrus. At the end of World War II, the British Ministry of Food made long-term agreements for the supply of orange concentrate to Great Britain. The arrangement was of particular importance to children in the United Kingdom during a period of continuing rationing. A factory was erected in the Stann Creek Valley which has achieved great success in canning grapefruit for export, particularly to the United Kingdom. Domestic exports of citrus products increased from $B.H.3·728 million in 1960 to $B.H.4·3 million in 1969.

The Colonial Development Corporation stated in its 1950 Report that the production of sugar in British Honduras was not commercially attractive. However, the colony was allocated an export sugar quota of 25,000 tons under the Commonwealth Sugar Agreement, of which it could only produce about 3,000 tons. The loss of the balance of the quota was threatened. The successful expansion of the industry commenced in 1955 when a group of private investors reorganized the small Corozal Sugar Factory, increasing its production to 27,500 tons in 1961. This dramatic increase, despite the interlude of a hurricane in 1955 which wrecked the factory, saved the sugar export quota for British Honduras. In 1963, the Corozal factory was sold to Tate and Lyle, who expanded it and built a second factory in the Orange Walk area. By 1970 the combined output of the two factories exceeded 66,000 tons of sugar. Production however had to be limited, since British Honduras joined the International Sugar Agreement formed to regulate world marketing. The substantial areas of level land suitable for mechanized cultivation and the high sucrose content of the cane make the country one of the most promising in the Caribbean for the economic production of sugar. The future of the sugar industry may lie more with those countries which have the most suitable conditions of terrain and labour.

Cacao has been planted unsuccessfully by the Hummingbird Development Company in the Sibun and Caves Branch valleys south-west of Belize. The cost of clearing the dense rain forest caused great problems. Finally, Hurricane Hattie in 1961 wrecked the young plantation and the company had to cease operations. Caribbean Investments Limited,

---

[1] *Colonial Development Corporation Report 1953* (H.M.S.O., London), p. 27.

with just over 1,000 acres under cacao, carried out a rehabilitation programme in 1970 to reduce the number of trees per acre.

The tourist industry holds potential. An extended Belize International Airport now handles jet aircraft which link British Honduras directly with the United States and thence Europe. Fort George Hotel, at Belize City, owned by the Commonwealth Development Corporation, made a profit of $B.H.47,716 in 1970, despite massive initial outlay costs.[1] As in other Caribbean countries, opinions differ over the advantages and disadvantages of uncontrolled tourist development. In addition too much of the profits goes on imported food, equipment and building materials.

Trade unions have actively developed and in 1962 no less than seven were registered and one Employers Association. Trade disputes have been limited in scope. Major industries, including sugar and citrus, afford employment which is partly seasonal: in consequence a relatively heavy incidence of seasonal unemployment occurs. In Belize City also the casual employment of stevedores and longshoremen results in many being out of work from time to time.

* * * *

British Honduras suffers economically from being a small country. For example, ships may have to be chartered to export the citrus and sugar. The lack of a good deep-water harbour adds to the cost of its import-export trade. However, the extremely interesting *Report of the Tripartite Economic Survey of British Honduras*[2] emphasizes the comparative success of the country, which had a *per capita* income of $437 in 1964, higher than that of many of the Commonwealth Caribbean islands and Central American Republics.[3] In fact, British Honduras has capitalized on its small population in relation to its land resources. Only about 5 per cent. of the cultivable land (over 2,000,000 acres) is in use. Historically the exploitation of its forests, particularly in areas near rivers, which provided the means of transport, only involved a small labour force. But the economy is capable of expansion.[4]

The views expressed by Jack Downie, the British Treasury Economist who advocated a positive immigration policy, appear to have been contradicted. He believed that only a large population could raise the

[1] Cf. *C.D.C. Report and Accounts 1970*, p. 56.
[2] Ministry of Overseas Development, London, May 1966.
[3] *Ibid.*, p. 2.
[4] The Government of British Honduras did not accept all the suggestions of the Tripartite Survey, but agreed with the main agricultural conclusions.

standard of living and provide a satisfactory income.[1] That a contrary policy has brought a substantial measure of success is significant, despite the drop in the production of lumber.

An annual rate of growth in aggregate gross domestic product of about 9 per cent. in real terms up to 1970 was estimated or a rise of just less than 6 per cent. per year on a *per capita* basis. The Report forecast, however, a serious balance of payments problem unless taxation was increased. It also stressed the need for an increasing supply of trained manpower.[2] To meet this need the Government have pressed ahead with expansion of the Belize Teachers' Training College aided by a Colonial Development and Welfare grant, while primary and secondary schooling is being developed.[3]

In August 1970 the seat of government moved from Belize City to Belmopan, some 50 miles inland, safe from the dangers of coastal flooding from hurricanes. The new capital city, built at a cost of approximately $B.H.25 million, houses the new National Assembly Building, Government Offices, Police Headquarters and the Public Works Department. Its big market with cold-storage facilities should prove of great advantage. In addition fully serviced commercial and industrial sites may stimulate local industry.

Membership of CARIFTA took effect in June 1971. Markets seemed possible for commodities such as corn, rice, peanuts, beef and citrus products.[4]

The boundary dispute of British Honduras with Guatemala has been reactivated and poses problems for both countries. Without a settlement, the entry of Belize after independence into the Organization of American States would be difficult.[5] Yet a solution for all parties is desirable. Certainly the Wyke treaty has proved unsatisfactory.

The 1859 solution, if impracticable at that time, might be reactivated in modern form for the long-term benefit of both Guatemala and an independent Belize. Guatemala has not unreasonably claimed that the

---

[1] "What I have in mind is a properly organized, sufficiently financed settlement scheme, intended essentially to establish new and concentrated peasant communities." J. Downie, *An Economic Policy for British Honduras* (Belize, 1959), p. 12.

[2] *Report of the Tripartite Economic Survey of British Honduras, May 1966*, p. 133.

[3] *Ibid.*, p. 78.

[4] Cf. *Caribbean Free Trade Association Ordinance*, 1971, May 26, 1971.

[5] In ratifying on March 18, 1955, the Charter of the Organization of American States drawn up at Bogotá in 1948, Guatemala reserved its assertion of rights over the territory of Belize.

development of its Petén Department has been held back by lack of an outlet to the sea. Instead of the "cart road" of those days, a modern highway might be constructed to link a reconstructed and deepened harbour and free port at or near Belize City, possibly internationally financed and managed.[1]

The advantages to both Guatemala and Belize would be considerable since existing facilities are limited. A fully independent Belize would in all likelihood develop more quickly with a modern port. Other interested parties, including the United States, Mexico (with ancient claims on part of Belize) and a Great Britain inside the E.E.C., might feel that the century-old problem had been solved.

To anyone familiar with the country, Belize appears to have one of the better futures in the Caribbean. Twice the size of Jamaica, its small population of around 100,000 makes possible an extensive economy of mechanized farming and cattle ranches requiring relatively little labour. The restrictions over mechanization of the sugar industry in countries like Jamaica—understandable as they are with chronic and high unemployment—do not exist. Its flat terrain lends itself to mechanized farming. With a stable government Belize should enter independence with trading outlets for part of its sugar to the E.E.C. through Great Britain as well as its U.S. quota. Its citrus industry in the fertile Stann Creek valley is perhaps the most efficient producer in CARIFTA.

Although the cost of clearing tropical forest remains high, as the Hummingbird Development Company was to find in the Sibun and Caves Branch Valleys, heavier mechanical equipment may provide the answer at a later date. In the meantime there remains plenty of scope for agricultural expansion.

[1] Although Belize City contains about one-third of the inhabitants of British Honduras, it is an unsatisfactory port with a shallow harbour. Sugar has to be sent by barge to Belize City and then transferred by lighter to a ship, a costly operation.

CHAPTER XII

THE FRENCH OVERSEAS DEPARTMENTS

MARTINIQUE AND GUADELOUPE

THE POLITICAL PATTERN

As a result of the French Revolution, French colonies were represented in 1790 in the Estates General. The Revolution, however, also paved the way for the slave revolt of 1791[1] in Haiti, led by Boukman, the very violence of which caused a reaction which enabled Napoleon, through General Antoine Richepanse, to reimpose in 1802 slavery in Martinique and Guadeloupe where it had been ended.[2] At the Treaty of Vienna in 1815 France put its signature to abolition of the slave trade; nevertheless French slavers, with those of other nations, continued the trade in black ivory from Africa to the Caribbean and North America, where slavery remained legal. Not until 1848 was slavery itself abolished in the French colonies, as a result of the efforts of Victor Schoelcher. Even then France's West Indian territories were in no sense a nation: planters and estate workers remained apart.

The eighteenth-century struggle with Great Britain for mastery of the Caribbean had been lost by France. French policy, however, continued Colbert's mercantilist doctrine of *l'exclusif* with trade tightly tied to the metropolis. At least an outlet was provided for the sugar and rum of the islands during a prolonged period of economic depression.

In the succeeding century, France's colonial ambitions were to turn mainly to Africa. Over its remaining West Indian territories, the original pattern of centralization continued; French colonies were given direct representation in the French Parliament in 1848. The concept had vision, for it meant that French culture, including the system of education, would be extended to the overseas territories, together with the right to French citizenship. The people of the Antillean departments were thus French citizens, even if in practice differences continued to exist.

During World War II, Martinique became a centre of world interest

[1] In the same year that the National Assembly decreed that persons of colour born of free parents were entitled to vote.

[2] Some 2,000 whites were massacred. The French even invited Britain and Spain in 1793 to invade Martinique and Guadeloupe to suppress revolution.

when the invasion of France in 1940 led the Banque de France to dispatch a large shipment of gold by cruiser via Halifax, Nova Scotia, to Fort-de-France, Martinique. Following the appointment, by the Vichy Government, of Admiral Georges Robert as High Commissioner for the French Antilles, a rigid blockade was enforced by British warships and later by those of the United States. The communications of the French Antilles with France were thus disrupted, and serious shortages of goods developed, while sugar became increasingly difficult to export to France.[1] During the period of Robert's governorship (1940-43), the French Antilles were brought to the verge of starvation.

France's centralized policy regarding its Antillean departments survived the crisis of World War II. Common citizenship permitted free movement between the overseas territories and the metropolis. Thousands of islanders in fact made their home in France. The Jamaican author W. Adolphe Roberts compared the French concept of colonies with that of ancient Greece; in contrast Britain and Spain followed the Roman plan of using overseas territories to enrich the colonizing power. Roberts believed that French culture was peculiarly suited to the Negro race, even though Negroes would not have accepted it as a thing imposed. "Intellectual tolerance by the masters, no matter how unjust their economic system, was what made it agreeable. Consequently we find colonies that have grown to be 95 per cent. negroid still passionately devoted to the country that shaped them and more aesthetically alert than other Africanised communities."[2]

World War II had paved the way for an ending of colonialism in French Africa and Indochina. In contrast, France's ancient West Indian colonies, together with Guyane and Réunion, were in 1946 reconstituted as four French departments, and became more tightly linked to the metropolis.[3] A prefect was to be appointed by the Minister of the Interior, while a General Council with limited powers was set up to deal with finance, including the departmental budget. The administrative services were modelled on those of France, and French laws were applied.

The experiment was novel and daring. To Professor Eugène Revert, writing shortly after its launching, the concept was a striking justification of France's policy of assimilation.[4] Victor Sablé, Mayor of Lamentin,

[1] The United States suspended food shipments to Martinique and Guadeloupe in 1943.
[2] *The French in the West Indies* (Indianapolis, 1942), pp. 66-7.
[3] Attached to Guadeloupe are several small dependencies: Marie Galante, La Désirade, Les Saintes, Saint Barthélemy and Saint Martin.
[4] *La Martinique* (Paris, 1949), pp. 504-5.

Martinique, was convinced that the greatest similarities should continue to exist between the political and social institutions of France and those of the Antillean departments. At the same time he thought it vital that economic planning and financial regulations should be moulded to the specific problems of the islands.[1] Many of the islanders shared his views. Unfortunately difficulties arose; the authority of the prefects gradually increased beyond that of the governors whom they had replaced, at the expense of the local authorities.[2] The General Councils proved to be ineffective.[3] Some of the officials and clergy in the French Antilles considered that the transition was too quick. Others found the change frustratingly slow. Even in 1948, the new departmental system was not yet fully in operation.[4] Much difficulty was caused by the lack of trained staff who could deal with the government departments in metropolitan France. Paris increasingly dominated the islands from both a cultural and an economic point of view.

The political concept of French citizenship presents undoubted benefits and attractions: France has given to the citizens of its overseas departments political rights on a basis of technical equality with the metropolis. A comparison with the constitutional organization of Puerto Rico, the Netherlands Antilles and Surinam emphasizes the difference. Failure has stemmed from the suspicion among the islanders that in practice a second-class citizenship has been offered.[5] Although many of the early errors were remedied, the stigma of discrimination lingered on to foster desire for an autonomy which might lead to independence.

In December 1959, serious rioting broke out in Fort-de-France. The French Government was on the point of dispatching a cruiser with metropolitan police on board when order was restored with the aid of police reinforcements from Guadeloupe. The most serious feature seemed to be the growing resentment against the French system, since the very nature of assimilation led to a far greater proportion of

---

[1] *La Transformation des îles d'Amérique en départements français* (Paris, 1955), pp. 176-7.

[2] Constitutional reform in the Netherlands Antilles in 1936 produced a similar result. *Vide* p. 293.

[3] The administration of the overseas departments was not identical with that of the departments of metropolitan France. Cf. Mitchell, *op. cit.*, p. 96.

[4] Cf. Georges Spitz, "La Martinique et ses institutions depuis 1948", *Developments towards Self-Government in the Caribbean* (The Hague, 1955), pp. 112-4.

[5] In Daniel Guérin's opinion, France's major mistake in 1946 lay in creating overseas departments which were deemed to be second-class ones. *The West Indies and Their Future* (London, 1961), p. 149.

"métropolitains" in official positions than of British in such positions in Trinidad or Jamaica prior to the granting of independence. In the police force, for example, this was very apparent to any visitor.

Much attention was given to the problems of the overseas departments as shown in the Caribbean visits of President de Gaulle in 1956 and 1960. During his travels de Gaulle had impressed on the public the importance of the links with France. Opposition from the Left, including that of an active Communist party, continued to be strong. The cantonal elections of June 1961, however, brought little change in the General Councils. The majority of the electors expressed their desire to retain the status of the islands as departments of France.

However, the struggle between those who favoured integration as part of France and those who desired either autonomy or independence continued in the Press and at elections. In a series of articles, Philippe Decraene emphasized the strong attachment to France throughout the French Antilles,[1] even though he compared the administration of the French half of the island of St. Martin unfavourably with that of the Dutch in their half.[2] The October 1962 issue of *Présence Africaine* of Paris was seized by order of the French Government which claimed that an article about the French Antilles and Guyane was subversive. In a joint letter commenting on Decraene's articles, E. Marie-Joseph, Edouard Glissant and Marcel Manville, who had recently written articles in *Esprit*, Paris, and *Présence Africaine*, declared that it was essential to remember that the masses in the French Antilles and Guyane refused to continue under the yoke of colonialism.[3]

Much of the criticism levelled against the French connection came from young men who did not want agricultural work but who found no other openings. Each year, over 400 scholarships were awarded in Martinique alone for secondary or higher education in France. The expansion in the number of those intellectuals who in due course returned to the island swelled the discontent.[4] A racist element also arose from the antipathy between the Negroes and the *békés* (white Creoles), who included many of the merchants and planters. Complaint was also voiced when the independence of Algeria led to the transfer

[1] "Terres françaises des Antilles", *Le Monde*, Paris, September 11, 12, 13 and 14, 1962.
[2] St. Martin, with an area of 36·63 miles, is divided between France and the Netherlands Antilles. The Netherlands Antilles portion is being actively developed for tourism. *Vide* p. 304.
[3] *Le Monde*, Paris, October 12, 1962.
[4] Max Clos, "Que se passe-t-il à la Martinique?", *Le Figaro*, Paris, February 25, 1960.

to the Antilles of officials who were regarded as having taken part in the repression in North Africa.

Military service in the French Army provided another source of grievance. Due to the lack of training facilities in the Antilles, many of the conscripts were transferred to France; some of these were ill-equipped psychologically and in consequence disliked their period of service. At the same time, the French Government introduced a realistic scheme based on the probability that the future of the overseas departments would be bound up with agriculture and tourism. The plan, named after General Nemo who commanded the West Indian forces, envisaged training the young soldiers in citizenship.[1] Work would be undertaken, at first in Guyane and later in the islands, on road construction, including tourist routes, the erection of buildings for small farms, and similar projects. Another purpose was to demonstrate to unemployed youth the value of manual work. Although doubts may have been raised in the minds of some who recalled youth training under totalitarian regimes, the project was democratic and aimed at breaking down racial and social barriers. In the outcome, however, Nemo admitted to de Gaulle that the results had been slight, since from 4 to 5 per cent. only of the young soldiers had of their own accord asked to remain in Guyane.[2]

In the November 1962 referendum, which sought to change the French Constitution in order to provide for direct election of the President, the Antillean departments strongly supported the French Government. In Martinique, for example, 63,679 voted in favour of the proposed change and only 9,295 against. In the General Election which followed, President de Gaulle's regime received strong support from the Caribbean, although author Victor Sablé had a narrow second-ballot win of only 648, in a poll of more than 20,000, over the Communist Georges Gratiant, who had led on the first ballot. In Guadeloupe, Médard Albrand (Union Nationale Républicaine) won easily at Pointe-à-Pitre, the largest town, while Pierre Monnerville (Union Socialiste de Gauche) easily defeated a Communist at Capesterre. The election showed that a majority favoured the retention of the existing association with France. However, a determined minority advocated autonomy or a separate state.

In the continuing debate over the future of the French Antilles, Jean-Marie Domenach, editor of *Esprit*, drew attention to press

---

[1] *Bulletin d'information du Ministère des Armées*, Paris, December 21, 1961. The scheme was also known as "Le Service Militaire Adapté". *Vide* p. 288.

[2] Cayenne, March 21, 1964.

265

restrictions including seizures of the Communist organ *Justice* of Martinique. However, *Match* of Guadeloupe attributed the cause of the repressive measures to the activities of members of the Organisation de la Jeunesse Anti-colonialiste à la Martinique, whose slogan was "Martinique for the people of Martinique". The newspaper observed that metropolitan France could equally well say "France for the French", in which event the problem would be not merely to find work for the 20,000 persons under 25 who were unemployed but also to house the 150,000 Antilleans living in France who would find themselves returned home.[1]

In April 1963, controversy continued when the General Council of Martinique requested the French Government to dissolve all organizations which, under the pretext of anti-colonialism, sought to take Martinique out of the French Republic and establish a nationalist government in the pay of foreign imperialism. The request claimed that a plot had been discovered by the police which implicated some young people. No details of the conspiracy were given. Cyprien Barrault attacked nationalism, claiming that anyone who demanded independence for Martinique or Gaudeloupe sought to exclude them from the national community of France with disastrous economic results.[2]

In the face of these pressures, in the same month the Front de Défense des Libertés Publiques was formed at Fort-de-France by a group of local organizations.[3] The group attacked the misuse of power by the Prefect of Martinique, who they alleged had created a restrictive regime. The Front declared that the administration was not in accord with the Constitution of 1958. It claimed that the Prefect was interfering in a manner which violated basic civil liberties, including on occasion the banning of public meetings, the seizing of newspapers and pamphlets and the interference with private citizens by the police. The group also criticized police examination of medical documents and the records of teachers, while it complained that the French radio in the Antilles had been transformed into a medium of propaganda. A frontal attack had been launched on the alleged suppression of the basic

---

[1] Pointe-à-Pitre, March 14, 1963.

[2] " 'Étroits sont les vaisseaux' ou l'entêtement colonialiste", *Match*, Pointe-à-Pitre, June 30, 1963.

[3] Amongst them were: Cercle Victor Schoelcher, Fédération des Conseils de Parents d'Élèves, Association Générale des Étudiants de la Martinique, Union Départmentale des Syndicats C.G.T., Union des Jeunesses Communistes de la Martinique, Parti Progressiste Martiniquais (Aimé Césaire, chairman), Fédération de la Martinique du Parti Socialiste Unifié.

rights of citizenship in Martinique by a regime presumably alarmed at the spread of Communism in the island.[1]

In May 1963, the Martinique authorities which had in April arrested twelve members of the O.J.A.M., transferred them to France, for security reasons, to stand trial on charges of conspiracy against the Government. The accused, whose ages ranged from 19 to 34, included a number of professional men. Deputy Aimé Césaire made a written protest to the National Assembly, questioning the legal grounds for the arrests and pointing out that the Martinique bar had protested the transfer of the men to France.[2] The trial in Paris was not held until November, more than six months after the arrests had been made. While the court admitted that the prosecutor had not produced sufficient evidence of any plot or attacks on the part of the O.J.A.M., throughout its verdict it insisted that the nature of the organization was clandestine and subversive. It also suggested ingratitude toward France on the part of the accused Martiniquais. Of the accused, five were found guilty. They received prison sentences of from three years to eighteen months.[3]

An appeal put down for hearing in March 1964 was postponed for six weeks, which caused the convicted autonomists to issue a communique protesting the delay, which they attributed to a forthcoming visit of President de Gaulle to the Antilles. Approximately a year after the arrests had been made, the appeal was heard. The accused argued that the O.J.A.M. was not a clandestine organization, adding "We merely say that we are not French; we do not say we are anti-French; we say we are Martiniquais". When the judge commented that Martinique had been French since 1635, Florent retorted, "Yes, but we had to wait until 1835 to acquire French citizenship".

The Court found the platform and manifestos of O.J.A.M. illegal, and the slogan "La Martinique aux Martiniquais" particularly offensive. It considered that the organization aimed at not just a new status but independence, and that its subversive efforts were directed towards the emotional masses, often unemployed, who might be moved to violent demonstrations. Although the Appeal Court raised the

---

[1] *Le Monde*, Paris, April 18, 1963.
[2] May 14, 1963.
[3] Hervé Florent, lawyer: 3 years; Henri Armougon, customs official: 3 years; Félix Lamotte, student: 3 years; Rodolphe Désiré, physician: 2 years; Victor Lessort, jeweller: 18 months. Witnesses for the accused included Senator Jean Geoffrey of the Section Française de l'Internationale Ouvrière (S.F.I.O.) who maintained that the overseas departments could not properly be termed departments of France.

sentences in each case by at least one year, they were suspended as a gesture of goodwill, in view of the youth, sincerity and visionary character of the defendants.

Meanwhile, doubtless concerned over the trial, conviction and sentences of five O.J.A.M. members, a meeting of some thirty persons, described by Le Monde as "leftists", was held at Pointe-à-Pitre.[1] The purpose of the discussion was to find an acceptable status which would best correspond to Guadeloupe's aspirations in order to preserve the heritage and to broaden its personality. The solution should correspond to social equality, history and to the common interests of Guadeloupe and the French nation. The situation in Martinique and Guadeloupe remained profoundly disquieting, despite the continued efforts of the French metropolitan authorities to minimize the problems while emphasizing the progress made.

Louis Jacquinot, Secretary for the Overseas Departments, had visited the French Antilles early in 1963. In May, a meeting of the overseas departments was held at the Elysée Palace with President de Gaulle presiding; Jacquinot and Premier Georges Pompidou were among those attending. The meeting decided to raise family allowances to the level of those in metropolitan France, a change which Martinique, Guadeloupe and Guyane had demanded since incorporation as departments of France in 1946. Industrialization would be encouraged. Martinique and Guadeloupe would each have a vocational school. Housing and television would be extended. De Gaulle's presence at this meeting tended to offset certain criticism since the measures, taken so soon after Jacquinot's return, appeared to be aimed at assuaging island criticism and countering autonomist propaganda. Instead, France was giving serious thought to the discontent in its overseas departments. In December of the same year, Jacquinot in a speech at Marseilles even took the line that no political problems existed in the Antillean departments and that assimilation with the metropolis would be pursued.[2]

In the curious criss-cross struggle between the supporters and opponents of adherence to the system of integration with France, Hector Dessout, Communist mayor of Pointe-à-Pitre, published a letter declaring himself against an autonomous Guadeloupe, notwithstanding that the Communist Party in Guadeloupe had declared itself to be in favour of autonomy.[3] Moreover, the Communist Party had

[1] Paris, January 29, 1964.
[2] Cf. Philippe Decraene, "M. Jacquinot réaffirme qu'il n'y a pas de problème politique aux Antilles", Le Monde, Paris, December 4, 1963.
[3] Match, Pointe-à-Pitre, January 2, 1964.

just denounced Raymond Guillod, Communist mayor of Bouillante, because he had signed a petition in favour of the retention of Guadeloupe's departmental system. Pressures against the Antillean newspapers continued, with seizures of issues of *l'Etincelle*, official organ of the Guadeloupe Communist Party, and of *Progrès Social*, also of Guadeloupe.

Supporters of the departmental system contrasted the generosity of France towards Martinique and Gaudeloupe after the series of hurricanes in 1963 with the inadequate aid given by Russia to Cuba.[1] Senator Lucien Bernier of Guadeloupe commented on the current status of Guadeloupe, emphasizing that like other overseas departments it shared the advantage of "adapted departmentalism".[2] With the right to review French policy which concerned its internal affairs, it was also the beneficiary of special credits and tax advantages. A new supporter of the departmental system in the Antilles appeared at Fort-de-France. In its maiden issue in January 1964, *France Toujours* supported the continuance of Martinique's association with France.

President de Gaulle visited Guadeloupe and Martinique in March 1964. When he addressed an enormous crowd at Pointe-à-Pitre, some fifty persons picketed the meeting with autonomist signs. Noting them, de Gaulle commented: "That small group will not change the magnificence of the demonstration".[3] He had an equally enthusiastic welcome at Fort-de-France, where the crowd of 25,000 broke the police cordon to greet him.

However, support for autonomy appeared to have grown in the French Antilles since 1960 when de Gaulle had last visited the area. No longer were the Communists the only supporters of autonomy. Deputy Aimé Césaire, one of the most influential leaders in the French Antilles, who in 1957 had dramatically broken with the Communists to lead his own Parti Progressiste Martiniquais, was now an outspoken autonomist.

To the autonomist slogans, de Gaulle countered that Martinique's only hope rested with France. He also contrasted the former French African territories which had retained their own languages and culture with the Antillean departments whose culture and institutions came from France. Soon after de Gaulle's return to Paris, further economic

---

[1] France gave some 40 million francs in aid to Martinique.

[2] "Sur le statut actuel de la Guadeloupe", *Match*, Pointe-à-Pitre, September 30, 1963, and October 14, 1963.

[3] *Hispanic American Report*, Vol. XVII, p. 235.

and social measures were taken in favour of the overseas departments. These, however, had a mixed reception.[1]

In May 1964, trade unionists, including teachers and civil servants, urged a repeal of the decree of October 15, 1960, under which civil servants and teachers in the French overseas departments could be prevented by the French administration from expressing political views. Nine teachers had been charged under the ordinance and expelled from Guadeloupe in 1961.[2]

These anxieties crystallized into action when in July 1964 an amendment to nullify the Ordinance of October 15, 1960, was sponsored by Senators Lucien Bernier and René Toribio of Guadeloupe and Paul Symphor of Martinique. However, the attempt at repeal failed when the National Assembly accepted the advice of former Premier Michel Debré to reject it. Undeterred, Bernier and his colleagues continued their opposition.

Discontent, often arising from economic causes, contributed to the rise of Communism. Although the movement was limited in extent, it caused anxiety to the authorities in both Antillean departments. For example, in 1953 the Communist Party won the municipal election at Le Moule, a small town in Grande Terre, Guadeloupe. Electoral fraud was charged. The departmental administration annulled the election and appointed a commission to run the small town.[3] A further election was held in 1957; again the Communists won easily.[4] For the second time the council was dissolved. In December 1962, a further election was held, only to be annulled the following month. Thus the municipal council of the town had been dissolved three times in nine

[1] Cf. "Le 'Plan Jacquinot' est diversement commenté aux Antilles", *Le Monde*, Paris, May 21, 1964.

[2] Edouard Glissant, the Martinique author, had also at this time been expelled from Guadeloupe because he had protested against the suppression of the Front Antillais et Guyanais pour l'Autonomie. For further details, cf. Mitchell, *op. cit.*, p. 104.

[3] Commenting on the Le Moule elections, Daniel Guérin strongly criticized the authorities, declaring that the Commune of Le Moule was prevented from choosing its councillors. "Falsification of the electoral lists paved the way for provoking fist-fights during which the urns were now simply smashed: the ballots, consequently, could not be counted this time." A second election was no better. "More frauds, more falsifications, more interference with the voting procedure were committed in the presence and under the protective supervision of the police and the gendarmerie." *The West Indies and Their Future* (London, 1961), p. 119. Cf. *Combat*, Paris, August 26, 1957; and *L'Humanité*, Paris, August 26, 1957.

[4] The Communists obtained 20 seats; the Rassemblement des Gauches Républicaines, 7. *Le Monde*, Paris, September 5, 1957.

years.[1] Charges of electoral corruption are frequent in the French Antilles[2]; nor are they unknown elsewhere in the Caribbean. The significance of the Le Moule affair resides in the continued pressure which the administration was prepared to exert on an insignificant and remote community.

President de Gaulle's visits to Martinique and Guadeloupe gave confidence to the Antilles. The Fifth Republic was showing interest in its islands: ministerial visits from France were becoming more regular. The installation of television was being speeded up. Income *per capita* had increased by 30 per cent. between 1962 and 1965. On the other hand, discontent was rife among agricultural labourers, and strikes had occurred on some estates, interrupting the cane harvest.[3]

At a press interview on the eve of the ministerial elections, Raphaël Petit, Prefect of Martinique, characterized 1964 as having been a difficult year because of the damage caused by Hurricane Edith. He was optimistic in regard to 1965, anticipating that the Common Market would be open to products from the French Antilles. Petit also detected a diminished drive for autonomy.[4]

At the Municipal elections in March 1965 Aimé Césaire was re-elected Mayor of Fort-de-France, while Henri Bangou, a distinguished heart specialist, won election to the mayoralty of Pointe-à-Pitre in Guadeloupe. Thus autonomists had won the two largest French Antillean towns. Nevertheless, the overall results did not suggest a surge towards self-government.[5]

However, the U.S. intervention in the Dominican Republic in May of that year resulted in protest meetings in Fort-de-France and criticisms in the local autonomist press.[6] In June, Rémy Bébel, editor

[1] *Le Monde*, Paris, February 12, 1963.

[2] "Pour qui a séjourné à la Réunion, par exemple, les Antilles françaises n'apportent dans le domaine aucun élément surprenant ni nouveau, et il suffit de dire que la combinaison et la fraude y sont constamment pratiquées, même par ceux qui n'auraient pas besoin d'y recourir pour conserver siège ou privilèges." Raymond Barrillon, "Les Antilles 'Poussières' sur l'océan", *Le Monde*, Paris, April 23, 1964.

[3] Cf. Gérard Viratelle, "L'autonomisme reste vivace, mais se manifeste moins", *Le Monde*, Paris, March 10, 1965.

[4] Fort-de-France, March 13, 1965.

[5] "L'audience du mouvement autonomiste ne s'est pourtant pas accrue si elle ne s'est pas atténuée. Durcissant aux extrêmes ses positions ou 'coopérant' presque dans le cadre de la départementalisation, et de la sorte très divisé, ce courant autonomiste donne plutôt l'impression d'être en sommeil et de rechercher un second souffle." Gérard Viratelle, "La situation aux Antilles paraît évoluer favorablement", *Le Monde Diplomatique*, Paris, May 1966.

[6] Gérard Viratelle, "L'intervention américaine a réveillé aux Antilles françaises des sentiments hostiles aux États-Unis". *Le Monde*, Paris, May 25, 1965.

of *Le Progrès Social,* was arrested. In three issues of his newspaper he had attacked the Guadeloupe administration more effectively than wisely.[1]

*   *   *   *

Despite their criticisms of the metropolis, Martinique and Guadeloupe were becoming more and more integrated with France. The very weakness of their economies, almost entirely agricultural, bound them to Paris, which in turn controlled the island administrations. France was showing increasing willingness to shoulder the burden of financing its historic territories. For example, 70 per cent. of the cost of new schools was borne by France; the balance, locally. Roads were categorized as in France: national (paid for by France), departmental and parochial. Numerous French civil servants helped to administer the overseas departments; in turn, many from Martinique and Guadeloupe worked in France.

The fact remains that many of the young men are autonomists. Some look with admiration to the Cuba of Fidel Castro. Both Guadeloupe and Martinique are flanked by British islands which have obtained from Great Britain substantial autonomy, at the least. Jamaica, Trinidad and Barbados already enjoy independence. The impact on the French islands should not be under-rated.[2]

Throughout his administration, President de Gaulle took a keen personal interest in the Antillean departments which again and again he had visited; nor did he ever hesitate to support the often strong policy of the French Government in Martinique and Guadeloupe. When he sought re-election as President in 1965, after failing to obtain a majority on the first ballot, a second was held. Although his victory was much narrower than had been expected, the response to his leadership was clear in the Antilles. De Gaulle obtained in the final ballot 86 per cent. of the votes cast in Guadeloupe and 90 per cent. of those cast in Martinique.

Results in the March 1967 General Election showed continued support for the de Gaulle Government. In Martinique, Victor Sablé, despite his narrow win in both ballots over Georges Gratiant, did better than he had done when opposing him in 1962. Camille Petit won easily in the northern district of the island. Nevertheless, in some areas there were growing indications of increasing Communist strength. Guadeloupe, as a result of Paul Lacavé's win at Capesterre, would have

---

[1] His arrest and subsequent imprisonment seemed to have been decided by Paris. Cf. *Le Monde,* Paris, June 20-21, 1965.

[2] Cf. "La cruche et la pierre", signed "JB", *La Montagne,* Clermont-Ferrand, January 8, 1966.

Martinique: a house at St. Pierre, destroyed in 1902 by the eruption of Mont Pelée shown in the background.

L'Office Départemental du Tourisme de la Martinique

Martinique: foreshore damage caused by Hurricane Edith in 1963.

Keystone

Cattle raising is increasing in the Caribbean. On this Martinique farm a Brahman (Zebu) herd illustrates the popularity of this hardy breed in the tropics.

Photo Platon, Marchés Tropicaux, Paris

SOCIPRESS, Paris

Guadeloupe: dock facilities at Basse-Terre, principal banana port. Behind, the volcano of Grande Soufrière.

Guadeloupe: oxen hauling sugar cane. Here as elsewhere in the Caribbean mechanization is steadily taking over.

Photo Platon, Marchés Tropicaux, Paris

Guadeloupe: the Old Harbour Market, Point-à-Pitre, where conchs are used for food as well as tourist souvenirs.

Photo Platon, Marchés Tropicaux, Paris

one autonomist representative in the Assembly.[1] Pointe-à-Pitre was narrowly won by M. Valentino for the Government with a majority of 934 over his Communist opponent who had led him on the first ballot.[2] The Government candidates fared better on the second ballot, perhaps suggesting that many of the electors were critical of the Government but also viewed with misgiving the policy of increased separation from France.

The 1968 Legislative Election again confirmed support for the de Gaulle Government. In Martinique, Sablé's majority over Gratiant rose from 1,348 in 1967 to 5,800 in 1968. Petit again won easily. In Guadeloupe Lacavé held Capesterre with a slightly increased majority, while Pointe-à-Pitre went to Léopold Hélène who increased his lead in the second ballot by nearly 4,000 over his Communist rival.

At the 1969 Presidential Election, Georges Pompidou received in Guadeloupe 82 per cent. of the votes and in Martinique 91 per cent. Compared with de Gaulle in 1965, he showed a slight falling off in the former island compensated by a marginal rise in the latter. A majority in both departments seemed to appreciate that their standard of living had risen following entry into the E.E.C., despite a vocal minority who clamoured for a loosening of the links with France.[3]

To assess the strength of the independence movement in the Antillean departments is difficult. On the surface, complaints against the status of a French overseas department are numerous. Yet the fear of separation is much stronger, even if few familiar with the French Antilles in the context of the Caribbean of our day can remain convinced that the official pattern of "departmentalism" will solve all the problems. The rate of population growth threatens the official solution. The very excellence of French education turns out critics who often become bitter when they fail to find acceptable employment; the distance from the shores of France (4,375 miles), compared with the distance from Cuba (1,250 miles) and from South America (275 miles), suggests that the technocrats from France may prove less appealing than the leaders of other Caribbean islands.[4] De Gaulle provided France with dynamic

[1] The seat formerly held by Pierre Monnerville. *Vide* p. 265
[2] *Le Monde*, Paris, March 14, 1967.
[3] *Vide* p. 264-9.
[4] Dr. Henri Bangou, in his address to the Conference on Economic Co-ordination in the Caribbean, stressed the failure of the French authorities to participate in the Conference as an illustration of their disapproval of what they considered an unnecessary *rapprochement* between the countries of the Caribbean. "Bref, tout cela peut se résumer dans le fait que chez nous il existe entre les pays légals et les pays réels une très grande différence." *Official Records*, San Germán, Puerto Rico, May 17-19, 1965, p. 57.

leadership; but not even Napoleon Bonaparte could maintain the link between the metropolis and Haiti.

France's disasters in Indochina and Algeria, which at the time caused bitterness, undoubtedly influenced its attitude towards its overseas departments in the Caribbean and to Réunion. In consequence, France has directed detailed attention to them. The Netherlands, which had a somewhat similar experience in Indonesia, reacted quite differently. The Dutch solution was to give the maximum autonomy compatible with avoiding complete separation, while the French made the interesting decision to intensify integration with the metropolis. In doing this, the bureaucratic attitude of Paris at first made failure more than likely. However, de Gaulle's personal interest in these small territories undoubtedly imposed his wider views on the Paris administration. The massive financial aid, recalling in some ways the U.S. approach to Puerto Rico, will become increasingly significant, integrating each year the overseas departments more and more with France.

Today issues are changing. Economic considerations often outweigh those of politics. Certainly strong forces oppose one another in the future of the "specks of dust", the beautiful and historic islands which are a little France in the Caribbean.

THE ECONOMIC PATTERN

Martinique's 425 square miles consist of much hilly country: Mont Pelée attains a height of 4,583 feet. Guadeloupe's 680 square miles are made up of two larger islands—Basse-Terre, which is mountainous, and Grande Terre, which is flat, the two separated by a narrow strait known as the Salt River—together with smaller dependent islands. The area of Grande Soufrière in Guadeloupe attains 4,812 feet. Martinique and Guadeloupe, together with the neighbouring islands, lie in the path of hurricanes. At times they have received heavy storm damage. For example, in 1963 Hurricane Edith swept Martinique, causing damage estimated at NF293,400,000, of which 60 per cent. was suffered by agriculture and 40 per cent. by housing. The often flimsy buildings were levelled: in southern Martinique only 15 per cent. of the houses were left standing. The French Government supplied food to prevent speculation. In this same hurricane, and in Hurricane Helen also in 1963, Guadeloupe lost 50 per cent. of its banana crop. Next year Hurricane Cleo, the most destructive since 1958, with winds of 100 miles an hour, struck Martinique, Marie Galante and Les Saintes, causing damage amounting to NF244·5 million. In 1966 Hurricane Inez occasioned some NF320 million worth of damage. In

August 1970 Hurricane Dorothy struck Martinique wreaking havoc, particularly in Fort-de-France. Damage in the island was estimated at some NF191 million.[1] The storm had sufficient force on its fringe to ruin part of the Guadeloupe banana crop.

The growing of sugar cane and the manufacture of sugar and rum were by far the most important factors in the economies of the French Caribbean islands. Like the British islands, the French Antilles suffered economically as the nineteenth century advanced, due to low sugar prices and competition from sugar beet. However, France's basic concept of its Caribbean territories as part of France assured a major outlet in the sheltered home market. After Martinique and Guadeloupe had been integrated into France as departments in 1946, wages had tended to rise. This encouraged mechanization in the sugar cane industry, when conditions returned to normal after the war. Another consequence was a reduced demand for labour. With no alternative local employment market, many islanders emigrated to France.[2] The old colonial concept continued: the metropolis bought the colonies' exports and in return supplied their manufactured and other requirements. France took two-thirds of the products of its Antillean islands, including sugar, rum and bananas, paying more than the world price.

A little more than a third of Guadeloupe's land is under agriculture: of the 150,000 acres which are farmed, some 67,000 are utilized for the growing of sugar cane. As in most other parts of the Caribbean, the growing of sugar cane is carried out partly by the owners of the sugar-mill, partly by individual farmers whose acreage may vary considerably, and the rest by peasant smallholders or share-croppers. Ten sugar-factories and 28 rum-distilleries process the cane of some 26,000 farmers and smallholders.[3] In 1963, a quota system was introduced to limit the amount of land which a factory could farm.[4] The effect of this has led to the sale by factories of 10,500 acres to cane farmers, including peasants.

In 1970 sugar cane and rum represented some 60 per cent. of Guadeloupe's exports. The nine factories produced 160,000 tons of sugar.

[1] *Le Monde*, Paris, October 14, 1970.

[2] From the overseas departments, there are about 150,000 living in France.

[3] Professor Guy Lasserre pointed out the poor rate of return shown by these smallholdings underlined the weakness of the Antillean economy. *Petite Propriété et Réforme Foncière aux Antilles Françaises*, Colloque International C.N.R.S., Paris, October 11-16, 1965, p. 11.

[4] Prefectoral decree No. 63-472, February 15, 1963.

Taking 20,000 to 30,000 tons of sugar per crop as the bare minimum quantity for a mill, Guadeloupe is not in a hopeless position thanks to the E.E.C. price, although the two largest Jamaica mills could process its total production. Since 1968 payment for cane by sucrose content has caused discontent among farmers since this depends to a large extent on the geographic location of the cane fields, something they could not alter.[1]

The weakness of Guadeloupe's sugar industry may be compared with that in other parts of the Caribbean. Its organization in many respects resembles that in Jamaica. Both countries are high-cost producers of sugar cane. Both depend on a particular market where they are protected by price, although the price is also linked to a quota.[2] France and Great Britain give these quotas for political as much as for economic reasons, even if this is not always admitted in the Caribbean or in Europe. Both recognize that the fragile economies of most of the Antillean islands depend on the growing of sugar cane and its manufacture. No other industry approaches that of sugar in terms of employment. There is therefore a strong political case for providing the maximum of employment. Great Britain may feel that, with the granting of independence to an increasing number of Caribbean countries, its responsibilities are reduced. France certainly remains committed to the hilt.

Unquestionably, the sugar industry in Guadeloupe could dispense with much more labour. The very legislation aimed at reducing the land holdings of the mills may well reduce the efficiency of cane growing. Yet a family on a smallholding in Grande Terre may be better placed there than seeking non-existent jobs at Pointe-à-Pitre. The future of the sugar cane industry in Guadeloupe will turn on its capacity to modernize. Loading remains a problem although improvements in roads and transportation have taken place.

In Martinique the position of the industry is much worse, though sugar and rum comprise only 42 per cent. of its exports. Total sugar production fell from 53,000 tons in 1966 to 27,000 in 1970, far short of its European market quota of 64,468 tons. In 1961 eleven factories produced sugar; by 1970 the number had shrunk to five.

Antiquated cultivation methods have retarded the cane industry. Mechanization, moreover, is difficult since little of the land is level. There can be no case for encouraging the continuation of poorly

[1] Cf. "L'Economie Sucrière", *Le Courrier du Parlement*, Paris, p. 7.
[2] To achieve the quota of 177,000 tons allocated under the E.E.C., Guadeloupe needed to increase its sugar production. Price per ton had fallen from NF58·50 in 1968 to NF51·50 in 1969. In 1970 it rose to NF52·90.

developed properties. The most effective way of eliminating them would probably be by taxation of land values. At the same time, there is nothing to suggest that the breaking up of land into small-holdings would improve the situation, at least so far as the production of sugar is concerned. If it led to the efficient production of other crops, especially food for local consumption, the case would be a strong one.

Although less successful than in the early 1960's, rum distilling took second place after bananas in the export figures for 1970. Twenty-five distilleries make rum although since 1967 their number has decreased. Exports fell from 69,000 hectolitres in 1965 to 61,000 in 1970. Local consumption however is considerable. Martinique pins its hopes on the high reputation of its product in the expectation that it will increasingly find customers in the markets of Europe.

The rise of bananas as an alternative crop to sugar cane in the Antilles, aided by the introduction of fast refrigerated ships, has characterized many islands of the Caribbean.[1] Cut-backs in sugar cane in Martinique have led to increased emphasis being placed on banana cultivation. By 1970 the area planted with this crop was 10,500 hectares as against 7,800 under sugar cane. As a crop it is much more suitable to the small farmer than sugar cane, particularly in a hilly island such as Martinique or on the acclivities above Guadeloupe's capital, Basse-Terre.[2]

Martinique's production of bananas had risen from 185,000 tons in 1961 to 225,000 by 1970. By agreement it shares with Guadeloupe that portion of the French market (two-thirds of the total consumption[3]) which is allocated to the Antilles. Guadeloupe, however, has not so far been able to fulfil its quota partly owing to hurricanes, and to a drought in 1967-68. Bananas from the Antilles are shipped in French vessels to Dieppe and Rouen.

A revolution is also taking place in the packing and transport of the fruit. Up-to-date packing in boxes using polyethylene covering is in general use. Guadeloupe has a modern banana wharf at Basse-Terre

[1] *Vide* p. 323.

[2] "In spite of the high rainfall and steep slopes, the soils are generally deep and fertile. In part, this apparently incongruous situation is explained by the youthfulness of the soils, their high porosity and great water-holding capacity which retard rapid leaching action, and a relatively rich parent material." Don R. Hoy, "The Banana Industry of Guadeloupe, French West Indies", *Social and Economic Studies*, Vol. 11, No. 3, Institute of Social and Economic Research, University of the West Indies, Jamaica, September 1962, p. 260.

[3] The remaining third is shared between the Ivory Coast, Cameroun and Madagascar.

where ships can dock, replacing the former system of loading by lighters. Although formerly Martinique was handicapped by poor port organization and installations at Fort-de-France, a new banana quay has been built. The port of Trinité on Martinique's east coast has been developed for the bulk loading of sugar.

Third in importance to Martinique, after sugar cane and bananas, pineapple production shows considerable development. From 1968 to 1970 some 20,000 tons of fruit were produced from 1,000 hectares in the north of the island. Three modern canneries process the crop which is exported fresh, as a conserve or as juice. Pineapples have the advantage of being less vulnerable than bananas to damage from storms. The crop is also suited to the often broken land in Martinique.

The pineapple industry in Martinique has however encountered serious competition, particularly from the Ivory Coast.[1] After a price fall of 30 per cent. in 1960-61, an improvement took place in 1962, but this did not last. By 1965 the position in the industry was serious, since the island could not compete in the Common Market to which the Ivory Coast had access, paying wages four to five times less than those of Martinique which were geared to those of France.[2] The situation illustrates the enormous difficulties of small industries in the Antilles where costs so often are higher than in competitive countries.

The Fifth Plan stressed the need for diversification of agriculture.[3] It advocated intense concentration on the production of foodstuffs and market gardening. While emphasizing the importance of the existing crops, it felt that little expansion could be expected from tea, tobacco, coffee and cacao.[4] During the transitional period of the Common Market, France would have to give consideration to the French-speaking territories in Africa. After that the agricultural products of the overseas departments would benefit from the community preference.[5] Little progress had been made with supplying the beef requirements from local sources. Dried milk was imported. Since cattle of Brahman (Zebu) stock—or European breeds crossed with Brahmans—do well in

[1] In 1965 the Ivory Coast received 9,500 tons, the same allocation for canned pineapples as Martinique out of a total French consumption of 22,000 tons.

[2] "L'ananas Martiniquais est-il condamné à disparaître?", Groupement des Producteurs d'Ananas de la Martinique, Le Courrier du Parlement, Paris, October 15-20, 1965, p. 6.

[3] The Plan was fifth in a series drawn up by the French Government to promote economic and social development in France and the overseas departments. Cinquième Plan de développement économique et social (1966-1970), Vol. I, No. 1278, Paris, 1965, pp. 138-139.

[4] Ibid., Vol. I, p. 139.

[5] Ibid., Vol. I, pp. 139-140.

tropical climates, it might be expected that the French islands would have become more nearly self-supporting. Even Indian cattle for milk are being bred, for example, in Brazil. The Fifth Plan did, however, stress the need for progress in livestock.[1]

A group of five French deputies, who had visited Martinique, Guadeloupe and Guyane, issued in June 1963 an important report.[2] The larger part was devoted to the Antilles, stressing the close attachment of these departments to France. It stated that in most fields the Antillean departments were not behind those in France; included were primary, secondary and technical education, hospitals, roads, port construction, urban development, sanitation and building.[3] The standard of living was rising in Martinique and Guadeloupe and was now as good as that in many departments of France.[4] The report added, however, that various factors had impeded advance, including delays by political vendettas and legal problems, together with a number of insufficiently qualified officials. On the economic side, the report emphasized that exports only covered imports to the extent of about 60 per cent. in the Antillean departments, and growth was slow.[5] In consequence the local financial position was not satisfactory. It also criticized the use of Antillean currency, suggesting that the introduction of French money was essential.[6]

The industrialization of the Antilles was indispensable, involving both capital and the will for action.[7] The report refrained from giving

---

[1] Cf. *Vème Plan, D.O.M. Elevage, Rapport Général*, p. 46.

[2] *Rapport d'Information . . . sur les départements français d'Amérique*, by MM. Jean-Paul Palewski, Pierre Baudis, Guy Ebrard, Roger Fossé, René Regaudie, Assemblée Nationale, No. 354, Commission des Finances de L'Economie Générale et du Plan, Paris, 1963.

[3] *Ibid.*, p. 21.

[4] Yet the Fifth Plan less optimistically stressed that effective progress would be made in the period 1966-70 towards harmonizing the standard of living of the overseas departments with that of continental France. *Cinquième Plan de développement économique et social (1966-1970)*, p. 138.

[5] Palewski, *et al., op. cit.*, p. 24.

[6] *Ibid.*, p. 27. France, like Great Britain and the Netherlands, followed a policy of using local currency in its Caribbean territories. On the other hand, the United States had made use of the dollar in Puerto Rico and also in the Virgin Islands of the United States, where American currency proved so popular that it established itself in the neighbouring British Virgin Islands. Different currencies between a Colonial Power and its colony may cause problems, such as the quarrel between Great Britain and British Honduras over the devaluation of the British Honduran dollar. *Vide* pp. 199 and 252.

[7] *Ibid.*, p. 36.

advice on the controversial subject of birth control; instead it suggested civic education and control of family allowances together with controlled immigration.[1] Excessive reference of decisions to Paris combined with unnecessary red tape prevented the development of an efficient local administration, thus alienating the local community.[2]

Only in 1964 was a regional development commission for the two Antillean departments and Guyane formed. Puerto Rico, in 1942, had been first to set up an Industrial Development Corporation followed by Jamaica in 1952 and Trinidad in 1959. The major difference was that in all these cases the Corporation was a Government body while France, following the pattern of Paris, wanted a private organization also in the metropolis. The capital, announced as NF2·5 million, seemed small. The Government offered special tax advantages, an inducement that existed in the other territories.

Of sixteen new smaller industries which should have started in Martinique and Guadeloupe during the period 1961-1965, only three in Martinique and five in Guadeloupe had commenced operation. By the time of the Fifth Plan, industrialization was recognized as one of the chief motivators of a developing economy.[3] The main objective of the Sixth Plan was to provide work locally as an alternative to emigration. Despite the difficulties of industrialization in the Overseas Departments, the Plan aimed at increasing manufacture locally of hitherto imported goods and the creation of an economic climate favourable to enterprises exporting to regional, European and American markets.[4]

As in other parts of the Caribbean, tourism presented the best long-term prospects. However, the beautiful beaches were usually without facilities for visitors. Early hopes of the success of a tourist industry

[1] "Ceux qui ont étudié ce problème estiment qu'il ne faut pas songer à introduire aux Antilles des méthodes de *birth control*. Trop de motivations psycho-sociologiques, notamment les convictions religieuses, s'y opposent." *Ibid.*, p. 40.

[2] *Le Journal de Genève* noted the same over-centralization. "Cette île [Guadeloupe], tout comme la Martinique et la Guyane, est administrée de Paris comme la Seine-et-Oise ou le Vaucluse." "Où débouchent les espoirs de la Guadeloupe?", Geneva, July 13, 1964.

[3] During a visit to the overseas departments, Jean Rigotard, Head of the Division for the Overseas Departments at the Commissariat Général du Plan, pointed out that a climate for industrial growth, particularly in the case of smaller industries, had by this time been created. Cf. *Le Monde*, Paris, January 26, 1966.

[4] *Le VIème Plan des Départements d'Outre Mer* (Texte de l'Annexe D.O.M. au Rapport du Gouvernement sur le VIème Plan), Commissariat Général du Plan d'Equipement et de la Productivité, Paris, May 1971, p. 4.

were unfulfilled in the period 1958-1964.[1] Despite tax concessions both to French and foreign enterprises, there had been very little foreign investment in the tourist industry.[2] This lack of progress over tourism was reflected in the modest forecasts made in 1964 of 1,000 rooms for Guadeloupe and 500 for Martinique in relation to the facilities offered by islands such as Puerto Rico, Barbados and Antigua.[3]

The Fifth Plan regarded tourist development as indispensable and, with industrialization, as one of its "twin pillars".[4] During the course of the Plan, hotel accommodation increased considerably while the number of visitors rose. However the Plan had concentrated too heavily on hotel development: a crisis arose because an average stay lasted only some three days and room occupancy proved to be about 60 per cent.[5] In consequence only 60 per cent. of the estimated new jobs were created. The tourist industry continued to suffer from poor publicity, insufficient organization of leisure facilities, such as water skiing, and too little interest on the part of the local inhabitants.[6] The weak overall planning led to a suggestion that a society should be formed to promote the tourist industry in the French Antilles. The proposal was turned down by the French Government. Although the Sixth

[1] Cf. *Troisième Plan 1958-1961, Rapport Général de la commission de modernisation et d'équipement des départements d'outre-mer*, Paris, 1959, pp. 75-6.

"Dès le IIIème Plan le tourisme figure ainsi parmi les secteurs à encourager. Les premières réalisations importantes, cependant, n'apparaissent qu'au cours du IVème Plan et sont restées inférieures, il faut le reconnaître, à ce qui avait été espéré et prévu." *Cinquième Plan 1966-1970, Rapport sur le tourisme dans les départements d'outre-mer*, Commissariat Général du Plan d'Equipement et de la Productivité, Paris, December 1965, p. 1.

[2] Tax concessions existed for new enterprises (both French and foreign) in the Overseas department which employed at least 10 permanent new persons. Ministerial Decree, June 17, 1961. Very little publicity was given to the encouragement of investors. "La propagande et la publicité ont été essentiellement dirigées vers la recherche des touristes et non vers la recherche des investisseurs." *Cinquième Plan 1966-1970, Rapport sur le tourisme dans les départements d'outre-mer*, p. 8.

[3] Cf. Raymond Barrillon, "Les Antilles 'Poussières' sur l'Océan", *Le Monde*, April 24, 1964. Moreover these forecasts were not realized, cf. Pierre Chauleur, "Il existe 1,000 chambres à Antigua, 1,300 à la Barbade, 6,000 à Porto-Rico, au regard de 400 chambres seulement à la Guadeloupe, la moitié moins à la Martinique." "Les problèmes des D.O.M. ne peuvent être résolus que dans un esprit d'active coopération", *Marchés Tropicaux et Méditerranéens*, Paris, June 18, 1966, p. 1679.

[4] " 'Pearl of Antilles' seeks New Luster", *The New York Times*, New York, January 28, 1966.

[5] *Rapport sur le tourisme dans les Départments d'Outre Mer*, Commissariat Général du Plan, VIème Plan-D.O.M., Phase de Programmation, Paris, April 1971, p. 14.   [6] *Ibid.*, p. 15.

Plan acknowledged the importance of tourism, it failed to grasp the urgency of need for professional organization if Martinique and Guadeloupe were to compete with the highly efficient operations in some other parts of the Caribbean, already long established.[1]

Both Martinique and Guadeloupe are heavily populated, probably overpopulated. At the end of 1970 the population was estimated at 340,000 in Martinique and 328,600 in Guadeloupe. The rate of growth is nearly four times that of metropolitan France. Notwithstanding this, the income *per capita* has risen, particularly in Martinique, from $288 in 1958 to $650 in 1969, no longer an under-developed figure by United Nations definition. This is about one-half of that in Puerto Rico.[2] Martinique's remarkable results have been achieved less from the growth or increase in value of production than from budgetary and social-service transfers from the metropolis. France is spending in the island three times what it collects. A very large part of this expenditure is utilised for national education designed to raise the cultural level of the youth. In addition to this expenditure, France absorbs a large deficit on Martinique's social security.

Martinique's example illustrates the determined effort which France is making to raise the standard of living in an overseas department. The cost of doing so also is apparent. Most of the complaints arise from the economic situation of these two departments, which depend too much on sugar, bananas and coffee. All of these commodities are subject to the prices in a world economy which seems to work against the products of tropical agriculture and in favour of those of the developed countries. Without doubt the link with France, which in turn gives entry to the European Common Market, has been a prop to the economy of these islands.

Professor Guy Lasserre clearly appreciated the difficulties that faced both France and its Antillean departments. He concluded that no tidy solution exists, and that autonomy would indeed lead to independence, in fact to the separation of the islands from France. He saw a grim alternative in the fate of Haiti. The crux of the partnership might be France's ability to provide economic aid for the development of the islands. Lasserre clearly felt that the continuation of the association with France was best for Martinique and Guadeloupe.[3]

[1] *Le VI Plan des Départements d'Outre-Mer*, Paris, May 1971, p. 3.

[2] Cf. Fuat M. Andic and Suphan Andic, *Fiscal Survey of the French Caribbean*, Special Study No. 2, Institute of Caribbean Studies, University of Puerto Rico, Río Piedras, Puerto Rico, 1965.

[3] "La France doit aider les Antilles à adapter les structures économiques des îles aux besoins d'une population nombreuse et démunie. Elle doit le faire au

The massive investment necessary for public works which could make a substantial impact on the numbers of unemployed had not appeared, despite the efforts of the economic planners. Uncertainty prevails as to the future after de Gaulle. The integration of the French Antilles into France may have even retarded their industrialization. Most underdeveloped countries have used tariffs and other devices to protect nascent industries. Examples of this may be seen in the development of Jamaica, which has not hesitated to impose tariffs against Great Britain, even if on a lesser scale than against non-Commonwealth countries, in order to protect new developments. Until the time of the Fifth Plan there had been little incentive for French firms to establish factories in Martinique or Guadeloupe. Unlike the British and former British islands, which have welcomed North American capital for the development of bauxite, hotels and other industries, France has done little to publicize investment opportunities to firms in other countries.[1]

In the thirteen years to 1967 (census year) the population of Guadeloupe increased by 36 per cent. and that of Martinique by 33 per cent. The forecasts in the Fifth Plan, which concentrated on this growth, fell far short of the actual figures. In the period 1971 to 1975 (as shown in the 1967 census), more than 22,000 men aged from 15 to 60 would be unemployed, 29,000 would only have temporary or part-time work, while out of a total permanent labour force of 190,000 men and 98,000 women, more than 10 per cent. would work only six hours a day with absenteeism at the rate of 1 out of 10 days.[2]

During the period of the Fifth Plan, out of an estimated 3,500 to 6,500 new jobs to be created in industry only 3,000 actually materialized and but 2,400 out of the proposed 3,400 in the tourist industry. The Commission Centrale des Départements d'Outre Mer, assuming that the Overseas Departments would remain for some time as part of France, considered emigration only as a contribution to the solution of the problem.[3] First and foremost it was vital that young people should remain in the overseas departments. This involved providing for them well-paid and appropriate work, particularly in industry. The economy should become productive rather than assisted.

---

moins à deux titres: d'abord parce que tous les Antillais se tournent spontanément vers elle, se reconnaissant d'abord comme Français; ensuite, parce que si la France reculait devant ses efforts et ses sacrifices, les Antillais seraient tentés d'entreprendre cette mutation sans elle, entraînés par des exemples africains ou caraïbes." La Guadeloupe, Vol. II (Bordeaux, 1961), p. 1067.

[1] Vide pp. 141-2, 161, 207-10.

[2] Rapport sur les options adoptées par la Commission Centrale des D.O.M. du VI Plan, Commissariat Général du Plan d'Equipement et de la Productivité, Paris, April 1970, pp. 6-7.   [3] Ibid., p. 10.

Neither the Fifth nor the Sixth Plans hesitated over the need for birth control. If family education, they claimed, was not given top priority the economic future of the overseas departments would be seriously prejudiced and the chance of raising the standard of living to that of the metropolis would be rendered impossible.[1] Government support should be given to any new or existing family planning centres. It was essential that the inhabitants themselves of the overseas departments should fully comprehend that their vital interests lay in curbing population growth.[2]

Martinique and Guadeloupe have a young population with about one half in the age group of less than 20 years. Education in the past has followed the pattern of metropolitan France, not necessarily the most suitable for the islands, although the Sixth Plan acknowledged the need for teaching to meet local requirements. Many young Martiniquais did not wish, as a result, to do the much-needed agricultural work. On the other hand, a well-founded education enables the inhabitants to realize their own problems. Sometimes, however, disappointed young intellectuals have tended to congregate in the towns, dissatisfied with their prospects and believing that a solution may lie in the weakening or breaking of the link with France: something which for the majority may well spell a disastrous fall in their standard of living. At the same time, the growth in the numbers of children of primary school age has resulted in a shortage of qualified teachers. In particular, the need to develop professional and technical education has been stressed.

After World War II, the start had been slow. France was not in a position to give the economic support that it now can. Too little was done to stimulate the tourist industry. Moreover, the islanders were disgruntled because at first they did not receive the full benefits of French social services. Experts voiced their misgivings over the unbalanced economy.[3]

[1] *Ibid.*, pp. 488 and 518. *Le VI Plan des Départements d'Outre-Mer*, Paris, p. 5.

[2] "Il est indispensable et urgent qu'une propagande active intervienne avec habileté et efficacité pour favoriser la limitation des naissances. La tâche est gigantesque, dans des départements où des facteurs traditionnels et religieux s'opposent à une transformation quelconque du mode de vie et de la mentalité populaire." "Les D.O.M. face à leur avenir", *Marchés Tropicaux et Méditerranéens*, June 18, 1966, p. 1767.

[3] "On peut prévoir le moment où les sucres et les rhums qui n'ont d'autres acheteurs que la Métropole et l'Union Française, vont se trouver en concurrence avec les produits similaires de France même. Il peut en résulter soit un effondrement des cours, soit le retour à de strictes mesures de contingentement." Eugène Revert (*Terres Lointaines*), *La France d'Amérique* (Paris, 1955), p. 247.

The position, however, appears to have changed. While island politicans argue with one another as to whether independence, self-government or the departmental *status quo* is desirable, the French Government, after a very careful survey of the position, has clearly determined to proceed with the complete integration of the overseas departments into France and to harmonize their standard of living with that of the metropolis. Moreover, elections have again and again supported such integration. Unquestionably, France, which has one of the world's strongest economies, can absorb the comparatively small island populations into the French system even if the cost is high.

Since their reconstitution in 1946 as French Departments, Martinique and Guadeloupe have made tangible progress. The somewhat narrow and bureaucratic attitude of Paris was substantially modified by the much wider and more sympathetic policy of de Gaulle who emphasized by his visits his personal interest. In return, the islanders gave strong political support to the General and afterwards to President Pompidou. French education and economic support have conferred real benefit. The weakness of the two overseas departments rests on a limited agriculture. However the sugar industry, not over-efficient by modern standards, has benefited from entry into the E.E.C. under the wing of France. Bananas have also shared in the sheltered French market.

On the other hand, the dominance of French imports has discouraged island industrial development, which in any event has limited prospects. Tourism, the one new industry likely to become significant, has advanced slowly.

Unemployment as elsewhere remains heavy. Yet the open door of France has provided an alternative which some 150,000 have chosen.[1] Despite a standard of living comparable to or above that of Spain, Portugal and Greece and better than that of some of the Commonwealth islands, considerable dissatisfaction has been displayed, especially by the younger age group. Nationalism directed against the metropolis has been fanned by the entry into independence of the major British colonies. This has overshadowed the economic benefits of French citizenship including sheltered trade, massive subsidies and unrestricted right of access to the metropolis. Aimé Césaire personifies such criticism even though his support for complete independence may have its limits. Others are more extreme.[2]

[1] Cf. Jean-Pierre Clerc, "Les Antillais sur le chemin de l'exil", *Le Monde*, Paris, September 18, 19-20, 1971.

[2] For example G.O.N.G. (Groupement des organisations nationalistes guadeloupéenes) appears to seek independence. Cf. Noel-Jean Bergeroux, "Les Antilles Françaises en quête d'un statut", *Le Monde*, Paris, May 8, 1971.

Criticism centres around too much control by France. The *békés* who control much of the trade have aroused antagonism. Although elections continue to show a sizeable majority in favour of the French connection, opposition creeps up.

Martinique and Guadeloupe have economies precariously poised on the French link. Should it be broken the sheltered sugar and banana industries would lose much of their present security. The concrete economic advantages of independence remain obscure and hypothetical. Nevertheless, in a world highly responsive to emotional appeal, too often solid fact makes less impact than mirage. Perhaps the needed compromise may be found in a new "créolisme" or nationalism within the framework of France.[1]

Formidable problems face both the central government and the departments. Despite heavy emigration to France, massive unemployment remains endemic.[2] Industrialization has made little progress, since the policy of local enterprises to replace imports (encouraged by the Commonwealth Caribbean governments) runs counter to the long-established pattern of open trade with metropolitan France. The economic dependence of the Antillean departments is complete. The very excellence of French education has increasingly provided critics of the existing system, especially among the youth of the islands. On a more vigorous policy of encouraging investment in the Antillean departments, including effective promotion of the tourist trade, may turn their economic future. Further decentralization would seem to be needed to assuage the rising criticism against the administration of Paris.[3]

GUYANE

THE POLITICAL PATTERN

Bounded by Brazil to the east and south and to the west by Surinam, Guyane has been a French possession since 1604, with minor Dutch and Portuguese interruptions, and is the largest of the overseas departments. Several offshore islands form part of the colony. More than two-thirds of the total population are of French extraction and the remaining third is made up of immigrants from St. Lucia and other

[1] Cf. Jean Lacouture, "Comment peut-on être Antillais?", *Le Monde*, Paris, August 26, 1970.

[2] *Vide* pp. 283.

[3] In a detailed article Claude Kiejman clearly senses increasing criticism of the existing system of government. "Martinique et Guadeloupe: Départements française ou terres étrangères," *Le Monde Diplomatique*, Paris, October 1971.

British islands together with Indians and the descendants of slaves, some of whom were brought in from neighbouring Surinam.[1]

Throughout the eighteenth and nineteenth centuries France attempted to colonize Guyane with varying degrees of failure. Each succeeding expedition proved more disastrous for the colony than the last. Bad management and an apparent blindness to existing conditions lie at the root of these mistakes. Many of the colonists died either on board ship or soon after landing. Others expelled from France for political reasons were totally unsuited to manual labour and many of these also perished. Finally, in 1854 after the discovery of gold, Guyane received a heavy influx of unsolicited immigrants. However, these too did little for the colony, for the gold workings proved disappointing.

From 1852 until 1946, Guyane was used as a prison colony. Shark-infested waters made escape from Devil's Island near impossible. Although the penal settlement was completely disassociated from the rest of the colony, Guyane's reputation suffered. The settlement was closed in 1946 but its influence has lingered on, not so much because some who had been freed continued to work in the country, as because the notorious settlement has left an insinuating and indelible mark on the minds of the people.

After 1854 Guyane had been governed according to the provisions of a senate decree of Napoleon III. In 1930 the country was divided into two: Guyane and the territory of Inini which comprised the hinterland. Since 1946 Guyane has enjoyed the same self-government at the municipal level, and departmental status, as have Martinique and Guadeloupe. Internally it is separated into fourteen *communes* each of which elects its local government. Like Martinique and Guadeloupe, Guyane has been thoroughly gallicized, and has remained fundamentally attached to France. But Guyane's attachment has been tinged with a certain unwillingness to shoulder its own problems, arising from the background of the penal settlement.[2]

Any movement for autonomy in Guyane appears to have faded out, unlike that in Martinique and Guadeloupe. Justin Catayée, leader of the Guyane Socialist Party, who had urged that the departmental status was worse than being a prison colony, was killed in an aeroplane crash in 1962. In the election of June 1961, however, Catayée had been defeated, although voting was close. No new leader of sufficient

---

[1] Theodore Sealy in an article in *The Sunday Gleaner*, commented on the difficulty in establishing who were the real Guyanese. "French Guiana where time stands still", Kingston, February 17, 1963.

[2] "C'est ensuite le fait que les Guyanais ont pris peu à peu la mentalité d'assistés habitués à recevoir sans contrepartie." Palewski, *et al.*, *op. cit.*, p. 20.

magnetism has yet arrived to take his place. General de Gaulle, during his visit to the Caribbean in March 1964, was given an even more enthusiastic welcome in Guyane than in either of the island departments.[1] He assured Guyane that, despite former neglect, better times lay ahead.

France itself has faced the problems of Guyane with a degree of ambivalence. Uncertain whether to regard Guyane as a sisyphean burden or to believe that economic viability could be achieved, it has tended to pursue both policies at the same time. Despite attempts to increase the population of Guyane and thus successfully to colonize it, by 1961 it remained more an empty tract of South America than a viable unit of the French nation. The Nemo Scheme, commenced in 1961, seemed to be the fulfilment of the idea put forward by Professor Eugène Revert that Guyane needed not individuals but groups to develop it.[2] To benefit both the French Antilles and Guyane in a single operation was an ingenious yet liberal concept. Although admirable in its intent and well received locally, the scheme met with limited success.[3] Two camps were established in Guyane, and the men were mainly employed in road building. Difficulties were numerous, chiefly on account of a shortage of under-officers to enforce discipline, lack of finance and the problems of providing suitable recreation for the young men. Added to this was the inborn disinclination of any Antilleans to go to Guyane as a result not only of its association with the penal settlement but also of earlier unfortunate experiences there in the twentieth century.

THE ECONOMIC PATTERN

Dense forests cover 90 per cent. of Guyane. Ten major rivers crisscross its 35,135 square miles with a network of tributaries. With a density some one to the square mile, over half the population live in

[1] Further support for the de Gaulle Government was shown in the results of the March 1967 elections.

[2] "Je suis maintenant très assuré qu'il faut désormais envoyer en Guyane non des individus, mais des groupes a priori assez nombreux pour constituer d'entrée du jeu des 'habitations' hiérarchisées, disciplinées, capables de se suffire sans tarder à elles-mêmes et de fournir rapidement un ou deux grands produits d'exportation." La France d'Amérique (Paris, 1955), p. 228. Cf. Mitchell, op. cit., pp. 102-3. Vide pp. 265.

[3] "Enfin il nous a été souvent dit que les espoirs d'implantation d'Antillais en Guyane par le biais du S.M.A. était fallacieux." Palewski et al., op. cit., p. 19. The Report, however, added that the economic and social interest of the S.M.A. ought to be encouraged to the full, even if only a small number of individuals were successfully transferred from the French Antilles to Guyane.

Photo Bossu-Picat, SOCIPRESS, Paris

Guyane: an Oyampis Indian.   Guyane's rivers lend themselves to fishing
rather than to navigation.

Guyane: handling the heavy timber.

SOCIPRESS, Paris

Photo Platon, Marchés Tropicaux,

Guyane: the Préfecture at Cayenne.   In the foreground two Traveller's Palms whose leaf stalks when cut yield water.

Guyane: President Charles de Gaulle greeting the Amerindian chief of the Oucouyenne tribe during a visit to Cayenne.

Keys

the capital, Cayenne, which is situated on the coastal strip, a small narrow belt containing much swampland.[1] The country almost totally lacks an economic structure. Few indigenous resources have been sufficiently developed. Guyane must import practically everything.[2] Guyane pays for barely 10 per cent. of its expenditure, although in 1970 the position improved slightly. France seemed to have continued to pour in money for the development of the country with little sign of positive results. Many projects had failed to produce an economic return. Whereas the cultural, social and public health sectors had been relatively well financed, the economic sector had not. In the fourteen *communes* the financial situation had been aggravated by excessive and often scandalous personnel expenditure, together with unnecessary outlay in the social sector, to the detriment of more pressing public needs.[3] Credit for new industries had not been readily forthcoming despite the obvious need of the country for full development. Under the Fourth Plan (1962 to 1965) the tax system was liberalized and new businesses benefited from an eight-year tax exemption. Newly developed land received a ten-year exemption. The Fifth and Sixth Plans gave to investors increased advantages.

Agriculture was neglected until the early 1960's when attempts were made to diversify the few existing crops. Rice is cultivated on the coast, sugar cane and bananas in the lowlands, and pineapples and cacao in the highlands. Rearing of livestock has been limited to hogs and poultry; cattle raising has been unsuccessful, due to the prevalence of disease.

As in many other tropical countries, little of the afforested areas can be commercially exploited because of the variety of trees.[4] The forests are virtually impenetrable except for the strips of land bordering the rivers. The rivers, as in Guyana and Surinam, are navigable only for a limited distance owing to rapids. Some varieties of wood are too heavy for the logs to float.[5] Labour shortages have compounded the difficulties. The successful mobilization of the resources of the forest depends to a large extent on considerable effort being made to improve

---

[1] The 1964 estimate was 35,000 people. Maurice Vaussard pointed out that the population which in 1875 had been about 60,000 in less than a century had fallen to about half that figure. "La Guyane peut-elle renaître?" *L'Aube*, Paris, May 9, 10, 11, 1950.

[2] "Il s'agit plutôt d'une absence de structure économique: la Guyane ne produit pas ou très peu de biens échangeables; elle dépend presque entièrement, non seulement pour son équipement, mais aussi pour sa subsistance, du marché extérieur. Il n'y a rien en Guyane, il faut tout y apporter." Palewski *et al.*, *op. cit.*, p. 6.

[3] Cf., Palewski *et al.*, *op. cit.*, p. 11.

[4] *Vide* pp. 242, 256 and 314.

[5] Revert, *op. cit.*, p. 209.

roads in the department.[1] Guyane faces no small task to secure for its timber a large and reliable market. In 1966 a consortium of French, Dutch and American interests launched a $12·25 million project to exploit nearly half a million acres on the eastern frontier with Brazil.[2]

Unlike Martinique and Guadeloupe, Guyane has a continental shelf stretching for more than 185 miles and an abundance of fish. Martinique and Guadeloupe, on the other hand, have the fishermen which Guyane lacks.[3] Following the discovery that the coastal waters of Guyane are rich in prawn, two fishing companies were formed in 1962 and 1963, both backed by North American capital. Unfortunately they employed few local people, preferring to import the necessary labour. Both have met with relative success.[4] Exports of fresh and frozen shrimps rose from some 1,700 tons in 1968 to 2,500 in 1970, much of it to Martinique.[5] Production was estimated to reach 4,000 tons in 1975.[6] The improvement of the port of Cayenne-ville is envisaged.[7]

The mineral wealth exploited in the nineteenth century has dwindled. Gold production has continued to fall. Deposits are scattered over a wide area and the ores have a complicated structure. Individual gold prospectors may do well, but as in Guyana no large-scale development has taken place.[8] The most interesting discovery has been bauxite in the Kaw Mountains, but this cannot be exploited commercially without the existence of a deep-water harbour. An American and French company has been formed to investigate the deposits.

Unemployment is low. In 1963, one out of five adults worked in the public service.[9] The problem is often one of underemployment rather than unemployment. The tribal population works only spasmodically, satisfied with about one-third of the legal minimum wage.[10] Literacy

---

[1] By 1965, Martinique and Guadeloupe had 1,494 and 1,912 kilometres of road whereas Guyane had only 735 (1,045, 1,095 and 459·3 miles respectively). *Vème Plan, D.O.M., Infrastructure Routière, Rapport Général*, p. 1.

[2] *The Financial Times*, London, July 19, 1966.

[3] Cf. *Vème Plan, D.O.M., Rapport Général, Pêche*, p. 26.

[4] In 1963 the shrimp-catch was valued at over $3 million. Walter Haidar, "Basic Data on the Economy of French Guiana", *Overseas Business Reports*, Washington, No. 111, September 1964, p. 2.

[5] *Guide Touristique (Caraïbes '71 Horizons du Monde)*, SOCIPRESSE, Paris 1971, p. 185.

[6] *Le VI Plan des Départements d'Outre Mer* Paris, p. 11.

[7] *Ibid.*, p. 11.   [8] *Vide* pp. 243-4.

[9] Palewski *et al.*, *op. cit.*, p. 13.

[10] Fuat M. Andic and Suphan Andic, "Economic Background of French Antilles", *Politics and Economics in the Caribbean*, Special Study No. 3, Institute of Caribbean Studies, University of Puerto Rico, Río Piedras, 1966, p. 113, n. 14.

is high; 98 per cent. of the children attend school. Public health facilities are good.

Strangely, the characteristics which made Guyane ideal for a penal settlement, namely its remoteness and small population density, made it an admirable choice for the site of a new missile research centre.[1] In 1964 the Centre National d'Etudes Spatiales decided to replace the missile base in the Colomb Béchar region of Algeria with a new one in Guyane. However the construction of the missile base at Kourou seems to have had small impact on the economic position of Guyane; the town of Kono may well develop in isolation from the rest of the country. Notwithstanding that Guyane claims the highest educational standard among the French Overseas Departments and Territories, many of those employed at the base are Brazilians, Bolivians and Colombians.[2]

Guyane's future would seem different from that of Martinique and Guadeloupe. Unlike these islands, it has no problem of over-population. Should one arise, it still has its rights of entry into metropolitan France —and indeed the E.E.C. countries—for any of its citizens who seek their fortunes abroad. The likelihood of agricultural development on a large scale would seem at present to be small. Its 44,000 inhabitants, mainly living in the coastal area, certainly benefit as French citizens both from the education and the freedom of movement that goes with it.

Guyane has one major advantage: it is thinly populated. Thus it could benefit from large-scale mechanized agriculture or mining, inevitably financed from beyond its shores. It has the choice of moving forward slowly, using France as an outlet for surplus population rather as Puerto Rico has done in relation to the United States, or alternatively, should it seek a rapid rise in its standard of living, of accepting overseas finance and expertise to open up the country. A resemblance with the problems of British Honduras (Belize) may appear, where the practice of an extensive agriculture has led to a rising standard of living in a very thinly populated country, which has been wise enough not to embark on heavy immigration and has substantially raised its standard of living.[3]

[1] Cf. Général Fondé "La Guyane encore méconnue", *Revue de Défense Nationale*, Paris, June-July 1968.

[2] Cf. Denise Gayet "Le racisme en Guyane Française", *Les Temps Modernes*, Paris, March 1968.

[3] *Vide* p. 260.

Chapter XIII

THE TRIPARTITE KINGDOM

THE NETHERLANDS ANTILLES

THE POLITICAL PATTERN

The nineteenth century proved to be a period of recession for the Netherlands possessions in the Caribbean. The Crown had succeeded the Dutch West India Company, and in 1828 the King appointed a Governor to administer the colonies.[1] Colonial officials were responsible to the King. As in the case of the British and French colonies, times were bad. The merchants of Amsterdam turned more and more to commerce with the extensive East Indies possessions of the Netherlands. The change in trade was further facilitated when the opening of the Suez Canal in 1869 shortened the voyage to Europe.

The Netherlands, like other European countries, was affected by the spirit of reform which swept Europe in 1848. Parliament gained increased control of the colonies at the expense of the Crown. In 1865, the Netherlands decided that the Netherlands Antilles should have a colonial parliament composed of officials and members all nominated by the Government. Taking into account the relatively high standard of education of both the white and coloured population, the solution was not a satisfactory one: protests were made in the Netherlands Legislative Assembly. The argument in favour of the measures was that the property qualification for voting disfranchised all but a handful of the population, which resulted in rule by an oligarchy of merchants and property owners. The reasoning was valid, but the remedy unsound. Universal suffrage had not yet been introduced in the Netherlands, although constitutional advance had been made. The obvious answer that the franchise in the Netherlands Antilles should have been steadily increased was no more acceptable to Ministers and their advisers than it was to their counterparts in Great Britain.[2] The solution adopted for the Netherlands Antilles followed the same general pattern of a

---

[1] Bernard H. M. Vlekke, *Evolution of the Dutch Nation* (New York, 1945), p. 299.

[2] *Vide* p. 121.

colonial parliament composed of officials and members nominated by the Governor. An additional reason advanced in favour of nominated members was that sea communications were slower and irregular and therefore elected members would have had difficulty in attending at Willemstad. Against that a nominated representative, for example from the Windward Islands, was equally remote from the people for whom he spoke.

An adverse balance of payments in the Netherlands Antilles led to increasing pressure from the mother country. Dutch Ministers had to defend the Netherlands legislature's expenditure in the Colonies. None of the Netherlands Antilles presented first-class possibilities for agricultural development. The enlargement of plantations in the nineteenth and twentieth centuries made the small islands less competitive. The Dutch investor in overseas development was much more readily attracted to the Netherlands East Indies than to the Caribbean.

In 1936, the Netherlands Government made an ineffective attempt to devolute more authority to the Netherlands Antilles. In attempting to do this, it loosened its former method of control over the Governor of the Netherlands Antilles, but failed to increase his responsibilities to the Netherlands Antilles Parliament. In consequence, the normal development of parliamentary government was in some ways retarded by the Governor's powers, and the changes did not contribute to the creation of more effective political parties.

Nevertheless, Dutch interest in economic expansion led to concentration on the efficient administration of their overseas territories. Young men were trained at Leiden University for government services overseas. Certainly the emphasis was mainly on the East Indies; however, the West Indies benefited too. The concept of a Greater Netherlands embracing all the Dutch overseas territories appeared to be valid.[1] These visions were overwhelmed when the Netherlands itself was submerged by the German attack in 1940. Two years later Japan conquered the Netherlands East Indies.

Queen Wilhelmina of the Netherlands had moved with her Government into exile in London. She emphasized that the Netherlands stood fast in the Allied cause from Curaçao to New Guinea. She also expressed the increasingly progressive ideas of her Ministers towards the Netherlands overseas territories, including those which had escaped invasion like the Netherlands Antilles. The Queen put forward the view that after the war the Kingdom of the Netherlands should be reconstructed on the solid foundation of complete partnership

[1] Cf. A. D. A. de Kat Angelino, *Colonial Policy* (The Hague, 1931), *passim.*

which would express the ideals for which the United Nations were fighting.[1]   She envisaged a future commonwealth in which the Netherlands, Indonesia, Surinam and Curaçao would participate.

The United States welcomed the Queen's expression of her Government's views as a constructive attempt to fulfil the aims of the Atlantic Charter.[2]   Under the Dutch plan, the partners would be brought closer to the mother country than in the case of the British Commonwealth.   Indeed the elastic and decentralized British system, which would a few years later permit an increasing number of republics to function within the Commonwealth, made little appeal to the legalistic and logical Dutch mind with its traditional interest in international law.

The dreams of a Greater Netherlands were not to be fulfilled. After World War II, Indonesia moved into independence and even absorbed Dutch New Guinea.   Only the ancient West Indian colonies remained for the interesting constitutional experiment.   The failure of the Dutch Government to find a solution of the Indonesian problem caused disillusionment and disappointment in the Netherlands.   Many Dutchmen believed that the future prosperity of their country was bound up with their association with the former colonies.   At a time when the Netherlands was still adversely affected by the effects of war damage and German occupation, the loss of Indonesia appeared to be a body blow.   The modern view that colonies are only too often a liability had hardly been considered.

The changed views on colonies developed gradually over a period of years.   The first reaction in the Netherlands to the break with Indonesia was that the relationship with the remaining colonies must be placed on a solid foundation.   The wartime speeches of Queen Wilhelmina had paved the way for the opening in 1946 of discussions between the Dutch Government, the Netherlands Antilles and Surinam. Negotiations, however, were overshadowed by the acute difficulties which had arisen in Indonesia.   The problem of translating political aspirations into a concrete document proved extremely difficult.   As the discussions dragged on, a temporary measure of self-government was given to the Netherlands Antilles and Surinam in 1948, granting universal franchise on the same basis as in the Netherlands.   Further revision was made for Surinam in 1949 and for the Netherlands Antilles in 1950 providing complete internal self-government.

The new Charter for the Kingdom of the Netherlands was agreed

[1] Radiooranje (Netherlands station), London, December 7, 1942.
[2] *Washington Post*, Washington, D.C., December 2, 1942, and *The Christian Science Monitor*, Boston, December 9, 1942.

and signed in 1954. As a result of eight years of intensive study, the Charter is a subtle and intricately balanced document. The problem which the Charter attempted to solve was how to make it possible, within the framework of a sovereign state, for two separate countries, separated by 4,000 miles from the Netherlands, to have the maximum amount of autonomy.

In the constitution, based on the principle of a constitutional monarchy, the King reigns over the Kingdom and over each of the countries.[1] The heart of the solution was the setting up of a Council of Ministers composed of the Netherlands Ministers together with the two Ministers Plenipotentiary appointed by the Netherland Antilles and Surinam respectively. Whenever matters concerning the Netherlands Antilles or Surinam come before the Dutch Cabinet, the respective Minister Plenipotentiary has the right to participate on an equal footing with the Netherlands Minister,[2] and has considerable powers of delaying legislation which he might consider detrimental to his country. The Minister Plenipotentiary would live normally at The Hague so as to be on hand for the task of resolving any problems or disagreements. This position resembles that of a Commonwealth High Commissioner in Great Britain, although the constitutional powers of a Minister Plenipotentiary are much greater.

Foreign affairs and defence are Kingdom matters: the Netherlands Antilles and Surinam make a financial contribution to the maintenance of independence and defence of the Kingdom.[3] Their residents cannot be compelled to serve in the armed forces or be put on compulsory civil duties, except by legislation passed by Country Statute (i.e. the Netherlands Antilles, or Surinam).[4]

In everything not deemed to be a Kingdom matter, the Netherlands Antilles is autonomous. Legislative power rests in a single chamber parliament of 22 members elected by a system of proportional representation. Curaçao elects 12 members, Aruba 8, Bonaire 1 and the three Windward Islands jointly 1. It is weighted in favour of the smaller islands, as was the West Indies Federation. A Prime Minister presides over a small cabinet of 5 or 6 ministers, who are responsible

[1] Article 2, *Charter of the Kingdom of the Netherlands*. Dr. Hans G. Hermans comments "The constitutions of both Surinam and the Netherlands Antilles stipulate that the ruler of the Netherlands is also the head of government in these countries. Surinam and the Netherlands Antilles thus are kingdoms in their own right. . . ." "Constitutional Development of the Netherlands Antilles and Surinam", *The Caribbean*, British, French, Dutch, United States, ed. A. Curtis Wilgus (University of Florida Press, 1958), p. 64.

[2] *Charter of the Kingdom of the Netherlands*, Article 10.

[3] *Ibid.*, Article 25.   [4] *Ibid.*, Article 32.

to parliament.[1]   There is further devolution of power to individual islands, or groups of islands.

The Governor-General of the Netherlands Antilles is appointed by the Sovereign on the advice of the Kingdom Cabinet. His position is somewhat delicate and ambiguous. He is responsible to the Crown. When he attends, which may be infrequently, meetings of the Cabinet of the Netherlands Antilles, he presides over it. But his power is symbolic only. He represents the Kingdom Government for police and military purposes, and also Netherlands nationals in any problems with the Netherlands Antilles Government. More recent governors, on instructions from Holland, have been reluctant to enter into local affairs.

Kingdom matters have been reduced to a minimum. The Caribbean territories accept the leadership and guidance of the Netherlands, while aiming at using their own independence as far as possible. Political leaders and the people for the most part have expressed satisfaction with the existing political situation. In the case of the Netherlands Antilles, the limited degree of self-government has at times been too onerous and the head of the Kingdom has been forced to refuse intervention in purely local matters.

A Kingdom parliament and government are clearly impossible. Consultation must take its place. On the Council of the Kingdom, the Dutch Cabinet, together with the Plenipotentiary Minister of the Netherlands Antilles and of Surinam, meet to discuss any problems affecting the two smaller countries.

The Netherlands Antilles and Surinam have in fact been satisfied with something less than independence. They do not handle their foreign policy, despite the careful provisions for consultation if their interests are affected. They are not directly represented at the United Nations. They have only modified responsibility for their national defence. Clearly the imbalance between the Netherlands and its overseas partners is enormous in terms of population and wealth.

However, by accepting an association with the Netherlands which is much closer than that of Jamaica or Trinidad with Great Britain, they have avoided a burden of costs arising from independence which they might have found hard to bear, particularly if they were to run into a period of economic difficulties. The ingenious and subtle constitution has given to each of the smaller partners the chance of influencing the major partner at the highest level. The Netherlands Antilles and Surinam have politically a far greater measure of

[1] An interesting feature in the Netherlands Antilles parliament has been the high proportion of officials who have been elected to parliament. They continue to serve as officials: there is no regular payment for members.

independence, both in theory and practice, than has Puerto Rico in relation to the United States. A Plenipotentiary Minister who attends by right the meetings of the Kingdom—in effect the Dutch Cabinet— has more status than Puerto Rico's Resident Commissioner who can speak but not vote in Congress. However, in terms of nationalism, Puerto Rico has Spanish as a first language, and a large University around which national aspirations have developed to compensate for its lack of political independence. In a period of strident nationalism in so many parts of the world, any association between countries is unlikely to be stronger than the goodwill which links the parties together. The mutual confidence which exists between the partners of the Tripartite Kingdom is the best augur of future success.[1]

The strength of the Tripartite Kingdom is not easy to assess. The intricate legal edifice of its Charter sometimes seems to be ambiguous. The Netherlands, with memories of Indonesian troubles and disappointments still alive, had not reached the point of seeking to abandon all colonial ties and made considerable effort to give continuing association a solid framework.

Internally, proportional representation modelled on the Dutch system has followed its usual pattern of leading to a number of different parties.[2] In contrast, the British system of voting which has been followed in the Commonwealth countries, has encouraged the two-party system of voting which is clearly the pattern in Jamaica, Trinidad and elsewhere. At that point the comparison with the former colonial powers seems to halt. In the Dutch islands as in the Commonwealth islands the image of parties has not crossed the Atlantic. Parties have evolved in the Netherlands Antilles dominantly on an island basis, and as a result of lack of strong federal organization, are not based on any political philosophy. Every party supports autonomy for the Netherlands Antilles, but each party is sufficiently honest not to advocate absolute independence from Holland. Local issues and local personalities tend to take precedence over matters of more general concern.

The 15-year majority coalition formed by the Democratic Parties of Curaçao, Bonaire and the Windward Islands together with the Aruba Patriotic Party was headed first by Dr. Efraim Jonckheer. On his appointment as Governor of the Netherlands Antilles he was succeeded by Ciro de Kroon. In May 1969 a march by several thousand petroleum workers, protesting against the effect of automation in the oil industry, suddenly erupted in violence. A weekend of riots engulfed Willemstad

---

[1] The term Tripartite Kingdom is used to signify the Kingdom of the Netherlands.

[2] *Vide* p. 231 n.2

causing many million dollars of damage in the capital. The clash appeared to be linked to the heavy unemployment in the island together with the disparity between the well-to-do white population, many of them Protestant or Jewish, and the impoverished workers, largely Roman Catholic.[1] Despite some Dutch criticism, Marines were flown to Curaçao from the Netherlands since the local police force could not contain the rioting. The precise origin of the outburst remains obscure although Kroon blamed foreign trained Communists.[2] To prevent further violence he resigned as Prime Minister.[3]

A period of interim government was followed in September 1969 by a General Election. Although Kroon's Democratic Party won 11 seats, for the first time a Socialist party, the Frente Obero, gained 3 seats in the Parliament. The Frente Obero, only three months old, had grown out of the troubles earlier in the year. Two of the victors, Wilson Godett, a Trade Union leader, and Stanley Brown, a journalist, were still in prison following their parts in the May riots. Because of pre-election pledges of non-co-operation, the new coalition Government under Ernesto Petronia was not set up until December 1969 after further strikes and unrest. In February 1970 the Government of the Kingdom of the Netherlands cancelled Jonckheer's appointment as Governor of the Netherlands Antilles following criticism in Curaçao supported by Surinam.[4] After further changes, by July 1971, the Coalition Government was headed by O. R. A. Beaujon of the Democratic Party as Minister President.

The overseas territories have not precisely the same aims. In the

---

[1] Cf. James Nelson Goodsell, "Curaçao violence traced to long discontent", *The Christian Science Monitor*, Boston, June 18, 1969.

[2] The Commission appointed to investigate the riots found the direct cause to be a labour dispute between Wescar, a building contractor, whose main employer was Shell, and the Federation of Curaçao Workers. The Commission criticized Wescar for by-passing the union and negotiating individual terms with the employees. In addition when a strike was threatened, it found that Wescar had paid scant attention to the explosive situation throughout the island and considered that its threat to dismiss all strikers was ill-judged. Both the Petroleum Workers Federation Curaçao and the dockers came out in sympathy. *De Meidagen van Curaçao*, Algemeen Culturele Maandblad "Ruku", Curaçao, 1970, pp. 9-18.

[3] The Commission criticized the Government for not sensing at once the seriousness of the dispute and for underestimating the general support it excited throughout the islands. *Ibid.*, p. 17.

[4] Surinam, however, denied accusations from the Netherlands Antilles Government that it had interfered in the internal affairs of the Netherlands Antilles or that it wished Jonckheer's appointment to be revoked. *Suriname news in brief*, Paramaribo, No. 7/1970.

forefront stands their desire to run their own affairs to the maximum degree possible. Yet they are sophisticated enough to realize that their resources would not suffice—at least for the present—to launch out on their own. They have, however, developed their own national consciousness.[1] Professor Logemann shrewdly deduced that there are positive and negative forces which hold the partners together. On the negative side, the Netherlands Antilles and Surinam are not large enough to stand on their own. Any movement for greater independence is found amongst young people, particularly those who have studied in Holland. Logemann's claim that there is no "state in their own geographic surroundings to which they would rather look for support"[2] is perhaps less true now than in 1955. The Netherlands Antilles shows interest in strengthening its links with Venezuela, a neighbour with whom in colonial days it was often at war and with which in modern times relations have often been difficult. Moreover Venezuela controls the oilfields which are the life-blood of Curaçao and Aruba. Former Prime Minister Jonckheer, after his nomination to the Governorship of the Netherlands Antilles had been rescinded, was appointed Ambassador at Caracas.

* * * *

Historically the Netherlands had never been able to mount the colonial drive that had resulted in the very extensive overseas empires of Spain, France and Great Britain. The small area of the mother country, often threatened with war and at times invaded by more powerful neighbours, did not provide the base for empire on the grand scale. The Dutch were essentially traders first: of less importance was the acquisition of new territories, even if at different times their dominion stretched far. The Netherlands flag had once flown from Pernambuco and Cape Town to Sumatra and New Guinea. They even acquired the tiny island of Palmas in the Pacific Ocean, which later they successfully defended against the United States at the International Court to become the classic case on territorial sovereignty.[3]

[1] J. H. A. Logemann, "The Constitutional Status of the Netherlands Caribbean Territories", *Developments towards Self-Government in the Caribbean* (The Hague, 1955), p. 57.

[2] Logemann, *op. cit.*, p. 58.

[3] The controversy arose in 1906 when the United States maintained that the island was included in the Philippine Archipelago ceded by Spain to the United States by the Treaty of Paris in 1898. The Netherlands claimed long and undisputed authority over the island. The case was referred to the Permanent Court of Arbitration, and the Arbitrator found that the island formed part of Netherlands territory. Cf. L. C. Green, *International Law through the Cases*, Second Edition (London, 1959), pp. 349-65.

Highly competent, they failed through lack of sympathetic perception to comprehend the rising force of nationalism in their territories. Great Britain was at the last moment able to come to terms with India; the Netherlands failed over Indonesia. At the very end of their distinguished and turbulent colonial history, they achieved one of the most interesting constitutional compromises with their Caribbean territories, something which might provide a pattern for other countries. "The new concept, which evolved and was applied in Dutch island possessions in the Caribbean, was in essence the commonwealth concept: voluntary association with political autonomy in the local affairs of the dependencies. In effect, the Netherlands has emulated the British example."[1] The association of the Dutch Caribbean territories with the Netherlands is not quite the same constitutionally as countries such as Jamaica, Trinidad and Barbados, which have independence within the Commonwealth and handle their own foreign policy and have overseas diplomatic representation. Professor Stoessinger has, however, put his finger on the touchstone of continued harmonious relations, namely, voluntary association.

A delegation from the Netherlands visited the Netherlands Antilles and Surinam during 1971. They appear to have made it plain that the Netherlands planned independence for their two partners within 4–5 years although the views of the Netherlands Antilles Government were that the period should be very much longer. "Politicians of the Netherlands Antilles were acutely alarmed at the proposals by the Netherlands that independence should be achieved with all due speed. The issue of independence has been raised at an awkward moment for the Netherlands Antilles, since its reliance on the Netherlands not only in terms of financial, but also of police, aid is at the moment absolute . . . education has relied wholly on the Netherlands."[2] On the whole, however, after nearly two decades, the Kingdom of the Netherlands has been a success. The Dutch Government has exercised both self-restraint and a liberal attitude to change towards its Caribbean partners.

THE ECONOMIC PATTERN

The six islands of the Netherlands Antilles are divided into two groups, some 550 miles apart. The Leeward group consists of Curaçao,

[1] John G. Stoessinger, *The Might of Nations* (New York, 1965), p. 79.

[2] *Handels-en Transport Courant*, Rotterdam, translation, September 8, 1971. Dr. H. R. Dennert, Vice-Minister-President of the Netherlands Antilles Government, stated: "Within the next twenty years there can be no question of an independent Netherlands Antilles". *Trouw*, Amsterdam, September 16, 1971.

Aruba and Bonaire; and the Windward group of St. Martin (southern part[1]), Saba and St. Eustatius. Altogether the Netherlands Antilles has an area of some 394 square miles and 222,000 inhabitants,[2] of which 94 per cent. of the entire population live on the two islands of Curaçao and Aruba. The birth rate is some 2·5 per cent. and the population a young one: both trends follow the general Caribbean pattern. The income *per capita* of the Netherlands Antilles, in decline from 1957 to 1964, had since 1967 made some recovery and was estimated at $1,000 in 1969:[3] somewhat less than Puerto Rico, yet among the highest in the Caribbean, and indeed in the Western Hemisphere.

In the Netherlands Antilles, as in most small islands, economics have usually dominated politics, a consideration which probably contributed to its decision to become part of the Tripartite Kingdom. Since the settling of Portuguese Jews early in the seventeenth century, trade has continued to be important. Agriculture was limited and only of local significance due to a shortage of water. Following oil discovery around and in Lake Maracaibo at a time when Venezuela was governed by Juan Vicente Gómez (1908-35), a ruthless but accommodating dictator, the Shell Oil Company in 1915 built a refinery for processing its Venezuelan oil on the more liberal and politically stable Dutch island of Curaçao.[4] The impossibility of large tankers entering Lake Maracaibo because of a sand bar also influenced the selection of the Curaçao site. In 1924 the project had been sufficiently successful to lead the Lago Oil and Transport Company in the Standard Oil group to choose the neighbouring Dutch island of Aruba for its refinery.[5]

These two decisions radically altered the economy of Curaçao and Aruba. The islands prospered from the employment generated by the refineries. So great was the demand that workers were brought in from abroad: technicians from Europe and the United States, and labour from other parts of the Caribbean and Surinam. When World War II disrupted Middle East oil supplies to Europe, the importance of the refineries in the Netherlands West Indies grew apace.

Thanks to the oil refineries, the commerce of the two islands rapidly expanded. As was the case in other parts of the Caribbean, the economy was based on a single industry. Just as some islands once

[1] The northern part is French. *Vide* 264.
[2] 1970 estimate.
[3] In the Netherlands a rise of 33 per cent. was registered.
[4] Venezuela had a tradition of international commercial quarrels during the rule of Gómez's predecessor Cipriano Castro.
[5] The refinery was not completed until January 1929.

prosperous, like little Nevis, had been ruined when the growing of sugar cane became no longer economic, the risks which faced Curaçao and Aruba were great. About 1954 the sand bar at the entry to Lake Maracaibo was successfully pierced to facilitate the entry of larger tankers.

Relations between the Netherlands Antilles and Venezuela had always been difficult. To the Latin American Republic the Dutch colonies were traditional bases for smuggling to the point that special tariffs had for long been directed against them just as they had been set up against Trinidad.[1] Moreover, during a period when increasing oil was being discovered, Venezuela saw no reason why its oil should be processed on foreign soil. Economic nationalism called for pressure against refining on the offshore islands.

A tacit understanding appeared to have been reached between the two countries that oil refining in the islands would not be unduly expanded. Meanwhile the companies, whose oil refineries were no longer modern, felt obliged to take all steps to bring them up to date. Modernization paid off in terms of the utilization of less labour. At Curaçao, for example, the replacement of process units of small capacity by larger ones enabled employers to make considerable reductions in manpower The operation of the Curaçao refinery was complex since it mixed Colombian and other oil with that of Venezuela to enable it to manufacture a wide range of products. In the decade following World War II, its personnel was about 10,000. Of the higher grade employees, some 900 came from outside the Netherlands Antilles (mainly from Holland), while foreign labourers amounted to 4,000 to 5,000. During the second decade (1956-66), however, Netherlands Antilles staff began to increase markedly in relation to foreign staff as a result of careful and extended training both in Curaçao and in overseas operations of the Royal Dutch Shell Group. By 1965, of 4,265 staff, some 3,528 (83 per cent.) were Antillean and most of the foreign labour had been eliminated.

Although the effect of these reductions was extremely serious, some of the work formerly done by the Company had been passed over to contractors. Fortunately for the Netherlands Antilles, the very large foreign labour force which was practically eliminated acted as a cushion to reduce the need for laying off local labour. However the personnel dispensed with, all well paid, affected the economy of a small community. Some of the small islands in the Eastern Caribbean who had supplied part of the labour force also suffered.[2]

[1] *Vide* p. 157.
[2] *Vide* p. 191.

In Aruba, a somewhat similar situation had arisen. The Lago Company also embarked on the modernization of equipment which until then had demanded excessive maintenance. Its employees were reduced from 8,000 in 1950 to 2,000 in 1966. Between 1950 and 1957, the labour force was reduced by some 2,000 because the new Lake Maracaibo channel had made both the lake tankers and the dry-dock facilities, and thus their staff, obsolete.

In fairness both to Lago and Shell, the Netherlands Antilles have a great deal for which to thank the oil companies. Not only did they arrive on essentially virgin islands but they themselves have provided and operated vital contingent services which strictly speaking should have already existed.[1] A large part of the redundant labour from outside the islands was repatriated and did not therefore swell the unemployment figures in Curaçao and Aruba. The oil companies took definite steps to find other employment for nationals and many near retirement age anyway were retired early with special benefits. Both Shell and Lago undertook new or further training of redundant staff. Antilleans were sent to the States or to the Netherlands for re-employment elsewhere. Dutch employment presented problems because of the already existing unemployment situation.[2] A navigational school, partly financed by Shell, opened in 1966 at a cost of some 200,000 N.A. guilders.[3]

Although employment in petrol refining was reduced by 15,000 people in 20 years, it remains the most important industry in terms of contribution to the gross national product and of numbers employed. Despite Government fears of further substantial reductions after 1966, the total number, at least of Shell employees, stayed fairly static at some 3,500. However, the high unemployment rate of about 20 to 22 per cent persisted.[4] New construction work at Esso's refinery on Aruba and Shell's on Curaçao afforded temporary employment but was no long-term solution.

[1] Lago, for example, operated three dining-halls, a vocational school, a bakery, a hospital, schools, a laundry, two commissaries, and housing facilities. Cf. *25 Years of refining at Lago*, Lago Oil and Transport Company Limited, Aruba, January 1954, pp. 16, 23, 26, 29-30.

[2] Cf. *Nos Isla*, Shell, Curaçao, N.V., Emmastad, May 16, 1964, June 13, 1964, and June 27, 1964.

[3] Cf. "Scheepvaartschool N.A. begint in September", *Amigoe di Curaçao*, Willemstad, July 4, 1966.

[4] The total number employed in 1971 was 29·5 per cent. of the population compared with 24·9 per cent. in 1966. *De werkgelegenheidssituatie op Curaçao en Aruba in Juli 1971 op grond van een gehouden steekproef onderzoek en een vergelijking met 1966*, Departement Economische Zaken Bureau voor de Statistiek, Curaçao, September 1971.

The mining of guano in Curaçao, commenced in 1876, provides a valuable export and employment for some 500 persons. Together with sea-salt and chalk it is the island's only natural resource. Phosphate has been formed out of sedimentary deposits from the excrement of innumerable seabirds on the Tafelberg. The soluble phosphatic salts percolated the coral limestone. From the adjacent harbour of Fuikbay, a protected lagoon, the product is exported. Thanks to its low fluorine content, it finds a ready market in the United States, Canada and Europe.[1] The Government, reluctant to increase the unemployment level, recently granted assistance to the N.V. Mijnmaatschappij when problems arose.[2]

Tourism affords the only likely alternative large-scale industry. Racial harmony and political stability have indirectly done much to encourage its growth. Already many visitors, mainly from America but also from other parts of the Caribbean and Europe, come, attracted by the old world Dutch character of Willemstad and Oranjestad, while the low tariffs which make these islands almost free ports appeal to those on cruise ships.[3] Since 1957 tourism's contribution to the national income has more than doubled and accounts for some 10 per cent. of the national income. By 1965 it took second place as a source of income after oil.

Despite the disturbances in Curaçao in 1969, in 1970 tourist figures showed an estimated 15 per cent. growth over the previous year. Even more significant was the increase in St. Martin, where a casino was opened, and Aruba. New hotels were opened and additions made to those already existing. Improvements to airport facilities at both Curaçao and Aruba estimated at some $25 million are being made to enable the largest aircraft to land. Although the Government has invested substantial sums in the tourist industry and has shown its willingness to improve communications, nevertheless the industry has been unable to absorb the large numbers out of work in the Netherlands Antilles.

The Netherlands Antilles were hit, however, when the United States in 1965 reduced to $100 per person duty-free purchases of

[1] About 120,000 tons of phosphate are produced each year: ¼ per cent. of world production.
[2] Cf. "Minder optimisme over verkoop 'Real Estate,'", *Het Financiëele Dagblad*, Amsterdam, December 27, 1971.
[3] Cruises to Curaçao had risen from 73 with 38,925 passengers in 1963 to 90 with 48,803 tourists in 1964. *Caribbean Monthly Bulletin*, Vol. II, No. 9, Institute of Caribbean Studies, University of Puerto Rico, Río Piedras, Puerto Rico, August 1965.

Netherlands Information Service

Willemstad, Curaçao: showing the oil installations and port facilities.

Saba: a steel band.

Netherlands Information Service

Smoke rising over Willemstad, Curaçao, after riots in 1969, pp. 297-8.

Associated Press

Surinam: the Affobakka Dam.

Netherlands Information Service

Paramaribo: out-patients waiting for public health service treatment.

Netherlands Information Service

goods. The islands had for long specialized in goods for tourists which in Curaçao alone amounted to $7 million annually.

Emigration appears to be no solution to the unemployment problem. There is already unemployment in South America. The limits to which the Netherlands is able to absorb its fellow-citizens satisfactorily may have been reached.[1] Immigrant numbers, more especially from Surinam, had increased alarmingly during the late 1960's.[2] In 1970 the Netherlands Government agreed with the Governments of the other two Kingdom members on the desirability of establishing an immigration policy both for the benefit of the immigrants themselves and for their countries of adoption and origin. More was required to be done to enlighten would-be immigrants as to the social and economic problems of working in the Netherlands. The provision of suitable accommodation posed a challenge.[3] So far the Dutch had avoided the overcrowding so often found in British industrial cities.[4] Employers were urged to provide living accommodation for immigrant employees before offering them jobs. Furthermore the policy of the Netherlands Government was to encourage repatriation wherever possible. This stemming of the "brain drain" was of vital importance since mainly skilled men and women came to the Netherlands. In addition to immigrants some 1,000 Antilleans study in the Netherlands.[5]

Laws were passed by the Netherlands Antilles Government to encourage the founding of investment and holding companies. However since 1954, due to changes in the Netherlands-American Tax

[1] Although Antilleans and Surinamers may freely visit, live and work in the Netherlands, no Dutch citizen may reside in either Surinam or the Netherlands Antilles without permission, and work permits are difficult to obtain.

[2] Some assess the number of Surinamese in Holland to be as high as 12 per cent. of the population of Surinam. A more conservative estimate would be 7-8 per cent., which showed a significant increase since 1965 when it was rated at 3·5 per cent. The percentage from the Netherlands Antilles was considerably less. Cf. *De Volkskrant*, Amsterdam, September 9, 1971.

[3] In an interesting article pointing out the many differences between life and customs for the immigrant from the Netherlands Antilles in the Netherlands, Dr. A. Meyer suggested a centrally organized professional body should handle the reception of immigrants, hitherto left to the employers. "Achtergronden en problemen van de emigratie van Antillianen naar Nederland", *Nieuwsbrief*, Ministerie van Cultuur, Rijswijk, Nr. 6-1971, pp. 152-6.

[4] Cf. J. Tholenaar-Van Raalte, "De Integratie van Westindische immigranten in Groot-Brittannië en in Nederland", *Nieuwe West-Indische Gids*, The Hague, No. 2, June 1968, and Renée Short "How the Dutch avoided the build-up of ghettoes", *The Times*, London, January 29, 1969.

[5] Grants for students from the Netherlands Antilles and Surinam amounted to over a million guilders in 1971.

Treaty, the attractions of the Antilles as a tax haven were partly lost.[1]

The Government of the Netherlands Antilles strove to attract new industries.[2] In the past decade many new factories, such as packing, paint, mattress, household goods and cigarette factories have been established together with a brewery, artificial fertilizer and fish-canning plants. A new petrochemical plant, owned by the Standard Oil Company of New Jersey and U.S., Bahamian and West German interests, was opened at the end of 1963 by Prince Bernhard of the Netherlands. A project for obtaining salt for industrial uses was due for completion on Bonaire by the end of 1971.

The need for mutual moral and economic support between the three autonomous countries of the Netherlands Kingdom was underlined in the Charter. Particular emphasis has been laid on co-operation between Surinam and the Netherlands Antilles, yet links between them remain considerably less than those between both countries and the Netherlands.

Nevertheless, these islands illustrate the danger of too heavy dependence on one industry, particularly in small islands with a fast-growing population. The high wages and standard of living do not make it easy to attract the sort of enterprise that would most quickly aid the unemployment problem such as factories with a heavy labour content. Moreover, the lack of rain and soil conditions in many of the islands limit agriculture. The small size of the home market is disadvantageous: any worthwhile industry must export abroad.

The Netherlands Antilles has, since October 1964, been an associate member of the European Economic Community.[3] While this opens up a large market of about 170 million people in Europe, it not only places reciprocal obligations on the Netherlands Antilles in regard to the entry of Common Market goods but also faces the islands with fierce competition. Although industries established in the Netherlands Antilles are given access to the E.E.C., France, for example, has objected to free imports of oil products and a ceiling has been set.[4] However, an emergent country may be permitted to impose some taxation on goods entering from the Common Market, and like Surinam

---

[1] Cf. F. P. de Vries, "Motieven en Perspectieven van de Nederlands-Antilliaanse Economie", *Nieuwe West-Indische Gids*, The Hague, No. 1-2, April 1965, p. 53.

[2] Cf. *Guide for the Establishment of enterprises in Curaçao*, Curaçao Bureau of Economic Affairs, July 1965.

[3] Surinam became an associate member of the E.E.C. in September 1962.

[4] Two million tons per annum.

the Netherlands Antilles is also able to draw from the Overseas Development Fund of the E.E.C.

The crux of the problem rests in what the Netherlands Antilles will be able to manufacture competitively. Its labour force is adequate with a much better record of industrial harmony than in many other parts of the Caribbean. Unlike some Caribbean countries, trade unions have not been linked to political parties. Wages, however, are much higher than in many competitive areas.

At a time when Venezuela is looking ever more critically at the refining of its oil in foreign offshore islands, the avoidance of strife in the refineries, which would disrupt outlet of mainland oil, has at all costs to be avoided. The riots in Curaçao in 1969 acted as a warning of the dangers that may lie ahead.

The Netherlands Antilles' population growth, unlike most of the other Caribbean islands, is not overwhelming its educational facilities. There are shortages, but on the whole expansion is adequate. Education is not compulsory but illiteracy is very slight. In 1970 there were 2,375 teachers in 278 schools with 71,217 pupils.[1] In addition to public, primary and secondary schools, there are various private institutions. Some of these are partially subsidized by the State, and of the total number of private schools 75 per cent. are run by Roman Catholic School Boards.

The language situation is complicated in the Netherlands Antilles where Curaçao, Aruba and Bonaire have about 200,000 Papiamento-speaking inhabitants, whilst in the Netherlands Windward Islands English is more commonly spoken. Dutch remains the official language of instruction in the schools. The teachers' training centre at Curaçao is symbolic of the present programme of appointing native teachers when possible. However, at present the majority of the teachers are Dutch and students from Curaçao still go to the Netherlands to train as teachers.

* * * *

The Netherlands Antilles afford a preview of the difficulties which the inevitable increase of automation may cause to other small countries where the economy does not expand fast enough to provide sufficient alternative employment.[2] Every allowance must be made for the complexity of the situation in Curaçao and Aruba. The immediate problem is

[1] Cf. *Het Onderwijs in de Nederlandse Antillen aan het begin van het Schooljaar 1970-71.* Departement van onderwijs examen-en statistiekbureau, December 1970.

[2] Cf. A. De Klerk, "Een Zonnig Probleemgebied", *Economisch Statistiche Berichten*, Rotterdam, April 27, 1966.

caused by the giant international oil organizations which have found it necessary to introduce, as they euphemistically call it, "streamlining". No one can quarrel with the modernizing of a refinery. To oppose it would be as hopeless as were the attempts of Luddites in England to destroy the new machinery in factories during the Industrial Revolution. Moreover, increasing pressure will undoubtedly be exerted from Venezuela against expansion of production. The situation might be compared to an isolated company town which depends on one industry such as a factory or mine. If the concern has to shut, the town has no other outlet. There appears, however, to be no risk of the refineries closing down.[1] Meanwhile the Netherlands Antilles optimistically rely on ever-continuing assistance from the Netherlands.

SURINAM

THE POLITICAL PATTERN

The territory now known as Surinam became a Netherlands possession at the Treaty of Breda in 1667. Dutch rule continued, apart from two brief periods of British administration during the Napoleonic Wars. From 1828 to 1845 it shared a Governor-General with the Netherlands Antilles. In 1865, Surinam received a Colonial Assembly of 13 members, of whom 9 were elected by some 800 voters, the remainder being nominated by the Governor. The administration was conducted by the Governor and his officials in conjunction with a Crown-appointed Advisory Council, mainly composed of officials.[2] Like Great Britain, the Netherlands believed that the Colonial Assembly with its small electorate composed largely of merchants and planters, would be less liberal in its outlook than a Governor appointed by the Metropolitan power.[3] Notwithstanding that the Netherlands extended its own franchise, that of Surinam remained oligarchical. The resemblance to Great Britain's attitude to Guyana is strong. When the Netherlands constitution was revised in 1922, the status of the colonies was changed to that of territories. Surinam's Assembly was increased to 10 elected and 5 nominated members. An Advisory Council of 5 members came into effect in 1937 to assist the Governor.

[1] The new Asphalt Bitumen project started in 1966, although not a sign of expansion, was at least an indication of normal progression. Cf. *Nos Isla*, Curaçao, June 24, 1966.

[2] Logemann, *op. cit.*, p. 49.

[3] *Vide* pp. 121-2.

Surinam attained internal autonomy in 1950; it became part of the Tripartite Kingdom of the Netherlands in 1954, as did the Netherlands Antilles by the Charter of the Kingdom of the Netherlands.[1] The Crown and the Kingdom Government are represented in Surinam by the Governor, who, after consultation with the Surinam Government, is appointed by the Monarch.[2] Executive power is exercised by a Parliament ("Staten van Suriname") of 39 members elected by universal suffrage every four years.[3] The country is divided into 12 electoral districts. Two-thirds of the Representatives are elected by majority vote from these districts and the remaining third by proportional vote from the entire country. The Executive Council of Ministers, headed by a Minister President, is responsible to this Parliament. Sandwiched between racially disrupted Guyana and backward Guyane, Surinam has succeeded where they have failed, although each country has similar basic resources. Surinam's recent rapid advance in the economic field is due partly to careful planning but also in large measure to the political and racial stability which the country has enjoyed. Its co-equal position in the Charter of the Tripartite Kingdom has increased its prestige. In consequence, Surinam appears less likely to press for separation from a European country with which it shares sovereignty. However, the very complexity of the racial groups which include East Indians, Creoles,[4] Javanese, Amerindians and Bush Negroes may have convinced these diverse peoples of the necessity of tolerance. The violence which has characterized Guyana has been avoided.

The desire for independence in Surinam appears to have racial links: the Creoles anxious to sever ties with the Netherlands, the East Indians to preserve the Dutch connection. The latter group realizes the economic danger of a break. In addition, the Bush Negroes have always favoured Surinam's ties with Holland. Surinam, like the Netherlands Antilles, has sought a greater control of its foreign affairs, together with membership of the United Nations and other international bodies.[5]

[1] *Vide* pp. 294-6.
[2] In March 1963, Archibald Currie was appointed Governor, the first native-born Surinamese to receive such an appointment. He was followed by Dr. H. L. de Vries, after leaving Surinam in September 1964.
[3] Eligible voters comprise resident male and female citizens of the Realm (Netherlanders, Surinamers and Netherlands Antilleans) who have attained the age of 23. Prior to the election in March 1967, the Staten was extended to 39 members instead of 36.
[4] Creoles in Surinam are Negroes, usually living in urban areas. The term excludes Bush Negroes.
[5] *Vide* pp. 296, 298-9.

Racial groups dominate politics in Surinam. The pattern, however, has changed in emphasis due to the faster growth rate of the Hindu population in comparison with the Creoles.[1] The Government elected in March 1963 consisted of a coalition between the National Party of Surinam, the United Hindustani Party and the Kaum Tani Persatuan Indonesia, a small racially oriented group. The election held in March 1967, and contested by 12 parties, ended in a victory for the N.P.S. and the U.H.P. with 18 and 11 seats respectively in the newly enlarged Staten. The K.T.P.I. which had gained 5 seats in 1963 contested the election alone and won no seats. The N.P.S. led by Johan Adolf Pengel, who was also the Minister President, drew its support from the Creole group who live predominantly in Paramaribo, the capital. The U.H.P., led by Jagernath Lachmon, was supported by East Indian small farmers around Paramaribo.

In March 1969, following a wave of strikes, Pengel resigned. An interim Cabinet was formed with Arthur J. May as Prime Minister. May had been Prime Minister of the First Cabinet of Surinam during the period leading to autonomy. At the elections held in October 1969, Lachmon's U.H.P. won 19 of the 39 seats in the Staten. To prevent possible trouble from the Creoles, who sought not only a complete break from the Netherlands but also a military settlement of the border dispute, Lachmon became Chairman of the new coalition with Dr. Jules Sedney of the People's National Party as Prime Minister, representing the Creoles. The N.P.S. gained 11 seats and the National Republic Party led by Edward Bruma, a lawyer, one.

Pengel, despite his skill as a politician, had finally lost his dominating leadership.[2] He had concentrated on the control of three key posts: general administration, finance and domestic affairs. To independence his attitude remained ambiguous; he realized the dangers of political instability. He sought time for Surinam to develop its own potential wealth with outside aid from the Netherlands and beyond. Lachmon on the other hand firmly supported continuation of the link with the Netherlands.[3]

During discussions between the Governments of the Netherlands, Surinam and the Netherlands Antilles in January 1970, Sedney stated that his Government did not aim at complete political independence within their period of office. Further talks would take place on the

---

[1] *Vide* p. 240.

[2] Pengel died in June 1970.

[3] Asked for his views on the outcome of a referendum on the issue in Surinam, Lachmon stated his conviction that 70 per cent. of the population would vote against independence. *Haagsche Courant*, The Hague October 4, 1971.

possible extension of independence within the Charter. Included would be the entry of Surinam and the Netherlands Antilles into international agreements which would remain the responsibility of the individual country, although the Crown would reserve the right of ratification. The introduction of both a Surinam and of an Antillean citizenship would also be considered.[1] More natives of Surinam and the Netherlands Antilles would enter the Dutch diplomatic service, especially with a view to service in countries such as those of South America whose connections were of particular significance to the area.

The problem of the border between Surinam and Guyana lingered on as a continuing headache until the current decade. In 1799, the west bank of the Courantyne River was settled by the Governors of Berbice and Surinam as the boundary between the two territories. The Courantyne thus became a Surinamese river. When the upper reaches of the river were in recent years thoroughly explored, a second branch of the Courantyne, now known as the New River or Upper Courantyne, was identified. In consequence, doubt has arisen as to which branch is the true Courantyne. The Netherlands Government, basing its claim on geographic features, argued that the New River, undoubtedly the larger, was the true Courantyne. Great Britain and later Guyana opposed any change in the existing boundary, despite the new discoveries.[2]

The importance of the triangle of land, amounting to some ten thousand square miles, derives from its potential mineral wealth. The Surinamers are a great deal further forward with their explorations than are the Guyanese, even to the extent of discovering diamonds in the area. Surinam has held out to Guyana possible benefits from the building of the Kabalebo hydro-electric plant in the area.[3]

In 1936 a mixed commission fixed the tri-junction point between Brazil, Guyana and Surinam, on the basis that the boundary defined in 1799 still held good. At this point the Netherlands might have been prepared to accept a settlement on historical grounds, but any decision was interrupted by World War II. As a result of their explorations, the Dutch attitude has changed.

Guyana was anxious to settle the problem after independence,

---

[1] *Protocol van te 's-Gravenhage gevoerde besprekingen in de tweede helft van de maand augustus 1970.*

[2] E. Sluiter, "Dutch Guiana—a Problem in Boundaries", *Hispanic Historical Review*, XIII, No. 1, Durham, North Carolina, February 1933, pp. 2-22.

[3] Cf. Hans J. A. Hansen, "Verkenningen in de West (No. 7)", *De Volkskrant*, Amsterdam, November 16, 1965.

despite the failure of talks with Great Britain, the Netherlands and Surinam. Surinam prefers minimal Dutch interference within the terms of the Charter. Well aware of the inflammability of the area, the Netherlands has sought to promote cordial relations. In 1964 rumours circulated that Cuban arms were being smuggled through Surinam into Guyana, although this was denied by Guyana.[1] Nevertheless, Pengel persuaded the Dutch Government to give him a special Marine patrol for the border area. As a last resort, Surinam could have intercepted shipping on the lower reaches of the Courantyne, which would have embarrassed the Guyanese Government.

In 1968 and 1969 Dutch restraint prevented Surinam from taking action against Guyana. Following talks in Trinidad in April 1970 between Prime Ministers Burnham and Sedney, both sides agreed to demilitarize the upper Courantyne border area and to co-operate in economic development. An official exchange of visits between the Prime Ministers sealed the compact. It was also agreed to reactivate the Surinam-Guyana Commission adjourned in London in 1966.[2]

* * * *

Politically Surinam is at a crucial stage in its development. Any outbreak of racial violence would gravely prejudice its economy. Possibly its leaders possess greater awareness of national over racial interests than do leaders of Guyana. Unlike France, which emphasizes the gallic nature of its overseas departments and seeks to strengthen ties with the metropolis, the Netherlands has encouraged the maximum use of Surinam's autonomy. It has facilitated Surinamese participation in foreign affairs and has agreed to consider modifications of the Charter, while avoiding any unwelcome pressure on its Kingdom partner.

THE ECONOMIC PATTERN

Surinam has an area of 55,643 square miles bounded by the Maroni River on the East and the Courantyne on the West. Like Guyana and Guyane, the country has a small, flat and fertile coastal belt. Forests cover some 80 to 90 per cent. of its land. The total population is about 374,000 of whom more than half live in Paramaribo, the only large town.

The prosperity of the country was built on a plantation economy which reached its zenith in the eighteenth century. Decline commenced in the nineteenth century; by the beginning of the twentieth

[1] Cf. *Hispanic American Report*, Vol. XVII, No. 6, pp. 528-9.
[2] *Suriname news in brief*, Paramirabo, June 27, 1970.

century many white planters had left the country.[1] After the emancipation of the slaves in 1863, East Indian and Javanese labour was introduced to avert a collapse of the economy. Surinam shared the fate of other Caribbean colonies, namely rule by a government whose main interest was in other areas of its empire, in this case the East Indies. At a time which was crucial in Surinam's economic development, the Netherlands Government did little to arrest the colony's decline. Its policy makers believed in the doctrine of *laissez faire*.[2] The final loss of Indonesia led to greater interest in its remaining territories.

In Surinam as in neighbouring Guyana and Guyane, farming is concentrated on the coastal plain. Less than one per cent. of the total land area is under cultivation. Almost half the farms are occupied by East Indians skilled in rice cultivation. Much of this coastal strip is below sea-level, involving the construction of polders. Irrigation is provided by a network of tidal rivers running seaward connected with canals which also provide transportation. Water control, however, sometimes complicates the growing of crops other than rice, which is the major farm product.

Surinam's Ten-Year Plan of 1954 emphasized the importance of broadening agricultural development, particularly to provide more supplies for the home market.[3] It concentrated on the small farmer rather than on large estates. However, encouragement of the trend towards small peasant holdings has resulted in less efficient agriculture. "All in all the new pattern of agricultural production, which grew at the cost of plantation farming, accounts for the very low income *per capita* in the agricultural sector."[4] Land clearance has been desultory with little attention to irrigation prospects. Farmers have been slow to adopt modern methods, while agricultural workers have moved to urban areas seeking higher wages.[5] Even projects such as that of

[1] R. A. J. van Lier, "Social and Political Conditions in Suriname and the Netherlands Antilles: Introduction", *Developments Towards Self-Government in the Caribbean* (The Hague, 1955), p. 126.

[2] Cf. J. H. Adhin, *Development Planning in Surinam in Historical Perspective* (Leiden, 1961), p. 39.

[3] The *Ten-Year Plan* was extended at the end of this period as the *National Development Plan*, of which the first phase was known as the *Five-Year Plan*. Sf80 million was added to the original Sf127 million approved for the Plan. Cf. *National Development Plan for Surinam*, 1, Stichting Planbureau Suriname, n.d., p. 35.

[4] R. M. N. Panday, *Agriculture in Surinam 1650-1950* (Amsterdam, 1959), p. 218.

[5] E. H. Jonkers, "Enkele facetten van de Economische ontwikkeling van Suriname", *Nieuwe West-Indische Gids*, No. 1-2, The Hague, April 1965, p. 38.

313

Wageningen in the Nickerie District, undertaken outside the Plan, with the object of improving rice production by the introduction of expert Dutch agriculturists to farm on a co-operative basis initially proved disappointing. Nevertheless, benefits resulted from the scheme including progress in pest control research and soil mechanization.

Decay continued in sugar cane until only two plantations remained producing sugar, one being in the Nickerie and the other in the Commewijne districts. The irrigation systems complicated the mechanization of the plantations. Efforts were made to better the workers' conditions by improvements in housing and medical welfare.

Surinam's banana industry increased by more than eight times between 1962 (4,047 tons) and 1967 (35,441 tons.) Freedom from hurricanes is a factor of great importance.[1] Competition in the export trade, however, remains strong. The Surinam Government has encouraged the growing of oranges which are popular in the Netherlands on account of their high juice content. Coffee is produced on small farms and on plantations for local and European markets.

Surinam has the usual timber problems met with in tropical forests in the Americas arising from the variety of the trees and the limited number of trees commercially exploitable. In consequence the cost is often high in supplying the plywood plant at Paramaribo. Competition from Africa is strong.

Bauxite is Surinam's most important natural resource. First discovered in 1915, it has increased in importance since 1922. By 1950, bauxite accounted for 80 per cent. of Surinam's exports, carried on by the Surinam Bauxite Company owned by the U.S. Alcoa and the Dutch Billiton mining companies. Production rose from 400,000 tons in 1938 to nearly $5\frac{1}{2}$ million tons in 1967 making Surinam the world's second largest supplier of bauxite. Among the proposals put forward by the International Bank for Reconstruction and Development Mission in 1951 was the important suggestion that Surinam's bauxite industry should be expanded for the production of aluminium.[2] The feasibility of this project turned on the possibility of a supply of cheap electricity. A suitable site was settled on at Brokopondo (Affobakka) to erect a dam, necessitating a lake of 600 square miles. An alumina plant and smelter to produce 40,000 tons of bauxite annually was planned.

In 1957, the Surinam Aluminum Company (Suralco) was formed by agreement between the Government of Surinam and the Aluminum Company of America. The enterprise was mainly a U.S. project but

---

[1] *Vide* pp. 329-30.

[2] *Surinam, Recommendations for a Ten-Year Development Program* (Johns Hopkins Press, Baltimore, 1952), p. 209.

the hydro-electric installation would revert after 75 years to the Surinam Government. The enterprise might be compared to the American and Canadian bauxite investments in Jamaica. In October 1965, Queen Juliana of the Netherlands officially inaugurated the hydro-electric plant and the aluminium smelter at Paranam. Surinam had become the first underdeveloped country to possess a fully integrated aluminium plant. In December, the first shipment of aluminium ingots was made. The main purpose of the Brokopondo project was the generation of cheap electricity but there were other advantages. The dam facilitated navigation of the Surinam river and widened the possibilities of irrigation for agriculture. Paramaribo received a cheaper supply of electricity.

The Suralco development is an important step towards the fulfilment of Surinam's aim to improve its economic position by increasing the value of the final export product. Although production at a reduced level only started during the third quarter of 1965, exports from the plants reached 7 per cent. of the country's total exports for that year. By 1967, 741,206 metric tons of alumina and 32,169 of aluminium were produced, although full capacity had not been reached.

Further discoveries of bauxite in the Bakhuis Mountains in 1963 led to the construction of a second dam on the Kabalebo river, still not completed[1], which would have ten times the capacity of the Brokopondo project. Unlike Jamaica which lacks a cheap source of power for further development of its bauxite, Surinam has an easily available source in its rivers.

After six years of research by international oil companies, oil was discovered in the Saramacca district in 1965. The possibilities of development of this oil have still to be determined.

Notwithstanding the bauxite expansion and the establishment of some small industries in the Paramaribo area, unemployment remains a problem due to a high rate of population increase.[2] As an example, the Brokopondo project, which was most impressive to watch in construction, afforded employment for 2,000 persons; after completion, only 50 were required.[3] An income *per capita* of some $U.S.430 compared favourably with other underdeveloped countries.

Emigration from Surinam to the Netherlands accelerated rapidly

---

[1] Since 1964 some 18 million Surinamese guilders had been invested in this project. *Opbouw '70*, Ministerie van Opbouw, Paramaribo, January 1971. United Nations support for the Kabalebo scheme was assured by early 1972.

[2] In 1971 the unemployment rate was some 15 to 20 per cent. compared with 7·5 per cent. in 1965, and the rate of population increase about 3·5 per cent.

[3] *Het Financiële Dagblad*, Amsterdam, August 22, 1966.

during the late 1960's.[1] The increased arrival of women and children suggested more permanent settlement.[2] Even so the rate of emigration remains much less than that from the French Overseas Departments to France.[3] Notwithstanding their Netherlands citizenship, many Surinamese encounter difficulties in obtaining work and, equally important, housing. Relatively few return to Surinam. At present more Surinamese doctors practise in the Netherlands than in Surinam.[4]

Like the Netherlands Antilles, Surinam has a well-organized system of education. In 1966 the Legislative Assembly passed a Bill for the establishment of a University at Paramaribo. The Universities of Leiden, Amsterdam and Wageningen volunteered assistance. An approach was made to the European Economic Community development fund for money to cover the construction of the university buildings. The country's primary and secondary educational system is reasonably efficient. Surinam suffers, however, from a shortage of classrooms and teachers. The Five-Year Plan allocated Sf10·5 million for education which included 82 classrooms, 25 living units for teachers, an advanced and a general technical school.

Surinam has benefited greatly from outside aid. In 1963 the country faced serious liquidity difficulties from which it was saved by the E.E.C. development fund. Surinam also accepts loans from the Agency for International Development, the United Nations Special Fund, and particularly from the Dutch Government. Infrastructural improvements and budgetary expenses are met and financed in this way in the hope that private investment, particularly from abroad, will follow. Other steps have been taken, such as the setting up of the Foundation to Promote Investments in Surinam, which aims particularly at attracting Dutch contractors. Dutch capital is more sought after because foreign enterprise to be of value to the country must be persuaded to reinvest at least part of its profits—not always an easy matter.[5]

Surinam faces problems of low wages and a sharply rising population together with considerable unemployment. Nevertheless it has advantages. Much less monocultural than Guyana, Surinam has land suitable for agricultural development. The integrated bauxite industry promises to continue as a valuable source of revenue. Even the tourist

[1] *Vide* p. 305.

[2] Cf. J. M. M. van Amersfoort, *Surinamese immigrants in the Netherlands*, The Hague, 1969, pp. 48-9.

[3] *Vide*, p. 285.

[4] Cf. Paul van Beckum, "Surinamers in Rotterdam", *Rotterdams Nieuwsblad*, Rotterdam, September 30, 1971.

[5] Cf. "Zoeklicht op Suriname", *Elseviers Weekblad*, The Hague, August 13, 1966.

industry, in a country that does not seem very favourably placed for easy development, has shown a substantial increase.[1] Its close association with the Netherlands gives it access to capital investment from one of Europe's shrewdest trading countries, while its participation in the E.E.C. has opened a potential market for its goods.

Like a number of countries with development potential Surinam faces very heavy unemployment which is accelerating dangerously. This comparatively small and still thinly populated country illustrates dramatically the grim future confronting such a large proportion of workers in today's world.

[1] In four years the number of visitors increased from 10,987 in 1966 to 17,389, in 1970. *Surinam S.A. Visitors Statistics 1970*, Surinam Tourist Bureau, Paramaribo, n.d.

CHAPTER XIV

AGRICULTURE IN THE CARIBBEAN

The Antilles are partially submerged mountain chains. The main east-west chain stretches from the Virgin Islands and Puerto Rico to Hispaniola where it divides. The northern portion passes through north Haiti and Cuba's Sierra Maestra; thence, submerged beneath the Caribbean with a momentary re-appearance in the Cayman Islands, it extends across British Honduras and Petén into southern Mexico. A roughly parallel range traverses southern Haiti to Jamaica's Blue Mountains; it re-appears in the Republic of Honduras and thence into Central Guatemala.[1] The continuity of the separated mountain chains may be clearly seen in a chart of the Caribbean. The mountains rise to over 10,000 feet in the Dominican Republic; they exceed 6,000 feet in Cuba and 7,000 feet at Jamaica's Blue Mountain Peak. Even in the smaller islands of the Eastern Caribbean, St. Kitts, Guadeloupe, Dominica, Martinique and St. Vincent, have summits over 4,000 feet; and Nevis, Montserrat, St. Lucia of 3,000 feet.[2]

The east-west mountain system which forms the northern boundary of the Caribbean Sea is connected to the continent of South America. The mountain systems of Central America, which contain the Caribbean to the west, are roughly parallel to the partly submerged system which bounds it to the east in a broken chain from the Virgin Islands to Venezuela.

In both chains active volcanoes occur. Professor Eugène Revert points out the apparent connection of the volcanoes of the Eastern Caribbean with those of Guatemala. This was particularly evident in 1902, when Mont Pelée erupted to destroy Saint Pierre in Martinique[3]; there was a corresponding activity in the volcanoes of Guatemala.

In the late summer and autumn much of the area is also subject to hurricanes which often cause severe damage and even loss of life. Since

[1] James, op. cit., p. 741.
[2] The fairly level and low-lying islands in the Eastern Caribbean, mostly small in size, are: the British Virgin Islands, Anguilla, St. Martin, St. Barthélemy, Barbuda, Antigua, Guadeloupe (Grande Terre, the eastern half only), Marie Galante, Barbados.
[3] Le Monde Caraïbe (Paris, 1958), p. 20.

318

the days of Columbus, who rode out a hurricane off Santo Domingo, the history of the Caribbean records the devastation of these storms.[1] In recent years, tropical storms have been numerous. For example, the town of Jérémie in southern Haiti was devastated in 1954. In 1955 a hurricane struck northern British Honduras causing a tidal wave to inundate the town of Corozal.[2] The sugar factory, principal source of employment in the area, was wrecked and had to be rebuilt. Hurricane Hattie in 1961 scourged British Honduras. Belize was damaged to a point that led the Government to decide to move the capital inland; parts of the city had been flooded by the sea to a depth of over six feet. Wooden houses, built on stilts, collapsed: the streets were blocked with debris. To commemorate the disaster, a village was constructed to house some of those who had lost their homes and appropriately named Hattieville.

In 1963, hurricanes proliferated. Edith caused heavy damage in Martinique.[3] Flora killed some 4,000 persons in Haiti and rendered 100,000 homeless, moving on to Cuba, where it caused the death of a further thousand and the destruction of 32,000 homes[4]; Helen then proceeded to devastate Guadeloupe. The next year, Cleo damaged Martinique, Marie-Galante and Les Saintes, while in 1966 Inez struck Martinique, Guadeloupe and Haiti. Hurricane Dorothy made 1970 a bad year for bananas. To St. Lucia, for example, it meant a loss of some $E.C.25 million. The Guadeloupe banana crop, although only on the edges of the hurricane which severely damaged Martinique, was badly hit.[5]

Lack of unity has characterized the development of this fragmented and contorted corner of the globe composed of hundreds of islands of which some are little more than small rocks. Most of them have only a comparatively small area of level land. In practice this area may be often further reduced due to lack of soil sufficient for agricultural crops and to rock points above or below the ground which impede mechanical cultivation. To judge the effective density of the population in these small communities by the measure of persons per square mile becomes extremely misleading.

The Greater Antilles (Cuba, Hispaniola, Jamaica and Puerto Rico)

[1] Samuel Eliot Morison, *Admiral of the Ocean Sea* (Boston, 1942), p. 591.

[2] One family, to whom the author spoke a few days after the storm, had been borne out to sea on the rebound of a wave, only to be deposited, still in their house, about a hundred yards along shore. The house, though battered, was still in use.

[3] *Vide* p. 274.

[4] *Hispanic American Report*, Vol. XVI, pp. 959 and 965.

[5] *Vide* p. 275.

comprise 90 per cent. of the land area of the Caribbean and of its population. With an area of over 44,217 square miles, Cuba is by far the largest.[1] Only about a quarter of its land is mountainous, mainly in Oriente. Cuba's agricultural potential probably exceeds that of all the other Caribbean islands combined.

The explanation of the present-day agriculture of the Antilles largely rests in the islands' past history. When Columbus reached the islands in 1492 he found a primitive Arawak agriculture. The man-eating Caribs, who were pushing northward from the Lesser Antilles, were no more advanced. The destruction of the Amerindian population of the Antilles as a result of the European conquest had little effect on agriculture. There were no significant community land-holdings such as the highly developed collective systems of the Incas, Mayas and Aztecs. Antillean agriculture had few attractions in those early days. The ablest of the Spaniards sought their fortunes in Mexico and Peru.[2] Those prepared to raise cattle in the Greater Antilles confronted the prospect of a narrow market. Equally the first British, French, Dutch and other settlers in the smaller islands faced a restricted outlet for their small production of tobacco, indigo and other crops. Probably the buccaneers, uncertain as was their trade, at times did better.

The rise of sugar-cane cultivation in the eighteenth century changed the outlook. Europe craved for sugar and was prepared to pay highly for it. Dutch skill gave Brazil an early lead in the production of this commodity. However, the final victory of the Portuguese compelled the Netherlanders to seek their fortunes elsewhere, including the Caribbean.

Absorbed in the wider task of developing the Spanish American mainland with its glamour of mining and greater agricultural possibilities, Spain nevertheless retained the Greater Antilles, the largest and most promising of the islands. Even there it lost Jamaica to Great Britain during the seventeenth century, and a third of Hispaniola to France by the Treaty of Ryswick in 1697. Strategic bases to control the narrow passages between the islands were an essential part of Spain's theory of strategy.[3] Trinidad in the far south-east was retained for its

[1] Cf. Hispaniola 29,843 square miles (Haiti 10,714 square miles and the Dominican Republic 19,129 square miles); Jamaica 4,411 squares miles; Puerto Rico 3,423 square miles. Cuba is approximately equal in area to the rest of the Antilles.

[2] A feature of those communities has been the small incentives for the more talented individuals, and a general inertia. Cf. Thomas F. Carroll, "The Land Reform Issue in Latin America", *Latin American Issues*, ed. Albert O. Hirshman (New York, 1961), p. 169.   [3] Cf. Mitchell, *op. cit.*, p. 1.

strategic value and was only ceded to Great Britain in 1802 by the Treaty of Amiens. Debarred by treaty from the Spanish and Portuguese tropical mainland, and usually unsuccessful in obtaining footholds by force, the rival European powers found in those islands of the Caribbean, which the Spanish could not effectively settle or garrison, strategic points for raiding the Spanish possessions or trafficking with them in contraband.

The shortage of labour in the canefields, which the Amerindian population could not satisfactorily fill, led to the establishment of the notorious African slave trade. Soon the slaves outnumbered the white population, while the Amerindians, a prey to European diseases, were in many of the islands almost eliminated. In the outcome, the descendants of the Negro slaves became the dominant element in the population in the larger part of the Antilles, just as on a wider pattern they were to populate the coastal fringe of the Americas, North, South and Central, from Washington, D.C., to Rio de Janeiro.[1] Agriculture has continued to be profoundly influenced by them.

The eighteenth century was the heyday of the Caribbean sugar plantations. The French rapidly developed Saint Domingue after taking it over from Spain at the end of the seventeenth century. They also transformed Martinique and Guadeloupe into important sugar exporters. British activity was centred in Jamaica and in the smaller islands of the Eastern Caribbean, including Antigua, St. Kitts and Barbados.

These developments would today be considered small. A plantation of a few hundred acres had its own mill. The coarse sugar, similar to the *panela* still made in parts of Latin America, was shipped in barrels from one of the nearby small harbours which in the days of sailing vessels made shipping easy. These farming conditions were particularly suited to the mountainous islands where large areas of flat land did not exist.

The Haitian slave revolt in 1791 destroyed what was at the time the most elaborate economy in the Caribbean. Although attempts were made by Dessalines to get the plantations going again, fragmentation won a victory to which the policy of President Alexandre Pétion, in other ways an enlightened ruler, contributed. To travel through Haiti today is a revealing experience. The erosion of the hillsides symbolizes the poverty of the inhabitants.

The enormous importations of slaves in the eighteenth century had shamed an influential portion of public opinion, particularly in Great

[1] Frank Tannenbaum, "Discussion", *Caribbean Studies: A Symposium*, ed. Vera Rubin (University of Washington Press, Seattle, 1960), p. 62.

Britain and France, into demanding an end of the system. Strong opposition came from the plantation owners in both countries. The writings of French philosophers like Diderot and Rousseau, the attacks of Adam Smith at Glasgow University, and Lord Mansfield's famous judgment of 1772 declaring slavery illegal in England, all contributed to the outlawing of the slave trade at the Treaty of Vienna.

Emancipation, which was passed in Great Britain in 1833, in France in 1848, in 1870 in Cuba, and in 1888 in Brazil, had its repercussions on the plantation economy, particularly in territories like Jamaica where, as in Haiti, there was a possibility of the former slaves obtaining land to cultivate for themselves. In some cases, the resulting labour shortage led to the introduction of indentured Asiatic labour from India.[1]

The struggle for the Caribbean in the eighteenth century had largely been for the economic prize of its main product, sugar. For Great Britain, the victor, which had made such sacrifices to retain its West Indian colonies, the position was little better than for France, the loser. France could regret a lost Haiti and strive to bolster up the commerce of Martinique and Guadeloupe: Britain could watch the decay of its great base at English Harbour, which was matched by the decline of the nearby sugar plantations until Antigua became a grant-aided colony.[2] To this day, however, in a number of the islands sugar remains the major crop.

The weakness of the plantation economy encouraged the establishment of central sugar factories. In this development, the larger islands led the way, favoured by greater blocks of level land which facilitated transport. For an island like Martinique, broken up by mountains, the problem was difficult; even more so for the formerly prosperous island of Nevis, once one of the best developed colonies in the Caribbean.[3]

Increasing investment of U.S. capital in Cuba and Puerto Rico followed the Spanish American War. The move to large-scale sugar operations was accelerated with the added attraction of preferential entry into the U.S. market. Development took place more slowly in the British and French islands, where the traditional, if fluctuating, policy was to afford preferential entry to colonial produce in return for similar facilities for the manufactures of the mother country.

Political instability operated against successful agriculture in Haiti and the Dominican Republic. In the latter country, it was not until

[1] Some delay inevitably occurred between the passage of legislation and the setting free of the slaves. *Vide* pp. 179 and 241.
[2] *Vide* p. 176.
[3] *Vide* pp. 179-80.

the era of Rafael Leonidas Trujillo's grim dictatorship that agriculture was effectively expanded.

In the twentieth century, the fickleness of the sugar market encouraged the development of the banana industry in some of the Caribbean islands and on the surrounding mainland. Bananas have the advantage of giving steady employment the year round. Like coffee and cacao, they can also be successfully grown, if the soil is suitable, on hilly ground. Mechanization is of less importance to the banana industry than to sugar, even though in some areas the spraying of plants is carried out by planes. Bananas require labour for picking the crop, whereas sugar cane is moving more and more towards mechanized harvesting. On the other hand, unless a steady supply of fruit is available in substantial quantities, it is impossible to justify a service of fast refrigerated ships to take the fruit to the markets of North America and Europe. This factor created great problems for the industry in the British Caribbean islands when shipping was no longer available in time of war.

When World War II ended, the Antilles had come through a period trying indeed for some of them, but which had in many cases also brought prosperity.[1] Sugar and its by-product rum were in strong demand. Lesser exports also commanded satisfactory prices. Nevertheless, as had also happened after World War I, agricultural prosperity was short-lived. The experiment of the Antilles was not dissimilar to that of Latin American countries whose buoyant war-time economies collapsed so disastrously when prices of farm products started to drop.

A great attraction for the grower of sugar cane in most of the Antilles is a protected, or at least partially sheltered, market. The United States has always been a large purchaser. Its quotas granted to different countries and related to its domestic sugar production from beet and cane, have been generously priced.[2] Cuba was the principal Caribbean supplier to the United States until the political quarrel between the two countries. After 1960, part of Cuba's former U.S. quota was distributed to other Caribbean producers, but most was allocated to other areas. Since Cuba's commercial break with the United States, most of its sugar has been purchased by the Soviet Union, China and other Iron Curtain countries. France purchases sugar and rum from its Antillean departments on terms favourable to them.[3] For Commonwealth countries, the 1951 Sugar Agreement, initially set up for a period of eight years to allow for long-term

[1] *Vide* pp. 62, 108-9 and 123
[2] Quotas were restored after World War II by the Sugar Act of 1948.
[3] *Vide* pp. 275

planning, continued to be re-negotiated from year to year for eight-year terms. The Agreement was not only an attempt to tailor the production of sugar in the Commonwealth countries to the United Kingdom market, but also to fix annually a fair price for export sugar. Unsold sugar in excess of the quota was offered in Commonwealth and other world markets.[1] The negotiated price was determined not by world market price but by a figure which was reasonably remunerative to efficient producers. At the same time it was intended to add stability to the sugar market. Together with the smaller U.S. quota which some of the Caribbean territories receive, this quota has been of immense value in keeping these producers in business.

Yet since 1965 sugar production in the Caribbean has fallen steadily. Barbados, St. Kitts and Jamaica suffer from a lack of cane cutters but have a comparatively high unemployment level. In addition, despite continuing experiment, more cane is still needed to produce a ton of sugar in the Caribbean than, for example, in Australia. Although a promising future for sugar is predicted, in general beet sugar producers are becoming more efficient and cane producers less.[2]

Britain's probable entry into the E.E.C. affected the Caribbean most significantly in terms of sugar. The current Commonwealth Sugar Agreement ends in 1974.[3] The E.E.C. already has a surplus of sugar as of many other agricultural commodities: it exports beet sugar in competition with cane sugar from the developing countries.[4] If Britain were to enter the E.E.C. without making special arrangements for sugar, the West Indies would automatically lose its guaranteed outlet in the United Kingdom.

France, which imports large quantities of raw sugar from its overseas departments, is also the largest exporter of refined sugar. All the sugar produced in Martinique and some 65 per cent. of that in Guadeloupe goes to France. The Treaty of Rome in 1957 safeguards the overseas

[1] Cf. A. C. Barnes, *The Sugar Cane* (New York, 1964), pp. 388-9, and Vladimir P. Timoshenko and Boris C. Swerling, *The World's Sugar* (Stanford University Press, Stanford, California, 1957), pp. 327-39.

[2] *The Daily Gleaner*, Kingston, editorial, January 7, 1971. C. Czarnikow Ltd. estimated that world sugar production needed to expand at around 2·5 million tons every year to keep pace with growing consumption needs. *Sugar Review*, No. 1001, London, December 17, 1970.

[3] Following negotiations in December 1971, developing countries received, in addition to a basic price of £50 a ton, a special payment agreed annually of £7 to £11 a ton, related inversely to the world sugar price. However, despite a high world price, Caribbean countries were still entitled to £61 a ton, if their quantity of exports fell short of a certain figure.

[4] For 1968-9 the surplus sugar production of the Six was over 900,000 tons with the likelihood of even greater increases.

departments because they are constitutionally part of metropolitan France. The 1968 system of marketing crops and stabilizing agricultural prices, established by the E.E.C., included sugar.[1] Thus the position of Martinique and Guadeloupe remains protected.

Already by December 1970 it seemed that in the event of British entry into the Common Market the Commonwealth Caribbean would seek association which would cover sugar and some other agricultural commodities. Pressure from these countries for a solution to the sugar dilemma continued. Postponement of a decision until 1974 was not feasible in view of the length of time required to plan sugar cane cultivation.

The proposals made by the Six on sugar to Geoffrey Rippon, Britain's chief negotiator on the Common Market, were badly received by the Commonwealth sugar producers. Along with an offer either of an association or a trade agreement went the statement that the enlarged E.E.C. would give special consideration to countries dependent on sugar exports.[2] At a conference with the Commonwealth Sugar Exporters under Rippon's chairmanship, which followed in London, the offer of the Six was interpreted to mean that there would be "a firm assurance of a secure and continuing market in the enlarged Community on fair terms for the quantities of sugar covered by the Commonwealth Sugar Agreement in respect of all its existing developing member countries".[3] On this basis the representatives of the Commonwealth countries connected with the Commonwealth Sugar Agreement accepted the results of the negotiation. Lord Campbell of Eskan, Chairman of the Commonwealth Sugar Exporters, associated himself with this acceptance. Tate and Lyle had earlier expressed their apprehension about the future of the refining industry unless access for sugar cane into an enlarged Community were safeguarded.[4]

The statement agreed at Lancaster House was reported by the British Government to Brussels and written into the record. The Government

[1] "Contrary to the general trend of the common agricultural policy, quotas were imposed on sugar production in each member state; but prices were fixed at levels which were tolerable for the high cost producers." John Southgate, *Agricultural Trade and the E.E.C.*, Fabian Research Series 294, Fabian Society, London, May 1971, p. 23.

[2] Statement by the Chancellor of the Duchy of Lancaster, House of Commons, May 17, 1971.

[3] *Consultations with the Developing Member Countries of the Commonwealth Sugar Agreement, 2-3 June 1971: Communiqué*, Foreign and Commonwealth Office, June 3, 1971.

[4] Cf. Anthony Rowley, "Six sugar policy seen as threat to Tate and Lyle operations", *The Times*, London, May 14, 1971.

White Paper in July 1971 stated that until 1974 beet sugar production would be limited. It reiterated that the enlarged Community would have "as its firm purpose the safeguarding of the interests of the developing countries concerned whose economies depend to a large extent on the export of primary products and in particular of sugar".[1]

In the outcome the export of sugar to the E.E.C. must turn on the policy of that body. British comment has been mixed, including both favourable editorials and sharp Opposition criticism in the House of Commons.[2] Some French interpretation of the negotiations differed widely from that expressed by the British Government.[3] In short, the commitment would appear to be mainly a moral one.

The problem of sugar is largely artificial. Developed countries such as the United States, Great Britain and France subsidize a limited home production of sugar beet, and then purchase the balance of sugar, also at a subsidized price, from selected tropical countries. Only a relatively small part of the total sugar production is sold on the world market. The narrowness of the market is an important factor in the violent price fluctuations which have for long characterized the commodity.

In a more rational world, the land used at present for growing sugar beet might be used for other agricultural purposes. The tropics in turn could supply more of the world's sugar at a stabilized but not excessive price to the benefit of the consumer.[4] The feasibility of the temperate countries moving from sugar beet into an alternative use for

---

[1] *The United Kingdom and the European Communities,* Cmnd. 4715,(H.M.S.O., London, June 1971.)

[2] *The Guardian,* London, editorial, May 14, 1971, *The Times,* London, editorial, May 14, 1971. Denis Healey, House of Commons, May 17, 1971. Lord Campbell of Eskan, *The Guardian,* London, May 20, 1971.

[3] "Enfin, on ajoute que, dans le cas où il ne serait pas possible de parvenir à un accord satisfaisant dans quatre ans, on s'en tiendra à une reconduction pure et simple du 'Commonwealth Sugar Agreement'. Comme on peut le constater, le dossier reste ouvert." "Les producteurs de sucre du Commonwealth se contentent de la 'ferme garantie' donnée par les 'Six' de la CEE", *Europe France Outremer,* Paris, July 1971, p. 40.

[4] "Perhaps there is an eternal and infernal triangle in the world of sugar. The old triangle of sugar, slaves and merchandise has been replaced by a new tensional triangle: the poor countries all too dependent upon agricultural exports; the rich countries all too bent upon self-sufficiency; and the industrial countries all too preoccupied with the balance of payments imperative to export manufactured goods. The trouble is, of course, that the poor agricultural countries, like their slave forbears, come off worst—because they can never call the tune." Lord Campbell of Eskan, "The Bitter Sweet World of Sugar—a Test-case for European intentions", *The Round Table,* London, April 1971.

land is much greater than for the tropical countries, including the Caribbean, finding crops other than sugar cane.

Other agricultural products in the Caribbean did not fare well after World War II. Banana production had in most areas suffered heavily from the ravages of Panama disease, which in some territories wiped out plantations. Although progress was made with the introduction of an immune variety of the fruit, increased competition from other countries, such as Ecuador and the Cameroons, had to be faced. Coconuts in several islands suffered both from disease and hurricanes, while the citrus industry in Jamaica and Trinidad, which had prospered under British Ministry of Food contracts during World War II, watched its profits diminish in the years that followed. Coffee prices, vital to Haiti, which had risen slowly from the low levels of the late 1930's, soared in the years following 1945. Here again world over-production, particularly in Latin American countries, led to a disastrous fall in prices, mitigated in some cases for Antillean farmers by sales to the mother country. Cacao, important to the Dominican Republic and Trinidad, also depended on world prices which were often un-favourable. The smaller crops, including sea-island cotton in the Eastern Caribbean, ginger and pineapples also met with difficulties.

The Antillean economy has remained basically one of exports. In favour of the system, the value of the sugar exports of the Common-wealth islands has roughly matched the cost of imported food. The cultivation of sugar cane in particular is very well understood and the crop is likely to suffer less damage in a hurricane than some others. The sugar-price hazard is substantially reduced, since most of the sales are made in sheltered markets.

In most other agricultural products, price fluctuations have been severe in the post-war period, just as in the earlier days. The Antilles have participated in the efforts being made to stabilize world prices of products such as coffee. However, due to their small production, their influence is limited in the commercial deliberations of the world. How far the Antilles can successfully change from an export economy, often monocultural, to diversification, with the emphasis on production for the home market, is questionable. The most ambitious attempt to diversify has been made by the Government of Cuba. Fidel Castro made promises of land distribution to the Cuban peasants in his early struggle against Batista. Later as Prime Minister these promises were not fulfilled, and his government operated almost without regard to its own 1959 agrarian reform law.[1] Castro was acutely aware of Cuba's

[1] Cf. Robert J. Alexander, "Agrarian Reform in Latin America", *Foreign Affairs*, Vol. 41, No. 1, October 1962, p. 195.

weakness, arising from its monocultural economy based on sugar, which was sold to a major producer, the United States, with whom Cuba's relations steadily deteriorated. Repeatedly Castro and his ministers stressed the need for crop diversification.[1]

The utilization and development of land creates much controversy. The rapid advance in population, a characteristic of the second half of the twentieth century and one which shows little sign of abating, has made the problem increasingly more acute. Land is limited in extent, though man-made works can improve its usefulness. That it should be used for the benefit of mankind rather than for the monopoly of a few commands general acceptance.

The agricultural problem has its paradoxes. The developed nations tend to have food surpluses, despite the fact that they are largely industrial countries. The famine areas appear worst in Asia, and the standard of living remains very near the danger point in parts of Latin America such as North East Brazil and the Andean countries.

The answer to the food problem could be the breaking up of *latifundia* which can be accomplished by legislation limiting land-holdings as in Puerto Rico: or by taxing land values as Jamaica has tried, using an Australian example: or by setting up peasant holdings such as President Juan Bosch unsuccessfully tried to organize in the Dominican Republic.

The *latifundium* of Latin America has been a target for international attack, sometimes, though not invariably, with justification. No one can defend the sterilizing of land which could be economically used. Frequently the owner may be unable to finance necessary development. In that case, change is clearly desirable. Much of the trouble in the Caribbean as elsewhere has been an antiquated system of taxation: sometimes even a failure to collect taxes. Thus the incompetent farmer has lingered on.

Probably there would be a general consensus that no single or simple solution to the large versus small farm controversy exists. Agriculture is not a single industry: rather is it a group of varied undertakings which have little resemblance one to another. A small farm may more easily be supervised. Much of the efficiency depends on attention to detail. To pay by results is more difficult than in a factory. In the Antilles, the broken nature of the ground may lend itself to a number of small farms rather than to large units. In some cases, the small farm is well suited to the intensive utilization of the land as in the rearing of poultry and pigs. Again dairy farming, one of the most exacting of businesses, may well suit the efficient owner-manager of a small unit.

[1] E.g., Castro's speeches at Havana, December 2, 1961, and August 18, 1962.

Hurricane damage in British Honduras.

Sugar loading in Cuba. In 196

of ten million tons was set, p. 47.

Cuban Embassy, London

Anne Bo

Citrus canning at a modern factory in the Stann Creek Valley, British Honduras.

Steep hillsides which do not lend themselves to mechanical cultivation may yet be used for specialized crops. Developments in the terracing of hillsides have been made in the Caribbean, one of the best known experiments being in the Yallahs Valley near Kingston, Jamaica. The difficulty has been the cost of terracing the land and preparing it for settlement, combined with problems of marketing.[1]

A politically contented peasantry has always been regarded as a stabilizing factor in a community. In the Antilles, the possibility frequently exists of part-time employment on a sugar cane or other plantation during the crop which may fit in with a family farm. Everything should be done to encourage the small family farm, particularly in technical training for the job.[2] More and more the successful small farmer will be the specialist. The State can help through credit services, marketing, processing his crop as in the case of coffee, making available services of artificial insemination for the dairy herd, advising on new types of cacao, coffee or sugar cane, and on the remedies for the various pests which plague the agriculturist in the Caribbean as elsewhere.

Leaving the inefficient and underdeveloped large estate as something which should least of all be permitted in an area of land shortage like the Antilles, the case of the large plantations must be considered. From the angle of the State, this group is of major importance in most of the islands. Sometimes these properties are family owned. The largest, particularly in the English-speaking countries, are usually joint stock companies which control a large proportion of the best land planted in sugar cane, in bananas or other crops.

The sugar-mills and plantations act as a relevant example since they fulfil four functions; they represent the major investment, employ the largest number of persons, pay substantial taxation and provide a very significant part of the exports of most of the Antillean countries. Whether so much of the best level land should be under one crop providing seasonal work remains debatable. An alternative in some cases would be the growing of bananas, which spreads work more evenly round the year. Price fluctuations, strong competition in the U.S. market from large Central and South American plantations, problems of disease necessitating costly spraying, are but three of the

[1] Cf. Yallahs Valley Land Authority, 1951-61, *Ten Years of Progress,* Kingston, Jamaica, n.p., n.d.

[2] Fidel Castro, commenting on the shortage of workers with technical knowledge of agriculture, claimed that Cuba would have 40,000 trained personnel by 1974. Speech at the Twelfth Congress of the Central Organization of Cuban Trade Unions, Havana, August 29, 1966.

disadvantages. In the case of a hurricane, loss of crop for a year may result. Even a strong windstorm will do severe damage.

Unless an alternative crop will yield more employment and bring in over the years more revenue, there is little national advantage in a change from sugar. It is, however, at least possible in some of the Antilles that areas of land at present under sugar cane may go out of production. Some of the small estates, for example, in Martinique may have an increasingly difficult time; similar situations exist in other islands.

Rice and cotton have some of the features which make them suitable for large-scale cultivation. An increase of rice-growing as a means of reducing imports of wheat or flour has an obvious economic attraction. Cuba, Guyana, Trinidad and Jamaica all aim at expansion of this crop.

An alternative to the sugar company growing sugar is the confining of its operations solely to sugar manufacture. In practice, there is a wide variation in the amount of cane farming undertaken by sugar-mill owners in the Caribbean. In Puerto Rico, for example, holdings are limited by law usually to 500 acres. In the islands forming part of the Commonwealth, frequently the sugar-mill owner produces at least one-third to one-half of the cane consumed. From the factory's point of view, greater efficiency can be obtained when control of a substantial part of the production ensures a steady supply of cane reaching the mill, something difficult to arrange from a large number of small farmers.

The cultivation of sugar cane has changed enormously. It is probable that in a few years most of the world's sugar cane will be cut and loaded mechanically. Weedicides are replacing the hand cleaning of cane. Tractors and transport are becoming heavier and therefore require a greater investment of capital, just as is happening in the earth-moving industries. Research on fertilizers and on new varieties of cane advances apace. These developments do not necessarily make the position of the small cane-farmer impossible. Through co-operative or Government services, he may keep abreast of the changes, always provided that he has the necessary education and zeal. At present, the yield per acre of the small farmer appears generally to be less than that of the larger farmer. Allowance must, however, be made for any differences in land. Perhaps the most that can be hoped for in the Antilles is a holding operation to try to keep existing peasant farmers at work on their land.[1] Large sums of money have been used towards this end in most of the developed countries. Unfortunately, few of the Caribbean countries can afford the luxury of such expenditure.

Some other Antillean crops, however, offer better possibilities for the small grower than sugar cane. Apart from bananas, already

[1] *Vide* p. 42.

discussed, cacao, coffee and citrus come into this category. Nevertheless from the grower's viewpoint they all suffer from the fluctuations of world markets, although they have the advantage of being less susceptible to mechanization than sugar cane.

It would be wise to retain large-scale enterprises unless more efficient production is assured by breaking them up. At the same time, the small farmer should be encouraged and aided unless the cost becomes prohibitive. In some parts of the Caribbean the miniscule holdings present a further problem.[1] For their owners, part-time alternative employment is the most hopeful solution. Meanwhile every effort should be made to encourage suitable new developments. Much may be learned from the experience of other countries. In an age of technological revolution in agriculture, there is little place for the poorly educated and even less for the illiterate man or woman.

Unlike some larger countries, the Caribbean islands do not have extensive areas of virgin land suitable for development. Areas that have once been cultivated and gone out of cultivation, sometimes termed in the Commonwealth islands "ruinate", may frequently be noted. Usually examination of these abandoned areas will show that the land is marginal: hilly, rocky or with an inadequate rainfall. The small and uncertain yield of these lands may once have given a marginal return because they were cultivated by slaves or miserably paid labour. When labour on these conditions was no longer available, the land went out of production. Irrigation, though far from easy in these often hilly regions, sometimes makes possible a more effective use of land. Puerto Rico, Guyana and other countries have successfully introduced water distribution in dry areas.

Agriculturally the Antilles are not underdeveloped in the sense of parts of Latin America and Africa. Accessibility to the sea rendered exploitation easy at an early date, just as it facilitated the transport of produce for export. The very profitability of sugar in the eighteenth century encouraged the merchants of London and Bristol, Bordeaux and Amsterdam to lend money to finance plantations.[2]

Problems of dividing land are extremely complex. In the first place, a decision must be made whether to pay compensation or not. Confiscation may seem simplest, since compensation is so costly. Yet

[1] Haiti presents the classic example of *minifundia* in the Caribbean. "The prevailing system of land tenure, indeed, is one of small holdings and not the classical *latifundia* of Latin America." Manigat, *op. cit.*, p. 6.

[2] Richard Pares gives an admirable account of the vicissitudes of financing plantations in the island of Nevis during the eighteenth and nineteenth centuries by the Bristol House of Pinney in *A West India Fortune* (London, 1950).

probably it will be accompanied by a collapse of confidence in the Government, by owners of property of any kind, landed or otherwise. In most countries these will include a substantial part of the educated population. The effects may be very far-reaching. If there are foreign owners, the destruction of a country's credit may be involved, the consequences of which are hard to foresee. In Cuba's case, the impact of Government intervention over property on its relations with its major customer, the United States, contributed to the break which in effect led Cuba to cross the Iron Curtain.

Professor Calvin B. Hoover notes the care needed in land distribution in Chile. He points out that many large estates in Chile could be farmed equally efficiently if they were divided up into, say, a quarter of the existing size. If, however, an estate is split up into smallholdings among several hundred labourers, the production may fall sharply. The question remains as to whether land is to be allotted to the former workers on the *latifundium*, or whether the owners of *minifundia*, whose holdings are too small to yield a reasonable living, are to be brought in.[1]

These questions must be faced. They strike more sharply in the Caribbean than in larger countries such as Chile, where there is a greater area of suitable land in relation to the population. To suggest that these problems are insoluble is defeatist. Rather they must be approached cautiously and gradually, bearing in mind the risk of damaging tax revenue and the food production through any over-hasty measures.

To the visitor from a temperate climate, tropical agriculture at first appears a miracle of nature; the lush, swift growth of vegetation astounds the eye. Moreover, wage costs appear low in comparison to those of the developed northern countries. Nevertheless, those who have spent their lives on tropical farms are only too aware of the other side of the coin.

Too often the land deceives. A magnificent rain forest may cover valley land. To cut the timber, selling the valuable hardwoods which will help to finance the undertaking, appears a feasible venture. The cleared land will then be planted with cacao, rubber, citrus or some other crop. Only when the undertaking has been launched do the difficulties develop. The hardwoods prove to be of numerous varieties,

[1] "Economic Reform vs. Economic Growth in Underdeveloped Countries", *Development: for what?*, ed. John H. Hallowell (Duke University Press, Durham, N.C., 1964), pp. 47-8. In one of its more radical moves the Allende Government planned to expropriate 1,000 farms during 1971. Some 3,800 estates would be taken over under a six-year plan. Cf. Richard Wigg, "Socialist Government in Chile to step up rate of farm takeovers", *The Times*, London, May 2, 1971.

all different, making the saw-milling operation impossible to operate economically, even if a suitable road exists to haul the sawn lumber to its destination which may be a distant port. The clearing cost, which probably far exceeds the purchase price of the land, may well surpass the estimate. Labour, which has had to be brought in from a distance, has to be housed and fed. The crop is planted. Trouble may arise from drought or flooding. Pests or diseases proceed to attack it. Finally a hurricane intervenes to compound the disaster.[1]

A major problem in the Antilles is the small size of the territories. General de Gaulle called the French Antilles "specks of dust", a remark which was not appreciated. "Emerald gems" might have been a happier and equally accurate designation. Whether named for Saint or ship, the small islands, as a result of the shortage of good agricultural land, put to use much second and third-class land. Frequently the experiment turns out to be a costly mistake; it is far easier to increase the yield of the first-class land.

By reason of their lack of large areas of first-class level land, the Antilles are becoming increasingly handicapped in the export markets of the world. To a significant extent present and past colonial connections enable them to sell a greater or lesser part of their farm produce in partly protected markets. In addition to the sugar quotas, the United States affords free entry to the products of Puerto Rico and the U.S. Virgin Islands. Great Britain provides a sheltered market for bananas as well as sugar. Similarly, bananas, like sugar, from the French Antilles departments have privileged entry to France. The European Common Market membership of France and the Netherlands also affords benefits to the Caribbean territories associated with them.[2]

Yet the Commonwealth islands have failed to hold their former position as exporters of bananas. Compared with the pre-war position their share of the world market has sharply declined. The sharp rise in production in the Windward Islands has been largely at the expense of Jamaica where prospects have been damaged by poor quality fruit.[3] Moreover, increasingly U.S. pressure is being exerted to open up the British citrus market to American competition. Despite the lower wages paid in the Caribbean, the efficiency backed by the technology of Florida might well make this competition irresistible.

[1] Lest this account appear exaggerated, the author has written it with an experience of a particular Caribbean development in mind.

[2] In an enlarged community, associated status alone would not sufficiently protect the United Kingdom's banana producers. If they were to retain their position in the British market they would have to be given quotas in addition to associated status. Cf. Southgate, *op. cit.*, pp. 11-12.

[3] Cf. *Hansard*, February 26, 1971, Cols. 1182-92. *Vide*, p. 147.

The inherent hazards and uncertainties of land account largely for one of the most urgent problems in Caribbean agriculture today, namely the difficulty in finding labour. In theory, the unemployment position may suggest that no shortage of labour exists: in practice, shortages constantly arise, particularly in the harvesting of crops. More and more people seek to move to the cities, even when there may be little prospect of obtaining employment and still less of adequate accommodation. The shanty suburbs that exist on the edge of too many Caribbean towns illustrate this movement, the counterpart of the terrible *favelas* of Rio de Janeiro, and the *barriadas* of Lima.

Partly the move from the country is revulsion from the historic link with forced labour on plantations. When slavery was abolished, usually the alternative to continuing on the plantation was the development of unpromising smallholdings in the hills. Bad housing conditions, the traditional barracks, can only be improved slowly. The imbalance in the terms of trade between the primary producers of tropical agricultural products and the developed countries discourages capital expenditure.

To poor accommodation is added a dreary life, with the weekly market as the only diversion. Infrequent and costly public transport too often complicates movement. Moreover, the village shop has little to attract the buyer. Probably the extension of hire purchase, despite its inflationary risks, may stimulate a desire to earn more. In many Caribbean countries absenteeism disrupts agricultural work.

Migration to the cities may also be observed in countries like Canada and the United States. Basically it is far cheaper and more efficient to house people in blocks of flats or on new urban estates. Roads, water drainage, electricity and shopping facilities, in short all services including transport, become simplified. More and more people also appear to prefer crowds and numbers.

On the other hand the people of the Antilles are naturally individualists. Even when a man does not want to work on the land, he will seek a house and garden. Often he will struggle on with a smallholding even when it cannot yield a reasonable living. Clearly any Government must try to improve the lot of the smallholder. The task, however, is becoming more difficult and costly as standards of living throughout the world tend to rise.

*   *   *   *

All evidence suggests that much of the agricultural production of the Antilles is marginal. Cuba, as the outstanding exception, depends on its extensive areas of good level land. On the other hand, Haiti, with its fragmented peasant holdings, presents the most hopeless case. The most successful islands, such as Puerto Rico, the Virgin Islands of the United States, Curaçao, Aruba and Trinidad, have moved away from agriculture as the major support for their economies. In Jamaica also, the revenue from bauxite and tourism in each case exceeds that of the sugar industry, formerly the mainstay of the island.

Probably the land of the Antilles can at best be expected to support its present rural population. Improvements by bringing into production neglected areas or marginal land may be matched by increasing mechanization to reduce the need for labour. Certainly the Antilles must not be defeatist over their land problem. The best use must be made of the existing cultivable ground, especially of the limited areas of first-class land. To break up efficient estates into less efficient units would be as disastrous as to permit the continuance of poorly run farms.

Diversification of crops may be desirable, including the greater production and processing of vegetables and fruit. At the same time, market gardening calls for a high degree of skill and technical knowledge. The revolution which is taking place in tropical agriculture can only be turned to advantage by highly trained management. Here the universities will play an increasingly important part. Much is being done at the large University of Puerto Rico, while the University of the West Indies is fortunate in having for its Agricultural Department the former Imperial College of Tropical Agriculture in Trinidad.[1]

In two years of CARIFTA agricultural exports had expanded by 29 per cent. The aims of the Agricultural Marketing Protocol, to assist the smaller, less-developed members of CARIFTA to dispose of their surplus agricultural products, such as eggs, poultry and pork, had been partially successful. A "rationalization" of agriculture concentrated on the diversification and specialization of agricultural products at regional rather than territorial level.[2]

In general the Caribbean continued to present a picture of most countries advocating small ownership on political grounds against a continuing stream of workers from the land to the cities. Everything suggested that this pattern, as in other parts of the world, would continue. Efforts to reduce food imports by increasing local production would be maintained. Yet the basic export crops so essential for the employment of labour and for the provision of foreign exchange remained under a cloud, whether sugar was being supplied by Puerto

[1] *Vide* p. 369.
[2] *CARIFTA and the New Caribbean*, Commonwealth Caribbean Regional Secretariat, Georgetown, Guyana, 1971, pp. 118-19.

335

Rico to the United States, by the Commonwealth Caribbean to Great Britain or by Cuba to the Soviet Union.

The violent fluctuations in the prices of sugar, coffee, cacao and other crops have over the years been disastrous. Great hardships have been brought to the producing countries. Price stabilization of the major crops would be the greatest gift which the world could offer to the peoples of the underdeveloped tropical countries.[1]

[1] Cf. Pierre Gourou, *op. cit.*, p. 177.

CHAPTER XV

THE ECONOMIC DEVELOPMENT OF THE CARIBBEAN

After the Spaniards had ransacked Hispaniola for gold, with little result apart from the destruction of most of the Amerindian population, they concentrated their efforts on the mainland. The staging and garrison character of the Greater Antilles became increasingly clear. The more adventurous Spaniards preferred to go to Mexico or South America where opportunity was greater. Those colonists who remained supplied the garrisons with food. The loss first of Jamaica to England in 1655 and later of Saint Domingue to France in 1697 did not change the Spanish attitude, even though Jamaica grew in importance until in the eighteenth century it was considered one of Britain's most important overseas possessions; while French agricultural and commercial skill turned Saint Domingue within a century into its most valuable colony and one of the largest world exporters of sugar.[1] Steadily sugar displaced in importance former Caribbean crops such as tobacco and indigo.

The different colonial powers, Spain, Britain, France, the Netherlands, Denmark and Sweden, operated a two-way trade in the Caribbean which was suited to the geography of the islands and to the economic beliefs of the day. As a by-product of the system, widespread smuggling developed during peace and contraband during the frequent periods of international conflict.

When the turmoil of the eighteenth century was followed by the tranquillity of the years after the Peace of Vienna, the established pattern of trade continued, even though modified by the new theories propounded by the liberal economists. The very cataclysm of the Napoleonic wars had sown the seeds of formidable competition for Antillean sugar. Final British victory, which included supremacy in the Caribbean, began to prove barren as the century advanced.

Mechanical development applied to sugar factories led to the installation of "centrals". Large sugar factories with newer processes of manufacture and modern machinery resulted in cane being hauled longer distances by improved methods. Many of the older and smaller

[1] Cf. Leyburn, *op. cit.*, p. 15.

mills which had often been driven by wind, water or even oxen, closed. Replacing the hogshead, the new factories bagged their sugar and shipped in large quantities; the steamship began to replace the sail ship. Larger vessels required deeper draft. Thus the picturesque little seaports of olden times fell into disuse. The half-abandoned harbours of Jamaica's north coast from Lucea to Annotto Bay symbolize this economic change. An entire island, such as Nevis, could be forced out of business, not being large enough for a central factory.

With quixotic change of fortune, the eighteenth century, which had channelled benefits largely to the mother countries,[1] was succeeded by the nineteenth century when the profits from sugar evaporated. Beet competition, which had been stimulated by the Napoleonic wars, increased. Spain's loss of its mainland colonies resulted in greater effort to produce sugar in Cuba. Capital and management from the United States and from Haitian planters who had fled the great slave revolt of 1791 contributed to this expansion. Increasingly Great Britain and France had to subsidize, albeit with reluctance, their once-prosperous colonies. When the United States took over Puerto Rico from Spain, and also Cuba for a time, favoured entry to its growing internal market followed. As the U.S. sphere of influence widened, aid was extended to other parts of the Caribbean, including the Dominican Republic and Haiti.

The industrialization of the nineteenth and twentieth centuries weighted the terms of trade against the West Indies. In the days when water transportation was usually cheaper than land, the proximity of small island plantations to the sea was of real advantage, coupled with a plentiful supply of small ships to transport the products to the markets in Europe or North America. In terms of haulage, Argentina with magnificent animal transport suffered a comparable disadvantage when the automobile succeeded the horse.

The Caribbean remained dominantly agricultural during the first four decades of the twentieth century. The riot-torn later "thirties" encouraged political consciousness. World War II hastened major change by stimulating nationalism.

Industrialization has conferred material benefits on the citizens of the leading developed countries which today are so pronounced that a modern worship of mammon threatens to outmode other cults. In

---

[1] Against this must be set off defence costs borne by each European power in respect of its West Indian possessions, particularly heavy during the wars of the eighteenth and early nineteenth centuries.

the forefront is the affluent society of the United States, whose achievement is beyond dispute. In education, in good living conditions and in generosity towards less-developed countries, history is likely to laud the accomplishment. Yet the very success of the United States in turning the scales to victory in World War II and in promoting with the Marshall Plan Europe's recovery has tended to oversimplify industrialization to citizens of less-developed countries as a solution to their problems. The hardships and sacrifices of the countries which first industrialized too often are forgotten.[1] Great Britain, first country to industrialize, exhibited them in the urban slums and miners rows grimly depicted by D. H. Lawrence. Saving is acknowledged by economists as being essential to successful advance. Great Britain achieved it by a ruthless holding down of conditions of employment, combined with a capitalism unenlightened socially but nevertheless prepared to save substantially for reinvestment. The early industrialization of other countries followed a somewhat similar pattern. Little foreign capital to finance development was available, unlike today.

The early economists of the era argued that development would breed further development, which indeed proved to be the case, though both John Stuart Mill and Karl Marx from different angles foresaw dangers. Saturation was partly alleviated by the fields for foreign investment which opened up, particularly in the Americas. U.S. investment in Cuba after the Spanish-American War provides an example. Great Britain, however, slanted its commercial drive to its other territories, and even to the mainland Americas, rather than to its ancient but impoverished Caribbean territories.

Of more significance than the development of new lands, industrialized countries expanded not only their internal trade but their commerce with one another. The substantial traffic between Great Britain and Germany before World War I provides an illustration, notwithstanding their relentless political rivalry.

Increasing technology kept on spawning new jobs, despite the rapid population increase. Malthus seemed to have been proved wrong. Electricity, automobiles, and later aeroplanes, in turn generated employment. Vast new food-producing areas came into production. The consecutive pattern whereby invention begot invention tended to sanctify and enshrine the system. Crises certainly occurred including

---

[1] "We have but to recall the long, hard years over which the development of the industrialised nations was spread, in order to put aside any false optimism. The process of industrial growth, and how to achieve it, is today better understood; but the difficulties are none the less formidable." *Aid to Developing Countries*, Cmnd. 2147 (H.M.S.O., London, 1963), p. 5.

the great crash of the early 1930's; but most people accepted the viability of the system. Even in our day the demand for labour has remained high. The United States, Great Britain, France, Germany, the Netherlands and Switzerland have all attracted immigrants or temporary workers in the post-World War II years. A shortage of labour in the industrialized countries has usually characterized the period.

In contrast, endemic unemployment has increasingly plagued the underdeveloped world. People seeking work flood the great cities of Latin America. The Antilles present in miniature an example of the greatest problem of our day, the need to provide for the people of a country steady employment at a fair wage. Mesmerized by the spectacular advances in the industrialized countries, the under-developed countries have too readily assumed that industrialization would prove the key to prosperity. The very ease of erecting a modern labour-saving factory, often financed with foreign capital, may prove a delusion. Too often new industries have turned out to be a cracked Aladdin's lamp for the transformation of a backward agricultural economy.

These industries import the latest labour-saving machinery, at the same time creating a capital debt. Usually protected by tariffs, unless they are extractive such as oil wells and bauxite mining, they are able to pay a relatively high rate of wages. Trade unions in the United States, perhaps with their tongues in their cheeks, press the desirability of this, as has occurred in Puerto Rico, Jamaica and Trinidad.[1]

The effect may often be to raise wages in existing industries. However, in agriculture, usually the largest employer of labour, topographical difficulties often raise costs dangerously in relation to world prices. In fact, the Antilles are high-cost producers. Still more serious, the employment of a small elite at unrealistic wages exerts an unsettling effect on workers in less favoured occupations. If wage rates in general are unduly low—and the margin of profit unduly high—the impact of the elite group could be beneficial. More often the result may be one of drawing labour to the perimeter of the cities in pursuit of the chimera of a non-existent high paid job.

In discussing Jamaica's economic problems, Professor Sir Arthur Lewis has clearly stated the dangers of an unbalanced wage structure which may hasten mechanization in the canefield or even in the house-wife's kitchen, when the former worker may join the ranks of the unemployed.[2] What may seem unreal in a country like the United

[1] *Vide* pp. 114-5, 143, and 159-60.
[2] "What Causes Unemployment", *The Daily Gleaner*, Kingston. September 7, 1964.

States or Great Britain presents an economic challenge in over-populated Caribbean countries with never-ending unemployment. The very mechanization results in a cash out-flow for the purchase of mechanical equipment to replace labour and adds additional strain to the balance of payments. Sir Alexander Bustamante, Jamaica's former Prime Minister, stated that he was not prepared to see labour thrown on the scrap heap of unemployment.[1] He introduced legislation to limit the further mechanization of the sugar industry in his island. In the long run, his action may make Jamaica's sugar industry uncompetitive in world markets. On the other hand, Great Britain would readily acknowledge that the purchase of much of the sugar under the Commonwealth Sugar Agreement does not constitute an economic proposition. If in fact there is an element of subsidy, a prime purpose of the aid would be to afford the maximum of employment.

Progress has been taking place in the industrialization of many parts of the Caribbean. The indications are that it will extend. Small markets, however, present a limiting factor. Infrequent shipping services and sometimes antiquated port facilities delay the interchange of goods; they discourage a change in the established pattern of trade which has been with Europe and North America.

Cuba possesses the greatest development potential. The American occupation was followed by the development of public utilities. Good roads and railways effectively linked different parts of an island much flatter than the remaining Greater Antilles. It had already attained one of the highest standards of living in Latin America before the Castro Revolution.[2] Despite a monocultural export economy, the basis for an advance had been laid. Some mineral development had taken place; more was envisaged. Proximity to the United States, plus good harbours, facilitated trade.

The Fidelista revolutionary government correctly grasped the need for commercial diversification. To encourage the production of more food was urgent; the development of industry was obvious. Conflict with the United States wrecked any chance of an easy change-over of Cuba's economy. If Castro had possessed the subtlety of a Nasser, he might well have obtained the help he needed from both sides of the Iron Curtain. In the outcome, an unnecessary degree of nationalism led him into a political quarrel which resulted in Guevara's misjudged

[1] September 2, 1964.
[2] *Vide* p. 33

341

attempt to hurry Cuba into an ill-considered factory programme dependent on Iron Curtain aid and advice. The neglect of the sugar industry, main source of the island's revenue, compounded the error.

Nevertheless, Cuba remains by far the most important potential market in the Caribbean. Development has taken place and will continue, even if the start was clumsy. In due course the country is likely to march ahead, particularly if it can achieve a *modus vivendi* with the United States. A basis for progress is provided for by a reasonably literate population which is without problems of excessive growth together with a government which concentrates on education.

In contrast, Haiti's population has the highest illiteracy rate in the Caribbean. From any angle the economic future looks grim. The swelling population confronts a diminishing standard of living, dependent on limited and eroded agricultural land. The country's economy has been wrecked by a century and a half of corrupt and incompetent government. Basic necessities like good systems of roads and railways do not exist. Public utilities, including an efficient system of water, electricity and telephones, are lacking. In Port-au-Prince the visitor quickly learns to keep a candle handy for the inevitable electricity cut. In the countryside, he is similarly struck with the backwardness of the agriculture, whether he journeys north-ward to the Artibonite Valley or southward to the shores of the Caribbean. Many Haitians tacitly recognize the hopeless situation by illegally emigrating, with all the attendant risks, to the Dominican Republic and the Bahamas. Outside aid to mitigate undernourish-ment and provide employment appears to be Haiti's immediate economic aim. Industrialization, local and foreign alike, has made little impact.

Despite political mismanagement almost as great, Haiti's neighbour, the Dominican Republic, shows more promise. Better roads and port facilities provide a foundation for modest advance. Trujillo established at Santo Domingo a trading estate with nascent industries. The layout is good. Agriculture provides more diversification than in Cuba and Haiti. The Dominican Republic is not overpopulated, though far too many of its inhabitants are illiterate and impoverished. If political stability can be permanently established, the United States is likely to continue its aid on a generous scale. A prosperous Dominican Republic oriented to the West would provide the most telling answer to a Communist Cuba.

Puerto Rico's high standard of living, thriving industries and well-educated population present a sharp contrast to the three Republics in the Antilles. The introduction of massive American aid and investment has been successfully married to enlightened administration introduced by Governors Tugwell and Muñoz Marín.[1] In the context of Cuba, Haiti and the Dominican Republic, charges levelled against Puerto Rico as being in thrall to colonialism ring hollow. Puerto Rico may find that industrial problems will develop out of increasing competition in island markets from the U.S. mainland; however, its industries are likely to make sufficient adjustments for the maintenance of continuing prosperity. None the less, Puerto Rico's economy is anchored to its special tax-favoured and free entry position in relation to the United States, strengthened by competition made possible by wage rates below those of the mainland United States.

The U.S. Virgin Islands have similarly benefited from association with the United States. To sugar production, helped by the American quota, has been added tourist development in recent years. An outlet for surplus population as in the case of Puerto Rico is afforded by right of entry to the United States. Despite the advantage of the American link, industrialization has not followed the successful pattern of Puerto Rico, a sure pointer to the weakness of very small islands as centres for manufacture. Nevertheless, the U.S. Virgin Islands have attained a standard of living much higher than the neighbouring British Virgin Islands and above that of Puerto Rico.

Jamaica has moved boldly and so far smoothly into independence. With an export economy divided between bauxite mining, sugar and tourism, the outlook would be promising but for the heavy rate of unemployment aggravated by the high birth rate characteristic of the Antilles.[2] The new industries developing around Kingston mark the progress of the country, even if they cannot provide enough jobs. The University of the West Indies has provided a focal point for education in the Commonwealth countries of the Caribbean. Inevitably its impact has been strongest upon Jamaica.

More industrialized than Jamaica, Trinidad has used its oil resources to good advantage. The processing of imported petroleum, a tribute to its competent and stable government, has expanded its refining by adding to the oil produced locally. Other industries have followed. The Trinidad Government has evinced continuing attention to education, increasingly since independence.

[1] *Vide* pp. 99-101 and 103.
[2] However family planning has been successfully established. *Vide* pp. 150 and 367-8.

Of the lesser islands, Barbados has made full use of its limited land resources. Densely populated, its sugar industry is fully developed though its units are small by international standards. The restricted size of its market of barely a quarter of a million persons limits industrialization. Tourism has been successfully encouraged. In the Commonwealth Caribbean, the people of Barbados have earned a high reputation for their standard of education and hard work.

The Leeward Islands and the Windward Islands typify the problems created by the lack of internal markets. Relatively worse-placed for the production of sugar or other crops than they were two hundred years ago with the passing of the small plantations, the future at best is uncertain. The new model of semi-independent political association with Great Britain is in operation.[1] At present almost all the islands are grant-aided by the United Kingdom. Whether this will continue indefinitely must remain a matter for speculation.

Other small groups including the British Virgin Islands fall into the same category. The Cayman Islands have already made creditable progress. Grand Cayman has established hotels on its magnificent beach, comparable with that of the Grande Anse in Grenada. Convenient air-services link it quickly to Florida and Jamaica. Keeping in view the pattern of the Bahamas and—outside the area under discussion—Bermuda, the Cayman Islands aim at an economy based on attracting foreign visitors, some of whom may acquire winter homes. A valuable addition to the revenue of the islands also comes from remittances often in hard currency from Cayman Islanders serving on ships, trading all over the world.

The Turks and Caicos Islands present the problem of an isolated community with little prospect of wealth. The salt industry has sharply receded. On the development already planned to attract tourists and foreign investors turns the future prosperity of the territory.

An equable climate, particularly attractive in the winter, and proximity to the coast of the United States, have presented opportunities which the Bahamians have turned to the advantage of their economy. In the case of several of the islands, particularly New Providence, prosperity has resulted from the development of what seemed an unpromising terrain. Industrialization is progressing effectively at Freeport in the Grand Bahama Island. The economy of the country represents a triumph of man over natural conditions.

The French Islands present a picture of inadequate development.

[1] *Vide* pp. 174-6 and 194-6.

344

France has invested heavily in Martinique and Guadeloupe, but not always wisely. The very excellence of French education has not been matched with opportunities for employment. Foreign capital has been insufficiently encouraged while French capital has sought outlets elsewhere. The surplus labour of islands which are considerably over-populated would seem to have its best chance in emigration to France, so long as that continues to be permitted. Independence might intensify rather than resolve these problems.

In contrast, the Netherlands Antilles reflect the intelligent approach by the Dutch and the islanders to the problem of territories with extremely limited natural resources. The great refineries of Curaçao and Aruba not only generated local employment; for a time they even drew labour from abroad, including the British islands. Industrialization and tourism are being pressed forward by the Netherlands Antilles Government in collaboration with the Netherlands. Diversification has become the more urgent since the oil refineries have tended in recent years to reduce their need for labour by increasing mechanization.[1]

The three Guianas present in some respects an economic contrast not only to the Antilles but also to one another. In every case a vast area of nearly empty land faces a coastal fringe development. Only in recent years has bauxite provided effective industrial development in the interior. The coastal plantation economy, despite good organization in Guyana and Surinam, might be termed a struggle of man against hard natural conditions of both climate and soil. The population of Guyane has shrunk compared with its nineteenth-century peak.[2]

Theoretically all three could be an outlet for the surplus population from Caribbean islands with which they have ethnic and linguistic links. In practice, such a policy remains suspect to many in the three mainland countries. The connotation evokes memories of slavery, indentured labour or convict prisons.

As patterns, the three countries provide an interesting political contrast. In time we may be able to judge the economic accomplishments of an independent Guyana, an autonomous Surinam in the Tripartite Kingdom, and the overseas French department of Guyane. All three are well placed to receive financial aid for development. All

---

[1] *Vide* pp. 302-3.
[2] Cf. Mitchell, *op. cit.*, p. 175.

three have hopes of increasing mineral finds. All three face a land composed to a significant extent of sterile rock formations not suited to agriculture and tropical jungle not easy to subdue.

To avoid the harsh pressures on the population which would otherwise be necessary for industrialization in any underdeveloped country, relying only on its savings, outside aid has become a well-established practice. Colonial powers have for long adopted this method. Great Britain contributed substantially to the financing of the railways of Canada and India. Much of the capital for such ventures was subscribed through the London Money Market. Colonial loans often arranged by the Crown Agents for the Colonies have been a continuing method of finance. In times of emergency or economic stress, grants-in-aid are made which normally involve the British Treasury keeping a close watch on the territory's expenditure. France, the Netherlands and later the United States have all participated in the financing of their colonies and dependencies.

A change of political climate has resulted in a new attitude towards the financing of the numerous underdeveloped countries, many of which have attained independence in recent years, and others which for long have had independence but have failed to "take-off". After World War II in all advanced countries there was a significant development in the attitude towards foreign aid. In Britain, as in France, the giving of aid to poor countries had its roots in colonial policy. At the Montreal Conference in 1958 Great Britain announced its new policy of extending development loans to independent members of the Commonwealth. By 1960 it had extended its interest to under-developed countries as a whole.[1] In 1963 France also expressed its responsibilities in regard to world development.[2] In the United States, the Marshall Plan had been the first major economic assistance pro-gramme, but it was in 1949 that development assistance as such

[1] *Assistance from the United Kingdom for Overseas Development*, Cmnd. 974 (H.M.S.O., London, 1960), p. 5.

[2] "La première raison, suffisante à elle seule, d'une politique française de coopération avec le Tiers Monde est le sentiment que la France a de ses devoirs envers l'humanité. D'autres motifs s'y ajoutent, qui tiennent à son besoin de rayonner au loin et à l'attente de certains avantages essentiels, encore qu'aléatoires ou lointains." *La Politique de Coopération avec les Pays en voie de Développement*, Ministère d'Etat chargé de la Réforme Administrative, Paris, 1963, p. 43.

became national policy.[1]   Over the next two decades the United States put forward the largest aid programmes.[2]

The creation of international organizations, such as the International Bank for Reconstruction and Development, the Food and Agricultural Organization, the World Health Organization and the United Nations Educational, Scientific and Cultural Organization, has focused attention on the needs of the underdeveloped countries and established new channels for obtaining financial assistance.   The word "aid", however, should be examined in the context of the underdeveloped countries. Usually the money advanced is for some purpose which, however sound, would not attract the private investor; yet its importance may be of the highest order.   An international institution can itself arrange a loan, repayable on terms often less onerous than could otherwise be obtained.   Such institutions are assumed to be non-political and impartial.   Their staff will include representatives of the aid-providing nations and presumably aid will be fairly administered.

Very often aid is given for political reasons, particularly by the participants in the Cold War.[3] "We will never know how many crises have been averted, how much violence avoided, or how many minds have been won to the cause of freedom in these years."[4] The attitude of the Soviet bloc towards economic assistance to the developing countries has changed since 1954 with the idea of "peaceful co-existence" growing and taking the place of the concept of economic isolation. As the Russians have aided Cuba, so too has the United States

---

[1] Goran Ohlin, *Foreign Aid Policies Reconsidered*, Development Centre of the Organization for Economic Cooperation and Development (Paris, 1966), p. 16. "Concern with the needs of other and poorer nations is the expression of a new and fundamental aspect of the modern age—the awareness that we live in a village world, that we belong to a world community." *Partners in Development*, Report of the Commission on International Development, (Chairman, Lester B. Pearson), London, 1969, p. 8.

[2] Next to America, France has the largest aid programme closely followed by Denmark and Japan.

[3] "As a rule, such aid is aimed at implementing definite imperialist and colonialist military-strategic plans.   Ultimately it is designed to keep the developing countries within the orbit of the world capitalist economy.   Since all the capitalist powers strive to utilize this 'aid' first and foremost to consolidate their own economic and political influence in the developing countries, competition between them is inevitable." Y. Grigoryan, "Rivals of the U.S.A. in Latin America", *International Affairs*, No. 12, Moscow, 1965, p. 48.

[4] President Johnson, Foreign Aid Message before the House Committee on Foreign Affairs, May 17, 1966. "Aid for development does not usually buy dependable friends." *Partners in Development*, p. 9.

aided Haiti, and both have given rival help to Egypt and Ghana.[1]

Aid may also take the form of a gift, the reasons for which may vary. A case, however, may be made that loans are preferable to gifts, as being more business-like and avoiding the recipient feeling humiliated or subservient to the donor. Apart from grants-in-aid, usually to colonies and ex-colonies, Britain has made a practice since 1960 of giving a "golden handshake" to a country on gaining its independence, something not always received like the traditional gift-horse.[2]

About two-thirds of all bilateral aid to developing countries is tied to purchases of goods or services from the donor country. So long as its own balance of payments problem remains unsolved, Britain, for example, ties a significant part of its aid to purchases from its own exporters.[3] In many of the Commonwealth countries the tying may be superfluous because traditional trading practices and contracts ensure that a large part of any loans or grants made will in any case be spent on British goods.[4] Naturally the monitoring of

[1] However Professor Peter T. Bauer comments: "But even if aid were much more productive than it is, it could not possibly affect living standards to an extent likely to influence political attitudes. Moreover, an inclination towards communism does not depend on living standards but on a number of quite different factors which encourage people to embrace a messianic faith, or encourage and enable some people to establish a communist regime." *Two Views on Aid to Developing Countries*, The Institute of Economic Affairs (London, 1966), p. 53.

[2] *Vide* pp. 157-8.
A similar situation had occurred in 1961 when Tanganyika moved to independence with the former colony bitterly disappointed with Britain's offer, the more so as Germany and the United States were offering aid: "On that occasion it took enormous personal pressure by Mr. Macleod to achieve some kind of patch-up in Anglo-Tanganyikan goodwill before the hand-over". Patrick Keatley, *The Guardian*, London, November 26, 1962.
Inevitably the financial needs of countries moving into independence would seem high to a British Government in a period of financial difficulty. At the same time recurring crises, as for example that of Lesotho (formerly Basutoland) provide a comparison. In October 1966, Chief Leabua Jonathan, the Prime Minister, complained that the aid offered by Britain was sufficient only for budgetary needs and not for development. Clearly Great Britain could not be expected to satisfy all financial demands, but the principle of the parting gesture seems to be one which in practice has adversely affected goodwill between the countries.

[3] Britain ties 60 per cent. of its bilateral financial aid. *Report from the Select Committee on Overseas Aid* (H.M.S.O., London, 1971), p. 21.

[4] Richard Bailey "Tied Aid not too helpful to Payments", *The Times*, London, June 7, 1966.

this money is not easy.[1] Even if the receiving country strictly carries out the letter of the agreement, it may often be able to switch other purchases away from the donor country to a competitor. Moreover, some of the goodwill of the aid may be lost to the donor country from the inconvenience caused to the recipient, which may well be precluded from purchasing in the cheapest market. The recipients feel these strings restrict their freedom of action and affront their competence.[2] To defend tied aid, donor countries point to countries from Haiti to the Congo which have misused funds. Moreover, the lending democracies of the West are forced to justify before their electors foreign loans, often in practice irrecoverable, while strong claims for financial expenditure at home remain unsatisfied. A candidate for election is unlikely to preface his election address with a programme of aid to underdeveloped countries.

Poor countries must assure political leaders in developed countries that the aid projects are sound and financially viable. If they are likely to yield an economic return, so much the better. The prestige plans for steel plants, international airlines, large dams, nuclear power plants or even new capital cities, examples of which may be found in the Caribbean, add to the difficulty of securing finance from abroad.[3]

In 1961 the Alliance for Progress claimed as one of its first objectives the bridging of the gap between the developed and underdeveloped countries of Latin America.[4] This statement was a declaration of the purpose of the United States, expressed by President John F. Kennedy and the other Western nations as an attempt to lift up the standard of living in the underdeveloped countries towards their own.

---

[1] The British Development Division was set up in Bridgetown, Barbados, in 1966 to organize the use of British aid.

[2] Recommending the halting and reduction of tied aid, the Pearson Report remarked: "Such tying has spread in a contagious fashion in the 1960's, and untied aid is now the exception rather than the rule." *Op cit.*, p. 172. Cf., Michael Wolfers, " 'Help with strings' seen as instrument of power politics", *The Times*, "Nations in Need", London, September 14, 1971.

[3] Escott Reid, "The Crisis in Foreign Aid", *The World Today*, London, August 1966, pp. 320-1. Cf. Ohlin, *op. cit.*: "It is also becoming clear that a need of great priority is for assistance in the use of assistance", p. 100.

[4] "To accelerate economic and social development, thus rapidly bringing about a substantial and steady increase in the average income in order to narrow the gap between the standard of living in Latin American countries and that enjoyed in the industrialized countries." *Declaration to the Peoples of America*, Punta del Este, Uruguay, August 17, 1961.

The failure fully to achieve such a noble goal is a measure of the challenge of the task.[1]

Differing points of view have discouraged the expansion of foreign aid.[2] The economic crises faced by the Western World in the 1960's compounded the difficulties. The rich countries lost the capacity, and indeed the will, adequately to help the developing world including areas such as Latin America.[3]

In August 1971 President Nixon, as part of his plan to revalue the dollar, announced a cut in overseas aid. In October the U.S. Senate's rejection of Nixon's Foreign Aid Bill came as a climax to years of growing disillusionment.[4] Guerrilla movements made the U.S. public critical of Latin American Governments unable to contain them.

In short, foreign aid which opened with brilliant success in the Marshall Plan had gradually met an increasing lack of achievement. Perhaps the rapid results in the developed countries, with their resources ready to flower again quickly after the damage of World War II, made the task look too easy.[5] In the underdeveloped countries the lack of sophisticated governments and technical expertise, something that may take years to develop, prevented similar rapid improvement. The world may have been too optimistic.

The simplest method of developing a backward country is often to introduce the established foreign company. Professor Sir Arthur Lewis put it succinctly: "The case for foreign investment is that it provides foreign exchange, raises domestic income, and increases domestic skills".[6] Brazil provides a good example. Although northeast Brazil remains backward, southern Brazil is one of the vibrant parts of Latin America. The city of São Paulo, second largest in

---

[1] "The Alliance was also plagued from the start by the vague expression which had been given to its ambitious goals and by the high expectations they had generated." *Partners in Development*, p. 245.

[2] "In some of the rich countries its feasibility, even its very purpose, is in question. The climate surrounding foreign aid programs is heavy with disillusion and distrust." Ibid., p. 4.

[3] Cf. George Bolton, Annual Review, *Bank of London and South America Review*, Vol. 4, No. 39, London, March 1970.

[4] Of the sixteen main donor countries, the United States ranks eleventh in scale of giving. Cf. *The Times*, London, editorial, November 1, 1971.

[5] Cf. Nigel Lawson, "Foreign aid: the wrong thing for the right reasons", *The Times*, London, November 3, 1971.

[6] *The Theory of Economic Growth* (London, 1955), p. 258. Cf. David Rockefeller "What Private Enterprise Means to Latin America", *Foreign Affairs*, Vol. 44, No. 3, Council on Foreign Relations, New York, April 1966, p. 412.

population and in industrialization in the Southern Hemisphere, derives its success to a significant degree from the numerous foreign firms which have established factories, and no less important, have supplied the "know how". Although many technicians may be imported at the start, in a remarkably short time they are usually replaced by residents. For one thing, the local man, even if he requires to be sent on a course to the United States, presents a far simpler problem of employment than that entailed in transporting and housing foreigners and their families. Moreover, the employment of foreigners increasingly affronts nationalism.

The cry against the foreign investor in underdeveloped countries is often a carry-over from bygone days.[1] Such an individual makes his contribution to the country's economy by creating employment. Since a successful business almost always demands more capital, part of any profits is likely to be reinvested. If the taxation system is inefficient, that is a matter for the Government itself to correct. The enemy of the economy is not the successful but the unsuccessful investor whose failure may damage others besides himself, and discourage further investment in the country.

Industrialization in the Caribbean tends to become a series of monopolies. Moreover, as automation advances, cheap labour becomes of decreasing value. Nevertheless, the advantage of securing the entry from abroad of a good firm already established in the trade often remains the best solution. Inevitably the cry of foreign dominance of industry will arise. Yet there may still be investment opportunity, since many foreign companies today wisely seek partnership with local capital.

One of the hardest tasks for the Finance Minister of any small Caribbean country will be the selection of the right industries. An unsuitable industry will simply raise costs to the consumer. Indeed, with industry dependent on tariffs for its survival, the highest degree of flexibility and skill alone will prevent an undue rise of cost or reduction of quality to the consumer. Probably a non-political permanent Tariff Commission is the most effective solution, as advocated for Jamaica by Sir Arthur Lewis.[2] Even so, a threat to remove or reduce a tariff may be difficult to carry out politically since the manufacturer may threaten to close his factory.

Small countries with sharply rising populations should never forget the importance of attracting industries which have in their costs a

---

[1] Cf. Rockefeller, *op. cit.*, p. 415.

[2] "Prospect for Industry", *The Daily Gleaner*, Kingston, September 11, 1964.

high labour content. Only thus can they hope to avoid a steady rise in the numbers out of work.

Of vital importance is good understanding between foreign-owned enterprises in any country and the local government and people. Nothing can exceed the importance not only of intelligent foreign management but equally of well-informed and sustained publicity to explain to the government and people of any country the value to them to develop agriculture and industry. Nothing can do more damage than the ill-advised, forcible taking-over of foreign concerns. The damage in bad publicity can extend far beyond the territory concerned and in the case of the Caribbean may well reach to the surrounding countries.[1] Jamaica, like Trinidad, has preserved a more balanced position, encouraging the "Jamaicanization" of industry hoping, with the aid of its new stock exchange, to widen island majority ownership in the developing industries.[2] At the end of the day the countries that handle foreign investment most successfully will be the ones to prosper most.

On December 15, 1965, at Dickenson Bay, Antigua, Guyana, and Barbados reached agreement over the setting up of a Caribbean Free Trade Area. The idea of a Commonwealth grouping on a wider scale was emphasized at the successful Commonwealth Caribbean-Canada Conference at Ottawa in July 1966.[3] However, this new free trade area called the Caribbean Free Trade Association was attacked by Guyana's opposition leader, Cheddi Jagan, who protested strongly against any limited trading bloc which did not include Cuba together with all Commonwealth and non-Commonwealth islands.[4] At a Conference of the heads of the Commonwealth Caribbean Governments in Barbados in October 1967, the opportunity of membership was afforded to other Commonwealth Caribbean territories.

On April 30, 1968, CARIFTA, which envisaged something not far short of a revival of the economic concept of the West Indies Federation, was formally launched.[5] It emerged as the first attempt of the Commonwealth Caribbean to form an economic unit independent of outside guidance. Nevertheless, rivalries appeared at the start: Jamaica, for example, was reluctant to accept the siting of the Regional Development Bank in Barbados.

[1] *Vide* p. 243.
[2] *Vide*, pp. 140-1.
[3] *Vide* p. 423.
[4] *The New York Times*, New York, December 31, 1966.
[5] *Agreement Establishing the Caribbean Free Trade Association*, Trinidad, 1968 .

The member territories,[1] which have a population of more than four and a half million, needed very heavy capital investment to develop their economies and maintain their standard of living. Poor communications remained a problem. Three years later the U.N. Economic Commission for Latin America found that the CARIFTA members still had neither the vessels nor the port facilities to handle increasing inter-island trade.[2]

The Caribbean Development Bank was inaugurated on January 31, 1970. Contributors included the United States, Canada and Britain, amongst others. The Bank covers not only CARIFTA countries but also the Bahamas, the British Virgin Islands, the Cayman Islands and the Turks and Caicos Islands. As a result of complaints by the less developed member territories of economic disparity between the larger and smaller countries, Sir Arthur Lewis, president of the Regional Development Bank, announced in February 1971 that Bank policy would concentrate that year on trying to identify the economic development needs of its lesser developed member territories.[3]

The constitution of CARIFTA does not limit it to Caribbean Commonwealth members. For example, the entry of the Dominican Republic, which has shown interest, would substantially enlarge CARIFTA in population, area and trade.[4] Venezuela has appeared interested, particularly in view of its close association with Trinidad and Tobago. The French Overseas Departments and the Caribbean components of the Kingdom of the Netherlands have already achieved access to Europe's Common Market, and intra-Caribbean economic links might be difficult for them to develop.[5] However, the dangers involved in widening CARIFTA without deepening and consolidating the achievements so far were acknowledged.[6]

Since 1968 CARIFTA has already made a considerable impact on the region. Its purposes are to encourage trade between member

[1] Antigua, Barbados, Dominica, Grenada, Guyana, Jamaica, Montserrat, St. Kitts-Nevis-Anguilla, St. Lucia, St. Vincent, and Trinidad and Tobago. British Honduras (Belize) joined in 1971.
[2] Cf. *The Financial Times*, London, April 22, 1971.
[3] Cf. *Jamaica Weekly Gleaner*, Kingston, February 10, 1971.
[4] Cf. *The Daily Gleaner*, Kingston, editorial, August 1, 1970.
[5] Fuat M. Andic concluded, however, that the relationship between the E.E.C. and its Caribbean Associates did not seem particularly fruitful. Both CARIFTA and the Caribbean Development Bank, he suggested, might constitute attractive alternatives for Surinam and the Netherlands Antilles. "The Development impact of the EEC on the French and Dutch Caribbean." *Journal of Common Market Studies*, Oxford, September 1969, pp. 47 and 49.
[6] *CARIFTA and the New Caribbean*, Georgetown, 1971, pp. 51 and 119.

territories in a closed market approximating to free trade, to stimulate the expansion of industry and to increase the cultivation of complementary foodstuffs. However, CARIFTA requires very substantial capital expenditure and expertise, which can only be provided by outside developed countries. The desire to build up nationalism as a bulwark to independence, which, in Jamaica, for example, results in strong pressure to control internally, say, 51 per cent. of shareholdings, may prove a deterrent to investment. Furthermore any action in one part of CARIFTA considered as detrimental by the outside world might have unfortunate repercussions on another; the nationalization in Guyana of Demba drew sharp criticism from Jamaica.[1] Many goods are not readily transported by air and are dependent on bad shipping communications. Very often, too, a monopoly supply exists with all the attendant risks of poor quality of goods and delays in replacement and service. In other words, there is a failure to supply the necessary competence, centre-piece of the Capitalist system. In some cases, it can also mean inferior quality. To attract industries, tax concessions usually have to be given to outside investors, in some cases for as much as 15 years.[2]

A good comparison can be made with the Central American Common Market, which started with remarkable expansion, supported by the United States. This had the advantage of good road connections between the member countries as well as sea and air links. There have been indications that the prosperity of the early years has flagged.[3] Behind the hostility between the Republics of Honduras and El Salvador lies the fact that Honduras, largest but poorest of these C.A.C.M. countries, benefited least. Relations with El Salvador, which had economically perhaps the most success, became strained. Large numbers of agricultural workers from El Salvador, working in Honduras, were sent back. Costa Rica, like Honduras, found the C.A.C.M. very disappointing and announced in January 1971 that it would have to re-examine its position within the Market.

It is not difficult to envisage that the smaller islands of the Eastern

[1] *Vide* pp. 243 and 352.

[2] Cf. Eric Williams, *From Columbus to Castro, The History of the Caribbean 1492-1969*, (London, 1970), p. 511.

[3] As a result of the closing of the main highway in the region, trade between the five member nations no longer rose at the rate prevailing up to 1968. *Central American Survey*, Barclays Bank Ltd., London, September 1970. Vincent Cable concluded that there was no reason to believe that the Common Market should in any way be written off. "The 'Football War' and the Central American Common Market", *International Affairs*, The Royal Institute of International Affairs, London, October 1969, p. 671.

Caribbean might run into great difficulties through being unable to obtain adequate and steady supplies from the industries in the larger islands. The advantages of the proximity of, say, the British Virgin Islands to the American Virgin Islands, with their access to the markets of the United States, might become even more obvious than they are at present. Similarly, Dominica might seek to exploit its geographical location between the French Overseas Departments of Martinique and Guadeloupe. The resentment of Anguilla has stemmed substantially from the feeling it had been neglected by the Government centred in far-off St. Kitts.

Nevertheless, the setting up of CARIFTA, hopefully, will continue to improve the economies of its members. This may not be easy or necessarily rapid, but the opportunities of attracting outside enterprises to manufacture within the market will increase. It will involve great concentration on improved communications of all kinds between the islands. Astute statesmanship will be called for. Excessive tariff erection against outside countries might result in the curtailment of present export advantages.

Whether this intra-Caribbean movement will ever pass beyond the stage of free trade remains to be seen. The Grenada Declaration published in 1971 envisaged a new West Indian state composed of CARIFTA members, Guyana, Dominica, Grenada, St. Kitts-Nevis, St. Lucia and St. Vincent, to be formed by 1973.[1] The initial response suggested delays in bringing this about might ensue. Disappointment was expressed that neither Trinidad and Tobago nor Barbados nor Antigua showed interest in joining.[2]

The very variety of the nations involved in the Caribbean has led to well-developed and competitive banking services. In addition to State banking facilities in these countries, a wide variety of commercial banks have been established. Puerto Rico, for example, is served by a selection of leading American and Canadian banks as well as local banks. In Jamaica, prior to the establishment by the Government of the Bank of Jamaica in 1963, the Bank of Nova Scotia, a Canadian bank, was the country's official bank. In both Jamaica and Trinidad, British, Canadian and American banks have been established. Throughout the small islands within the Commonwealth, banking is well developed. For example, the small population of the Cayman Islands

[1] *The Grenada Declaration, 1971, on West Indian Political Unity*, Commonwealth Caribbean Regional Secretariat, Press Release No. 46/1971, October 30, 1971.
[2] *The Times*, London, editorial, November 2, 1971.

(some 10,000 persons) is served by three major banks, British and Canadian. In the French Antilles, banking is dominantly French, usually local. The Netherlands too have a similar situation. In the Greater Antilles, Cuba was served prior to the Revolution with a variety of local and foreign banks. The position has changed due to the closed economy, strictly Government controlled. In Haiti, local banks and a Canadian bank provide facilities. The Dominican Republic, besides local firms, has a choice of the U.S. and Canadian banks.

To small communities like those in the Caribbean, a modern banking service, preferably competitive, is vital. Sometimes foreign can supplement local banks. The relatively high development in many of the Antilles, compared with mainland Latin American countries with their much greater natural resources, has been partly due to the attraction to investors, local and overseas alike, of competitive banking. The businessman who is developing a factory or seeks crop finance for a farm wants to know quickly whether a loan is available or not. Nothing holds back a great country more than the impossibility of getting credit. Brazil provides an example, even on what in most countries would be termed unreasonably high terms. The practice in Jamaica of encouraging banks to form a local subsidiary company including Jamaican shareholders appears to work well. As a whole, banking facilities in the Caribbean are good.

Few world industries have brighter prospects than tourism. A combination of rising wages and salaries, together with the introduction of holidays with pay in the developed countries of the world, has rapidly accelerated the desire to travel. Certainly the aeroplane has played a major part. Travel costs have been reduced: they are likely to be cut still more. Giant planes, already in service, are further transforming the industry. Massive advertising to fill them has necessarily followed. The aeroplane has proved to be an effective and even deadly competitor to the passenger-liner trade. Many of these vessels have been diverted, partially or completely, to tourist cruising, a change which has greatly benefited the Caribbean with its diversity of countries and ports. In living memory the automobile industry had limited importance; today in the United States it ranks as an industrial giant. Tourism may be the Titan of the future.

In so far as it caters for foreigners, tourism is an export industry. Underdeveloped countries depend on overseas visitors, who alone usually have the money to spend and the desire for the holiday attractions provided. Some countries, however, have been curiously slow to realize the economic possibilities of tourism. The most outstanding world failure is Latin America as a whole, with the notable exception of Mexico.[1]

The construction by the United States of military airfields during World War II, which were later used for civilian purposes, proved to be an unexpected but major contribution to the development of tourism in the Caribbean. Many of these countries have made striking progress in the last two decades. The disappointments encountered in the three Antillean republics have arisen from political causes outside the tourist industry itself. Cuba, Haiti and the Dominican Republic indicate how quickly tourism wilts when any sign of political instability or lack of welcome appears. The existence of this sanction, unconsciously applied by the public, should cause any country with a significant tourist trade to hesitate from embarking on revolution or major industrial disturbance. The Cuban imbroglio in 1961 and 1962 when commercial planes for a time avoided flying over Cuba, even temporarily adversely affected the tourist trade of Jamaica, its neighbour to the south.[2] In due course, Cuba's former tourist business moved to other more stable Caribbean territories. Puerto Rico was undoubtedly aided by the protection of the American flag in at once attracting some of these people to its shores. The Bahamas suffered a temporary setback in 1969 due to civil unrest in the islands.

The residential visitor is becoming a regular feature of the tourist industry. In Jamaica and the Bahamas, as in other parts of the Caribbean, the tourist of today is becoming the house-owner of tomorrow, returning year after year: even when he is away he disburses money, often in hard currency, for the employment of staff. These salary rates are usually in excess of those prevalent in the territory.

Caribbean tourist statistics present difficulties in interpretation, and are not always comparable. Cruise ships often complicate an accurate assessment. At present the tourist trade of the Caribbean is predominantly from the United States and Canada. Probably this pattern will continue. Distance militates against an extensive European trade, although airlinks are numerous and increasing. A further source of tourists may in due course develop from adjacent parts of

---

[1] In one year (1968-1969) Mexico's visitors increased from 1,664,474 to 2,064,733. *International Travel Statistics*, International Union of Official Travel Organizations, Geneva, 1970.

[2] Jamaica's visitors fell from 224,492 in 1961 to 206,838 in 1962, a drop of 7·8 per cent. In 1963 a further small fall occurred to 202,329. Recovery did not take place until 1964 when the figure rose sharply to 227,417. *Report of Tourist Travel to the Caribbean for 1965*, The Caribbean Travel Association, New York, n.d.

Latin America. This could be of particular importance to the Spanish-speaking islands of the Caribbean.

On the whole, the Caribbean has been quick to appreciate the potentiality of the tourist trade. Moreover, as the industry has largely developed since World War II, the standard of accommodation is modern. Rooms with bath or shower are the rule, aimed at the North American market. In this respect, the Caribbean surpasses most resort areas in the British Isles and Europe.

Despite an enlightened tax policy towards tourist development by Caribbean governments, resort hotels as elsewhere in the world have often proved highly speculative as an investment, due to the short period of full occupancy. The greatest measure of success has arisen from the realization, thanks to intelligent publicity and promotion, that the summer in the Caribbean can be very pleasant, particularly at resort areas on the north coasts of the islands exposed to the trade winds. Reduced summer rates are beginning to fill the hotels. Moreover, increasingly people are learning to take holidays out of season, so that year-round occupancy is growing, aided by the increasing travel from groups and conventions.

The crux of the problem is whether or not an island can achieve continuing economic success based primarily on tourism. For some of the Eastern Caribbean islands which have little else to look forward to, tourism would seem to present perhaps the only hope of the future. Bermuda provides an example of a successful economy resting solely on tourism. Fresh water in Bermuda must be caught from the heavens or distilled from the sea; the lack of soil in most parts precludes extensive farming. The population density of over 3,000 to the square mile exceeds even that of Barbados. The island has made good use of its exiguous resources, namely an attractive climate and a warm sea, both derived from the Gulf Stream. Less than two hours by air from the Eastern United States, it has developed a major tourist industry. Initiative at home, combined with skilful and effective promotion abroad, has created one of the soundest tourist industries in the world; political stability and a population which understands and welcomes the visitor has compounded the success. Certainly the construction of an airport by the United States greatly aided the island; but no one can claim that President Franklin D. Roosevelt did other than drive a hard bargain over bases in 1941. Tourism has created for Bermuda's population, in origin one-third European and two-thirds African, a standard of living probably higher today than that of Great Britain, thus refuting the arguments advanced against overdependence on the tourist industry. Bermuda is fortunate in having an annual population growth rate of about 2·1 per cent. aided by active encouragement of birth control. No serious unemployment exists.

The example of Bermuda is of major interest to other small islands like the British Virgins, once prosperous Nevis, or Montserrat. The progress of tourism in the Cayman Islands, Antigua and the out-islands of the Bahamas, all of which have realized the importance of the tourist dollar, will be of particular interest in coming years.

However much tourism may be under-rated as a potential factor in the economy of the Caribbean and beyond, clearly it must remain in most territories only a factor. The development of industries remains vital, largely to replace imports. The chances of building significant export trades are illusory. Exceptions happily there will be; but the idea of cheap factory labour in the Caribbean is a myth while port services are often both exorbitant and dilatory. The manufacturers may well be impeded in obtaining their imports of raw materials and machinery. The legacies of different colonial customs administration have been disastrous to efficiency particularly in Latin American countries in the Caribbean and beyond.

A small home market and an export market costly to reach form a fragile base for any extensive industrialization. Nevertheless, increasingly opportunities for new industries will arise, which in turn may lead to others. The larger islands will remain the better placed. The selection of the right industries remains one of the most vital tasks for an enlightened government. It must resist the siren voices of promoters who may seek to establish unsuitable industries which can only flourish under tariffs or subsidies that will burden the community as a whole. At the same time, the increasing labour force in every Caribbean country makes the provision of new jobs ever more urgent.

CHAPTER XVI

POPULATION AND EDUCATION

No social problem threatens the well-being of the world more ominously than the progressive rise in population. No other criterion, be it *per capita* income, urbanization, literacy or industrialization, defines the dichotomy between developed and developing areas so sharply as the level of human reproductivity.[1] Already in country after country the problem threatens to retard improvement in living conditions. Should inconclusive disarmament conferences end in a holocaust, population pressure may well have contributed to the disaster: it is not yet possible to contemplate a world in which population control is exercised by law, and families regulated by heavy taxation.[2]

The mid-1971 population of the world was estimated at 3,706 million[3]; by the end of the century it may well be 6,494 million. The area of the fastest growth over the 40-year period from 1920 to 1960 was Latin America, with an estimated increase of 136 per cent. It had the highest rate of population growth in every decade from 1920[4]; the pattern is likely to continue.

The fastest growing populations of any major world region are found in Central America and Tropical South America, where the increase is 3·2 per cent. a year.[5] Brazil, largest country in Latin America, has reduced its rate from 3·6 per cent. in 1964 to 2·8 per cent. in 1971. These countries have sharply improved their vital statistics as a result of the spectacular advance in tropical medicine.

---

[1] *Provisional Report on World Population Prospects as Assessed in 1963*, United Nations, New York, 1963, pp. 15-16.

[2] ". . . this may be the last generation which has the opportunity to limit population growth on the basis of free choice." Richard M. Gardner, White House Conference on International Co-operation, Washington, D.C., November 1965.

[3] *1971 World Population Data Sheet*, Population Reference Bureau, Washington, D.C., June, 1971. The U.N. estimated world population growth at 2 per cent.

[4] *Provisional Report on World Population Prospects as Assessed in 1963*, pp. 37 and 39.

[5] I.e., all South America, excluding Argentina, Chile, Uruguay and Paraguay. *1971 World Population Data Sheet*, June, 1971.

Unfortunately any method of control must be slow.[1] Countries with the greatest population growth are least able to deal with it. The concept that national strength lies not in quantity but in quality is difficult for underdeveloped countries to grasp. Moreover, in the Caribbean the problem is complicated by a high proportion of Roman Catholics, and also by deeply rooted cultural forces which oppose efforts made to restrain fertility.

The major problem is not how to feed people, although this presents complications enough. Much graver loom the enormous difficulties of improving and extending the education of these growing numbers of world inhabitants. Some success has been achieved: in twenty years the number of literates has reached 600 million, keeping ahead of the rate of population growth.[2] In Latin America the percentage of illiterates has been cut by more than a quarter to 23·6 per cent.[3]

Many reasons have prevented action to control population. Thomas Malthus recommended abstinence to check the birth rate. He could not foretell the great technological advances including the production and distribution of foodstuffs which would follow. Yet when we look at India, parts of Brazil and the Amerindian areas of Latin America, or certain West Indian territories, especially Haiti, the basis for Malthus' fears are more real than they appeared to be half a century ago.

One common point of agreement shared by informed leaders on both sides of the Iron Curtain is the basic view that unless the general standard of education can steadily advance, the efforts of the human race will be stultified. With especial force this applies to the Western democracies. So far they have reacted extremely slowly to the dangerous

[1] "In India, which was the first of the developing countries to take official action to encourage smaller families, comparatively little success has been achieved. Religion, illiteracy and lack of contraceptive knowledge or availability have been the obstacles." *New Commonwealth*, London, editorial, No. 7, 1966.

[2] The criterion of illiteracy adopted by the United Nations for estimated statistical purposes is the ability both to read and write: "Hence, persons who can read but not write, are considered as illiterate". *Statistical Yearbook, 1964*, U.N.E.S.C.O., p. 13.

Illiteracy, and even more so, literacy, is extremely hard to define. An adult may, if the above criterion is accepted, have no more than the reading and writing ability of a child of 6 and yet be classified as literate. However, for the purposes of this chapter, in which most of the illiteracy estimates quoted are from U.N. sources, with 15-plus as the age level, the criterion has been accepted.

[3] Latin America includes in this case the Caribbean area. U.N.E.S.C.O., Paris, September 1, 1971.

problem which rising populations present and which their own technology has made possible. Only their world leadership in industrial advance has enabled them for the moment to surmount the problem. New additions to the labour force have usually been absorbed. Immigration from less developed countries has often been encouraged. Shortage of labour may at times exist.

These facts have obscured the wider scope of the problem. Asia alone contains one half of the world's population.[1] The problem of overpopulation is an ever-increasing threat in Africa. Probably nothing menaces the survival of Western democratic institutions more than the challenge of excessive population. Instead many continue to live in the not-so-distant past when legislation was passed in countries like Great Britain and France to encourage an unrestricted rise in population.[2]

Historically population increased slowly in the Caribbean. The impact of European discovery led to the near extinction of the Arawaks in the Greater Antilles and of the Caribs in the smaller islands. The conditions of slavery, abolished during the nineteenth century at different dates in the various islands, militated against a population rise, notwithstanding the desire of slave-owners to encourage breeding for the continuance of a labour force. A preponderance of imported males was adverse to increase, as were miserable living conditions. Moreover, disease played a major role in holding down population increases up to the end of the nineteenth century. The garrison church at Port Royal, Jamaica, with its memorials and tombstones, bears witness to the number of young officers who died from yellow fever in the prime of life.

The dramatic medical discoveries of the twentieth century have revolutionized life in the tropics. The recognition of the mosquito as the vector of yellow fever and malaria and the modern insecticides made available to mankind by science have led to increasingly effective control. Yaws, a disease widespread in the tropics, has been greatly reduced, as has hookworm. National health organizations have been aided by the United Nations and the Rockefeller Foundation.[3]

---

[1] Asia in mid-1971 had a population of 2,104 million. *1971 World Population Data Sheet*, June, 1971.

[2] By 1971, however, a note of alarm was sounded: the steady drop in the birth rate in Europe could lead to a decline in population. The average family size in Europe was just over two children, whatever the parents' religion.

[3] Cf. Dr. Philip R. Lee, "The Role of Health Programs in International Development", *Population Bulletin*, Vol. XXI, No. 2, May 1965, pp. 21-4.

The effect on population in the Caribbean has been startling.[1] In addition to lengthening life, infant mortality has been strikingly reduced.[2] In considering population statistics, especially in an area such as the Antilles which is fragmented into tiny units, the resources of any territory must be kept in mind. Those of the Caribbean have so far proved to be strictly limited.

Movement of population has characterized the Antilles from the days of the early Spaniards who used Cuba and Santo Domingo as a base for the conquest of Mexico and the Spanish Main. Even before the arrival of Columbus, Caribs were pressing northwards from the Lesser Antilles to the Greater. European invasion resulted in the elimination of a large part of the Arawak population from disease and enslavement, particularly in the Greater Antilles. The disappearance of the Amerindian population was followed by the importation of African slaves, who soon outnumbered in most islands the early European settlers. The ending of slavery and the consequent shortage of labour in some islands led to considerable introduction of indentured labour from India.

Political as well as economic events have caused population movements in the Caribbean. The Haitian slave revolt led to substantial emigration of French planters with their families and slaves across the Windward Passage to Cuba's Oriente, adding to the Negro content of that province.

Ailing agriculture and increasing population resulting in the demand for more jobs encouraged emigration from the end of the nineteenth century. For example, thousands of Jamaican labourers helped to build the Panama Canal. Later farm labour in the United States provided seasonal employment. Considerable inter-island movements (often seasonal) of population took place; large numbers of Jamaicans found work in the canefields of Cuba during the expansion of the sugar industry for the protected American market. Thousands of

---

[1] The rate of population growth in the Caribbean islands during the past thirty to forty years is shown by the following: in 1930 there were 12 million people; in 1940, 14 million; in 1950, 17 million; in 1960, 20 million; and in 1969, 25 million. Thus in nearly 40 years the population in the Caribbean islands area had more than doubled. *Demographic Yearbook, 1969*, Table 1, p. 115.

[2] Statistics available for the islands of the Caribbean show that infant mortality rates have decreased sharply: in Jamaica for example, in 1932 the infant mortality rate was 141 per thousand and only 35·2 in 1960-65. In Barbados it dropped from 198 in 1932 to 45·7; in Trinidad from 108·9 to 35·8 in the same period, and in Puerto Rico from 132·3 to 28·3 in 1968. *Demographic Yearbook, 1951*, and *Demographic Yearbook, 1969*.

these emigrants have remained in Cuba. Lesser population movements may be seen such as from the British Virgin Islands to the more prosperous U.S. Virgin Islands.[1] With slender resources at home, the Cayman Islanders have gained renown all over the world as merchant seamen.[2]

The early settlement of Baymen in British Honduras later received additions from Caribs, who, driven from the Windward Islands after rebellion, had also settled in the Bay Islands off the coast of Honduras.[3] Again the development of the oil refineries at Curaçao and Aruba has attracted labour from outside areas, including the Eastern Caribbean.[4] Their subsequent loss of jobs in many cases has, however, been less tragic than the lot of those Haitians who have fled a dictatorship or that of the Cubans who intermittently arrive in small boats to seek asylum in Jamaica. From September 1965, America opened its doors to refugees from Cuba. During the first two months some 2,800 people left Cuba for the United States; in the next four months some 12,500 more made the journey. Priority was given to families who already had one or more members in the United States, and after that to political refugees. Cuban refugees also make their way in significant numbers to Europe and especially to Spain.[5] When flights were curtailed in 1971 over 245,000 Cubans had left Cuba.

Emigration has too often originated from compulsion or bitter necessity, nor have emigrants always found a welcome. Reluctance to accept the free movement of labour within the West Indies Federation caused major disagreement between Trinidad and the other federated islands of the Eastern Caribbean. With difficulty the dispute was settled by agreement to phase free population movement between the islands over a period of nine years. However, the collapse of the Federation left each territory free to impose restrictions.

Modern history has thus shown a reverse trend so that the most important population movements in recent years have been away from the Caribbean to the developed countries of Europe and North America. An unfortunate feature of this emigration is that dominantly skilled workers obtain employment in developed lands.[6] In most

---

[1] *Vide* p. 199.   [2] *Vide* p. 214.   [3] *Vide* pp. 215-6.   [4] *Vide* p. 301.

[5] Cf. Paul Hofmann, "Spain is the Goal of 37,000 in Cuba", *The New York Times*, New York, April 3, 1965, and "14,000 Cubans find Refuge in Spain", *The Times*, London, January 28, 1965.

[6] ". . . we find that the richest countries generate an almost insatiable demand for skills and brains. They enter a spiral growth of education, health services and consumer provision which is faster than even the fast-growing universities can meet." "Two-way Movement of World's Skill", *The Times*, London, July 16, 1965.

cases where immigrants are admitted, choice is limited to, or heavily weighted in favour of, those with skills. The exceptions have been underdeveloped territories with close political links to another country, such as Puerto Rico to the United States, the Antillean departments to France, and the Netherlands Antilles and Surinam to the Netherlands.

Industrial expansion in Great Britain drew labour from less to more skilled work, leaving gaps to be filled. At the same time, it followed a policy of free entry for Commonwealth citizens. Aided by cheap air and steamship fares, West Indian immigration rose from 2,000 in 1953 to over 50,000 in 1960.[1] Public opinion in Great Britain played its part in the introduction of the Commonwealth Immigrants Bill into the House of Commons in 1961.[2] Before passing into law, the measure was hotly debated in Parliament and in the columns of the Press. To many, the restrictions struck at the ideal of a Commonwealth with freedom of movement from end to end,[3] despite the current flaw in this concept occasioned by the restrictions on immigrant labour which had already been imposed by almost every Commonwealth territory. Probably opposition in Great Britain arose not so much on grounds of colour as through fear of unemployment in the event of a trade recession. Following on parliamentary criticism of the measure, a paper was issued by the Home Office to emphasize that no discrimination against coloured Commonwealth citizens was intended.[4] Large numbers of immigrants remain in Britain, helping to man the railway stations and buses and filling a hundred other jobs in London and other major cities.[5]

The 1971 Immigration Act superseded most immigration legislation before it. All existing quotas for admission into the United Kingdom from Commonwealth countries were abolished and unless an applicant

---

[1] "The massive migration of Jamaicans to the United Kingdom, which began on a large scale in 1953 and was sharply curtailed in 1962 with the passage of the British Commonwealth Immigrants Act, provides one of the few examples in recent history of an economically motivated population movement of significant size." Gene Tidrick, "Some Aspects of Jamaican Emigration to the United Kingdom 1953-1962", *Social and Economic Studies*, Vol. 15, No. 1, University of the West Indies, Jamaica, March 1966.

[2] This was finally passed in 1962 and became the *Commonwealth Immigrants Act, 1962. Vide* p. 142.

[3] *The Daily Telegraph*, London, November 2, 1961.

[4] The paper states: "Immigration officers will, of course, carry out their duties without regard to race, colour or religion of Commonwealth citizens who may seek to enter the country". *Instructions to Immigration Officers,* Cmnd. 1716 (H.M.S.O., London, 1962).

[5] Cf. *The West Indian comes to England*, ed. S. K. Ruck (London, 1960).

could establish a "right of abode" in Britain, he would be admitted only if he had a specific job to go to.[1] In the event citizens of the Republic of Ireland were entitled not only to enter Great Britain freely to work, but also to vote, while citizens of the Commonwealth, including the Caribbean, were treated as aliens. One of the most provocative clauses, whereby Commonwealth Caribbean immigrants were obliged to report to the police or employment exchanges, was later amended.[2]

Great Britain's decision became inevitable when India and Pakistan, which had for years discouraged emigration to Great Britain, changed their policy. Yet the situation of the West Indies is historically different. Britain brought many of the forebears of West Indians by force from Africa to work on British owned plantations. Today, particularly in the smaller islands, the land can no longer support the population. The claims of the West Indians for special treatment are strong. Confusion with the much wider question of immigrants from India and Pakistan distorted the issue into one of race. Morally the claims are not the same. Probably the West Indian Governments made a mistake in linking the issue too much to these large countries and stressing colour discrimination rather than historic justice. At least their claims to entry should not be less than those of immigrants from the Republic of Ireland.

The grim underlying factor to these population movements is the endemic high rate of unemployment in many of the islands. Precise statistics are not generally available. A rate of 12 to 20 per cent. of the labour force without regular and steady employment would probably be a fair estimate. Family work in smallholdings complicates any estimate but also probably gives the scantiest of livelihoods.

*   *   *   *

Different educational systems in the United States and Latin America have resulted in divergent political developments. North American education had its roots in the movement of many colonists from Europe because they sought toleration of their views. Very considerable freedom was granted to the colonists by England. A visit to the Capitol at Williamsburg immediately conjures up a miniature House of Commons.

The concept that every child has a right to carry its education as far as its ability permits is basic to U.S. democracy. The vast expansion of universities in the United States brings an ever increasing influence

[1] *Immigration Act 1971*, Chapter 77 (H.M.S.O., London, 1971), Part I, 2 (1) and 3 (1).
[2] Cf. Lord Constantine, *Hansard*, House of Lords, March 10, 1971, Col. 90.

to bear on national life. Education tends to be locally controlled within a national framework; thus great variety exists. On the whole it is pragmatic and utilitarian. An example of this may be observed in the numerous business schools, pioneered in the United States, which have made a powerful contribution to the economic world leadership of the United States. The importance attached to education not only in the United States but also in Great Britain, France and the Netherlands continues to have a strong impact on the whole Caribbean area.[1]

From earliest times, the Church closely controlled Latin American education. In the nineteenth century, France, whose philosophy had inspired the revolutionary movements in Latin America, became an additional influence. That inspiration has continued into the twentieth century.[2] Directed towards the few rather than the many, it prepared scholars for the universities, including the lawyers and philosophers who have been so numerous in Latin America. Education was essentially culture for culture's sake.[3]

Throughout the Caribbean, different patterns may be observed. The old Latin influence was strong in Cuba up to the Castro Revolution. Haiti still remains culturally attached to France. The Dominican Republic has followed a pattern similar to the rest of Latin America. The modern French system is most clearly reflected in Martinique and Guadeloupe. In some ways these islands provide the best primary and secondary education in the Caribbean, but it is an education not always attuned to the particular environment and demands of the Caribbean islands. The British islands have been strongly influenced by the Free Church tradition which took a lead in education in the days of slavery and afterwards. This influence remains particularly strong, for example in Jamaica. As a result Family Planning has progressed much further in such islands than in those whose population is predominantly Roman Catholic and where a great many of the

[1] "The Government affirms its belief in education not only for its inestimable social value in enabling every individual, for his own sake, to develop his personality and his talents to the fullest extent, but equally that each individual might be enabled to make a maximum contribution to society in every respect." *Five-Year Independence Plan 1963-1968*, Government Printer, Kingston, Jamaica, 1963, p. 159.

". . . a liberal education is an end in itself in that it permits the development of human personality—the ultimate aim of all programmes of social and economic development." *Draft Second Five-Year Plan 1964-1968*, National Planning Commission, Government of Trinidad and Tobago, 1963, p. 123.

[2] As for example in the formation of the University of São Paulo.

[3] Cf. Galo Plaza, "Problems of Education in Latin America", *Latin America: Evolution or Explosion*, ed. Mildred Adams (New York, 1963) p. 160.

private schools are sponsored by Roman Catholic bodies. However, many nominal Roman Catholics pay little attention to their Church's stand on birth control.[1] Protestant Jamaica's birth rate is in fact higher than Catholic Puerto Rico's[2]; it is tempting therefore to conclude that a higher *per capita* income and standard of living is more relevant to Planned Parenthood than religious teaching.[3]

Adult literacy campaigns recommended by the International Conference on Public Education in 1965 have shown increasing success in Latin America.[4] Asia and Africa, by comparison, have only recently begun to tackle the problems of providing primary education, let alone adult literacy instruction.[5] This latter course of action is especially applicable to the Caribbean, where in some cases, due to recent independence, increased emphasis has been placed on literacy as essential to economic progress. Moreover, the preponderance of youth in the Caribbean islands makes a proportionally greater number of teachers necessary than in the more developed countries where the age-groups are comparatively evenly spread. This demand for teachers cannot always be met due to the limited number of educated adults available. The development of Caribbean universities has changed the

---

[1] Professor Ronald Hilton pointed out that in Puerto Rico "the supposedly Catholic women of the people would sooner face the ire of the priests than a lifetime of misery brought about by the bearing of excessively large families". "The Population Explosion in Latin America", reprinted from *The Population Crisis and the Use of World Resources*, World Academy of Art and Science No. 2, The Hague, 1964, p. 201.

[2] The 1969 birth rate was 40·0 per thousand in Jamaica and 26·0 per thousand in Puerto Rico. United Nations findings reveal that: "Part of the decline of the birthrate in Puerto Rico since 1950 may be due to modified age composition as a result of emigration". Furthermore, estimates anticipating quinquennial percentage increases reveal those of Puerto Rico will exceed those of Jamaica during the period 1965 to 1980. *Provisional Report on World Population Prospects as Assessed in 1963*, pp. 265, 268.

[3] Professor Hilton, however, highlights the dangers of the general application of such a theory. In the case of Haiti which is poor, and the Dominican Republic which is less poor, a "differential in birth rate based on income levels would be hard to verify, since the Dominicans have not reached the economic level at which the rate of reproduction seems to decline". *Op. cit.*, pp. 202-3. Trinidad does not support the theory. It has one of the highest standards of living in the Caribbean and also a high birth rate of 3 per cent. Some 40 per cent. of its population is Roman Catholic.

[4] *International Conference on Public Education XXVIII Session, 1965*, International Bureau of Education, Geneva, and U.N.E.S.C.O., Paris, 1965, p. 175.

[5] Despite the cuts in illiteracy rates in Africa and the Arab States 73·7 per cent. of the adult population were unable to read or write in 1971.

former pattern of seeking higher education abroad. Today the major problem is to retain the student after graduation to fill important posts at home.

The University of Puerto Rico, at Río Piedras on the outskirts of San Juan, is situated on a beautiful campus recalling that of Stanford University. Modelled on the U.S. system of education, to which it is linked, it has nevertheless retained many island characteristics reflected in some of the buildings. With a student body of more than 34,000 and a wide choice of Faculties, it is well equipped to serve Puerto Rico's population of more than 2·7 million. Together with the smaller Inter-American University of San Germán, the availability of university education plays its part in the successful industrialization of the island.

The University College of the West Indies was incorporated in 1949 and received full University status in 1962. It was established on a beautiful site at Mona above Kingston, where the Faculties of Arts, Education, Natural Sciences, Medicine and Social Sciences are situated, together with a fine teaching hospital. From 1958 the University became the responsibility of the West Indies Federal Government. The collapse of the Federation created a difficult situation, but the individual territories have continued financial contributions which are assured until 1972. Guyana withdrew its suppport in 1963 to concentrate on its own University. On the other hand, the Bahamas were affiliated to the University of the West Indies in the same year.

In view of the wide distances which separate the Commonwealth Caribbean territories, decentralization of the University was adopted. In 1960 the Imperial College of Tropical Agriculture at St. Augustine in Trinidad was incorporated into the University College. Faculties of Agriculture and of Engineering were established there, and also the John F. Kennedy College of Arts and Sciences, whose students take General Degrees of the University and degrees and diplomas in the social sciences. In Barbados, the U.W.I. has established the College of Arts and Sciences at Cave Hill. By 1969 the number of students exceeded 4,000 between the three centres. Although not yet large in numbers in regard to the extensive area which it serves, the U.W.I. has preferred the wiser policy of gradual expansion combined with the retention of a high standard of teaching. It has had the original advantage of being linked to British education through its early association with the University of London, combined with close contact with leading Universities in the United States.

In Cuba Castro's ultimate goal was the "universalization" of the university: the turning of the whole country into a university.[1] In 1970 the number of students exceeded 35,000. By 1972–73, young people educated under the Revolution would reach the universities.[2] The Castro Government concentrated on the Sciences instead of as before on Law and the Arts. The number of students at Havana University enrolling in Medicine and Technology almost doubled between 1962 and 1968. The Academy of Sciences expanded rapidly, aided by the Soviet Union.[3] Two new universities were opened in the province of Havana.

The ancient University of Santo Domingo was made autonomous in 1962. Its enrolment two years later was 4,932 students and 278 professors. It includes Faculties of Medicine, Law, Economics, Engineering and Philosophy. In 1964 the Agency for International Development extended a loan to cover partially a university development programme including a School of Agriculture and Animal Husbandry, and the creation of a General Studies Centre. The student body, as in most Latin American universities, is politically active.

In contrast, the new Catholic University, Madre y Maestra, founded in Santiago in 1962, has been unusually apolitical. In January 1967 it moved to a new campus which had cost $2 million and could accommodate 900 students. Law, Education, Engineering, Electromechanics and Business Administration formed the curriculum in 1967 with new fields being constantly added.[4]

In addition to its newly created University, Surinam has a Medical College, founded at the end of the nineteenth century, and a Law School which was incorporated two decades ago. A Law School opened in Curaçao in the early 1970's.

Cuba, Haiti and the Dominican Republic contain two-thirds of the population of the Caribbean area: Haiti and the Dominican Republic carry the bulk of the illiterate population. Cuba, with a population exceeding 8·6 million and an island largely flat with good communications, discounting political problems, has potentially the strongest economy in the Caribbean. A density of 185 persons per square mile cannot

[1] "The universalization of the University is the result of the mass education policy", *Granma*, Havana, December 7, 1969.
[2] Cf. Didier Dacunha-Castelle, "L'Enseignement universitaire veut lier la production et la formation", *Le Monde*, Paris, March 29-30, 1970.
[3] Ronald Hilton, *The Scientific Institutions of Latin America*, (California Institute of International Studies, Stanford, 1970), pp. 155-158.
[4] Cf. *Caribbean Educational Bulletin*, Institute of Caribbean Studies, for the Association of Caribbean Universities, May 1969.

be considered excessive. Since Fidel Castro came to power in 1959, the island's population has increased by about two million, despite the departure of at least 245,000 during the same period. The rate of growth is about 1·9 per cent. a year: a rather lower rate than in the other Caribbean islands. Parroting the Marxist line, Castro has decried birth control as the solution of "capitalists and exploiters", stressing the fact that Cuba has enough land to support a much greater population than it has now. He claims to have turned Cuba into a "giant school" and to have reduced illiteracy from 23 per cent. to 3·9 per cent. in less than three years.[1] Educational progress has not been confined only to urban areas: Castro has nationalized education throughout the island. The campaign to eliminate illiteracy in 1961 had impressive results.[2]

With a population density of some 476 persons to the square mile, more than double that of Cuba and with a much smaller proportion of land suitable for cultivation, Haiti presents the most serious population problem in the Antilles. The improvement of public health has contributed to the population increase. The country affords an example of the much greater difficulty of creating employment than of controlling or eliminating disease. So strong has been the pressure of population on the eroded soil combined with little progress with industrialization that there has been for years a stream of illicit emigration from the island.[3] Little has been done to reduce the high rate of illiteracy, and thus any check to the population by birth control methods is virtually non-existent.[4]

Nearly double the size of Haiti, and with a population density less than half that of Haiti (about the same as Cuba), the demographic problem of the Dominican Republic is less acute.[5] The country's resources are more solid and diversified than in many other Caribbean countries, although the standard of living remains pitifully low. Industrialization has begun and a start has been made with developing the tourist trade. Given internal stability and initiative, the population growth should not prove an impossible handicap. Nevertheless, the

[1] This figure is supported by U.N.E.S.C.O. Cf. *Literacy 1967-1969*, Paris, 1970, p. 32.
[2] *Cuba: A Giant School*, Information Department, Ministry of Foreign Affairs, Havana, n.d. *Vide* p. 46.
[3] *Vide* pp. 65-6.
[4] *Vide* pp. 65-7.
[5]

	Area sq. m.	Population (mid-1971 estimate)
Dominican Republic	19,129	4·4 million
Haiti	10,714	5·4 million

371

high amount of illiteracy illustrates the need for educational re-organization.[1]   The cost may well prove to be prohibitive.

Most favoured of the Caribbean countries by reason of its link with the United States, Puerto Rico, despite emigration, which at times has been massive, has shown an increase in population.   Its population density of 789 persons to the square mile is the second highest in the Antilles.   Emigration to the United States, which is unrestricted, was most marked in the period 1947 to 1960.[2]   Since then, the flow has changed, with large numbers of Puerto Ricans returning to the island, a tribute to its prosperity.   The phase of heavy emigration appears to have passed, although should economic conditions deteriorate, doubtless the flow would recommence.

Instead, the movement of population has become dominantly internal, from the country districts to the towns.[3]   Perhaps the most disturbing fact about Puerto Rico is that notwithstanding the massive financial aid from the United States and the opportunity for Puerto Ricans to obtain work in that country, considerable unemployment still exists, illustrating the deep seated problems facing small communities. Since the reduction in emigration, more than 20,000 additional persons are seeking work each year.   Already the population has exceeded two and a half million.

A non-official birth control movement was started in the middle 1950's, but the Government, although sympathetic to the programme, was wary of the opposition.   The issue of birth control caused much conflict in the 1960 election, when the Roman Catholic Church announced that it was a sin to vote for Muñoz, and some priests aided the organization of a new political party against him.   Although Muñoz won easily, the Church's position made it extremely difficult for the Government to act on this matter.   As a result of the failure to persuade the public to accept contraception, the non-official birth control movement lost what little ground it had previously gained.[4]

Those in favour of the project regained hope momentarily when

[1] Illiteracy was estimated at 35·5 per cent. in 1960.   *Literacy 1967-1969.* Former President Juan Bosch estimated the figure at 50 per cent.   *The Unfinished Experiment* (London, 1966), p. 111.

[2] The Puerto Rican population on the United States mainland has grown from 1,513 in 1910 to 892,513 in 1960.   United States Census Bureau, quoted by *The New York Times*, New York, September 8, 1963.

[3] George C. Myers, "Migration and Modernization: the case of Puerto Rico", United Nations World Population Conference, Belgrade, August 30 to September 10, 1965.

[4] *Look*, New York, March 24, 1964.

the Planning Board's economic report of 1963 included for the first time a special section on the island's population statistics which seemed to indicate that the Government was at last going to take a stand.[1] However, much of the general optimism subsided when the International Planned Parenthood Federation held a conference in Puerto Rico in the spring of 1964. In the welcoming address delivered by the Secretary of Health, Guillermo Arbona, the words "birth control" and "family planning" did not appear. Arbona simply agreed that the population explosion posed a problem.[2] The Government was not yet willing to assume responsibility in this field.

Jamaica's 408 persons to the square mile exhibit a crude density a little less than that of Haiti. Both countries have extensive mountainous areas impossible for agriculture. Jamaica's economy has developed dramatically since World War II.[3] Nevertheless, the high rate of unemployment and the heavy reduction of emigration to Great Britain cloud the economic future of the island. Despite development, the population increase has impeded any amelioration of the unemployment problem and has accelerated the immigration to the towns, particularly Kingston.[4]

Jamaica has faced its problem much more openly and courageously than most countries: few countries are being made more population-conscious, due to active interest in birth control displayed by the two main political parties and by leading members of the medical profession.[5] The effect of this cannot yet be assessed. Whether the majority of Jamaicans have reached a high enough level of education fully to comprehend and appreciate the advantages, indeed the necessity, of family planning, remains to be seen. This level varies from country to country; sometimes the mere attainment of literacy is sufficient, sometimes it requires a minimum of high school education.[6]

On the question of population, the example of Jamaica presents one of the situations most worthy of study in the Caribbean. The

---

[1] A. W. Maldonado, "Population Explosion", *The San Juan Star*, San Juan, February 5, 1964.

[2] A. W. Maldonado, "Muñoz and the Church", *The San Juan Star*, April 23, 1964.

[3] *Vide* pp. 141-2.

[4] In 1971 the current rate of population increase was 2·1 per cent. in Jamaica compared with 1·4 per cent. in Puerto Rico and 2·5 per cent. in Haiti. *1971 World Population Data Sheet*, June, 1971.

[5] *Vide* p. 150.

[6] United Nations findings reveal that the educational attainment of women is more significant than that of men in this respect. *World Population: Challenge to Development*, United Nations, New York, 1966, p. 16.

country has taken steps to reduce the number of illiterates. The need for upgrading the skills of the adult population is fully recognized, and four teacher-training colleges are to be expanded.

Less than half the size of Jamaica and with a somewhat greater crude density of 555 persons to the square mile, Trinidad and Tobago has an annual population growth rate of 1·8 per cent. The success of Trinidad's industrialization has given it the highest *per capita* income in the Commonwealth islands of the Caribbean. As in Jamaica, the adoption of the English system of education was not altogether successful; the curriculum failed to meet local requirements. Nevertheless Trinidad, when compared with the Caribbean republics, does not have a high rate of illiteracy. Since the attainment of independence the need for more highly qualified teachers has been partially remedied through the Emergency Teachers' Course. Trinidad, however, continues to battle with a shortage of school places and an ever-increasing school-age population, particularly at the elementary level. Family planning, although recognized as essential, is, as in Jamaica, a question of individual decision, and the same problems arise.

Of the lesser Commonwealth islands, Barbados with 1,807 persons to the square mile has the highest density of population in the Antilles.[1] Although it would be only fair to point out that the island is basically flat, with a substantial part devoted to agriculture, nevertheless it faces a difficult situation. Tourist development and some emigration in the past have helped to ease the situation. A high standard of education has aided the island's development and also the chances for its citizens to obtain jobs abroad.

Martinique and Guadeloupe with crude densities of 753 and 460 present extremely difficult cases. The post-war history of both islands underscores the problems, notwithstanding substantial aid from France.[2] Mountains severely reduce the area of arable land. The uncontrolled population surge compounds the problem.[3] The safety valve of emigration to France has so far been restricted by the cost. With the probability of reduction in Atlantic fares in future years, emigration may accelerate on a massive scale. In this event, France, which has had to absorb a large population of émigrés from Algeria, would face a situation fraught with difficulty.

During the period of the Fourth Plan a new realization of the

[1] The annual rate of population growth of 0·8 per cent. is the lowest in the world outside Europe.

[2] *Vide* pp. 261-86.

[3] *Vide* p. 282.

necessity of population control had come about.[1] This was clearly shown by the number of articles and editorials appearing in the local press, by conferences and by study groups working in the overseas departments. The overseas departments of France, Guadeloupe, Martinique, Guyane and Réunion, had a population of nearly a million to be added to France's 50·0 million. Of the overseas million, Martinique and Guadeloupe together numbered more than half. France also was faced with a rising population, although the problem was thrown into sharper relief in the overseas departments. Fears for the future of the islands, which in 1985 might have to support a population of more than a million, seemed to be well founded on statistical evidence.[2]

The Netherlands Antilles differ in some respects from the rest of the islands. The significant islands of Curaçao and Aruba containing much the greater part of the population of the Netherlands Antilles have prospered from the establishment of oil refineries. The age composition of a population which has been largely built up by immigrant labour is partly reflected by very low death rates. Emigration to the Netherlands does not take place on the same scale as it does to France from Martinique and Guadeloupe. Family planning has been initiated but not been carried as far as in Jamaica or Trinidad. Religion, as in Martinique and Guadeloupe, presents difficulties. Education, although not compulsory, is good and illiteracy negligible. Supported by considerable industrialization, a population density of 818 to the square mile in the Netherlands Antilles does not appear excessive. Yet the outlook for employment from the oil refineries remains uncertain. Future prosperity will turn on the establishment of new industries and tourism.[3]

No amount of capital investment in the Caribbean, however, is likely to match the population growth with sufficient new jobs. In most of the islands the most pressing problem remains the control of population increase.

Neither a low standard of living nor religious beliefs are at the root of the population rise. Medical skill has outstripped practical thinking: in consequence, the great benefits from science have bred new problems. In the Caribbean and beyond, birth control stands out as a

[1] "Un phénomène extrêmement important et nouveau a marqué, à cet égard, les années d'application du 4ème Plan: les responsables locaux comme la majorité de la population ont pris clairement conscience du problème démographique et de la nécessité d'y apporter une solution efficace sortant, au besoin, des conceptions traditionnelles de l'action en la matière." *Vème Plan. D.O.M. Politique Démographique, Rapport General*, p. 18.

[2] *Ibid.*, p. 23.

[3] *Vide* pp. 304-5.

major political and social problem. Unless the full influence of the State is used to inform the public on the issues, the menace of population will overshadow all others before the end of the century.[1]

Population and education are tightly linked. Nothing hinders effective education more than a population which is expanding over-quickly. In these conditions, a shortage of teachers will normally exist. Lack of finance may result in salary rates too low to attract the best talent. Moreover, as world educational standards rise, the *per capita* cost of educating a child soars. At high school and university level finance presses increasingly on the State. New buildings, class-rooms, laboratories and the transportation of pupils mount. A substantial part of the Caribbean population lives in country districts with poor communications. Too often bus services are infrequent and irregular. In most of the smaller islands, a student must move abroad to enter a university.

Excessive population growth magnifies all these difficulties. Parental unemployment compounds them; and no quick solution is in sight. The subject bristles with economic and political problems. Independence has not solved them; indeed, excessive nationalism may be a complicating factor.

[1] In a number of Latin American countries the interest in family planning was mainly from the health point of view. *Human Fertility and National Development*, United Nations, 1971, p. 90.

Chapter XVII

NATIONALISM IN THE CARIBBEAN

Nationalism is one of the most dynamic, sometimes dangerous, forces in the mid-twentieth century. No significant area of the world has remained unaffected by it. In the Caribbean, it has gained great impetus, notably in the years since the end of World War II. In few parts of the world has man more profoundly changed the ethnic composition of a group of islands. The advent of Columbus tolled the death knell for the majority of the Amerindians, Carib or Arawak alike. New races with new ideas displaced them. The civilization came from Europe; the manpower from Africa. The amalgam of the two has produced something different from both, with even an Asian flavour added.

At the end of the eighteenth century, the gathering of clouds could be observed. The centralized European states had outpaced democracy: the fury of the storm was about to burst. But the two forces, national and international, had continued to grow, entwined together. So far neither has crushed the other, even in the drama of the twentieth century.

Nationalism is not easy to define. Immediately it leads to the consideration of what constitutes a nation. All sorts of ingredients may contribute to that complex body: language, religion, history, geographic boundaries, minimum area, and natural resources. Yet none of these is basic. We do not need to look beyond some of the established successful nations to see that they lack many of these unifying norms. Switzerland breaks many of the suggested standards. Yet so successful has it been that a quarrelling world uses it as a prime mediator, while its cities provide centres for many international organizations. Its neighbour Italy, fulfilling most of the obvious requirements, took longer to achieve nationhood. Norway and Sweden, like the Netherlands and Belgium, had many of the ingredients for successful nationhood, but in each case dissolved their unions, created originally at the Treaty of Vienna, as was the modern Swiss Confederation.

John Stuart Mill in his celebrated Essay on Bentham and Coleridge sums up the basic essentials for a state, as apt today as when he wrote more than a century ago. First he places a system of education to train the human being to subordinate his personal impulses and aims to the considered ends of society. Next, in securing permanence of political society, he suggests allegiance to the constitution of the state so that whatever internal conflicts of opinion take place, the fundamental principles of the system of social unison are not destroyed. His third necessity for the state is a strong and active principle of cohesion among the members of the same community. In examining the Caribbean, and indeed many other areas of the world, the dangers that arise from the breaching of these precepts stand forth for all to see.

The islands of Hispaniola and Cuba, discovered by Columbus, were the springboard for the conquest of the Spanish Main. Strangely, it was also in Hispaniola that took place the first effective uprising against the European domination of Latin America. Revolting against Napoleon, Saint Domingue (afterwards Haiti) obtained its independence in 1803, and its new government encouraged the great Simón Bolívar. Spain's mainland Empire was finally destroyed at Junín and Ayacucho in 1824. Nevertheless, for almost three-quarters of a century, until 1898, the red and gold flag of Spain still flew over the Caribbean islands of Cuba and Puerto Rico from the mighty fortresses named El Morro at Havana, Santiago de Cuba and San Juan. Ultimately surrender was forced on Spain, not by the local revolutionaries, who had for long borne the brunt of the fighting, but by the overwhelming power of the United States.

Already in the eighteenth century there had been occasional revolts against the highly organized colonial rule of Spain and the less rigorous one of Portugal. In the uprisings of Tupac Amaru in Peru between 1780 and 1781 and of Tiradentes in Minas Gerais, Brazil, in 1788, the seeds of revolution were sown.

The strong centralized states which had crushed feudalism in Western Europe provided the foundation for nationalism. The intellectual background was put forward by new thinkers who attacked the limitations of a state in which so many of the citizens had only an illusory participation. The philosophy of the English revolution of 1688, supported by the writings of Locke, and the French encyclopaedists, influenced both the American and the French Revolutions, and through them Spanish and Portuguese America.

Not unnaturally, the influence of French philosophy was most marked in Saint Domingue, the western portion of the island of Hispaniola, which had been ceded to France by Spain at the Treaty

378

of Ryswick in 1697, a clear indication of the rise of power in one monarchy and its decline in the other. The wealth of the colony facilitated frequent visits of the planters to Paris, and of the merchants to Bordeaux. There was no barrier of language, such as handicapped the introduction of French literature to the Spanish colonies, reinforced by a strict censorship of French books. By the end of the eighteenth century, French commercial ability had transformed the agriculture of Saint Domingue. At the outbreak of the French Revolution, the colony's combined annual exports and imports exceeded $140 million. Nearly two-thirds of the foreign commercial interests of France centred in this territory. The trade in sugar, coffee, indigo and cotton in a good year employed 700 ocean-going vessels and 80,000 seamen.[1]

The cultivation of the plantations, some of which were irrigated, required large numbers of labourers. Saint Domingue competed strongly with the British colonies for the African slave cargoes. In consequence, the racial composition of the territory changed radically. By 1790, this formerly poor and empty territory, inherited from the buccaneers, had a population of more than 450,000 slaves, 40,000 whites and 28,000 free persons of colour.[2] Many of the free coloured group had acquired wealth. They probably owned at this period about a fifth of the land and the slaves, and their affluence was increasing rapidly. With prosperity fanning the jealousy of the whites, colour prejudice mounted. As the French Revolution developed, each section sought to turn its doctrines to its own end and to further its own desire for power. While the two factions quarrelled, in 1791 the slaves revolted. The pent-up anger of years of ill-treatment burst out. White men, women and children were slaughtered: the plantations of the fertile Plaine du Nord were largely laid waste.

Order was gradually restored by Toussaint l'Ouverture, a former slave who proved a remarkable national leader and an effective military commander. He succeeded in gaining the goodwill of President John Adams of the United States, who sent ships and supplies. So violent was the revolution that not even Napoleon at the height of his power could stem the tide. His troops, commanded by General Charles Leclerc, his brother-in-law, gained a temporary success. Toussaint l'Ouverture, "the gilded African", was finally deported to a Jura

[1] Leyburn, op. cit., p. 15, quoting Pamphile de Lacroix, Mémoires pour servir à l'histoire de la Révolution de Saint Domingue (Paris, 1820), II, p. 277. Cf. Herring, op. cit., p. 249.

[2] The free persons of colour arose from the Code Noir of Louis XIV which permitted a slave to secure liberty by a cash payment or by the gift of his master.

fortress, where he died. But as a result of yellow fever, which killed Leclerc and played havoc with his army, the French finally withdrew and Haiti achieved its independence in 1803.[1]

Yet the very freedom declaimed in the "Rights of Man" was to degenerate into licence and even anarchy, despite the ability of the early Haitian leaders. Toussaint l'Ouverture was followed by Dessalines and Henri Christophe, the fantastic king of Northern Haiti, who created his own nobility, printed books and built one of the most remarkable fortresses in the Americas.

These men were all Negroes. Alexandre Pétion, who ruled Southern Haiti from Port-au-Prince, was a mulatto who had been educated in the military school of Paris. His views were liberal. Influenced perhaps by the then novel theories of Adam Smith, that the more freedom an entrepreneur has, the more he will produce, he abolished the tax on sugar cane of a quarter of the crop.[2] Under his regime, land was subdivided and peasant proprietors were created to replace serfs. His political objectives and those of Jean-Pierre Boyer, his successor, were theoretically admirable. Unfortunately, they resulted in the impoverishment and near collapse of Haitian agriculture.

The slaves who revolted in Haiti were not a nation. During a century or more they had been transported from Africa, drawn from different tribes and speaking different languages. The rebellion was more than an uprising caused by cruelty and suppression. It was a foretaste of the "wind of change" of British Prime Minister Harold Macmillan, in the guise of a tropical hurricane.

In the first half of the nineteenth century, a large standing army was maintained by Haiti through fear of French invasion,[3] a fear which may itself have contributed to the development of nationalism. Pétion favoured the nascent political movement in Spanish America. In particular, he gave moral and material support to Bolívar, who visited him when in exile. The Venezuelan in return promised to abolish slavery in his own country. Negroes and mestizos fought under Bolívar.[4] When, after initial failure, Bolívar returned to Haiti, it was Pétion who gave him encouragement and aid.[5]

---

[1] *Vide* p. 49.

[2] Leyburn, *op. cit.*, p. 55.

[3] In 1825 Haiti agreed to pay France 60 million francs over a period of years. Consequently the Haitian army was sharply reduced in numbers.

[4] Fred J. Rippy, *Latin America* (University of Michigan Press, Ann Arbor, 1958), p. 140.

[5] Cf. Salvador de Madariaga, *Bolívar*, 3rd edition (Buenos Aires, 1959), Vol. I, pp. 558-60, and A. B. Thomas, *Latin America* (New York. 1956), p. 231.

Like the Haitian revolution, the revolts in South America had their origin in European thoughts and events. With Bourbons ruling Spain since the beginning of the eighteenth century, the French connection, strengthened by alliances, was close drawn. Prosperous colonials like Francisco de Miranda and later Bolívar travelled extensively in Europe, meeting statesmen and philosophers. In 1794, Antonio Nariño published in Bogotá a Spanish translation of the French Declaration of the Rights of Man. The influence of the Freemasons helped to extend the ideas of the *philosophes* in Spain and ultimately to undermine the power of kings.

Professor C. H. Haring describes the Spanish West Indian islands as one of the most backward regions of the Empire. He considers that "The revolutions in America were the work of a comparatively few enlightened, keen-witted leaders, who in many areas represented the ambition of the educated creole class to supplant the peninsular Spaniards in government and trade, and in whose hands the ignorant classes were a ready tool for the accomplishment of their aims".[1] To this, he attributes some of the political troubles that subsequently arose in Latin America.

Germán Arciniegas, the liberal Colombian diplomat, professor and author, writes: "These conflicts were only natural. Spain, whose power had been absolute during the colonial epoch, had not prepared the Creoles for self-government. In the United States, where the North Americans had, for all practical purposes, been governing themselves since before the Revolutionary War, nothing serious happened. But in Spanish America everything had to be improvised, done by the trial-and-error method, and all this when the masses were excited by the wars of Independence. . . ."[2]

In the nineteenth-century struggle for independence, José Martí, journalist, writer and thinker, is regarded as the Cuban national hero. Much of his life was spent in exile in the United States, though he died leading a Cuban revolutionary force against the occupying Spanish army. He pleaded the cause of Cuban independence both in the United States and in the columns of the great South American newspaper *La Nación* of Buenos Aires. One of his most celebrated speeches, "Los Pinos Nuevos", was delivered in Florida on the twentieth anniversary of the execution by Spain of a group of Havana medical students, a beautiful and moving piece of prose which has not dated. Jorge Mañach declares that in the final analysis all modern political thought turns on an axis whose poles are Thomas More and Machiavelli,

[1] *The Spanish Empire in America* (New York, 1947), p. 346.
[2] *Caribbean, Sea of the New World* (New York, 1946), p. 369.

381

the idealistic Utopia and *Realpolitik*. He considers that Martí represented the romantic-positivist compromise between these two extreme positions.[1]

In eighteenth-century Cuba may be seen the interplay of nationalism and internationalism. The fervour of revolutionary freedom spread through Latin America from the United States boundary to the Antarctic. Alone of the former Spanish colonies in the Americas, Cuba and Puerto Rico remained "faithful". To this various factors contributed. Most important were the relatively large Spanish garrisons, and the sea barrier which prevented the mainland colonies from giving aid. The British fleet, supreme in the Caribbean as elsewhere, had no desire to ferment revolution in territories adjacent to British Islands. The excesses of the Haitian slave revolt had shocked opinion in Britain which had fears that the revolution might spread to Jamaica. Many French families had fled across the Windward Passage from Haiti where they had settled in Cuba's Oriente, strong opponents of emancipation. Moreover, many loyalist Spaniards had moved to the Spanish Islands from Spanish America just as opponents to the American Revolution had in the preceding century emigrated to Canada. Against such a background in favour of preserving the *status quo*, supplemented by immigration from Spain into Cuba, the revolutionary path was a stony one.

Cuba's repeated attempts to throw off the Spanish yoke were gallant, but had failed. Finally the intervention of the United States, on the doubtful ground of sabotage to its battleship *Maine*, destroyed the Spanish grip. The United States was very conscious of the strategic importance of Cuba. The very course of the Spanish American War, which had involved the transfer of U.S. warships from the Pacific to the Atlantic, a long and hazardous operation, had opened the eyes of the American Government and public to the need for an inter-ocean Canal. Cuba occupied a key position between the United States and the sea approaches to Central America. The base at Guantánamo Bay became in the twentieth century to the United States what the forts of El Morro at Havana and Santiago de Cuba had been to the Spaniards from the sixteenth century.

Nationalism was strong in the United States, with an expansionist flavour. Captain Mahan stressed the need for sea-power; President Theodore Roosevelt, himself a veteran of the Cuba War, was convinced of the strategic importance of the Caribbean to the United States. Emergent Cuban nationalism, which had vainly struggled against Spain,

---

[1] "José Martí Rompeolas de América", *Combate*, San José, Costa Rica, March/April 1961, p. 70.

was still further frustrated by the terms of the Platt Amendment which restricted Cuba's sovereignty.[1]

On the economic side, America moved in to help rehabilitate a country devastated by war and riddled by disease. American investment followed. The development of Cuba was rapid, and could certainly not have been accomplished so quickly by the Cubans themselves. Unfortunately, when the American military government left in 1902, Cuba failed during the succeeding years to elect competent administrations. Corruption was excessive. No attempt was made to introduce a modern system of taxation. The glaring disparities between rich and poor appeared everywhere. Perhaps the shock to Cuban nationalism in living in association with a new master—however beneficent—discouraged a flowering of national talent. To be fair to the United States, a study of the first decades of independence in other Latin American countries suggests that these countries fared no better, as Argentina, Venezuela, Mexico and the neighbouring Hispaniolan Republics bear witness. Cuba's failure to set up honest and democratic government cannot be laid at the door of the United States.

Cuba, in fact, made better economic than political progress during the first part of the twentieth century. Roads and railways were built; public utilities were organized; the sugar industry had claims to be among the most efficient in the world. There had, however, been a nineteenth-century tradition among the commercially important urban Spaniards of strong opposition to Cuban nationalism.[2] In the twentieth century, Spanish and other immigrants settled in Cuba together with U.S. investors. They continued the tradition. Cuba became one of the more developed countries in Latin America, though little was done by successive governments to bridge the excessive gaps between the wealth of some in the cities and the poverty, particularly in the countryside. Certainly the glamour and the corruption associated with the casinos in the capital emphasized these disparities and prepared a climate ready for change.

The advent of Fidel Castro was regarded by many as a breath of fresh air. He symbolized a youthful, honest and nationalistic Cuba. The very fact that his philosophy in the first years was vague made it easier for him to captivate the country. The Sierra Maestra period gave a romantic touch. The final march from the Oriente to Havana was dramatic though devoid of heavy fighting.

Castro made his appeal as wide as possible, from his first followers, the middle class in the cities, to the peasants in the Oriente. The

[1] *Vide* pp. 7-8.

[2] Draper, *Castroism: Theory and Practice* (New York, 1965), p. 107.

move to a Communist system came later in 1960, with the joining of Castro's twenty-sixth of July party to the Communists. Castro made effective use of every method of communication, particularly television and radio. His technique was to develop Cuban nationalism, particularly by representing it as being menaced by the United States. The Bay of Pigs affair, the American flights over Cuba, the missile crisis, all aided this aspect of the nationalistic image.

Events, however, relentlessly showed the impossibility of a self-contained Cuba directing its development unfettered. In the name of nationalism, the economic links with the United States were severed. Not only was the normal interchange of goods terminated but even basic supplies, such as spare parts for U.S. machinery in Cuba, were cut off by the United States. Cuba's only course then was to negotiate trade, much of it not for cash, with Russia and other Iron Curtain countries. Moreover, Cuba which was following a policy of swift industrialization was forced to equip the new factories with a great deal of the plant coming from Communist countries thousands of miles away.

Cuba soon found itself in a vice even tighter than the former U.S. grip. At least the Americans had paid for their purchases of Cuban sugar in cash, but Cuba's new trading partners favoured barter deals. Ernesto ("Che") Guevara, internationally oriented and Cuban only by naturalization, had been in charge of the unsuccessful industrialization policy. Much more interested than Castro in Communist ideology, his disappearance from Cuba in 1965 may have strengthened Castro's basically nationalistic views.

Although Castro had embraced Communism, he strove for independence. He tried to steer a path between the struggle of Russia and China, even if his commercial dependence on Russia drew him ultimately to the Russian side. In theory, Cuba remained a member of the group of unaligned countries. Yet its history showed the difficulty of an Antillean island retaining effective independence, notwithstanding that its resources were the best in the Antilles. From being a Spanish colony, it had become a near U.S. dependency, and finally largely bound to the Soviet Union. The forces of internationalism seemed stronger than those of nationalism. The Cuban experience may be a pointer to the ultimate weakening of nationalism, perhaps disappointing at first to new nations, but a tendency which may ultimately aid world unity. In the long run, the most important effects of Castro's Revolution may be found in the better education of the Cuban people, and in the higher standards of honesty in the administration. His nationalism in Cuba was not racial. Indeed, the

Oriente, which was his base in the years of guerrilla warfare, had a substantial Negro population together with many persons of French descent who had escaped from Haiti at the time of the great Slave Revolt.[1] Anyone in Havana following the 1959 Revolution could not fail to notice the considerable numbers of Negroes in Castro's army.

Haiti presents Negro nationalism at its strongest in the Caribbean. Stemming from the Code Noir of Louis XIV, French rule had separated the inhabitants into the white French population, the mulattoes, who likewise could own property and slaves, and the African Negro slaves. Intense hostility, not only to Europeans but to mulattoes, was evinced after the rebellion which led to independence, even if the mulattoes survived in a divided country with a distinguished President in Alexandre Pétion at Port-au-Prince, while the Negro king, Henri Christophe, ruled in the North. Nationalism from the days of Dessalines has been linked with Negro dominance in a country which has the highest percentage of African blood in the Caribbean. The prosperity of the mulatto section of the community, often educated in France or at French oriented schools in Haiti, stood out in contrast to the Negro villages of the interior. Although at times power rested with the mulattoes, force of numbers swung politics in the opposite direction.

As a result of the twenty-year American occupation, power was handed back to the mulattoes and not the Negroes. However, after independence returned to Haiti with the departure of the U.S. Marines in 1934, the reasonable Magloire Government was followed by the election of Duvalier. Haiti was now to experience nationalism in its crudest form. Duvalier drew his support from the country villages. A clever psychologist, he knew how to impose his image as the father of the country, "Papa Doc", on the illiterate peasantry who composed the larger part of the four million inhabitants of the country. He was thought to believe in voodooism, as did most of the Haitians, and his grip on Haiti, backed by the Tonton Macoute, was relentless.

The outside world meant not much more to him than it did to Dr. José Francia, the nineteenth century dictator of Paraguay. Duvalier was prepared to accept a U.S. Military mission to train his forces, theoretically against Cuban interference, in practice to support the Duvalier regime. The economic development of Haiti interested him little. Haiti's membership of the O.A.S. was on occasion a political convenience to the United States and at the same time an economic one to Haiti. Duvalier effectively exploited nationalism in the interest of personal power.

[1] *Vide* pp. 6 and 32.

With a record of internal turmoil and corruption no less than that of Haiti, the Dominican Republic had not the same racial hatreds as its near neighbour. Family political feuds replaced them. President Rafael Trujillo governed his country as egotistically as Duvalier. He had certainly used the image of nationalism to mirror that of himself as the Benefactor of his country. Trujillo's nationalism had expressed itself in the massacre of some 10,000 Haitians who had entered his country to seek work. Even after his death, quarrels between the two Hispaniolan countries brought them to the brink of war.[1]

A series of dictatorships interrupted by the U.S. occupation (1916-24) which was succeeded by over thirty years of *La Era de Trujillo* inevitably militated against the formation of a modern state. For example, the creation of a sound Civil Service, basic to any progress, was impossible. This contributed to the failure of a democratic state after Trujillo's assassination. The divisions within the Republic emerge clearly from the events of 1965.[2] At the start of the seventies U.S. intervention appeared to some extent justified by six years of peace in the island.

To many Puerto Ricans, the results of the Spanish-American War were disappointing despite the welcome that most of the colonists had given to the U.S. conquerors. The long period of U.S. rule seemed to be a change of masters. Despite American expenditure and money, unemployment, stimulated by a rapidly increasing population, created hardship.

Prosperity began during World War II and continued afterwards. Even so there were many who regarded the island's position with misgiving, historically forced from a Spanish past to a U.S. present and an uncertain future.[3] Great changes, however, would transform the fortunes of the island.

The organization of Puerto Rico as a Commonwealth or *Estado Libre Asociado* is expressed inaccurately in both English and Spanish —perhaps deliberately. The word Commonwealth has no connection with the present (former British) Commonwealth, nor with the earlier colonial usage of the word in North America, nor is Puerto Rico an "associated free state". It is in no sense federated with the United States. Indeed, it can only intervene in U.S. policy through its

[1] *Vide* pp. 55-6 and 75.

[2] *Vide* pp. 80-6.

[3] "Somos una generación fronteriza, batida entre un final y un comienzo, sin saber a dónde dirigir las requisiciones necesarias para habilitar nuestra responsabilidad. Al empezar el siglo XX, huérfanos ya de la madre histórica, quedamos al cuidado de un padrastro rico y emprendedor." Antonio S. Pedreira, *Insularismo* (Puerto Rico, 1957), p. 210.

representative at Washington who can speak but not vote in the House of Representatives. Puerto Rico's foreign policy is in the hands of the United States, as is its Customs Service and national defence.

Notwithstanding these substantial limitations of sovereignty, for practical purposes Puerto Rico has very substantial autonomy. With its own elected Governor, Senate and House of Representatives, it manages its own affairs. Certainly the United States has military bases in the island. Besides saving Puerto Rico the cost of a defence force, the U.S. forces are, as it were, by their expenditure, a permanent addition to Puerto Rico's tourist revenue. On the other hand, Puerto Rico's financial gains from its exemption from U.S. Federal taxation are very substantial.[1] This unusual arrangement was largely created by the far-sighted ability of Luis Muñoz Marín co-operating with Governor Rexford Tugwell.

The impact of Puerto Rican nationalism makes an interesting study. How far will a territory sacrifice independence for material gain? Without doubt the benefits have been striking, placing Puerto Rico highest of Latin American countries in regard to income *per capita*. Moreover, the distribution of the income *per capita* would compare favourably with Latin American competitors for first place, such as Venezuela.

On the other side, a case may be made that Puerto Rico is sacrificing its Spanish heritage and culture for commercial reasons. Some will say that independence must rank first of all national considerations. There are also those who claim that Puerto Rico should, like Alaska and Hawaii, seek entry as a state into the United States. Since the island's inhabitants are debarred from participation in U.S. elections, there is a limitation on its citizenship.

So far the supporters of the Commonwealth have carried the day. They can point to practical progress. Spanish culture and language have not been destroyed. Indeed, the appointment of Teodoro Moscoso, one of the island's foremost planners, to the Alliance for Progress programme was intended as a tribute to Puerto Rico's own dramatic advance. The University of Puerto Rico, with more than 26,000 students, has a commanding position in the Caribbean area.[2] The diversification and industrialization of the island lend force to the economic benefits which have accrued. To the Puerto Ricans, the solution arrived at is a special one. They do not suggest that it can be applied elsewhere. Nor are there many countries which could emulate the United States in its generosity.

[1] *Vide* p. 119.
[2] *Vide* p. 369.

387

Both World Wars I and II profoundly modified Great Britain's attitude towards the overseas territories with which it was associated. The very words "British Empire" became "Commonwealth". An early act of the powerful Coalition Government of Ramsay MacDonald and Stanley Baldwin was to pass the Statute of Westminster which clarified the independence of the Dominions and was a declaration of Great Britain's intent for the future. World War II greatly accelerated the move towards independence inside, or even in some cases outside, the Commonwealth. The increase of nationalism was natural. A new country looks to nationalism as something which will give it internal strength, particularly in the difficult formative years.

The political leaders in the British Caribbean islands were nationalistic, but not to an exaggerated degree. In Jamaica, Sir Alexander Bustamante was throughout his career a strong supporter of Jamaica's association with Britain, and of the link with the Sovereign. Norman Manley, politically influenced by British statesmen like Sir Stafford Cripps and with a profound knowledge of British law, also was sympathetic to British ties. In Trinidad, Eric Williams was probably intellectually more critical of Great Britain.

Curiously nationalism in the British Caribbean worked most strongly against the West Indies Federation, to whose collapse it contributed. None of these three leaders would serve in the Federal Government, probably because they realized that the feelings of the people they represented were not in tune with the concept of Federation. The inevitable consequence was the emergence of Jamaica and Trinidad as independent countries and later Barbados, even smaller in area and population. The Leeward and Windward Islands sought to work out with Great Britain some viable solution to their very difficult political and economic problems, resulting in associated statehood.

In the French Antilles, island nationalisms have been submerged by the force of Gaullist French Nationalism. Substantial benefits have come to Martinique and Guadeloupe from integration with France. In the field of education this has been outstanding, though it has meant that at university level students must go to France. Economic integration with France, providing entry to the European Market, has been of major importance. The very serious population problem has been alleviated by the right of the islanders to enter France to find employment, comparable to the position of Puerto Ricans coming to the United States. Moreover, citizens of the Antillean departments have full political rights and representation in the government of France.

Notwithstanding the advantages, the movement in favour of local nationalism, pointing to independence, remains strong even if partly concealed. The very excellence of the French education has resulted in many young men in Martinique and Guadeloupe finding no suitable employment for their talents in a largely agricultural community. Dissatisfaction has been expressed in riots and also by the substantial Communist vote in some districts.[1] There is probably more sympathy for Cuba in the French Antilles than in the British or Dutch islands, resulting from a history of antagonism.[2] The opposition to separatism had been dominant, particularly with the strong and itself highly nationalistic government of de Gaulle. The weakness of local nationalism rests in the probable plight of the islands, should the bond with France be broken.

Small in area and population, the Netherlands Antilles has accepted the far-reaching political accommodation with the Netherlands which gives them a much greater participation in Dutch policy than has Puerto Rico in that of the United States. Surinam, however, has aspirations towards independence. Access to the capital market in one of Western Europe's most successful countries is important to both the Netherlands Antilles and Surinam. As in the case of Puerto Rico and the French Antilles, the cost of defence and of diplomatic representation has been removed. Some will feel that the sacrifice of independence is a price worth paying.

* * * *

Black nationalism in the Caribbean has taken a different form from that which developed in the United States. It can be traced back to the writings of Haiti's Jean Price Mars and to the work of Marcus Garvey in the 1920's. Until the late 1960's Black nationalism was not, in the Caribbean, synonymous with Black Power: instead it consisted of an emotional desire to reinstate the values of an African heritage during a period when independence, in some cases, was gradually being achieved.

It was a call to black peoples "to throw off white domination and resume the handling of their destinies".[3] To the Commonwealth Caribbean, Castro was the hero of the Black Power movement. Cubans having achieved their rights were able to forget the category "black" and think simply as "Cuban citizens, as Socialist equals and as men".[4] In its less extreme forms Black Power was not racially intolerant. The Caribbean, however, presented a particular case: in every country where a majority of black people occurred there was a black Cabinet and black

[1] *Vide* pp. 270-1 and 272-3.   [2] *Vide* p. 272.
[3] Walter Rodney, *The Groundings with my Brothers* (London, 1969), p. 24.
[4] *Ibid.*, p. 31.

Head of Government. But Black Power did not mean "merely putting black faces in office".[1] Black visibility was not Black Power. Heavy overseas investment, the control of businesses and industry by foreign companies, what was in other words, White Power, was anathema to many.

Tourism, if it made invaluable contributions to the economy of many territories, also highlighted the gap between rich and poor. The Caribbean saw itself becoming a nation of servants. To the young, university educated Trinidadian or Jamaican, or the worker employed by the large foreign firm, money poured in to sustain a society which they could not tolerate. The style of Black Power was a young style: politically and psychologically it was a phenomenon of youth.

Although in the early seventies Black Power was still in its infancy there, the economic basis for its growth was widespread. Any future disorder or unrest might be exploited by the movement, such as the 1969 rioting in Curaçao in May which had specifically concentrated on white-owned businesses. The expulsion of Rodney from Jamaica in October 1968 had led to student riots used by Black Power insurgents; in Trinidad a Latin American type *cuartelazo* took place in 1970.[2]

To expect no more trouble would be optimistic. The dangers would be greater if world Black Power movements synchronized.[3] Unemployment figures in countries such as Jamaica, Trinidad and Curaçao, are precariously high.[4]

The potential danger of Black Power, not least in the Caribbean, is the breadth of its interpretation. The Trade Unions equate it with higher wages and better living conditions; island leaders and the entrenched middle classes equate it with Communism; students with almost anything. Unfortunately its exponents often present it as destructive and not constructive. A revolution might facilitate the seizure of property and plant. Yet property loses its value if it cannot be effectively managed: a danger of greater significance each year as technology advances. Moreover, the need for attracting ever more capital to these countries is a clamant and continuing one.

Charismatic qualities in leaders have characterized the Caribbean. Sir Alexander Bustamante, Norman Manley, Cheddi Jagan, Fidel

[1] Stokely Carmichael and Charles V. Hamilton, *Black Power* (Harmondsworth 1969), p. 60.
[2] *Vide* pp. 154-5.
[3] Stokely Carmichael indicated the existence of a movement to coordinate Black Power movements in Africa, Asia, Britain, the United States and the Caribbean. Georgetown, Guyana, May 3, 1970.
[4] *Vide* pp. 150, 162 and 302-3.

Castro and Johan Pengel provide examples, of which the most remarkable is Fidel Castro. In such cases leadership is based on a racial or nationalistic appeal. President François Duvalier's propaganda, linked to voodooism, made a formidable impact on the Haitian peasants. How far is the proliferation of small countries practicable? Can a country be independent if it is economically dependent for its survival on another either because of the direction of its trade or by the necessity of a subsidy, in one form or another? More and more the independence of one country will seem to depend on the actions and tolerance of others.

Nationalism continues to dominate the Caribbean. Racial and linguistic differences, combined with different systems of education, law and religion stemming from the past, have contributed to this characteristic. The very water frontiers of the islands are self-containing as anyone knows who has lived on one.

The Commonwealth islands which have moved into independence have shown few signs of reuniting since the West Indies Federation collapsed. Certainly CARIFTA is a vigorous attempt at economic cooperation even if effective implementation may prove exceedingly difficult. The division of the Caribbean is further exemplified by Cuba, economically detached from the Western Hemisphere and now dependent for its economic survival on the Soviet Union. The French islands have been increasingly absorbed as parts of France notwithstanding a vociferous minority who seek independence, which would carry little likelihood of economic success. They may be compared with Puerto Rico whose high standard of living substantially depends on its links with the United States and the taxation favours which flow from this relationship.

Yet it would be unrealistic to deduce that a union of the Caribbean would necessarily increase prosperity. All the factors, including distance, language and tradition, which exist would impede an effective union. Indeed some of the islands such as Puerto Rico, the Netherlands Antilles, the French Overseas Departments and Trinidad compare favourably from the point of view of standard of living with much larger neighbours in Latin America.

Economic factors indicate danger signals.[1] Unemployment may be increasing, not only from the growth of population but from the difficulties in agriculture where costs rise and mechanization reduces the number of workers.[2]

[1] Cf. *The Observer*, London, editorial, April 26, 1970.
[2] Cf. Manuela Semidei, "Pouvoir noir et décolonisation dans les Caraïbes", *Le Monde Diplomatique*, Paris, January 1971.

Clearly no obvious solutions suggest themselves. A new nation should be proud of its heritage and moreover seek to improve it. That is something which provides a challenge, particularly to the young men emerging in ever greater numbers from the universities. Nationalism can and should be constructive: something which holds a nation together but is not directed against other countries. The heritage of Black culture, like other cultures, can fortify and inspire a people.

For the majority, whose forebears have come from far-off lands, the future provides a great challenge. In co-operation with the peoples of other countries in trade and commerce and in communication lies the best chance for the Caribbean's future.

CHAPTER XVIII

FOREIGN INFLUENCES ON THE CARIBBEAN

EUROPE

The nineteenth century pattern suggested that the European powers had not abandoned their colonial aspirations but rather that they were directing them to more promising spheres in Africa and Asia.[1] From time to time, colonialist acquisitiveness broke through during that century. The United States succeeded in taking over peacefully from Spain Florida and Louisiana; but other problems arose, many of which were connected with Caribbean territories as well as those of the successor Republics on the surrounding mainland.

France still hankered after Haiti, and for long received payments from that island. Great Britain, France and the Netherlands retained colonies in South America. The ill-defined boundaries of the Guianas were in due course settled peacefully with Brazil and Venezuela.

Central America, after the final collapse of its Federation in 1847, split into a group of small quarrelling Republics, providing fertile ground for international intrigue. Great Britain claimed possession of the Bay Islands off the coast of the Republic of Honduras.[2] Moreover, it had settlements at Belize and elsewhere in the coastal area which later became British Honduras. In 1859 Great Britain relinquished its claims on the Bay Islands but successfully asserted its sovereignty over Belize, which became British Honduras.

As the nineteenth century drew to a close, Britain had clearly decided that its major colonial interests lay elsewhere. Meanwhile the concept of Empire, which in due course would be transformed into Commonwealth, had become well established. Britain, however, clung

[1] From different angles, European policy in the Caribbean has been already examined in the preceding territorial chapters. A brief résumé is given here. It is considered in more detail in the author's *Europe in the Caribbean*. In view of the lessening influence of Europe and the increasing influence of the United States in the area, and the problems of the relationship of the new independent Commonwealth countries in relation to Latin America and the O.A.S., more space has been devoted in this chapter to these topics.

[2] *Vide* p. 216.

tenaciously to its territorial rights if it deemed them threatened, as in the case of the Venezuela boundary dispute over Guyana.[1] As the world's leading trading nation of the day, Britain gradually realized that its prospects in the Caribbean had become extremely limited in contrast to its expanding commerce in greater territories like India, Canada, parts of Africa and Australia.

France, which was in the process of forming the most extensive colonial empire in the world, equally perceived that its Caribbean interests were withering. For a moment in the mid-nineteenth century Victor Schoelcher had aroused his country's interest over the issue of emancipation of the slaves. However, larger territories such as Algeria and Indochina absorbed its energies. In 1863, Napoleon III had attempted to foist Maximilian, his puppet Emperor, on Mexico. The intervention, at first facilitated by the engagement of the United States in civil war, soon ended in failure.

The Netherlands, once interested in Curaçao as a pawn in its early struggle against Spain, devoted its major effort to the development of its East Indies. Apart from the expansion of oil refineries in its Caribbean islands, the Dutch interest was small.

In addition to their varied colonial possessions, the industrialized countries of Europe, including Great Britain, were heavily involved in economic developments all over the world. Entrepreneurs soon sensed that the larger underdeveloped countries with increasing discoveries of natural resources held more promise than the sugar islands of a bygone day.

At the opening of the twentieth century, the United States was moving rapidly into a dominant position in the Caribbean. The Spanish-American War had convinced the U.S. public of the strategic importance of the Antilles, the more so as the project of constructing a trans-isthmian canal took shape.

Nevertheless Europe, imbued with the tradition of defending its interests and influenced by its policy of trading enclaves and treaty ports in Asia, did not easily retire from the Caribbean. Sweden and Denmark at different times indeed disposed of their small and unprofitable Antillean possessions,[2] but Great Britain and France, and also Germany which owned no territory in the Caribbean, reacted strongly when their commercial interests were threatened. Examples were the Venezuelan dispute of 1902[3]; and the claims against the

[1] *Vide* pp. 237-9.
[2] Sweden sold St. Barthélemy to France in 1877. Denmark sold its West Indies to the United States in 1916-17.
[3] *Vide* p. 404.

Dominican Republic in 1904[1] and Haiti in 1915.[2] The political weakness of Spain and Portugal during the nineteenth and twentieth centuries increasingly restricted their interference in Latin America.

World War II accelerated the transformation of these former colonies into independent nations. The Caribbean territories, older and more sophisticated than many of their counterparts in Asia and Africa, hesitated to separate from the metropolitan powers to whom they were linked both by tradition and by commerce. When Great Britain's attempted solution of Federation failed, British interest however waned due in part to its post-war financial difficulties. As soon as Jamaica, for example, entered independence, the small British garrison was withdrawn. Naval bases had been closed at an earlier date. What defence there was, outside the slender resources of the new countries themselves, became more obviously a U.S. matter.[3] America reduced its World War II bases in size but usually retained them.

Great Britain's cultural and economic interest remained, however. Substantial help was given to the University of the West Indies, including the handing over to it of the former Imperial College of Tropical Agriculture in Trinidad. In commerce, Great Britain continued to aid in different ways the entry of West Indian products including sugar, bananas and citrus. Nevertheless, its share of the Commonwealth market in the Caribbean was shrinking in competition with the United States.

The Colonial Development Corporation was established by Great Britain in 1948 to assist the economic development of the then dependent Commonwealth territories.[4] The setting up of permanent resident organizations in the areas of operation ensured first-hand knowledge of these territories. Enterprises such as forestry, fishing, mining, transport and hotels were undertaken by the C.D.C. either by itself or in conjunction with other bodies. The C.D.C. had declared its desire to work closely with private enterprise but claimed a measure of freedom which had in its early days led to substantial losses. It experienced a severe setback during the Korean War

---

[1] *Vide* pp. 69-70.
[2] *Vide* p. 50.
[3] *Vide* p. 137.
[4] Overseas Resources Development Act, 1948 and 1959. The regions covered in the Caribbean are British Honduras, Guyana, Jamaica, Trinidad, and all other British West Indian islands together with the Bahamas.

owing to rising costs which adversely affected many of the projects which it was developing. Financial difficulties increased; by 1952 the total deficit was £8,399,807.[1]

Increasingly the C.D.C. found itself operating in countries which had gained independence. By the Commonwealth Development Act of 1963, its name was changed to the Commonwealth Development Corporation and as such it was given power to operate in all countries which had gained independence since 1948. With Government approval, the Corporation could also act in a managerial or advisory capacity in any independent Commonwealth country. In January 1965, under a Labour Government, the Minister of Overseas Development took over responsibility for the C.D.C. in place of the Secretaries of State for Commonwealth Relations and for the Colonies.

At the end of 1970 the C.D.C. had 51 projects established in the Caribbean region with a capital of over £40 million. These included new housing estates in Guyana, the Fort George Hotel at Belize, power stations in Dominica, St. Lucia and St. Vincent, harbour developments in Jamaica and a mortgage fund in Trinidad.[2] New projects in 1970 were mainly in the Eastern Caribbean.

The C.D.C., created by a Labour Government and continued by successive Conservative and Labour Governments, had become the major vehicle used by Great Britain to provide development aid in its present and former colonies. After a stormy start, the Corporation was playing a significant part in the development of the Caribbean.

As Great Britain prepared to enter the Common Market, problems of the future of the Commonwealth Caribbean loomed ominously, particularly in regard to the sugar industry, largest employer of labour in the area. The short-term arrangement negotiated by the British Government by no means gave a certain guarantee for the future. Great anxiety was expressed in the Commonwealth Caribbean while opinion in Great Britian was divided on the interpretation of the offer which had been obtained after long negotiation with the Six.[3]

Of all the European countries, France has involved itself most

---

[1] *Colonial Development Corporation Report and Accounts 1952*, p. 3. Cf. Mitchell, *op. cit.*, p. 83, n. 3.

[2] In Dominica and St. Vincent, for example, the C.D.C. had owned and managed the Electricity Services since 1953 and at the end of 1970 some $E.C.5·5 million was employed in their development. *Commonwealth Development Corporation Report and Accounts, 1970*, pp. 57, 64.

[3] *Vide* pp. 324-6.

closely with its Caribbean territories by incorporating them in the metropolis. The French Government shows no reluctance to incur expenditure on the Antillean departments. Notwithstanding earlier difficulties of integration with the metropolis, a position seems to have been reached where the alternative of independence has become economically impossible.

Despite France's efforts, the problems of employment remain as acute in Martinique and Guadeloupe as in Jamaica and Trinidad. At least the overseas departments benefit from unrestricted entry of their citizens to France, where many thousands have found employment. Whether French zeal to keep the Antillean link will continue since the demise of de Gaulle cannot be determined. The islanders themselves are divided on the issue. Entry to the European Common Market, derived from France's membership, has proved of increasing value. Sugar, rum and bananas have a promising outlet, as have canned fruits. Not even the energy of de Gaulle made much impression on Guyane's stagnant economy. Again and again France has attempted to activate its Latin American territory but always without success. The Nemo Scheme appears to have had small results.[1]

The Netherlands had made its cautious choice to form the Tripartite Kingdom following its Indonesian disaster. As in the case of France, the cost was not prohibitive. Indeed these two countries, together with Belgium, had proved that a major colonial liquidation could be advantageous to their economies.

The Netherlands helped the Netherlands Antilles to build up one of the strongest economies in the Caribbean. Unfortunately, changes in the situation of world oil in which the great reserves of the Persian Gulf overshadow even those of Venezuela, have led to heavy pressures on Caribbean refineries to reduce costs. The once prosperous Dutch islands face critical times as a result of unemployment. In consequence, their bond with the Netherlands in the Tripartite Kingdom takes on increasing importance.[2]

Surinam, which has a more diversified economy, still seeks to retain its European link. As a vital source of capital investment the Netherlands is valuable to it. Combined with aid from international sources, the country shows promising growth.[3] Some of the people look to a time when economic development may make possible political independence. For the time being at least, the union between the members of the Tripartite Kingdom remains firm.

[1] *Vide* pp. 265 and 288.
[2] *Vide* pp. 302-7.
[3] E.E.C. funds were used for the new University at Paramaribo. *Vide p.* 316.

Despite Spain's loss of its remaining Caribbean colonies more than half a century ago, it has retained ties with Spanish-speaking countries. Of particular significance is its friendly relation with Cuba, notwithstanding the different ideologies of the two governments. Spain retains full diplomatic representation at Havana. Alone in Western Europe, it operates a regular air service to Havana from Madrid which functions smoothly. It has developed its trade with Cuba which is substantial. Notwithstanding a trade dispute in the autumn of 1971, which nearly led to a break in diplomatic relations, the two countries continued to co-operate.[1]

The Caribbean countries' trade links with Europe necessitate voyages of thousands of miles, with all the consequent delays. The commerce, once highly valuable to the eighteenth-century Colonial Powers, today has often to be protected or subsidized by them. The Caribbean markets to which they may have preferential entry are small. The purchasing power of the population is limited.

Everything points to increasing commercial links between the United States and the Caribbean. Certainly Europe will continue to seek trade outlets and in fact at least one leading European country, the Federal Republic of Germany, which has no historic ties with the Caribbean, is actively promoting its trade. Nevertheless, easy communications and proximity favour the American market.

THE UNITED STATES OF AMERICA

During the half century following the Treaty of Utrecht (1713), the American colonies prospered. Prices for colonial products in Great Britain and Europe rose. The American colonies, which had an expanding manufacture of rum, imported the molasses for its manufacture from the British and French West Indian islands. After Great Britain in 1733 placed a heavy duty on foreign molasses, widespread smuggling tempered the impact of the Act and made possible the continuance of the trade.[2] To merchants in the northern colonies who sold goods to the French, Spanish and Dutch Caribbean territories, the commerce was of consequence. "Against the Molasses Act, Americans had only their smugglers to depend upon—but these redoubtable gentry proved more than a match for the British."[3] The

[1] *The Times*, London, October 29, 1971.
[2] Samuel E. Morison and Henry S. Commager, *The Growth of the American Republic*, Vol. I (New York, 1960), pp. 100, 147-8.
[3] John C. Miller, *Origins of the American Republic* (Stanford University Press, 1959), pp. 13, 99.

Revenue Act of 1764 halved the duty on foreign molasses, but it placed additional duties on sugar. Much worse, it put pressure on customs officers who had failed to enforce the earlier Act.[1] The tightening by Great Britain of the Mercantile system undoubtedly contributed to the break with the American colonies.

In the ensuing struggle, the Caribbean played a significant part. War disrupted the profitable trade between the American Colonies and the Caribbean. Great Britain lost the war; nevertheless it retained its hold in the Caribbean largely through Admiral Rodney's victory at the battle of the Saints in 1782.

Louisiana and Florida were of importance to the United States, not least in a Caribbean context. France colonized Louisiana from the end of the seventeenth century, and in due course controlled the Mississippi from the upper waters to the mouth. However, disaster in the Seven Years' War had led France a year before the close of the war to present Louisiana to Spain, presumably to compensate Spain for the impending loss of Florida to Great Britain.

The Peace of Paris (1763) boundary between British and Spanish territories followed the Mississippi from its source to a point just below Baton Rouge: then it turned eastwards to reach the Gulf of Mexico, leaving New Orleans on the Spanish side. Great Britain created two new colonies—East Florida (the peninsula) and West Florida, the region between the Apalachicola River on the east and the Spanish frontier on the West. Spain, however, recovered the Floridas in 1783. The territory was finally purchased by the United States from King Ferdinand VII of Spain in 1821.

The Mercantile system, cornerstone of Colonial trade, was badly dented by the American and French Revolutions and the revolt of the Spanish American colonies. The United States, which had no colonies but possessed an active mercantile marine, sought outlets wherever it could, including the traditional Caribbean markets. The disruption of trade caused by the European wars from 1793 until the Peace of Vienna in 1815 resulted in British and French ports being opened to American ships, though both belligerents restricted neutral rights. Saint Domingue, France's richest colony, had already in 1803 fought its way to independence to become the Republic of Haiti. Although the opening of these ports was spasmodic and dependent on local conditions, the neutral shipping of the United States reaped great advantages, until the position changed after the opening in

[1] Morison and Commager, *op. cit.*, p. 147.

399

1812 of war with Great Britain.[1] Neither side won a complete victory.[2]

Commerce between the United States and Great Britain remained unsatisfactory after the Napoleonic wars since the commercial treaty of 1815, which placed their trade on a most-favoured nation basis, did not extend to the British West Indies. The colonial powers re-imposed their monopolistic practices. In consequence, U.S. trade with the Caribbean slumped. The policy aided shipping from Canadian ports to the West Indies. The United States retaliated against British shipping from colonial ports. By 1830, the tedious dispute which stemmed from the mercantile system was beginning to fall from favour.[3]

The Doctrine which bears the name of President James Monroe stems from his message to Congress on December 2, 1823. At the time much of the significance of the pronouncement originated from the diplomatic conversations with the British Government which had preceded it. George Canning, British Foreign Secretary, suggested to Richard Rush, American Minister in London, that the two countries should jointly affirm certain principles which particularly affected Spain's colonies in the Americas. Both agreed that Spain had a negligible chance of regaining its lost colonies in the New World. While the two powers did not seek any portion of the former Spanish Territories for themselves, they were opposed to the transfer of these lands to any other power. The United States accepted existing European colonies in the Americas. It declared its opposition to any extension. The question of recognition of the new Latin American Republics was a matter of time and circumstances. President Monroe favoured a joint declaration, and this was also the view of former Presidents Thomas Jefferson and James Madison, whom Monroe consulted. However, Secretary of State John Quincy Adams opposed a joint declaration on the grounds that it placed the United States in the position of following a British policy. Adams prevailed and Rush was instructed to decline the British invitation. Monroe's independent action annoyed Canning. The British Foreign Secretary had however previously received assurance from France that it did not seek to acquire any of the Spanish possessions in America.

---

[1] Samuel F. Bemis, *A Diplomatic History of the United States* (New York, 1957), pp. 292-3.
[2] C. S. Forester gives a vivid and well-balanced account of the sea war, part of which took place in Caribbean waters. *The Age of Fighting Sail* (New York, 1956).
[3] Cf. Pratt, *op. cit.*, pp. 186-8.

The President's statement was not approved by the House of Representatives or by the Senate. It remained as the pronouncement of the President of the United States. Without the co-operation of Great Britain with its navy, there was little that could be done to implement it. Indeed the Powers concerned soon transgressed it. Great Britain forcibly re-occupied the Falkland Islands in 1833 and expanded its interest in British Honduras, the Bay Islands off the coast of Spanish Honduras, and at Greytown (San Juan del Norte) on the coast on Nicaragua. France put pressure on Mexico to pay its debts by blockading Veracruz in 1838.

Nevertheless, the episode crystallized the American belief that the destiny of the island continent of the Americas, bounded by the Atlantic and Pacific Oceans, must remain apart from the rest of the world. The concept of isolation ended only when the United States emerged from World War II as the most powerful world Power.

The Monroe Doctrine had a limited impact on the world at the time.[1] Its importance grew during the nineteenth and particularly the twentieth centuries, when the expansion of U.S. naval power made the implementation of the Doctrine practicable.

The American Civil War affected U.S. policy in the Caribbean. The policy of Manifest Destiny had been closely, though not exclusively, linked to the Democratic Party.[2] The Republican Party could claim that the successful completion of the Union Pacific-Central Pacific railroad in 1869 reduced the urgency for Isthmian transport to connect the Eastern seaboard with California.

France's intervention in Mexico (1861-67), at a time when the United States was locked in Civil War, presented a much more serious challenge to the Monroe Doctrine.[3] Napoleon III could not even advance former ownership of the country in defence of France's action. The dramatic collapse of Maximilian's empire, which the French had set up, added emphasis to the Monroe Doctrine. Meanwhile Spain's attempt to re-annex the Dominican Republic after a troubled four years had ended in 1865.

[1] "His famous proclamation of December 1823, later known as the Monroe Doctrine, caused a momentary excitement, but it was soon made plain that the United States would not interfere if Spain or Portugal attempted a reconquest. Thus most of the liberators felt that the northern republic had let them down throughout their long trials." John E. Fagg, *Latin America* (New York, 1963), p. 1004.

[2] Secretary of State William H. Seward was a supporter of expansion to the South.

[3] The affair began as an Anglo-Franco-Spanish expedition to enforce the payment of debts. Great Britain and Spain soon withdrew.

In its efforts to track down Confederate cruisers, the wartime Navy of the North had been handicapped by a lack of Caribbean bases. The United States sounded out the Danish Government as to a possible purchase of St. Thomas, St. John and St. Croix in the Virgin Islands. Negotiations were continued after the war and a purchase for $7,500,000 agreed. However, opposition developed in the United States and finally the Senate Committee on Foreign Relations recommended rejection of the purchase.

Secretary of State William H. Seward also negotiated with the Dominican Republic for the lease or purchase of Samaná Bay, whose deep harbour commands the Mona Passage separating the Dominican Republic from Puerto Rico.[1] President Ulysses S. Grant (1868-76) finally agreed with President Buenaventura Báez in 1869 that the Dominican Republic should be incorporated as a territory of the United States, a step to be followed in due course by entry into statehood. The Dominican Republic confirmed the Treaty by plebiscite, but the U.S. Senate refused its ratification. Had the project gone through, the future of the Dominican Republic—and easily of Haiti too—might have been very different. A loss of identity might have been compensated by an increase in prosperity, even if deferred as in the case of Puerto Rico.

The Spanish-American War resulted in the emergence of the United States as a major world power. In particular it had gained control of the approaches to an Isthmian canal. The United States had achieved a position of dominance in the Caribbean, aided by the lessening interest of Great Britain. The anxieties of the war, including the problem of uniting in the Caribbean the U.S. fleet split between the Atlantic and Pacific, had emphasized the need for U.S. bases in the Antilles to control the approaches and defend the planned trans-Isthmian canal. The very success of the Spanish fleet in reaching Santiago de Cuba after coaling en route in the Caribbean emphasized the limits of U.S. Naval power, despite the enemy fleet's subsequent destruction.

Just as Spain had controlled from the Antilles and Florida the routes to Middle and South America,[2] the United States as its successor followed a similar policy, in each case partly at the dictates of geography. Professor Louis J. Halle points out that the United States

---

[1] In 1854 President Franklin Pierce had attempted to negotiate a commercial treaty and for the use of Samaná Bay. Great Britain and France however put sufficient pressure on President Pedro Santana to secure the withdrawal of the treaty.

[2] *Vide* p. 97.

began to take a major interest in Latin America only late in the nineteenth century after its expansion to the Pacific had been completed; and after it had begun to compete self-consciously for world trade. "A change in our position from an Atlantic coast nation to a continental nation with two ocean fronts to defend suddenly made Central America and the Caribbean an area of vital strategic importance for us."[1] In 1901, Theodore Roosevelt succeeded to the Presidency. His advocacy of a large navy was already well known. He had taken part in the Cuban campaign in command of a regiment. Roosevelt was convinced of the need for a forward-looking Caribbean policy. Inevitably the United States pressed on to the achievement of an Isthmian canal. Arguments between Nicaragua and Panama regarding the selection of a site ended with the dramatic secession of Panama from Colombia. The building of the canal under U.S. direction and control in a Zone leased by the United States enormously increased American power and prestige in the Caribbean and beyond. At the same time, the United States became increasingly sensitive to the financial mismanagement in many Central American and Caribbean countries. The attempts of European powers to enforce the collection of debts in these countries caused sharp reaction in the United States and in Latin America. Luis M. Drago, Foreign Minister of Argentina, proposed that international debts should never be collected by force. His Doctrine met with no acceptance from the European powers.[2] The essentially practical American President put forward as an extension of the Monroe Doctrine the theory that the United States should itself put pressure on the smaller Latin American countries if, as a means of avoiding interference from the European powers, they defaulted on their obligations. The Roosevelt Corollary, as it was in due course termed, led to extensive and prolonged U.S. interventions in the Antilles.[3]

Professor Julius W. Pratt detected in the Platt Amendment, set up for the purpose of restricting Cuba's borrowing powers and of permitting the United States to intervene to preserve orderly government, an interpretation of the Monroe Doctrine which would involve certain policing powers of the United States.[4] The Amendment had foreshadowed the Corollary.

[1] *American Foreign Policy* (London, 1960), pp. 163-4.

[2] The Pan-American Conference in 1906 endorsed the Drago Doctrine. The Second Hague Peace Conference in 1907 agreed to a convention to prohibit the use of force for debt collection. Cf. Philip C. Jessup. *A Modern Law of Nations* (New York, 1958), p. 113.

[3] *Vide* pp. 50 and 70.   [4] *Op. cit.*, p. 416. *Vide* pp. 7-8.

In 1903-04, a test came over a proposed economic blockade of Venezuelan ports by Great Britain and Germany to enforce the payments of debts. The United States vigorously protested. Finally President Cipriano Castro agreed to submit the question to arbitration. Much more drastic action was in due course taken by the United States against the Dominican Republic in 1905 and against Haiti in 1915, involving occupation by American Marines.

Unquestionably the implications of the Monroe Doctrine were applied most stringently in the Caribbean Republics and the surrounding Latin American countries. The region was of increasing importance to the United States once it was committed to the giant task of constructing the Panama Canal. Unfortunately these small Republics were too often corruptly governed. Frequently they invited foreigners of dubious ability to undertake development projects, many of which ran into difficulties. The financial mismanagement of these countries invited foreign intervention. The United States remained determined at all costs to prevent this. On the whole it achieved its purpose. The cost, however, was high; for the United States by its actions gravely damaged its image in the eyes of Latin America. There were many occasions when force was used in lieu of persuasion. Moreover, the calibre of U.S. diplomatic representation in these countries was often poor.[1]

Since earliest days, the Caribbean has acted on the United States as a magnet, from the field of which the Republic has at times attempted to withdraw. Always the force of isolation has been overcome by the pull to the south. The ebb and flow of the pattern in the nineteenth century has been already referred to. The full force was seen in the Spanish-American War, in the events leading up to the construction of the Panama Canal, in the U.S. policy towards Cuba and even more in the Hispaniolan interventions. President Theodore Roosevelt personified his country's concern with the Caribbean. President Woodrow Wilson, whose international philosophy was utterly different, also felt compelled to resort to interventions in the most high-handed fashion. As usually happens in the case of a great power, continuity of foreign policy over-rode party politics.

A basic change in U.S. policy towards Latin America came about with the election as President of Franklin D. Roosevelt in 1933. His Good Neighbour Policy proved far-reaching. In the Caribbean the American occupation of Haiti was ended, while the Platt Amendment, which restricted Cuba's sovereignty, was abrogated. A new era of

[1] Cf. Munro, *op. cit.*, pp. 543-6.

co-operation with Latin America was ushered in. The policy harmonized with the isolationist sentiments of many Americans at this time, who reacted strongly against involvement in the spreading threats of European conflict.

These very threats forced the United States to look southward after the outbreak of World War II. After the fall of France in 1940, the dispatch of part of the French gold reserves to Martinique in the same year and the continuing attachment of the island's Governor Admiral Georges Robert to the French Vichy Government, caused the United States to blockade Martinique and Guadeloupe.[1] The destroyer deal of 1941 between Roosevelt and Churchill still further involved the United States in the Caribbean since the bases stretched from Jamaica to Trinidad.[2]

From the American policy of adding additional bases to those at Guantánamo Bay in Cuba, Puerto Rico and the American Virgin Islands, flowed far reaching consequences. The large airfields constructed at the bases proved to be of particular significance: after the war they were used to develop civil aviation, which then rapidly expanded to improve inter-island communications. One of the arguments advanced for launching the ill-fated West Indies Federation was the speeding up of travel. The increase of air traffic also revolutionized the tourist trade. Even those islands which had no American bases constructed small airfields as links to those which possessed them.

The bases which had been leased for ninety-nine years continued after the termination of World War II, though in a depleted state. The increase in nationalism which was evident in the Caribbean led to criticism of the bases as infringing island sovereignty; the benefits which had flowed from them had been forgotten. Finally, after substantial pressure, spearheaded by Premier Eric Williams of Trinidad, the United States gave up a substantial part of its leased areas in the British Islands and made substantial *ex gratia* gifts, presumably having in mind that the island governments had hardly been consulted in the base deal and that the destroyers, believed to be of great value in 1941, contributed nothing to the prosperity of the islands in the post-war period.[3]

---

[1] *Vide* p. 262.

[2] The Caribbean bases were in Jamaica, Antigua, St. Lucia and Trinidad. The bases outside the Caribbean were in the Bahamas, British Guiana, Bermuda and Newfoundland. The agreement is thoughtfully considered by Philip Goodhart, M.P., *Fifty Ships that Saved the World* (London, 1965) pp. 216-35.　　　　　[3] Mitchell, *op. cit.*, pp. 64-5.

The American partial relinquishment of its Caribbean bases in 1961 took place at a time when the strategic significance of the Panama Canal was increasingly being questioned. Although the U.S. Navy believed in the importance of the bases, having in mind not only the Panama Canal but also the defence of the approaches to the vital oil reserves of the Maracaibo Basin in Venezuela, the critics were many.[1]

The first effective reversal to a more liberal Latin American policy, as demonstrated by Roosevelt, had been shortlived. The disaster of World Wars I and II, which the late Professor Wilhelm Röpke used to term European Civil Wars, left the United States as the major world power. Yet with unexpected speed a threat began to develop from Soviet Russia: the Cold War had begun. The United States, traditionally adverse to political action at least outside the Americas, was compelled to expand the armaments which it had with the arrival of peace begun to reduce. The challenge of the Soviet Union, however, was made not only with vast battalions, but with propaganda both open and undercover which leapfrogged frontiers.

To meet it the United States, which had pioneered open diplomacy, which encouraged press conferences in which its leaders from the President downwards participated, and which believed that a minimum of information should be withheld from the public, was compelled to take covert action. Most opponents of Communism would agree that the Soviet drive had to be countered, or at least contained. Events involving threats to security proliferated in the United States, Great Britain, Canada and other countries causing public scandal. The Government of President Harry S. Truman gave consideration to the problem. The Eisenhower Administration developed numerous Government security bodies with the Central Intelligence Agency as a nucleus.

The Caribbean clearly had great significance for the international network which quickly expanded. Guatemala provided an early C.I.A. training ground. In 1951, Jacobo Arbenz succeeded Juan José Arévalo as President. The new Head of State was the son of a Swiss immigrant who had married a Guatemalan and had set up business as a druggist in Quetzaltenango, second city of the Republic. Jacobo had served as a professional army officer, and subsequently as a member of the Arévalo Government. The new President quickly collided with much local

---

[1] Cf. Martin B. Travis and James T. Watkins, "Control of the Panama Canal: An Obsolete Shibboleth?", *Foreign Affairs*, Vol. XXXVII, No. 3, New York, April 1959, reprinted by Stanford University, Political Science Series, No. 64.

opinion and with the United States over land reform, including expropriation of large holdings of the United Fruit Company. Probably much more than land reform, which many believed to be essential, Arbenz alarmed American opinion by surrounding himself with some advisers who were believed to be Communists, and by arranging in 1954 for a shipment of arms from the Communist bloc into Guatemala.

The Eisenhower regime had set its face against the spread of Communism. Guatemala City had a large airport which the United States had expanded and made use of in World War II. It was an important fuelling point on the route to the Panama Canal.

The C.I.A., operating from Honduras, actively promoted a change of government in Guatemala. Their effort was facilitated by the unpopularity of Arbenz with many Guatemalans. The choice of John E. Peurifoy as U.S. Ambassador to Guatemala has been alleged to have been arranged by the C.I.A.[1] After a dramatic, but almost bloodless, invasion of Guatemala by Colonel Carlos Castillo Armas supported by a C.I.A. airforce,[2] the victor, who had finally arrived at Guatemala City in Peurifoy's embassy plane, entered the capital in triumph and was appointed President by the Junta in control on July 8, 1954.

The Cold War increasingly forced the United States and the Soviet Union further apart, embittered by the Korean War, the Hungarian and Suez crises, and the continuing struggle over Berlin. In its remarkably successful endeavour to restore the economy of Western Europe with the Marshall Plan, the United States had made a major contribution to the cause of democracy. Unfortunately, success in one area bred jealousy in another. Latin America had accepted the Good Neighbour Policy of Franklin D. Roosevelt. With few exceptions it had supported the Allied cause during World War II. High prices for the commodities which it exported during the war and post-war years were succeeded by a period when the terms of trade moved sharply against Latin America. In short, criticism began to mount that the United States in its position as world leader was forgetting its old friends in the Americas. The dissatisfaction was demonstrated in different ways, and in several countries. The symbolic climax was the rough reception accorded to Vice-President Richard M. Nixon during his 1958 Latin American tour. Concerned with these events, the U.S. Government scanned the Latin American continent with increasing anxiety. However dangerous Communism might be

[1] Wise and Ross, *op. cit.*, p. 171.
[2] Allegedly "sold" by the U.S. Air Force to the Government of Nicaragua. *Ibid.*, p. 178.

in the Far East, the implications of it were even grimmer nearer home.

The Bay of Pigs highlighted the dilemma that the Caribbean presented to the United States.[1] President Eisenhower's Government had failed to come to terms with Castro. To do so may well have been impossible. The Cuban's lack of political experience in these first years, combined with his apparent over-confidence, made negotiation extremely difficult.

President Kennedy learned much from the Bay of Pigs. He made changes in his advisers, particularly in the C.I.A. When in October 1962, a second and infinitely graver crisis developed, the President was far better equipped to handle it.[2] His timing in the Cuban missile crisis was cool and shrewd. Indeed he allowed the Soviet ships to do most of the Atlantic crossing until Russian nerves gave way under the strain. He was able to effect a settlement which the world interpreted as a signal victory for the West.

On this occasion the Latin American states did not consider that U.S. action constituted unilateral action in violation of the non-intervention cornerstone of the O.A.S.[3] Kennedy's success in the Cuban rocket crisis of 1962 was underscored by Russia's unwillingness, or inability, to guarantee unreservedly defence to a country attempting to break away from U.S. influence.[4]

Kennedy had made it clear in 1961 that the United States would not tolerate an offensive base in the Western Hemisphere.[5] He had advanced Eisenhower's policy. Neither President had used United States troops on foreign soil. Any intervention had been under the cover of exile groups.

How far Kennedy was aided in his handling of the Cuba missile crisis by detailed information smuggled out of Russia cannot be exactly assessed. During the critical first years of his Presidency, a remarkable flow of information from a source within the Soviet Union

---

[1] *Vide* pp. 15-17.   [2] *Vide* pp. 17-20.

[3] Larman C. Wilson, "International Law and the United States Cuban Quarantine of 1962", *Journal of Inter-American Studies*, Vol. VII, No. 4, University of Miami Press, Florida, October 1965, p. 491.

[4] Cf. Celso Furtado, "U.S. Hegemony and the Future of Latin America", *The World Today*, Vol. 22, No. 9, London, September 1966, p. 377.

[5] "But a nation of Cuba's size is less a threat to our survival than it is a base for subverting the survival of other free nations throughout the hemisphere. It is not primarily our interest or our security but theirs which is now, today, in the greater peril. It is for their sake as well as our own that we must show our will." "The Lesson of Cuba", Address by President Kennedy, Washington April 20, 1961, *Department of State Bulletin*, Washington, D.C., May 8, 1961, p. 660.

was reaching Washington and London. Oleg Penkovsky, a Colonel of Military Intelligence in the Soviet Army, appears to have supplied the West with vital information.[1]

Penkovsky was arrested in Moscow on October 22, 1962, just before the culmination of the U.S.-Soviet confrontation over the installation of missiles; he appears to have continued to supply information to the West almost up to the time of his apprehension. "In out-facing the Soviet regime over the Berlin issue and in the Cuban missile crisis, the West used Penkovsky's information to decisive effect."[2] Moreover, Penkovsky had knowledge in the field of nuclear weapons and missiles as is clear from the text of his papers.[3]

Probably Penkovsky's greatest service to the West was his reasoned and stated conviction based on his own observations and those of his military colleagues that, notwithstanding Khrushchev's boasts and threats, the Soviet Union was not capable of carrying on a long war. He knew from his friends on the General Staff how critical many of them were of Khrushchev and how much they distrusted his policy of a lightning military strike. If the success of Kennedy's policy saved a holocaust, the Soviet Union may also in retrospect have cause to be thankful. The Penkovsky affair also illustrated that fanatical ideology can be a far more powerful motive in espionage than monetary reward.

In Kennedy's brief but striking presidency, Cuba was the scene both of his major failure and of his most dramatic and lasting success. The anguish of the Bay of Pigs in 1961 had helped to temper the mind of the young statesman occupying the most powerful position in the democratic world, enabling him to meet and defeat the blackmail of the nuclear confrontation a year later. The Caribbean had lived up to its reputation as a storm centre of nature and man alike.

Meanwhile the United States actively opposed any extension of Communism to other countries in the Caribbean. Haiti, separated from Cuba by the narrow Windward Passage, presented an obvious trouble spot. Although the U.S. Government strongly disapproved of the Duvalier regime, it maintained, not without interruption, its financial aid and its military missions fearing lest an American withdrawal might usher in Communism.[4]

The Dominican Republic presented a different although no less

[1] At Penkovsky's trial in May 1963, the Soviet prosecutors alleged that he had handed over to Western intelligence some 5,000 separate items of secret military, political and economic intelligence. *The Penkovsky Papers*, ed. Frank Gibney (London, 1966), p. 26.

[2] *Ibid.*, p. 28.   [3] *Ibid.*, pp. 233-47.   [4] *Vide* p. 57.

serious problem. The long-drawn-out rule of President Rafael Leonidas Trujillo offended democracy at every point.[1] After his assassination in 1961, the United States co-operated with the Bosch Government and gave it aid. When Bosch in turn was overthrown in 1963, the United States somewhat unwillingly and belatedly recognized the succeeding Triumvirate and watched anxiously as events went from bad to worse.[2] Whereas in Guatemala under Arbenz and in Cuba under Castro, a President and Government sympathetic to Communism and hostile to the United States were in power, in the Dominican Republic a state of near civil war between factions existed.

The objective of American policy was to retain its influence in those countries, even when a government uncongenial to American policy and ideals ruled. Cuba's proximity was ever in mind. The policy of the United States, however, fluctuated in its dealings with both Haiti and the Dominican Republic.[3]

In regard to Cuba, the United States showed no such ambivalence. The Johnson administration continued its pressure on Cuba to the point that the island was effectively isolated from the rest of the Americas.

The reaction of President Johnson to the Dominican revolution of 1965 was remarkable in its strength and its speed. At a time when he had increasing anxieties in Vietnam, where the involvement of more and more U.S. troops appeared inevitable, an additional military commitment must have been most unwelcome. At best, opinion in the United States would be divided, while the breach of the O.A.S. Charter, together with memories of former Marine interventions not only in the Caribbean but in Santo Domingo itself, would alienate Latin America.[4] The explanation may again be found in U.S. fears of another Communist regime being established in the Caribbean.[5] Had the Dominican Republic succumbed to Communism, its nearest

[1] "In short, during the period 1933-1940 the Trujillo dictatorship was the complete antithesis of what the United States claimed itself to be—the bastion of democracy." Raymond H. Pulley, "The United States and the Trujillo Dictatorship, 1933-1940: the High Price of Caribbean Stability", *Caribbean Studies*, Vol. 5, No. 3, Institute of Caribbean Studies, University of Puerto Rico, October 1965, p. 31.

[2] *Vide* pp. 78-81.

[3] *Vide* pp. 52-8, 74-5 and 78.

[4] Cf. Herbert L. Matthews, "Santo Domingo and 'Non-intervention' ", *The New York Times*, New York, May 10, 1965. Cf. *The Times*, London, editorial, May 3, 1965.

[5] "I only wish to say that the problem of Communist subversion in the hemisphere is a real one. It should not be brushed aside on a false assumption that American states are prohibited by inter-American law from dealing with it." Thomas C. Mann, Under Secretary of State for Economic Affairs,

neighbour, dictator-ridden Haiti, might also have fallen, an easy prey sandwiched between two Communist-oriented countries. Venezuela, Colombia and Guatemala all bordered Caribbean waters: all three faced Communist subversion.[1]

Foreign opinion, which was ready to accept limited Marine landings to protect U.S. citizens, increasingly criticized the use of larger forces. To Marcel Niedergang, it reflected the Bay of Pigs mentality, with Johnson surrounded by the men who had advised Kennedy over that ill-fated project.[2]

Meanwhile criticism mounted that the United States was overtly favouring the Imbert regime, which in turn was backed by the larger part of the Dominican army—sourly dubbed by *The Guardian* "Trujillo's legacy to the Republic".[3] In 1905 the turbulence of the Dominican Republic had forced the addition of the Roosevelt Corollary to the Monroe Doctrine[4]; six decades later it had become the scene of the Johnson variant.

The meeting of the Security Council of the United Nations on May 3-4, 1965, brought the matter into focus. Adlai Stevenson stated the new doctrine clearly when he claimed that the United States had summoned the resources of the entire Western Hemisphere to prevent Communism from gaining control of the Dominican Republic.[5]

---

address to the Inter-American Press Association, San Diego, California, October 12, 1965, *Department of State Bulletin*, Washington, D.C., November 8, 1965, p. 731.

R. T. Bohan gives a different interpretation. Cf. "The Dominican Case: Unilateral Intervention", *The American Journal of International Law*, Vol. 60, No. 4, Washington, D.C., October 1966, p. 810.

[1] "What pentagonism learned in Vietnam and perfected in the Dominican Republic, and what it learned in the Dominican Republic and perfected in Vietnam is going to be put into practice in other countries in Latin America, especially in those in which there are guerrilla movements." Juan Bosch, *Pentagonism: A Substitute for Imperialism* (New York, 1968), p. 120.

[2] Including Dean Rusk, Robert McNamara, Thomas Mann, Vice-Admiral William F. Raborn, Jr., "Et demain Cuba?", *Le Monde*, Paris, May 4, 1965. The Washington Correspondent of *The Financial Times* thought that much of President Kennedy's work to improve relations with Latin America might be lost by the U.S. intervention in the Dominican Republic. London, May 4, 1965.

[3] London, editorial, May 22, 1965. Cf. Gordon Connell-Smith, "In spite of her continued protestations that she was neutral in the struggle and wanted only that the Dominican people should have freedom to choose a new government, her very presence denied them such a choice and her actions, whether consciously or inadvertently, favoured the military junta". *The Inter-American System* (London, 1966), p. 340.

[4] *Vide* pp. 69-70.

[5] Speech at the Security Council of the United Nations, May 3, 1965.

Johnson had followed up and crystallized the policy of Kennedy at the time of the Cuba crisis in 1962 to curb an extension of Communist power in the Western Hemisphere.

The United States regarded the Dominican crisis as an O.A.S. matter, a view supported by Lord Caradon for Great Britain and Fernando Ortiz Sanz for Bolivia. Carlos María Velázquez of Uruguay, the other Latin American member of the Security Council, held that the affair should be handled by the United Nations, a view shared by the Soviet and French representatives. Criticism was strongly voiced by Latin American countries which considered that the U.S. Government was departing from the principles to which it had agreed in the Rio de Janeiro Treaty of 1947 and the Bogotá Charter of 1948.[1]

In the Dominican controversy, the relationship not only of the United States to the O.A.S. but also of the United Nations to the O.A.S. came under international debate. While the U.N. Charter recognizes regional organizations, only usage and experience can interpret an article with any precision.[2] The United Nations appeared ineffective when it sent an observer to Santo Domingo. Awkwardly placed, with the O.A.S. already directly involved in the settlement of Dominican problems, the mission achieved little.[3]

Starting from the even more difficult situation of an apparent U.S. infringement of Article 15 of its Charter, the O.A.S. succeeded in setting up a mediating authority. Without the active assistance of Brazil which supplied both a substantial military contingent and a general to command the international forces, including those of the United States, the weakness of the O.A.S. would have been more apparent. In effect the co-operation of Brazil combined with minor aid from some other members, papered the cracks in the framework

[1] The Latin American reaction is clearly set out by J. Halcro Ferguson, "How L.B.J. united his friends against him", *The Observer*, London, May 9, 1965.

[2] Articles 52, 53 and 54. "In the era of the cold war, regional organizations are the chosen instruments of the great antagonists locked in political conflict. Those antagonists will not permit their instruments to be held in check by the United Nations." *International Conciliation*, No. 547, New York, March 1964, p. 63.

[3] Lucien Nizard, however, considered the intervention of the Security Council in sending an observer to Santo Domingo as a significant precedent on the part of the U.N. His article sets out the French point of view, sharply critical of the United States. "O.N.U., si! O.E.A., no!", *Le Monde*, Paris, May 27, 1965. The U.N. observer was José Antonio Mayobre, executive secretary of the United Nations Economic Commission for Latin America.

of the Organization. Nevertheless, many O.A.S. members were clearly not in agreement with what had been done.[1]

Whether the O.A.S. would strengthen its constitution in the light of the Dominican crisis, was likely to influence its own effective future; and perhaps on a wider front, the whole concept of regional organizations.[2] There were some who felt that the United States was trying to use the O.A.S. as its tool.[3]

While this might have been an occasion for the United Nations to intervene strongly, the ruinous Congo affair over-shadowed the minds of all. To add another controversial and costly dispatch of troops to grapple with the Dominican tangle was uninviting, while the eight-year former occupation of the country by U.S. troops was a discouraging precedent. However, the O.A.S. began to play an increasingly significant role in the Dominican affair, notwithstanding the domination of its activities by the United States, when José A. Mora, Secretary-General of the O.A.S., arrived with a team of mediators in June 1965.

The effectiveness of the O.A.S. was weakened by the criticisms of the Presidents of Mexico, Chile and Venezuela; nor did Peru, Ecuador or Uruguay favour its role.[4] The O.A.S. seemed to have been called in belatedly to extricate the United States from an awkward

[1] During the Security Council discussion on the Dominican crisis on May 13, 1965, Carlos María Velázquez expressed the view that the U.N. should not abdicate too much of its authority to the O.A.S.

[2] "What the O.A.S. has done is to grant later approval to unilateral intervention by the United States, a return to unilateralism in the Hemisphere. It has, by its action, largely abandoned its rôle as a juridicial organization and a force for harmony and law in the Hemisphere." Bohan, *op. cit.*, p. 812.

[3] Teodoro Moscoso, former Coordinator of the Alliance for Progress, clearly had great misgivings over the U.S. Dominican policy. "There is little point in arguing the pros and cons of what has or has not been done in the Dominican Republic except as a take-off point for a full fledged re-evaluation of the facts of life in the new Latin America, and for recasting United States policy in the light of these facts." *The New York Times*, New York, June 2, 1965.

"The 'legitimacy of multilateralization' is of great importance in sustaining her self-image; in staving off criticism of her intervention as aggression comparable with that of which she has consistently accused the Communists; and in limiting the role of the United Nations in hemispheric affairs." Connell-Smith, *op. cit.*, p. 341.

[4] "For one thing, the five dissenting members states—Mexico, Uruguay, Chile, Ecuador, and Peru—account for more than a quarter of the total population of Latin America. For another, the only vote to spare was cast by the Dominican representative—and in the continuing chaos in Santo Domingo, no one knew just how validly or firmly his government held power". "Dominican Crisis: Help from the O.A.S." *Newsweek*, Dayton, Ohio, May 17, 1965.

predicament.[1] However, since the United States was meeting the wage bill of the Junta—and sometimes of both sides[2]—the O.A.S. could exert effective financial pressure by threatening to cut off funds.

As the Dominican affair dragged on, France, Uruguay and Jordan suggested to the Security Council that the representation in the Dominican Republic of the Secretary-General of the U.N. should be increased and his mandate widened to check on alleged violations of human rights and to investigate the breach of the cease fire.[3] Against this was the feeling of frustration and paralysis in other U.N. quarters which led some to favour an extension of regionalization. Great Britain supported the United States' contention that matters should be left in the hands of the O.A.S. The United States now commenced changing its attitude towards the problem of who was to govern the Dominican Republic. It could start to extract itself from "the most dangerous form of quicksand".[4] Under President Balaguer a strong U.S. link including economic support continued.

The new turn given to President Monroe's pronouncement of 1823 had quickly been named the Johnson Doctrine. In a critical editorial, *The Guardian* suggested that the United States intervention invited comparison with that of Russia in Hungary in 1956, though it saw a significant difference in that the American Government did not support any faction.[5] Looking at the affair from the official viewpoint of the United States, Thomas Mann regarded American intervention as an attempt to facilitate a political compromise acceptable to both factions.[6] Perhaps it would be fair to say that the Johnson Doctrine was an extension and

[1] Cf. *The New York Times*, New York, editorials June 14 and July 22, 1965.

[2] "In the Dominican Republic last week the U.S. found itself in the novel and anomalous position of financing both sides to a civil war. This, of course, was not avowed U.S. policy; ostensibly, the financing was to be done by the Organization of American States, which announced that it would pay the salaries of all Dominican civil servants and soldiers, whether loyal to junta leader Gen. Antonio Imbert or to rebel Col. Francisco Caamaño Deño. But there was scant doubt in anyone's mind as to where this solomonic scheme or the $6 million necessary to carry it out had originated." *Newsweek*, International Edition, London, editorial June 7, 1965, p. 28.

[3] United Nations Security Council debates, June 8 and 9, 1965.

[4] *The New York Times*, New York, editorial, May 18, 1965.

[5] London, May 5, 1965. Cf. John Rettie, "A Hungary in the Caribbean?" *New Statesman*, London, May 7, 1965.

[6] "Latin Americans do not want a paternalistic United States deciding which particular political faction should rule their countries. . . . This explains why, in the case of the Dominican Republic, we refrained during the

intensification of the policies of Presidents Eisenhower and Kennedy. Despite the different attitudes of the three men, all were influenced, and had to be influenced, by considerations of security in a world armed to the teeth with new and deadly weapons whose full scope in warfare could not be precisely assessed but had implications of the grimmest character.

Johnson himself denied that he had formulated a new doctrine, claiming that Communism was incompatible with the principles of the O.A.S. He declared his policy to be one of support for the O.A.S., with the object of establishing a broadly-based government acceptable to the Dominican people and to the O.A.S. followed by a reconstruction and development programme for the country.[1] Yet in the disturbed conditions elsewhere in Latin America, his actions had a significance beyond the Caribbean, and indeed the Americas.[2]

Professor Salvador de Madariaga considered that the United States by its Dominican intervention had seriously impaired its moral authority. He believed that "the consequences of this deplorable move" might be disastrous for the issue of the Cold War.[3] However, a substantial body of responsible opinion was also prepared to give Johnson the benefit of the doubt on the grounds that if there indeed were a Communist take-over risk, he must act with speed.[4]

World statesmanship faced the problem as to how far the United States was entitled to go to prevent the Communist bloc from

first days of violence from 'supporting' the outgoing government or 'supporting' either of the factions contending for power. It explains why we and others thought it best to work for a cease-fire and to encourage the rival Dominican factions to meet together and agree on a Dominican solution to a Dominican problem." *Department of State Bulletin*, Washington, D.C., November 8, 1965, p. 731.

[1] Press Conference, Washington, D.C., June 1, 1965.

[2] "If any group or any movement with which the Communists associate themselves is going to be automatically condemned in the eyes of the United States, then we have indeed given up all hope of guiding or influencing even to a marginal degree the revolutionary movements and the demands for social change which are sweeping Latin America". Senator J. William Fulbright, *Congressional Record*, 89th Congress First Session, No. 198, Part 2, October 22, 1965, pp. 2-4. Cf. Jerome Slater, "The United States, the Organization of American States, and the Dominican Republic, 1961-1963", *International Organization* Vol. XVIII, No. 2, World Peace Foundation, Boston, Spring 1964, pp. 290-1.

[3] *The New York Times*, New York, May 7, 1965.

[4] "The risk of a second Cuba was not to be taken lightly. Had it come to that Mr. Johnson would have been blamed for failure to act in time; he can reasonably claim the benefit of the doubt for preventive action which has removed that risk." *The Daily Telegraph*, London, editorial, May 4, 1965.

promoting Communism in Latin America.[1] Presumably the flow of
Communist ideology was permissible. In any event propaganda could
only be countered effectively by counter-propaganda. The shipment
of arms, probably smuggled in the best Caribbean tradition, might be
considered to constitute unwarranted intervention. Yet the role of
indoctrination, for example, of students, or in more extreme form
the training of men to be repatriated later as guerrilla fighters in
their own countries, had also to be evaluated.

In its later colonialist days Spain had tried to censor the flow of
revolutionary ideas originating in France and other countries. If
Spain failed then, it was questionable whether greater success would
crown the efforts of the United States. In a century and a half, widespread popular education and expanded communications, which
included transistor radios, had profoundly changed the world. The
United States might argue that the Monroe Doctrine of hemisphere
defence had also to be adjusted to meet the perils of the day.

The O.A.S. Conference which was held at Rio de Janeiro in the
autumn of 1965 was expected to voice recriminations over the U.S.
role in the Dominican Republic. However, a critical resolution on the
unilateral armed intervention earlier in the year was, with the aid of
Chile and Mexico, two opponents of intervention, directed to a drafting
committee which was studying reform of the O.A.S. charter. Thus
the United States came through without formal censure.

The conference demonstrated the primary importance of the
Alliance for Progress. Secretary of State, Dean Rusk, announced
that the United States would extend the Alliance beyond its original
ten years. The statement was immensely important for Latin America,
even if it implied that there had been delay in reaching the targets
which had been laid down. Latin American countries may have
silently assented to U.S. political leadership in the Cold War in
exchange for the expectation of great material benefits.[2] Already the

[1] Tad Szulc comments: "The implications of the Dominican episode on
the whole U.S. posture in Latin America and the world, particularly at the
time of the Vietnam war, are immensely disturbing to our friends and allies
everywhere—even if one is to accept the explanation that there is no 'Johnson
Doctrine' providing for U.S. armed interventions whenever the danger of a
Communist take-over is suspected." *Dominican Diary* (New York, 1965),
p. 305.

[2] "This is the most serious bid yet to scotch further Communist and
neutralist developments in the area. The Latins virtually agree to co-operate
politically with the United States, provided their chief banker and benefactor
doesn't let them down. . . ." Michael Field, "New Directions in South
America", *The Daily Telegraph*, London, December 7, 1965.

Alliance for Progress, which had started badly, was beginning to produce substantial results which would be some justification for the $20 billion in public aid and private investment pledged by the United States to supplement an estimated $80 billion of Latin American expenditure on development.[1]

Despite an apparent softening of its attitude towards Cuba at the beginning of 1969, the United States maintained its boycott with increasing effect. The deterioration of Cuba's economy was highlighted by the failure to reach the 1970 ten million ton sugar crop target: the arrival of Soviet technicians in the island, apparently on an economic salvage operation, suggested Moscow's misgivings. Whether improved U.S.-Soviet relations will lead to modification of Nixon's policy towards Havana remains obscure, complicated by the rapprochement between the United States and Communist China. Senator Edward Kennedy has urged the resumption of diplomatic relations with Cuba.

* * * *

Jean-Jacques Servan-Schreiber's *Le Défi Américaine* made a substantial impact on the Western World.[2] Latin American leaders detected a similar pattern of American corporative infiltration into their economic life which seemed to them a threat to their self-rule.[3] The nationalization of U.S. interests in Chile in July 1971 following on action in Peru expressed nationalistic feeling against foreign investment manifested throughout the world.

During his 1968 Presidential campaign and in his inaugural speech President Nixon made no specific reference to Latin America. On April 14, 1969, Pan American Day, at the meeting of the O.A.S. Assembly, he acknowledged that the Alliance for Progress, although "a great concept", had been far from successful. The rate of growth in Latin America during the period of the Alliance was approximately the same as before: a result which Nixon termed "very disconcerting". By appointing Charles Meyer, an able businessman, as Assistant Secretary

[1] Cf. Juan de Onis, "Hemisphere: Rio Plus and Minus", *The New York Times*, New York, December 5, 1965.

[2] (Paris, 1967).

[3] Cf. Covey T. Oliver, "Despite the author's [Servan Schreiber] disclaimer of any intent to deal with Latin America, and his precise distinction between 'challenge' and 'threat', the book is widely accepted as a warning against North American 'imperialism' through private sector investment." "Foreign and Human Relations with Latin America", *Foreign Affairs*, New York, April 1969, p. 526.

of State for Latin America, Nixon emphasized his preference for trade rather than aid.

Nelson Rockefeller's fact-finding mission to Latin America in 1969 resulted in turbulence in several of the countries visited. However in the Caribbean area, as might be expected, Rockefeller was welcomed in Haiti; Jamaica, Barbados and Guyana also acclaimed him, but he had a nerve-wracking 24-hour tour of the Dominican Republic.

For the first time, in May 1969, a united Latin America confronted the United States in the Viña del Mar document.[1] Handed to Nixon by the Chilean Minister of Foreign Affairs the document coincided with Rockefeller's departure on the third leg of his Latin American mission. Its contents, by no means new, stressed employment problems and called for unrestricted loans. Nowhere was birth control mentioned although two of the newest members of the O.A.S., Barbados and Jamaica, had made substantial progress in this field, with strong Government backing.

Nixon's response to the Viña del Mar document in October 1969 confirmed the reduction of U.S. efforts in Latin America: he called for a more balanced partnership rather than an American-dominated alliance.[2] Nixon promised continued aid, no longer on a tied basis, but with the provision that the money could only be spent in the United States or in Latin America. Most Latin American nations sought the option of purchasing in Europe and Japan. On the difficult problem of private investment in Latin America, Nixon stressed that this would not be encouraged where it was not wanted, although he emphasized its vital role. In general it was obvious that the United States was encouraging the Latin American nations to play an ever more active part in their own development.[3]

The discouraging conclusions of the Rockefeller Report foresaw increased authoritarian solutions: all weakening to democracy. The document acknowledged the difficulties of controlling the urban guerrilla. Commenting on malnutrition it pointed out that only five nations main-

[1] *The Latin American Consensus of Viña del Mar*, Comisión Especial de Coordinación Latinoamericana, Viña del Mar, May, 1969. The Caribbean signatories of the document were Barbados, Haiti, the Dominican Republic and Trinidad and Tobago. Cf. Luciano Tomassini, "Towards a Latin American nationalism", *The World Today*, London, December 1969, pp. 544-556.

[2] ". . . the principal future pattern of this assistance must be U.S. support for Latin American initiatives . . .", Washington, October 31, 1969.

[3] In a severely critical editorial, *The Washington Post* stated "The Kennedy-Johnson judgement was compassionate; it has been supported, in our view, by the weight of a decade's testing. The Nixon judgement is clinical: we fear it is wrong." Quoted by *International Herald Tribune*, Paris, November 3, 1969.

tained a diet considered by the World Health Organization as adequate: in Haiti more than 80 per cent. of the people were under-nourished.[1] Although it contrasted Russia's economic hold over Cuba with Communist Party protestations of peaceful co-existence and of disassociation from Castro's programme for violent revolution in Latin America, it found Communism, contrary to current U.S. opinion, remained a serious factor in the Western Hemisphere.[2]

Undoubtedly a misunderstanding had grown up between the two groups in the Alliance: the United States believed that the advent of its businessmen with their modern expertise had contributed to the development of Latin America. Yet to the Latin American, money paid out in dividends was looked at askance as if Latin America was being milked by the United States. As far as the United States was concerned the Alliance for Progress seemed to have been founded more on goodwill than on good sense. Exemplified by the U.S. Senate's rejection of Nixon's Foreign Aid Bill in October 1971, the goodwill was obviously running out.[3] Moreover, from a Latin American viewpoint, increasing criticism of North American society as a model was beginning to be expressed.[4]

The Caribbean remains an area of vital strategic importance to the United States. Its recent concern over the possibilities of a submarine base in Cuba, evoking all too strongly memories of 1962, bears witness to this.[5] Certain problems, such as Anguilla, could be left to Britain to resolve, even if sections of the U.S. press were strongly critical of British action. Yet the troubles in Trinidad in April 1970 led the United States, as well as Britain, discreetly to despatch warships into the area, which would once have been considered mainly a British zone of influence.[6]

British, French and Dutch links with the Caribbean remain significant, sometimes with political ties. Yet much of the relationship is supported

[1] *The Rockefeller Report on the Americas* (Chicago 1969), p. 131.

[2] "At the moment, there is only one Castro among the twenty-six nations of the hemisphere; there can well be more in the future. And a Castro on the mainland, supported militarily and economically by the Communist world, would present the gravest kind of threat to the security of the Western Hemisphere and pose an extremely difficult problem for the United States." *Ibid.*, p. 38. Despite Rockefeller's concentration on Communism, Nixon made no mention of it in his October 1969 speech.

[3] *Vide* p. 350.

[4] Cf. Mariano Grondona, "The role of the United States in the world: a Latin American point of view", *Atlantic Conference*, Puerto Rico, November 12-15, 1970, p. 17.

[5] *Vide* p. 25.

[6] *Vide* pp. 154-5.

by subsidies and a special relationship. The very enlargement of the Common Market may orient the United States more and more towards those areas outside this rapidly expanding body. The Caribbean, like Canada and Australia, would seem a likely field for U.S. commercial expansion. Its proximity to U.S. markets, supported by excellent communications, remains a factor of major commercial significance, emphasized by Cuba's plight.

CANADA

Notwithstanding its long relationship with the Caribbean, Canada has never sought political influence in the area. As a member of the Commonwealth, Canada's interests were directed mainly towards the British islands. After World War I Great Britain, although anxious for commercial reasons to encourage closer co-operation between Canada and the British West Indies, did not advocate the political union of these two members of the Empire. The West Indian islands themselves seemed equally unenthusiastic, and Canada showed no interest in such an association.

When the British West Indies were seeking to federate after World War II, Canada remained a supporter from the outside. The great disparity in economic levels between the countries, together with the problems that would result from free entry as citizens into Canada of thousands of West Indians, suggested circumspection.

Canada has shown the same caution in weighing the advantages and disadvantages of membership in the Organization of American States. In 1943, Howard Green, Secretary of State for External Affairs, favoured Canadian entry into the Pan American Union, predecessor of the O.A.S., which would have involved a change in Canada's traditional policy. The United States opposed the move to join. However, Latin American interest in Canadian entry increased. The United States mistrusted this apparent enthusiasm, believing that British influence in Latin America might increase through this channel.[1]

After World War II, Canada maintained friendly relations with Latin America, but its interest in joining the O.A.S. waned. During these years Canada was more interested in the newly formed United Nations than in any regional organization which might compromise it.

[1] Cf. Douglas G. Anglin, "United States Opposition to Canadian Membership in the Pan American Union: A Canadian View," *International Organization*, Vol. XV, No. 1, World Peace Foundation, Boston, Winter 1961, p. 12.

However, when the Conservative Party took office in 1957, interest in Latin America revived, alerted by the interjection of the Cold War into the Caribbean.[1] Canadian investment in the area was considerable and Canada supplied aid through the Inter-American Bank. The U.S. attitude to Canadian entry also changed. The United States was beginning to realize that Canada might share the economic burden, despite apprehension lest Canada might on occasion side with the Latin American countries against the United States, bearing in mind Ottawa's traditional policy of independence. Like many Latin American countries, Canada had misgivings over the intervention of the United States in the Dominican Republic.[2]

In November 1965, Canada displayed its interest in the O.A.S. by sending observers to the Conference at Rio de Janeiro, as did Jamaica and Trinidad. At the Commonwealth Caribbean-Canada Conference at Ottawa in July 1966, the participants emphasized the great value they attached to their relationship with the United States and with Latin America. It was agreed that either a joint study, or national studies, should be made by those eligible for membership and that mutual consultations should take place.[3] The entry of Trinidad into the O.A.S. in 1967 was quickly followed by that of Barbados and Jamaica. They may yet influence Canada's entry.[4]

[1] ". . . the introduction of the 'cold war' into the Caribbean may, paradoxically increase rather than diminish Canadian interest in O.A.S., despite the criticism in Canada of Washington's handling of the Cuban situation and the natural Canadian reluctance to become needlessly embroiled in it. As long as Latin America remained relatively a backwater area in world politics, it was bound to be of only marginal political concern to Canada." *Ibid.*, p. 19.

[2] Cf. "The Dominican Republic adventure is fresh in Canadians' memory. It demonstrated—if a demonstration was necessary—that the O.A.S. is not the voice of the 'inter-American system', but the voice of what Washington believes the 'inter-American system' should be." *The Globe and Mail*, Toronto, editorial, September 4, 1965.

[3] *Final Communiqué*, Ottawa, July 8, 1966, pp. 4-5. The countries represented were Guyana, Trinidad, Jamaica, Barbados and Canada.

[4] "Merely joining the O.A.S. will not in itself work wonders; what will matter most is the extent to which we show ourselves prepared to cooperate in practical ways with other countries in the hemisphere. We can do—and in fact are doing—a good deal even without being a member." Paul Martin, Secretary of State for External Affairs, 2nd Annual Conference on World Development, the Canadian Institute of International Affairs, and the United Nations Association in Canada, in co-operation with the University of Alberta, Banff, August 24, 1964. Canada might have to change its relations with Cuba before seeking entry into the O.A.S. Cf. John W. Holmes, "Canada and Pan America", *Journal of Inter-American Studies*, Vol. X, No. 2, Miami, April, 1968, p. 180.

For long Canada has used its influential position in the Commonwealth as a balancing factor. An example of this independence was Canada's maintenance of diplomatic relations with Cuba.[1] Canadian banks, like other foreign banks, have withdrawn from the island, but Canada has firmly continued its trade. Its attitude has been similar to that of Great Britain and France, which have not acceded to the pressure that the United States has exerted on its N.A.T.O. allies to terminate trade with Cuba. Canada is in a position to supply goods which Cuba is no longer able to purchase from the United States.[2] Significantly, Cuba participated in the Montreal Exposition in 1967.

French Canadians are attracted to association with Latin America by reason of the common Latin cultural heritage. To learn Spanish and Portuguese comes more easily to them than to Anglo-Saxons. Moreover, the Quebec legal system is founded on Roman law and is largely codified in accordance with the common model of the Code Napoléon. Some French Canadians regard closer association with Latin America as a counterpoise to excessive Anglo-American influence.

Trade between Canada and the Caribbean is long established. Canadian fish and lumber were shipped in exchange for sugar and rum. After the establishment of the United States of America, Canada's links with the British Caribbean colonies continued and its commerce strengthened.[3] The importance of trade between the two areas was finally recognized by a series of bilateral trade agreements negotiated in 1912, 1920 and 1925, which provided for preferences advantageous to both sides.[4] Canada's preferences under the Commonwealth Sugar Agreement were also of great value to the West Indian islands.[5] During recent years, Canada has sold an increasing range of manufactured goods to the Caribbean.

Trade between Canada and the Commonwealth Caribbean has presented difficulties. Immediately after World War II, Canada took over 15 per cent. of the exports of these countries, but by 1963 this

---

[1] Canada also has diplomatic representation in Guyana, Trinidad, Jamaica and Haiti. It closed its mission to the Dominican Republic at the end of 1969.

[2] Cf. John D. Harbron, "Canada in Caribbean America", *Journal of Inter-American Studies and World Affairs*, Vol. XII, No. 4, Miami, October 1970, p. 482.

[3] *Vide* p. 400.

[4] At the Ottawa Conference in 1932, the West Indies colonies were included in the framework of the agreement.

[5] *Vide* p. 146 n. 4.

share had dropped to about 11 per cent.[1] West Indians complained that their products in many cases did not receive preference in the Canadian market unless shipped directly to a Canadian port. Furthermore, valuation of their exports of manufactures to Canada received only arbitrary estimates thus often increasing the rate of import levied. Rum sales were alleged to be restricted by unfair labelling practices. Sugar suffered from beet competition and increased Canadian purchases from other foreign sources. Citrus and banana exports had considerably diminished.[2]

However, at the 1966 Commonwealth Caribbean-Canada Conference, the participants decided that it was in their mutual interest to strengthen their commercial ties. West Indian shippers would now be allowed to use less expensive U.S. routes; the banana trade was reviewed; and the origin and content of any rum marketed in Canada clearly marked. Canada undertook to grant a duty-free quota of sugar equivalent to the overall volume of exports to Canada over the preceding five years. The possibility of a free trade area would be studied.[3]

In the spring of 1970 the Trudeau Government decided to replace the annual payment of a tariff rebate on sugar imports from the Commonwealth Caribbean with a Canadian $5 million Agricultural Development Fund. This proposal evoked much criticism from the Caribbean. Despite concessions, Canada paid considerably less than Britain under the Commonwealth Sugar Agreement and the United States on its quota system.[4]

The problem arose at a time when deterioration in Canada-Caribbean relations seemed to have occurred. A special Canadian Senate Committee was in the process of investigating Canada's position in the

[1] *Business Review*, Bank of Montreal, January 29, 1965.

[2] Cf. Eric Williams, "Canada in the West Indies—A Force for Island Unity", *The Round Table*, London, January 1967, pp. 57-8. Premier Errol Barrow of Barbados asserted that Canadian business men switched to other markets, such as Cuba, before attempting to negotiate prices with their trading partners in the West Indies with whom their trade was diminishing. "We also find it difficult to believe . . . that the unfavourable trends which have been developing should not only continue but appear to be actively encouraged." "A Role for Canada in the West Indies", *International Journal*, Vol. XIX, No. 2, Canadian Institute of International Affairs, Toronto, Spring 1964, p. 177.

[3] *Report of the Chairman of the Trade Committee, Final Communiqué*, Commonwealth Caribbean-Canada Conference, July 8, 1966, pp.1-3.

[4] Sir Robert Kirkwood stated that the price paid by Canada for West Indian sugar bore "no relationship whatsoever to the cost of sugar production in the West Indies". Press Release, Kingston, October 6, 1970.

Caribbean, more particularly the Commonwealth Caribbean.[1] The Committee stressed the need for a clear determination by the Canadian Government of its future policy in the area, which hitherto had lacked consistency.[2] The Commonwealth-Caribbean Free Trade Area, discussed at the 1966 Conference, seemed to have only limited scope. The Committee's recommendations included intensified efforts to increase two-way trade involving private enterprise preferably associated with Caribbean investors. During a visit to the area in the autumn of 1970, Senator Paul Martin smoothed out some of the misunderstanding over the Agricultural Development Fund.[3] The withdrawal of the rebate on sugar was delayed for a further period.[4]

Canada had also substantial trade with Puerto Rico, the Dominican Republic, Haiti and Cuba. Its exports reflected the development of the Caribbean. Machinery sales, both agricultural and industrial, had expanded. The industrial growth of the islands created a demand for materials similar to those which Canada already supplied to the vast North American market. A substantial export trade to the French islands was being developed.[5] Canadian imports of oil and oil products from Trinidad and the Netherlands Antilles had increased since 1958.

Canadian banking has from long experience earned a high reputation throughout the Caribbean. In the Bahamas alone there are four Canadian banks, and in Barbados three of the four commercial banks are Canadian. Banking in Jamaica was pioneered from Canada. Canadian banks are represented in both Haiti and the Dominican Republic.

Investment from Canada has greatly assisted the expansion of the Caribbean economy. Guyana's bauxite was first developed by a Canadian company in 1917.[6] Canadian capital played a major part in the development of Jamaica's bauxite.[7] Any visitor to the Ewarton works cannot fail to be impressed with the undertaking. Canada has

[1] "The first concern of this Committee has been to ascertain whether or not Canada-Caribbean relations have subsequently developed along the close consultative lines envisaged in 1966. Regrettably, the conclusion is that they have not. The dramatic success of that Conference may have created unwarranted expectations of future results." *Report of the Standing Committee on Foreign Affairs of The Senate of Canada on Canada-Caribbean Relations*, Ottawa, 1970, p. 3.

[2] *Ibid.*, p. 6.

[3] *Hansard*, Ottawa, December 8, 1970, p. 295.

[4] Cf. *The Daily Gleaner*, Kingston, June 27, 1970.

[5] C.-J. Saint-Pierre, "Des Produits Canadiens sont fort bien accueillis aux Antilles", *Les Affaires*, Montreal, February 7, 1966.

[6] *Vide* pp. 242-3.   [7] *Vide* p. 141 n. 4. Cf. Mitchell, *op. cit.*, p. 90.

also imported the products of its Caribbean mining ventures. In Jamaica a tax treaty was signed in early 1971 preventing double taxation of certain categories of incomes. This example may be followed in other Caribbean countries thereby encouraging investment.[1]

Airline connections from Canada to Trinidad, Barbados, Antigua, Jamaica and the Bahamas have assisted the tourist industry in these islands. Reduced excursion fares are offered during the winter months. After the United States, the largest number of tourists to the Commonwealth islands have come from Canada.

Immigration problems involving discrimination created difficulties between Canada and the West Indies. After 1962 Canada accepted only immigrants whose standard of education and training were such that they were capable of self-support, regardless of racial origins. As a result only a few from the West Indies obtained entry. Yet by 1969 the number had risen to 14,468, over four times that of 1965. What intangible effect this loss of skill may have had on the developing countries they have left deserves thought. Since 1967 the seasonal entry of agricultural workers from the West Indies has proved successful.

In 1958 Canada introduced an assistance programme of $10 million to be used over a five-year period by the West Indies Federation then in process of formation. After the collapse of the Federation, this programme was continued; aid was fragmented for use in schemes put forward by the individual units. In 1963, over $2 million was made available for the succeeding year. During these first six years, the Canadian programme of aid was primarily concerned with financing two inter-island ships, which had been proposed by the island governments. Canada also provided educational and technical assistance. Aid was further increased to $10 million for the period 1965-66. At the 1966 Conference the Canadian Government announced that it would strengthen its aid efforts in the countries of the Commonwealth Caribbean with which it had special links. Between 1966 and 1970 Canadian assistance reached $76 million.

Tourist travel to the Caribbean and the presence of many West Indian students at Canadian universities has increased Canada's interest in the area, particularly since 1965. The number of students increased to the point where a special liaison officer had to be established for them.[2] However, the provision of undergraduate scholarships for study at the University of the West Indies by the Canadian International Development

[1] Cf. *The Daily Gleaner*, Kingston, January 13, 1971.
[2] Cf. Robin W. Winks, *Canadian-West Indian Union: A Forty-Year Minuet*, (University of London, 1968), p. 42.

425

Agency may lessen student entry. The serious rioting at Sir George Williams University in Montreal in 1969 was particularly unfortunate.[1]

As Canada develops, increasingly Canadian capital is likely to become available for the development of those Caribbean countries who welcome it. An obvious field is that of the extension of the tourist trade, although in some countries the number of tourists that can be absorbed without damaging consequences may have been reached.[2] Canada showed its confidence in Jamaica and Guyana by its bauxite investments, though, in the case of Guyana, this appears to have been rejected.[3]

Events such as Prime Minister Lester B. Pearson's visit to Jamaica and Trinidad at the end of 1965, followed by Commonwealth-Canada Conference, the Report of the Senate Standing Committee and Senator Paul Martin's Caribbean tour have fostered co-operation between these countries and helped to correct misunderstandings. Canada is likely, within or without the framework of the O.A.S., gradually to extend its influence in the Caribbean.

LATIN AMERICA

The Organization of American States was conceived out of the history of the Americas. The purpose of the O.A.S. was to polarize and preserve the traditional concept of the Americas as being apart from the rest of the world. The germ of the idea may be seen in the Monroe Doctrine. The O.A.S. is essentially devoted to upholding the freedom and independence of the Americas and its members.

Inevitably the United States as the largest and by far the wealthiest member has to a considerable extent dominated the O.A.S. Yet it is easy to detect a divergence of interest between the United States and the Latin American countries over their attitude to the O.A.S. By the United States the O.A.S. has been used as a weapon to prevent the infiltration of Communism. The other members, however, have regarded the O.A.S. as a bulwark against this interference of the United States in their affairs.[4]

[1] *Vide* pp. 154-5.
[2] *Report of the Standing Committee on Foreign Affairs of the Senate of Canada-Caribbean Relations*, p. 47.   [3] *Vide* pp. 242-3.
[4] Commenting on the cumbersome working of the O.A.S., Gordon Connell-Smith observes: ". . . the truth is that the Latin Americans do not regard the inter-American system as an instrument for furnishing swift endorsement of United States policy. Rather they look to it to impose a measure of restraint upon their powerful neighbour: to maintain the principle of non-intervention." *op. cit.*, pp. 341-2.

Since the two groups had divergent interests, inevitably the O.A.S. failed to satisfy the aspirations of either. That nevertheless it has had some measure of success is a tribute both to its constitution and to its staff. Moreover, neither group wishes to destroy it, though there is a consensus that its constitution should be modified to meet modern conditions. However, the sponsors of change are not agreed as to what should be done. The Latin American nations vary widely in national aims and outlook. These differences emerge sharply in a study of their history.[1]

The Caribbean has been the forge where the O.A.S., a regional organization, and the United Nations have tempered their relationship. In the Cuban missile crisis, the United States called in the O.A.S. to defeat what it deemed a threat to the hemisphere. On the whole, the O.A.S. responded in a most favourable manner. Ships were even supplied as a token to join the blockade of Cuba.

At the height of this crisis, however, the United States and the Soviet Union negotiated directly with one another. With Soviet ships carrying missiles on their way across the Atlantic, both superpowers sensed that time was too short to introduce a third party, whether the O.A.S. or Cuba. To a considerable extent the U.N. was bypassed; on the whole the O.A.S., spearheaded by the United States, seemed to have asserted itself in the crisis somewhat more than the U.N.

In the Dominican crisis of 1965, the U.N.-O.A.S. relationship was tested once more. The United States belatedly managed to turn its unilateral intervention into an O.A.S. operation, although the cover of a Brazilian general nominally in command of U.S. troops, and a handful of others besides a substantial Brazilian contingent, seemed thin.[2]

The U.N. endeavoured to mediate discreetly and sent an observer; again the O.A.S. clearly had the more dominant role. Probably the massive scale of the U.S. intervention had set a pattern which was difficult to change. Moreover, the U.N. must have had in mind the heavy cost of its intervention in the Congo and the financial embarrassment which resulted.

Notwithstanding that the O.A.S. intervention in the Dominican

[1] "Actually, the states of the hemisphere are united by very little. They differ among themselves in most important ways; as we have seen, even the geographically contiguous states of Central America, among which some transnational forces are at work, diverge from one another in crucial political, economic, social and even racial respects." John H. Plank, "The Caribbean: Intervention, When and How", *Foreign Affairs*, Vol. 44, No. 1, Council on Foreign Relations, New York, October 1965, p. 44.

[2] *Vide* p. 82.

crisis was tardy, it did contribute to a peaceful solution. A general election, generally deemed to have been fair, was held in June 1966.[1] Moreover, the world's most powerful nation had found it expedient to bring in a regional organization to provide some international backing for a very dubious initial operation. To that extent the international standing of the O.A.S. was strengthened.

After independence the new Commonwealth Caribbean nations had to consider the question of joining the O.A.S. Trinidad and Barbados were accepted as members in 1967 and Jamaica in 1969. Guyana may be precluded from doing so at present by reason of its boundary problem with Venezuela, not yet finally settled.[2]

The argument against the recently independent Caribbean countries joining includes the fact that they are members of the British Commonwealth. There is, however, a precedent in that the United States is a member of the North Atlantic Treaty Organization and other defence organizations with much more precise obligations than the very wide and indefinite Commonwealth.

Another reason advanced against joining was that the newly independent Caribbean countries are all small. They have close links with the United States which has military bases in some of them. As members of the O.A.S., they may have to make a choice over some issues which might offend their powerful neighbour. Canada, perhaps for similar reasons, has as yet preferred not to join despite opportunities of doing so. Notwithstanding, its reputation in Latin America stands high.

Against these arguments, a regional organization clearly is less effective if there are potential members in its area who do not join. Moreover, the Caribbean lies in the heart of the Americas, and some countries in it already belong to the O.A.S.; Canada's geographic position is remote from other members except the United States.

The new nations of the Caribbean added to the international aspect of the O.A.S. In terms of population, the Organization's Spanish flavour was overemphasized. In recent years, the Amerindian character received increasing expression, for example in Mexico. The voices of persons of European descent were heavily represented, however, not only by most Spanish-speaking countries but by the United States and Brazil. The new entrants from the Caribbean will express the views of those whose forebears came from Africa, in a manner more explicit than either the United States or Brazil could easily do. To those who believe that the future of the world will result more and more in

[1] *Vide* pp. 84-5.
[2] An analogous situation exists in the case of British Honduras. *Vide* pp. 259-260.

racial miscegenation, the advent to the O.A.S. of a country like Trinidad, with a population composed mainly of persons of African and Indian origin, seems logical.

From another angle, the countries of the Commonwealth Caribbean may have a practical political contribution to make to the O.A.S. In all of them democracy has functioned reasonably since independence. Trinidad in 1966 and 1971 and Jamaica in 1967 and 1972 held General Elections. In every case but one, after elections democratically conducted, the incumbent government was returned, largely on its economic record.[1] At the same time, well-organized opposition parties provided the possibility of alternative government.

In 1970, under its newly elected Marxist President, Salvador Allende, Chile re-established trade relations and later full diplomatic ties with Cuba. Although directly opposed to O.A.S. and hence U.S. policies, Chile exercised its right as a sovereign state to establish relations with whom it liked. Peru and Bolivia also indicated a change of policy. Concern grew over the future of the O.A.S. The Nixon administration, having offered no alternative to the unsuccessful Alliance for Progress programme, may have affected the morale of the O.A.S.[2]

Notwithstanding indications within the O.A.S. that Cuba might be reinvited, Castro reiterated his intent to remain outside unless the United States was expelled from membership.[3] In November 1971 Castro visited Chile, his first journey to South America for twelve years. Some saw beginnings of a new era of relationships with Latin America.[4] Although the atmosphere in Chile remained far from that of Cuba in the early sixties, nevertheless the General Secretary of the Socialist Party of Chile openly acknowledged that the historic objectives of both movements were identical.[5]

On the economic side, the immediate prospects of greatly increased trade between South and Central America and the Caribbean appear limited. The pattern is already established in the Latin American Common Market and the Central American Common Market. Although the Caribbean countries might find it difficult to participate

[1] *Vide* pp. 153, 155-6, 138-9 and 140.
[2] Cf. William C. Selover, "Allende cracks O.A.S. unity", *The Christian Science Monitor*, Boston, November 14, 1970.
[3] Havana, April 22, 1970.
[4] Cf. Richard Wigg, "Dr. Castro welcomed to Chile", *The Times*, London, November 11, 1971.
[5] Dr. Carlos Altamirano, *Granma*, Havana, June 6, 1971.

in either body separately, the possible future merger of L.A.F.T.A. and C.A.C.M. would provide more compelling reasons.

The initial advance of the C.A.C.M. in particular was impressive. A group of small nations increased its internal trade to $128 million in 1965, a threefold increase in four years. Moreover, the population of the Central American Republics is small even by Caribbean standards. Setting aside Cuba, which has its trade oriented in another direction, Haiti has a larger population than any of the five C.A.C.M. members, and Jamaica is larger than two of them.

Communication is a major difficulty, however. If the Caribbean countries joined either L.A.F.T.A. or C.A.C.M., they might experience serious shipping delays in obtaining from mainland factories import-substitution goods and also in delivering exports to the mainland. Unless a substantial two-way trade of this nature could be built up, the association between the two areas would not be mutually profitable. It would seem that, under present conditions, the Caribbean countries would be wise to foster their present trade outlets with North America and Europe while working to develop CARIFTA.

During World War II the Anglo-American Caribbean Commission had been formed. Four years later, with French and Netherlands support, it became the Caribbean Commission, with the improvement of the economic and social well-being of the Caribbean peoples as its aim. In order to devolute more authority to the Caribbean, the Caribbean Commission gave way in September 1961 to the Caribbean Organization. With its headquarters in San Juan, Puerto Rico, the Caribbean Organization was destined to be a regional advisory and consultative body for all its members in the fields of economics, social and cultural development. In 1962 a Clearing House on Trade and Tourist Information was set up to facilitate trade between the Caribbean countries.[1] However, political complications, arising from difficulties involved in getting decisions from capitals as far apart as Washington, Paris, London and The Hague, as well as from the legislatures of the territories themselves, resulted in the collapse of the Caribbean Organization.[2] Instead, Puerto Rico sponsored informal inter-Caribbean co-operation and in the summer of 1965 the Caribbean

[1] Cf. "The Development of Trade in the Caribbean", *The Caribbean Organization—The First Three Years*, Central Secretariat, Hato Rey, Puerto Rico, 1964, pp. 13-16.

[2] ". . . its effectiveness is likely to be limited by the fact that it was founded by the wrong people, in the sense that it originated with the metropolitan powers and for a time it was dominated by them." Sir Philip Sherlock, "Prospects in the Caribbean", *Foreign Affairs*, Council on Foreign Relations, New York, July 1963, p. 753.

Economic Development Corporation was established. C.O.D.E.C.A. achieved more success in a few months than the other organizations had in a period of years.[1] Creating a suitable climate for inter-Caribbean trade was one of its main functions. In 1968 the C.O.D.E.C.A. experiment ended.[2]

The disastrous pattern of price fluctuations has bedevilled the economies of Latin America as it has of the Caribbean. Attempts are being made to regulate and stabilize some major commodities such as coffee and sugar. So far the difficulties of doing so appear to be formidable. The International Coffee Organization faced the greatest obstacles in making effective its policy of quotas.[3] That the outlook for sugar is even more unpromising was expressed by the largest sugar enterprise in the Commonwealth Caribbean. Its misgivings were emphasized by the announcement that it would extend its diversification away from sugar.[4]

Clearly the long-term outlook for tropical produce seems uncertain. Despite industrialization, agriculture remains a basic part of the Caribbean economies. So long as world prices for their agricultural production remain out of gear with the capital and other goods which must be imported, a condition of difficulty in these underdeveloped countries will continue.

The United States clearly prefers to deal with one large rather than a number of small units in matters of aid. That was a major factor in its support of the C.A.C.M. The Commonwealth Caribbean countries, despite the dissolution of their Federation, have formed CARIFTA and some even look to political union in the future.[5] Undoubtedly those Caribbean countries that have joined the O.A.S. sought also to establish closer ties with the United States.[6]

Since 1967 the disillusionment of the U.S. Congress and people over

[1] "San Juan plans Neighbourly Help", *The New York Times*, New York, January 16, 1966.
[2] "With its death would perish, also, at least temporarily, the hope of creating for Puerto Rico a role as leader and innovator in Caribbean integration". Herbert Corkran, *Patterns of International Co-operation in the Caribbean 1942-1969*, (Dallas, 1970), p. 194.
[3] Cf. John Woodland, "Coffee Man faces a Tough Job", *The Times*, London, March 20, 1967.
[4] Cf. "Tate and Lyle Looking Past Sugar", *The Daily Telegraph*, London, March 23, 1967. *Vide* p. 325.
[5] *Vide* p. 355.
[6] Cf. Roy Preiswerk, "The Relevance of Latin America to the Foreign Policy of Commonwealth Caribbean States", *Journal of Inter-American Studies*, Vol. XI, No. 2, Miami, April 1969.

development aid has grown still further.[1]   Should the United States increasingly withdraw its interest in Latin America the complex problem of the future remains.   Ties to Europe may not prove strong enough to resist pressure from the Soviet bloc.   The future of L.A.C.M. and C.A.C.M., strongly sponsored by the United States, remains uncertain. Already some question integration as the panacea for Latin America. Even Felipe Herrera, President of the Inter-American Development Bank, admitted that the faith of Latin Americans in regional interest had waned.[2]   A satisfactory response is required to the fundamental challenge from within the different Latin American societies.[3]   External economic ties with North America and Europe will probably continue to play a greater role in the economy of Latin America than an integrated internal market.   Possibly narrower free trade areas like the Andean group may meet with more success.[4]

The failure of the United States to develop the Latin American economy unaided may result in the whole area being increasingly opened to other countries.   Post-war Britain has been slow to expand in Latin America.   Other countries such as France, Germany and Switzerland have shown keenness to enter these markets while Japan, too, presses ahead.   Fidel Castro's visit to Chile may presage more activity and interest by the Communist countries in an area from which they have for long been excluded.

[1] *Vide* p. 350.

[2] *Nacionalismo Latinoamericano* (Santiago, Chile, 1968).

[3] William Woodruff and Helga Woodruff, "The Illusions about the role of integration in Latin America's future", *Inter-American Economic Affairs*, Washington, Spring 1969, p. 76.

[4] President Nixon stressed his support of regional economic integration, Washington, October 31, 1969.

CHAPTER XIX

CONCLUSION

THE POLITICAL PATTERN

The islands of the Caribbean have many common problems. During three centuries all these territories have been largely repopulated from outside the Americas: Africa, Europe and Asia. Intermarriage has softened some of the racial asperities so violently expressed in the United States. The cultures of various origin have been blended, which should contribute in the long run to harmony. So far the Commonwealth territories have entered into independence with nationalism usually tempered by tolerance. The concept of CARIFTA, which could be extended to other Caribbean countries, suggests the value of co-operation.

Many of the Caribbean's most pressing problems surge within the economic sphere. Whether the area, fragmented by distance, history, language and ideology, will coalesce remains uncertain. At least it is reasonable to hope that its role as an international battleground has ended, despite the memory of the 1962 crisis.

Any assessment of the Caribbean political situation must remain speculative. In Cuba, Fidel Castro has stressed Cuban nationalism to weld together his people, including those of Spanish and Negro origin. His very educational experiment in his much advertised campaign to eliminate adult illiteracy provided at the same time an opportunity for the propagation of his faith. No alternative to his highly centralized one-party government, buttressed by propaganda and by the emigration of disgruntled citizens, is in sight. Castro has provided a façade of equality, at the price of food rationing and queues, and the discipline of a police state, strongly supported by his very sizeable and well equipped army. More and more Cuba seems to be coming under Russian influence: the power of the paymaster.

Haiti too has set aside democracy for another form of totalitarian government, stressing strongly the nationalism and folklore of the Haitian people, while the Tonton Macoute lurk in the background. Young President Jean-Claude Duvalier faces a formidable task; he seems to be ill-prepared to follow his father.

The Dominican Republic has struggled to recover a vestige of

2 E   433

democracy after the long and grim Trujillo years. Under President Balaguer, who won a much criticized election, the country maintains an uneasy calm.

From a political standpoint the Commonwealth Caribbean has entered independence successfully. The powerful influence of long-term association, albeit colonial, with Great Britain, has engendered the development there of British political and judicial institutions.

The Trinidad General Election of May 1971 was the first threat to democracy in the Commonwealth Caribbean. Although the party system enshrined in the British political concept still exists, it has been damaged by the refusal of the major opposition leaders to co-operate.

Guyana, which in past years had appeared far more vulnerable, has so far won through under its dynamic Prime Minister, Forbes Burnham. Jamaica, which had suffered the unexpected loss of Prime Minister Donald Sangster at a critical moment and had felt the impact of Black Power earlier than Trinidad, appears nevertheless to have an entrenched and viable two-party system as it prepares for a general election in 1972.

If some doubts had arisen over the viability of Associated Statehood in the smaller territories, no one seemed more anxious than Great Britain to see those islands move into independence. Anguilla provided an uncomfortable reminder of remaining colonial problems. The decision of Guyana to become a Republic had many precedents in other parts of the Commonwealth. British Honduras and the Bahamas both seemed likely to follow the same path into independence.

As part of France, the French Overseas Departments in the Caribbean derived considerable benefits from entry to the European Common Market. Economics provided a counter-weight to nationalism. Nevertheless some would prefer a Black Power independence to a more prosperous "colonialism". So far the ballot boxes have suggested that the economic pull remains the strongest.

As parts of the Tripartite Kingdom, Surinam and the Netherlands Antilles have benefited. Nevertheless, serious unemployment in Curaçao and Aruba resulted in riots.

The Caribbean, country by country, has been seeking its identity. CARIFTA remains essentially economic: political union seems far off. Membership of the Organization of American States has not necessarily drawn these countries closer to one another.

The role of the Black Power movement is complicated in some of the countries with a multinational background. Perhaps the overriding factor in the Caribbean is the multitude of cultural influences which has formed the character of its diverse population. In a pessimistic summary of the issue, Prime Minister Eric Williams saw the only bright spot in a bleak picture as "the apparent success in Castro's Cuba with the full integration of the black population into his society".[1]

Despite the successful functioning of democracy in much of the area, rumblings of press control began to be heard in the 1970's. The newly elected Government of Antigua proposed substantial deposits and annual licensing fees for its press.[2] Nearby St. Kitts-Nevis passed a Press and Publications Act which the Attorney General claimed was necessary since the press in the Caribbean lacked responsibility.[3] Antigua in 1968 had already taken measures aimed at prohibiting undesirable publications. More ambitious, the Government of Guyana announced that it was entering the field with its own daily newspaper, part of a large publishing complex.[4] "If the press in all these countries is only to be allowed to exist at the price of being beholden to the Governments or being absorbed by them then the prospect of democracy surviving in any of them is very dim indeed."[5]

All these countries have entered into recent independence carrying with them the strongly entrenched British system of a free press. It may well be that newly established free legislatures are more sensitive to criticism than the hardened Parliament of Westminster or Congress of Washington. Yet it would be a tragedy if independence which has so far worked in democratic fashion should fail in so important a field. Latin America provides only too many examples of newspapers shackled and gagged by politics.

THE ECONOMIC PATTERN

The crucial problem for the islands lies in limited natural resources linked to a burgeoning population. Despite the active promotion of birth control in some of these countries, the problem has an urgency far greater than in, say, Brazil or Canada. Emigration to Panama, Cuba, the United States or Great Britain once provided a solution, even if not a very satisfactory one. To some degree, Puerto Rico and the American Virgin Islands through their link with the United States, and Martinique and Guadeloupe, as overseas departments of France,

[1] *From Columbus to Castro, The History of the Caribbean 1492-1969*, (London, 1970) p. 503. *Vide* pp. 389-90.

[2] *Antigua Times*, Antigua, editorial, July 10, 1971.

[3] Cf. *The Times*, London, October 14, 1971.

[4] *The Advocate-News*, Barbados, July 30, 1971. Alfred Baburam commented "The Press in the Caribbean . . . is going through a heart-rending and soul-searching exercise." "The Press and the new Carib society", *Sunday Graphic*, Georgetown, June 27, 1971.

[5] *The Daily Gleaner*, Kingston, editorial, November 24, 1971.

435

have a built-in outlet for surplus population at a time when traditional emigration appears to be coming to an end.

However successful CARIFTA may be, it is unlikely to solve the unemployment which plagues much of the area. In Jamaica and Trinidad it may well reach 20 per cent. while underemployment is much higher still. The dense numbers in Haiti or in Barbados also presage danger. On the other hand the Caribbean has so far avoided the over-sized cities that unbalance so many other parts of the world. Yet the flow from the countryside to the towns increases too fast, luring the youth to the glamour of a non-existent urban job. The mechanization of agriculture linked to higher wages has had little effect on stemming the move to the cities, an occurrence that may be observed from Brazil to Canada.

In the developed countries education opens an increasing number of administrative and technical jobs. The Caribbean, despite improvements, remains handicapped by inadequate educational facilities in comparison with the United States or the Common Market. No one familiar with the education of children from rural districts can under-rate the problems that face these countries.

To envisage a substantially self-contained Caribbean offering a reasonable standard of living to the average citizen requires a high degree of optimism. The population explosion, as in many other parts of the world, would seem to exclude this: nevertheless improvement may be achieved. The advantage of the area rests in its agreeable climate and in its location in the heart of the Americas, which are still perhaps the most rapidly developing world area.

Change is in the air. The sugar industry, basis of so much of the Caribbean economy, has at best a limited future depending on protection from world competition. Many Caribbean farms, efficient in earlier days, struggle for survival in competition with vast areas of flat land in larger countries, better suited to mechanization.

A changed agriculture may produce specialized produce for export. Fresh fruit, vegetables and flowers suggest possibilities. As air-freight expands, new markets will open. The field is one requiring high specialization and skill, both in growing and marketing. Moreover, in a perhaps expanded CARIFTA, the islands may supply themselves with many things, manufactured goods as well as foodstuffs.

Of all the industries, tourism offers the greatest future. The expansion of air travel, with ever larger groups arriving in ever larger planes, seems likely to continue. Fortunately for the Caribbean its climate makes possible a nearly all-year-round season. Objections are often advanced that people do not wish to work for tourists; and that disparity in wealth between the visitors and the local inhabitants causes ill-feeling. Intelligent explanations of the nature of the tourist trade can do much to overcome these criticisms. The widespread advantages to communities as a whole—far beyond hotel employees—gradually become appreciated. Thanks to tourism, Bermuda, with a population density of nearly 3,000 persons per square mile—more than that of Barbados or Haiti—has a higher standard of living than any Caribbean island, including Puerto Rico and the U.S. Virgin Islands, where in turn the standard of living is higher than in any Latin American country. An expanding trade in "winter visitors", many of whom may own houses which they occupy for only part of the year, begins to appear. These people provide a useful addition to the tourist industry as has been proved in Barbados and Jamaica; one much less volatile than tourism and affording continuing employment.

Clearly some countries will move ahead faster than others. Size is by no means the only criterion for economic prosperity. Cuba and Hispaniola (Haiti and the Dominican Republic), the two largest islands with some of the best land, exemplify that. Solutions may be found by compromise which the people of these countries are sometimes prepared to accept: one advantage derived from the racial mixture. Industrialization may focus on specialized industries, including those which replace imports. The successful attraction of capital will depend on the treatment it receives.

In one way the whole area is sensitive to outside happenings. The Cuban Revolution, which terminated Castro's tourist trade with North America, also at first adversely affected Jamaica, even though a little later when the public realized that Cuba's problems did not touch Jamaica that island probably gained in tourism as Puerto Rico certainly did.

In the same way the overseas businessman, increasingly sophisticated and concerned with happenings in various parts of the world, is becoming more selective as to where he invests his money. Undoubtedly those countries which welcome the foreign investor—not just when he first makes his investment but in the long term—will succeed in attracting the funds without which any chance of long-term development and consequent increase of employment appears remote.

Here is something where islands have an equal chance. Political stability and intelligent handling of the important art—for it is that more than a precise science—of presenting to foreigners their attractions as a home for investment or recreation will pay dividends, not least to the islanders themselves.

The day of the manual worker is passing, though he must for some time have an important role. The problem is to satisfy the aspirations of the adult inadequately equipped to hold a skilled job—probably through no fault of his own—and simultaneously to employ the talent which is bursting from the schools and universities.

Criticism of the establishment, be it in the Americas or Europe, is salutary. Rigidity and dislike of change may wreck a major enterprise or even a government. Nevertheless, criticism must be constructive. Life is always a choice, not necessarily of evils but of alternatives. In tribal days wars and unrest had a limited impact. Today the vast communities of the world, who pay little attention whence their food and necessities originate, depend for survival upon an immensely complex system of international trade. It is easy for Frantz Fanon, a West Indian, to write off Europe and work out new concepts. North Africa does not face the population pressure of his native Martinique.[1] Regardless of the advantage of being a department of France, which provides the consequent population outlet, Martinique has not the space of Algeria, though it has a substantially higher standard of living.

Two differing approaches appear sharply in the Caribbean as in other parts of the world. Prime Minister Forbes Burnham has put forward actively the philosophy of a Guyana that will be nationally controlled, though obviously requiring very substantial foreign investment from public or private sources. He considers, rightly, that his country has made a substantial effort to help itself, but he also claims that if Guyana has friends, "those friends may justly and properly be asked to assist in financing our programme to a higher degree than has been the case in the past".[2] He also, not unreasonably, criticizes the tying of aid to the purchase of goods and services from the donor country.

This argument overlooks the problems that donor countries themselves face. Democracies like the United States, Great Britain and Canada have to justify their policy to their own elected representatives. At a time when taxation is rising and unemployment exists also in these "developed" countries, appeals for overseas aid are far from popular: they believe that they are themselves still developing.[3] Should there be a background of expropriation or unfair treatment of foreign investment, pressure against further investment will inevitably mount in the

[1] "Come, then, comrades, the European game has finally ended; we must find something different. We today can do everything, so long as we do not imitate Europe, so long as we are not obsessed by the desire to catch up with Europe." *The Wretched of the Earth* (New York, 1968), p. 312.

[2] *A Destiny to Mould* (London, 1970), p. 185.

[3] The emergency 10 per cent. cut in aid to underdeveloped countries announced by President Nixon on August 15, 1971, was significant even if only intended as a temporary measure.

donor country. Moreover, in a world of nervous investors, public and private alike, bad news travels fast. Competition between under-developed countries for investment funds will continue to exceed the funds readily available. Economic difficulties certainly contributed to making Cuba more financially dependent on Russia than ever it was on the United States.[1]

Guyana, for example, by its nationalization of the Demerara Bauxite Company may well have damaged its prospects of attracting further outside capital. Significantly, protest came from Jamaica, a fellow CARIFTA member, on the grounds that it would also discourage in-vestment in other parts of the Caribbean.[2] Nothing is more certain than that the mistreatment of foreign capital may backfire sharply. Unquestionably those countries which handle foreign investment wisely will gain. A reputation for long-term stability counts in the long run far more than extended tax holidays.

The approach of Jamaica and Trinidad appears more realistic than that of Guyana. Both countries advocate local participation in major island industries, often combined with stock exchange quotations. As in other parts of the world, the Caribbean relies heavily on tax incentives to attract new industries. The method has its merits, although it obviously means that others must carry a tax load which is not shared by all. Prime Minister Williams himself refers to the excessive tax holiday, amounting sometimes to 15 years, being granted in some parts of the Caribbean.[3]

It will become increasingly necessary to develop technology as well as natural resources, but ever more costly. Labour-saving machinery and methods continue to reduce the total numbers employed. At the same time manual work involving heavy physical labour, as for example in the cutting of sugar cane, becomes increasingly unpopular. The pace of world population expansion may well retard or even reverse the rise in standards of living in many countries. Co-operation becomes the important factor for developed and underdeveloped countries alike.

Robert S. McNamara, a shrewd observer, pinpoints the dilemmas of the small underdeveloped country which seeks to industrialize. Though attractive in early years, once imports of any product have been re-placed, that industry's expansion is limited to the growth of the domestic market. "To maintain industrial momentum requires import

[1] *Vide* pp. 47-48.

[2] *Vide* p. 243.

[3] *From Columbus to Castro, the History of the Caribbean, 1492-1969*, (London, 1970), p. 511.

substitution in continually new products." This may lead to products increasingly unsuited to the size of the market or economy.[1]

The real problem for underdeveloped countries in the Caribbean as in other parts of the world is to raise their standard of living quickly by the only known means, namely the heavy injection of capital. To obtain this capital from within the country is well nigh impossible. Even Cuba, well endowed in Caribbean terms, has signally failed in its economic development. "Che" Guevara and the economic Ministers who succeeded him could not match the former flow of U.S. capital linked to U.S. markets. Even the support of Communist countries has not proved sufficient to expand the economy at an acceptable rate, despite heavy rationing which presses hard on the standard of living.[2]

As more and more countries seek to industrialize, the temptation to expropriate or take over foreign-owned concerns increases. Yet at the end of the day the only large sources of capital and of expertise rest in the developed countries. This position is unlikely to change in the near future. Foreign investors will become increasingly selective in which countries they invest. Those who may feel that they have been unfairly expropriated will inevitably discourage other investors—as well as their own elected governments—from providing funds to the ex-propriating country.

No simple panacea exists for the Caribbean. Territorial diversity impedes close union. Yet by developing wisely their special opportunities these countries may succeed in raising their living standards, while at the same time giving expression to their national culture. Patterns will change and modify, adding to the interest and indeed the charm of this enigmatic area of the world.

No area of the world has more to offer to the student of political science or economics. Democracy, autocracy, dictatorship, Marxism, all have their Caribbean examples. Great variation exists in the standards of living.

Few areas of the world have experimented more with different religions which themselves often exert a marked political impact. Languages and cultures afford a variety just as nature has provided widely different land and sea scapes. The Caribbean is learning the real as well as the commercial value of its different heritages.

The variety of its systems of education from Puerto Rico to Curaçao and from Martinique to Jamaica add to the cultural charm and provide endless material for research. Yet the major challenge rests in the

[1] *Address to the Board of Governors*, World Bank Group, Washington, D.C., September 27, 1971.
[2] *Vide* pp. 44-5.

provision of acceptable employment: the problem in small scale as the world approaches the third millennium of the Christian era. The limited area highlights urgency more sharply than in larger countries. Ahead of much of the world several Caribbean governments have accepted the need for action to steady population growth. Jamaica[1] and Barbados[2] are examples: and, perhaps more unexpectedly, the Roman Catholic overseas departments of France.[3]

Nowhere more than in the Antilles is the need for trained workers more acute. The sophisticated new industries without which CARIFTA cannot succeed: the market gardening, scarcely yet touched, which could enter the markets of countries with less favoured climates: the skills needed for the import substituting industries: the ever-increasing complexity of the highly competitive tourist trade: here lies employment for the educated worker, the man and woman of the future.

[1] *Vide* p. 150.
[2] *Vide* p. 171.
[3] *Vide* p. 284.

BIBLIOGRAPHY

COMMONWEALTH TERRITORIES

FRENCH OVERSEAS DEPARTMENTS

THE TRIPARTITE KINGDOM

GENERAL

The Bibliography has been grouped into seven main sections: Cuba, Haiti, the Dominican Republic, Puerto Rico and the Virgin Islands of the United States, the Commonwealth Territories, the French Overseas Departments, and the Tripartite Kingdom. A General Section has been added which relates to more than one territory. Sources and studies mentioned in the text have been included together with others of relevance.

443

ABBREVIATIONS

Cmd./Cmnd.	British White Paper.
Hansard	Parliamentary Reports.
H.M.S.O.	Her Majesty's Stationery Office, London.
n.d.	No date.
n.p.	No publisher.

CUBA

SOURCES

(a) *Documents*

Agrarian Reform Law, May 17, 1959, Official Gazette, Special Issue No. 7, Havana, Cuba, June 3, 1959.

CASTRO, FIDEL, *La Historia me Absolverá*, Mendez y Cia., Havana, 1964.

C.I.A. attacks the Cuban people, The Cuban Embassy, London, n.d.

Cuba: A Giant School, Information Department, Ministry of Foreign Affairs, Cuba, n.d.

Cuba: Public Health and Socialism, Department of Information, Ministry of Foreign Affairs, Republic of Cuba, n.d.

Cuba at the Second Conference of non-aligned nations, October 1964, The Foreign Ministry, Republic of Cuba.

Cuban protest to the United Nations, Political Document No. 4, Ministry of Foreign Relations, Republic of Cuba, March 4, 1963.

Development of Cuban Foreign Trade, Ministry of Foreign Affairs, Republic of Cuba, n.d.

Economic Aggression, Ministry of Foreign Relations, Republic of Cuba, n.d.

Letter from Premier Castro to Secretary General of the U.N., January 1966, *Cuba Information Bulletin*, No. 5/66, Cuban Embassy, London.

Letter sent by Prime Minister Fidel Castro to the Public Prosecutor in the trial of Cubelas and his accomplices, March 8, 1966, *Cuba Information Bulletin*, No. 6/66, Cuban Embassy, London.

Manual para el Alfabetizador, Ministerio de Educación, Havana, 1961.

Methods and Means Utilized in Cuba to eliminate Illiteracy, U.N.E.S.C.O. Report, Editora Pedagógica, Havana, 1965.

Procedures established for Movement of Cuban Refugees to United States, *Department of State Bulletin*, Washington, D.C., November 29, 1965.

Proceedings of the trial of C.I.A. agents at La Cabana fortress, starting on March 7, 1966, *Cuba Information Bulletin*, No. 8/66, Cuban Embassy, London.

Profile of Cuba, Information Department, Ministry of Foreign Relations, Havana, n.d.

Reply by Fidel Castro, February 5, 1966, to the declarations of the Chinese Government, *Cuba Information Bulletin*, No. 2/66, Cuban Embassy, London.

Reply of Prime Minister Fidel Castro to the statements of the President of Chile, Eduardo Frei, March 23, 1966, *Cuba Information Bulletin*, No. 9/66, Cuban Embassy, London.

Report by the Ministry of the Revolutionary Armed Forces, May 1966, *Cuba Information Bulletin*, No. 10/66, Cuban Embassy, London.

Report on Cuba, 1950, International Bank for Reconstruction and Development, Washington, D.C., Johns Hopkins Press, Baltimore, 1951.

Report to the XXIX International Conference on Public Instruction convoked by O.I.E. and U.N.E.S.C.O., Geneva (Switzerland), July 7-16, 1966, *Cuba 1965-1966, The Educational Movement*, Ministry of Education, Havana, 1966.

Speech by Fidel Castro, Havana, December 2, 1961.

Speech by Fidel Castro, "Cuba's Agrarian Reform", Havana, August 18, 1962.

Speech by Fidel Castro, Closing Session of First Conference of Solidarity of the Peoples of Asia, Africa and Latin America, Havana, January 15, 1966.

Speech by Fidel Castro, Closing Session of the 12th Congress of the Central Organization of Cuban Trade Unions, August 29, 1966.

Speech by Fidel Castro, marking the beginning of the 10-million ton sugar harvest, Puerto Padre, Oriente Province, July 14, 1969.

Speech by Fidel Castro, 17th Anniversary of the Attack on the Moncada, Havana, July 26, 1970.

Speech by Fidel Castro, Tenth Anniversary of the Committees for the Defence of the Revolution, Havana, September 28, 1970.

Speech by Ernesto ("Che") Guevara, "Colonialism is doomed", before the General Assembly of the United Nations on December 11, 1964.

Speech by President John F. Kennedy, "The Lesson of Cuba", Washington, D.C., April 20, 1961, *Department of State Bulletin*, Washington, D.C., May 8, 1961.

Speech by Dr. Raúl Roa, Minister of Foreign Relations, United Nations, October 18, 1966.

Text of the Law on Loafing, March 17, 1971, *Granma*, Havana, March 28, 1971.

The Cuban Revolution and the Peasantry, Ministry of Foreign Affairs, Republic of Cuba, n.d.

¡Venceremos!, Comisión Nacional de Alfabetización, Ministerio de Educación, Imprenta Nacional de Cuba, Havana, 1961.

(b) *Newspapers, Periodicals and Year Books*

Cuba, Havana.
Cuba Azúcar, Havana.
Cuba Information Bulletin, Cuban Embassy, London.
Cuba Socialista, Havana.
Educación en Cuba, Havana.
El Mundo, Havana.
Granma, Havana.
Hoy, Havana.
Revolución, Havana.

STUDIES

(a) *Books and Pamphlets*

ABEL, ELIE, *The Missile Crisis*, J. B. Lippincott Co., Philadelphia, 1966.

BARAN, PAUL A., *Reflections on the Cuban Revolution*, Monthly Review Press, New York, 1961.

445

BATISTA, FULGENCIO, *Respuesta* . . ., Mexico City, 1960.
BENÍTEZ, FERNANDO, *La Batalla de Cuba*, Ediciones Era, Mexico, 1960.
BONSAL, PHILIP W., *Cuba, Castro and the United States*, University of Pittsburgh Press, Pennsylvania, 1971.
BRENNAN, RAY, *Castro, Cuba and Justice*, Doubleday & Co., Garden City, New York, 1959.
BUCHAN, DAVID, *Cuba the star that fell*, The Economist, Brief 25, London, August 1971.
"Cuba", *World Survey*, The Atlantic Education Trust, London, No. 9, September 1969.
DEWART, LESLIE, *Christianity and Revolution: The Lesson of Cuba*, Herder and Herder, New York, 1963.
DRAPER, THEODORE, "Castro's Communism", *Encounter*, Pamphlet No. 6, London, n.d.
DRAPER, THEODORE, *Castroism: Theory and Practice*, Frederick A. Praeger, New York, 1965.
DRAPER, THEODORE, *Castro's Revolution: Myths and Realities*, Frederick A. Praeger, New York, 1962.
DUBOIS, JULES, *Operation America*, Walker and Company, New York, 1963.
DUMONT, RENE, *Cuba est-il socialiste?*, Editions du Seuil, Paris, 1970.
DUMUR, JEAN A., *Cuba*, Editions Rencontre, Paris, 1962.
EDUARDO RUIZ, RAMON, *Cuba, the Making of a Revolution*, W. W. Norton and Co., New York, 1970.
FAGEN, RICHARD R., RICHARD BRODY and THOMAS J. O'LEARY, *Cubans in Exile, Disaffection and the Revolution*, Stanford University Press, Stanford, 1968.
FAGEN, RICHARD R., *The Transformation of Political Culture in Cuba*, Stanford University Press, 1969.
GILLY, ADOLFO, *Inside the Cuban Revolution*, translated from the Spanish by Felix Gutierrez, Monthly Review Press, New York, 1964.
GOLDENBERG, BORIS, *The Cuban Revolution and Latin America*, Frederick A. Praeger, New York, 1965.
GONZÁLEZ PEDRERO, ENRIQUE, *La Revolución Cubana*, Escuela Nacional de Ciencias Políticas y Sociales, Mexico, 1959.
GUERRA Y SÁNCHEZ, RAMIRO, *Sugar and Society in the Caribbean*, Yale University Press, New Haven and London, 1964.
GUEVARA, ERNESTO "CHE", *Guerrilla Warfare*, Monthly Review Press, New York, 1961.
HALPERIN, ERNST, *Nationalism and Communism in Chile*, MIT Press, Cambridge, Mass., 1965.
History of an Aggression, Ediciones Venceremos, Havana, 1964.
HUBERMAN, LEO and PAUL M. SWEEZY, *Socialism in Cuba*, Monthly Review Press, New York, 1969.
KENNEDY, ROBERT R., *13 Days: The Cuban Missile Crisis, October 1962*, Macmillan, London, 1969.
JOLLY, RICHARD, *Cuba: The Economic and Social Revolution*, ed. Dudley Seers, "Education", The University of North Carolina Press, Chapel Hill, 1964.
JOHNSON, HAYNES, *The Bay of Pigs*, W. W. Norton & Company, New York, 1964.

446

Julien, Claude, *La Révolution Cubaine*, René Julliard, Paris, 1961.

Karol, K. S., *Guerrillas in Power*, Jonathan Cape, London, 1971.

López-Fresquet, Rufo, *My fourteen months with Castro*, The World Publishing Company, Cleveland and New York, 1966.

MacGaffey, Wyatt, and Clifford R. Barnett, *Twentieth Century Cuba*, Doubleday & Company, Inc., Garden City, N.Y., 1965.

Matos, Almir, *Cuba: A Revolução na América*, Editorial Vitória, Rio de Janeiro, 1961.

Matthews, Herbert L., *Castro: A Political Biography*, Allen Lane, The Penguin Press, London, 1969.

Matthews, Herbert L., *Cuba*, The Macmillan Company, New York, 1964.

Matthews, Herbert L., "Return to Cuba", *Hispanic American Report*, Special Issue, Stanford University, Stanford, California, 1964.

Matthews, Herbert L., *The Cuban Story*, George Braziller, New York, 1961.

Merle, Robert, *Moncada, premier combat de Fidel Castro*, Robert Laffont, Paris, 1965.

Miller, Warren, *The Lost Plantation*, Secker & Warburg, London, 1961.

Mills, C. Wright, *Listen, Yankee*, McGraw-Hill Company, Inc., New York, 1960.

Moncada's Program Achievements, Havana, 1966.

Otero Echeverría, Rafael, *Reportaje a una Revolución*, Editorial del Pacífico, S.A., Santiago de Chile, 1959.

Phillips, R. Hart, *Cuba, Island of Paradox*, McDowell, Obolensky, New York, n.d.

Political, Economic, and Social Thought of Fidel Castro, Editorial Lex, Havana, 1959.

Rodriguez Morejón, G., *Fidel Castro, Biografía*, P. Fernández & Cia., Havana, 1959.

Sartre, Jean-Paul, *Furacão Sôbre Cuba*, Editora do Autor, Rio de Janeiro, n.d.

Scheer, Robert, and Maurice Zeitlin, *Cuba, an American Tragedy*, revised edition, Penguin Books, Harmondsworth, Middlesex, 1964.

Smith, Robert F., *What Happened in Cuba?*, Twayne Publishers, Inc., New York, 1963.

Sweezy, Paul M., and Leo Huberman, *Cuba, Anatomy of a Revolution*, Monthly Review Press, New York, 1960.

The Complete Bolivian Diaries of Ché Guevara and Other Captured Documents, ed. Daniel James, Stein and Day, New York, 1968.

Thomas, Hugh, *Cuba or the Pursuit of Freedom*, Eyre and Spottiswoode, London, 1971.

Tretiak, Daniel, *Cuba and the Soviet Union: The Growing Accommodation*, The R.A.N.D. Corporation, Santa Monica, California, 1966.

Urrutia Lleó, Manuel, *Fidel Castro & Company, Inc.*, Frederick A. Praeger, New York, 1964.

Venceremos! The speeches and writings of Che Guevara, ed. John Gerassi, Panther Modern Society, London, 1969.

Yglesias, Jose, *In the Fist of the Revolution: Life in Castro's Cuto*, Penguin, Harmondsworth, 1968.

447

(b) *Articles*

AIROY, GIL CARL, "The peasantry in the Cuban Revolution", *The Review of Politics*, Vol. 29, No. 1, The University of Notre Dame, Notre Dame, Indiana, January 1967.

ALSOP, JOSEPH, "Soviet Exodus from Cuba", *The New York Times*, New York, November 13, 1963.

ARON, RAYMOND, "Césars Fous", *Le Figaro*, Paris, May 4, 1971.

ARON, RAYMOND, "Fidel Castro et sa révolution", *Le Figaro*, Paris, March 7, 1961.

BATES, JULIEN, "Castro Keeps Eye on U.S. Changes", *The Christian Science Monitor*, Boston, December 18, 1963.

BEATON, LEONARD, "Cuba crisis: how close to nuclear war?", *The Times*, London, February 6, 1969.

BEESTON, RICHARD, "Cuba plans work camps for loafers", *The Sunday Telegraph* London, January 31, 1971.

BERLE, ADOLF A., "It had to be faced", *The Reporter*, New York, January 8, 1962.

BERNER, WOLFGANG W., "Soviet Strategy Toward Cuba, Latin America and the Third World", *Bulletin*, Vol. XV, No. 7, Institute for the Study of the USSR, Munich, July 1968.

"Blacklist Amended to Aid Shipowners", *The Journal of Commerce*, New York, December 17, 1963.

BONSAL, PHILIP W., "Cuba, Castro and the United States", *Foreign Affairs*, Vol. 45, No. 2, Council on Foreign Relations, New York, January 1967.

CARR, RAYMOND, "Cuban Dilemmas", *The World Today*, Vol. 23, No. 1, The Royal Institute of International Affairs, London, January 1967.

"Castro's Seven Years", Latin American Correspondent, *The Times*, London, May 12 and 13, 1966.

CHAYES, ABRAM, "Law and the Quarantine of Cuba", *Foreign Affairs*, Council on Foreign Relations, New York, April 1963.

CHONCHOL, JACQUES, "Bringing About the Revolutionary Processes", *The New York Times*, New York, January 25, 1971.

CLAXTON, ROBERT H., "Some recent images of Cuba in the United States Leftist Press", *South Eastern Latin Americanist*, Vol. XIV, No. 3, Southeastern Conference on Latin-American Studies (SECOLAS). University of Alabama. Alabama, December 1970.

CONNELL-SMITH, GORDON, "Fidel Castro's challenge: Ten Years On", *The World Today*, Vol. 25, No. 1, The Royal Institute of International Affairs, London, January 1969.

COOKE, ALISTAIR, "Bay of Pigs put the press in a dilemma", *The Guardian*, London, June 4, 1966.

"Cuba—a Soviet Colony", *Swiss Press Review and News Report*, Berne, Switzerland, May 11, 1970.

"Cuba call for more guerrilla violence", *The Times*, London, August 2, 1967.

"Cubans wait for their number to come up", Latin American Correspondent, *The Times*, London, November 28, 1963.

DACUNHA-CASTELLE, Didier, "L'Enseignement universitaire veut lier la production et la formation", *Le Monde*, Paris, March 29-30, 1970.

DANIEL, JEAN, "Ben Bella and Castro", *The New Republic*, Washington, D.C., October 5, 1963.

DE GRAMONT, SANCHE, "Cuba al Borde del Desastre", *Listín Diario*, Santo Domingo, December 11-16, 1963.

DE ONIS, JUAN, "Castro's Cuba—After Six Years", *The New York Times*, New York, January 3, 1965.

DEVLIN, KEVIN, "The Permanent Revolutionism of Fidel Castro", *Problems of Communism*, Washington, January-February 1968.

DINERSTEIN, HERBERT S., "Soviet and Cuban Conception of Revolution" *Studies in Comparative Communism*, Vol. 4, No. 1, School of Politics and International Relations, University of Southern California, January 1971.

DIUGUID, LEWIS H., "Report from Cuba, where Revolution is on the Farm", *The Washington Post*, Washington, D.C., March 26, 1967.

DIUGUID, LEWIS H., "Touristless Havana Readjusts", *The Washington Post*, Washington, D.C., March 27, 1967.

DIUGUID, LEWIS H., "Cuba Tackles its Teacher Shortage in the Castro Manner", *The Washington Post*, Washington, D.C., March 28, 1967.

DIUGUID, LEWIS, H., "U.S. Boycott Fits Castro's Need for a Scapegoat", *The Washington Post*, Washington, D.C., March 30, 1967.

DRAPER, THEODORE, "Castro, Krushchev, and Mao", *The Reporter*, New York, August 15, 1963.

DRAPER, THEODORE, "The Confused Martyr", *Encounter*, London, August 1964. [Reply to Herbert L. Matthews, "Dissent over Cuba", *Encounter*, London, July 1964.]

DRAPER, THEODORE, "Castro and Communism", *The Reporter*, New York, January 17, 1963.

EDER, RICHARD, "Castro as King Lear", *The New York Times*, New York, March 20, 1966.

EDER, RICHARD, "Cuba Again Tightens its Belt", *The New York Times*, New York, January 16, 1966.

FAGEN, RICHARD R., "International Politics and the Making of Citizens: The Case of Cuba", Annual Meeting, The American Political Science Association, Chicago, Illinois, September 9-12, 1964.

FERGUSON, J. HALCRO, "Poorer than 'before' but proud as ever", *The Observer*, London, January 3, 1965.

"14,000 Cubans find refuge in Spain", *The Times*, London, January 28, 1965.

FRAYN, MICHAEL, "Castro and Che", *The Observer Review*, London, January 26, 1969.

GALL, NORMAN, "How Castro Failed", *Commentary*, Vol. 52, No. 5, American Jewish Committee, New York, November 1971.

GOODSELL, JAMES NELSON, "Cuba goes fishing—for food and profit", *The Christian Science Monitor*, Boston, October 4-5, 1970.

GOODSELL, JAMES NELSON, "Result of unfulfilled dreams," *The Christian Science Monitor*, Boston, August 28, 1970.

GOTT, RICHARD, *The Guardian*, London, October 14, 15, 16, 1970.

GRAHAM, JOHN, "The Russians press on at Cienfuegos", *The Financial Times*, London, January 21, 1971.

GREENE, GRAHAM, "Fidel—an Impression", *Weekend Telegraph*, London, December 2 and 9, 1966.

"Guerillas turn to urban terrorism", *The Financial Times*, London, October 29, 1969.

GUEVARA, ERNESTO "CHE", "The Cuban Economy", *International Affairs*, Vol. 40, No. 4, The Royal Institute of International Affairs, London, October 1964.

HALCRO FERGUSON, J., "Apostle of Revolution", *The Observer*, London, August 13, 1967.

HALCRO FERGUSON, J., "Havana's hymn of hate", *The Observer*, London, August 6, 1967.

HARSCH, JOSEPH C., "The Cienfuegos base", *The Christian Science Monitor*, Boston, October 27, 1970.

HART PHILLIPS, R., "Cuban refugees restive under U.S. restrictions", *The New York Times*, New York, April 8, 1967.

HARTLEY, ANTHONY, "Cuba and the Intellectuals", *Encounter*, London, August 1961.

HILTON, RONALD, "Castrophobia in the United States", *Yearbook of World Affairs, 1964*, London Institute of World Affairs, London, 1964.

HOFMANN, PAUL, "Spain is the goal of 37,000 in Cuba", *The New York Times*, New York, April 3, 1965.

HORELICK, ARNOLD L., "The Cuban Missile Crisis", *World Politics*, Vol. XVI, No. 3, Princeton University, April 1964.

"Is Cuba a typical Soviet Satellite?", *Report, An Analysis of developments*, Vol. 1, No. 2, ed. Ronald Hilton, Stanford, January 1971.

JOHNSON, LELAND L., "U.S. Business Interests in Cuba and the Rise of Castro", *World Politics*, Vol. XVII, No. 3, Princeton University, April 1965.

JULIEN, CLAUDE, "Sept Heures avec M. Fidel Castro", *Le Monde*, Paris, March 22 and 23, 1963.

JULIEN, CLAUDE, "M. Fidel Castro et le socialisme", *Le Monde*, Paris, March 3, 4, 5, 6, 7/8, 1965.

KNORR, KLAUS, "Failures in National Intelligence Estimates, The Case of the Cuban Missiles", *World Politics*, Vol. XVI, No. 3, Princeton University, April 1964.

"Kuba unter dem Regime der permanenten Revolution", *Neue Zürcher Zeitung*, Zürich, September 11, 18, 24, 25, 28, October 1, 8, 1966.

MAIDENBERG, H. J., "Latins Accelerate Tempo of Revolution", *The New York Times*, New York, January 25, 1971.

MARCHANT, SIR HERBERT, "Cuba hamstrung by economic troubles", *The Times*, London, February 6, 1968.

MATTHEWS, HERBERT L., "Dissent over Cuba", *Encounter*, London, July 1964.

MATTHEWS, HERBERT L., "The revolution Guevara died for lives on in Cuba", *The Times*, London, November 1, 1967.

MOORHOUSE, GEOFFREY, "The manana mob", *The Guardian*, London, January 17, 1970.

NIEDERGANG, MARCEL, "A la Conférence de la Havane", *Le Monde*, Paris, January 18, 1966.

NIEDERGANG, MARCEL, "Citoyen de l'Amérique Latine . . .", *Le Monde*, Paris, October 12, 1967.

NIEDERGANG, MARCEL, "Cuba à l'âge de raison", *Le Monde*, Paris, May 12,13, 14, 15, 17, 1966.

NIEDERGANG, MARCEL, "Le 'Che' ou la révolte permanente. . .", *Le Monde*, Paris, October 17, 1967.

NOURRY, PHILIPPE, "Conférence Précontinentale de la Havane", *Le Figaro*, Paris, January 24, 1966.

NOURRY, PHILIPPE, "Cuba 1968: La guérilla au pouvoir", *Le Figaro*, Paris, April 19, 23, 24, 1968.

O'CONNOR, JAMES, "On Cuban Political Economy", *Political Science Quarterly*, Faculty of Political Science, Columbia University, New York, June 1964.

O'SHAUGHNESSY, HUGH, "Castro curbs the Party", *The Financial Times*, London, October 1, 1970.

PLANK, JOHN, "We should start talking with Castro", *The New York Times Magazine*, New York, March 30, 1969.

RAYMONT, Henry, "Castro's Revolution Remains", *The New York Times*, New York, December 22, 1963.

RAYMONT, HENRY, "U.S. Allies Resist Strong Cuba Curb", *The New York Times*, New York, July 16, 1963.

ROBERTS, CHALMERS M., "A Decade Later—Echoes from the Bay of Pigs Continue", *International Herald Tribune*, Paris, April 12, 1971.

ROBERTS, CHALMERS M., "The 'Understanding' on Cuba", *International Herald Tribune*, Paris, November 25, 1970.

RODRIGUEZ, CARLOS RAFAEL, "The Cuban Economy in 1970", *New Times*, Moscow, March 3, 1970.

ROUCEK, JOSEPH S., "Pro-Communist Revolution in Cuban Education", *Journal of Inter-American Studies*, Vol. VI, No. 3, University of Miami, Coral Gables, Florida, July 1964.

SAUVAGE, LEO, "Fidel Castro dix ans après...", *Le Figaro*, Paris, January 8, 1969.

STONE, I. F., "The spirit of Che Guevara", *New Statesman*, London, October 20, 1967.

SUCHLICKI, JAIME, "El Estudiantado de la Universidad de la Habana en la Política Cubana, 1956-1957", *Journal of Inter-American Studies*, Vol. IX, No. 1, University of Miami, Coral Gables, Florida, January 1967.

SZULC, TAD, "Cuban Confrontation—A Look One Year Later", *The New York Times*, New York, October 20, 1963.

TAYLOR, HENRY J., "Our Allies should think twice", *New York World Telegram and Sun*, New York, October 10, 1962.

"The lorry makers do battle for sales", *The Financial Times*, London, January 8, 1971.

"The Reds in Latin America", *The Round Table*, No. 209, London, December 1962.

"The universalization of the University is the result of the mass education policy", *Granma*, Havana, December 7, 1969.

THOMAS, HUGH, "Paradoxes of Castro's Cuba", *New Statesman*, London, August 26, 1966.

THOMAS, HUGH, "Saints and sacrifices—another side of Castro's Cuba", *The Times*, London, March 1, 1969.

TIDMARSH, KYRIL, "Cuba manifesto hits at Soviet Policy", *The Times*, London, May 3, 1967.

TRETIAK, DANIEL, "China and Latin America", *Current Scene*, Vol. IV, No. 5, Hong Kong, March 1, 1966.

TRETIAK, DANIEL, "Cuba and the Communist System: the Politics of a Communist Independent, 1967-1969", *Orbis*, Vol. XIV, No. 3, Foreign Policy Research Institute, Philadelphia, Fall 1970.

451

Urrutia Lleó, Manuel, "Cuba está en ruinas", *Diario Las Américas*, Miami, July 17, 1963.

Valier, Jacques, "L'Economie Cubaine: quelques problèmes essentiels de son fonctionnement", *Les Temps Modernes*, No. 262, Paris, March 1968.

Van Der Vat, Dan, " 'Che' Guevara: the man and his legend", *The Times*, London, October 10, 1967.

Vanhecke, Charles, "Cuba: de l'utopie aux réalites", *Le Monde*, Paris, March 17, 18, 19, 20, 1971.

Vanhecke, Charles, "M. Fidel Castro entreprend de 'démocratiser' la révolution", *Le Monde*, Paris, October 17, 1970.

Volkov, V., "Cuba faces seaward", *New Times*, Moscow, January 1972.

Volsky, George, "Castro sees little hope for Cuban Economy in '71", *The New York Times*, New York, January 2, 1971.

Wigg, Richard, "A Soviet foot in the door of Latin America", *The Times*, London, July 27, 1970.

Wigg, Richard, "Cuba's future rests on rapid educational growth", *The Times*, London, July 16, 1968.

Wigg, Richard, "Dr. Castro welcomed to Chile", *The Times*, London, November 11, 1971.

Wigg, Richard, "Dr. Castro's utopian hopes that failed", *The Times*, London, July 29, 1970.

Windass, G. S., "The Cuban Crisis and World Order", *International Relations*, Vol. III, No. 13, The David Davies Memorial Institute of International Studies, London, April 1966.

HAITI

Sources

(a) *Documents*

Bulletin Trimestriel de Statistique, Institut Haïtien de Statistique, Port-au-Prince, March 1957.

"Enquêtes sur les terres et les eaux dans la plaine des Gonaïves, et le Département du Nord-Ouest," *Haiti, Rapport Final*, Vol. 1 General, U.N. Development Programme and F.A.O. of the United Nations, Rome, 1968.

La production des fruits et leur transformation industrielle en Haïti, M. J. Del Matto, Mission effectuée pour le compte de l'Institut de Développement Agricole et Industriel, 26 Janvier-24 Février 1963—Société d'Assistance Technique et de Crédit Social, Paris.

Plan and Program for Development of the Artibonite Valley, Organisme de Développement de la Vallée de l'Artibonite, Port-au-Prince, September 1952.

Plan d'action économique et sociale 1968-1969, Conseil National de Planification, Port-au-Prince, 1969.

(b) *Newspapers, Periodicals and Year Books*

La Phalange, Port-au-Prince.

Panorama, Port-au-Prince.

The Haiti Sun, Port-au-Prince.

STUDIES

(a) *Books and Pamphlets*

BELLEGARDE, DANTÈS, *Haïti et son peuple*, Nouvelles Éditions Latines, Paris, 1953.

BRAND, Professor W., *Impressions of Haiti*, Mouton and Co., The Hague, Netherlands, 1965.

DARTIGNE, MAURICE, *Conditions Rurales en Haiti*, Imprimerie de l'Etat, Port-au-Prince, 1938.

DAUMEC, GÉRARD, *Salut! Témoignage, pour Célébrer les 60 Ans d'un Glorieux Leader: Docteur François Duvalier*, Editions Edilite, Port-au-Prince, n.d.

DEROSE, RODOLPHE, *Caractère Culture Voudou*, Bibliothèque Haïtienne, Port-au-Prince, 1956.

DIEDERICH, BERNARD and AL BURT, *Papa Doc (Haiti and its Dictator)*, introd. Graham Greene, Bodley Head, London, 1970.

DORSINVILLE, ROGER, *Toussaint Louverture*, René Julliard, Paris, 1965.

DUVALIER, FRANÇOIS, *Eléments d'une Doctrine*, 2 vols., Collections Œuvres Essentielles, Port-au-Prince, 1966.

GOURAIGE, GHISLAIN, *Histoire de la Littérature Haïtienne*, Imprimerie N. A. Theodore, Port-au-Prince, 1960.

GREENE, GRAHAM, *The Comedians*, Bodley Head, London, 1966.

LATORTUE, FRANÇOIS, *Le Droit du Travail en Haïti*, Les Presses Libres, Port-au-Prince, 1961.

LEYBURN, JAMES G., *The Haitian People*, Yale University Press, New Haven, Connecticut, 1941.

MANIGAT, LESLIE F., *Haiti of the Sixties, Object of International Concern*, The Washington Center of Foreign Policy Research, Washington, D.C., 1964.

MAXIMILIEN, LOUIS, *Le Voudou Haïtien*, Imprimerie de l'Etat, Port-au-Prince, n.d.

MÉTRAUX, ALFRED, *Haiti, Black Peasants and their Religion*, translated from the French by Peter Lengyel, George G. Harrap & Co., London, 1960.

MORAL, PAUL, *L'Economie Haïtienne*, La Cour Supérieure des Comptes, Imprimerie de l'Etat, Port-au-Prince, 1959.

PATTEE, RICARDO, *Haiti*, Ediciones Cultura Hispánica, Madrid, 1956.

POMPILUS, PRADEL, *Pages de Littérature Haïtienne*, 2ème édition, Imprimerie Theodore, Port-au-Prince, n.d.

PRICE-MARS, Dr. JEAN, *La République d'Haïti et la République Dominicaine*, 2 vols., Collection du Tricinquantenaire de l'Indépendance d'Haïti, Port-au-Prince, 1953.

ROTBERG, ROBERT I., with Christopher K. Clague, *Haiti, the Politics of Squalor*, Twentieth Century Fund Study, Houghton Mifflin Co., Boston, 1971.

SCHARON, FAINE, *Toussaint Louverture et la Révolution de St. Domingue*, Imprimerie de l'Etat, Port-au-Prince, 1957, 2 vols.

WOOD, HAROLD A., *Northern Haiti*, University of Toronto Press, 1963.

(b) *Articles*

BALL, IAN, "Exquisite cruelty of Papa Doc's dictatorship", *The Daily Telegraph*, London, April 23, 1971.

BRADSHAW, JON, "Haiti: A Black Comedy", *The Daily Telegraph*, London, June 13, 20, 1969.

453

BUELL, RAYMOND LESLIE, "The American Occupation of Haiti", *Foreign Policy Association Information Service*, Vol. V, Nos. 19-20, Foreign Policy Association, New York, n.d.

COLLIER, BARNARD L., "François Ièr of Haiti? Duvalier mulls over idea", *The New York Herald Tribune*, New York, March 11, 1965.

CORLEY SMITH, G. T. "The grim chronicle of Papa Doc's rule in Haiti", *The Times*, London, March 26, 1970.

CORY, M.-I., "Le Vatican a signé un accord avec Duvalier", *Journal de Genève*, Geneva, September 5, 1966.

CRASSWELLER, ROBERT D., "Darkness in Haiti", *Foreign Affairs*, Council on Foreign Relations, New York, January 1971.

"Diminishing returns from extortion", *The Financial Times*, London, May 29, 1968.

"Dr. Duvalier as Emperor of Haiti?", Latin America correspondent, *The Times*, London, March 12, 1965.

DRUMMOND, ROSCOE, *The New York Herald Tribune*, New York, May 3, 1963.

EDER, RICHARD, "U.S. Said to Lose Prestige in Haiti", *The New York Times*, New York, December 6, 1964.

EDER, RICHARD, "Haitian Mysteries", *The New York Times*, New York, December 5, 1964.

EDER, RICHARD, "Haiti—Land of the big 'Tontons'", *The New York Times Magazine*, New York, January 24, 1965.

EVANS, CHRIS, "Se Crea Problema en Nassau por el Exodo de Haitianos", *Diario Las Américas*, Miami, August 7, 1963.

GINIGER, HENRY, "Duvalier—a Lion at Bay in a Political Jungle", *The New York Times*, New York, August 13, 1967.

GOLD, HERBERT, "Haiti, Land of Voodoo and Papa Doc's Bogeymen", *The Daily Telegraph*, London, June 11, 1965.

GREENE, GRAHAM, "Nightmare Republic", *The Sunday Telegraph*, London, September 29, 1963.

GROSSBERG, LYNN, "President Duvalier Stands on the Record", *The Haiti Sun*, Port-au-Prince, February 15, 1959.

HOAGLAND, JIM, "Haiti: Papa Doc's Heir—Chaos", *The International Herald Tribune*, Paris, June 9, 1969.

HOLDEN, DAVID, "Bogymen of Port-au-Prince", *The Guardian*, London, April 26, 1962.

HUXLEY, FRANCIS, "Haiti's Search for a Social Order", *The Times*, London, May 1, 1963.

J.-L. P., "Haiti: Une décolonisation manquée", *Journal de Genève*, Geneva, July 3, 1967.

JOHANSSON, BERTRAM B., "Haiti Rumbles", *The Christian Science Monitor*, Boston, Mass., April 30, 1963.

JULIEN, CLAUDE, "Haiti ou la dictature pour rien", *Le Monde*, Paris, August 7, 1964.

KREBS, ALBIN, "Haiti's Duvalier: Medicine, Voodoo, Dictatorship", *International Herald Tribune*, Paris, April 23, 1971.

"La responsabilité de l'institut de développement", *Panorama*, Port-au-Prince, July 16, 1962.

LATORTUE, GERARD R., "Haiti et les institutions économiques Caraïbéenes",

Caribbean Studies, Vol. 10, No. 3, Institute of Caribbean Studies, University of Puerto Rico, October 1970.

"Le régime haïtien devant l'orage", *Le Monde*, Paris, August 24, 1963.

Lettre d'Haiti, A. R., "Sous la dictature de M. Duvalier, la république noire des Caraïbes s'enfonce dans l'anarchie", *Le Monde*, Paris, May 26/27, 1963.

LEWIS, NORMAN, "Haiti—The Caribbean Africa", *The Sunday Times*, London, February 16, 1958.

LUBIN, MAURICE A., "Où en sommes-nous avec l'élite intellectuelle d'Haïti", *Journal of Inter-American Studies*, University of Florida, Gainesville, January 1961.

MASSOCK, RICHARD, "An explosion is building up under Haiti's dictator", *The Times*, San Mateo, California, March 8, 1963.

NICHOLLS, DAVID G., "Embryo-Politics in Haiti", *Government and Opposition*, A Journal of Comparative Politics, Vol. 6, No. 1, London School of Economics, London, Winter 1971.

NIEDERGANG, MARCEL, "Haiti continue de connaître la terreur et l'arbitraire", *Le Monde*, Paris, January 23, 1965.

NIEDERGANG, MARCEL, "La Mort de l'Ubu Noir", *Le Monde*, Paris, April 24, 1971.

O'SHAUGHNESSY, HUGH, "Haitian Exports: The unknown goods", *The Financial Times*, London, October 19, 1970.

O'SHAUGHNESSY, HUGH, "Papa Doc leaves a legacy of violence", *The Financial Times*, London, April 23, 1971.

"Papa Doc rides out the storm", *The Financial Times*, London, June 30, 1967.

RANDAL, JONATHAN, "Duvalier Retains Tight Grip in Haiti", *The New York Times*, New York, May 9, 1966.

RAYMONT, HENRY, "U.S. Quietly Seeks Better Haiti Ties", *The New York Times*, New York, May 24, 1964.

ROPER, CHRISTOPHER, "The day that Guede got Doc", *The Guardian*, London, April 23, 1971.

SCOTT, IAN, "Haiti refugees a big social problem", *The Financial Times*, London, April 1, 1969.

SZULC, TAD, "Beautiful, Cruel, Explosive—Haiti", *The New York Times Magazine*, New York, June 9, 1963.

SZULC, TAD, "O.A.S. Unit to urge rights for Haitians as a key to peace in Americas", *The New York Times*, New York, June 10, 1963.

UCHITELLE, LOUIS, "Haiti: Land where chaos reigns", *The Latin American Times*, New York, September 13, 1965.

"Une Crise Permanente", *Le Monde*, Paris, September 25, 1963.

WELCH, COLIN, "The Waste that is Haiti", *The Daily Telegraph*, London, May 27, 1963.

DOMINICAN REPUBLIC

SOURCES

(a) *Documents*

Background Information Relating to the Dominican Republic, Committee on Foreign Relations, United States Senate, U.S. Government Printing Office, Washington, D.C., 1965.

455

Basic Data on the Economy of the Dominican Republic, Overseas Business Reports, U.S. Department of Commerce, Washington, D.C., June 1964.

(b) *Newspapers, Periodicals and Year Books*
El Caribe, Santo Domingo.
Listín Diario, Santo Domingo.

STUDIES

(a) *Books and Pamphlets*

BOSCH, JUAN, *The Unfinished Experiment*, The Pall Mall Press, London, 1966.
BOSCH, JUAN, *Trujillo: Causas de una Dictadura sin Ejemplo*, Populibros Peruanos, Lima, n.d.
CRASSWELLER, ROBERT D., *Trujillo: The Life and Times of a Caribbean Dictator*, The Macmillan Company, New York, 1966.
DE GALÍNDEZ, JESÚS, *La Era de Trujillo*, Editorial del Pacífico, S.A., Santiago, Chile, 1956.
MARTIN, JOHN BARTLOW, *Overtaken by Events*, Doubleday & Company, Inc., Garden City, New York, 1966.
ORNES, GERMÁN E., *Trujillo: Little Caesar of the Caribbean*, Thomas Nelson & Sons, New York, 1958.
RODMAN, SELDEN, *Quisqueya: A History of the Dominican Republic*, University of Washington Press, Seattle, 1964.
SLATER, JEROME, *Intervention and Negotiation: the United States and the Dominican Revolution*, Harper and Row, New York, 1970.
SZULC, TAD, *Dominican Diary*, Delacorte Press, New York, 1965.
WIARDA, HOWARD J., *The Dominican Republic, Nation in Transition*, Pall Mall Press, London, 1969.

(b) *Articles*

ASCOLI, MAX, "Hispaniola", *The Reporter*, New York, July 15, 1965.
BERESFORD, JO, "The legacy of violence", *The Financial Times*, London, July 9, 1971.
BOHAN, R. T., "The Dominican Case: Unilateral Intervention", *The American Journal of International Law*, Vol. 60, No. 4, Washington, D.C., October 1966, p. 810.
BONAFEDE, DOM, "Freedom after Trujillo: The Dominican Elections", *The Nation*, New York, January 12, 1963.
BOSCH, JUAN, "Two Roads for America: Constitutionalism or Occupation", *Los Angeles Times*, Los Angeles, California, June 13, 1965.
BOSCH, JUAN, "Why I was Overthrown", *The New Leader*, New York, October 14, 1963.
BOURNE, RICHARD, "Dominican Consequences", *The Guardian*, London, July 6, 1965.
CLOS, MAX, "The Four Musketeers of the Dominican Revolution", *The Guardian*, London, June 8, 1965.
CLOS, MAX, "Santo Domingo's Activist Adventurers", *The Reporter*, New York, June 17, 1965.

CONNELL-SMITH, GORDON, "The O.A.S. and the Dominican Crisis", *The World Today*, The Royal Institute of International Affairs, London, June 1965.

DE LA SOUCHERE, ELENA, "La campagne pour l'élection présidentielle se déroule dans un climat d'extrême tension", *Le Monde Diplomatique*, Paris, May 1970.

"Dominican Crisis: Help from the O.A.S.", *Newsweek*, Dayton, Ohio, May 17, 1965.

DRAPER, THEODORE, "Bosch y el Comunismo", *Cuadernos*, Paris, January 1964.

DRAPER, THEODORE, "Los Origenes de la Crisis Dominicana", Supplement, *Cuadernos*, Paris, n.d.

DRAPER, THEODORE, "The Dominican Crisis, A Case Study in American Policy", *Commentary*, Vol. 40, No. 6, American Jewish Committee, New York, December 1965.

EVANS, ROWLAND, and ROBERT NOVAK, "The Dominican Headache", *The New York Herald Tribune*, New York, March 1, 1966.

FERGUSON, J. HALCRO, "How LBJ united his friends against him", *The Observer*, London, May 9, 1965.

FIELD, MICHAEL, "Five years after the Marines went in", *The Daily Telegraph*, London, April 21, 1970.

GALL, NORMAN, "Ferment in the Caribbean", *The New Leader*, New York, June 10, 1963.

GALLUP, GEORGE, "U.S. Majority favors Policy in Santo Domingo", *The New York Herald Tribune*, New York, June 2, 1965.

GARDINER, C. HARVEY, "The Japanese and the Dominican Republic", *Inter-American Economic Affairs*, Vol. 25, No. 3, Washington, Winter 1971.

HENNESSY, ALISTAIR, "Background to the Dominican Coup", *The World Today*, The Royal Institute of International Affairs, London, June 1965.

LIPPMANN, WALTER, "Solidarity of the Americas", *The New York Herald Tribune*, New York, May 7, 1965.

LOWENTHAL, ABRAHAM F., "The United States and the Dominican Republic to 1965: Background to Intervention", *Caribbean Studies*, Vol. 10, No. 2, Instituto de Estudios del Caribe, Universidad de Puerto Rico, July 1970.

MAS, FERNANDO, "En la Dominicana, la mecha sigue encendida", *Visión*, Mexico City, September 26, 1969.

MATTHEWS, HERBERT L., "Santo Domingo and 'Non-intervention' ", *The New York Times*, New York, May 10, 1965.

MEEKER, LEONARD C., "The Dominican Situation in the Perspective of International Law", *Department of State Bulletin*, Washington, D.C., July 12, 1965.

MONTGOMERY, PAUL L., "U.S. Vastly Expands Embassy in Santo Domingo", *The New York Times*, New York, June 19, 1966.

NIEDERGANG, MARCEL, "Et demain Cuba?", *Le Monde*, Paris, May 4, 1965.

NIEDERGANG, MARCEL, "Saint-Domingue ou l'illusion lyrique . . .", *Le Monde*, Paris, June 3, 4, 6/7, 8 and 9, 1965.

NIZARD, LUCIEN, "O.N.U., si ! O.E.A., no!", *Le Monde*, Paris, May 27, 1965.

PREWETT, VIRGINIA, "Hemisphere Searchlight", *The Latin American Times*, New York, July 7, 1965.

PULLEY, RAYMOND H., "The United States and the Trujillo Dictatorship 1933-1940: the High Price of Caribbean Stability", *Caribbean Studies*,

Vol. 5, No. 3, Institute of Caribbean Studies, University of Puerto Rico, Río Piedras, October 1965.

"Recipe for renewed violence", *The Financial Times*, London, May 15, 1970.

RETTIE, JOHN, "Bosch Essential to any Solution", *The Guardian*, London, May 7, 1965.

RETTIE, JOHN, "A Hungary in the Caribbean?", *New Statesman*, London, May 7, 1965.

RODMAN, SELDEN, "A Close View of Santo Domingo", *The Reporter*, New York, July 15, 1965.

"Santo Domingo: The Voice of Rifles", *Tricontinental*, Havana, March/April 1970.

SCHUMACH, MURRAY, "Dominican Rebels said to hide arms", *The New York Times*, New York, July 5, 1965.

" 'Statu Quo' et terreur à Saint-Domingue", *Le Monde*, Paris, May 19, 1970.

WELLS, HENRY, "The O.A.S. and the Dominican Elections", *Orbis*, Vol. III, No. 1, Foreign Policy Research Institute, University of Pennsylvania, Spring 1963.

WIARDA, HOWARD J., "The Development of Labor Movement in the Dominican Republic", *Inter-American Economic Affairs*, Vol. XX, No. 1, Washington, D.C., Summer 1966.

WIARDA, HOWARD J., "Trujilloism without Trujillo", *The New Republic*, Washington, D.C., September 19, 1964.

PUERTO RICO AND THE VIRGIN ISLANDS OF THE UNITED STATES

SOURCES

(a) *Documents*

Annual Report, 1970, Government Development Bank for Puerto Rico, n.d.

A Summary in Facts & Figures 1964/1965, Migration Division, Department of Labor, Commonwealth of Puerto Rico, New York.

Annual Report 1964-65, Department of Health, Commonwealth of Puerto Rico.

Economic Development Administration, Office of Economic Research, San Juan, Puerto Rico.

Electric Revenue Bonds (Series 1971), Puerto Rico Water Resources Authority, December 1970.

Final Report of the United States—Puerto Rico Status Commission, August, 1966, Stacom Supplement, *The San Juan Star*, Puerto Rico, August 6, 1966.

Informe Anual, 1963-64, Departamento de Agricultura, San Juan, P.R.

Informe Anual, 1965-1966, Administración de Terrenos de Puerto Rico, Santurce, Puerto Rico.

Monthly Economic Report: Virgin Islands, First National City Bank, New York, September 1970.

Puerto Rico, International Economic Survey, Chemical Bank International Division, New York, June 1970.

Selected Indices of Social and Economic Progress: Fiscal Years 1939-40, 1947-48 to 1964-65, Bureau of Economic and Social Analysis, Puerto Rico Planning Board, n.d.

Speech by Roberto Sánchez Vilella at inauguration, Puerto Rico, January 2, 1965.

Speech by Roberto Sánchez Vilella to first session of the 5th Legislative Assembly, San Juan, Puerto Rico, January 29, 1965.

Speech by Roberto Sánchez Vilella to the House of Representatives, San Juan, Puerto Rico, February 2, 1966.

STEAD, WILLIAM H., *Fomento—The Economic Development of Puerto Rico*, National Planning Association, Washington, D.C., 1958.

Virgin Islands 1970 Annual Report to the Secretary of the Interior, U.S. Government Printing Office, Washington, D.C.

World Business—14—Country Reports: Puerto Rico, January 1969.

(b) *Newspapers, Periodicals and Year Books*

El Mundo, San Juan.

Progress in Puerto Rico, Banco Popular de Puerto Rico, Hato Rey.

Revista de Ciencias Sociales, University of Puerto Rico, Río Piedras.

The Daily News, St. Thomas.

The Home Journal, St. Thomas.

The San Juan Star, San Juan.

STUDIES

(a) *Books and Pamphlets*

AITKEN, THOMAS, Jr., *Luis Muñoz Marín, Poet in the Fortress*, The New American Library of Canada, Toronto, 1965.

ANDERSON, ROBERT W., *Party Politics in Puerto Rico*, Stanford University Press, Stanford, 1965.

BABIN, MARÍA TERESA, *Panorama de la Cultura Puertorriqueña*, Las Américas Publishing Co., New York, 1958.

CLARK, VICTOR S., and Associates, *Porto Rico and its Problems*, Brookings Institution, Washington, D.C., 1930.

COCHRAN, THOMAS C., *The Puerto Rican Businessman*, University of Pennsylvania Press, Philadelphia, 1959.

CREQUE, DARWIN D., *The U.S. Virgins and the Eastern Caribbean*, Whitmore Publishing Co., Philadelphia, 1968.

D'ESTEFANO, MIGUEL A., *Puerto Rico: analysis of a plebiscite*, Tricontinental, La Habana, 1968.

EASTMAN, SAMUEL EWER, and DANIEL MARK, Jr., *Ships and Sugar: An Evaluation of Puerto Rican Offshore Shipping*, University of Puerto Rico Press, Río Piedras, Puerto Rico, 1953.

GALBRAITH, JOHN KENNETH, and RICHARD H. HOLTON (and others), *Marketing Efficiency in Puerto Rico*, Harvard University Press, Cambridge, Mass., 1955.

GRUBER, RUTH, *Puerto Rico, Island of Promise*, Hill and Wang, New York, 1960.

459

HANCOCK, RALPH, *Puerto Rico, a success story*, D. Van Nostrand Company, Inc., Princeton, N.J., 1960.

HANSON, EARL PARKER, *Transformation: The Story of Modern Puerto Rico*, Simon and Schuster, New York, 1955.

HENLE, FRITZ, *Virgin Islands*, Hastings House, New York, 1949.

LEWIS, GORDON, K., *Puerto Rico, Freedom and Power in the Caribbean*, Monthly Review Press, New York, 1963.

LEWIS, OSCAR, *La Vida*, Random House, New York, 1965.

LLORENS, WASHINGTON, *El Español de Puerto Rico*, Editorial Club de la Prensa, San Juan, Puerto Rico, 1957.

MACCOBY, ELEANOR E., and FRANCES FIELDER, *Saving among Upper-income Families in Puerto Rico*, University of Puerto Rico, Río Piedras, Puerto Rico, 1953.

MORALES-CARRIÓN, ARTURO, *Puerto Rico and the Non-Hispanic Caribbean*, University of Puerto Rico Press, Río Piedras, Puerto Rico, 1952.

MYERS, GEORGE C., *Migration and Modernization: The Case of Puerto Rico, 1950-60*, United Nations World Population Conference, Belgrade, Yugoslavia, August 30 to September 10, 1965.

PEDREIRA, ANTONIO S., *Insularismo*, Biblioteca de Autores Puertorriqueños, San Juan, Puerto Rico, 1957.

PERLOFF, HARVEY S., *Puerto Rico's Economic Future*, The University of Chicago Press, Chicago, Ill., 1950.

PICÓ, RAFAEL, *The Geographic Regions of Puerto Rico*, University of Puerto Rico Press, Río Piedras, Puerto Rico, 1950.

THORNE, ALFRED P., *The Caribbean in Transition*, "Foreign Sector Lessons of the Puerto Rican Development Experience", edited by F. M. Andic and T. G. Mathews, Institute of Caribbean Studies, University of Puerto Rico, 1965.

TÍO, AURELIO, *Fundación de San Germán*, Biblioteca de Autores Puertorriqueños, San Juan, Puerto Rico, 1956.

TUGWELL, REXFORD, *Art of Politics*, Doubleday & Co., Toronto, 1958.

VIVAS, JOSÉ LUIS, *Historia de Puerto Rico*, Las Américas Publishing Co., New York, 1960.

WAGENHEIM, KAL, *Puerto Rico, A Profile*, Pall Mall Country Profile Series, Pall Mall Press, London, 1971.

WELLS, HENRY, *The Modernisation of Puerto Rico, A Political Study of Changing Values and Institutions*, Harvard University Press, Cambridge, Mass, 1969.

(b) *Articles*

"Bargains in the Sun", *Time*, New York, April 7, 1967.

BILL, AL., "St. Croix and St. Thomas . . . Squabbling Sisters?", *The Home Journal*, St. Thomas, June 6, 1971.

"Church softens population stand", *People*, Population Reference Bureau, Inc., Washington, Vol. 1., No. 1, May 1970.

CROCKER, JOHN, "Puerto Rico's future in balance", *The Scotsman*, Edinburgh, June 5, 1965.

CURTIS, THOMAS D., "Employment and Land Reform in a Labor-Surplus Economy: A Case Study of Puerto Rico", *Land Economics*, Vol. 43, Madison, Wisconsin, November 1967.

"Ferré Sees Labor OK for Wage Exemptions", *The San Juan Star*, San Juan, June 8, 1971.

FRYE, WILLIAM R., "Operation Bootstrap Suffers From Some Foot-Dragging", *The Hartford Courant*, Hartford, Connecticut, March 5, 1967.

GINIGER, HENRY, "Puerto Rico Vote Will Split 3 Ways", *The New York Times*, New York, March 20, 1967.

GRUBER, RUTH, "Puerto Rico Oils its Economy", *The New York Herald Tribune* (European Edition), Paris, August 25, 1965.

HARMAN, JEANNE P., "Businessman-Governor Spurs Commerce in the Virgin Islands", *The New York Times*, New York, January 6, 1964.

KONSTANT, Ed., "Badillo Hits House OK of Sugar Slash", *The San Juan Star*, June 11, 1971.

LEWIS, GORDON K., "An introductory note to the study of the Virgin Islands", *Caribbean Studies*, Vol. 8, No. 2, Institute of Caribbean Studies, University of Puerto Rico, July 1968.

LEWIS, OSCAR, "The Culture of Poverty", *Scientific American*, Vol. 215, No. 4, New York, October 1966.

LUKAS, J. ANTHONY, "We have been encroached on, invaded, engulfed", *The New York Times Magazine*, New York, April 18, 1971.

MALDONADO, A. W., "The Puerto Rican Tide Begins to Turn", *The New York Times Magazine*, New York, September 20, 1964.

MALDONADO, A. W., "Status Commissions", *The San Juan Star*, San Juan, Puerto Rico, February 25, 1964.

MALDONADO, A. W., "Commonwealth and Congress", *The San Juan Star*, San Juan, Puerto Rico, August 24, 1963.

MALDONADO, A. W., "Muñoz and the Church", *The San Juan Star*, San Juan, Puerto Rico, April 23, 1964.

MALDONADO, A. W., "Population Explosion", *The San Juan Star*, San Juan, Puerto Rico, February 5, 1964.

MALDONADO DENIS, MANUEL, "Efectos de la Revolución Cubana en la Política Puertorriqueña", *Revista de Ciencias Sociales*, Vol. VIII, No. 3, University of Puerto Rico, Río Piedras, Puerto Rico, September 1964.

MARQUÉS, RENÉ, "El Puertorriqueño dócil", *Cuadernos Americanos*, CXX, Mexico, 1962.

MATHEWS, THOMAS G., "La Próxima Década en la Política Puertorriqueña", *Revista de Ciencias Sociales*, Vol. IX, No. 3, University of Puerto Rico, Río Piedras, Puerto Rico, September 1965.

MERCADO, JOAQUÍN O., "Revela demanda empleos aumenta 23,300 por año", *El Mundo*, San Juan, Puerto Rico, January 17, 1964.

OBER, RALPH, "Island Trade Deficit Grows Serious", *The San Juan Star*, San Juan, May 31, 1971.

OLDMAN, OLIVER and MILTON TAYLOR, "Tax Incentives for Economic Growth in the U.S. Virgin Islands", *Caribbean Studies*, Vol. 10, No. 3, Institute of Caribbean Studies, University of Puerto Rico, Río Piedras, October 1970.

PICÓ, RAFAEL, "Growing with Tight Money", *Progress in Puerto Rico*, Vol. II, 4, Banco Popular de Puerto Rico, Hato Rey, 1966.

"Puerto Rico: colony in revolution", *Tricontinental Bulletin*, 48, Havana, March 1970.

RAMOS, FRANK, "Collision Course", *San Juan Star*, San Juan, June 13, 1971.

461

ROSENN, KEITH S., "Puerto Rican Land Reform: The History of an Instructive Experiment", *The Yale Law Journal*, New Haven, Conn., December 1963.

SÁNCHEZ VILELLA, Governor ROBERTO, "Puerto Rico's Growth in Fiscal 1967 to Approach 11%", *American Banker*, New York, February 3, 1967.

"Should the Island Join the States?", Special Correspondent, San Juan, *The Financial Times*, London, November 9, 1965.

STONE, LEROY O., "Population Redistribution and Economic Development in Puerto Rico, 1950-1960", *Social and Economic Studies*, Vol. 14, No. 3, Institute of Social and Economic Research, University of the West Indies, Jamaica, September 1965.

"Tourism—Clouds over Puerto Rico", *Time*, New York, May 24, 1971.

"Two bright spots in the troubled Caribbean", *U.S. News and World Report*, Washington, March 15, 1971.

UNGER, HARLOW, "Why Puerto Rico's Bootstrap is all hung up", *The Sunday Times*, London, June 15, 1969.

WALKER, RONALD, "St. Thomas has its eye on Jet Airport", *The New York Times*, New York, October 25, 1964.

WELLS, HENRY, "Puerto Rico's Association with the United States", *Caribbean Studies*, Vol. V, No. 1, Institute of Caribbean Studies, University of Puerto Rico, April 1965.

WICKER, TOM, "In the Nation: 'Estadidad Jibara' in the Caribbean", *The New York Times*, New York, April 28, 1970.

COMMONWEALTH TERRITORIES

SOURCES

(a) *Documents*

Agreement Establishing the Caribbean Free Trade Association, Government Printery, Trinidad, 1968.

Anguilla Act 1971, H.M.S.O., London, 1971

Antigua, Report for the years 1959 and *1960*, H.M.S.O., London, 1963.

Antigua, Report for the years 1961 and *1962*, H.M.S.O., London, 1964.

Antigua Sugar Industry, Interim Report—July/August 1966, British Ministry of Overseas Development, London, August 1966.

Associated States, The Dominica Constitution Order 1967, No. 226, H.M.S.O., London, 1967.

Associated States, The Grenada Constitution Order 1967, No. 227, H.M.S.O., London, 1967.

Associated States, The Saint Christopher, Nevis and Anguilla Constitution Order 1967, No. 228, H.M.S.O., London, 1967.

Associated States, The Saint Lucia Constitution Order 1967, No. 229, H.M.S.O., London, 1967.

Associated States, The West Indies Associated States Supreme Court Order 1967, No. 223, H.M.S.O., London, 1967.

A Teacher's Guide to Jamaica, Ministry of Education, Kingston, Jamaica, 1970.

Barbados, Reference Pamphlet 74, Central Office of Information, H.M.S.O., London, 1966.

Barbados Development Plan 1965-68, Government Printing Office, Barbados, n.d.

Barbados Development Plan 1962-1972, Barbados Government Printing Office, St. Michael, Barbados, n.d.

Barbados Independence Act 1966, H.M.S.O., London, 1966.

Barbados, Report for the years 1962 and 1963, Government Printing Office, Barbados, 1965.

Britain and Education in the Commonwealth, Reference Pamphlet 66, Central Office of Information, H.M.S.O., London, 1964.

British Guiana, An Economic Survey, Barclays Bank, D.C.O., London, April 1965.

British Guiana Conference 1963, Cmnd. 2203, London, 1963.

British Guiana Constitutional Commission, 1950-51, *Report and Despatch from Secretary of State of the Colonies, 6th October 1951*, Colonial No. 280, H.M.S.O., London, 1951.

British Guiana (Guyana) Development Programme (1966-1972), The Government Printery, Guyana, 1966.

British Guiana, Report by the Commonwealth Team of Observers on the Election in December 1964, Colonial No. 359, London, 1965.

British Honduras, Report for the years 1962 and 1963, H.M.S.O., London, 1965.

British Virgin Islands, Report for the years 1963 and 1964, H.M.S.O., London, 1966.

British Virgin Islands, Report of the Constitutional Commissioner 1965, Colonial No. 361, London, 1965.

Caribbean and North Atlantic Territories, The Bahama Islands (Constitution) Order in Council, 1963, No. 2084, H.M.S.O., London, 1964.

Caribbean and North Atlantic Territories, The Bahama Islands (Constitution) Order 1969, No. 590, H.M.S.O., London, 1969.

Caribbean and North Atlantic Territories, The Guyana Independence Order 1966, No. 575, H.M.S.O., London, 1966.

Caribbean and North Atlantic Territories, The Jamaica (Constitution) Order in Council, 1962, No. 1550, H.M.S.O., London, 1962.

Caribbean and North Atlantic Territories, The Montserrat Order 1967, No. 230, H.M.S.O., London, 1967.

Caribbean and North Atlantic Territories, The Saint Vincent Electoral Provisions Order 1969, No. 1064, H.M.S.O., London, 1969.

Caribbean and North Atlantic Territories, The Trinidad and Tobago (Constitution) Order in Council, 1962, No. 1875, H.M.S.O., London, 1962.

Caribbean and North Atlantic Territories, The Virgin Islands (Constitution) Order 1967, No. 471, H.M.S.O., London, 1967.

Caribbean Free Trade Association Ordinance, 1971, May 26, 1971.

Carifta and the New Caribbean, Commonwealth Caribbean Regional Secretariat, Georgetown, Guyana 1971.

Cayman Islands, an Economic Survey, Barclays D.C.O., London, March, 1971.

Cayman Islands, Despatch from the Secretary of State, Foreign and Commonwealth Office, on Proposals for Constitutional Advance, Foreign and Commonwealth Office, H.M.S.O., London, 1971.

Cayman Islands, Proposals for Constitutional Advance, Report by the Constitutional Commissioner, the Rt. Hon. the Earl of Oxford and Asquith, K.C.M.G., Foreign and Commonwealth Office, H.M.S.O., London, 1971.

Cayman Islands, Report for the years 1961 to 1965, H.M.S.O., London, 1967.
Colonial Development Corporation Report and Accounts, 1952, 1953, 1958, 1961, 1962, H.M.S.O., London.
Commonwealth Development and its financing, No. 8, Jamaica, H.M.S.O., London, 1964.
Commonwealth Development Corporation, Caribbean Region, 1969, 1970, Commonwealth Development Corporation, London.
Commonwealth Development Corporation Report and Accounts, 1964, 1965, 1969, 1970, H.M.S.O., London.
Commonwealth Development Corporation, Partners in Development 1970, C.D.C., London.
Commonwealth Immigrants Act, 1962, H.M.S.O., London, 1962.
Constitutional Proposals for Antigua, St. Kitts-Nevis-Anguilla, Dominica, St. Lucia, St. Vincent, Grenada, Cmnd. 2865, London, 1965.
Consultations with the Developing Member Countries of the Commonwealth Sugar Agreement 2-3 June 1971: Communiqué, Foreign and Commonwealth Office, June 3, 1971.
Development Strategy for the next decade, A submission made to the Meeting of Commonwealth Finance Ministers in Barbados on September 26, 1969, by Hon. Edward Seaga, M.P., Minister of Finance and Planning.
Dominica, Report for the years 1961 and 1962, H.M.S.O., London, 1965.
Dominica, Report for the years 1963, 1964 and 1965, H.M.S.O., London, 1967.
DOWNIE, J., *An Economic Policy for British Honduras*, Belize, British Honduras, 1959.
DOXEY, GEORGE V., *Survey of the Jamaican Economy*, Commissioned by the Jamaica Chamber of Commerce, Kingston, 1969.
Draft Second Five-Year Plan 1964-1968, Government of Trinidad and Tobago, National Planning Commission, Trinidad, 1963.
Draft Third Five-Year Plan 1969-1973, Government of Trinidad and Tobago, Government Printer, Trinidad and Tobago, 1968.
Draft Treaty between Great Britain and Guatemala relating to the Resolution of the Dispute over British Honduras (Belize), Submitted by the Mediator on 26th April 1968.
Economic Survey and Projections: Turks and Caicos, British Development Division in the Caribbean, Ministry of Overseas Development, November 1969.
Economic Survey, Jamaica 1969, Central Planning Unit, Government Printer, Kingston, 1970.
Federation of East Caribbean Territories, Report of the Fiscal Commissioner, Cmnd. 1991, London, 1963.
Final Communiqué, Commonwealth Caribbean-Canada Conference, Ottawa, July 6-8, 1966.
Five-Year Independence Plan, 1963-1968, Central Planning Unit, Ministry of Development and Welfare, Jamaica, July 1963.
Grenada, Report for the years 1963 and 1964, H.M.S.O., London, 1966.
Guyana, an Economic Survey, Barclays Bank D.C.O., London, 1969.
Guyana, Reference Pamphlet 71, Central Office of Information, Reference Division, H.M.S.O., London, 1966.

464

Instructions to Immigration Officers, Cmnd. 1716, London, 1962.
JACOBS, K. C., C.B.E., *British Guiana Report on the Financial Position, August 1963*, Colonial No. 358, London, 1964.
Jamaica (Banana Trade), *Hansard*, Vol. 812, No. 93, Cols. 1182-1192, February 26, 1971.
Jamaica Election Factbook, Operations and Policy Research, Inc., Washington, D.C., February 1967.
Jamaica Today, A Brief Survey, Jamaica Information Service, Jamaica, n.d.
Jamaica, Trinidad and Tobago, Leeward Islands, Windward Islands, Barbados and British Guiana, Projected Levels of Demand, Supply, and Imports of Agricultural Products, to 1975. Foreign Relations Analysis Division, Economic Research Service, U.S. Department of Agriculture, E.R.S. Foreign 94, Washington, D.C., n.d.
Joint Statement issued on Wednesday 21 May after the conclusion of the talks between the Foreign and Commonwealth Secretary and the Premier of St. Kitts-Nevis-Anguilla, Verbatim Service 124/69, London Press Service, May 22, 1969.
Memorandum on Statutory Boards, Farquharson Institute of Public Affairs, Jamaica, July 1965.
Monthly Visitor Report, Bahamas Ministry of Tourism, December 1970.
Montserrat Development Plan 1966-1970, Advocate Commercial Printer, Plymouth, 1966.
Montserrat, Report for the years 1961 and 1962, H.M.S.O., London, 1964.
Montserrat, Report for the years 1965 and 1966, H.M.S.O., London, 1968.
"New Status of Association with Britain for Six Eastern Caribbean Islands", Colonial Office, Information Department, May 26, 1966.
1969 Bahama Islands Visitor Statistics, Ministry of Tourism, Nassau, n.d.
Official Gazette Bahamas, Supplement Part 1, No. 4 of 1970, Nassau, March 16, 1970.
O'LOUGHLIN, Dr. CARLEEN, *A Survey of Economic Potential and Capital Needs of the Leeward Islands, Windward Islands and Barbados*, Department of Technical Cooperation, H.M.S.O., London, 1963.
Progress Report to January 1967, The Grand Bahama Port Authority, Ltd., Grand Bahama Island, n.d.
Property and Tourist Development in the Turks and Caicos Islands (Sir Derek Jakeway), Foreign and Commonwealth Office, London, March 1970.
Proposals for a Federation of East Caribbean Territories, Colonial No. 360, London, 1965.
Protocol between the Government of the United Kingdom of Great Britain and Northern Ireland, the Government of Guyana and the Government of Venezuela relative to the Agreement to resolve the Controversy over the Frontier between Venezuela and British Guiana, signed at Geneva on 17 February 1966, Port of Spain, 18 June 1970, Treaty Series No. 75 (1970) Cmnd. 4446, H.M.S.O., London, 1970.
Report from the Prime Minister of Trinidad and Tobago on his good offices Mission, to the Premier of British Guiana, June 12, 1964.
Report of a Commission of Inquiry into Disturbances in British Guiana in February 1962, Colonial No. 354, London, 1962.
Report of Royal Commission appointed 1938 (Moyne Report), Cmd. 6607, London, 1945.

Report of the Antigua Constitutional Conference 1966, Cmnd. 2963, London, 1966.

Report of the Bahamas Constitutional Conference 1968, Cmnd. 3792, H.M.S.O., London, 1968.

Report of the Barbados Constitutional Conference 1966, Cmnd. 3058, London, 1966.

Report of the British Guiana Commission, April, 1927, Cmd. 2841, London, 1927.

Report of the British Guiana Commission of Inquiry, "Racial Problems in the Public Service", International Commission of Jurists, Geneva, 1965.

Report of the British Guiana Independence Conference 1965, Cmnd. 2849, London, 1965.

Report of the British Honduras Constitutional Conference, Cmnd. 2124, London, 1963.

Report of the Commission of Enquiry appointed by the Governments of the United Kingdom and St. Christopher-Nevis-Anguilla to examine the Anguilla Problem, Miscellaneous No. 23 (1970), Cmnd. 4510, H.M.S.O., London, 1970.

Report of the Commission of Enquiry into the Control of Public Expenditure in Grenada during 1961 and subsequently, Cmnd. 1735, London, May 1962.

Report of the Commission of Enquiry into the Operation of the Business of Casinos in Freeport and Nassau, H.M.S.O., London, 1967.

Report of the Commission of Enquiry on the Sugar Industry of Jamaica, January 1960, Goldenberg, H. Carl, O.B.E., Q.C., Chairman, Jamaica, 1960.

Report of the Royal Commission appointed to inquire into the public revenues, expenditures, debts, and liabilities of the Islands of Jamaica, Grenada, St. Vincent, Tobago and St. Lucia, and of the Leeward Islands, 1844, C. 3840, London.

Report of the Royal Commission appointed on the Recommendation of the Bahamas Government to Review the Hawksbill Creek Agreement, Vols. 1 and 2, H.M.S.O., London, 1971.

Report of the St. Kitts-Nevis-Anguilla Constitutional Conference 1966, Cmnd. 3031, London, 1966.

Report of the Sugar Enquiry Commission (1966) Jamaica, Government Printer, Kingston, October 1967.

Report of the Tripartite Economic Survey of British Honduras, May 1966, Ministry of Overseas Development, London.

Report of the Tripartite Economic Survey of the Eastern Caribbean, January-April 1966, Ministry of Overseas Development, H.M.S.O., London, 1967.

Report of the Windward Islands Constitutional Conference 1966, Cmnd. 3021, London, 1966.

Report on Closer Association of the British West Indian Colonies, Cmd. 7120, Colonial Office, London, 1947.

Representation of the People's Act, 1968, Georgetown, 1968.

Statistical Abstract 1969, Commonwealth of the Bahamas, Department of Statistics, Nassau, Bahamas, October 1970.

St. Kitts-Nevis-Anguilla, Report for the years 1959-1962, H.M.S.O., London, 1966.

St. Lucia Five Year Development Plan 1966-1970, Development Planning and Statistics, Premier's Office, 1966.

St. Lucia, Report for the years 1961 and 1962, H.M.S.O., London, 1966.

St. Lucia, Report for the years 1963 and 1964, H.M.S.O., London 1967.
St. Vincent Development Plan 1966-1970, Government Printer, 1968.
St. Vincent, Report for the years 1962 and 1963, H.M.S.O., London, 1966.
Speech from the Throne, Nassau, June 14, 1971.
The Bahama Islands (Constitution) Order 1969, No. 590, H.M.S.O., London, 1969.
The Caribbean, a survey for businessmen, Report of the London Chamber of Commerce, Trade Mission to Jamaica, Trinidad and Tobago, Guyana, and Barbados 1967, London, 1968.
The Commonwealth Caribbean and the E.E.C., A Study by the West India Committee, London, 1967.
The Commonwealth Caribbean and the E.E.C., The West India Committee, London, revised edition 1970.
The Economic Development of British Guiana: Report of a Mission organized by the International Bank for Reconstruction and Development at the request of the Government of British Guiana, Johns Hopkins Press, Baltimore, 1953.
The Economic Development of Jamaica, Report by a Mission of the International Bank for Reconstruction and Development, Johns Hopkins Press, Baltimore, 1952.
The Federal Negotiations 1962-1965 and Constitutional Proposals for Barbados, The Barbados Government Printing Office, Barbados, n.d.
The Future of Tourism in the Eastern Caribbean, H. Zinder and Associates Inc., Washington, under contract with the Agency for International Development and sponsored by the Regional Development Agency, May 1969.
The Grenada Declaration, 1971, on West Indian Political Unity, Commonwealth Caribbean Regional Secretariat, Press Release No. 46/1971, Georgetown, October 30, 1971.
The Saint Vincent Electoral Provisions Order 1969, H.M.S.O., London, August 1969.
Trinidad and Tobago: The Making of a Nation, Reference Pamphlet 53, Central Office of Information, H.M.S.O., London, 1962.
Tripartite Banana Talks, Ministry of Agriculture, Fisheries and Food, London, July 1966.
Turks and Caicos Islands, Report for the years 1961 and 1962, H.M.S.O., London, 1963.
Turks and Caicos Islands, Report for the years 1963 and 1964, H.M.S.O., London, 1966.
United Nations General Assembly, *British Guiana*, Working paper prepared by the Secretariat, April 25, 1966.
United Nations General Assembly, *Implementation of the Declaration on the Granting of Independence to Colonial Countries and Peoples: Reports of the Special Committee: British Guiana*, December 7, 1965.
Yallahs Valley Land Authority, 1951-1961, Ten Years of Progress, Jamaica, n.p., n.d.

(b) *Newspapers, Periodicals and Year Books*

Antigua Star, St. John's, Antigua.
Antigua Times, Antigua.

467

Bahamas Handbook and Businessman's Annual, Nassau, Bahamas.
Bahamas Out Island Guide, Nassau, Bahamas.
Barbados Advocate, Bridgetown, Barbados.
Booker News, Georgetown, Guyana.
Daily Argosy, Georgetown, Guyana.
Daily Chronicle, Georgetown, Guyana.
Democrat, Basseterre, St. Kitt's.
Dominica Chronicle, Roseau, Dominica.
Guyana Graphic, Georgetown, Guyana.
Handbook of Jamaica, Kingston, Jamaica.
Jamaica Times, Kingston, Jamaica.
Mercantile News, Freeport, Bahamas.
Public Opinion, Kingston, Jamaica.
Spotlight, Kingston, Jamaica.
Sunday Chronicle, Georgetown, Guyana.
Sunday Gleaner, Kingston, Jamaica.
Sunday Graphic, Georgetown, Guyana.
Sunday Guardian, Port of Spain, Trinidad.
The Advocate News, Bridgetown, Barbados.
The Belize Billboard, Belize City, British Honduras.
The Belize Times, Belize City, British Honduras.
The Daily Gleaner, Kingston, Jamaica.
The Jamaican Weekly Gleaner, Kingston, Jamaica.
The Nassau Guardian, Nassau, Bahamas.
The Nation, Port of Spain, Trinidad.
The Sunday Argosy, Georgetown, Guyana.
The West Indian Economist, Kingston, Jamaica.
Thunder, Georgetown, Guyana.
Torchlight, St. George's, Grenada.
Trinidad Guardian, Port of Spain, Trinidad.
Trinidad and Tobago Year Book, Port of Spain, Trinidad.
Vincentian, Kingstown, St. Vincent.
Voice of St. Lucia, Castries, St. Lucia.
West Indian, St. George's, Grenada.
West Indian Review, Kingston, Jamaica.
Who's Who in Jamaica, Kingston, Jamaica.

STUDIES

(a) *Books and Pamphlets*

ABRAHAMS, PETER, *Jamaica, An Island Mosaic*, H.M.S.O., London, 1957.
A Destiny to Mould, the speeches of Forbes Burnham, Longman Caribbean, London, 1970.
AYEARST, MORLEY, *The British West Indies*, George Allen & Unwin Ltd. London, 1960.
BEACHEY, R. W., *The British West Indies Sugar Industry in the late 19th Century*, Basil Blackwell, Oxford, 1957.
BELL, WENDELL, *Jamaican Leaders*, University of California Press, Berkeley and Los Angeles, 1964.
BETHEL, JEANETTE, *A National Accounts Study of the Economy of Barbados,*

Social and Economic Studies, Vol. 9, No. 2 (Special Number), Institute of Social and Economic Research, University College of the West Indies, Jamaica, June 1960.

BLACK, CLINTON V., *The Story of Jamaica*, Collins, London, 1965.

BREWSTER, HAVELOCK, *Wage-Policy Issues in an Underdeveloped Economy: Trinidad and Tobago*, Institute of Social and Economic Research, University of the West Indies, Jamaica, 1969.

BRYCE, WYATT, *et al.*, *Historic Port Royal*, Tourist Trade Development Board, Kingston, Jamaica, 1952.

BURNS, Sir ALAN, *History of the British West Indies*, George Allen & Unwin Ltd., London, 1954.

CAIGER, STEPHEN L., *British Honduras*, George Allen & Unwin Ltd., London, 1951.

CALLENDER, CHARLES VICTOR, *The Development of the Capital Market Institutions of Jamaica, Social and Economic Studies*, Supplement to Vol. 14, No. 3, Institute of Social and Economic Research, University of the West Indies, Jamaica, 1965.

CARIFTA and the Caribbean Economic Community, Government of Trinidad and Tobago, July 1968.

CARLEY, MARY MANNING, *Jamaica, The Old and the New*, Frederick A. Praeger, New York, 1963.

CARMICHAEL, GERTRUDE, *The History of the West Indian Islands of Trinidad and Tobago*, Alvin Redman, London, 1961.

CASSIDY, FREDERICK G., *Jamaica Talk*, Macmillan & Co., London, 1961.

CLARKE, S. ST. A., *The Competitive Position of Jamaica's Agricultural Exports*, Institute of Social and Economic Research, University College of the West Indies, Jamaica, 1962.

COLLART, YVES, "Regional Conflict Resolution and the Integration Process in the Commonwealth Caribbean", reprinted from *Regionalism and the Commonwealth Caribbean*, Institute of International Relations, University of the West Indies, Trinidad, n.d.

CRATON, MICHAEL, *A History of the Bahamas*, Collins, London, 1962.

CUMPER, G. E., *The Economy of the West Indies*, Institute of Social and Economic Research, University College of the West Indies, Jamaica, 1960.

CURTIN, PHILIP D., *Two Jamaicas*, Harvard University Press, Cambridge, Mass., 1955.

D'AGUIAR, PETER, *Highways to Happiness*, United Force, n.d.

DAVISON, R. B., *West Indian Migrants*, Oxford University Press, London, 1962.

EDWARDS, DAVID, *An Economic Study of Small Farming in Jamaica*, Institute of Social and Economic Research, University College of the West Indies, Jamaica, 1961.

EISNER, GISELA, *Jamaica 1830-1930*, Manchester University Press, Manchester, 1961.

EMERUWA, LINDA, *The West Indies*, Longmans, London, 1962.

FARLEY, RAWLE, ALLAN FLANDERS, and JOE ROPER, *Industrial Relations and the British Caribbean*, University of London Press, London, 1961.

GLASS, RUTH, *Newcomers, the West Indians in London*, George Allen & Unwin Ltd., London, 1960.

HALPERIN, ERNST, *Racism and Communism in British Guiana*, Massachusetts Institute of Technology, Cambridge, Mass., 1964.

HAMILTON, B. L. ST. JOHN, *Problems of Administration in an Emergent Nation,* Frederick A. Praeger, New York, 1964.

HENRIQUES, FERNANDO, *Jamaica,* MacGibbon & Kee, London, 1957.

HOYOS, F. A., *Barbados, Our Island Home,* Macmillan & Co., London, 1961.

HUGHES, MARJORIE, *The Fairest Island,* Victor Gollancz, London, 1962.

HUMPHREYS, R. A., *The Diplomatic History of British Honduras 1638-1901,* The Royal Institute of International Affairs, Oxford University Press, London, 1961.

JAGAN, Cheddi, *The West on Trial,* Michael Joseph Ltd., London, 1966.

JOSHUA, M. S., *Politics and Economics in the Caribbean,* "Government and Politics of the Windward Islands", Special Study No. 3, Institute of Caribbean Studies, University of Puerto Rico, Río Piedras, 1966.

KEENAGH, PETER, *Mosquito Coast,* Chatto & Windus, London, 1938.

KERR, MADELINE, *Personality and Conflict in Jamaica,* Collins, London, 1963.

KLASS, MORTON, *East Indians in Trinidad,* Columbia University Press, New York, 1961.

KNOWLES, WILLIAM H., *Trade Union Development and Industrial Relations in the British West Indies,* University of California Press, Berkeley and Los Angeles, 1959.

LE PAGE, R. B., and DAVID DE CAMP, *Jamaican Creole,* Macmillan & Co., London, 1960.

LEWIS, Professor Sir ARTHUR, *The Agony of the Eight,* Advocate Commercial Printery, Barbados, n.d.

LOWENTHAL, DAVID, *The West Indies Federation,* Columbia University Press, New York, 1961.

LOWENTHAL, DAVID, *Federation of the West Indies,* ed. H. D. Huggins, "Two Federations", *Social and Economic Studies,* Vol. 6, No. 2, Institute of Social and Economic Research, University College of the West Indies, Jamaica, June 1957.

Manley and the New Jamaica, Selected speeches and writings 1938-1968, ed. Rex Nettleford, Longman Caribbean, London, 1971.

MARSHALL, W. K., *The Caribbean in Transition,* ed. F. M. Andic and T. G. Mathews, "Social and Economic Problems in the Windward Islands, 1838-65", Second Scholars Conference, Mona, Jamaica, April 14-19, 1964, Institute of Caribbean Studies, University of Puerto Rico, Río Piedras, Puerto Rico, 1965.

MARTEN, NEIL, *Their's not to reason why,* A study of the Anguillan Operation as presented to Parliament, Conservative Political Centre, London, July 1969.

MAUNDER, W. F., *Employment in an Underdeveloped Area,* A sample survey of Kingston, Jamaica, Yale University Press, New Haven, 1960.

MCFARLANE, DENNIS, *A Comparative Study of Incentive Legislation in the Leeward Islands, Windward Islands, Barbados and Jamaica, Social and Economic Studies,* Supplement to Vol. 13, No. 3, Institute of Social and Economic Research, University of the West Indies, Jamaica, 1964.

MORDECAI, JOHN, *The West Indies: The Federal Negotiations,* Allen and Unwin, London, 1968.

NEWMAN, PETER, *British Guiana,* Institute of Race Relations, Oxford University Press, London, 1964.

OLDMIXON, JOHN, *The History of the Isle of Providence*, John Culmer, London, 1949.

OLIVIER, LORD, *Jamaica, The Blessed Island*, Faber & Faber, London, 1936.

OTTLEY, CARLTON, *Spanish Trinidad*, n.p., Port of Spain, 1955.

PALMER, RANSFORD W., *The Jamaican Economy*, Pall Mall Press, London, 1969.

RAMPERSAD, FRANK, *Growth and Structural Change in the Economy of Trinidad and Tobago 1951-1961*, Social and Economic Studies, Institute of Social and Economic Research, University of the West Indies, Jamaica.

RENO, PHILIP, *The Ordeal of British Guiana*, Monthly Review Press, New York, 1964.

REUBENS, EDWIN P., *Migration and Development in the West Indies*, Studies in Federal Economics No. 3, Institute of Social and Economic Research, University College of the West Indies, Jamaica, n.d.

ROBERTS, E. ADOLPHE, *Jamaica, The Portrait of an Island*, Coward-McCann, Inc., New York, 1955.

ROBERTSON, E. ARNOT, *The Spanish Town Papers*, The Cresset Press, London, 1959.

RUCK, S. K., editor, *The West Indian comes to England*, Routledge & Kegan Paul Ltd., London, 1960.

SCOTT, MICHAEL, *Tom Cringle's Log*, J. M. Dent & Sons Ltd., London, 1928, reprint.

SHERLOCK, PHILIP, *Jamaica Way*, Longmans, London, 1962.

SIMEY, T. S., *Welfare & Planning in the West Indies*, Clarendon Press, Oxford, 1946.

SIMMS, PETER, *Trouble in Guyana*, George Allen & Unwin Ltd., London, 1966.

SINGHAM, A. W., *The Hero and the Crowd in Colonial Policy*, Yale University Press, 1968.

SMITH, M. G., and G. J. KRUIJER, *A Sociological Manual for Extension Workers in the Caribbean*, The Extra-Mural Department, University College of the West Indies, Kingston, Jamaica, 1957.

SMITH, RAYMOND T., *The Negro Family in British Guiana*, Routledge & Kegan Paul Ltd., London, 1956.

SMITH, RAYMOND T., *British Guiana*, The Royal Institute of International Affairs, Oxford University Press, London, 1962.

"Some Caribbean Problems", *World Survey*, incorporating *The British Survey*, The Atlantic Education Trust, London, No. 6, June 1969.

SPRINGER, HUGH W., *Reflections on the Failure of the First West Indies Federation*, Occasional Papers in International Affairs, No. 4, Harvard University, Center for International Affairs, Cambridge, Massachusetts, July 1962.

SPURDLE, F. G., *Early West Indian Government*, Palmerston, New Zealand, n.d.

THOMAS, CLIVE YOLANDE, *Monetary and Financial Arrangements in a Dependent Monetary Economy—A study of British Guiana, 1945-1962*, Social and Economic Studies, Supplement to Vol. 14, No. 4, Institute of Social and Economic Research, University of the West Indies, Jamaica, December 1965.

THORNTON, A. P., *West-India Policy under the Restoration*, Clarendon Press, Oxford, 1956.

VOELKER, WALTER D., *Survey of Industry in the West Indies*, Studies in Federal Economics No. 1, Institute of Social and Economic Research, University College of the West Indies, Jamaica, n.d.

"Where did the money go"—The Demba Record in Guyana 1919-1960, Demerara Bauxite Company Ltd., Guyana, September 1970.

WILLIAMS, ERIC, *Britain and the West Indies*, Noel Buxton Lecture, 20 March 1969, University of Essex, Longmans, London 1969.

WILLIAMS, ERIC, *British Historians and the West Indies*, P.N.M. Publishing Co. Ltd., Port of Spain, 1964.

WILLIAMS, ERIC, *History of the People of Trinidad and Tobago*, Andre Deutsch, London, 1964.

WISEMAN, H. V., *A Short History of the British West Indies*, University of London Press, London, 1950.

(b) *Articles*

ABBOTT, GEORGE C., "Political Disintegration: The Lessons of Anguilla", *Government and Opposition*, A Journal of Comparative Politics, Vol. 6, No. 1, London School of Economics, London, Winter 1971.

"A clash of Commonwealth commercial interests", *The Financial Times*, London, April 2, 1970.

"A Sleepy Caribbean Isle Awakens to Tourism", *The New York Times*, New York, March 15, 1964.

ALLSOPP, S. R. R., "British Honduras—The Linguistic Dilemma", *Caribbean Quarterly*, Vol. II, Nos. 3 and 4, University of the West Indies, Jamaica, September and December 1965.

ARCHIBALD, CHARLES, "Trinidad . . . Cross Roads of the Caribbean", *New Commonwealth*, London, November 1962.

"Bahamas, a special report", *The Times*, London, Supplement, September 17, 1970.

"Bahamas: Trouble in Paradise", *The Economist*, London, October 15, 1966.

BALL, IAN, "Anguilla: almost all forgiven", *The Daily Telegraph*, London, September 20, 1969.

"Bauxite becomes a major industry", Georgetown correspondent, *The Financial Times*, London, April 27, 1966.

BELL, E.-A., "La bauxite en Guyane", *Chemische Rundschau*, Solothurn, Switzerland, June 23, 1966.

BENN, BRINDLEY, "British Guiana—Labour's responsibility", *The Daily Worker*, London, January 25, 1965.

BEST, LLOYD, "Black demands for economic power", *The Sunday Gleaner*, Kingston, Jamaica, April 13, 1969.

"Bid for real co-operation", *The Financial Times*, London, January 30, 1970.

"Bid to close the poverty gap", *The Financial Times*, London, January 6, 1970.

BLOOD, Sir HILARY, "And Now—Jamaica", *New Commonwealth*, London, August 1962.

BOBB, LEWIS E., "The Federal Principle in the British West Indies", *Social and Economic Studies*, Vol. 15, No. 3, Institute of Social and Economic Research, University of the West Indies, Jamaica, September 1966.

BOWDEN, ALAN, "Jamaica—A Stable Island", *New Commonwealth*, London, No. 8, 1965.

472

BOWDEN, ALAN, "A Vast Potential", *New Commonwealth*, London, No. 9, 1965.

BRADLEY, JOHN H., "Banking in the Commonwealth Caribbean, *The Banker*, London, August, 1970.

BRADLEY, JOHN H., "Modern legislation offers a complete tax haven", *The Financial Times*, London, February 6, 1969.

BRODERICK, MARGARET, "Associated Statehood—a new form of decolonisation", *The International and Comparative Law Quarterly*, Vol. 17, part 2, The British Institute of International and Comparative Law, London, April 1968.

BROWN, Hon. G. ARTHUR, Address, Jamaica Chamber of Commerce, Kingston, February 16, 1971.

BROWNRIGG, E., "Bright Future forecast for Bahamas", *New Commonwealth*, London, February 1962.

BUCKLEY, THOMAS, "Rivals in British Guiana Decline to Meet in Effort to End Strife", *The New York Times*, New York, June 1, 1964.

BUCKLEY, THOMAS, "Racial Hatred Deepens Between British Guiana's East Indians and Negroes", *The New York Times*, New York, May 29, 1964.

BUCKMASTER, MICHAEL, "Tax-free-port and land the asset", *The Times*, London, August 8, 1970.

BYRNE, JOYCELIN, "Population Growth in St. Vincent", *Social and Economic Studies*, Vol. 18, No. 2, Institute of Social and Economic Research, University of the West Indies, June 1969.

"Carifta", *World Business*, No. 17, The Chase Manhattan Bank, October 1969.

"Cayman Islands, a special report", *The Times*, London, Supplement, August 8, 1970.

"Changed Pattern in British Guiana", *The Times*, London, June 8, 1964.

"Choice of a tax haven demands careful study", *The Financial Times*, London, September 17, 1971.

"Citrus—new goal set for the industry", *The Jamaican Weekly Gleaner*, Kingston, May 20, 1970.

CLEMONS, D. H., "Guyana—the New British Guiana—Becomes Independent", *Foreign Trade*, Ottawa, Canada, May 14, 1966.

COGGINS, J. C., "Race, Economics, and Politics in Trinidad", *The Round Table*, The Commonwealth Journal of International Affairs, London, January 1971.

COLLINS, B. A. N., "Independence for Guyana", *The World Today*, Vol. 22, No. 6, The Royal Institute of International Affairs, London, June 1966.

COLLINS, B. A. N., "The Civil Service of British Guiana in the General Strike of 1963", *Caribbean Quarterly*, Vol. 10, No. 2, University of the West Indies, Jamaica, June 1964.

COLVIN, IAN, "Warship sent to West Indies Island", *The Daily Telegraph*, London, December 24, 1966.

"Commonwealth sugar and the Six", *The Economist*, London, May 22, 1971.

"Covetous neighbours—but many friends", Caribbean Correspondent, *Statist*, London, May 27, 1966.

COZIER, Tony, "Rising exports of a wide range of crops", *The Financial Times*, London, August 21, 1970.

473

CROCKER, JOHN, "Unemployment an Election Issue for Trinidad", *Observer Foreign News Service*, London, September 2, 1966.

CROSBIE, A. J., and P. A. FURLEY, "Los Problemas de la Capacidad de la Tierra en Honduras Británica", Union Geográfica Internacional, Conferencia Regional Latinoamericana, Sociedad Mexicana de Geografía y Estadística, Tomo II, Mexico City, 1966.

CROSBIE, A. J., and P. A. FURLEY, "The New Belize—Prospects for British Honduras", *Scottish Geographical Magazine*, Vol. 83, No. 1, Edinburgh, April, 1967.

DAVIES, ROSS, "A place in the sun", *The Times*, London, April 19, 1971.

DAVIS, HORACE B., "The decolonization of sugar in Guyana", *Caribbean Studies*, Vol. 7, No. 3, Institute of Caribbean Studies, University of Puerto Rico, October 1967.

DAVIS, WILLIAM, "A place in 'paradise' and it's tax free", *The Guardian*, London, January 24, 1966.

DECRAENE, PHILIPPE, "La plus anglaise des Antilles", *Le Monde*, Paris, August 7, 1962.

"Dominica", Survey by *The Financial Times*, London, August 21, 1970.

"Eastern Caribbean—a special report", *The Times*, London, Supplement, September 7, 1970.

"E.C.M. talks—causes for hope and doubt", *The Jamaican Weekly Gleaner*, Kingston, Jamaica, September 24, 1969.

EDELMAN, MAURICE, "Cayman Islands link with the Crown", *The Times*, London, January 22, 1966.

EDER, RICHARD, "Election Brings Guiana no Closer to Racial Unity", *The New York Times*, New York, December 16, 1964.

EDER, RICHARD, "British Guiana, Racial Friction Keeps the Land in Turmoil", *The New York Times*, New York, July 14, 1963.

EDSON, LEE, "Barbados keeps its distance to resist change", *The New York Times*, New York, February 7, 1971.

"Effects of new registration systems on elections", *The Daily Gleaner*, Kingston, February 27, 1967.

"Empire Builders 1964", Insight, *The Sunday Times*, London, May 24, 1964.

EVANS, PETER, "Cloudy distinction between immigrants and aliens", *The Times*, London, September 2, 1971.

EVANS, ROWLAND, and ROBERT NOVAK, "Communist Guiana", *The New York Herald Tribune*, New York, August 13, 1963.

FABER, MICHAEL, "A 'Swing' Analysis of the Jamaican Election of 1962: A Note", *Social and Economic Studies*, Vol. 13, No. 2, Institute of Social and Economic Research, University of the West Indies, Jamaica, 1964.

FIELD, MICHAEL, "The Flag comes down in South America", *The Daily Telegraph*, London, May 25, 1966.

"Focus Jamaica", *New Commonwealth*, London, March 1969.

FORBES, URIAS, "The West Indies Associated States: some aspects of the Constitutional Arrangements", *Social and Economic Studies*, Vol. 19, No. 1, Institute of Social and Economic Research, University of the West Indies, Jamaica, March 1970.

FURLEY, PETER, "A capital waits for its country", *The Geographical Magazine*, Vol. 43, No. 10, London, July 1971.

"Fyffes poised to abandon Jamaica banana industry", *The Financial Times*, London, February 5, 1970.

GINIGER, HENRY, "Americans Decide to Press Plan for Anguilla Despite Opposition", *The New York Times*, New York, August 28, 1967.

GOODSELL, JAMES NELSON, "Anguilla action stirs other British islands", *The Christian Science Monitor*, Boston, March 26, 1969.

GOODSELL, JAMES NELSON, "Anguilla votes for independence", *The Christian Science Monitor*, London edition, July 18, 1967.

GOODSELL, JAMES NELSON, "Support wanes for Trinidad and Tobago chief?", *The Christian Science Monitor*, Boston, May 27, 1971.

GOSSET, PIERRE and RENEE, "Bahama", *Journal de Genève*, Geneve, October 5, 6, 7, 8, 9, 1968.

GRANT, C. H., "The Politics of Community Development in British Guiana", *Social and Economic Studies*, Vol. 14, No. 2, Institute of Social and Economic Research, University of the West Indies, Jamaica, June 1965.

"Grenada personages and politics", *The Nation*, Port of Spain, September 21, 1962.

GRUNEWALD, DONALD, "The Anglo-Guatemalan Dispute over British Honduras", *Caribbean Studies*, Vol. 5, No. 2, Institute of Caribbean Studies, University of Puerto Rico, Río Piedras, Puerto Rico, July 1965.

" 'Guyana'—rich potential with a spice of risk", *Business Week*, New York, May 28, 1966.

HARBRON, JOHN D., "Jamaica—not yet a Caribbean nation", *The Jamaican Weekly Gleaner*, Kingston, August 5, 1970.

HAREWOOD, JACK, "Population Growth in Grenada in the Twentieth Century", *Social and Economic Studies*, Vol. 15, No. 2, Institute of Social and Economic Research, University of the West Indies, Jamaica, June 1966.

HAREWOOD, JACK, "Population Growth of Trinidad and Tobago in the Twentieth Century", *Social and Economic Studies*, Vol. 12, No. 1, Institute of Social and Economic Research, University of the West Indies, Jamaica, March 1963.

"Here are Pindling's 'Answers' for the Bahamas", Excerpts from recorded interview with Bahamas Premier Lyndon Pindling, *The Miami Herald*, Miami, February 18, 1968.

HENFREY, COLIN, "Guyana's uncertain independence", *The Listener*, London, June 2, 1966.

HILL, KEN, "Comment", *The Nation*, Port of Spain, December 7, 1962.

"How lasting the joy", *The Economist*, London, May 25, 1966.

"How the CIA got rid of Jagan", Insight, *The Sunday Times*, London, April 16, 1967.

HUGHES, ALISTER, "What Protection is there for Small Islands", *Antigua Times*, Antigua, May 29, 1971.

INCE, BASIL A., "The Venezuela-Guyana Boundary Dispute in the United Nations", *Caribbean Studies*, Vol. 9, No. 4, Instituto de Estudios del Caribe, Universidad de Puerto Rico, January 1970.

"Indians in Guiana", *The Hindu*, Madras, June 7, 1964.

"Is it 'silly' that Anguilla does not want to become a nation of bus boys", *The New York Times*, New York, August 14, 1967.

"Islandwide birth control drive launched", *The Daily Gleaner*, Kingston, March 18, 1965.

475

"It's great if you're rich", *The Observer*, London, June 15, 1969.

JACOBS, H. P., "What Future for the Cayman Islands?", *New Commonwealth*, London, January 1962.

JAGAN, CHEDDI, "British Guiana under U.S. shadow", *The Daily Worker*, London, November 15, 1965.

"Jamaica—a special report", *The Times*, London, Supplement, September 14, 1970.

"Jamaicanization—how far, how fast?", *The Jamaican Weekly Gleaner*, Kingston, March 31, 1971.

"Jamaican switch makes a $ worth more than a buck", *The Financial Times*, London, June 17, 1969.

"Jamaica Pasture Land Pays Off in Bauxite", *Business Week*, New York, April 19, 1952.

JOHNSON, THOMAS A., "Caribbean Uproar is Fired by Economic Exploitation", *The International Herald Tribune*, Paris, April 24, 1970.

KEATLEY, PATRICK, " 'Derisory' Amount Loan Offer to Trinidad", *The Guardian*, London, November 26, 1962.

KENDALL, W. O. R., "Guyana in World Trade", *International Trade Forum*, No. 2, Geneva, June 1966.

KEEGAN, WILLIAM, "Where not only tourists are important," *The Financial Times*, London, June 2, 1967.

KEY, IVOR, "Now hatred sweeps those islands in the sun", *The Daily Express*, London, April 23, 1970.

"Lack of profits yields a bitter crop", *The Financial Times*, London, May 13, 1969.

LASCELLES, DAVID, "When the flying had to stop", *The Financial Times*, London, October 15, 1970.

LEAPMAN, MICHAEL, "The Bahamas must decide what they want to be", *The Times*, London, October 16, 1970.

LEWIS, Professor Sir ARTHUR, "Industrialization of the British West Indies", *Caribbean Economic Review*, Vol. II, No. 1, Caribbean Commission, General Secretariat, Port of Spain, May 1950.

LEWIS, Professor Sir ARTHUR, "Jamaica's Economic Problems", seven articles, *The Daily Gleaner*, Kingston, September 1964.

LEWIS, GORDON K., "British Colonialism in the West Indies: the Political legacy", *Caribbean Studies*, Vol. 7, No. 1, Institute of Caribbean Studies, University of Puerto Rico, Río Piedras, Puerto Rico, April 1967.

LEWIS, ROY, "Britain's little Anguillas of the future", *The Times*, London, March 28, 1969.

LINTON, NEVILLE, "Regional Diplomacy of the Commonwealth Caribbean", *International Journal*, Canadian Institute of International Affairs, Toronto, Spring 1971.

MANLEY, MICHAEL, "Overcoming insularity in Jamaica", *Foreign Affairs*, Council on Foreign Relations, New York, January 1971.

MARTIN-KAYE, P. H. A., "Prosperous Future for Minerals", *The Financial Times*, London, Supplement on Guyana, May 26, 1966.

McFARLANE, DENNIS, "The Future of the Banana Industry in the West Indies", *Social and Economic Studies*, Vol. 13, No. 1, Institute of Social and Economic Research, University of the West Indies, Jamaica, March 1964.

McGlashan, Colin, "The Two Jamaicas", *The Observer*, London, November 23, 1969.

Merritt, I. K., "That 'Safari' ", *The Nation*, Port of Spain, April 3, 1964.

Merry, Cyril A., "Trinidad-Tobago Attract Investors", *International Trade Review*, Dun and Bradstreet, New York, May 1963.

Miles, Keith, "An unholy alliance in British Guiana", *The Daily Worker*, London, June 12, 1963.

Montgomery, Paul L., "Enter Guyana, Struggling", *The New York Times*, New York, May 22, 1966.

"Mrs. Jagan Resigns from British Guiana Cabinet", Latin American Correspondent, *The Times*, London, June 2, 1964.

Mulchansingh, Vernon C., "The Oil Industry in the Economy of Trinidad", *Caribbean Studies*, Vol. 11, No. 1, Institute of Caribbean Studies, University of Puerto Rico, Río Piedras, Puerto Rico, April 1971.

"New look U.K. aid programme", *The Financial Times*, London, May 12, 1970.

Newman, Peter, "Epilogue on British Guiana", *Social and Economic Studies*, Vol. 10, No. 1, Institute of Social and Economic Research, University College of the West Indies, Jamaica, March 1961.

"New personalities come to the fore", *The Financial Times*, London, March 5, 1969.

"New Sugar Authority—different in form as well as substance", *The Jamaican Weekly Gleaner*, Kingston, April 22, 1970.

Nicholls, David G., "East Indians and Black Power in Trinidad", *Race*, Institute of Race Relations, London, April 1971.

"No Eldorado—but progress", Caribbean Correspondent, *Statist*, London, September 30, 1966.

O'Loughlin, Carleen, "Problems in the Economic Development of Antigua", *Social and Economic Studies*, Vol. 10, No. 3, Institute of Social and Economic Research, University College of the West Indies, Jamaica, September 1961.

"On the Horns of a Dilemma", *The Nation*, Port of Spain, Grenada Supplement, October 5, 1962.

"More Troops Being Sent to British Guiana", Latin American Correspondent, *The Times*, London, May 27, 1964.

O'Neale, H. W., "The Economy of St. Lucia", *Social and Economic Studies*, Vol. 13, No. 4, Institute of Social and Economic Research, University of the West Indies, Jamaica, December 1964.

O'Shaughnessy, Hugh, "Bananas the mainspring of the economy", *The Financial Times*, London, August 21, 1970.

O'Shaughnessy, Hugh, "Prospects for agriculture the brightest ever", *The Financial Times*, London, March 12, 1970.

Oulahan, Richard, and William Lambert, "The Scandal in the Bahamas", *Life Magazine*, New York, February 3, 1967.

Oxaal, Ivar, "Neo-nationalism in the West Indies", *New Society*, London, February 10, 1966.

Persaud, Bishnodat and Lakshmi Persaud, "The impact of Agricultural Diversification Policies in Barbados and the Post-war Period", *Social and Economic Studies* Vol. 17, No. 3, Institute of Social and Economic Research, University of the West Indies, Jamaica, September 1968.

477

PILGRIM, FRANK, "Guiana Strikers Agree to go Back", *The Observer*, London, July 7, 1963.

PILGRIM, FRANK, "Jagan Fights to stop new Premier", *The Observer*, London, December 13, 1964.

PILGRIM, FRANK, "Blood and Fire in El Dorado", *Observer Foreign News Service*, London, June 8, 1964.

"Pressures under the bubble", *The Economist*, London, March 22, 1969.

RICHARDS, ROY, "A Challenge for our Manufacturers", *Sunday Guardian*, Port of Spain, April 12, 1964.

RICHARDSON, LEIGH, "Three choices for British Honduras", *The Daily Telegraph*, London, June 4, 1968.

RICHARDSON, LEIGH, "Uncle Gairy Still Casts a Long Shadow", *Sunday Guardian*, Port of Spain, September 23, 1962.

RICKARDS, COLIN, "Bahamas airline bacchanal", *Caribbean Business News*, Toronto, December 1970.

RICKARDS, COLIN, "Caribbean federalists soldier on", The *Daily Telegraph*, London, October 30, 1969.

ROBERTS, G. W., and N. ABDULAH, "Some Observations on the Educational Position of the British Caribbean", *Social and Economic Studies*, Vol. 14, No. 1, Institute of Social and Economic Research, University of the West Indies, Jamaica, March 1965.

ROBINSON, A. N. R., "Economic Potential", *New Commonwealth*, London, No. 12, 1966.

RUTHERFORD, MALCOLM, "Mr. Joshua finds the walls too strong", *The Financial Times*, London, July 16, 1968.

SANGER, CLYDE, "Black Power on Jamaica", *San Francisco Sunday Examiner & Chronicle*, San Francisco, August 3, 1969.

SANOWAR, LEE, "Plan to win back tourists", *Sunday Guardian*, Port of Spain, February 2, 1964.

SCOTT, IAN, "Haiti refugees a big social problem", *The Financial Times*, London, April 1, 1969.

SCOTT, RICHARD, "U.S. Support for Britain over Guiana", *The Guardian*, London, July 13, 1963.

SEGAL, AARON, "Economic integration and Preferential Trade: the Caribbean Experience", *The World Today*, Vol. 25, No. 10, The Royal Institute of International Affairs, London, October, 1969.

"Shearer's Tour—crucial for our future", *The Sunday Gleaner*, Kingston, October 8, 1967.

SHERLOCK, PHILIP, "Crisis in Education", *The Times*, London, Supplement on Jamaica, February 21, 1966.

SIMMONDS, K. R., "Anguilla—An interim settlement," *The International and Comparative Law Quarterly*, Vol. 21, Part 1, London, January 1972.

SKELTON, DOUGLAS, "A more profitable approach comes to tourism", *The Financial Times*, London, August 12, 1969.

SMITH, CHARLES, "Anguilla looks for a partner", *The Financial Times*, London, June 20, 1967.

SMITH, E. P., "Mechanization of the Trinidad Sugar Industry", *New Commonwealth*, London, No. 8, 1966.

SMITH, PAUL, "Bahamas on the brink? Mr. Pindling's Government faces major problems", *The Royal Gazette*, Bermuda, December 16, 1970.

478

SMITH, RAYMOND T., "Race and Political Conflict in Guyana", *Race,* Institute of Race Relations, London, April 1971.

SMYTH, PETE, "Casuarinas & Croupiers", *Panam Magazine,* November-December 1969.

"St. Lucia", *West Indies Chronicle,* Supplement, London, January 1971.

"Sugar, Canada and the Commonwealth Caribbean", *The Jamaican Weekly Gleaner,* Kingston, June 3, 1970.

SPACKMAN, ANN, "Constitutional Development in Trinidad and Tobago", *Social and Economic Studies,* Vol. 14, No. 4, Institute of Social and Economic Studies, University of the West Indies, Jamaica, December 1965.

"Tackling adult illiteracy problem in Jamaica", *The Jamaican Weekly Gleaner,* Kingston, September 30, 1970.

TAYLOR, FRANK, "Race Madness in the Sugar Belt", *The Daily Telegraph,* London, June 6, 1964.

TAYLOR, FRANK, "Violent prelude to British Guiana Poll", *The Sunday Times,* London, April 26, 1964.

"Technical education—what should concern us", *The Nation,* Port of Spain, January 11, 1963.

"The Cayman Islands—sophisticated tax haven", *Caribbean Business News,* Toronto, October 1970.

"The Economy: A review of 1970 and a look at 1971", *The Jamaican Weekly Gleaner,* Kingston, March 17, 1971.

"The economy's first bad year since Independence", *The Financial Times,* London, April 18, 1968.

"The Finance Bill and Sugar Mechanization stimulate Controversy in Trinidad", *Chronicle of the West India Committee,* London, September 1966.

"The Future of our Cocoa Industry", *The Nation,* Port of Spain, March 1, 1963.

"The National Banks of Jamaica", *The Daily Gleaner,* Supplement, Kingston, Jamaica, October 1, 1970.

"The secret banana war", *The Sunday Times,* London, January 24, 1971.

TIDRICK, GENE, "Some Aspects of Jamaican Emigration to the United Kingdom 1953-1962", *Social and Economic Studies,* Vol. 15, No. 1, Institute of Social and Economic Research, University of the West Indies, Jamaica, March 1966.

"Too little, too late", *The Observer,* London, June 7, 1964.

TOPPING, DENNIS, "Alcan plays it cool", *The Times,* London, October 28, 1971.

"Tourist Industry's Place in the Sun", Special Correspondent, *The Times,* London, Supplement on Jamaica, February 21, 1966.

"Towards the Point of No Return", Special Correspondent, *The Times,* London, July 5, 1963.

"Trade Union developments—year of the splinter movement", *The Sunday Gleaner,* Kingston, Jamaica, January 25, 1970.

"Trades Unions Militant", *The Times,* London, Supplement on Trinidad and Tobago, January 25, 1966.

TRAVERS, NICOLAS, "Steering the Bahamas to a financial future", *The Times,* London, November 24, 1969.

"Turks & Caicos", Survey by *The Financial Times,* London, October 22, 1970.

479

'U.K. sales wilting in the hot Caribbean sun", *The Financial Times*, London, September 20, 1968.

"Un nouveau pays indépendant: la Guyane", *Informations du Commerce Extérieur*, Brussels, May 25, 1966.

"Valuable finds of natural gas", *The Financial Times*, London, Supplement, May 19, 1971.

VERRIER, ANTHONY, "The Need for Statesmanship in British Guiana", *The World Today*, Vol. 19, No. 8, The Royal Institute of International Affairs, London, August 1963.

VIEIRA, PHIL, "State of uncertainty hits coffee industry", *Trinidad Guardian*, Port of Spain, May 2, 1964.

WEST, RICHARD, "Footpads in Georgetown", *The Sunday Times*, London, November 28, 1965.

WHITTAM SMITH, ANDREAS, "Opportunities galore for British investors in Jamaica", *The Daily Telegraph*, London, August 7, 1968.

"Will Proportional Representation Work", Caribbean Correspondent, *The Financial Times*, London, November 20, 1964.

WILLIAMS, DOUGLAS, "Two Flags or One in the Virgin Islands?", *The Daily Telegraph*, London, April 15, 1964.

WILLIAMS, ERIC, "Together we have achieved, together we must aspire", *The Nation*, Port of Spain, August 28, 1964.

WINSLADE, H. A., "British Guiana's Tragic Farce", *The Daily Telegraph*, London, June 26, 1963.

WINSLADE, H. A., "British Guiana: Time to Act", *The Daily Telegraph*, London, July 16, 1963.

WINSLADE, H. A., "Jagan says U.S. pressure delaying Independence", *The Daily Telegraph*, London, July 1, 1963.

WODDIS, JACK, "Government and the Unions in British Guiana", *The Daily Worker*, London, May 13, 1963.

YOUNG, JOHN, "Boost for Trinidad's opposition", *The Times*, London, October 22, 1970.

YOUNG, JOHN, "Caribbean search for a common cause", *The Times*, London, December 16, 1970.

FRENCH OVERSEAS DEPARTMENTS

SOURCES

(a) *Documents*

Banque de la Guyane, Cayenne, Assemblée Générale Ordinaire du 23 Mars, 1963.

Bulletin de statistique des départements et territoires d'outre-mer, Institut National de la Statistique et des Etudes Economiques, Paris, n.d.

Bulletin d'information du Ministère des Armées, Paris, 1961.

Bulletin Statistique, Commissariat général au tourisme, Paris, No. 9 and 10—septembre-octobre 1969.

Cinquième Plan de développement économique et social (1966-1970), Vols. I and II (Annexes), Imprimerie des Journaux officiels, Paris, 1965.

Cinquième Plan 1966-1970, Rapports des Sous Commissions, Commissariat Général du Plan d'équipement et de la Productivité, Paris, n.d.

Comptes Economiques de la Guadeloupe, Institut National de la Statistique et des Etudes Economiques, Paris, 1969.

Comptes Economiques de la Martinique, Institut National de la Statistique et des Etudes Economiques, Paris, 1969.

Les Cahiers Français, "La démographie guyanaise", No. 223, Documents d'Actualité, La documentation française, Paris, No. 127, June 1968.

Les Cahiers Français, "La démographie dans les départements français des Antilles (Martinique et Guadeloupe)", No. 205, Documents d'Actualité, La Documentation Française, Paris, No. 125, March 1968.

Le Sixième Plan des Départments d'Outre Mer (Texte de l'Annexe DOM au Rapport du Governement sur le VIe Plan), Commissariat Général du Plan d'Equipement et de la Productivité, Paris, May 1971.

Les Départements d'Outre Mer, Ministère d'Etat chargé des Départements et Territoires d'Outre Mer, Paris, December 1964.

Rapport d'Information sur les départements français d'Amérique, by MM. Jean-Paul Palewski, Pierre Baudis, Guy Ebrard, Roger Fossé, René Regaudie, (Deputés), Assemblée Nationale, No. 354, Commission des Finances de l'économie générale et du Plan, Imprimerie de l'Assemblée National, Paris, 1963.

Rapport sur les options adopté par la Commission Centrale des D.O.M. du VIème Plan, Commissariat Général du Plan d'Equipement et de la Productivité, Paris, April 1970.

Rapport sur le tourisme dans les départements d'outre mer, Commissariat Général du VIème Plan—D.O.M., Commissariat Général du Plan, Phase de Programmation, Paris, April 1971.

Troisième Plan 1958-1961, Rapport Général de la commission de modernisation et d'équipement des départements d'outre-mer, Paris, 1959.

(b) *Newspapers, Periodicals and Year Books*

Combat, Paris.

Europe-France-Outremer, Paris.

Esprit, Paris.

France Toujours, Fort-de-France, Martinique.

Guide Touristique Illustré, Antilles Guyane Françaises et Barbade (Caraïbes 71 Horizons du Monde), Societé de Création Internationale de Publicité et de Presse, Paris, 1971.

Horizons du Monde, Paris.

Journal des Finances, Paris.

Justice, Martinique.

La Montagne, Clermont-Ferrand.

L'Aube, Paris.

Le Courrier, Martinique.

Le Courrier du Parlement, Paris.

L'Etincelle, Guadeloupe.

L'Humanité, Paris.

Le Progrès Social, Guadeloupe.

Livre d'Or des Antilles et Guyane Française, Collection France, No. 4, Société Edition Publicité Antillaise, Saint Barthélemy, n.d.

Marchés Tropicaux et Méditerranéens, Paris.
Match, Pointe-à-Pitre.
Paris-Presse, Paris.
Présence Africaine, Paris.
Radio Presse, Guyane.
Revue de Défense Nationale, Paris.
Rivarol, Paris.

STUDIES

(a) *Books and Pamphlets*

ANDIC, FUAT M., and SUPHAN ANDIC, *Fiscal Survey of the French Caribbean*, Special Study No. 2, Institute of Caribbean Studies, University of Puerto Rico, Río Piedras, Puerto Rico, 1965.

ANDIC, FUAT M., and SUPHAN ANDIC, *Politics and Economics in the Caribbean*, "Economic Background of French Antilles", Special Study No. 3, Institute of Caribbean Studies, University of Puerto Rico, Río Piedras, Puerto Rico, 1966.

GRATIANT, GILBERT, *Ile Fédérée Française de la Martinique*, Editions Louis Soulanges, Paris, 1961.

GUÉRIN, DANIEL, *Les Antilles décolonisées*, Présence Africaine, Paris, 1956.

HALIAR, ANDRÉ, *Dans les Départements d'Outre-mer*, Editions Louis Soulanges, Paris, 1965.

JOROND, ANTOINE-VICTOR, *La Guadeloupe et ses îles*, Editions Les Beaux Livres, Basse-Terre, n.d.

LACOUR, M. A., *Histoire de la Guadeloupe*, in 4 vols., Société d'Histoire de la Guadeloupe, Basse-Terre, reprinted 1960.

LASSERRE, GUY, *La Guadeloupe*, 2 vols., Union Française d'Impression, Bordeaux, 1961.

LASSERRE, GUY, *Petite Propriété et Réforme Foncière aux Antilles Françaises*, Colloque International, Centre National de la Récherche Scientifique, Paris, October 1965.

Les Départements d'Outre-mer, La documentation française illustrée, Paris No. 256, Avril 1970.

LUCHAIRE, FRANÇOIS, *Droit d'outre-mer et de la Coopération*, Presses Universitaires de France, Paris, 1966.

MÉTRO, HENRY, *K. et M.* (*Guadeloupe-Martinique*) *filles de France*, Editions Louis Soulanges, Paris, 1965.

POUQUET, JEAN, *Les Antilles Françaises*, Presses Universitaires de France, Paris, 1960.

REVERT, EUGÈNE, (*Terres Lointaines*) *La France d'Amérique*, Editions Maritimes et Coloniales, Paris, 1955.

REVERT, EUGÈNE, *La Martinique*, Nouvelles Editions Latines, Paris, 1949.

ROBERT, AMIRAL GEORGES, *La France aux Antilles*, Librairie Plon, Paris, 1950.

ROBERTS, W. ADOLPHE, *The French in the West Indies*, Bobbs Merrill, New York, 1942.

SABLÉ, VICTOR, *La transformation des îles d'Amérique en départements français*, Larose, Paris, 1955.

SALANDRE, H., and CHEYSSAC, R., *Histoire et Civilisation des Antilles Françaises*, Guadeloupe et Martinique, Fernand Nathan, Paris, 1962.

Spitz, Georges, *Developments towards Self-Government in the Caribbean,* "La Martinique et ses institutions depuis 1948", Van Hoeve, The Hague, 1955.

(b) *Articles*

Barrault, Cyprien, " 'Etroits sont les vaisseaux' ou l'entêtement colonialiste", *Match,* Pointe-à-Pitre, June 30, 1963.

Barrillon, Raymond, "Les Antilles 'Poussières' sur l'Océan", *Le Monde,* Paris, April 23, 24, 1964.

Bergeroux, Noel-Jean, "Les Antilles Françaises en quête d'un statut", *Le Monde,* Paris, May 7, 8, 1971.

Bernier, Lucien, "Sur le statut actuel de la Guadeloupe", *Match,* Pointe-à-Pitre, September 30 and October 14, 1963.

Chauleur, Pierre, "Les Problèmes des D.O.M. ne peuvent être résolus que dans un esprit d'active coopération", *Marchés Tropicaux et Méditerranéens,* Paris, June 18, 1966.

Clerc, Jean-Pierre, "Les Antillais sur le chemin de l'exil", *Le Monde,* Paris, September 18, 19, 20, 1971.

Clos, Max, "Que se passe-t-il à la Martinique?", *Le Figaro,* Paris, February 25, 1960.

Cornec, Jean, "Libres opinions S.O.S.", *Le Monde,* Paris, May 10, 11, 1971.

Decraene, Philippe, "Terres Françaises des Antilles", *Le Monde,* Paris, September 11, 12, 13, 14, 1962.

Decraene, Philippe, "M. Jacquinot réaffirme qu'il n'y a pas de problème politique aux Antilles", *Le Monde,* Paris, December 4, 1963.

Florent, Claude, "Les Antilles, îles incertaines", *Le Monde,* Paris, January 6, 7, 8, 1970.

Fonde, General, "La Guyane encore méconnue", *Revue de Défense Nationale,* Paris, June-July 1968.

Gayet, Denise, "Le racisme en Guyane Française", *Les Temps Modernes,* Paris, No. 262, March 1968.

Giraud, Raymond, "Où en est le tourisme en Guadeloupe", *Horizons du Monde,* Paris, March-April 1966.

Haidar, Walter, "Basic Data on the Economy of French Guiana", *Overseas Business Reports,* No. 111, Washington, D.C., September 1964.

Hoy, Don R., "The Banana Industry of Guadeloupe, French West Indies", *Social and Economic Studies,* Vol. II, No. 3, Institute of Social and Economic Research, University of the West Indies, Jamaica, September 1962.

J.-A. D. "Une psychosociologie des Antilles françaises", *Le Monde,* Paris, September 3, 1969.

Jouandet-Bernadat, R., "L'économie des Antilles Françaises", *Caribbean Studies,* Vol. 7, No. 2, Institute of Caribbean Studies, University of Puerto Rico, July 1967.

Kiejman, Claude, "Martinique et Guadeloupe, Départements français ou terres étrangeres?", *Le Monde Diplomatique,* Paris, October 1971.

Lacouture, Jean, "Comment peut-on être Antillais?", *Le Monde,* Paris, August 26, 27, 1970.

"La cruche et la pierre", J.B., *La Montagne*, Clermont-Ferrand, January 8, 1966.

"L'Economie Sucrière", *Le Courrier du Parlement*, Paris, March 5-11, 1971.

LEGRIS, MICHEL, "Les Antilles: nœud de contradictions", *Le Monde*, Paris, November 20, 21, 1968.

"Le 'Plan Jacquinot' est diversement commenté aux Antilles", *Le Monde*, Paris, May 21, 1964.

"L'ananas Martiniquais est-il condamné à disparaître?", Groupement des Producteurs d'Ananas de la Martinique, *Le Courrier du Parlement*, No. 158, Paris, October 14-20, 1965.

"Les D.O.M. face à leur avenir", *Marchés Tropicaux et Méditerranéens*, Paris, June 18, 1966.

MARIE-ANNE, GEORGES, "Vérités sur la conjoncture Martiniquaise", *Le Courrier du Parlement*, No. 155, Supplement, Paris, September 23-29, 1965.

"Martinique May Make Demand to France", Barbados correspondent, *The Times*, London, November 3, 1965.

"Martinique: un volcan", *Journal de Genève*, Geneva, July 14, 1964.

M.S., "Le Centre Spatial Guyanais est devenu operationnel cette année", *Europe-France-Outremer*, Paris, August 1968.

M.S., "L'exploitation de la forêt se développe en Guyane", *Europe-France-Outremer*, Paris, August 1968.

NAVARRE, PIERRE, "Derrière les biguines pour touristes", *Rivarol*, Paris, April 28, 1966.

O'SHAUGHNESSY, H., "A French Caribbean prospect", *The Financial Times*, London, March 16, 1971.

"Où débouchent les espoirs de la Guadeloupe?", *Journal de Genève*, Geneva, July 13, 1964.

" 'Pearl of Antilles' seeks New Luster", *The New York Times*, New York, January 28, 1966.

R. Mo., "Le Marché commun est devenu la 'nouvelle frontière' des Antilles—Guyane", *Le Figaro*, Paris, September 7, 1966.

SABLÉ, VICTOR, "Marché Commun et production tropicale européenne", *Le Courrier du Parlement*, No. 158, Paris, October 14-20, 1965.

SAINT-YVES, YVON, "Le Port de Fort-de-France", *Le Courrier du Parlement*, No. 158, Paris, October 14-20, 1965.

SEALY, THEODORE, "French Guiana—Where Time Stands Still", *The Sunday Gleaner*, Kingston, Jamaica, February 17, 1963.

"Un grand espoir: le tourisme", *Marchés Tropicaux et Méditerranéens*, Paris, June 18, 1966.

VANVES, JACQUES, "Les Antilles Françaises et le Marché Commun", *Journal des Finances*, Paris, January 14, 1966.

VAUSSARD, MAURICE, "La Guyane peut-elle renaître?", *L'Aube*, Paris, May 9, 10, 11, 1950.

VIRATELLE, GÉRARD, "L'autonomisme reste vivace, mais se manifeste moins", *Le Monde*, Paris, March 10, 1965.

VIRATELLE, GÉRARD, "L'intervention américaine a réveillé aux Antilles françaises des sentiments hostiles aux Etats Unis", *Le Monde*, Paris, May 25, 1965.

VIRATELLE, GÉRARD, "La situation aux Antilles paraît évoluer favorablement", *Le Monde Diplomatique*, Paris, May 1966.

THE TRIPARTITE KINGDOM

SOURCES

(a) *Documents*

Charter of the United Kingdom of the Netherlands, The Hague, 1954.
Continental Shelf, Government Information Services, Surinam, n.d.
De Meidagen van Curaçao, Algemeen Culturele Maandblad "Ruku", Curaçao, 1970.
De werkgelegenheidssituatie op Curaçao en Aruba in Juli 1971 op grond van een gehouden steekproef onderzoek en een vergelijking met 1966, Departement Economische Zaken Bureau voor de Statistiek, Curaçao, September 1971.
Die Assoziierung der Niederländischen Antillen mit der EWG, The Hague, n.d.
Economic Review Surinam, Hollandsche Bank-Unie N.V., Amsterdam.
Economische Voorlichting Suriname, Economic Information Division of the Ministry of Economic Affairs, Surinam.
Education in the Netherlands Antilles, Department of Education, n.d.
ESSED, Dr. IR. F. E., *Opbouw, Ontwikkelingsstart der Zeventiger Jaren I*, Ministerie van Opbouw, Paramaribo, January 1971.
Guide for the establishment of enterprises in Curaçao, Curaçao Bureau of Economic Affairs, July 1965.
Het onderwijs in de nederlandse antillen aan het begin van het school jaar 1970/71, Departement van onderwijs examen-en statistiekbureau, December 1970.
Investment Factors, Netherlands Antilles, Netherlands Antilles Department of Social and Economic Affairs, Willemstad, March 1966.
National Development Plan for Surinam, Stichting Planbureau, Suriname, n.d.
Netherlands Antilles, Economic Survey, Barclays Bank International Limited, London, October 1971.
Nota inzake het prijsbeleid, Departement Sociale en Economische Zaken, April 1971.
Staatsblad van het Koninkrijk der Nederlanden, 17 januari 1968, Stb. 28, 29, 1968.
Statistische Mededelingen Nederlandse Antillen, Departement Sociale en Economische Zaken Bureau voor de Statistiek, May 1971.
Surinam, Recommendations for a Ten Year Development Program, International Bank for Reconstruction and Development, The Johns Hopkins Press, Baltimore, 1954.
Surinam S.A. Visitors Statistics 1970, Surinam Tourist Bureau, Paramaribo, n.d.
Verslag Over Het Jaar 1965, N.V. Mijnmaatschappij Curaçao, Amsterdam, n.d.
Verslag Over 1969, Centrale Bank Van Suriname.
Werknemers-en Werkqeversorqanisaties in de Nederlandse Antillen, Samengesteld door de Regeringsvoorlichtingsdienst van de Nederlandse Antillen, Curaçao, February 1970.
Zitting 1969-70—10 734, *Beknopt verslag van het bezoek van een parlementaire delegatie aan Suriname en van een daarop gevolgd kort bezoek aan de Nederlandse Antillen (12 mei-27 mei 1970)*, Geleidende Brief, Nr. 1, The Hague, July 1, 1970.

(b) *Newspapers, Periodicals and Year Books*

Algemeen Handelsblad, Amsterdam.
Amigoe di Curaçao, Willemstad.

485

Antilliaanse Nieuwsbrief, The Hague.
Dagblad de Telegraaf, Amsterdam.
De Nederlandse Industrie, The Hague.
De Volkskrant, Amsterdam.
De Ware Tijd, Paramaribo.
Echo of Aruba, Aruba.
Economisch Statistische Berichten, Rotterdam.
Elseviers Weekblad, The Hague.
Haagsche Courant, The Hague.
Handels-en Transport Courant, Rotterdam.
Het Financiële Dagblad, Amsterdam.
Holland Herald, Amsterdam.
Maandblad Belastingbeschonwingen, Leiden.
Nieuwe Rotterdamse Courant, Rotterdam.
Nieuwe West-Indische Gids, The Hague.
Nieuwsbrief, Rijswijk.
Nos Isla, Shell Curaçao, N.V., Curaçao.
Rotterdams Nieuwsblad, Rotterdam.
Statistisch Jaarboek, 1965, Bureau voor de Statistiek, Curaçao, 1965.
Statistisch Jaarboek 1970, Nederlandse Antillen Departmente van Sociale en Economische Zaken Bureau voor de Statistiek, Curaçao, 1970.
Statistische Mededelingen, Nederlandse Antillen, Bureau voor de Statistiek, Curaçao.
Surinaams Nieuws, Paramaribo, Surinam.
Suriname News in Brief, Government Information Service, Paramaribo, Surinam.
Trouw, Amsterdam.

STUDIES

(a) *Books and Pamphlets*

ADHIN, Dr. J. H., *Development Planning in Surinam in Historical Perspective*, H. E. Stenfert Kroese, N.V., Leiden, 1961.
DE KAT ANGELINO, A. D. A., *Colonial Policy*, Martinus Nijhoff, The Hague, 1931.
Doing Business in Surinam, Foundation for the Promotion of Investment in Surinam, Amsterdam, 1969.
DONNER, W. R. W., *The Financial Mechanism of The Netherlands Antilles*, Uitgeverij Weto, Amsterdam, 1961.
GASTMANN, ALBERT L., *The Politics of Surinam and the Netherlands Antilles*, Institute of Caribbean Studies, University of Puerto Rico, Río Piedras, Puerto Rico, 1968.
HELLINGA, W. Gs., *Language Problems in Surinam*, North-Holland Publishing Company, Amsterdam, 1955.
HERMANS, Dr. HANS G., *The Caribbean, British, French, Dutch, United States*, "Constitutional Development of the Netherlands Antilles and Surinam", University of Florida Press, Gainesville, 1958.
HOETINK, Dr. H., *Het Patroon Van de Oude Curaçaose Samenleving*, Van Gorcum, Assen, 1958.

HOUBEN, PETRUS-HENRICUS JOHANNES MARIA, *De Associate van Suriname ende Nederlandse Antillen Med de Europese Economische Gemeenschap*, Sijthoff for Europa-Instituut, Rijksuniversiteit te Leiden, Leiden, 1965.

KASTEEL, Dr. ANNEMARIE, *De Staatkundige Ontwikkeling der Nederlandse Antillen*, Van Hoeve, The Hague, 1956.

KRUUER, Dr. G. J., *Suriname en zun Buurlanden*, J. A. Boom & Zoon, Meppel, 1960.

LAMPE, W. F. M., *In de Schaduw van de Gouverneurs*, De Wit, N.V., Aruba, 1968.

LOGEMANN, J. H. A., *Developments Towards Self-Government in the Caribbean*, "The Constitutional Status of the Netherlands Antilles Caribbean Territories", Van Hoeve, The Hague, 1955.

MATHEWS, THOMAS G., *Politics & Economics in the Caribbean*, "Politics and Government of the Netherlands Antilles", Special Study No. 3, Institute of Caribbean Studies, University of Puerto Rico, Río Piedras, Puerto Rico, 1966.

MATHEWS, THOMAS G., *Politics & Economics in the Caribbean*, "The Political Picture in Surinam", Special Study No. 3, Institute of Caribbean Studies, University of Puerto Rico, Río Piedras, Puerto Rico, 1966.

NYSTROM, J. WARREN, *Surinam, A Geographic Study*, The Netherlands Information Bureau, New York, n.d.

PANDAY, R. M. N., *Agriculture in Surinam, 1650-1950*, H. J. Paris, Amsterdam, 1959.

25 Years of refining at Lago, Lago Oil & Transport Co., Aruba, January 1954.

VAN AMERSFOORT, J. M. M., *Surinamese immigrants in the Netherlands*, Government Printing and Publishing Office, The Hague, 1969.

VAN LEEUWEN, Dr. W. C. J., *Verslag aan de staten van de Nederlandse Antillen omtrent onze toekomstige Staatkundige structuur*, Willemstad, 1970.

VAN LIER, R. A. J., *Developments Towards Self-Government in the Caribbean*, "Social and Political Conditions in Suriname and the Netherlands Antilles: Introduction", Van Hoeve, The Hague, 1955.

VLEKKE, BERNARD H. M., *Evolution of the Dutch Nation*, Roy, New York, 1945.

(b) *Articles*

"Algemeen Overzicht", Verslag van de President, *Verslag over 1965*, Centrale Bank van Suriname.

"Beleid gericht op toeneming van werkgelegenheid", *De Nederlandse Industrie*, The Hague, April 1, 1966.

"Bevredigend jaar 1965 in Suriname", *Het Financiële Dagblad*, Amsterdam, July 23/25, 1966.

"Bosnegers van Suriname willen graag in Koninkrijk blijven", *Algemeen Handelsblad*, Amsterdam, October 18, 1966.

BRYSON, ALBERT E., "Long Term Lumber Operations actively solicited in Surinam", *International Commerce*, No. 24, Washington, D.C., June 13, 1966.

DE BRUIJNE, G. A. "Surinam and the Netherlands Antilles: their Place in the world". *K.N.A.G. Geografisch Tijdschrift* V (1971) Nr.4, Wolters-Noordhoff, Groningen.

487

DE KLERK, A., "Een zonnig Probleemgebied", *Economisch Statistiche Berichten*, Rotterdam, April 27, 1966.

DE VRIES, F. P., "Motieven en Perspectieven van de Nederlands—Antilliaanse Economie", *Nieuwe West-Indische Gids*, No. 1-2, The Hague, April 1965.

"Economische Samenwerking met de Nederlandse Antillen", *Surinaams Nieuws*, Paramaribo, October 22, 1966.

"Economische Samenwerking Suriname-Antillen", *Nieuwe Rotterdamse Courant*, Rotterdam, October 4, 1966.

FAUGHT, MILLARD C., and ARTHUR FAIRWEATHER, "Where Free Enterprise is Building a new Frontier", *Nation's Business*, The Chamber of Commerce of the United States, Washington, D.C., June 1965.

Foreign Economic Trends and their implications for the United States, U.S. Dept. of Commerce, Bureau of International Commerce, Washington, February 17, 1971.

GOODSELL, JAMES NELSON, "Curaçao violence traced to long discontent," *The Christian Science Monitor*, Boston, June 18, 1969.

GORDON, ROBERT, "Scenic 'Jungle Cruise' for Caribbean Tourists", *The New York Times*, New York, October 25, 1964.

HANSEN, HANS J. A., "Verkenningen in de West", *De Volkskrant*, Amsterdam, October 28, 30, November 3, 6, 9, 12, 16, 1965.

"Infrastructuur wordt beter", *Het Financiële Dagblad*, Amsterdam, August 20, 22, 1966.

JACOB, CARL, "Pengel's Surinam on the brink of economic boom", *Sunday Guardian*, Port of Spain, Trinidad, February 7, 1965.

JONKERS, E. H., "Enkele facetten van de economische ontwikkeling van Suriname", *Nieuwe West-Indische Gids*, No. 1-2, The Hague, April 1965.

KOCH, ERIC G., "De waarheid over onze Surinamers", *Dagblad De Telegraaf*, Amsterdam, February 15, 1966.

MEYER, Dr. A., "Achtergronden en problemen van de emigratie van Antillianen naar Nederland", *Nieuwsbrief*, Voorlichtingsdienst Ministerie van Cultuur, Recreatie en Maatschappelijk Werk, Rijswijk, Nr. 6-1971.

"Minder optimisme over verkoop, 'Real Estate'," *Het Financieële Dagblad*, Amsterdam, December 27, 1971.

"Ontsluiting van West Suriname belangrijk voor ontwikkeling van natuurlijke hulpbronnen", *De Ware Tijd*, Paramaribo, August 25, 1966.

O'SHAUGHNESSY, HUGH, "Tinted Tourists and Black Power", *The Financial Times*, London, February 1970.

"Racialism comes to the fore", *The Financial Times*, London, July 11, 1969.

"Scheepvaartschool N.A. begint in September", *Amigoe di Curaçao*, Willemstad, July 4, 1966.

SHORT, RENEE, "How the Dutch avoided the build-up of ghettoes", *The Times*, London, January 29, 1969.

SLUITER, E., "Dutch Guiana—A Problem in Boundaries", *Hispanic American Historical Review*, Vol. XIII, No. 1, Durham, N.C., February 1933.

STAHL, JOEL, "Surinam as manufacturing site offers good future prospects", *International Commerce*, No. 24, Washington, D.C., June 13, 1966, p. 28.

"Surinaamse partijen steken Pengel naar de kroon", *Algemeen Handelsblad*, Amsterdam, August 23, 1966.

"Surinam faces Independence issue", *The New York Herald Tribune*, New York, August 2, 1966.

"The Netherlands Antilles", *The New York Times*, advertising supplement, New York, May 2, 1965.

THEUNS, H. L., "Hulpverlening aan de Nederlandse Antillen", *International Spectator*, Het Nederlandsch Genootschap voor Internationale Zaken, The Hague, Het Koninklijk Institut voor Internationale Betrekkingen, Brussels, March 8, 1971.

"Trying to stay rich", *The Economist*, London, December 24, 1966.

"Unemployment the main scar", *The Financial Times*, London, December 4, 1970.

VAN BECKUM, PAUL, "Surinamers in Rotterdam", *Rotterdams Nieuwsblad*, Rotterdam, September 30, 1971.

VAN RAALTE, J. THOLENAAR, "De integratie van Westindische immigranten in Groot-Brittannie en in Nederland", *Nieuwe West-Indische Gids*, Martinus Nijhoff, The Hague, No. 2, June 1968.

VAN WAARDENBURG, D. A., "De Nederlandse Antillen en Engeland; uitbreiding van het nieuwe verdrag", *Maandbald Belastingbeschouwingen*, Nederlandsche Uitgeversmaatschappij, N.V., Leiden, No. 4, April 1971.

"Zoeklicht op Suriname", *Elseviers Weekblad*, The Hague, August 13, 1966.

GENERAL

SOURCES

(a) *Documents*

Aid to Developing Countries, Cmnd. 2147, London, September 1963.

Alliance for Progress, Declaration to the Peoples of America, Punta del Este, Uruguay, August 17, 1961. Pan American Union, Washington, 1961.

Assistance from the United Kingdom for Overseas Development, Cmnd. 974, London, 1960.

British Aid, Ministry of Overseas Development, H.M.S.O., London, 1966.

Bulletin of Labour Statistics, 1966 (2nd quarter), International Labour Office, Geneva.

Caribbean: a market report, London Chamber of Commerce, London, 1970.

Caribbean '66 Latin America, Report of the British Pump Manufacturers' Association, March 4-26, 1966.

Charter of the Organization of American States, Pan American Union, Washington, D.C., first printed in 1957, fourth printing 1962.

Charter of the United Nations and Statute of the International Court of Justice, United Nations, New York.

Congressional Record, 89th Congress First Session, No. 198, Part 2, October 22, 1965.

Cuba, Dominican Republic, Haiti, Puerto Rico, Quarterly Economic Review, The Economist Intelligence Unit, London.

Debates of the Senate, 3rd Session, 28 Parliament, Vol. 119, No. 22, *Official Report (Hansard), December 8, 1970*, Ottawa, 1970.

Documents on International Relations in the Caribbean, ed. Roy Preiswerk, Institute of Caribbean Studies, University of Puerto Rico, Río Piedras, 1970.

External Financing in Latin America, Department of Economic and Social Affairs, United Nations, New York, 1965.

Final Act, Second Special Inter-American Conference, Rio de Janeiro, Brazil, November 17-30, 1965. Pan American Union, Washington, D.C.

Financial and Technical Aid from Britain, Reference Pamphlet 62, Central Office of Information, H.M.S.O., London, 1964.

HAUCH, CHARLES C., *Educational Trends in the Caribbean: European Affiliated Areas*, U.S. Department of Health, Education, and Welfare, Washington, D.C., 1960.

Human Fertility and National Development, United Nations, 1971.

Immigration Act 1971, H.M.S.O., London, 1971.

International Conference on Public Education XXVIII Session, 1965, International Bureau of Education, Geneva, and U.N.E.S.C.O., Paris, 1965.

International Travel Statistics, 1969, International Union of Official Travel Organizations, Geneva, 1970.

La Politique de Coopération avec les pays en Voie de Développement (Rapport et Annexes), Jean-Marcel Jeanneney, Ministère d'Etat Chargé de la Réforme Administrative, La Documentation Française, Paris, 1963.

Literacy 1967-1969, U.N.E.S.C.O., Paris, 1970.

1971 World Population Data Sheet, Population Reference Bureau, Washington D.C., June 1971.

Official Records, Conference on Economic Coordination in the Caribbean, San Germán, Puerto Rico, May 17-19, 1965.

Overseas Development; The Work of the New Ministry, Cmnd. 2736, London, 1965.

Provisional Report on World Population Prospects as Assessed in 1963, United Nations, New York, 1963.

Report from the Select Committee on Overseas Aid, Session 1970-71, H.M.S.O., London, 1971.

Report of The Standing Committee on Foreign Affairs of The Senate of Canada on Canada-Caribbean Relations, Queen's Printer for Canada, Ottawa, 1970.

Report of the Uganda Relationships Commission, Government Printer, Entebbe, Uganda, 1961.

Text of President Nixon's Speech on Latin America, October 31, 1969, Washington, November 3, 1969.

The Caribbean Organization—The First Three Years 1961-1964, Caribbean Organization, Central Secretariat, Hato Rey, Puerto Rico, 1964.

The Capital Development Needs of the Less Developed Countries, Department of Economic and Social Affairs, United Nations, New York, 1962.

The Latin American Consensus of Viña del Mar, Comisión Especial de Coordinanción Latinoamericana, Viña del Mar, May 1969.

The Rockefeller Report on the Americas, The New York Times edition, introduced by Tad Szulc, Quadrangle Books, Chicago, 1969.

The Senate of Canada Proceedings of the Standing Senate Committee on Foreign Affairs, respecting the Caribbean area, No. 12, June 9, 1970, June 16 1970, Queen's Printer, Ottawa, 1970.

The United Kingdom and the European Communities, Cmnd. 4715, H.M.S.O., London, 1971.

United Nations, *Security Council Debates*, June 1965.

World Illiteracy at Mid-Century, U.N.E.S.C.O., Paris, 1957.

World Population: Challenge to Development, United Nations, New York, 1966.

World Population Data Sheet, Information Service, Population Reference Bureau, Washington, D.C., December 1965.

(b) *Newspapers, Periodicals and Year Books*

American Banker, New York.
Asta Travel News, New York.
Barclays Caribbean Bulletin, Barclays D.C.O., London.
Barclays International Review, Barclays Bank International Limited, London.
Bulletin, Institute for the Study of the U.S.S.R., Munich.
Business Review, Bank of Montreal, Montreal.
Business Week, New York.
Caribbean Business News, Toronto.
Caribbean Economic Review, Caribbean Commission, Port of Spain.
Caribbean Educational Bulletin, Institute of Caribbean Studies for the Association of Caribbean Universities, University of Puerto Rico, Río Piedras, Puerto Rico.
Caribbean Monthly Bulletin, Institute of Caribbean Studies, University of Puerto Rico, Río Piedras, Puerto Rico.
Caribbean Quarterly, University of the West Indies, Jamaica.
Caribbean Studies, Institute of Caribbean Studies, University of Puerto Rico, Río Piedras, Puerto Rico.
Central American Survey, Barclays Bank Ltd., London.
Chemische Rundschau, Solothurn, Switzerland.
Combate, San José, Costa Rica.
Commentary, American Jewish Committee, New York.
Cuadernos, Paris.
Cuadernos Americanos, Mexico.
Current History, Philadelphia.
Current Scene, Hong Kong.
Demographic Year Book, United Nations, New York.
Department of State Bulletin, Washington, D.C.
Diario las Américas, Miami.
El Universal, Caracas.
Encounter, London.
Expreso, Lima, Peru.
Foreign Affairs, Council on Foreign Relations, New York.
Foreign Economic Trends, Washington.
Foreign Policy Association Information Service, Foreign Policy Association, New York.
Foreign Trade, Ottawa.
Government and Opposition, London School of Economics, London.
Hispanic American Historical Review, Durham, N.C.
Hispanic American Report, Stanford University, California.
Hsinhua News Agency, Peking.
Informations du Commerce Extérieur, Brussels.
Inter-American Economic Affairs, Washington, D.C.
International Affairs, The Royal Institute of International Affairs, London.
International Affairs, Moscow.
International Commerce, Washington, D.C.

International Conciliation, New York.
International Journal, Canadian Institute of International Affairs, Toronto.
International Organization, Boston.
International Relations, London.
International Spectator, The Hague.
International Trade Forum, Geneva.
International Trade Review, New York.
Izvestia, Moscow.
Journal de Genève, Geneva.
Journal of Common Market Studies, Oxford.
Journal of Inter-American Studies and World Affairs (To January 1970, *Journal of Inter-American Studies*), Center for Advanced International Studies, University of Miami, Coral Gables, Florida.
Land Economics, Madison, Wisconsin.
Latin America, Latin America Newsletters Ltd., London.
Latin American Business Highlights, Chase Manhattan Bank, New York.
Le Figaro, Paris.
Le Monde, Paris.
Le Monde Diplomatique, Paris.
Les Affaires, Montreal.
Les Temps Modernes, Paris.
Life Magazine, New York.
Look, New York.
Los Angeles Times, Los Angeles, California.
Monthly Bulletin of Statistics, United Nations, New York.
Monthly Review, The Bank of Nova Scotia, Toronto.
Moorgate and Wall Street Review, Hill Samuel and Co., Ltd., London.
Morning Star, London (formerly *The Daily Worker*).
Nation's Business, The Chamber of Commerce of the United States, Washington, D.C.
Neue Zürcher Zeitung, Zürich.
New Commonwealth, London.
New Society, London.
New Statesman, London.
New Times, Moscow.
New York World Telegram and Sun, New York.
Newsweek, Dayton, Ohio (International edition, London).
Observer Foreign News Service, London.
Orbis, Foreign Policy Research Institute, University of Pennsylvania.
Overseas Business Reports, Washington, D.C.
Panam Magazine.
People, Population Reference Bureau, Washington.
Petroleum Press Service, London.
Political Science Quarterly, Columbia University, New York.
Population Bulletin, Population Reference Bureau, Washington, D.C.
Population Profile, Population Reference Bureau, Washington, D.C.
Pravda, Moscow.
Problems of Communism, Washington, D.C.
Quarterly Economic Review, The Economist Intelligence Unit, London.
Quarterly Review, Bank of London and South America, London.

Race, Institute of Race Relations, London.
Report of Tourist Travel to the Caribbean, the Caribbean Travel Association, New York.
San Francisco Sunday Examiner and Chronicle, San Francisco.
Scientific American, New York.
Scottish Geographical Magazine, Edinburgh.
Social and Economic Studies, Institute of Social and Economic Research, University of the West Indies, Jamaica.
South Eastern Latin Americanist, Southeastern Conference on Latin American Studies, University of Alabama, Alabama.
Statist, London.
Statistical Yearbook, U.N.E.S.C.O., Paris.
Studies in Comparative Communism, University of Southern California.
Sugar Review, C. Czarnikow Ltd., London.
Sugar Year Book, International Sugar Council, London.
Swiss Press Review and News Report, Berne, Switzerland.
The American Journal of International Law, Washington, D.C.
The Banker, London.
The Christian Science Monitor, Boston, Mass.
The Daily Express, London.
The Daily Telegraph, London.
The Economist, London.
The English Periodical Service of the Center of Intercultural Documentation, Cuernavaca, Mexico.
The Financial Times, London.
The Geographical Magazine, London.
The Globe and Mail, Toronto.
The Guardian, London.
The Hartford Courant, Hartford, Conn.
The Hindu, Madras.
The International and Comparative Law Quarterly, The British Institute of International and Comparative Law, London.
The International Herald Tribune, Paris.
The Journal of Commerce, New York.
The Journal of Politics, University of Florida, Gainesville.
The Latin American Times, New York.
The Listener, London.
The Miami Herald, Miami.
The Nation, New York.
The New Leader, New York.
The New Republic, Washington, D.C.
The New York Herald Tribune, New York.
The New York Herald Tribune (European Edition), Paris.
The New York Times, New York.
The OAS Chronicle, Pan American Union, Washington, D.C.
The Observer, London.
The Oil and Gas Journal, Tulsa, Oklahoma.
The Reporter, New York.
The Review of Politics, The University of Notre Dame, Notre Dame, Ind.
The Royal Gazette, Bermuda.

The Round Table, London.
The Scotsman, Edinburgh.
The Sunday Telegraph, London.
The Sunday Times, London.
The Times, London.
The Times, San Mateo, California.
The Travel Agent, New York.
The Wall Street Journal, New York.
The Washington Post, Washington, D.C.
The Weekly Review, Cheltenham.
The World Today, The Royal Institute of International Affairs, London.
The Yale Law Journal, New Haven, Conn.
The Year Book of World Affairs, London.
Time, New York.
Tricontinental, Havana.
U.S. News and World Report, Washington, D.C.
Ve Venezuela, Caracas.
Visión, Mexico City.
West Indies and Caribbean Yearbook, London.
West Indies Chronicle, London (formerly *Chronicle of the West India Committee*).
World Business, Chase Manhattan Bank, New York.
World Politics, Princeton University, New Jersey.
Yearbook of National Accounts Statistics, United Nations, N.Y.

STUDIES

(a) *Books and Pamphlets*

ALEXANDER, ROBERT J., *Government and Politics in Latin America*, "Organized Labor and Politics", ed. Harold E. Davis, The Ronald Press Company, New York, 1958.

AMADO, JORGE, *Terras do Sem Fim*, Livraria Martins, São Paulo, 1959.

ARCINIEGAS, GERMÁN, *Caribbean, Sea of the New World*, Alfred A. Knopf, New York, 1946.

ASPINALL, Sir ALGERNON, *The Pocket Guide to the West Indies*, Methuen & Co., London, 1960, reprint.

AUGIER, F. R., and S. C. GORDON, *Sources of West Indian History*, Longmans, London, 1962.

AUGIER, F. R., S. C. GORDON, D. G. HALL, and M. RECKORD, *The Making of The West Indies*, Longmans, London, 1960.

BARNES, A. C., *The Sugar Cane*, Leonard Hill, London, 1964.

BEMIS, SAMUEL FLAGG, *The Latin American Policy of the United States*, Harcourt, Brace and World, New York, 1943.

BEMIS, SAMUEL FLAGG, *A Diplomatic History of the United States*, Henry Holt and Company, New York, 1957, 4th edition.

BLANSHARD, PAUL, *Democracy and Empire in the Caribbean*, the Macmillan Company, New York, 1947.

BLOOD, Sir HILARY, *Parliament as an Export*, "Parliament in Small Territories", ed. Sir Alan Burns, George Allen & Unwin Ltd., London, 1966.

BOSCH, JUAN, *Pentagonism, a substitute for Imperialism*, Grove Press Inc., New York, 1968.

494

BUTLAND, GILBERT J., *Latin America: a Regional Geography*, Longmans, Green & Co., London, 1960.

CARLSON, FRED. A., *Geography of Latin America*, Prentice-Hall, Englewood Cliffs, New Jersey, 1952.

CARMICHAEL, STOKELY and CHARLES V. HAMILTON, *Black Power*, Penguin, Harmondsworth, 1969.

CARROLL, THOMAS F., *Latin American Issues*, "The Land Reform Issue in Latin America", ed. Albert O. Hirshman, The Twentieth Century Fund, New York, 1961.

CONNELL-SMITH, GORDON, *The Inter-American System*, Oxford University Press, London, 1966.

CORKRAN, HERBERT, *Patterns of International Cooperation in the Caribbean*, Southern Methodist University Press, Dallas, 1970.

COULTHARD, G. R., *Race and Colour in Caribbean Literature*, Oxford University Press, London, 1962.

CLARK, GERALD, *The Coming Explosion in Latin America*, David McKay Company, Inc., New York, 1962/1963.

COHEN, R., *The Economics of Agriculture*, Cambridge University Press, 1959.

DE MADARIAGA, SALVADOR, *Bolívar*, Editorial Sudamericana, Buenos Aires, 3rd edition, 1959, 2 vols.

DE MADARIAGA, SALVADOR, *Latin America between the Eagle and the Bear*, Hollis & Carter, London, 1962.

DEMAS, WILLIAM G., *The Economics of Development in Small Countries with Special Reference to the Caribbean*, McGill University Press, Montreal, 1965.

Developments Towards Self-Government in the Caribbean, A Symposium held under the auspices of the Netherlands Universities Foundation for International Cooperation, at The Hague, September 1954, Van Hoeve, The Hague, 1955.

ENSOR, Sir ROBERT, *The New Cambridge Modern History*, "Political Institutions in Europe: Political Issues and Political Thought", Cambridge University Press, 1960.

ESQUEMELING, JOHN, *The Buccaneers of America*, George Allen & Unwin Ltd., London, 1951.

FAGG, JOHN E., *Cuba, Haiti and the Dominican Republic*, Prentice-Hall Inc., New Jersey, 1965.

FAGG, JOHN E., *Latin America*, The Macmillan Company, New York, 1963.

FANON, FRANTZ, *The Wretched of the Earth*, Grove Press, New York, 1968.

FARÍAS, ARCILA, *Economía Colonial de Venezuela*, Fondo de Cultura Económica, Mexico, 1946.

FERMOR, PATRICK LEIGH, *The Traveller's Tree*, John Murray, London, 1955.

FORBES, ROSITA, *Islands in the Sun*, Evans Brothers Limited, London, 1950.

FORESTER, C. S., *The Age of Fighting Sail*, Doubleday, New York, 1956.

FREYRE, GILBERTO, *Casa-Grande y Senzala*, Livraria José Olympio, Rio de Janeiro, 1954.

GAULD, CHARLES A., *The Last Titan*, Special Issue *Hispanic American Report*, Institute of Hispanic American and Luso-Brazilian Studies, Stanford University, 1964.

GOODHART, PHILIP, *Fifty Ships that Saved the World*, Heinemann, London, 1965.

GOUROU, PIERRE, *The Tropical World*, John Wiley & Sons Inc., New York, 1966, fourth edition. Translated by S. H. Beaver and E. D. Laborde.

GREEN, L. C., *International Law Through the Cases*, Stevens and Sons Ltd., London, 1959.

GUÉRIN, DANIEL, *The West Indies and their Future*, Dennis Dobson, London, 1961.

HALLE, LOUIS J., *American Foreign Policy*, Allen and Unwin, London, 1960.

HARING, C. H., *The Spanish Empire in America*, Oxford University Press, New York, 1947.

HART, FRANCIS RUSSELL, *Admirals of the Caribbean*, George Allen & Unwin Ltd., London, 1923.

HAYTER, TERESA, *Aid as Imperialism*, Penguin, Harmondsworth, 1971.

HERRERA, FELIPE, *Nacionalismo Latinoamericano*, Editorial Universitaria, Santiago, Chile 1968.

HERRING, HUBERT, *A History of Latin America*, 2nd edition revised, Alfred A. Knopf, New York, 1961.

HILTON, RONALD, "The Population Explosion in Latin America", reprinted from *The Population Crisis and the Use of World Resources*, Uitgeverij Dr. W. Junk, World Academy of Art and Science No. 2, The Hague, 1964.

HILTON, RONALD, *The Scientific Institutions of Latin America*, California Institute of International Studies, Stanford, 1970.

Histoire des Relations Internationales, Tome Septième, ed. Pierre Renouvin, Hachette, Paris, 1957.

HOOVER, CALVIN B., *Development: For What?*, "Economic Reform vs. Economic Growth in Underdeveloped Countries", ed. John H. Hallowell, Duke University Press, Durham, N.C., 1964.

Intervention in Latin America, ed. C. Neale Ronning, Alfred A. Knopf, New York, 1970.

IRELAND, GORDON, *Boundaries and Conflicts in South America*, Harvard University Press, Cambridge, Mass., 1938.

JAMES, PRESTON, *Latin America*, 3rd edition, The Odyssey Press, New York, 1959.

JESSUP, PHILIP C., *A Modern Law of Nations*, The Macmillan Company, New York, 1958.

KENNEDY, SENATOR JOHN F., *The Strategy of Peace*, Harper and Brothers, New York, 1960.

Khrushchev Remembers, ed. Edward Crankshaw, André Deutsch, London, 1971.

KOTT, JAN, *Shakespeare our Contemporary*, Methuen and Co. Ltd., London, 1964, translated by Boleslaw Taborski.

LAZO, MARIO, *American Policy Failures in Cuba*, Twin Circle Publishing Co., Inc., N.Y., 1970.

LEIP, HANS, *The Gulf Stream Story*, Jarrolds, London, 1957, translated by H. A. Piehler and K. Kirkness.

LEWIS, Professor Sir ARTHUR, *The Theory of Economic Growth*, George Allen & Unwin Ltd., London, 1955.

MACPHERSON, JOHN, *Caribbean Lands*, A geography of the West Indies, Longmans Green and Co., London, 1963.

MCNAMARA, ROBERT S., *Address to the Board of Governors*, World Bank Group, Washington D.C., September 27, 1971.

MAHAN, ALFRED THAYER, *The Influence of Sea Power upon History*, 8th edition, Little, Brown and Company, Boston, 1894.

MARIGHELLA, CARLOS, *Minimanual of the Urban Guerrilla*, Spade, n.p., n.d.

MARRERO, LEVI, *Venezuela y sus Recursos*, Cultural Venezolana, Caracas, n.d.

MATHEWS, T. G., G. LATORTUE, M. S. JOSHUA, F. M. ANDIC, S. ANDIC, and A. P. THORNE, *Politics and Economics in the Caribbean*, Institute of Caribbean Studies, University of Puerto Rico, Río Piedras, 1966.

MAY, STACY, and GALO PLAZA, *The United Fruit Company in Latin America*, National Planning Association, Washington, D.C., 1958.

MENDEZ-AROCHA, ALBERTO, *La Pesca en Margarita*, Estación de Investigaciones Marinas de Margarita, Fundación La Salle de Ciencias Naturales, Caracas, 1963.

MILLER, JOHN C., *Origins of the American Republic*, Stanford University Press, Stanford, 1959.

MITCHELL, Sir HAROLD P., *In My Stride*, W. & R. Chambers, Ltd., Edinburgh, 1951.

MITCHELL, Sir HAROLD P., *Europe in the Caribbean*, W. & R. Chambers, Ltd., Edinburgh, 1963.

MITCHELL, Sir HAROLD P., *Co-operation in the Caribbean*, Address to the Antillean Students' Association at Delft, Netherlands, October 31, 1963.

MITCHELL, Sir HAROLD P., *L'agriculture aux Antilles*, Colloque International Centre National de la Récherche Scientifique, Paris, October 1965.

MITCHELL, Sir HAROLD P., *The Caribbean in Relation to the Integration of Latin America*, The California Institute of International Affairs, May 1968.

MORGENTHAU, HANS J., *Politics Among Nations*, Alfred A. Knopf, New York, revised third edition, 1960.

MORISON, SAMUEL ELIOT, *Admiral of the Ocean Sea*, Little, Brown and Company, Boston, 1942.

MORISON, SAMUEL E., and HENRY S. COMMAGER, *The Growth of the American Republic*, 2 vols, Oxford University Press, New York, 4th edition, 1958.

Movement Towards Latin American Unity, ed. Ronald Hilton, Praeger, New York, 1969.

MUNRO, DANA G., *Intervention and Dollar Diplomacy in the Caribbean*, Princeton University Press, Princeton, N.J., 1964.

NAIPAUL, V. S., *The Middle Passage*, Andre Deutsch, London, 1962.

NIXON, RICHARD M., *The Challenges We Face*, McGraw-Hill Book Company, New York, 1960.

OGILVY, DAVID, *Confessions of an Advertising Man*, Dell Publishing Co. Inc., New York, 1964.

OHLIN, GORAN, *Foreign Aid Policies Reconsidered*, Development Centre of the Organization for Economic Cooperation and Development, Paris, 1966.

OLIVERA, OTTO, *Breve Historia de la Literatura Antillana*, Ediciónes de Andrea, Mexico, 1957.

PARES, RICHARD, *A West India Fortune*, Longmans, Green & Co., London, 1950.

PARRY, J. H., and P. M. SHERLOCK, *A Short History of the West Indies*, Macmillan & Co., Ltd., London, 1960.

Partners in Development, Report of the Commission on International Development (Chairman Lester B. Pearson), Pall Mall Press, London 1969.

Patterns of Foreign Influence in the Caribbean, ed. Emanuel de Kadt, Royal Institute of International Affairs, Oxford University Press, 1972.

PENKOVSKY, OLEG, *The Penkovsky Papers*, ed. Frank Gibney, Collins, London, 1966.

PIPPIN, Professor LARRY, *The Remón Era*, special issue *Hispanic American Report*, Institute of Hispanic American and Luso-Brazilian Studies, Stanford University, 1964.

PLAZA, GALO, *Latin America: Evolution or Explosion*, "Problems of Education in Latin America", ed. Mildred Adams, Dodd, Mead & Co., New York, 1963.

PRATT, JULIUS W., *A History of United States Foreign Policy*, Prentice-Hall, Inc., Englewood Cliffs, N.J., 1958.

PROUDFOOT, M., *Britain and the U.S.A. in the Caribbean*, Frederick A. Praeger, New York, 1953.

QUARRY, JOHN, *The Land and People of the West Indies*, Adam and Charles Black, London, 1956.

REVERT, EUGÈNE, *Le Monde Caraïbe*, Les Editions Françaises, Paris, 1958.

REVERT, EUGÈNE, *Les Antilles*, Collection Armand Colin, Paris, 1954.

RICKARDS, COLIN, *Caribbean Power*, Dennis Dobson, London, 1963.

RIPPY, FRED J., *Latin America*, University of Michigan Press, Ann Arbor, 1958.

RODNEY, WALTER, *The Groundings with my Brothers*, The Bogle-L'Ouverture Publications, London, 1969.

RUBIN, SEYMOUR, *The Conscience of the Rich Nations*, Council on Foreign Relations, New York, 1966.

SCHLESINGER, Jr., ARTHUR M., *A Thousand Days*, Andre Deutsch, London, 1965.

SERVAN-SHREIBER, JEAN-JACQUES, *Le Défi Americaine*, Denoël, Paris, 1967.

SILBERMAN, CHARLES E., *Crisis in Black and White*, Jonathan Cape, London, 1965.

SMITH, M. G., *West Indian Family Structure*, University of Washington Press, Seattle, 1962.

"Some Caribbean problems", *World Survey*, The Atlantic Education Trust, London, June 1969.

SORENSEN, THEODORE C., *Kennedy*, Hodder and Stoughton, London, 1965.

SOUTHGATE, JOHN, *Agricultural Trade and the E.E.C.*, Fabian Research Series 294, Fabian Society, London, May 1971.

STOESSINGER, JOHN G., *The Might of Nations*, Random House, New York, 1965.

STUART, GRAHAM H., *Latin America and the United States*, 5th edition, Appleton-Century-Crofts, New York, 1955.

SUBERO, JESÚS MANUEL, *Cien Años de Historia Margariteña*, Impresora Delta C.A., Caracas, 1965.

Symposium Intercolonial, juin/juillet, 1952, Organisé par la Faculté des Lettres de Bordeaux et l'Institut de la France d'Outre-Mer, Imprimeries Delmas, Bordeaux, 1954.

TANNENBAUM, FRANK, *Ten Keys to Latin America*, Alfred A. Knopf, New York, 1964.

TANNENBAUM, FRANK, *Caribbean Studies: A Symposium*, "Discussion", ed. Vera Rubin, University of Washington Press, Seattle, 1960.

The Caribbean, ed. A. Curtis Wilgus, University of Florida Press, Gainesville, 1950-1966.

THOMAS, A. B., *Latin America: A History*, Macmillan, New York, 1956.

TILLYARD, E. M. W., *Shakespeare's History Plays*, Chatto and Windus, London, 1961.

TIMOSHENKO, VLADIMIR, and BORIS C. SWERLING, *The World's Sugar*, Stanford University Press, Stanford, California, 1957.

TRAVIS, MARTIN B., and JAMES T. WATKINS, "Control of the Panama Canal: an Obsolete Shibboleth?", *Foreign Affairs*, Vol. XXXVII, No. 3, April 1959, reprinted by Stanford University, Political Science Series, No. 64.

VASCONCELOS, JOSÉ, *La Raza Cósmica*, Colección Austral, Mexico, 1948.

WARD, BARBARA, and P. T. BAUER, *Two Views on Aid to Developing Countries*, Occasional Paper 9, The Institute of Economic Affairs, London, 1966.

WAUGH, ALEC, *A Family of Islands*, Doubleday and Company, Inc., Garden City, New York, 1964.

WILLIAMS, ERIC, *Documents of West Indian History, 1492-1655*, P.N.M. Publishing Co., Port of Spain, Trinidad, 1963.

WILLIAMS, ERIC, *Capitalism and Slavery*, Andre Deutsch, London, 1964.

WILLIAMS, ERIC, *From Columbus to Castro, The History of the Caribbean 1492-1969*, Andre Deutsch, London, 1970.

WINKS, ROBIN W., *Canadian-West Indian Union: A Forty Year Minuet*, University of London, Athlone Press, 1968.

WISE, DAVID, and THOMAS B. ROSS, *The Invisible Government*, Jonathan Cape, London, 1965.

WORCESTER, D. E., and W. G. SCHAEFFER, *The Growth and Culture of Latin America*, Oxford University Press, New York, 1956.

YOUNG, EVERILD, and KJELD HELWEG-LARSEN, *Rogues and Raiders*, Jarrolds, London, 1959.

(b) *Articles*

ALEXANDER, ROBERT J., "Agrarian Reform in Latin America", *Foreign Affairs*, Vol. 41, No. 1, Council on Foreign Relations, New York, October 1962.

ANDIC, FUAT M., "The development impact of the E.E.C. on the French and Dutch Caribbean", *Journal of Common Market Studies*, Oxford, September 1969.

ANGLIN, DOUGLAS G., "United States Opposition to Canadian Membership in the Pan American Union: A Canadian View", *International Organization*, XV, No. 1, World Peace Foundation, Boston, Winter 1961.

BABURAM, ALFRED, "The Press and the new Carib society", *Sunday Graphic*, Georgetown, Guyana.

BAILEY, RICHARD, "Tied Aid Not Too Helpful to Payments", *The Times*, London, June 7, 1966.

BARROW, ERROL, "A Role for Canada in the West Indies", *International Journal*, Vol. XIX, No. 2, Canadian Institute of International Affairs, Toronto, Spring 1964.

BENÍTEZ, Dr. JAIME, "Developing Nations in the International Arena", Caribbean Conference on International Affairs, University of the West Indies, Jamaica, March 17, 1966.

"Black against black", *The Economist*, London, April 25, 1970.

"Black Power on the Beach", *Time*, New York, October 19, 1970.

499

BLUMENTHAL, W. MICHAEL, "A World of Preferences", *Foreign Affairs*, Council on Foreign Relations, New York, April 1970.

BOSSHARD, ANTOINE, "Le face à face des riches et des pauvres", *Journal de Genève*, Geneva, August 28-29, 1971.

CABLE, VINCENT, "The 'Football War' and the Central American Common Market", *International Affairs*, The Royal Institute of International Affairs, London, October 1969.

CAMPBELL OF ESKAN, LORD, "The Bitter Sweet World of Sugar", *The Round Table*, London, April 1971.

"Caribbean Agriculture", Survey, *The Financial Times*, London, April 29, 1970.

Caribbean Integration, papers on Social, Political and Economic Integration, 3rd Caribbean Scholars' Conference, Georgetown, Guyana, 4-9 April, 1966, Institute of Caribbean Studies, University of Puerto Rico, Río Piedras, Puerto Rico, 1967.

"Charity at 6½%", *The Economist*, London, October 1, 1966.

"Chinese Efforts in Latin America", *The Times*, London, Latin American Correspondent, January 5, 1966.

CONNELL-SMITH, GORDON, "Inter-American Relations Today", *Quarterly Review*, Vol. VI, No. 2, Bank of London and South America Ltd., London, April 1966.

DE ONIS, JUAN, "Hemisphere: Rio Plus and Minus", *The New York Times*, New York, December 5, 1965.

DE ONIS, JUAN, "A Latin Revolution: Birth-Control Pills", *The New York Times*, New York, April 12, 1967.

DOXEY, G. V., "Canada takes the Initiative", *The Round Table*, London, October 1966.

DOXEY, G. V., "Canada and the Organisation of American States", The Caribbean and Latin America: Political and Economic Relations Conference, University of the West Indies, Jamaica, March 13-17, 1967.

DUNNE, S. J., The Reverend GEORGE H., "World Peace and the Population Crisis", *Population Bulletin*, Vol. XXI, No. 1, Population Reference Bureau, Inc., Washington, D.C., February 1965.

DYKE, LORNE D. R., "Take Two Weeks in the Eastern Caribbean", *Foreign Trade*, No. 4, Ottawa, August 21, 1965.

FIELD, MICHAEL, "Black Power's itchy palm", *The Daily Telegraph*, London, May 28, 1970.

FIELD, MICHAEL, "Black Power in the Caribbean", *The Daily Telegraph*, London, May 15, 1970.

FIELD, MICHAEL, "New Directions in Latin America", *The Daily Telegraph*, London, December 7, 1965.

FRASER, PROFESSOR D. G., "Canada deserting the Caribbean?", *West Indies Chronicle*, London, July 1970.

FURTADO, CELSO, "U.S. Hegemony and the Future of Latin America", *The World Today*, Vol. 22, No. 9, The Royal Institute of International Affairs, London, September 1966.

GALL, NORMAN, "Mao-type War in the Andes", *The Observer*, London, January 16, 1966.

"Getting the West Indies into Order", *Statist*, London, April 29, 1966.

GIRVAN, NORMAN, and OWEN JEFFERSON, "Institutional Arrangements and

The Economic Integration of the Caribbean and Latin America", The Caribbean and Latin America: Political and Economic Relations Conference, University of the West Indies, Jamaica, March 13-17, 1967.

GRIGORYAN, Y., "Rivals of the U.S.A. in Latin America", *International Affairs*, No. 12, Moscow, 1965.

GRONDONA, MARIANO, "The role of the United States in the world: a Latin American point of view", *The Working Papers from the 1970 Atlantic Conference*, Dorado Beach, Puerto Rico, November 12-15, 1970, The Centre for Inter-American Relations, New York, 1971.

HAAR, CHARLES M., "Latin America's Troubled Cities", *Foreign Affairs*, Vol. 41, No. 3, Council on Foreign Relations, New York, April 1963.

HARBRON, JOHN, "Canada in Caribbean America: technique for involvement", *Journal of Inter-American Studies and World Affairs*, Vol. XII, No. 4, University of Miami, October 1970.

HASSON, JOSEPH A., "Latin American Development: The Role of the Inter-American Committee for the Alliance for Progress", *Orbis*, Vol. IX, No. 4, Foreign Policy Research Institute, University of Pennsylvania, Winter 1966.

HAWTIN, GUY, "The Commonwealth without us", *The Times*, London, June 16, 1971.

HERRERA, FELIPE, "The Inter-American Bank: Catalyst for Latin American Development", *The World Today*, Vol. 20, No. 11, The Royal Institute of International Affairs, London, November 1964.

HOLMES, JOHN W., "Canada and Pan America", *Journal of Inter-American Studies*, Vol. X, No. 2, University of Miami, April 1968.

HUMPHREY, HUBERT H., "U.S. Policy in Latin America", *Foreign Affairs*, Vol. 42, No. 4, Council on Foreign Relations, New York, July 1964.

"Industrial Ports of the Caribbean", Survey, *The Financial Times*, London, August 27, 1969.

"Investments in the Caribbean", Survey, *The Financial Times*, London, February 4, 1970.

KHAN-PANNI, AZIZ, "Sugar: bitter-sweet balance", *The Sunday Times*, London, May 16, 1971.

KRASSOWSKI, ANDRZEJ, "Aid and the British Balance of Payments", *Moorgate and Wall Street Review*, Hill Samuel and Co. Ltd., London, Spring 1965.

LAWSON, NIGEL, "Foreign aid: the wrong thing for the right reasons", *The Times*, London, November 3, 1971.

LEE, Dr. PHILIP R., "The Role of Health Programs in International Development", *Population Bulletin*, Vol. XXI, No. 2, Population Reference Bureau, Washington, D.C., May 1965.

LERCHE, CHARLES O., "The Crisis in American World Leadership", *The Journal of Politics*, Vol. 28, No. 2, Southern Political Science Association together with the University of Florida, May 1966.

"Les producteurs de sucre du Commonwealth se contentent de la 'ferme garantie' donnée par les 'Six' de la C.E.E.", *Europe-France-Outremer*, Paris, July 1971.

LLERAS CAMARGO, ALBERTO, "The Alliance for Progress: Aims, Distortions, Obstacles", *Foreign Affairs*, Vol. 42, No. 1, Council on Foreign Relations, New York, October 1963.

LODGE, GEORGE C., "Revolution in Latin America", *Foreign Affairs*, Vol. 44, No. 2, Council on Foreign Relations, New York, January 1966.

MALABRE, Jr., ALFRED L., "Curbing Latin Births", *The Wall Street Journal*, New York, April 7, 1967.

MAÑACH, JORGE, "José Martí Rompeolas de América", *Combate*, San José, Costa Rica, March/April 1961.

MANIGAT, LESLIE F., "Les Etats-Unis et le Secteur Caraïbe de l'Amérique Latine", *Revue française de science politique*, Paris, June 1969.

MARTIN, PAUL, "Latin America: Challenge and Response", 2nd Annual Conference on World Development, The Canadian Institute of International Affairs, and the United Nations Association in Canada, in co-operation with the University of Alberta, Banff, August 24, 1964.

"Micro-states loom large", *The Financial Times*, London, April 10, 1969.

MIRÓ CARDONA, Dr. JOSÉ, "La Infiltración Comunista en América", *Diario Las Américas*, Miami, November 8, 1963.

MIRÓ CARDONA, Dr. JOSÉ, "El Comunismo en el Caribe", *Diario Las Américas*, Miami, June 21, 23, 24, 1964.

MITCHELL, Sir HAROLD P., "Conflict and Cooperation in Tomorrow's Caribbean", *International Journal*, Vol. XXIV, No. 3, Canadian Institute of International Affairs, Toronto, Summer, 1969.

MITCHELL, Sir HAROLD P., "Islands of the Caribbean", *Current History*, Philadelphia, February 1970.

OLIVER, COVEY T., "Foreign and Human Relations with Latin America", *Foreign Affairs*, Council on Foreign Affairs, New York, April 1969.

PACKENHAM, KEVIN, "A sugar-free Caribbean", *The Times*, London, June 2, 1971.

PARKINSON, F., "The Alliance for Progress", *The Year Book of World Affairs, 1964*, The London Institute of World Affairs, London, 1964.

PATTERSON, WILLIAM D., "The Big Picture 1963-1964", reprinted from the March, April, May and June, 1964, editions of *Asta Travel News*, New York.

PERSAUD, BISHNODAT, "An Enlarged E.E.C. and the Commonwealth Caribbean", *The Round Table*, London, October 1971.

PLANK, John N., "The Caribbean: Intervention, When and How", *Foreign Affairs*, Vol. 44, No. 1, Council on Foreign Relations, New York, October 1965.

PREISWERK, ROY, "La coopération régionale dans les Caraïbes", *Le Monde Diplomatique*, Paris, August 1968.

PREISWERK, ROY, "The Relevance of Latin America to the Foreign Policy of Commonwealth Caribbean States", *Journal of Inter-American Studies*, Vol. XI, No. 2, University of Miami, Coral Gables, Florida, April 1969.

REID, ESCOTT, "The Crisis in Foreign Aid", *The World Today*, Vol. 22, No. 8, The Royal Institute of International Affairs, London, August 1966.

REIRSON, ROY L., "Why the Dollar Worries Europe", *U.S. News and World Report*, Washington, D.C., October 3, 1966.

ROCKEFELLER, DAVID, "What Private Enterprise Means to Latin America", *Foreign Affairs*, Vol. 44, No. 3, Council on Foreign Relations, New York, April 1966.

ROWLEY, ANTHONY, "Six sugar policy seen as threat to Tate and Lyle operations", *The Times*, London, May 14, 1971.

RUNGE, SIR PETER, "Sugar—the world and the Caribbean" Address, New York Sugar Club, New York, February 29, 1968.

SAINT-PIERRE, C.-J., "Des Produits Canadiens sont fort bien accueillis aux Antilles", *Les Affaires*, Montreal, February 7, 1966.

"San Juan plans neighbourly help", *The New York Times*, New York, January 16, 1966.

SANZ DE SANTAMARÍA, CARLOS, Statement, The Caribbean and Latin America: Political and Economic Relations Conference, University of the West Indies, Jamaica, March 13-17, 1967.

SEGAL, AARON, "Economic Integration and Preferential Trade: the Caribbean Experience", *The World Today*, The Royal Institute of International Affairs, Chatham House, London, October 1969.

SELOVER, WILLIAM C., "Allende cracks O.A.S., unity", *The Christian Science Monitor*, Boston, November 14, 1970.

SEMIDEI, MANUELA, "Pouvoir noir et décolonisation dans les Caraïbes", *Le Monde Diplomatique*, Paris, January 4, 1971.

SHERLOCK, Sir PHILIP, "Prospects in the Caribbean", *Foreign Affairs*, Council on Foreign Relations, New York, July 1963.

SLATER, JEROME, "The United States, The Organization of American States, and the Dominican Republic, 1961-1963", *International Organization*, Vol. XVIII, No. 2, World Peace Foundation, Boston, Spring 1964.

SMITHERS, DAVID, "The American umbrella: is it letting in the rain?", *Chronicle of the West India Committee*, London, February 1967.

SYLVESTER, ANTHONY, "Caribbean Imperatives", *The Scotsman*, Edinburgh, January 19, 1972.

TANNENBAUM, FRANK, "The United States and Latin America", *Political Science Quarterly*, Vol. LXXVI, No. 2, Columbia University, New York, June 1961.

"Tate and Lyle Looking Past Sugar", *The Daily Telegraph*, London, March 23, 1967.

"The Expanding 'Universe of the Untutored' ", *Population Profile*, Population Reference Bureau Inc., Washington, D.C., September 26, 1966.

"The Latin American offshore", *Petroleum Press Service*, Vol. 38, No. 3, London, March 1971.

"The 'Liberal' Break with Johnson", *U.S. News and World Report*, Washington, D.C., May 24, 1965.

"The Paradox of Canadian foreign policy", *The Times*, London, December 30, 1966.

TOMASSINI, LUCIANO, "Towards a Latin American nationalism", *The World Today*, The Royal Institute of International Affairs, London, December 1969.

"Tourism in Latin America", *Latin American Business Highlights*, Chase Manhattan Bank, New York, 3rd Quarter 1964.

TRETIAK, DANIEL, "Sino-Soviet Rivalry in Latin America", *Problems of Communism*, Vol. XII, No. 1, Washington, D.C., Jan.-Feb. 1963.

"Two-Way Movement of World's Skill", *The Times*, London, July 16, 1965.

VAUGHAN, JACK H., "U.S. Trade Policy in Latin America", *Department of State Bulletin*, Washington, D.C., October 4, 1965.

WIGG, RICHARD, "Socialist Government in Chile to step up rate of farm takeovers", *The Times*, London, May 2, 1971.

WILLIAMS, ERIC, "Canada in the West Indies—a Force for Island Unity", *The Round Table*, January 1967.

WILSON, LARMAN C., "International Law and the United States Cuban Quarantine of 1962", *Journal of Inter-American Studies*, Vol. VII, No. 4, University of Miami, Coral Cables, October 1965.

WILSON, LARMAN C., "The Monroe Doctrine, Cold War Anachronism: Cuba and the Dominican Republic", *The Journal of Politics*, Vol. 28, No. 2, Southern Political Science Association together with the University of Florida, May 1966.

WIONCEZEK, MIGUEL S., "The Rise and Decline of Latin American Economic Integration," *Journal of Common Market Studies*, Vol. 9, No. 1, Oxford, September 1970.

WOLFERS, MICHAEL, " 'Help with strings' seen as instrument of power politics", *The Times*, London, Supplement, September 14, 1971.

WOODLAND, JOHN, "Coffee man faces a tough job", *The Times*, London, March 20, 1967.

WOODRUFF, WILLIAM and HELGA WOODRUFF, "The illusions about the role of integration in Latin America's future", *Inter-American Economic Affairs*, Washington, Spring, 1969.

WOODS, GEORGE D., "The Development Decade in the Balance", *Foreign Affairs*, Vol. 44, No. 2, Council on Foreign Relations, New York, January 1966.

CURRENCY CHART[1]

Country	Currency	*Sterling* £1 *equivalent in local currency*	*U.S.* $1 *equivalent in local currency*
Cuba	Peso	2.21	0.90
Haiti	Gourde (1 Haitian Dollar = 5 Gourdes)	12.25	5.00
Dominican Rep.	Gold Peso or R.D. Dollar	2.45	Par
Puerto Rico and Virgin Islands of the United States, also British Virgin Islands	U.S. Dollar	2.45	Par
Bahamas	Bahamian Dollar	2.36	0.97
Jamaica Turks and Caicos Islands	Jamaican Dollar	2.00	0.815
Cayman Islands	Cayman Islands Dollar	2.00	0.815
Antigua St. Kitts-Nevis- Anguilla Montserrat Dominica St. Lucia St. Vincent Barbados	East Caribbean Dollar[2]	4.80	1.96
Trinidad and Tobago Grenada	Trinidad and Tobago Dollar[2]	4.80	1.96
Guyana	Guyana Dollar[2]	5.21	2.13
British Honduras	British Honduras Dollar	4.00	1.63
Martinique Guadeloupe Guyane	Martinique Franc Guadeloupe Franc Guyane Franc	12.26	5.00
Netherlands Antilles	N.A. Florin/Guilder	4.30	1.75
Surinam	Surinam Florin	4.29	1.75

[1] As at August 10, 1972. Values subject to fluctuation.
[2] British West Indian Dollar until 1965.

INDEX

bananas in—*contd.*
  Guyane, 289
  Haiti:
    as Haiti's second crop, 62
    contract with Standard Fruit and
      Steamship Co., 62, 63
    expansion of, 61
    in Artibonite Valley, 62
    rise and fall of, 62-3
    ruined by Haitian politics, 62-3
  Jamaica:
    competition in, 174, 333
    continuing problems of, 147, 150
    depression in, 147
    disease, 174
    hazards of growing, 174n
    hurricane damage to, 174
    land used for, 145
    shipping of, 147
  Martinique, 277-8, 282, 285
  St. Lucia, 188, 189
  St. Vincent, 190
  Surinam, 314
  Windward Islands, 174, 174n, 186, 333
Bangou, Henri, 271, 273n
banking:
  in Haiti, 49, 356, 424
  in Puerto Rico, 108, 355, 356
  in the Bahamas, 212, 424
  in the Caribbean, 353, 355-6
Banque Nationale de la République
  d'Haïti:
  establishment of, 49
  United States control of, 50
Barbados:
  agriculture:
    Agricultural Development Corpora-
      tion, 169
    cattle, 170
    dairying, 170
    diversification of, 171
    government land-ownership, 169
    intensive use of land, 170, 374
    smallholdings, 169, 170
    sugar, 169, 187, 321, 344
    value of products, 170
  banking in, 424
  Bridgetown Deep Water Harbour, 170
  Canada and, 424, 425
  CARIFTA and, 169n, 170, 171, 352,
    353n
  cattle, 170
  civil service, 168
  constitution:
    adult suffrage, 167
    House of Assembly, 168
    length of British government, 97, 167
    machinery for change in, 168
    nominated Senate, 168
    parliamentary government, 167, 171
    retention of original constitution,
      122, 221
    self-government, grant of, 167-8

Barbados—*contd.*
  dairying, 170
  democracy, 96
  Eastern Caribbean Federation, pro-
    posal for, 167
  economic:
    attempt to reduce imports, 170
    pattern, 169-71
    success of, 122
    use of resources, 344
  education:
    College of Arts and Sciences, 170,
      369
    high standard of, 170, 344, 374
    illiteracy rate, 170
    importance of University, 369
    teacher training, 170
    technical, 170
    University of the West Indies campus,
      149, 170, 173, 369
    withdrawal of British Council aid,
      149n:
  election of:
    1966, 168
    1971, 169
  emigration, 171, 374
  external affairs, 300
  family planning, 171, 418, 441
  federation with Windward Islands,
    123n
  fishing, 170, 171
  future of, 170
  geographical position of, 167
  harbour, 170
  independence:
    constitution under, 168
    desire for, 131, 167, 388
    effect of, on French Antilles, 272
    grant of, 167, 172
  industrialization:
    concessions for, 170
    Industrial Development Corpora-
      tion, 170
    industrial estates, 170
    industrialization policy, 170, 171
    limitations on, 170, 344
    Operation Beehive, 170
  judiciary, 168
  Marketing Corporation, 170
  Operation Beehive, 170
  Organization of American States:
    entry into, xvii-xviii, 5, 169, 421, 428
    observer sent to conference, 421
    tourism and, 170
  political:
    pattern, 167-9
    success of two-party system, 167, 231
  population:
    age of, 170
    density, 167, 170, 344, 358, 374, 436
    food production and, 170
    growth of, and unemployment, 170-1
    size of, 167

2 K   513

514

British Honduras—*contd.*
British:
settlement in, 250, 393
transgression of Monroe Doctrine,
401
cacao:
damage by Hurricane Hattie, 257
Hummingbird Development Co.,
257, 260
rehabilitation programme, 258
CARIFTA:
membership, 259, 353n
prospects, 259, 260
cattle, 260
citrus:
expansion of, 252, 256, 257, 260
shipping for, 258
Clayton-Bulwer Treaty, effect of, 216,
250
Colonial Development Corporation aid
for, 237, 259, 396
constitution:
abolition of Legislative Assembly,
251
Crown Colony government, 251
franchise, 251, 254
of 1954:
provisions of, 251-2
of 1964:
House of Representatives, 254
Senate, 254
restoration of elections, 251
currency:
sterling devaluation:
and West Indies Federation, 252-
253, 254
controversy, 252, 254, 279n
importance of parity, 252
defence, 254, 255
economic:
Caribbean Investments Ltd., 257-8
future, 259-60
pattern, 256-60
education, 259
elections of:
1954, 253
1957, 253
1969, 255
foreign investment in, 256
free port, attractions of, 260
future of, 255-6, 259-60
grapefruit, 257
gross domestic product, 259
harbour, need for deep-water, 258, 260
houses, 2, 319
hurricane hazards, 259, 319
immigration policy, 258-9
imports, 251
income *per capita*, 258
independence:
advocated by People's United Party,
253, 255, 256
grant of, 191n, 434

British Honduras: independence—*contd.*
name under, 255
prospects under, 256
Organization of American States and,
259
origins of, 250, 393
political parties:
absence of pull between rural and
urban, 256
Honduran Independence Party, 253,
255n
People's United Party:
control of Belize City Council,
252
imprisonment of leaders, 253
independence campaign, 253
success in elections, 253, 255
union associations, 232, 253
quality of leaders, 253
political pattern, 250-6
population, 255, 256, 260
racialism, avoidance of, 253-4, 256
shipping, problems of, 252, 258, 260n
Spanish dominance in, 250, 255
sugar:
Colonial Development Corporation
view of, 257
Commonwealth Sugar Agreement:
aid through, 254, 257
quota, 257
Corozal Sugar Factory, 257
expansion of, 252, 256, 257
export of, 257
hurricane damage to factory, 257,
319
International Sugar Agreement, 257
mechanization, 257, 260
Orange Walk Factory, 257
quality of, 257
shipping for, 258
timber:
diversity of forests, 256
drop in, 256
expansion of, 258
exports, 256
logwood, 250, 256
lumbering, 256
mahogany, 250, 256
tourism:
Colonial Development Corporation
aid for, 258, 396
expansion of, 258
hotel, 258
trade unions, 253, 256, 258
unemployment, 258
West Indies Federation:
fear of Jamaican immigration, 254n
fear of unemployment, 254n
issue of, in 1957 elections, 253
refusal to join, 124, 254
sterling devaluation and, 253
British North America Act, 221-2
Brookings Institution, 108

517

Canada: investment in—*contd.*
  Caribbean, 421, 424-5
  Haiti, 46
Jamaican export of bauxite to, 141
lumber trade, 112n
membership of Organization of American States, 420, 421
migration to cities, 334
oil trade, 424
rum trade, 423
Senate Standing Committee, 423-4, 426
sugar:
  Commonwealth Sugar Agreement, 423
  competition from beet, 428
  trade, 422
tourism, 425, 426
trade with:
  Caribbean, 422-3, 424
  Cuba, 36, 39, 422, 423
visit of Prime Minister to Jamaica and Trinidad, 426
visit of Senator Paul Martin, 424, 426
West Indian students in, 425-6
Canning, George, 400
Cantave, Léon, 56
Capildeo, Rudranath, 153, 154
Caracas:
  agreement of 1954, 55
  Dominican exiles in, 77
Caradon, Lord, 182, 412
Cardona, Dr. Miró:
  elected provisional president of Cuba, 14
  resignation from Revolutionary Council, 20
  views on American Cuban policy, 20
Cargill, Morris, 128
Caribbean:
  as the American Mediterranean, 3-4
  historical links with other countries, xvii
  situation of, 1
  use of term, 1
Caribbean Cement Co., 144
Caribbean Commission, 430
Caribbean Development Bank, 141, 353
Caribbean Economic Development Corporation, 430-1
Caribbean Free Trade Association, *see* CARIFTA
Caribbean Organization, 430
Caribbean Patterns, 1st Edition, xvii
Caribs:
  extinction of, 362, 377
  movements of, 320, 363, 364
CARIFTA:
  Agricultural Marketing Protocol, 335
  agriculture, 335, 436
  aims of, 391
  Barbados, 169n, 170, 171, 352, 353n
  British Honduras, 259, 260
  Caribbean Development Bank, 141, 353
  constitution of, 353

CARIFTA—*contd.*
  creation of, xviii, 4-5
  criticism by Jagan, 352
  Dominican Republic, 95, 141
  economic integration, 391, 434
  Expo '69, 194
  future of, 355, 430, 431, 433, 436
  Guyana, 248-9
  Haiti, 141
  impact of, 353-4
  industry, encouragement of, 5
  Jamaica and, 95n, 150
  launching of, 352-3
  member countries, 353
  Montserrat, 185
  need for, xviii
  Oils and Fats Agreement, 186, 188
  origin of, 352
  problems, 354
  purpose of, 5
  St. Lucia, 188
  St. Vincent, 190
  significance of, 4-5
  trade and, 5
  Trinidad, 95n
  unemployment and, 436
Carlisle, Lord, 167
Carmichael, Stokeley, 155, 390n
Caroni, 163
Carriacou, 191, 192
Casiano, Manuel A., 115n
Castro, Angel, 26
Castro, President Cipriano, 301n, 404
Castro, Fidel:
  accession to power, 9-10
  admission of failure, 26
  agrarian policy, 10, 27, 327-8
  agricultural policy, xviii, 42, 327-8
  alignment with U.S.S.R., 22, 23
  appeal of, 10-11, 103, 383-4
  as a *caudillo* in modern setting, 21, 31
  attempted capture of Moncada Barracks, 9
  Bay of Pigs affair:
    action against invaders, 15
    foreknowledge of, 15
    enhancement of prestige after, 16, 22
    treatment of prisoners, 16-17
  censorship of press and broadcasting, 29, 31
  character of, 26
  charismatic qualities of, 26, 30, 390-1
  compared to Jagan, 26
Communism:
  Castroism and, 24
  desire to spread system to Latin America, 23, 25, 52
  influence of action, 83, 383-4
  of Castro, 21, 24, 26-7
  paving the way for, 77
  preference for militant, 23
  relations with Cuban, 22, 25-6, 31
  support of guerrillas, 24

519

Castro, Fidel—*contd.*
decline of prestige outside Cuba, 29
decline of revolutionary spirit, 25
denunciation of:
American policy in Dominican Republic, 23
American policy in Vietnam, 23
desire for independence, 29, 384
dislike of foreign investment, 26
disregard of dogma, 21
domestic policy, 22-3, 29
education policy, 29, 30, 46, 369-70, 371
elections:
promise of, 27
refusal to hold, 29, 31
execution of Batista followers, 10, 16
explanation of Guevara's disappearance, 23
expropriation policy, 10, 11
forced labour camps, 29, 31
honesty of, 29, 30, 39, 383, 384
idealism of, and Cuban materialism, 26
imprisonment and release of, 9, 27
increasing domination of Cuban policy, 21
indifference to economics, 26, 34
installation as Premier, 10
interest in Algeria, 40
interest in China, 19, 20, 384
lack of permitted opposition, 29
missiles crisis:
demand for withdrawal of American naval base, 19
humiliation of, 20, 21
part in, 17-18
refusal of inspection of sites, 19
Russian relations and, 17-18
nationalist policy, 383-4
part in "Bogotazo" riots, 26
part in Tricontinental Conference, 23
permission for disaffected Cubans to leave, 30, 68
personality of, 26, 28, 30
philosophy in early years, 26-7, 384
political ideals of, 9, 21, 22, 24, 26, 383-384
popularity with Cubans, 16, 20, 26, 30, 31, 48, 384
racialism, absence of, 384-5
speech at trial, 9, 27
struggle in Sierra Maestra, 9-10, 26-7, 383
successor, failure to appoint, 31
Twenty-sixth of July Movement, 10, 22
use of army, 31
use of television and radio, 30
U Thant's visit to, 19
views on birth control, 371
views on Organization of American States, 429
visit to Chile, 429, 432
visit to Moscow, 21, 39, 40

Castro, Fidel—*contd.*
visit to United States, 11, 226
withdrawal of Soviet ambassador, 22
world opinion of, 10, 27-8
Castro, Raúl:
as head of armed forces, 31
inexperience of economics, 34
representative at Moscow meeting of Communist parties, 21
visit to Moscow, 18
Castroism, 24
Cat Island, 209
Catayée, Justin, 287
Cato, Milton, 190
cattle in:
Bahamas, 209
Barbados, 170
Brazil, 279
Caribbean, 320
Cuba, 44, 95
Dominican Republic:
Bosch's advocacy of development of, 74
breeding under Trujillo, 95
destruction of pedigree herds, 95
French Antilles, 278
Guyana, 242
Guyane, 289
Haiti, 63
Puerto Rico, 112, 116
St. Lucia, 187
St. Vincent, 190
Cayman Islands:
airport, 214
air services to, 214, 344
as a dependency of Jamaica, 213
as a tax haven, 214, 344
association with Bay Islands, 216
banking, 355-6
Cayman Brac, 213
cession by Spain, 213
constitution, 213-14
development of, 214-15
economy of, 214-15
emigration from, 364
financial centre, 214-15
fishing, 214
Grand Cayman, 194, 213, 364
links with United States, 214
local industries, 214
merchant seamen, 214, 344, 364
Little Cayman, 213
population, 214
position, 213
refusal to enter the West Indies Federation, 213
tourism, 185, 214, 344, 354
Central African Federation, 174
Central America:
collapse of confederation, 134, 216, 393
Common Market, 134, 217, 354, 429-430, 431, 432

521

Columbus—*contd.*
  naming of:
    Margarita, 218
    St. Vincent, 189
  quest for treasure, 2
Commonwealth and CARIFTA, 89n
Commonwealth Caribbean-Canada Conference, 352, 421, 423
Commonwealth Development Corporation, 396
Commonwealth Immigrant Act, 142n
Commonwealth Sugar Agreement, *see* sugar
Communism:
  activities in Latin America, 21, 23, 89
  divided opinion on means of spreading, 22-3
  dividing American States, 89
  failure to spread Revolution, 22, 23
  in:
    Cuba, 22, 23, 24, 25, 30, 41-2, 47, 52, 53, 83, 240
    French Antilles, 264, 268-9, 270, 272
    Guadeloupe, 265, 268-9, 270-1, 272-273
    Haiti, 42, 52, 53, 59
    Martinique, 265, 267
    United States' fear of, 406, 407-8, 409, 410-11, 412, 415-16, 419, 426
  World Conference on, 25
constitutions, diversity of, 1
copra in:
  Dominica, 186
  Leeward Islands, 173
  Windward Islands, 173
Cortés, Hernán, 21
Costa Rica:
  C.A.C.M. and, 354
  reliance on police force, 255
  withholding of recognition of Dominican Republic Triumvirate, 78
cotton in:
  Caribbean, 327, 330
  Grenada, 192
  Haiti, 63, 379
  Leeward Islands, 173
  Montserrat, 184
  Nevis, 180
  St. Kitts, 179
  St. Lucia, 187
  Windward Islands, 173, 174
Coxin's Hole, 215
cricket, 1
Cripps, Sir Stafford, 388
Cromwell, Oliver, 135
Cuba:
  absenteeism, problem of, 36, 45
  agrarian reform:
    problems of, 38
    promises of, 10, 38, 327, 332
  agriculture:
    as the central work of the Revolution, 42

Cuba: agriculture—*contd.*
    beginnings of, 32
    call for increased production, 36-7
    cattle, 44, 95
    Cordon de Habana, 44
    development of, 61-2
    diversification policy, 37
    effects of monocultural economy, 32, 33, 37, 41, 42, 43, 328
    equipment for, 41
    expansion of, 6
    extension of nationalization to, 37, 38n
    failure of policy, 43-4, 47, 48
    failure to appreciate importance of, 95
    Instituto Nacional de Reforma Agraria (I.N.R.A.), 35-6
    labour shortage, 42
    lack of efficiency, 38
    land available for, 6, 32, 47, 334
    mechanization of, 1, 42
    need for diversification, 32-3, 327-8
    new projects, 44
    percentage of nationalized land, 39
    potential of, 47, 320
    rice, 44, 330
    Russian interest in Cuba's return to, 41
    smallholdings, 42, 47
    State farms, 38, 47
    sugar, 2, 6-7, 8, 10, 11, 12, 25, 32, 33, 35, 36, 37, 38, 39-40, 42, 43, 47-8, 95, 122, 322, 323-4, 327-8, 338, 341, 363
    tobacco, 44-5
  Algeria and, 40
  American dominance of:
    economic:
      access to markets, 8, 11, 32
      benefits of, 12, 28, 32-3, 62, 338, 383
      investment in, 32, 108, 339
    political:
      American naval power in the Caribbean, 7-8
      departure of mission, 383
      effects of, 383
      effects of Spanish-American War, 7, 27, 28, 32, 378, 404
      health improvements, 383
      institution of civil government, 98
      intervention in Cuba, 8, 50
      military control of, 7-8
      naval bases, 8, 19
      Platt Amendment, 7-8, 28, 29, 104, 383, 403, 404
      resentment against, 8
      trans-isthmian canal, 7, 8
      Treaty of 1903, 8
      Treaty of 1934, 8
      United States strategy and, 382
  area of, 240, 320
  Army, xviii, 16, 31, 385, 433

education in—*contd.*
Barbados:
College of Arts and Sciences, 170, 369
high standard of, 170, 344, 374
illiteracy rate, 170
importance of University, 369
teacher training, 170
technical, 170
University of the West Indies campus, 149, 170, 173, 369
withdrawal of British Council aid, 149n
Caribbean:
association with problem of population, 3, 4, 367-8
family planning and, 367-8
financing of, 3, 376
French influence in, 367
International Conference on Public Education, 368
Latin American concept of, 366, 367
literacy campaign, 368
nationalism and, 376, 378
need for better education, 4, 441
need for teachers, 368-9, 436
North American concept of, 366-7
population growth, unemployment and, 361, 376
transport problem, 376
University, 368-70
University of the West Indies, 369
variety of systems of, 440
Cuba:
adult, 46-7
appropriation from budget, 35
Centro Escolar, 46
concentration on, 29, 45, 384
higher, 30, 369-70
illiteracy:
drive to eliminate, 30, 46, 371, 433
percentage of, 46, 342, 371
importance attached to, by Revolutionary government, 46, 342, 369-370
Latin American pattern of, in pre-Castro Cuba, 45, 437
nationalization of, 371
number of graduates, 45
overconcentration on Arts, 45
pre-Revolution, 45-6, 367
propagation of Revolutionary ideas through, 46, 433
reform of, 46, 371
Russian aid for, 370
significance of advance in, 46-7
technological, 38, 45
under Castro, 369-70
University, 45, 46, 369-70
Curaçao:
Law School, 370
Navigational School, 303
Teachers' Training College, 307

education in—*contd.*
Dominican Republic:
effects of Haitian occupation, 69
financing of, 93
illiteracy:
among adults, 74
among youth, 94, 96
rate of, 94, 342, 370, 371
Latin American tradition in, 367
schools, 94
University:
aid for, 370
development of, 370
of Santo Domingo, 69
School of Agriculture and Animal Husbandry, 370
French Antilles:
aid for, 176, 272, 282
benefits of, 288, 289
discontent from, 268, 273, 284, 286
employment and, 284, 345, 389
French culture and the Negro race, 262
French type of, 261, 284, 267, 385
1963 Report, 279-80
Sixth Plan, 284
teacher shortage, 284
technical, 279, 284
Guadeloupe:
discontent of youth, 284, 389
French type of, 284, 367
services, 176, 345
technical, 284
Guyana:
aid for:
Booker Brothers, 247
United Nations, 247
Bishop's High School, 247
Queen's College, 247
St. Stanislaus College, 247
schools:
building of, 245
state of, 247
Teachers' Training College, 247
University of:
Guyana, 247, 369
the West Indies, 369
urban, 245-6
Ursuline Convent School, 247
Guyane:
illiteracy rate, 290-1
state of, 291
Haiti:
allocation from budget, 67-8
curriculum, 66
effects of reduction of American aid, 66
failure to use qualified Haitians, 68
financing of, 67-8
French basis of, 48, 66, 68, 367
illiteracy:
"écoles d'analphabétisation", 67
in rural areas, 66

education in Haiti: illiteracy—*contd.*
    need to solve problem of, 68
    percentage of, 49, 65, 66, 66n, 342,
        370, 371
    lack of technological, 67
    medium of instruction, 66-7
    monopoly of elite, 66
    primary, 67
    University, 67, 370
Jamaica:
    Free Church tradition in, 367
    G.C.E. results, 149
    illiteracy:
        campaign to reduce, 373-4
        percentage of, 148
    improvement in, 148
    infant schools, 149
    in rural areas, 148
    plans for extension, 148-9
    state of, 148-9
    teachers:
        number of, 148-9
        training of, 149n, 374
    technical:
        availability of, 145, 373
        emphasis on, 149
        in University of the West Indies,
            142
    U.N.E.S.C.O. help in planning, 149
    University of the West Indies:
        aid to, 395
        benefits of, 148, 173, 343, 369
        Black Power riots, 140
        expulsion of Walter Rodney, 140,
            390
        financing of, 369
        influence of graduates, 173
        medical faculty, 149
        number of students, 149
        technical education, 142
        withdrawal of British Council aid,
            149
        World Bank aid for, 149
Martinique:
    aid for, 282
    discontent of youth, 264, 389
    French type of, 261, 284, 367
    number of scholarships for study in
        France, 264
    services, 176, 367
Netherlands Antilles, 307, 316, 375
Puerto Rico:
    building of schools, 108
    emphasis on, 117
    expenditure on, 117n
    illiteracy rate, 111
    improvement in, 111
    numbers attending school, 111
    population movements and, 111
    private schools, 111
    standard of, 343
    state of, 107
    technical, 111-12

education in Puerto Rico—*contd.*
    University of:
        as a centre of national inspiration,
            297
        campus riots, 106
        impact of, 335, 369
        places, 112
        situation, 369
        size of, 100, 369, 387
    University of San Germán, 369
Surinam:
    Medical College, 270
    state of, 316
    under Ten Year Plan, 316
    University of Paramaribo, 316, 370,
        397n
Trinidad and Tobago:
    attention to, 165-6, 343
    Emergency Teachers' Course, 374
    financing of, 165-6
    higher, 166
    illiteracy rate, 374
    Imperial College of Tropical Agri-
        culture, 335, 369, 395
    Institute of International Relations,
        166
    John F. Kennedy College of Arts and
        Sciences, 369
    John S. Donaldson Technical Insti-
        tute, 166
    libraries, 166
    Maurice Committee, 165
    number of places, 165
    organization of, 165
    San Fernando Technical Institute, 166
    schools, improvement in, 161, 165
    technical, 166
    University:
        aid for, 158
        establishment of College, 149, 166,
            173
        failure of graduates to return, 166
        withdrawal of British Council aid,
            149n
Egypt, aid for, 40, 348
Eisenhower, President:
    belief in foreign investment, 11
    efforts to restore world economy, 28
    policy on:
        Caribbean, 406-7, 408, 415
        Cuban exiles, 13
    support on American intervention in
        Dominican Republic, 83
    use of C.I.A., 406-7
    views on the Cuban situation, 12
    withdrawal of military supplies to
        Cuba, 10
El Salvador, 56n, 78, 354
Eldemire, Herbert, 150
Eleuthera:
    agriculture in, 209
    prosperity of, 212
    tourism in, 207

533

534

French Antilles—*contd.*
  elections:
    Le Moule, 270-1
    support of integration, 285
  emigration, 262, 266, 272, 275, 280,
    283, 316, 345, 365, 435-6
  family allowances, 268, 280
  foreign investment in, 283, 286
  housing, 268
  hurricane damage, 269, 271, 274-5
  in World War II, 261
  income *per capita*, 271
  independence, 264, 265, 273-4, 282,
    286, 345, 389, 434
  industrialization:
    Development Corporation, 280
    in 1963 Report, 279
    Jacquinot Plan, 268
    new industries, 280
    progress of, 285
    under Fifth Plan, 280
  Jacquinot Plan, 268
  legal system, 262
  military service, 265
  nationalism in, 388-9
  Nemo Scheme, 265
  police force, 264
  population:
    birth control, 280, 284, 372-3, 441
    control of, 374-5
    growth of, 273, 345
    problem of, 374-5
    size of, 374-5
  press, restrictions on, 265-6
  racialism in, 264-5
  referendum of 1962, 265
  resentment at transfer of Algerian
    officials, 264-5
  riots in, 263-4, 389
  rum, 275, 397
  social:
    family allowances, 268, 280
    services, 176, 268, 270, 284
  standard of living, 273, 279, 282, 285, 391
  strikes, 271
  sugar:
    competition from sugar beet, 275
    dependence on, 282
    difficulties of exporting in World
      War II, 262
    market, 285, 322, 323, 397
    mechanization, 275
    prices, 275
    production, 275
  television, 268, 271
  tourism:
    advertising, 281
    desire to improve, 265
    hotel accommodation, 281
    length of stay, 281
    need to develop, 282
    slow development of, 280-1, 284, 285
    tax concession, 281

French Antilles—*contd.*
  trade, 261, 275
  trade unionism, 270
  unemployment, 283, 285, 286, 345, 397
  views expressed in *Présence Africaine*,
    264
  see also Guadeloupe, Martinique
French Revolution, effect on colonies,
  261, 378, 379
Fuentes, Ydígoras, 13

Gairy, Eric, 192, 193, 194, 195-6
Galíndez, Jesús de, 71-2
Gall, Norman, 77
gambling:
  in Bahamas, 208, 210
  in Cuba, 9, 33
García, Laútico, 74
Garvey, Marcus, 140, 389
Geoffrey, Jean, 267n
geography of the Caribbean, 1, 2, 3,
  318
geology of the Caribbean, 1
Germany:
  and Haiti, 48
  as a creditor in the Dominican fraudu-
    lent loans case, 70n
  benefit from foreign troops, 118
  trade with:
    Caribbean, 394, 398
    Latin America, 432
    Puerto Rico, 107
    Venezuela, 404
  United States fear of influence of, 88
Ghana:
  aid for, 40, 348
  attempted mediation in the Guyana
    crisis, 231-2
ginger, 327
Glissant, Edouard, 264, 270n
Godber, Joseph, 182
Godett, Wilson, 298
Godoy, Hector García:
  career of, 83-4
  death of, 86
  proposed as provisional governor, 83
  removal of top military leaders, 84
  supporters of, 89
gold, 187-8, 243-4, 287, 290
Gomes, Albert, 132
Gómez, Juan Vicente:
  administrative efficiency of, 72, 88
  compared with Trujillo, 72-3
  oil industry under, 73, 301
  ruthlessness of, 72, 73
  suppression of human liberties, 73
Grand Bahama, 205, 207, 209, 342
Grand Cayman, 194, 213
Grand Mechanism:
  assassination, 88
  democracy of the exiles, 88
  in Hispaniola, 88-9

Haiti: army—*contd.*
    loyalty to Duvalier, 56
    maintenance of, against French invasion, 380
    size of, 55
    training by American Marines, 52
Artibonite Valley:
    banana industry in, 62
    crops to be grown in, 63
    development scheme, 63, 342
    electrical scheme, 63
    French plantations in, 65
    irrigation scheme, 63, 64
as part of Hispaniola, xvii
bananas:
    as Haiti's second crop, 62
    contract with Standard Fruit and
      Steamship Co., 62, 63
    expansion of, 61
    in Artibonite Valley, 62
    rise and fall of, 62-3
    ruined by Haitian politics, 62-3
banking, 49, 356, 424
bauxite, 66
bibliography, 452-5
cacao, 66
Canadian relations with, 66, 69, 424
CARIFTA and, 141
cattle, 63
civil wars, 49
coffee:
    cheap labour factor in, 62
    export of, 62, 66
    French market for, 62
    prices, 62, 63, 66, 327
    production, 379
    threat of competition to, 62, 65, 327
communications, 342
Communism:
    American fear of, 52, 53, 59
    lack of response to, 42
    use of threat of, 59
constitution:
    amendment to, 59
    installation of President for life, 57-8,
      59
    reorganization of Cabinet, 52
corruption of government, 49, 57n, 386
cotton, 63, 379
Cuban invasion of, 52
Cul de Sac, 65
cultural differences, 68
dictatorships of, 49, 51, 53, 58, 59-60,
    88
distance from neighbouring territories,
    3, 52, 59, 137
division into two states, 49
economic:
    absence of prosperity, 61, 99, 342
    aid:
      American: Alliance for Progress
        programme, 64, 347-8; desire to
        advance, 52-3, 57; extent of, 57n,

Haiti: economic aid—*contd.*
    63; nature of, 57n, 63, 67, 409;
    reduction of, 64; reliance on,
    59-60, 64; resumption of, 57, 64;
    vacillating policy on, 64; withdrawal of, 57
    French, 49, 90, 379
    Haitian defalcation of funds, 64
    Import-Export Bank, 63
    International, 68
    International Monetary Fund, 64
    need for, 59-60, 64, 342
    political mismanagement of, 65
    United Nations, 65
average family income, 53n
disinterestedness of Duvalier in economic problems, 68, 385
effect of bad government on, 61, 63,
    64, 68
exports and imports under French
    dominance, 379
financial problems, 63, 67-8
foreign investment in:
    discouragement of, 61
    reversal of policy, 62
future, 68, 342
graft, 63n, 65
hurricane damage, 2, 319
importance of Banque Nationale de
    la République d'Haïti, 49, 50
income *per capita*, 42, 63, 65
pattern, 61-8
political domination, 65
poverty of peasantry, 49, 61n, 63, 65,
    348n
problems, 63
public debt, 51n
standard of living, 51n, 52-3, 90,
    342
under French dominance, 379
education:
    allocation from budget compared
      with military, 67-8
    curriculum, 66
    effects of reduction of American aid,
      66
    failure to use qualified Haitians, 68
    financing of, 67-8
    French basis of, 48, 66, 68, 367
    illiteracy:
      "écoles d'analphabétisation", 67
      in rural areas, 66
      lack of technological, 67
      need to solve problem of, 68,
      percentage of, 49, 65, 66, 66n, 342,
        370, 371
    medium of instruction, 66-7
    monopoly of elite, 66
    number of schools, 66, 67
    primary, 67
    University, 67, 370
emigration, 65-6, 68, 342, 363, 364, 371
exiles, amnesty for, 68

Haiti: relations with
United States (*economic*)—*contd.*
    57n, 63; nature of, 57n, 63, 67,
    409; reduction of, 64; resumption
    of, 57, 64; vacillating
    policy, 64; withdrawal of, 57
  airport, provision of, 53, 64
  Haiti's insistence on employment
    of personnel, 63
  hospital, promise of, 53
United States (*political*):
  action in Haitian-Dominican
    crisis, 56
  appeal to America, 59
  attitude to dictatorship, 27
  attitude to Duvalier's installation
    for life, 58
  complications with Organization
    of American States, 53
  criticism of American policy, 57
  effect of Bay of Pigs affair on, 53
  effect of Cuban Revolution on, 52,
    53, 409
  embarrassment at Duvalier's dictatorial
    methods, 52, 57
  fear of Communism in, 52, 53, 409
  fear of Cuban intervention in, 53
  influence of Marines, 50, 51, 52,
    52n, 55, 81, 385, 400
  military mission in, 52, 56, 57, 385,
    409
  opportunism of policy, 57
  political considerations behind,
    52-3
  question of C.I.A. involvement, 58
  retention of Air Force Mission,
    10n, 56
  retention of Military Assistance
    group, 56
  Rockefeller visit, 59, 418
  securing of Haitian vote on
    Organization of American
    States, 53
  training of Haiti's armed forces,
    52, 385
  vacillating policy of, 10n, 52-3, 58,
    64, 78, 410
Vatican:
  action of the Vatican, 53
  Duvalier's attempt to lacquer
    Voodooism with Roman
    Catholicism, 53-4
  expulsion of church dignitaries,
    53-4, 60
  nationality of priests in Haiti, 54n
  Papal Nuncio in Haiti, 53-4, 58
  re-establishment of relations, 58,
    60
  seizure of Catholic newspaper, 53
Venezuela:
  political asylum controversy, 54-5
  requested recall of chargé
    d'affaires, 55

Haiti: relations with Venezuela—*contd.*
  threat to denounce Haiti before
    Organization of American
    States, 55
religion:
  African character of, 68
  controversy with Vatican, 53-4, 58
  Voodooism, 2, 52n, 53-4, 56, 385,
    391
resistance to Western civilization, 68
Revolt:
  association with Bolívar, 378
  effect on agricultural economy, 6, 61,
    65
  fear of spread of, 261n
  inability of Napoleon to suppress,
    274, 379
  influence of French philosophy on,
    378-9
  intervention by Great Britain in, 6
  numbers killed in, 261n
  restoration under l'Ouverture, 379-80
  significance of, 378
  violence of, 6, 61, 379
rice, 63
secret police, *see* Tonton Macoute
sisal, 66
slavery, 90, 322, 379
sugar:
  difficulties in establishing factories,
    65n
  history of, 65n, 321
  Pétion's abolition of tax, 380
  production, 66, 337
  replaced by coffee as principal crop,
    62
  under French dominance, 61, 65n, 90,
    321, 337, 379
tobacco, 63
Tonton Macoute:
  action in Haitian-Dominican controversy,
    55
  allocation from budget, 64
  display by, 58
  Duvalier's use of, 50, 52n, 58, 60
  institution of, 51
  meaning of, 52n
  protest against use of, 54
  suggested abolition of, 55
  use of, 385, 433
tourism:
  effect of unsettled conditions, 64, 357
  extent of, 63-4
  foreign divorce business, 64
  Office National du Tourisme, 64
  tax concessions, 63
unemployment, 65, 90
Voodooism:
  Duvalier's appeal to, 56, 60, 68, 385,
    391
  Duvalier's attempt to lacquer Roman
    Catholicism with, 53-4
  Duvalier's play on, 52n, 53, 60

missile research centre, 291
missiles crisis, xvii, 17-20, 31, 384, 408-9, 427
Molina Urena, Rafael, 80, 81
Mona Passage, 3
Moncada Barracks, 9, 43
Monnerville, Pierre, 265
Monroe, President James, 400
Monroe Doctrine:
  application of, 404
  as a deterrent to European interference in the Caribbean, 98
  Clayton-Bulwer Treaty as an expression of, 217
  Communism and, 12
  Haitian intervention and, 50
  isolation concept, 401, 404
  Johnson doctrine as a variant of, 89, 411-12, 414-15
  Organization of American States and, 426
  origin of, 400
  Roosevelt Corollary as addendum to, 70, 403, 411
  strategy and, 404
  transgressions of, 400
Montserrat:
  agriculture, 184, 185
  Antilles Radio Corporation, 184
  area of, 183
  association with Great Britain, 183-4, 185
  CARIFTA and, 185, 353n
  cotton, 184
  discovery of, 183
  emigration, 184
  formation, 183, 318
  French in, 184
  fruit and vegetables, 184
  hurricane damage, 184
  inclusion in the Leeward group, 172n
  industry, 185
  political parties, 184-5
  population, 183
  position, 183
  rentals, 184
  settlement of, 184
  share cropping, 184
  sugar, 184
  tomatoes, 184
  tourism, 184, 185, 359
  West Indies Federation, representation on, 124
Mora, José A., 73n, 413
moral leadership as aspiration of Caribbean countries, 4
Morales, President Carlos F., 70
Morillo, Pablo, 218
Moscoco, Teodoro, 74, 104, 118n, 387
Mosquitia, 216
Mosquito Coast, 215, 216
Mosquito Indians, 216
Moyne Commission, 123

Muñoz Marín, Luis:
  ability of associates, 104, 119
  achievements of, 100, 103
  administrative ability, 100, 119, 343, 387
  advertising campaign, 118n
  agreement with Kennedy on need to clarify constitutional position, 101-2
  appeal of, 100, 103
  appointed governor, 100
  belief in honest politics, 103
  career of, 103
  character of, 100
  compared to Bosch, 77
  emphasis of policy, 117
  extension of industrialization to other parts of Puerto Rico, 110-11
  industrialization policy, 109
  Operation Bootstrap, 109
  organization of Partido Popular Demo-crático, 99, 103
  political acumen, 100, 103
  political views of, 103
  question of birth control, 372
  resignation of, 104-5
  sugar industry policy, 113
  transformation of the Puerto Rican political scene, 103
  unique qualities of, 102-3
  use of aid, 119
Muñoz Rivera, Luis, 98, 99

Napoleon, 378
Napoleon III, 394, 401
Nariño, Antonio, 381
Nasser, 341
nationalism:
  as a world force, 377
  Black, 389-90
  constructive, 392
  difficulty of defining, 377-8
  domination of politics, 391
  education and, 378
  European thought and, 378-9, 381
  independence and, 391-2
  internationalism and, 391-2
  in:
    Caribbean, xvii, 122, 123, 200, 338, 377-92, 433
    Cuba, 341, 382-5, 433
    French Antilles, 388-9
    Haiti, 61, 68, 378-80, 385, 433
    Netherlands, 377
    Netherlands Antilles, 389
    Puerto Rico, 101, 107n, 119, 386-7
    Trinidad and Tobago, 154
    Spanish, 297, 387
natural resources of the Caribbean, 3, 4
naval power in the Caribbean, 6, 98, 121, 337, 382
négritude, 60n

555

Nemo Scheme:
  effect of, 265, 288, 397
  object of, 265
Netherlands:
  aid to:
    colonies, 346
    Surinam, 316
  attraction of Dutch East Indies for
    trade, 292, 293, 313, 394
  colonial policy, xvii, 299-300
  Dutch architecture, 1
  economy of, 4
  effect of loss of:
    Dutch New Guinea, 294
    Indonesia, 274, 294, 297, 300, 313,
      397
  European Economic Community, ad-
    vantages of, 306-7
  extent of empire, 299
  failure to comprehend force of nation-
    alism, 300
  financial aid, 419-20
  idea of voluntary association, 300
  interest in the nineteenth-century
    Caribbean, 394
  nationalism in, 377
  Palmas, acquisition of, 299
  possession of the U.S. Virgin Islands,
    200
  primary interest in trade, 299
  sugar plantations in Brazil, 61
  trade with Caribbean, 337
  use of colonies, 3
      see also Netherlands Antilles,
        Netherlands Windward Is.
Netherlands Antilles:
  administration, 293
  agriculture, limitations of, 301, 306
  aid to, 307
  area, 277
  associate membership of E.E.C., 306-
    307
  autonomy movement in, 274, 279, 389
  banking, 356
  civil disturbances, 297-8, 307
  constitution:
    Charter of 1954:
      constitutional monarchy concept,
        295
      Council of Ministers, 295
      Council of the Kingdom, 296
      degree of independence, 296-7
      formulation of, 294-5
      lack of representation on United
        Nations, 296
      Ministers Plenipotentiary, 295, 296
      partnership concept, 293-4, 297,
        299, 300
      reception of, 296
    colonial parliament of 1865, 292-3
    constitution of 1936, 263n, 293
    Federal Legislative Council:
      coalition government, 297-8

Netherlands Antilles constitution:
  Federal Legislative Council—*contd.*
    differing aims of constituents,
      298-9
    electoral procedures, 295
    Governor-General, 296
    influence of smaller islands, 296
    number of officials elected, 296
    Prime Minister, 295-6
    reasons for unity, 299
    relation to Tripartite Kingdom,
      389
    representation at The Hague, 175
    representation on, 295
    West Indies Federation compared
      with, 295
  Tripartite Kingdom:
    concept of, 293-4
    in accordance with Atlantic Char-
      ter, 294
    nature of the association, 296-7,
      397, 434
    strength of, 297
    success of, 300
  defence, 295, 296
  democracy in, 96
  Dutch West India Co., 220, 292
  economic:
    adverse balance of payments, 293
    concentration on development, 293
    encouragement of investment, 305-6
    future of, 345
    lack of investment, 393
    need for mutual support, 306
    one-sidedness of the economy, 301-2,
      306
    pattern, 300-8
    training of youth in Leiden, 393
    wages, 307
  education:
    illiteracy rate, 307, 375
    state of, 307, 316, 375
    Teachers' Training College, 307
  elections of 1969, 298
  emigration:
    from Grenadines, 191
    to Netherlands, 305, 365
  European Economic Community, pros-
    pects of, 306-7, 353
  external affairs, 295, 296, 300
  future of, 307-8
  groups of, 300-1
  immigration:
    from Surinam, 305
    policy, 305
  income *per capita*, 301
  independence:
    cost of, 296, 297, 300
    desire for, 299
    proposed, 300
  industrialization:
    encouragement of new industries,
      306, 375

556

poverty in the Caribbean, 2-3
Pratt, Professor Julius, 8n, 69n, 217, 403
press control, 435
Preston, Amias, 218
Price, George:
  ability of, 253-4, 256
  accusation of Guatemalan negotiations, 253
  compared with Williams, 256
  independence question, 255
  leadership of People's United Party, 253
  relations with Richardson and Pollard, 253
Pringle, John, 147-8
Proudfoot, Dr. Mary, 199
Providence Island, 210
Puerto Cabezas, 15
Puerto Rico:
  advertising campaign, 118
  agrarian reform, limitation of holdings, 328
  agriculture:
    area suitable for, 108
    based on American pattern, 119
    cattle, 112, 116
    coffee, 107, 111n, 113, 116
    dairying, 112, 116
    development under American aid, 107-8
    diversification of, 104, 113
    drift to towns, 110-11, 117
    education for, 111-12
    employment, 108
    fruit and vegetables, 113
    irrigation, 331
    move from, 335
    poultry, 112, 116
    production, 116
    soil conservation, 108
    sugar, 98, 99, 103, 104, 107-8, 109, 111n, 112-13, 116, 117n, 322
    tax concessions, 113
    under Spanish dominance, 97
    unstable land, 120
  area, 320n
  as a model for the Caribbean, 96, 118, 119, 123
  as an island fulcrum, 97
  banking in, 108, 355
  bibliography, 458-62
  cattle, 112, 116
  coffee:
    depression in, 113, 116
    prices, 108
    production, 111n
    trade, 107
  communications, 107, 111, 111n
  constitution:
    amendment to, 100
    as an *Estado Libre Asociado*, 100, 101, 386-7
    as a special case, 387

Puerto Rico: constitution—*contd.*
  citizenship:
    and virtual independence, 100
    compared to French, 263
    employment and, 99, 107, 117
    grant of, 99
    ineligibility to vote in Congressional elections, 99, 101, 387
    liability for American military service, 99, 101
    Netherlands citizenship and, 388
    question of voting in Presidential elections, 106
  Committee on Status, 106
  Commonwealth status:
    ambiguity of term, 101, 386
    economic attraction of, 101, 118-119
    endorsement of, 104
    grant of, 100
    question of, 102, 105, 106n, 203
  criticism:
    in the 1930s, 99
    in the post World War II period, 100, 101
  diplomatic representation, 118
  Executive, powers of, 101
  Governor:
    elected by popular vote, 100, 387
    Muñoz appointed, 100
    powers of, 99n, 105
  incorporation argument, 101, 105, 203, 389
  independence, degree of, 175-6, 297, 387
    question of, 98, 101, 102, 104, 105, 106n, 119
  Kennedy-Muñoz agreement, 101-2
  nature of relations with United States, 386-7
  Organic Act, 100
  plebiscite, 102, 105-6
  price of status, 107
  provincial status, 98
  Resident Commissioner, powers of, 202, 297, 386-7
  self-government:
    degrees of, 100
    question of, 99
    under Spanish dominance, 98
  separationist argument, 101, 106n, 119, 203
  statehood question, 102, 105, 387
  Status Commission, 102
  status question, continuation of, 106-7
  under American dominance:
    constituted a territory of the United States, 99
    Executive, 98, 99
    Foraker Act, 98
    Jones Act, 98-9
    Legislature, 99, 387
  under Spanish dominance, 98

2 N   561

565

573

West Indies Federation—*contd.*
taxation, inequalities of, 125
Trinidad and:
  attitude to smaller islands, 126
  choice of as capital, 124
  criticism of, 126
  customs negotiations with Venezuela,
    127
  effects of collapse, 152
  fear of immigration, 126, 127-8, 226
  financial burden on, 124, 132-3
  number of immigrants entering, 128
  percentage of population, 126
  percentage of revenue, 157
  proposal to invite Guyana to join,
    128
  representation on, 124
  victory of the Democratic Labour
    Party, 125
Virgin Islands, refusal to join, 198
voting, inequalities of, 125
Williams' appreciation of weakness of,
  153
Whitlock, William, 181
Wilberforce, William, 122
Wilhelmina, Queen, 293-4
Willemstad, 1
Williams, Dr. Eric:
  ability of, 158
  and the question of British aid, 152-3,
    157-8
  appeal of, 103
  appreciation of gap between have and
    have-not countries, 159
  avoidance of racialism, 152
  Black Power problems, 154-5, 166
  career of, 152
  character of, 152
  criticism of British policy, 152, 388
  decision to remain in island politics,
    125, 133, 388
  dynamism of, 152
  education of, 152
  grasp of international politics, 152
  independence policy, 130, 151-2
  industrial policy, 158, 439
  leadership of the People's National
    Movement, 151, 152, 153
  offer of co-operation with other parts
    of the Caribbean, 152, 192
  part in Venezuelan-Guyanese dispute,
    238
  participation policy, 154, 160
  position between state and private
    ownership, 158, 166
  pragmatism, 154
  pressure over United States base, 153,
    405
  request to mediate in Guyana, 232
  success in 1966 elections, 153-4
  success in 1971 elections, 156
  suggested economic ties with Cuba, 30
  tolerance of, 152

Williams, Dr. Eric—*contd.*
tour of:
  Africa, 159
  European Economic Community, 158
  Middle East and Europe, 152
trade policy, 157, 158
Venezuelan customs question, 127
view of Trinidad in world context, 153
views on Black Power, 434-5
views on foreign aid, 152-3
West Indies Federation:
  policy on, 127
  realization of weakness of, 153
  secession from, 152
  support of Federal Labour Party, 124
Willis, Robert, 230
Wilson, Harold, 152, 237
Wilson, President Woodrow, 70, 404
Windward Islands:
British:
  agriculture, 173-4
  aid for, 173, 175
  area, 172
  association with Bay Islands, 217
  association with Great Britain, 175-6,
    344, 388
  bananas, 174, 174n, 186, 333
  banking, 172
  British citizenship, 176
  cacao, 172
  Caribs driven from, 364
  charm of, 172
  constitution:
    adult suffrage, 175
    associated statehood, 194-5
    House of Assembly, 175
    nature of, 175
    Regional Supreme Court of Judi-
      cature, 175
    self-government, 174-6
    wisdom of political solution, 194-5
  copra, 173
  cotton, 173, 174
  currency, 172
  defence, 175, 195
  Eastern Caribbean Federation, 167,
    173
  economic conditions, 344
  education, 173
  external affairs, 175, 195
  federation, 123n, 173
  history of, 172
  islands in the group, 172n
  language differences, 172
  police in, 206
  politics and leaders, 173
  proposed federation with Barbados,
    123n, 173
  religious differences, 172
  slavery in, 172, 173
  Spanish dominance in, 172
  sugar, 173-4, 344
  trade unions, 173

582

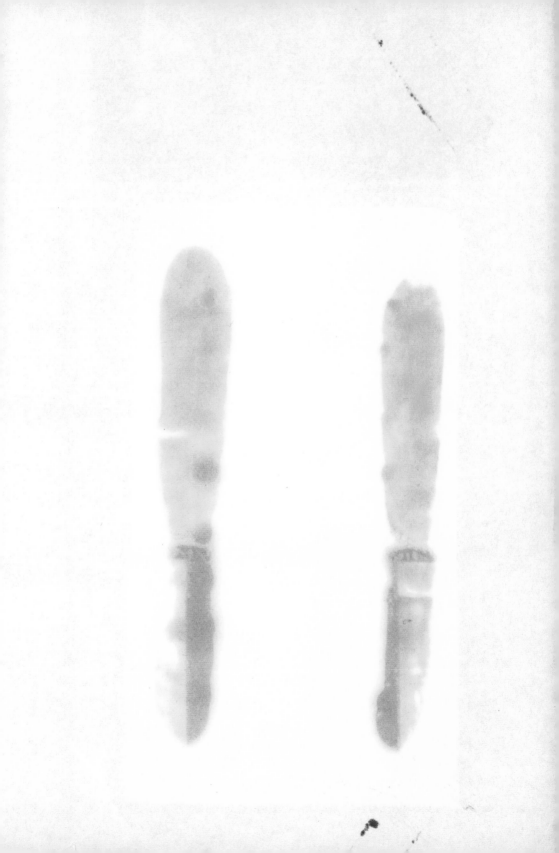